PERGAMON INTERNATIONAL LIBRARY
of Science, Technology, Engineering and Social Studies

The 1000-volume original paperback library in aid of education,
industrial training and the enjoyment of leisure

Publisher: Robert Maxwell, M.C.

Self-Management and Behavior Change

(PGPS-106)

THE PERGAMON TEXTBOOK
INSPECTION COPY SERVICE

An inspection copy of any book published in the Pergamon International Library
will gladly be sent to academic staff without obligation for their consideration for
course adoption or recommendation. Copies may be retained for a period of 60 days
from receipt and returned if not suitable. When a particular title is adopted or
recommended for adoption for class use and the recommendation results in a sale
of 12 or more copies the inspection copy may be retained with our compliments.
The Publishers will be pleased to receive suggestions for revised editions and new
titles to be published in this important international Library.

Pergamon Titles of Related Interest

Anchin/Kiesler HANDBOOK OF INTERPERSONAL PSYCHOTHERAPY

Hersen/Bellack BEHAVIORAL ASSESSMENT: A Practical Handbook, Second Edition

Kanfer/Goldstein HELPING PEOPLE CHANGE: A Textbook of Methods, Second edition

Rachman/Wilson THE EFFECTS OF PSYCHOLOGICAL THERAPY, Second Edition

Rathjen/Foreyt SOCIAL COMPETENCE: Interventions for Children and Adults

Walker CLINICAL PRACTICE OF PSYCHOLOGY: A Guide for Mental Health Professionals

Related Journals*

ADDICTIVE BEHAVIORS
BEHAVIOR RESEARCH & THERAPY
BEHAVIORAL ASSESSMENT
CLINICAL PSYCHOLOGY REVIEW
PERSONALITY & INDIVIDUAL DIFFERENCES
PHYSIOLOGY & BEHAVIOR

*Free specimen copies available upon request.

Self-Management and Behavior Change
From Theory to Practice

Edited by
Paul Karoly
University of Cincinnati

Frederick H. Kanfer
University of Illinois

PERGAMON PRESS
New York   Oxford   Toronto   Sydney   Paris   Frankfurt

Pergamon Press Offices:

U.S.A.   Pergamon Press Inc., Maxwell House, Fairview Park,
                     Elmsford, New York 10523, U.S.A.

U.K.   Pergamon Press Ltd., Headington Hill Hall,
                     Oxford OX3 0BW, England

CANADA   Pergamon Press Canada Ltd., Suite 104, 150 Consumers Road,
                     Willowdale, Ontario M2J 1P9, Canada

AUSTRALIA   Pergamon Press (Aust.) Pty. Ltd., P.O. Box 544,
                     Potts Point, NSW 2011, Australia

FRANCE   Pergamon Press SARL, 24 rue des Ecoles,
                     75240 Paris, Cedex 05, France

**FEDERAL REPUBLIC   Pergamon Press GmbH, Hammerweg 6
OF GERMANY**   6242 Kronberg/Taunus, Federal Republic of Germany

Library of Congress Cataloging in Publication Data
Main entry under title:

Self-management and behavior change.

    (Pergamon general psychology series ; v. 106)
    Includes indexes.
    1. Behavior modification. 2. Behavior therapy.
3. Self-control. I. Karoly, Paul. II. Kanfer, Fred-
erick H., 1925-   . III. Series.
BF637.B4S44   1982   158'.1   81-17730
ISBN 0-08-025987-1   AACR2
ISBN 0-08-025986-3 (pbk.)

Printed in the United States of America

For my wife, Linda
(P.K.)
For Ruth – and the future of psychology
(F.H.K.)

Contents

Preface

In the mid 1960s, the rapid development of behavioral technologies inspired the enthusiasm of a generation of psychologists about the potential of conditioning paradigms for the treatment of a wide variety of adjustment disorders. The behavioral paradigm seemed to herald an era in which clinical interventions could be standardized, programmed, and rigorously applied. However, there were those who doubted the comprehensiveness of this technological approach. Some questioned the ethics of rearranging environmental contingencies and controlling reinforcers without the client's consent or active participation. Others believed that exclusive use of these techniques would be insufficient, not for change, but for maintenance of newly established behaviors once the client would return to the same unfriendly world in which the original symptoms had been developed. Others believed that the early operant technology overlooked the critical contributions to the change process of the individual's cognitive and self-regulatory activities. Gradually the task for all interested parties became clearer. It was not a question of choosing between theoretical paradigms or multipurpose clinical methods. The important task was the careful integration of various approaches toward the aim of achieving a comprehensive theoretical model as well as the development of effective clinical strategies matched to the complexity of human problems.

The issues concerning the client's contribution to the therapy process became the natural focus for convergence of several different research areas. Interest was increased by the fact that an essential part of the controversy between humanistic and behavioral approaches had long been the potential of the individual to guide his or her own fate and future. In the 1960s, learning theorists whose work had provided the major support for the new behavioral change technology began to question the appropriateness of the conditioning paradigms for all human learning and attacked the methodological narrowness of the radical behavioral approach. Development of information processing and cognitive learning theories lent further support to the need for inclusion of covert cognitive events in any thorough account of human behavior. At the same time, the increasing influence of systems theories in psychology emphasized the interactive and reciprocal nature of persons and environments, pointing once again to the type of field approach that had so deeply affected social psychology under the leadership of Kurt Lewin. Finally, sociopolitical, economic, and technological changes on the American scene provided the context for the emergence of new attitudes toward scientific inquiry and toward health professionals. Greater interest in citizen participation on all levels, a decreased belief in the infallibility of professionals, be they physicians, psychologists, or social workers, and an increased awareness of the potential uses of psychological change methods led to a decreased willingness to submit passively to professionals for care and treatment. With greater public information came an increased willingness to assume some responsibility in the treatment process. These and many influences seem to have worked together to set the stage for an acceptance of the theories and methods describing the processes by which humans guide, regulate, correct, or control their own behavior.

Despite the power of conditioning-based clinical procedures, it was apparent that continuous verbal interactions, in interviews as in thinking and self-talk, would remain significant features of most treatment programs. From the work on verbal conditioning, it had become clear that a simple operant paradigm was insufficient for modification of verbal-symbolic and other cognitive behaviors. The studies clearly indicated the important role of the subject's self-generated cues, responses, and reinforcers in guiding behavior. They also demonstrated the strong impact of learning by observation and modeling. The shift to the study of self-regulatory processes was a logical next step in efforts to supplement and expand the behavioral paradigms. The rapid expansion of research in cognitive psychology made available a body of empirical knowledge about variables affecting memory, perception, and organization of information and other intraperson processes. Recent research and theorizing about cognitive-behavioral interventions and strategies on the one hand and intensified research on self-processes on the other have provided a firm basis for the development of a psychology of self-regulation and its applied counterpart, a psychology of self-management.

The present volume provides an overview of divergent theoretical approaches. It testifies to the wide influence that the emphasis on client participation and self-management has already had in stimulating research and the use of new intervention techniques in many different clinical areas. The reader will surely be struck by the fact that, despite the differences in the theoretical points of view expressed in the first section of the volume, there is a common thread of agreement concerning the need for careful analysis and research on component processes and skills that make up the complex called self-regulation or self-management. While earlier models of self-regulatory processes rooted in psychophysiology, cognitive psychology, and behavioral psychology remained isolated "minitheories," current approaches seem to take cognizance of the interrelationships between these areas. They attempt to deal with the complexities of the phenomena under scrutiny and address the interface between various levels on which different subdivisions of psychology concentrate. Most importantly, unlike earlier theories about intrapersonal processes, they maintain a commitment to rigorous experimental methodology at the research level of operation. This desire for rapprochement seems to have helped theoreticians from different areas to become increasingly aware of the need to consider the constant interplay of cognitive, motivational, physiological, and behavioral components in a full explanation of human functions.

In the second and third sections of the book the reader will note the youth and vigor of the research and the clinical methods based on these theoretical models. To date, almost all of the clinical intervention procedures described here are still in a stage of development and refinement. As has often been the case in clinical psychology, effective procedures have been developed and have preceded clear explanatory formulations about the underlying processes. Nevertheless, in less than a decade, the recognition of the importance of self-regulatory processes in clinical change has resulted in a variety of widely researched and applied procedures for treatment of a range of clinical problems. In almost all of the clinical intervention methods described in the second and third sections of the volume, one notes the increased emphasis on the integration of attained change into the total life pattern of the individual. Such integration is sought for the purpose of enhancing durability of therapeutic effectiveness and for increasing the client's resilience under the varying environmental conditions and conflict situations which the client is sure to encounter after therapy terminates.

No single volume can encompass the large body of knowledge that contributes to a full understanding of self-management. We have attempted to select as contributors those persons whose originality, creativity, and productivity have marked them as leaders in their respective areas of competence. We have also limited the volume to contributions that deal with the self-regulatory phenomena at the psychological-behavioral level. Despite the importance of the biological and societal levels of self-regulation and of their interface with psychological processes, research and theories at these levels have not been afforded representation here. Space limitations and our primary concern with individual behavior and with the clinical utility of current work in the area have imposed practical limitations on the scope of the volume.

The major incentive for assembling these original contributions into one volume has been the need felt by us to offer students, researchers, and clinicians a sampler of the exciting work in the area. Readers will find many suggestions for their own work, be it in theorizing, research, or clinical practice. In the spirit of the importance of self-management, however, the volume is not offered as a definitive, authoritative prescription on theory or clinical practice, but as a stimulant for the reader's further self-development and growth.

We are deeply indebted to the excellent cooperation of our contributors, their patience in listening to our suggestions, and their willingness to maintain a degree of structure so as to give coherence to the book. Finally, to Diane Kopriwa we extend our thanks for excellent clerical assistance.

Part I:
Basic Concepts and Foundations

1
Perspectives on Self-Management and Behavior Change
Paul Karoly

Freedom of the will means being able to change those premises for the sake of which we behave. Personal responsibility means that we acknowledge our role in the fixing of premises. There are obvious limitations to such freedom.

— Joseph Rychlak (1979)

Man is not and never will be the master of his fate: His very reason always progresses him by leading him into the unknown and unforeseen where he learns new things.

— F. A. Hayek (cited in Weimer, 1980)

The circuitous route from theory to practice in the helping professions has traditionally been a source of debate, disappointment, confusion, and excitement for researchers and practitioners alike. Some observers, like Jerome Frank (1973), believe that there is little substantive distance between prescientific and theory-directed thought in clinical psychology and psychiatry; so, to them, the existence of a "scientist-practitioner gap" is interpreted as a testament to disciplinary arrogance rather than as a sign of a ripening clinical enterprise. To others, who recognize that psychology has yet to achieve paradigmatic consensus, the frustrating divergences between textbook logic and clinical practice represent a major portion of the motiva-tional fuel that incites the creative juices of young (and even not-so-young) mental health professionals.

On balance, both perspectives own a piece of the truth. Yet neither folk wisdom nor humanitarian artistry can long serve without the assistance of a scientific stance that seeks to both identify and manipulate patterns of regularity in human behavior (Weimer, 1980). Unfortunately, because the worlds of the clinical practitioner and the clinical researcher are often so dissimilar, the search for workable regularities soon reverts to posturing and philosophizing. Indeed, there is sufficient orthodoxy *within* each camp to ensure multiple "gaps" and to inspire intrepid bridge builders with diverse motives and talents. The brief history of the self-management psychologies illustrates these points clearly.

THE UBIQUITY OF ADVERSARY ADVISORS

Regardless of one's absolute power, strength, or influence, every human be-ing confronts constraints on the exercise of personal decision making. While certain people feel freer than others, and some persons within any society are actually presented with a larger set of decisional options, it is nonetheless necessary that all social animals recognize the *relativity of control*—that no single source of control is absolute, that the stage for our lives is set (by history and biology) before we are born, and that survival re-quires cooperation. Such a simple truth as is embodied in the relativity of control principle has *not* been translated into consensual viewpoints regard-ing the conditions of human life. Philosophy, science, and religion have all laid claim to having some authority in the interpretation of the meaning of control and its corollaries, responsibility and freedom. Indeed, there is good reason to assert that the truth value of the relativity assumption (i.e., that people are neither 100 percent free to act and choose, nor 100 percent deter-mined) has been eclipsed by the *principle of relative interpretation of the meaning of control*. This principle states that when approached from the perspectives of logic (philosophy), manipulation (science), and human values (religion), the concept of control becomes three separate and ap-parently irreconcilable entities. While this is not the place for a review of the historical or philosophical underpinnings of the concepts of control, freedom, and/or responsibility (interested readers may consult Harré & Secord, 1972; Klausner, 1965; Rychlak, 1979; among others), it is impor-tant to note that the conflict between empirical, philosophical, and ethico-religious concerns has continued to serve as a source of division and contro-versy within clinical psychology and psychiatry.

One cannot ask questions about the methods of control without also asking why, by whom, and with what authority. The possibility of even incomplete control by the individual over the varied forces of nature (the environment) carries with it the apparent need to understand formally the controlling agency—that is, the self, ego, proprium, or mind. Twentieth-century psychology has not so much transcended earlier preoccupations as it has absorbed and reorganized them.

Psychology exists because all people behave and some people observe and want to know why. In observing people, one group of investigators has sought to approach their subject via what has come to be called "the scientific method." This basically implies that the investigator adopts an attitude toward his or her "subject," which presupposes (1) that the subject doesn't care about and isn't influenced by being observed, and (2) that the "scientific" observer is objective in his or her viewing. The second major group of investigators has sought to learn about their subjects by participating with them in the business of living (behaving, thinking, and feeling). Not surprisingly, each group has developed its own methods as well as its own criteria for judging the goodness of its efforts.

One might imagine that the study of self-management would have forced both groups to work together. After all, it should be clear to the "participators" that while many subjects claim to want to alter problematic behavior patterns or to be more goal directed, the subjective intent, belief, or plan often falters, and in ways that baffle the subject. Clearly, then, neither the participant observers nor their subjects have access to all the relevant information. Similarly, the "objectifiers" would have to acknowledge that because people will, on occasion, influence the visible, countable, or tangible forces that determine their behavior in ways that are not totally predictable on the basis of previous observations, they might have to be approached at least partly from the "subjective" point of view. Unfortunately, it has only been recently that the phenomenologists (the participators) and the behavioral investigators (the objectifiers) have occupied the same scientific platform.

THE TWO DISCIPLINES

The specific problems and issues of concern to self-management theorists of all persuasions (from Freud to Skinner) have involved the same psychological dimensions of choice, commitment, intentionality, and the behavioral enactment of internalized goals. Yet there have always been at least two, seemingly clear but divergent, routes to the identification and manipulation of the "determinants" of these regulating factors: the environment and the person. Self-management has traditionally been approached as a serious topic from within each of the two disciplines of scientific psychology (e.g., Cronbach, 1957): the experimental-manipulative and the clinical-descriptive-correlational. In the absence of a genuine desire for integration of perspectives, the topic has (until very recently) lived a double life: as a personality construct (with such aliases as ego, conscience, character, and social intelligence) and as an acquired behavioral competency, under the "ultimate control" of the individual's past and present learning as well as current enabling conditions. Perhaps because each of the camps felt that it was making progress in explicating the features of human self-sufficiency, no cross-fertilization occurred. From our present perch, we can see that both the S-R and the personological model builders were, in fact, flexing their respective muscles, carving their niche, and, by and large, *defining progress in terms that best suited their own purposes* (see Kanfer & Karoly, in this volume, for a further discussion of philosophy of science in self-management psychology). Purposes derive from metatheoretical commitments. And with respect to the metatheoretical question of *where* the control of organismic goal-directedness originates, the behaviorists maintained the neatest psychological house by keeping the traffic outside—in the settings that cue and reinforce action. Person-oriented psychologists have offered at least two alternatives (both logistically "messy" ones): conscious versus unconscious control.

Freudianism and Ego Psychology

Surrounded by the technical and philosophical benefits of the "age of reason," the clinician-scientist Sigmund Freud challenged the prevailing wisdom at its most basic level. For this iconoclast, instinct, rather than conscious mentation, was the primary steering mechanism for the human adventure. This is not to say that Freud believed in irrational control. Rather, the id (storehouse of innate biologic drives) was said to give rise to a self-regulatory system, dominated by the ego, which takes external reality into account in such a way as to permit the maximal expression of instinct at the least risk of punishment from the agents of society.

In his early writings, such as *The Interpretation of Dreams* (1900), Freud used the notion of ego as the mental structure responsible for reality-based perception and thought. Psychoanalysis was, in the early days, primarily an id (or drive-discharge) psychology, and the ego was less prominent than it is today. The introduction of the *structural* theory, with the publication of *The Ego and the Id* in 1923 ushered in the beginnings of what is, in fact, called "ego psychology." The ego became part of a team of constructs (working with the id and superego) and took on unconscious and conscious components as well as the added responsibility of serving the id (instinctual gratification), but without offending the internalized moral sense (the superego). When the child deliberately stops himself from aggressing or defers some immediate gratification, it isn't just because that's the logical thing to do. It is also because such a response is the best way to bring about a balance between the ego, the id, and the superego.

The ego is the executive over the structural divisions of the personality. And the assumption is made that, over time, the individual develops an habitual style of dealing with the tasks of adaptation, including self-management. In this view, ego and *character* become almost synonymous concepts (Fenichel, 1945).

Broadly conceived, the function of the ego is to manage the process of adaptation. Of the functions attributable to the ego apparatus, I shall restrict this discussion to the delay of gratification and tolerance of tension (self-control) capacities and the propensity toward self-initiated and self-directed activity (self-regulation).

Initially, biological and social reality force the developing infant into learning how to "tame" instincts which cannot readily be satisfied. He or she must be able to interpose some form of mediation between impulse and action, and do so without the assistance of socializing agents. When an impulse is aroused but no outlet for "discharge" is available, the infant is said to "bind time" by means of gross motor movement and "hallucinatory" images. Such "archaic ego" functions are believed to be quite important, since the primitive drive-reducing capacity of fantasy sets the stage for more mature, synthetic capacities such as judgment, anticipation of future consequences, and planning. Postponement of gratification or tolerance of bodily tension are accomplished because the images, fantasies, and daydreams of the preverbal child do eventuate in the discharge of small amounts of energy; they act as a kind of mental drainage system. With the emergence of language, the child can use more abstract and elaborated methods for binding time and "retarding automatic id functions." Whereas Freud emphasized the discharge function of the infant's fantasy life, others have suggested that the primitive ego's capacity to delay contributes in a circular fashion to its own development via a process labeled *neutralization*. That is, whenever the infant succeeds in taming impulses, some of the energy involved becomes transferred to the ego, invested in a kind of restricted bank account: energy to be used for ego building (structuralization). Thus, a structure (ego) is built up by means of external stimulation, but becomes capable of enhancing itself, somewhat autonomously.

The ego functions as more than a mere impulse monitor, however. The story of the emergent ego and its role in adaptation is yet incomplete. The finishing touches await the child's resolution of the Oedipal complex and the birth of a new structural component—the superego.

The child, it is reasoned, must learn to defer or postpone gratification of aggressive and sexual drives, as well as consummatory activity. If the child is to derive pleasure, he or she must now satisfy not merely the constraints of reality, but the prohibitions of parents, teachers, and the society at large. Through the process of identification, the child takes in (introjects) the social point of view. The ego then has another source of potential conflict with which to contend: the internalized agent of civilization, which, "like a garrison in a conquered city," uses a powerful weapon—guilt—to enforce the inhibition of antisocial behavior.

In learning to deal with "social realities," the ego is said to evolve to even higher levels of autonomous functioning. The ego is charged not only with the job of delay, tolerance, postponement, and inhibition, but with the responsibility of organization, integration, and what we know as self-regulation. It was even presumed that some of the inborn capacities of the ego (perception, memory, etc.) do *not* derive from instinctual or conflictual sources. The so-called conflict-free functions of the ego were largely the creations of the ego psychologists. For present purposes, I will concentrate on the self-regulatory model developed by George Klein.

Klein (1976) viewed the ego as providing "a source of independent motivation for contacting the environment and of developing adaptive controls—a 'third force', on par with drive and social reality" (p. 142). Klein sought to develop models and measures of the consistent styles or strategies by which individuals organize their experiences and perceptions of the world, and thereby direct and control their behavior. Cognitive controls, as they are called, are specific and measurable mechanisms which are believed to be activated by current environmental stimulation and by the "adaptive intentions" of the individual.

For example, Klein and his associates (Gardner, Holzman, Klein, Linton, & Spence, 1959) have identified, among others, a dichotomous style called "leveling-sharpening" which does not depend upon anxiety for its activation (as do defenses) and which denotes a method that the person (ego) actively uses to make sense of the world—either by widening or narrowing conceptual (information-processing) focus. Klein (1968) also introduced the notion of "peremptory ideation," suggesting a model for the ways in which a "train of thought" can take on momentum and guide perception and behavior. His formulation depended not upon drive as a motivator, but upon cognition: "What is motivating about behavior and what is cognitive about motivation are one and the same thing" (Klein, 1968, p. 5).

Perhaps his most interesting concept, however, in view of our present concerns, is the "Principle of Self-Initiated Active Reversal of Passive Experience" (Klein, 1976, chapter 8). Consistent with his deemphasis of instinctual and unconscious motivational forces, Klein noted that Freud's principle of "repetition compulsion" (based upon observations of children's play) seemed to reflect a fundamental tendency of the developing child to reproduce actively a pattern of behavior that was initially experienced passively. Repudiating Freud's explanation that compulsive repetition reflected a desire to recapture a previous state (ultimately linked to the "death instinct"), Klein argued that the child's tendency to repeat is an act of "recreation with the aim of *resolution* or mastery"; and that a fundamental tendency of development is to "make sense" of experience, particularly to achieve inner consistency. Thus, in creating a cognitive motive for self-regulation, Klein was aligning the functioning of the ego with familiar social psychological themes, such as self-perception and cognitive dissonance, and with nonanalytic personality theories, such as those of Carl Rogers (1961) and George Kelly (1955).

The reader may well interpret this brief review of psychodynamic theory as pointing to a softening of a *strict intrapsychic* position. Interestingly, revisionism within the Freudian ranks has been paralleled by a liberalization within the S-R tradition. Therefore, before considering the "conscious processing" view of self-management (recall that consciousness was one of the two logistically messy concepts referred to earlier), I shall overview the traditional environmental perspective(s) so as to illustrate the other explanatory extreme along the control continuum.

The Learning Theory Tradition

One of the clear and distinctive contributions of the learning perspective has been its characterization of self-management, not as a quality or a personality construct, not as an innate biologic given (or potential), but as the end product of a series of behavioral enactments most of which are learned. Tied to this functional-response-class approach has also been a single-minded dedication to the development of intervention procedures designed to assist the individual in altering an array of maladaptive behavior patterns (Goldfried & Merbaum, 1973).

However, describing the assumptive world of the learning theorist as stimulus-response, empty organism, *tabula rasa*, or mechanistic fails to capture the variety of interpretations of the self-management process that are possible or the host of "mechanisms" that have been invoked. In the space available, I shall present the behavioral versions under three general headings—the aversive conditioning, the instrumental, and the modeling paradigms—and try to underscore the precursors of contemporary cognitive, cybernetic, or interactionist conceptions.

Aversive Conditioning Conceptions. Early formulations in the learning tradition were concerned with specifying the determinants of "internalization." Simply put, the child was expected to learn to experience fear or anxiety at the mere thought of rule transgression, and to feel pleasure (anticipation of parental love) when obedient. Self-control was therefore considered to be a conditioned response, associated with a history of parent-mediated punishment or reward for "bad" versus "good" behavior, respectively.

Although positive as well as aversive affective states are capable of being conditioned and can, theoretically, serve as mediators of prosocial behavior, negative emotions (such as fear, guilt, and shame) and punishment contingencies tended to garner the major share of the young experimental market. Perhaps this was so because, in the most critical training situations, parents are more likely to resort to tactics of punishment. Or, it may have been because the aim of self-control-related socialization practices is usually suppression, inhibition, or delay—outcomes which all seem to call forth punishment as a "natural" mode of influence. Further, doing the "right thing" is in many cultures "its own reward," while transgression is expected to elicit aversive aftereffects such as self-criticism, confession, and reparation (Aronfreed, 1968).

Apparently, not having a tyrant-like, pain-administering conscience is worse than having one (Mowrer, 1972). Therefore, the experimental analysis of the effects of punishment and avoidance conditioning was expected to clarify the processes of healthy adjustment.

Studies of child rearing and parental disciplinary methods conducted during the 1950s suggested that the common parental practice of withdrawing love (a form of negative punishment) contingent upon child misbehavior may have the effect of suppressing that behavior and strengthening the so-called identification with parents (Sears, Maccoby, & Levin, 1957). Whiting (1959) believed that the withholding of love or material pleasures fostered *status envy* in the child, a supposed mediator (in the Freudian tradition) of conscience development.

Among the most interesting attempts to wed learning theory and conscience development, however, was the research of R. L. Solomon, who brought socialization into the animal laboratory. Using what they called a "taboo-training" procedure, Solomon and his colleagues taught young dogs to avoid a preferred meat by hitting them on the snout with a rolled-up newspaper, while permitting access to a dry dog food. Later the animals were placed into a "temptation-testing" situation, with free access to both kinds of food and with the experimenter absent. In this context their choice behavior was observed. Resistance to temptation (choosing the nonpreferred food) was found to be conditionable, stable (with short delay of punishment times), and generalizable (Solomon, Turner, & Lessac, 1968).

Much of the early work on punishment and self-control went unnoticed in the larger research community because, as G. C. Walters and Grusec (1977) noted, "virtually no research was being done on punishment in learning laboratories," and the child developmentalists of the day were strongly committed to a Freudian model of childhood personality. The influential writings of Skinner (1938) and Estes (1944), to the effect that punishment is a transitory phenomenon with damaging side effects, was certainly partly responsible for the lack of widespread research interest.

However, during the 1960s the picture changed somewhat. Reviews by Azrin and Holz (1966), Church (1963), Solomon (1964), and others reawakened interest in punishment and suggested that under the proper conditions, its suppressive effects on behavior could be durable and without harmful side effects. Analogue research with children examined such parameters of punishment as timing, severity, quality, schedules of delivery, and their interaction (Aronfreed, 1968; Cheyne & Walters, 1970). Results were supportive of the general role of punishment as a mediator of children's resistance to temptation, but the level of complexity of the child experiments was such that investigators soon abandoned the hope of unqualified application of animal models. Researchers also began to note that punishers used in their experiments could have an informational as well as an aversive impact. And the effects of what can be called cognitive structuring (explicitly via instructions, or implicitly through experimental demand characteristics) were not only unavoidable; they were found to be exceedingly powerful. Punishment research gradually defected from the ranks of the aversive conditioning model to take up asylum in the interactionist domain. As Parke (1974), a leader in research on punishment effects, concluded:

> The model of the child as a passive recipient of adult controlled input is no longer adequate. . . . An interactive model of response inhibition in which both the cognitive capacities of the child and the social situational factors are recognized would offer the greatest promise for understanding the development of self-control in childhood. (p. 141)

The Instrumental Paradigm. The behavioral view of self-control is almost synonymous with the Skinnerian emphasis upon the functional relationship between responses and their consequences. The individual controls himself or herself, said Skinner (1953), "precisely as he would control the behavior of anyone else—through the manipulation of variables of which behavior is a function" (p. 228). Skinner (1953) introduced the notion that the positive and negative consequences of an action might give rise to two responses, a controlling and a controlled response. "The controlling response may manipulate any of the variables of which the controlled response is a function; hence, there are a good many different forms of self-control" (p. 231).

Among the techniques which Skinner suggested to accomplish self-control were: physical restraint and physical aid, changing the discriminative cues, removing the discriminative cues, extinguishing responses to discriminative stimuli, deprivation and satiation, manipulating emotional conditions, aversive conditioning (self-administered punishment), and use of drugs to reduce the impact of tempting or painful stimuli (in the resistance and tolerance situations, respectively). Whatever was done, however, Skinner noted that the person's history and the environmental contingencies were *ultimately* responsible. An "inner originating and determining agent" was deemed unnecessary.

Contemporary advocates of the operant model (e.g., Ainslie, 1975; Goldiamond, 1976; Rachlin, 1974; Risley, 1977; Stuart, 1972) have vigorously defended the operant perspective against the onslaughts of the cognitivists and the social-learning revisionists. Parsimony and operationalization have provided powerful counterarguments against the reintroduction of the person as an active agent. Some illustrations should help to concretize for the reader the operant version of self-control.

Risley (1977; Risley & Hart, 1968), for example, discussed the correspondence paradigm as an alternative to the familiar stimulus generalization approach designed to ensure that certain behaviors occur in settings where there are no functional reinforcers immediately available for their support. Risley observed that an individual's verbal statements about what he or she would like to do typically bear little relationship to actual or "real life" behavior. The ability to enhance the correspondence between words and deeds would be the tangible objective of all those who claim to be interested in establishing the vague qualitative dimensions of *altruism*, *honesty*, *character*, the *Protestant ethic*, or *self-control*. The formula for correspondence training is, in principle, quite straightforward. Whereas verbal commitments to action are often unsystematically reinforced, and certain prosocial or desirable activities (self-controlling actions included) are sometimes reinforced, the clinician's goal should be to establish a *generalized behavior class of correspondence* (a predictable relationship between one's commitments and subsequent actions) by systematically reinforcing correspondence only.

Suppose one is confronted with a young "delinquent" who makes frequent promises about engaging in cooperative or school-related behavior, but who never follows through. In contrast to the view that ego-enhancing experiences must be provided, or that specific reasoning or instrumental skills must be taught, the *operant-correspondence* approach calls for the clinician to gain access to valued rewards and to be in a position to observe both the *promise* and the actual *nondelivery* (or the emission of some response other than the one promised). Promises might be prompted and an instruction given to the effect that emission of the intended act shall merit reward. Noncorrespondence is, then, ignored (or punished). Correspondence, and only correspondence, is followed consistently by reinforcement.

Indices of self-management often involve measures other than the sheer frequency with which a particular response is emitted or omitted. Many investigators focus upon children's choices or values as a means of determining the success of socialization. For example, children are labeled as mature or moral who prefer large delayed rewards to immediately available but smaller outcomes. Children who choose to spend more time studying than fishing are considered to be future oriented and self-regulating. Similarly, when in a setting that potentially supports aggressive and cooperative responding to an equal degree, the selection of the aggressive alternative supposedly indicates a deficiency in judgment. Can an instrumental conditioning framework accommodate such abstract dimensions of self-management as unconstrained choice or an individual's differential time allocation across activities? Many learning theorists have answered in the affirmative.

One operant method for assessing value or choice which is free of self-report bias is the behavior ratio. Assuming A is the "moral," the more difficult, or the less hedonistic behavioral alternative in a two-choice situation, then:

$$\frac{\text{Behavior on alternative } A \text{ (i.e., frequency or duration)}}{\text{Behavior on } A + \text{Behavior on } B}$$

represents the formula for computing a behavior ratio. A behavior ratio of 1 would suggest maximal reaction tendency; a ratio of 0, the minimal level; and a .5 ratio, the point of indifference.

To truly appreciate the instrumental model of self-management, the reader must recognize some additional phenomena. First, consider the *Matching Law*. According to this formulation, behavior ratios are said to match the proportion of rewards that are concurrently available for each of the behavioral alternatives. Thus:

$$\frac{\text{Behavior on } A}{\text{Behavior on } A + \text{Behavior on } B} = \frac{\text{Reinforcement obtained by choosing } A}{\text{Total reinforcements } (A + B)}$$

Experiments have been performed across a variety of animal species with varied parameters of reward (e.g., amount, schedule of delivery, delay, mode of delivery), and the matching law has been remarkably accurate (Rachlin, 1976).

Descriptive schemes, developed originally to account for choice reversals among animals, suggest a form of the matching law to account for a human's seemingly nonhedonistic choice. According to Rachlin and his colleagues (Baum & Rachlin, 1969; Rachlin & Green, 1972), the ratio of values of two rewarded alternatives that differ in delay and in amount is the product of the ratio of the amounts multiplied by the inverse ratio of the delays:

$$\frac{V_1}{V_2} = \frac{A_1}{A_2} \cdot \frac{D_2}{D_1}$$

Let's assume that the amount of reward for studying (A_1) is quite high (including the value of receiving good marks, improving chances for college admission, loving responses from mother and father, the self-satisfaction that comes from doing a job well). We can arbitrarily attach a monetary value to it of $100. Let's also assume that the value of a game of baseball (A_2) is also high; but only $10 worth. If there were a 1-hour delay involved in obtaining the small reward associated with baseball playing, but a 20-hour delay before the posting of grades, then according to the formula

$$\frac{V_1}{V_2} = \frac{100}{10} \cdot \frac{1}{20}$$

and the baseball game is preferred two to one. However, if both rewards were delayed by an additional 100 hours, the child would then be expected to prefer studying by more than eight to one (assuming that the value of hours and money is numerically proportional).

The instrumental perspective, thus, explains the occasional preference for delay without recourse to special qualities of cognition or judgment. Similarly, the absence of delay choice is explained algebraically rather than clinically. According to Rachlin's view, there are situations in which the child (as well as laboratory animals participating in choice experiments) will wait for a delayed payoff even if a smaller immediate payoff is available. What is required is that at an earlier point in time (say 101 hours prior to the baseball game, which is 120 hours prior to the posting of grades) the child engages in some activity that *commits* him to studying. For example, the child might call his baseball companions at this earlier time and tell them he definitely does *not* want to be called to play baseball later. "When we label these behaviors as self-control, the part that should be attributed to the self is the invention of the commitment strategy. Once this is done, subsequent behavior would be predicted by the matching formula and the contingencies" (Rachlin & Green, 1972, pp. 21–22).

Modeling. Thus far, the learning theory approach has explained "internalization" by means of conditioned emotional responding and the planful manipulation of cues and contingencies. In both instances, the routes to self-management lie in the exploitation of rewards and punishers. Yet, self-control and regulation obviously require more than the mechanical inhibition of a deviant action or robot-like adherence to a desirable course, for it must take place across a variety of times and places and be enacted in a multitude of forms. Children must know when to do what, and for how long. Even Rachlin and Green (1972) noted the importance of the "intervention of the commitment strategy" (cf. also Brigham's chapter in this volume).

In their classic *Social Learning and Personality Development* (1963), Bandura and Walters presented a compelling case in support of the necessity of modeling influences in the "development of children's habits of self-control." Whether through words, pictures, or concrete actions, models inform and motivate, prescribe and proscribe, allowing the child to extract the rules for creative interaction with a world that becomes increasingly complex as the child grows older.

Bandura and Walters' distinction between the acquisition and performance of modeled actions provided a significant point of departure from previous response-centered conceptualizations (e.g., Baer & Sherman, 1964; Miller & Dollard, 1941). The observational learning of any complex behavior was considered by Bandura and Walters to be more than the mere copying of what has been seen, or the acquisition of a generalized tendency to copy.

> It involves exposure to the responses of others, learning and recalling what one has seen, abstracting classes of behavior, and subsequently accepting the modeled behavior, sometimes after substantial generalization or sophisticated assessment of "what it tells you," as a guide for one's own actions. (Liebert, Poulos, & Strauss, 1974, p. 149)

How does this S-S formulation apply to self-management? Let us examine delay of gratification, but this time from the perspective of an experiment by Bandura and Mischel (1965). These investigators assessed the delay preferences (for either smaller immediate or delayed larger rewards) of fourth- and fifth-grade children, and identified a "high-delay" and a "low-delay" group on the basis of extreme scores. These children were then exposed to one of three conditions, two of which were designed to alter already existing self-control-relevant preferences. In a live modeling condition, an adult demonstrated the reverse of the observing child's previous preference (choosing the immediate reward in the presence of high-delay children, and the delayed reward in the presence of children who seemed to prefer immediate reward). In a symbolic modeling condition, the same sort of manipulation occurred, except the adult model's preferences were presented in written form. A no-model control condition was also included. The results supported the investigators' contention that children's exposure to adult models (live or in symbolic form) could dramatically alter children's judgmental behavior. Other experiments have likewise shown that models can influence children's choice of performance standards and their self-administered reinforcement practices (Bandura, 1977).

FROM ENVIRONMENT CONTROL TO ARTIFACT CONTROL: THE SOCIAL LEARNING VIEW

If self-control is viewed not as operant or a conditioned response, nor as a stable trait or unconscious structure, but rather as the outcome of a relatively long sequence of behaviors (i.e., as may be involved in successful dieting or smoking cessation), then it becomes necessary to look to the person to provide the continuity for long-term "program" adherence (Karoly, 1981). The person's conscious experience of goals (incentives) and the means of their achievement must be taken into account. But how, if we are to remain loyal to the scientific credo of intersubjectivity and avoid the known pitfalls of introspectionism ?

With the so-called cognitive revolution of the late sixties and early seventies (Dember, 1974) came a softening of hardline behaviorism and an awareness that the difficulties wrought by any examination of the flow of consciousness need not forever impede the study of imagination, memory, or the personal experiences of an individual (Pope & Singer, 1978). The fact that no subjective observation can ever be verified by a second observer led Klinger (1978) to ask: "How severely does this special limitation handicap observation of inner experience?" (p. 226). His answer was typical of the new "cognitive-behavioral" trend in assessment (see also Kendall & Hollon, 1981).

> The relevant question is not of handicap but of what special burdens this feature of introspective observation places on an investigator to validate the observations. The burden does not seem appreciably different from that placed on most sciences in practice. Whereas astronomy requires that observations be validated by direct confirmations of newly observed phenomena, it is a rare comparative psychologist whose observations are confirmed by another comparative psychologist observing the selfsame event. No comparative psychologist knows what is going on in the inner experience of his or her colleague . . . the real criterion even here is replicability not traceable to artifact. Thus, in observation of inner experience as in such other procedures, the validating process resides in ruling out artifacts, in replications, and, ultimately, in the usefulness of data or theory for making possible other forms of prediction and perhaps control. (Klinger, 1978, pp. 226–227)

In a social learning analysis, cognitive control determinants are afforded equal attention and the same explanatory potential as the antecedent and consequential influences with which they interact.

Mediation is not considered to be composed simply of physiological responses, subvocal speech, or similar forms of mediate response in a chain anchored by observable stimuli on one end and motor responses on the other. The environment is subject to the effects of attention, expectancy, internal representation and transformation, the vagaries of storage and retrieval processes, language mediation, and experiential feedback (Mahoney, 1974; Rosenthal & Zimmerman, 1978; Staats, 1975). Self-management becomes anything but an epiphenomenon, the mere fallout of external control procedures. However, defining the unique properties and mechanisms of self-management has not been a simple matter. Although the richness of the social learning theoretical superstructure has not been matched by congruent procedural refinements in the laboratory or by clinical breakthroughs, the comparative potency of this relatively recent ideology is quite creditable. A brief overview should communicate the salient features of the evolving cognitive social learning perspective.

Ironically, one of the most influential paradigms, the *three-stage* model (Kanfer, 1970; Kanfer & Phillips, 1970; Kanfer & Karoly, 1972) is an outgrowth of the Skinnerian external-influence tradition.

The experimenter who would shape the behavior of a pigeon in an operant chamber must observe the bird's actions in regard to the response level, decide on some criterion for the delivery of a food reward (i.e., establish a schedule), and arrange for the machine to provide the rewards contingent upon the requisite tempo or frequency of responding. When the purveyor and recipient of shaping efforts are the same person (as in human self-control), then the subjectively administered program is built upon the processes of self-observation, self-evaluation (criterion- or standard setting) and self-consequation (self-reward or self-punishment). No arcane intrapsychic agent is implied; merely the individual doing double duty.

Over the years, this three-stage conception has generated a vast amount of research, dealing with such topics as: differentiating the reactive and therapeutic effects of self-observation; establishing the therapeutic parameters of self-observation (e.g., the type and timing of self-recording), exploring the socialization (via direct tuition and modeling) of self-evaluative standards; examining the factors accounting for the disengagement of performance standards; discovering the determinants of self-reward rates in the immediate context and in the actor's previous experience; and investigating the parameters of motivationally effective self-reward and self-punishment (e.g., Bandura, 1977; Kanfer & Duerfeldt, 1967; Karoly & Kanfer, 1974a, 1974b; Kazdin, 1974; Kirschenbaum & Karoly, 1977; Mischel & Liebert, 1966; Thoresen & Mahoney, 1974).

Also, it became evident that the three-stage model was in need of supplementation. Kanfer (1977) noted the increased reliance upon cognitive constructs to enhance the predictive accuracy of the model. Among the variables coming under increased scrutiny are: attributional processes, physiological mediators, social influences, developmental determinants, motivational factors, language, and self-instructional processes (Kanfer, 1977; Kanfer & Hagerman, 1981; Karoly, 1981; Meichenbaum, 1977; Staats, 1975).

Of course, other conceptual models have relied much less upon a behavioral or S-R learning framework and have dealt directly with many of the aforementioned cognitive and personality-oriented concerns in the analysis of self-control and self-regulation. Among the outstanding systematizers is Walter Mischel, whose contributions in three major subareas will be summarized, to complete this selective review of the social learning literature.

Determinants of Delay Choice

Social learning theory has long relied upon an Expectancy × Value model as a basis for integrating the cognitive and the direct reinforcement views of behavior control (Rotter, 1954). Conceptualizing self-control as the tendency to prefer delayed larger over immediate smaller rewards, social learning researchers naturally looked to differential expectancies and/or differential reward values as potential mediators of children's delay choices. Mahrer (1956), a student of Rotter, published the first experiment clearly linking children's expectancy of future reward delivery (i.e., their trust in the promises of the adult experimenter) to stated preferences for delayed rewards over immediate smaller rewards. Mischel, also a student of Rotter, has demonstrated, via the most fully integrated and imaginative series of studies on children's delay preferences, that choice is a complex function of situational, personal, temporal, and consequential factors.

As summarized by Mischel (1974), children's willingness to defer immediate gratification varies partly as a result of:

- Positive expectations that the delayed rewards will actually be available
- Stability of the subjective value of the anticipated rewards
- The length of the delay (with longer delays apparently reducing the desirability of postponing gratification)
- Individual difference dimensions, such as age, general intelligence, socioeconomic status, and achievement orientation (all correlating positively with delay choice)
- Prior reward for waiting (i.e., the receipt of promised delayed rewards)
- Exposure to models who are consistently rewarded for self-imposed delays
- The child's momentary emotional state prior to the choice between immediate or delayed outcomes (i.e., children feeling "good" or "successful" are more willing to pick large delayed rewards)

Cognitive Transformations

Dealing not just with delay choice, but with actual (measured) propensities to sustain or "tolerate" a waiting period, Mischel and his colleagues have actively investigated the psychological "mechanisms" hypothesized to facilitate self-imposed delay in children. In one of the early studies, Mischel and Ebbesen (1970) asked preschoolers to pay attention either to the delayed or to the immediately available reward, or to neither, in an effort to determine which tactic would enhance their delay times. Attention to the delayed reward was expected to assist the children in "time-binding." The results proved not to support such a contention, as children's attention to rewards interfered with their ability to successfully wait for them. Speculating that the delay might in fact be an aversive or frustrating event, Mischel, Ebbesen, and Zeiss (1972) suggested that "delay of gratification should be enhanced when the subject can readily transform the aversive waiting period into a more pleasant nonwaiting situation" (p. 205).

Self-distractive mechanisms thus became the objects of study. In a series of experiments, Mischel and his co-workers determined that overt or cognitive distractions tended to enhance delay; that what the child thought about or imaged made a difference (fun thoughts facilitated, sad thoughts reduced the delay); that symbolically presented rewards (pictures) enhanced delay, as opposed to exposure to the actual rewards themselves; and that children who cognitively transformed symbolic rewards to "real" acted much like those who were confronted with real rewards—that is, they evidenced shortened delay times. These findings led to speculations about the mechanisms of cognitive transformations during delay. Mischel and his associates reasoned that it may not matter whether the rewards are real or symbolic, but rather that the child's transformation allows him or her to maintain a focus upon the *informational* as opposed to the *arousal* aspects of the tempting stimuli (Mischel & Baker, 1975; Moore, Mischel & Zeiss, 1976; Moore, 1977).

Plans

The fact that a cognitive focus upon the information value of rewards facilitates the child's ability to delay suggests that an active stance with regard to the environment may be a fundamental requirement of successful adaptation. However useful the three-stage (self-observation, self-evaluation, self-administered consequences) model may have been in the early development of a social-learning conception of self-management, it has become clear that it can be supplemented by an information-processing view point, with its emphasis on continuous representational processes. Mischel and his colleagues (particularly Charlotte Patterson) have therefore undertaken a program of basic experiments dealing with *plans* as they influence children's performance on complex and repetitive self-control tasks. The importance of this line of investigation lies in its potential for uncovering the specific elements that impede or facilitate task completion, in contrast to the search for global or unitary correlates of self-management (like IQ or ego strength).

Most of the *planning* experiments have been structured as follows: Preschoolers are seated at a table, before a large machine called "Mr. Clown Box." Also in the room are two sets of toys, "fun toys" and "broken toys," either of which will be available for the children's amusement later in the experiment. All of the children, when asked, indicate a desire to play with the fun toys. However, before doing so, the children are presented with another task, usually a rather dull and repetitive one. The children are told that they must work at the boring task until the experimenter returns, at which time, if the children have followed instructions, they shall have the opportunity to play with the fun toys. What about the Clown Box? This apparatus simulates the "devil" in real-life temptation situations. That is, while the children are working in order to earn the privilege of playing with interesting toys, the Clown Box calls to them, beckoning the children to play with it, to watch and listen to it instead of working. The experimental questions deal with determining what "cognitive-attentional" activities the child might employ to successfully resist the persistent Clown Box, and continue working. Note that both the self-control *and* self-regulatory aspects of self-management are included in such an arrangement.

Patterson and Mischel's (1975) first study demonstrated that nursery school children could make use of preselected "plans" for structuring their time during the work and temptation periods. Children with plans spent proportionally more time working than did those without plans. The specific attentional focus of children's plans was investigated next. Patterson and Mischel (1976) found that a self-instructional plan which directed children away from the tempting Clown Box facilitated performance to a greater degree than plans focussing on how to continue working on the repetitive task. Mischel and Patterson (1976) later demonstrated that "reward-oriented plans" (i.e., plans that focus the children's attention on the payoff associated with continued work) are likewise facilitative of appropriate performance and that "elaborated" plans, wherein the experimenter specified the wording and the nature of the self-instruction, are important determinants of effective self-management.

Most recently, Mischel and his associates have focused their research efforts on children's knowledge or understanding of the strategies for effective delay of gratification. Such an emphasis is consistent with the movement within cognitive psychology toward the exploration of basic data structures (scripts, frames, metamemory, schemata, etc.) underlying information processing. According to the results of their laboratory experiments (e.g., Mischel, Mischel, & Hood, Note 1) children younger than age 5 tend, for the most part, to think (counterproductively) about what they cannot immediately have. But by the third grade, most youngsters can spontaneously produce a number of "waiting strategies" that (according to previous laboratory findings) should work for them. Sixth-grade children, according to Mischel, are quite sophisticated in their understanding of what it takes to effectively delay gratification. Of course, the connecting links between knowledge and action remain to be more fully explored, in adults as well as in children (Fishbein, 1980; Karoly, 1981).

THE CURRENT STATUS OF THEORY AND PRACTICE

In clinical psychology generally and in the area of self-management specifically, the extent of the cross-fertilization between the laboratory and the clinic has been disappointing. In particular, the needs of the practitioner have chronically gone unattended (e.g., Barlow, 1981). However, if the separation between the researcher and the service-provider were total or irreconcilable, the journals would continue to insist primarily upon statistical significance and adherence to procedural fine points and clinicians would largely ignore the books, audio cassettes, and continuing education opportunities offered by their academic colleagues. Clearly, communication does exist; indeed, many of the so-called ivory tower academic types are themselves practicing clinicians. The fact that professional journals are beginning to insist upon follow-ups to therapy outcome studies, to expect that improvements be indexed normatively rather than just statistically, to look askance at college-freshmen-based therapy programs, and to call for the analysis of clinical failures, client-therapy congruence, cost-effectiveness of treatment, and the durability of change all suggest that the broad criterion of ecological validity has not been completely lost on the academic community.

It would appear that unworkable theory (that is, theoretical views that are either too broad or too narrow) doesn't survive indefinitely. The brief historical overview I have just provided illustrates the sometimes subtle movement away from extreme viewpoints in both psychoanalysis and S-R psychology and the concomitant nurturance, especially over the last 15 years, of a clinically workable cognitive-social learning position. Despite the fact that the essence of the psychodynamic viewpoint has not been altered radically (so that many of its adherents continue to treat mainly their own constructions of their clients' problems) and that a nonmediational, natural-science model of learning is flourishing within behavior modification, the trend in self-management psychology is definitely toward both a conceptual and practical allegiance to the tenets of interactionism.

We have come a long way since willpower, abreaction, catharsis, and self-actualization were considered as useful explanatory concepts. And, for many of us, the heritage of what I like to call *Kansas Common Law* (that all events are externally caused unless proven otherwise) has now been put into its proper historical perspective. But there is really very little justification for complacency. We have a long way yet to travel.

In parts II and III of this volume, a distinguished group of clinician-researchers provide a detailed accounting of the state of the art in clinical self-management. The reader may be impressed by both what is and isn't contained in these chapters.

First, on the positive side of the ledger is the sheer scope of the self-management enterprise. Self-direction is a basic component of a *com-*

petence or *skills* approach to personality, psychopathology, rehabilitation, education, and prevention as well as being essential to the new look in psychotherapy. In fact, in a recent poll of 36 therapist-researchers (Prochaska & Norcross, Note 2), responding to a 100-item survey on the future of psychotherapy, self-change methods emerged as the top ranked form of "intervention" predicted to increase in use over the next 10 years. Also among the top 12 modalities predicted as growing in popularity were cognitive restructuring, problem-solving, imagery-based methods, self-control procedures, homework assignments, behavioral contracting, and biofeedback. The respondents to the survey expected to find that, on average, 60 percent of therapy outcome would be determined by or attributable to the clients' efforts. Despite the admittedly biased sampling of prognosticators, their predictions certainly reflect a growing interest in active problem solving, self-reliance, and "consumerism" among the general public as well as among professionals.

A related dimension of the self-change and self-maintenance perspective is a movement away from prepackaged therapies toward *treatment tailoring*. While not an exclusive concern of self-management adherents, a trend is nonetheless evident in the assessment and treatment models described in Parts II and III of this book that places a premium upon the determination of specific client needs and abilities and the role of the client's unique social environment as facilitative and/or disruptive of therapeutic goals. As the field has developed beyond its early vision of self-control and self-regulation as unitary states of the organism, amenable to *before-after* comparisons, clinical investigators have begun to move toward multilevel and continued assessments of both personal and environmental "readiness" to support self-management efforts.

Another important shift in focus is captured by the concept of *lifestyle*. Self-management requires more than a temporary change in setting conditions or the acquisition of specific strategies. For therapeutic change to be maintained, the individual must be prepared, by virtue or his or her mode of information processing, the adequacy of active coping skills, and by dint of having selected a supportive social setting (friends, co-workers, spouse, etc.) to deal with unforeseen challenges, conflicts, periods of deprivation, and/or the periodic malfunctioning of "best laid plans." A person's lifestyle may alter a problematic pattern, but at the cost of setting the stage for a new source of difficulty. Thus, there is never a guarantee of perpetual success; and clinicians can do no more than help their clients anticipate the future, insofar as that is possible, and assist their clients in evaluating the pros and cons of varied activities and in knowing how to decide what is in their best interests. Self-management efforts are unlikely to be maintained if clients are merely learning how to behave in accordance with standards that are foreign to them. Therefore, an essential ingredient of a sophisticated *self-*

management as lifestyle treatment program, notably with clients who are ambivalent about their choices, is a process of value(s) clarification. Similarly, for individuals who are strongly committed to incentives associated with behavior patterns that are "high risk" (e.g., the adventuresomeness that often accompanies drug exploration, criminal activities and gambling or the relief from discomfort that sometimes accompanies smoking, drinking, truancy, etc.), there is no reason to assume that the mere teaching of specific strategies (self-instruction, self-administered relaxation, and the like) will have any lasting impact. For those persons committed to "maladaptive" values, the process of therapy becomes decidedly less collaborative or "negotiable" than is characteristic of the self-management model.

A decade ago, the analogy of a "lion's den" was used to illustrate the trepidation with which empirically minded investigators entered into the study and supposed manipulation of the covert processes underlying self-direction (Kanfer & Karoly, 1972). Today, the diversity of self-management approaches and their popularity among students and professionals would seem to suggest that the den has been all but cleared of dangers. This new "fearlessness" has produced some clear advantages over first generation behavior modification techniques (as well as some problems, to be discussed later in this chapter). First, what has been termed cognitive-behavior modification (or CBM; see Meichenbaum, 1977) has sought to encourage clinicians to be jointly concerned with the mechanics of training (practice, feedback, reinforcement contingencies, and so forth) as well as with the client's readiness to learn (as indexed by attentional parameters, outcome expectancies, language skills and deficiencies, intellectual boundaries, values, and understandings and misunderstandings of the causes and consequences of current behavior and its alteration, among other things). The client simply cannot be viewed as a passive responder; particularly not when long-term, self-maintained change is the desired goal. When the client's perceptions and interpretations are considered "responses" to be predicted and/or controlled, the empty-organism image of behavioral psychology tends to dissipate, and clinicians are "permitted" to study what common sense has repeatedly offered as potentially important data.

The CBM movement has encouraged the expansion of the clinical measurement model to include "not only overt motor acts but also the client's thoughts, beliefs, values, and any other aspects that help the behavioral change agent to understand the client's objectives" (Nay, 1979, p. 2). Thus, in addition to the use of observational methods, the assessor interested in a comprehensive view of the client makes use of interview data, analogue or simulation tests, free-response written materials, standardized psychological tests, psychophysiological recording, reports by "significant others" in the client's life, the examination of contextual "baserates" and critical performance levels, and the analysis of theoretically or empirically derived component skills (see also Karoly, 1977, 1981). It is interesting to consider that CBM psychologists did not invent the multiplicity of procedures now considered legitimate. Rather, most of the methods have been recalled from the exile imposed by the behavioral movement. We are therefore reminded of what Heinz Werner used to say to his students about "advances" in psychology; namely, that psychologists "were in the habit of putting obstacles in their path, and then as they removed them, one by one, of calling attention to the progress they were making." The real test of progress in the assessment of covert processes and individual difference factors in self-management will require the demonstration of measurement reliability as well as the ability of assessors to integrate observational and subjective data into the stream of ongoing performance, so as to improve predictability and the power of clinical intervention.

And thus, we move to a fuller appraisal of the *it remains to be seen* aspects of human self-management psychology. It is the view of the editors and contributors to this volume that a great deal remains to be demonstrated before self-management can be considered a truly substantive clinical model.

The fundamental shortcoming of the contemporary cognitive-behavioral assault on clinical self-management problems is the paucity of evidence that a genuine integration of the psychologies of thought and action has in fact occurred, or that the largely technological approach to enhancement of self-directiveness has produced durable and generalizable outcomes in the extra-laboratory world. In addition, much of what is done in the name of self-control or self-regulation therapy remains relatively inexplicit, subject to alternative interpretations, and vague in regard to whether those strategies trained (often covert in nature) are actually employed over time and, if so, whether changes in outcome can be directly attributable to their use by clients (see also Hall, 1980; Jeffrey, 1974; Karoly, Note 3; Mahoney & Arnkoff, 1978).

The fact that contemporary clinician-researchers do not consider the notion of a "cognitive-behaviorism" to be a self-contradiction (Mahoney & Arnkoff, 1978) does not imply that inferences can be managed as easily as operants. As Hollon and Kendall (1979) have asked: "To what extent can cognitive processes be treated as covert behavioral phenomena? To what extent will their incorporation require new models and procedures?" (p. 448). Additional questions can be posed. Does calling a process interactive, holistic, or cognitive-behavioral provide any pragmatic clues as to the nature of the interface between inner (cognitive) and outer (environmental), between cause and effect, or between the forces for continuity versus the forces for change within a system? How do we access the relevant process data when one cognitive event is invoked to alter the presumed consequence of another cognitive event? Can we establish firm linkages between cues, mediating events, and behavioral consequences to be able to affirm the existence of the mediators? Can any fixed or reconstructive approach to assessing the interaction of thoughts, images, and affective responses (i.e., association techniques, simulations, multidimensional scaling, multiple regression analyses, and the like) yield an accurate account of the moving or dynamic nature of these processes as they occur in the natural environment? What are the limits to cognitive control? Under what circumstances should the clinician look to setting factors, biological or physiological processes, or social forces to "carry the individual through" a behavioral impasse? It should be clear that at this point in the evolution of self-management via cognitive-behaviorism, the integration is largely between the epistemology of cognitivism and the procedures of behaviorism. Over the long run, only a conceptual synthesis with its own, congruent clinical procedures will qualify cognitive-behaviorism as a truly viable foundation for understanding and/or influencing self-direction (see Kanfer & Karoly's discussion in Chapter 16 for a further consideration of these issues).

There are also a number of problems with the clinical self-management literature that result simply from a narrowness of focus attributable, in part, to the apparent linearity of the process in the early behavioral accounts. Despite the message that self-management involves the ongoing evaluation of situational antecedents, internal stimuli, and the feedback from behavioral enactments upon the environment, the so-called sequential stages of self-monitoring, self-evaluation, and self-reward (self-punishment) became abstracted out as the necessary and sufficient instrumental steps toward self-directiveness. Little regard was shown (either in the laboratory or in the clinic) for the personal and environmental factors that might predispose the individual toward relapse, the motivational counterforces that might interfere with long-range success, or the multidimensional nature of the adaptive tasks of naturalistic self-management and/or of the therapeutic strategies needed to engineer and support self-control or self-regulation. The boundary conditions set by the person's unique history or biological-genetic makeup were largely downplayed by virtue of the questionable belief in the infinite *plasticity* of human behavior. The psychology of generalization was presumed to follow from the psychology of acquisition, and both were viewed primarily from the perspective of the laboratory rather than from the real world of alcoholic, drug addicted, chronically anxious, or mentally retarded clients.

Fortunately, we have been attuned to the data. And they have not supported the narrow-band approach. Reviewing the findings of self-management programs for obesity, cigarette smoking, alcohol abuse, and related disorders, Hall (1980) has noted:

Outcomes using self-management treatments, either alone or in combinaton with other techniques, are often superior to controls. However, although the course or relapse is slower, relapse rates remain high. We may find that they are equivalent to those noted in traditional treatments in the long term . . . we have not generated dramatic changes in the shape of the relapse curve for these disorders. (p. 287)

PLAN OF THE BOOK

In general, the chapters in Part I of this volume are directed toward filling the lacunae in our conceptions, while the chapters in Parts II and III address some (though certainly not all) of the assessment and treatment issues neglected by the first generation of self-management researcher-clinicians.

We shall discover, for example, that the notion of organism-environment reciprocity is central to definition of self-management—even from a "radical behavioral" perspective—as is the need to move beyond a static conception of the environment (Chapter 2). The "biopsychosocial" view of self-management, based on the concept of *homeostasis*, is introduced as providing a guiding framework for clinical intervention (above and beyond specific *techniques*), particularly in the ongoing management of internal and external cues that signal a discrepancy from an optimum bodily state (Chapter 3). In Chapter 4 the implications of an hierarchical, control-systems conception of information processing (likewise built upon a negative feedback loop) are addressed as applied to normal adult functioning. Both practitioners and researchers will find the authors' speculations about impediments to the complete functioning of the self-regulatory system, especially failures at the "higher levels of abstraction," to be of particular interest. The challenge of translating these ideas into workable interventions remains. The individual's capacity for the management of affect, mood, and attention (topics too long neglected in both the traditional psychodynamic and the learning theory accounts of self-direction) are addressed in Chapter 5. In the final conceptual contribution, the topics of self-monitoring, self-evaluation, and self-reward are examined within the context of child development, and a new understanding of motivation, commitment, and mastery (now often called *efficacy*) emerges. The editors sincerely hope that, to the extent that students and professionals deem it appropriate, new and creative efforts will be forthcoming to make practical use of the concepts discussed in Part I of this book.

Finally, in Parts II and III, a sampling will be presented of the most sophisticated programs of assessment and treatment of child, adolescent, and adult self-regulatory and self-control disorders currently available. Covered in these chapters are individual difference factors; component analysis and training procedures for developmentally delayed as well as normal children and adolescents; the application of the relapse prevention model to addictions; the use of the interpersonal skills model; the variety of methods for the self-mediated control of anxiety; and the role of self-regulation in the treatment of sexual dysfunctions and depression.

In the editors' epilogue (Part IV), attention is focused upon the lingering questions of how best to define the domain of self-management, the possible advantages of a dialectical view, the dangers of a retreat to pure cognitivism, and an assortment of practical concerns of the would-be self-management psychologist.

Let us therefore begin our journey of discovery with the view that human self-management consists of nothing less than the processes by which the individual controls the sources of variation in his or her own behavior. The sources of variability can be cognitive, affective, biophysical, chemical, or environmental, and all are time bound and context specific. The means of achieving control are largely through the enactment of intellective and behavioral skills. And the *fundamental prerequisites* for success include not only a task-specific instrumental repertoire, but a reasonably well defined internal goal or standard, the ability (or opportunity) to relate current functioning (cognitive, affective, behavioral, etc.) to the standard, and an accurate knowledge of the larger system (the peer group, family, vocational setting, etc.) within which compatible and/or incompatible standards may be operating in support of and/or opposition to the individual's pursuits.

An overview of the applied literature in self-control and self-regulation reveals that, at best, clinicians have assisted their clients toward the attainment of short-term success at self-management. An analysis of why the field has not achieved its hoped-for long-range results would, I believe, reveal that training efforts have largely focused on the building of task-specific repertories, ignoring the development and individual expression of the "fundamental prerequisites" cited above.

The present volume reflects both the current state of the art/science and the efforts that are being made to push back the borders of the discipline, however slowly and cautiously, so as to encompass all the hypothesized elements in human self-directiveness. The volume offers a balanced presentation of concepts, methods, and accomplishments along with philosophical debates, procedural discontinuities, and the clinical limitations of contemporary self-management psychology. By examining the past and the present, it is hoped that the future can be addressed, if only tentatively. By asking more questions than we answer, the contributors to this volume require neither faith in nor blind allegiance to the ideas expressed. Instead, the intent is to prime the reader's problem-solving capacities and to set in motion a self-correcting process of continuing inquiry, theory building, clinical application, rigorous self-scrutiny, and, of course, healthy skepticism.

REFERENCE NOTES

1. Mischel, W., Mischel, H. N., & Hood, S. Q. *The development of knowledge of effective ideation to delay gratification.* Unpublished manuscript. Stanford University.
2. Prochaska, J. O., & Norcross, J. C. *The future of psychotherapy: A Delphi poll.* Unpublished manuscript, University of Rhode Island.
3. Karoly, P. *On the failures of self-control interventions: Review and speculation.* Unpublished manuscript, University of Cincinnati.

REFERENCES

Ainslie, G. Specious reward: A behavioral theory of impulsiveness and impulse control. *Psychological Bulletin*, 1975, *82*, 463–496.

Aronfreed, J. *Conduct and conscience.* New York: Academic Press, 1968.

Azrin, N. H., & Holz, W. C. Punishment. In W. K. Honig (Ed.), *Operant behavior: Areas of research and application.* New York: Appleton-Century-Crofts, 1966.

Baer, D. M., & Sherman, J. A. Reinforcement control of generalized imitation in young children. *Journal of Experimental Child Psychology*, 1964, *1*, 37–49.

Bandura, A. *Social learning theory.* Englewood Cliffs, N.J.: Prentice-Hall, 1977.

Bandura, A., & Mischel, W. Modification of self-imposed delay of reward through exposure to live and symbolic models. *Journal of Personality and Social Psychology*, 1965, *2*, 698–705.

Bandura, A., & Walters, R. H. *Social learning and personality development.* New York: Holt, Rinehart & Winston, 1963.

Barlow, D. H. On the relation of clinical research to clinical practice: Current issues, new directions. *Journal of Consulting and Clinical Psychology*, 1981, *49*, 147–155.

Baum, W. M., & Rachlin, H. Choice as time allocation. *Journal of Experimental Analysis of Behavior*, 1969, *12*, 861–874.

Cheyne, J. A., & Walters, R. H. Punishment and prohibition: Some origins of self-control. *New directions in psychology.* New York: Holt, Rinehart & Winston, 1970.

Church, R. M. The varied effects of punishment on behavior. *Psychological Review*, 1963, *70*, 369–402.

Cronbach, L. J. The two disciplines of scientific psychology. *American Psychologist*, 1957, *12*, 671–684.

Dember, W. N. Motivation and the cognitive revolution. *American Psychologist*, 1974, *29*, 161–168.

Estes, W. K. An experimental study of punishment. *Psychological Monographs*, 1944, 57(3, Whole No. 263).

Fenichel, O. *The psychoanalytic theory of neurosis.* New York: Norton, 1945.

Fishbein, M. A theory of reasoned action: Some applications and implications. In H. E. Howe & M. M. Page (Eds.), *Nebraska Symposium on Motivation 1979: Beliefs, Attitudes, and Values.* Lincoln: University of Nebraska Press, 1980.

Frank, J. D. *Persuasion and healing.* Baltimore: Johns Hopkins University Press, 1973.

Freud, S. *The interpretation of dreams.* London: Hogarth, 1900.

Gardner, R. W., Holzman, P. S., Klein, G. S., Linton, H. B., & Spence, D. P. Cognitive control: A study of individual consistencies in cognitive behavior. *Psychological Issues*, Monograph 4. New York: International Universities Press, 1959.

Goldfried, M. R., & Merbaum, M. (Eds.), *Behavior change through self-control.* New York: Holt, Rinehart & Winston, 1973.

Goldiamond, I. Self-reinforcement. *Journal of Applied Behavior Analysis.* 1976, *9*, 509–514.

Hall, S. M. Self-management and therapeutic maintenance: Theory and research. In P. Karoly & J. J. Steffen (Eds.), *Improving the long-term effects of psychotherapy: Models of durable outcome.* New York: Gardner Press, 1980.

Harré, R., & Secord, P. F. *The explanation of social behavior.* Totowa, New Jersey: Rowman & Littlefield, 1972.

Hollon, S. D., & Kendall, P. C. Cognitive-behavioral interventions: Theory and procedure. In P. C. Kendall & S. D. Hollon (Eds.), *Cognitive-behavioral interventions: Theory, research, and procedures.* New York: Academic Press, 1979.

Jeffrey, D. B. Self-control: Methodoligical issues and research trends. In M. J. Mahoney & C. E. Thoresen (Eds.), *Self-control: Power to the person.* Monterey, Calif.: Brooks/Cole, 1974.

Kanfer, F. H. Self-regulation: Research, issues, and speculation. In C. Neuringer & J. L. Michael (Eds.), *Behavior modification in clinical psychology.* New York: Apple-Century-Crofts, 1970.

Kanfer, F. H. The many faces of self-control, or behavior modification changes its focus. In R. B. Stuart (Ed.), *Behavioral self-management: Strategies, techniques, and outcome.* New York: Brunner/Mazel, 1977.

Kanfer, F. H., & Duerfeldt, P. H. Motivational properties of self-reinforcement. *Perceptual and Motor Skills,* 1967, *25,* 237–246.

Kanfer, F. H., and Hagerman, S. The role of self-regulation. In L. P. Rehm (Ed.), *Behavior therapy for depression: Present status and future directions.* New York: Academic Press, 1981.

Kanfer, F. H., & Karoly, P. Self-control: A behavioristic excursion into the lion's den. *Behavior Therapy,* 1972, *3,* 398–416.

Kanfer, F. H., & Phillips, J. S. *Learning foundations of behavior therapy.* New York: Wiley, 1970.

Karoly, P. Behavioral self-management in children: Concepts, methods, issues, and directions. In M. Hersen, R. M. Eisler, & P. M. Miller (Eds.), *Progress in behavior modification* (Vol. 5). New York: Academic Press, 1977.

Karoly, P. Self-management problems in children. In E. J. Mash & L. G. Terdal (Eds.), *Behavioral assessment of childhood disorders.* New York: Guilford Press, 1981.

Karoly, P., & Kanfer, F. H. Situational and historical determinants of self-reinforcement. *Behavior Therapy,* 1974, *5,* 381–390. (a)

Karoly, P., & Kanfer, F. H. Effects of prior contractual experiences on self-control in children. *Developmental Psychology,* 1974, *10,* 459–460. (b)

Kazdin, A. E. Self-monitoring and behavior change. in M. J. Mahoney & C. E. Thoresen (Eds.), *Self-control: Power to the person.* Monterey, Calif.: Brooks/Cole, 1974.

Kelly, G. A. *The psychology of personal constructs.* New York: Norton, 1955.

Kendall, P. C., & Hollon, S. D. (Eds.), *Assessment strategies for cognitive-behavioral interventions.* New York: Academic Press, 1981.

Kirschenbaum, D. S., & Karoly, P. When self-regulation fails: Tests of some preliminary hypotheses. *Journal of Consulting and Clinical Psychology,* 1977, *45,* 1116–1125.

Klausner, S. Z. (Ed.), *The quest for self-control.* New York: Free Press, 1965.

Klein, G. S. Peremptory ideation: Structure and force in motivated ideas. In R. Jessor & S. Feshbach (Eds.), *Cognition, personality, and clinical psychology.* San Francisco: Jossey-Bass, 1968.

Klein, G. S. *Psychoanalytic theory: An exploration of essentials.* New York: International Universities Press, 1976.

Klinger, E. Modes of normal conscious flow. In K. S. Pope & J. L. Singer (Eds.), *The stream of consciousness.* New York: Plenum, 1978.

Liebert, R. M., Poulos, R. W., & Strauss, G. D. *Developmental psychology.* Englewood Cliffs, N.J.: Prentice-Hall, 1974.

Mahoney, M. J. *Cognition and behavior modification.* Cambridge, Mass.: Ballinger, 1974.

Mahoney, M. J., & Arnkoff, D. B. Cognitive and self-control therapies. In S. L. Garfield & A. E. Bergin (Eds.), *Handbook of psychotherapy and behavior change* (2nd edition). New York: Wiley, 1978.

Mahrer, A. R. The role of expectancy in delayed reinforcement. *Journal of Experimental Psychology*, 1956, *52*, 101–106.

Meichenbaum, D. *Cognitive-behavior modification.* New York: Plenum, 1977.

Miller, N. E., and Dollard, J. *Social learning and imitation.* New Haven, Conn.: Yale University Press, 1941.

Mischel, W. Processes in delay of gratification. In L. Berkowitz (Ed.), *Advances in experimental social psychology* (Vol. 7). New York: Academic Press, 1974.

Mischel, W., & Baker, N. Cognitive appraisals and transformations in delay behavior. *Journal of Personality and Social Psychology*, 1975, *31*, 254–261.

Mischel, W., & Ebbesen, E. B. Attention in delay of gratification. *Journal of Personality and Social Psychology*, 1970, *16*, 329–337.

Mischel, W., Ebbesen, E. G., & Zeiss, A. R. Cognitive and attentional mechanisms in delay of gratification. *Journal of Personality of Social Psychology*, 1972, *21*, 204–218.

Mischel, W., & Liebert, R. M. Effects of discrepancies between observed and imposed reward criteria on their acquisition and transmission. *Journal of Personality and Social Psychology*, 1966, *3*, 45–53.

Moore, B. S. Cognitive representation of rewards in delay of gratification. *Cognitive Therapy and Research*, 1977, *1*, 73–83.

Moore, B. S., Mischel, W., & Zeiss, A. Comparative effects of the reward stimulus and its cognitive representation in voluntary delay. *Journal of Personality and Social Psychology*, 1976, *34*, 419–424.

Mowrer, O. H. On the delights, and dire consequences of conscience killing. In R. C. Johnson, P. R. Dokecki, & O. H. Mowrer (Eds.), *Conscience, contract, and social reality.* New York: Holt, Rinehart & Winston, 1972.

Nay, W. R. *Multimethod clinical assessment.* New York: Gardner Press, 1979.

Parke, R. D. Rules, roles, and resistance to deviation: Recent advances in punishment, discipline, and self-control. In A. Pick (Ed.), *Minnesota Symposia on Child Psychology* (Vol. 8). Minneapolis: University of Minnesota Press, 1974.

Patterson, C. J., & Mischel, W. Plans to resist distraction. *Developmental Psychology*, 1975, *11*, 369–378.

Pope, K. S., & Singer, J. L. (Eds.), *The stream of consciousness: Scientific investigations into the flow of human experience.* New York: Plenum, 1978.

Rachlin, H. Self-control. *Behaviorism*, 1974, *2*, 94–107.

Rachlin, H., & Green, L. Commitment, choice, and self-control. *Journal of the Experimental Analysis of Behavior*, 1972, *17*, 15–22.

Risley, T. R. The social context of self-control. In R. B. Stuart (Ed.), *Behavioral self-management.* New York: Brunner/Mazel, 1977.

Risley, T. R., & Hart, B. Developing correspondence between the non-verbal and verbal behavior of preschool children. *Journal of Applied Behavior Analysis*, 1968, *1*, 267–281.

Rogers, C. R. *On becoming a person.* Boston: Houghton-Mifflin, 1961.

Rosenthal, T. L., & Zimmerman, B. J. *Social learning and cognition.* New York: Academic Press, 1978.

Rotter, J. B. *Social learning and clinical psychology.* Englewood Cliffs, N.J.: Prentice-Hall, 1954.

Rychlak, J. F. *Discovering free will and personal responsibility.* New York: Oxford University Press, 1979.

Sears, R. R., Maccoby, E. E., & Levin, H. *Patterns of child rearing.* Evanston, Ill.: Row Peterson, 1957.

Skinner, B. F. *The behavior of organisms.* New York: Appleton-Century-Crofts, 1938.

Skinner, B. F. *Science and human behavior.* New York: Macmillan, 1953.

Solomon, R. L. Punishment. *American Psychologist,* 1964, *19,* 239–253.

Solomon, R. L., Turner, L. H., & Lessac, M. S. Some effects of delay of punishment on resistance to temptation in dogs. *Journal of Personality and Social Psychology,* 1968, *8,* 233–238.

Staats, A. W. *Social behaviorism.* Homewood, Ill.: Dorsey, 1975.

Stuart, R. B. Situational versus self-control. In R. D. Rubin, H. Fensterheim, J. D. Henderson, & L. P. Ullmann (Eds.), *Advances in behavior therapy.* New York: Academic Press, 1972.

Thoresen, C. E., & Mahoney, M. J. *Behavioral self-control.* New York: Holt, Rinehart & Winston, 1974.

Walters, G. C., & Grusec, J. E. *Punishment.* San Francisco: W. H. Freeman, 1977.

Weimer, W. B. Psychotherapy and philosophy of science: Examples of a two-way street in search of traffic. In M. J. Mahoney (Ed.), *Psychotherapy Process.* New York: Plenum, 1980.

Whiting, J. W. M. Sorcery, Sin, and the superego: A cross-cultural study of some mechanisms of social control. In M. R. Jones (Ed.), *Nebraska Symposium on Motivation.* Lincoln: University of Nebraska Press, 1959.

2

Self-Management: A Radical Behavioral Perspective*
Thomas Brigham

> We know already that there is a time when the female fly
> prefers protein, which cannot nourish her own body, to
> sugar, which is an adequate food for her but useless for her
> eggs. Here is an example of survival of the individual being
> subordinated to survival of the species. *In some quarters it
> would be hailed as maternal instinct, and by so naming it
> we would be no nearer an understanding of what it is.*
>
> — V. G. Dethier, 1962, emphasis added

It may seem odd to begin a chapter on self-management with a quote concerning the eating patterns of the common fly, but Dethier's point is a general one about language and explanation, which is germane to the analysis of human behavior as well. In this instance, the editors of the

*The analysis of self-management presented here is a result of reading and interpreting the work of many investigators. In most instances I have not cited positions similar to mine. The reader will recognize the liberal borrowing from such theorists as Skinner, Rachlin, Catania, our editors Kanfer and Karoly, and even those theorists whose overall positons I have rejected such as Bandura and Mahoney. Parts of earlier papers on self-control appear in this analysis of self-management. Prose and one table from "Self-control," which was originally published in A. C. Catania and T. A. Brigham (Eds.), *The Handbook of Applied Behavior Analysis* (New York: Irvington Press, 1978) is reprinted with the permission of the editors and publisher. Prose from "Self-control Revisited," originally published in *The Behavior Analyst*, is reprinted with the permission of the Association for Behavior Analysis.

volume have chosen to use the term "self-management" in the title rather than "self-control." Presently no general consensus exists in the general area of research and treatment that dictates how each term should be used. From a radical behavioral perspective, however, there are good reasons for using "self-management" to describe a particular type of response repertoire displayed by an individual and for reserving the term "self-control" solely to denote certain types of response contingencies which cause difficulties for the individual.

A major reason for preferring the term "self-management" to describe the behavior of the individual has to do with word usage. Clearly, the manner in which words are utilized has important implications for the analysis of the phenomenon in question. As Dethier (1962) and others (e.g., Rapaport, 1953) have noted, labeling often tends to be confused with explanation; especially when the label appears in the noun form rather than the adjective form. In common usage the term "self-control" is consistently employed as a noun while "self-management" more frequently appears as an adjective. For example, the sentence "Sally has a great deal of self-control," seems complete and stands on its own. Further, the statement can be easily interpreted as an explanation of Sally's behavior. On the other hand, "Sally has a great deal of self-management," is an awkward sentence and needs another word to complete it. The sentence is better rewritten as, "Sally displays a great many self-management responses or self-management skills." The term "self-management" itself tends to force the focus of the analysis on what the individual does. In contrast, the term "self-control" implies existence of a special entity called the self. After hypothesizing the self, the question "What does the self control?" follows. Again by implication, the self controls the individual's behavior. This interpretation of the term logically leads investigators to pursue an internal search for the self and its parts.

A related difficulty is that by focusing on the self, well-documented behavioral processes become transformed from observable environmental events to inferred cognitive events. Similarly, behavioral principles change from accounts of these observable events to speculations about hypothesized cognitive processes. The following illustration of self-reinforcement appears in a well-known text on self-control, after a careful and well-done presentation of positive reinforcement:

A professor we know reported that he developed the bad habit of bluntly telling others when he thought they were not acting very intelligently. "What do you think reinforces this behavior?" he was asked. "I guess it's the feeling that I have that I am smart. By showing others when they do something dumb, it shows them that I am smart. The trouble is, of course, that it makes them angry." We suggested that he could gain the same reinforcer (feeling intelligent) by intelligently choosing a positive statement instead of making some deprecating remark. (Watson & Tharp, 1972, pp. 102–104).

Although the professor of the anecdote may have taken an initial step in a behavioral analysis of his actions (i.e., the observation that this particular response makes others angry), the difficulty is that here, apparently without notice, the definition of a reinforcer has changed from the observation of an environmental event to the identification of a feeling about behavior. Similarly, the basis for identifying a reinforcer has changed from a functional demonstration of an increase in the frequency of a behavior to an introspective analysis.

Clearly this manner of defining and identifying reinforcers alters the basis of explanation from behavior/environment interactions to the functioning of the internal self. Self-reinforcement is controlled not by environmental events, but by self-determined standards of performance, and those standards are inside the organism mediating the influence of environmental variables on behavior (Bandura, 1977). Whether the standard is inside the self is unclear at this time; but the opportunity to develop a new set of ids, egos, and superegos certainly exists here. Also apparently inside are self-instructions and discriminations. And what are these things? Thoughts, cognitions, cognitive states, and/or cognitive structures are some of the major candidates for the status of explanatory concepts (Meichenbaum, 1974). As cognitive events rather than behavioral processes become the target of therapeutic interventions, the clarity of the behavioral analysis is lost. Such ambiguity, however, could be avoided if investigators attend to the responses in question. From a radical behavioral perspective, the theoretical issue for psychologists should not be "What is self-control?" but rather "How does the individual manage his or her behavior?"

Obviously there are a number of issues concerning self-management where there is a divergence of approach and analysis between cognitive behaviorists and radical behaviorists. As a first step in the elaboration of a radical behavioral position on self-management, three areas where a radical behavioral position clearly differs from that of current cognitive approaches to self-management will be examined in detail. They are: self-reinforcement, reciprocity, and the role of conscious private events.

SELF-REINFORCEMENT

As an interest in self-management approaches to dealing with behavior problems evolved in the late sixties and early seventies, not unexpectedly, one of the first procedures to be applied in this new approach was positive reinforcement. In many ways, this choice was not unreasonable. Positive reinforcement has proven to be an extremely powerful technique in behavior modification programs, and the extention of the procedure to instances where the individual provides positive reinforcement for his or her own behavior seemed to be the next logical step. The logic and rhetoric of self-reinforcement have proven to be very popular; and current self-reinforcement is a key if not the major theoretical and procedural component of most conceptualization of self-management. Nonetheless, at this time, the focus of self-management systems on self-reinforcement appears to be overly simplistic. There are both theoretical and practical reasons why this emphasis seems misplaced. First, the origins of the concept of self-reinforcement are at least in part based on a misinterpretation of Skinner's discussion of the possible role of positive reinforcement in self-control (Skinner, 1953). For instance, a fairly common attribution to Skinner is found in the following passage: "Skinner (1953) suggests that one of the ways in which individuals control their own behavior is by the administration of rewards to themselves without environmental restrictions and contingent upon certain behavior" (Rehm & Marston, 1968). The most straightforward interpretation of this passage is that Skinner advocates self-reinforcement as a method of changing behavior. Skinner's actual verbal behavior was somewhat less positive.

After describing a possible example of self-reinforcement, Skinner goes on to analyze the example:

> Something of this sort unquestionably happens, but is it operant reinforcement? It is certainly roughly parallel to the procedure in conditioning the behavior of another person. *But it must be remembered that the individual may at any moment drop the work in hand and obtain the reinforcement. We have to account for his not doing so.* It may be that such indulgent behavior has been punished—say, with disapproval—except when a piece of work has just been completed. The indulgent behavior will therefore generate strong averse stimulation except at such a time. The individual finishes the work in order to indulge himself free of guilt. (Skinner, 1953, chapter XII, emphasis added)
>
> The ultimate question is whether the consequence has any strengthening effect upon the behavior which precedes it. Is the individual more likely to do a similar piece of work in the future? It would not be surprising if he were not, although we must agree that he has arranged a sequence of events in which certain behavior has been followed by a reinforcing event. (Skinner, 1953, chapter XV, p. 238)

It is difficult to interpret these passages from Skinner as a suggestion that self-reward or self-reinforcement is likely to be an effective procedure for modifying one's own behavior. Skinner has noted the procedural similarity between operant reinforcement and self-reinforcement, but he has also recognized that some other process is required to account for the self-reinforcement behavior itself. Because this issue has been the focus of the exchanges between Bandura and Catania and those between Goldiamond and Mahoney, rather than continue the discussion here, the reader is referred to those authors' papers (see References).

Leaving aside the theoretical arguments concerning self-reinforcement procedures, there is the practical question raised by Skinner: Do they work? Currently, there seems to be a general consensus in the field that they are effective behavior-change techniques. O'Leary and Dubey (1979), writing in the *Journal of Applied Behavior Analysis*, concluded that "Self-reinforcement is clearly one of the most powerful self-control procedures—effective when used alone, incremental when added to other procedures, and equal to or better than external reinforcement." This is certainly a ringing and definitive endorsement of self-reinforcement. However, the evidence they muster in support of this conclusion does not appear to warrant such a positive assessment. In all, 10 studies are cited to support the thesis. Of these, only two were conducted in applied settings (see Baer, 1979 on the importance of applied research for testing principles) and neither of these met the Bandura and Mahoney (1974) criterion on self-reinforcement—that the reinforcer be freely and continuously available to the subject whether the response is emitted or not. Most of the other studies are only tangentially related to the author's conclusions. For instance, the authors cite a study by Kanfer, Karoly, and Newman (1975) as demonstrating that the statement "I am a brave boy (girl); I can take care of myself in the dark" was a self-reinforcer which increased the time children spent in the dark. Kanfer et al., however, referred to the "I am a brave boy (girl)" statement as a verbal controlling response. The statement was not voluntarily emitted by the subjects contingent on any behavior, but rather was elicited by the experimenters on cue in the treatment condition. In fact, Kanfer et al. report that the statement was never verbalized by the subjects in the subsequent test sessions. They speculate that the children may have covertly emitted the response, but they indicated there was no evidence to suggest that the students actually did so. A careful reading of the study's procedures indicates that the statement was never used as a contingent stimulus, and, as Kanfer et al. note, it more likely functioned as some form of antecedent instruction to set a high criterion for staying in the dark. Such antecedent statements have been consistently demonstrated to affect behaviors (e.g., Hartig & Kanfer, 1973; Karoly & Briggs, 1978), and in the current analysis would fit within the context of environmental restructuring or commitment responses. Irrespective of the precise theoretical interpretation of the procedures, the statement clearly had antecedent and not reinforcement functions. It is probably the case that O'Leary and Dubey inferred that the statement was a reinforcer because of its content, and not because of how it actually functioned in the study. To date, unequivocal empirical evidence to support the notion of self-reinforcement as an effective applied procedure is almost nonexistent and certainly does not justify the major role that self-reinforcement has been given in most treatments of self-management.

RECIPROCITY

Another notion that has created controversy between radical behaviorists and cognitive behaviorists is that of reciprocity. Simply stated, reciprocity refers to the mutual effects of two variables on each other: A may be viewed as the cause of B, while from a different perspective, B may be analyzed as the cause of A. In psychology, cognitive behaviorists have suggested that the analysis of behavior as a function of environmental events is arbitrary and that changes in the environment may be analyzed in terms of changes in the organisms's behavior (Bandura, 1971; Mahoney, 1974). Reciprocity, in and of itself, is not a concept antithetical to a radical behavioral analysis of behavior. Skinner's basic definition of the operant consists of the effects that a response has on the environment and how those changes in turn influence the frequency of that particular response. The fact that psychologists generally concern themselves with manipulating the environment to produce behavior change does not rule out the possibility of other relations holding. The environment of an older nonlanguage child is considerably different from that of a chid possessing functional language. If the nonlanguage child acquires functional language, that acquisition alters his or her environment in that what was noise is now the discriminative stimuli or reinforcement for words. Although applied behavior analysts may be more interested in the environmental changes that produced the language acquisition, it may be equally important to examine the environmental changes produced by the new language responses. In the second case, it is appropriate to plot the environmental changes as a function of behavior change. By doing so, it might be discovered that some classes of language responses produce greater environmental change than others. Such a finding, in turn, could be important for designing language-acquisition programs.

Upon analysis, then, the concept of reciprocity or the desirability of sometimes analyzing environmental change as a function of behavior change is not in question between the radical behaviorists and the cognitive behaviorists. Rather, how the cognitive behaviorists use the concept is in dispute. Mahoney (1974) correctly argues that the notion of reciprocity need not result in the "mental way stations" so eloquently opposed by Skinner. Unfortunately, though, the cognitive-behavior concept of reciprocity centers not on the behavior/environment interactions, but rather on the role of the individual's conscious cognitions in these interactions. For instance, the extensive locus-of-control literature often employs reciprocity as an explanatory concept, but, here, the individual's actual abilities to affect the environment are not of major importance; instead, it is the individual's perceptions. Mahoney (1974) illustrates the importance of personal belief with the following example:

> A child's poor school performance, for example, may be partly affected by his personally inferred incompetence. By systematically altering that perception, academic performance may improve. The future direction taken by the belief-behavior cycle may then be a function of myriad influences — whether the child incorporates his new experiential feedback into a modified pattern of self-statements, whether success experience are appropriately scheduled to induce and maintain a resistant and enduring "internal" belief pattern, and so on. (p.216)

In the past, the behavior analysis of phenomena proceeded and succeeded at the level of responses and environmental events. As the center of concern changes from such easily identified events, the likelihood of producing functional relations decreases. Clearly within the theoretical perspective espoused by Mahoney, the concern shifts from individual skills to vaguely identified individual beliefs, and in turn, the possibility of developing useful relations between variables diminishes. Thus reciprocity, a reasonable and possibly valuable concept, becomes a vague conception of the relations between conscious events and behavior-environment changes.

CONSCIOUS PRIVATE EVENTS

The appropriate role of conscious events in the analysis of behavior is another important area of dispute between radical behaviorists and cognitive behaviorists. As Skinner has frequently argued, the individual's verbal report of private events may reveal to the community at large the external events of which the behavior in question is a function. Unfortunately, imprecise conditioning operations produce the verbal repertoire for describing private events. Many times in the process of acquiring a verbal repertoire, the relation between private events and external events is lost. As a consequence, both the individual and community frequently fail to understand communications about private events. Speaking colloquially, however, the individual's verbal behavior can be used as an indication of that individual's current understanding about how he or she interacts with the environment (that is, why the person believes he acts as he does). But do those reported beliefs cause the individual to act in that specific manner? The quasi-mediational position of the cognitive behaviorists implies that beliefs, ideas, feelings, and so on do indeed cause one to act in a particular manner. But these private events themselves must be accounted for: "To say that a man strikes another because he feels angry still leaves the feeling of anger unexplained" (Skinner, 1953). Further, after the analysis of the antecedents of such behavior, one must once again ask, what role do they actually play? Rachlin (1977) has argued that conscious events do not cause behavior, but instead tell about behavior/environment interactions. Similarly, Jaynes (1977), in an extensive analysis of consciousness, suggested that consciousness is not the same as thinking, but rather metaphorically represents the individual's experience a la a road map. Although road maps contain much useful, often essential, information, the road map per se does not cause the driver to engage in any particular behavior; it simply provides information about the alternatives. Upon analysis, the metaphors chosen by cognitive behaviorists similarly lend themselves to a "road-map" or informational function for consciousness rather than a causal one. For instance, Meichenbaum, in discussing the internal dialogue, argues that it allows individuals to monitor their thoughts, wishes, feelings, and actions. This monitoring in turn causes them to behave in a particular manner. But to monitor means to observe or record the condition(s) of a particular system at a particular time. One does not say that a gauge measuring the changes of pressure in a system causes those changes. On the other hand, an observer discriminating the reading on the gauge may move to adjust some components of the system, thus changing the pressure. To elaborate, in the area of nuclear reactor safety, how a technician reads the dials in the control room affects his or her behavior and possibly our future. It is not, however, the dials that cause a particular behavior by the technician, but rather the technician's prior experience and training with regard to those specific dial readings. Further, those dials must accurately reflect the condition of the system. The resultant difficulties in the recent reactor breakdowns were not caused by the technician's attributions, but by the fact that the dials did not accurately reflect the environment. Analyzing the problem from this perspective, while the technicians must know how to react to various dial readings, the major therapy for nuclear safety would focus on making sure the dials accurately reflected the conditions of the reactor. Similarly, it is likely that many reports of private events do not accurately reflect environment-behavior interactions, and again the therapy would consist of teaching the appropriate discriminations to the individual. Because such an operation would involve the individual's verbal behavior, it might be interpreted as "cognitive." The individual's verbal behavior, however, changes, not because of some independent private event, but because of the changes in behavior/environment contingencies.

The literature on cognitive self-instruction seems particularly susceptible to the mislabeling of procedures modifying behavior/environment interactions as cognitive ones. For instance, a recent study compared cognitive self-instructions with contingency awareness and found that the self-instructions produced greater change in the target behavior of aggressive delinquent adolescents (Snyder & White, 1979). Although conservative, the authors concluded that "this suggests that treatment focusing on both external contingencies for desired behaviors and internal control of behavior by the use of private speech may be a potent behavior change strategy for aggressive delinquent adolescents" (p. 234). The interpretation of these results as a function of cognitive variables or causes seems to be a misinterpretation of the procedures due to the verbal nature of the manipulations. The cognitive self-instructions group was trained to identify specific problem situations by emitting a verbal response chain and then to behave in a manner consistent with the instructions. The authors provide the following example: Situation—a cottage counselor says, "time to get up." Verbalization—"Already, damn. It feels good to stay in bed, but if I get up I'll get the points I need for cigarettes. OK, just open my eyes, get up. Good, I made it." Subjects were also reinforced with tokens for appropriate behavior. In contrast, the contingency awareness group simply discussed the various contingencies in the token system. Thus, the cognitive self-instruction group learned to respond to immediate and specific stimuli within the problematic situations, while the contingency awareness group lacked such rehearsed stimuli or responses. The difference does not appear to be one of behavioral variables versus cognitive ones, but again, to use Jaynes' (1977) metaphor, one of the scale of the map. The self-instruction group had the equivalent of a city street map, whereas the discussion group was given a correct but less specific road map for the state. It is easier to get around London with a street map of London than with a map of England that includes only the major streets of London. The verbal nature of the training operations and the label "self-instructions" led the authors to interpret the causal variables as cognitive. From a radical behavioral perspective, to be valuable, private events must tact (i.e., serve a naming function) or be discriminative for behavior/environment interactions. In summary, cognitive discriminative stimuli undoubtedly were involved in the observed changes in the adolescents' behavior. However, those factors developed as a function of behavior/environment relations and will continue to serve only so long as the relations hold.

SELF-CONTROL PROBLEMS

Rather than focusing an analysis of self-management on the private events of individuals, from a radical behavioral perspective, it appears more logical to begin with an analysis of those situations which cause individuals difficulties. It was suggested earlier that these situations be labeled self-control problems. The majority, if not all, of the situations where the individual is said to have a self-control problem involve some difference between the immediate consequences of a response and its delayed consequences. Smoking is a good example of a response, the immediate consequences of which are positive for most smokers, but the accumulated delayed consequences of which are clearly negative. Smoking is further complicated because even when the delayed negative consequences occur, they are not easily discriminated by the individual. That is to say, not only are there no clear immediate aversive consequences, but the delayed consequences for each response (identified by medical research) are so small that they cannot be disciminated by the individual. Later, when consequences such as coughing, sore throat, and shortness of breath do appear, smoking has been additionally strengthened by other behavioral processes to the point where the response is still difficult to eliminate when the consequences change. A process that contributes to self-control problems is antecedent stimulus control. In the case of smoking, the response is easy to emit concurrent or in conjunction with other responses in a wide variety of settings. As smoking occurs consistently in many situations, these stimuli set the occasion for subsequent smoking. For example, many people smoke while drinking coffee. Because the two responses occur together, engaging in one may become a cue for the other. Later, when the smoker attempts to quit, the coffee provides powerful antecedent stimuli for smoking.

Another example of a self-control problem based on a difference between immediate and delayed consequences involves going to the dentist. This instance appears to consist of immediate aversive stimuli and larger delayed aversive consequences. Here the individual may not go to the dentist because the response is followed by some pain or discomfort and is therefore punished. Such small immediate aversive consequences are apparently sufficient to reduce the likelihood of going to the dentist until the delayed consequences of not going are felt. The resulting painful stimulation then forces the person to visit the dentist to escape that pain. If the individual had simply gone to the dentist in the first place, the delayed aversive painful consequences could have been avoided. These two examples indicate that the difference between the immediate and delayed consequences is a major variable in self-control problems.

To reiterate, in a self-control problem, there is some immediate consequence that has a controlling effect on the response, while there are later consequences for the response or alternative incompatible responses that have opposite effects from the immediate consequences. The student who goes out to drink beer with his friends instead of finishing a term paper is emitting responses that have immediate positive consequences (e.g., drinking beer, talking to friends, escaping the term paper), but that may also have delayed aversive consequences (staying up all night to finish the paper, turning in a poor quality paper, not getting it in at all, and/or receiving a poor grade on the paper). Even though the student may swear he will never do that again (an apparent commitment response), it is likely that he will engage in similar responses in the future. If such behavior occurs often, we would say that this student has a self-control problem with studying. As was the case with smoking, this particular example involves immediate positive consequences and delayed aversive consequences. Most problems of over-consumption (i.e., eating, drinking, smoking) appear to fit this particular set of contingencies. Both component contingencies must be present to produce self-control problems. If it were not for heart disease, lung cancer, emphysema, and the like, few people would worry about smoking. Thus, smoking, would no longer be a self-control problem.

There are three other basic variations of these contingencies. A response may have immediate aversive consequences, but failure to make the response may have even larger delayed aversive consequences, as in the dental example. A similar set of contingencies are in effect when an individual whose initial social interactions been punished in the past is, as a consequence, less likely to make social advances. Here the reduction of important behavior by small immediate aversive consequences may lead to the long-range loss of greater positive social interactions with an increased sphere of friends and acquaintances (i.e., if the individual had emitted the approach responses, they may have have led to the development of new friends and enjoyable activities). Finally, a response may produce a small immediate positive consequence, but not emitting that response and instead emitting an alternative response may produce a larger delayed positive consequence. Behavior such as saving money in small amounts may eventually result in the purchase of a large reinforcer, while spending that same amount immediately might produce only small reinforcers.

Although behavioral psychologists have tried to avoid analyzing phenomena in terms of nonresponding, it appears that nonresponding is an important component in analyzing self-control problems. In every self-control situation, the problem is a particular response that is either occurring or not occurring. As a consequence, it is important to examine the contingencies for both the occurrence and the nonoccurrence of the target response. The four sets of immediate and delayed consequences for the target response are summarized in table 2.1. The first two instances are situations where the self-control problem is the occurrence of the target response, while in the second two it is the nonoccurrence of a particular response that constitutes the problem. The contingencies in the table are identified in terms of both stimulus and operation; a response can affect either a reinforcing or an aversive stimulus.

An important feature of self-management is made explicit by these examples. The immediate contingencies involve small consequences, either

Table 2.1. Responding (R_1) and Not-responding (R_0) Alternatives in Self-control, and Consequences for Each Alternative. The Problem Response is Indicated by an Asterisk (*).

Response	Example	Immediate consequence	Delayed consequence
*R_1	Smoking	Minor reinforcing event	Major aversive event
R_0	Not smoking	No reinforcing event	No aversive event
*R_1	Spending money	Minor reinforcing event	No reinforcing event
R_0	Not spending (saving)	No reinforcing event	Major reinforcing event
R_1	Going to dentist	Minor aversive event	No aversive event
*R_0	Not going to dentist	No aversive event	Major aversive event
R_1	Making new friends	Minor aversive event	Major reinforcing event
*R_0	Not meeting new people	No aversive event	No reinforcing event

Source: From T. A. Brigham, Self-Control. In A. C. Catania & T. A. Brigham (Eds.), *Handbook of Applied Behavior Analysis*. New York: Irvington, 1978. Reproduced with permission.

positive or negative, while the delayed consequences are all major but potential. Cases are well documented of individuals who smoked two packs of cigarettes a day throughout their adult life and who died of old age at 95 without any health problems related to smoking. Similarly, regular visits to the dentist will not guarantee the avoidance of serious dental problems.

A less obvious aspect of self-management follows from the nature of the consequences for the responses that need to be changed. The required direction of change is a function of the immediate consequences: when the immediate consequences are positive (e.g., smoking, or spending rather than saving), the target response needs to be decreased in frequency; when the immediate consequences are negative (e.g., going to the dentist, or fighting shyness), the target response needs to be increased. To accomplish these changes, the individual obviously must use different strategies. When decreasing the frequency of a response, a twofold approach appears to be effective. First, alternative incompatible responses which will produce reinforcement need to be found, and the individual must avoid situations that in the past were discriminative for the target behavior. In the case of increasing the frequency of a response, the environment must be analyzed and restructured to make both the occurrence and the reinforcement of the response more probable. (See the later section on teaching self-management for more details. Further, note that the intuitively obvious self-punishment and self-reinforcement approaches both have been rejected on the logical and empirical grounds presented earlier.)

THE CHANGING ENVIRONMENT

The analysis of the contingencies involved in self-control problems, not unexpectedly, suggests that the environment plays a major role in self-management. A logical examination of the functioning of the environment in regard to the solution of self-control problems does, however, indicate that the usual conception of the environment and the corollary assumptions about how to change behavior are in need of modification. To indicate how the conception of the environment needs to be changed, the common assumptions concerning the role of the environment must be reviewed. Presently, the authors of introductory psychology texts often begin the section on behaviorism and learning theory with the equation $B = f(E)$. The generally accepted translation of the equation is that behavior is a function of the environment. This, of course, is a difficult statement to argue with. It is also totally gratuitous, because it does not specify *how* behavior is controlled by the environment. Most writers then go on to give examples from laboratory research of how the responses of an organism in an experimental chamber may be changed by manipulating aspects of the organism's environment. These instances of behavioral principles are extremely powerful, and by the end of the exposition the author has built a case for what may be called the behavior-modification or controlling-environment model of behavior. Greatly oversimplified, the major assumption of this model is that to change an individual's behavior, you simply change that individual's environment. The student comes away with the impression that the environment is somehow a monolithic, immutable force that molds behavior irrespective of other factors.

The concept of the controlling environment is either explicitly or implicitly held by many psychologists both within and without operant psychology. What is wrong with this concept of the environment and behavior? Simply put, it is incorrect in its view of the environment. The usual criticism at this point is to say that the real environment is infinitely more complex than the laboratory one. That may be true, but it is not the critical error. The error is in how the typical laboratory environment is designed to be a primarily static one in which the organism's responses have no direct effect on the basic contingencies that the experimenter has scheduled. This is by necessity: in order for an experimenter to evaluate the effects of a particular variable on behavior, an experimenter must carefully control that variable and others. But the natural environment is not impervious to the effects of the responding organism; it changes.

At this point the reader may object that the animal's behavior *does* interact with the experimenter's. The experimenter designs the environment, monitors the animal's responses in that environment, and changes the environment when appropriate. These activities of the experimenter represent a major advance in the methodology of the experimental analysis of behavior. This interaction of the investigator with the experimental organism is an important feature of inductive research (Sidman, 1960; Skinner, 1956a). Careful monitoring of the organism's responses allows the investigator to manipulate an independent variable and directly observe the effects on the animal's responding. Thus, the laboratory environment does change in a systematic manner related to the organism's responses. But there are two differences between changes in the laboratory environment and those in the natural environment. The first is simply the immediacy of change. In the nonlaboratory situation, the relations between the individual and the environment are constantly and immediately changing in both small and large ways. This, of course, is mainly a difference of degree, but the importance of immediacy of a consequence contingent on a response is well documented. Similarly, it is likely that the immediacy of change plays an important role in the functioning of the natural environment.

The second difference is again one of degree and has to do with a behavioral interpretation of the concept of reciprocity. It is clear that the relations between the organism and its environment are dynamic and reciprocal. The environment changes the organism's behavior, but it is changed by that behavior in turn. This is especially true for humans, where the important environment consists for the most part of other humans. In these situations, the organism-environment distinction changes with perspective: one individual's responses most likely are another individual's stimuli.

There is, of course, a similar reciprocal relation between the experimenter's behavior and that of the experimental organism. But there is a form of insulation between the experimenter's responses and the changes in the organism's behavior; changes in the organism's behavior are systematically transformed, quantified, and analyzed, and therefore may have an impact on the experimenter's behavior only in remote and indirect ways. Although these processes may carry the weight of scientific method, they can lead to the view that changes in the environment are separate from changes in the experimenter's behavior. The conclusion is that the environment has changed the organism's behavior, but it ignores the complementary change in the environment (the experimenter's behavior) produced by the changes in the organism's responses.

Although this concept of the interaction between behavior and the environment is not a radical departure from current operant theory, the differences are important for the analysis of self-management. Skinner, in his analysis of operant behavior, has often focused on the effects of responses on the environment. One reason he selected the term "operant" was because the response *operates on* the environment. By implication, to operate means to affect, to produce results, to change. Therefore, this informal definition of the operant implied that the response changes the environment (Skinner, 1953). In his more formal discussion of the operant, however, Skinner chose to give a heavier weight to the role of the environment. Here it is the environment that affects the response, that is, changes its frequency. Thus, the operant becomes a response whose future probability of occurrence is a function of its stimulus consequences. But again, in his discussions of countercontrol (Skinner, 1948; 1974) and self-control (Skinner, 1953), he takes the position that the individual can change his or her own environment. But Skinner contends that, in the ultimate, the environment determines behavior:

> If this is correct, little ultimate control remains with the individual. A man may spend a great deal of time designing his own life—he may choose the circumstances in which he is to live with great care, and he may manipulate his daily environment on an extensive scale. Such activity appears to exemplify a high order of self-determination. But it is also behavior, and we account for it in terms of other variables in the environment and history of the individual. It is these variables which provide the ultimate control. (p. 240)

What is to be made of these apparent inconsistencies in Skinner's position on the role of the environment? The problems are resolved by recognizing that these statements represent different levels of description in Skinner's analysis of behavior. As a consequence, it is possible to hold as a major theoretical assumption that in the ultimate, it is the environment that controls behavior, but still to assert that in the day-to-day operation of the environment, the individual can change the environment by behaving.[1]

Unfortunately, both critics and practitioners of the analysis of behavior too often focus on Skinner's statements about the environment as the ultimate source of control and ignore other aspects of his analysis of behavior. For the applied behavior researcher, however, Skinner's positions on countercontrol and on the ability of the individual to change the environment are as important as his assumptions concerning the ultimate role of the environment in controlling behavior. To elaborate, when someone is taught a new skill, two things happen: the individual's behavior is changed by an environmental manipulation, but it also becomes possible for the individual to change the environment. In self-management, augmenting an individual's ability to deal with the environment should be of more concern to the behavior analyst than changing behavior by manipulating the environment directly.

The behavior modification conception of the environment continues to be widely held because of its manipulative and explanatory power. When an experimenter places an organism in a particular environment arranged in a specific manner, it is an extremely powerful reinforcer for the experimenter if the organism's behavior conforms to a predicted outcome. Likewise, the application to human problems of those principles and procedures derived from the laboratory has been extremely successful in many instances. Numerous examples of such successes can be found in the *Journal of Applied Behavior Analysis, Behavior Therapy, Behavior Research and Therapy*, and other journals. Also, there has been a very practical reason for the environmental emphasis in both laboratory and applied research: to date, it has been easier to manipulate the environment directly because more knowledge is currently available for isolating and manipulating environmental variables than for dealing with individual variables.

This position, however, appears to be reaching a point of diminishing returns as the sole basis for behavioral research and programs. An examination of many successful behavior modification research programs shows that they have involved powerful consequences in relatively constrained environments. For example, Lovaas's (1973) research with autistic children used powerful reinforcers and punishers in an extremely controlled environment. This in no way negates the achievements of Lovaas and his associates, but simply puts that research into the context of the behavior modification model. Violating the constraints and assumptions of the model greatly reduces the applicability of behavior modification procedures if innovative corrections are not undertaken. Reppucci and Saunders (1974) found just these sorts of difficulties in their research at the Connecticut School for Boys. Their initial conception of the project was to design an environment that they would control to "shape up" the boy's behavior. In designing their programs, they appear to have assumed that their work with the boys represented a closed system, in that no one would interfere with their control of the boys' environment. Unfortunately, the behavior of a variety of individuals—boys, administrators, politicians, and others—failed to match the investigators' expectations and impeded the operation of their controlled environment. Because they were unable to manipulate the environment as they had expected, they then concluded that the assumptions of the operant model about how to change behavior did not work and that what was needed was a new form of social psychology. Such an out-of-hand rejection of an operant approach appears inappropriate, because many programs, such as Achievement Place, have overcome these difficulties. In the Achievement Place program (Fixsen, Philips, & Wolf, 1978), environmental changes are considered and adaptive self-management skills are taught. But as a consequence, this overall program and its procedures more closely fit the proposed model of the changing environment than that of the controlling one. Similarly, until the recent work on self-management procedures, the adult with minor to moderate adjustment problems who was still operating in the natural environment was generally outside the domain of behavior modification or behavior therapy. This was the case primarily because the assumptions about how to change behavior (i.e., making systematic changes in the environment) could not be made to operate in that individual's environment. A further important but distinct issue, not adequately considered in most early behavior modification models, is the question of generalization. Clearly there is no guarantee that behavior changed as a function of controlling the environment in one situation will be maintained in subsequent situations. The problem of generalization of behavior modification programs such as token economies became an important theoretical and practical issue. But because it is not of central concern to this analysis, persons concerned with generalization should read Stokes and Baer (1977), Goldstein and Kanfer (1979), or Karoly and Steffen (1980) for detailed treatments of the issues.

In general, because the model used in much behavior modification research has not adequately considered the interaction between the client and the modifier, the method for dealing with problems in applied projects has been to attempt to gain more control of the environment. As indicated earlier, however, such attempts have been counterproductive. Because of its emphasis on the reciprocal interactions between organism and environment, an analysis of the environment as proposed here makes it possible to anticipate these difficulties and to develop noncoercive procedures for dealing with them. For example, when the teacher is no longer considered an impervious controlling environment for the children in a class, the teacher will be taught in advance how to respond appropriately to the countercontrolling responses of the students, the principal, and other teachers. The logic of a changing environment and the corollary emphasis on the individual's ability to change the environment is a major premise of a behavioral model of self-management.

Finally, the conception of the environment presented here does not, in the last analysis, question the Skinnerian assumption that the environment controls behavior, but rather questions the degree to which someone can directly intervene in the environment to change behavior. The distinction can be illustrated by considering the problems presented to the psychologist by a behavior-problem child versus a predelinquent adolescent. In the case of the younger child, it can be (and has been) reasonably assumed that the child's parents and teachers control a significant portion of his or her environment. The strategy typically adopted in such a situation is to teach the parents and teachers how to modify the child's behavior. The success of such an approach is well documented. On the other hand, a number of investigators have ruefully found that such a strategy has little chance of success with the adolescent. The environment of the adolescent is not as circumscribed as that of the young child. No single adult or set of adults control all or a major portion of the adolescent's environment; a wide variety of consequences are available from a heterogeneous peer group. Also, the adolescent's ability to engage in countercontrol behaviors is much greater than that of the young child. As a consequence, the intervention strategy must change from a behavior modification focus on directly changing the environment to change behavior, to one of changing behavior to modify the broader patterns of behavior/environment interactions. This strategy may be called *indirect behavior modification* or, in this instance, self-management training.

For indirect behavior modification, or self-management training, the environment must be viewed as consisting of two parts, that of the therapeutic setting and that of the larger environment where the new behaviors must be maintained. In the therapeutic environment, the therapist has much less powerful techniques available to influence behavior, modeling, logical analysis, and social reinforcers and therefore, somewhat paradoxically, must teach clients more powerful techniques for modifying their own behavior: self-management skills.

A MODEL OF SELF-MANAGEMENT BEHAVIOR[2]

The preceding sections have detailed the differences between a radical behavioral perspective on self-management and that of other approaches. It is now time to specifically outline the implications of these differences for a model of self-management. Self-management is the ability of the individual to interface his or her behavior with the environment. Self-management, as conceptualized in this manner then, is simply the application of behavior analysis principles and procedures to modify the behavior/environment interactions *of* the individual *by* the individual. That is, rather than behavior modification being viewed from the perspective of the environment, the person whose behavior is being changed and the person doing the changing are one and the same. The target of the analysis and modification at any one time can be the individual's response repertoire, his or her environment, or frequently both.

The following model of self-management behavior involves some basic assumptions about the environment implicit in the previous discussion which, for clarity, will be made explicit here. The abilities to analyze, modify, and evaluate behavior/environment interaction will not be utilized unless there are sufficiently good reasons to do so. That is, motivational contingencies for self-management responses must be present in the environment. Negative reinforcement (escape or avoidance of some aversive condition) was suggested by Skinner (1953) as the major reason for engaging in self-management behavior. People frequently have self-control problems because they lack the required skills to deal with those problems. However, occasionally an individual will simply lack the "motivation" to engage in self-management responses. Irrespective of the theoretical interpretation of this lack of motivation, in those instances, the procedures proposed here will be ineffective. Further, if the new behaviors (products of self-management efforts) do not make contact with appropriate contingencies, they will not be maintained. Consequently, it is assumed in the following treatment of self-management that the proposed skills will all be developed and maintained as a function of the individual's interaction with his or her environment.[3]

The most important component of a behavioral analysis approach to changing behavior is reinforcement. A central task of self-management, then, is to learn to analyze the environment in terms of reinforcement contingencies. Catania (1976) interpreted the research on self-reinforcement in terms of discrimination. Simply put, he argued that the self-reinforcement per se is largely peripheral and that the important component is learning to discriminate when a response is good enough (appropriate) that it will eventually be reinforced by others. Returning to the example from Skinner, the student may indulge himself in some reinforcing activity after completing a task because he has learned to discriminate when that work will be reinforced by others. The interaction of the individual's behavior with the consequences in the larger environment maintains both the working behavior and the "self-reinforcement" behavior. From this perspective, the first component in self-management is the ability to discriminate (analyze) the various behavior/environment interactions in one's own life. Without this set of analytical responses, the individual cannot effectively utilize any of the other self-management skills. The major behavior for analysis in self-management is self-observation. Self-observation can consist of the systematic recording of behavior and its antecedents and consequences to analyze the behavior/environment interdependencies or simply noting another person's reaction to a particular response or set of responses as a way of determining how to interact with the person. The individual with many self-management responses is skillful at analyzing his or her own behavior and that of others. An important part of analyzing the other person's responses is the ability to understand what things reinforce the person's responses. The individual can then discriminate the various contingencies for both his or her own responses and those of others in the environment and can emit the appropriate responses.

Related to the ability to observe one's own behavior/environment interactions is the recognition of mutual influences of the individual's responses on the environment and the effect of the environment on his or her responses. This, of course, is again the concept of reciprocity. In the case of self-management, it refers, in the first person, to the recognition that how I behave affects the way people react to me, and vice versa. Although this may appear to be an overly simple point, people vary tremendously in the degree that they understand it. In general, individuals characterized as lack-

ing self-management skills or having self-control problems display little or
no understanding of this essential interdependency.

Finally, an important product of the ability to objectively observe one's
own behavior is the understanding of personal, private events. The individual skillful at self-observation can discriminate the relations between
behavior/environment interactions and private feelings. The individual who
can recognize the source of his or her feelings of anger in the behavior/en-
vironment interplay has a much greater chance of dealing with the problem
than the individual who can only report feeling angry.

The person who possesses these analytical skills will then be able to
recognize the various immediate and delayed contingencies involved in self-
control problems discussed earlier. The student's recognition that he or she
is not studying enough because other incompatible responses are immediately reinforced by some friends, while the consequences for studying
are delayed, constitutes the first step in solving the self-control problem.
Similarly, the adolescent's ability to understand that some friends provide
the immediate consequences for illegal drinking by encouraging and reinforcing those behaviors may then be able to take steps to change the problem behavior. The person characterized as having many self-management
skills will be able to analyze the immediate and delayed contingencies in the
environment and deal with self-control problems accordingly.

Obviously the ability to analyze would do the individual little good
without the complementary skills of being able to modify behavior/en-
vironment interactions. How does one modify the personal environment?
Although a wide variety of procedures might occasionally be used, the core
of modification skills consist of the reinforcement, extinction, and shaping
of other people's behavior and restructuring of the physical/psychological
environment. An example of environmental change by reinforcement and
extinction is provided by special-education students who were taught to
change their social and educational environments (Graubard, Rosenberg, &
Miller, 1974). Special-education children often interact with a hostile environment that has labeled them deviant and, therefore, as people who can
be treated with less respect, subjected to more ridicule, or given more
negative comments. Graubard et al. taught a group of special-education
children some simple reinforcement and extinction techniques. They
showed them how to reinforce the positive comments of teachers and "normal" students. For example, the children were taught to make the "uh huh"
("I understand") response when a teacher carefully explained something to
them, and to thank the teacher and praise the teacher's efforts. On the other
hand, the students broke eye contact after the teacher's negative comments
and were generally unresponsive to them. Similar procedures were used with
other students in the school. These procedures involved the systematic
manipulation of the therapeutic environment, which in turn made the

students more skillful in manipulating their environment. For instance, when the special-education children used their new social skills, there was an increase in positive comments and approaches and a complementary decrease in negative ones by the teachers and "normal" students toward the special-education children. The special-education students, by changing the way they used reinforcement and extinction, changed their environment and made further positive changes possible. In addition, their changed behavior changed the teacher's environment and that of other students, because the special-education children were now a source of social reinforcers. It is appropriate to reiterate here that such an approach will only succeed if the new behaviors fit the environment. If, for some reason, there had been other powerful contingencies on the behavior of the teachers or other students to maintain their negative responses to the special-education students, then the procedure would not have worked. Graubard et al. (1974) appropriately labeled their approach an environmental or ecological one. Because the special-education students were not taught how to analyze their environment and behavior, the Graubard et al. study is not an example of self-management per se. Rather, it represents the successful implementation of one component of the self-management model. Individuals can, however, be taught these skills within the context of self-management training with similar positive results (e.g., Gross, Brigham, Hopper, & Bologna, 1980).

In summary, one set of procedures utilized to modify the environment, and thus the individual's own responses, consists of the techniques of behavior modification. An additional important set of self-management skills not usually considered within the context of behavior modification or behavior therapy involves restructuring the physical/psychological environment. Skinner's initial analysis of self-control focused heavily, not on consequences per se, but on environmental structuring involving either the physical or psychological environment. It was assumed that the individual could arrange the environment so that the probability of particular responses would be increased or decreased. In line with the earlier analysis of the environment, he further assumed that if these changes were successful, there would be environment consequences to maintain the new behaviors. Although this approach to self-management has not been systematically examined with humans, there is animal and anecdotal evidence to support the analysis.

For example, Kanfer and Phillips (1970) relate the story of Odysseus and the sirens as an instance of arranging the physical environment to prevent a particular response. Odysseus, of course, plugged his sailors' ears with wax and then had himself lashed to the mast so that he could hear the sirens' song without losing his life or his ship. A more recent anecdote involves a personal problem solved by a rearrangement of the environment. After many years of setting up reinforcement or punishment contingencies for the automobile riding behavior of our children with limited success, an analysis of the environmental situation suggested an alternative approach.[4] Although the goal of strong familial affection that transcends situational variables is a desirable long-term objective, a realistic assessment of the probability of such behavior under the stimulus situation of a crowded back seat suggests it is extremely low. The obvious solution (obvious is a *post hoc* term, it took many years of trying contingencies before a restructuring approach was taken) was simply to change the adult/child seating patterns. Now the driver and one child sit in the front while the second child and adult sit in the back.

Many miles have been covered in relative comfort and peace maintained by small reinforcers, in contrast to the small amount of control exerted by contingencies employed in the past. The difference is that the change in the environment eliminated the "accidental" kick or bump, the "friendly" poke, and so on which had led to retaliation and escalated verbal and/or physical violence. These behaviors were the key to the self-management problem. When they occur, the probability of disruptive inappropriate responses is increased irrespective of whatever consequences may be programmed. Recently, to check if the observed changed behavior was due to increased maturity on the part of the children, a *brief* reversal was instituted. While they did behave somewhat better than in years past, there was nonetheless an easily discriminated increase in disruptive behaviors.

This quasi experiment convinced the author that environmental restructuring can often be more efficient and effective than the manipulation of consequences. Similarly, the impact of environmental changes on behavior can be seen in the simple instruction to smokers to keep all cigarettes and ashtrays put away before and after smoking. The manipulation changes the environment by removing stimulus factors that in the past had cued smoking and it introduces a delay between the "desire" to smoke and the availability of a cigarette. These small steps consistently result in a 25 to 35 percent reduction in the smoking frequency below baseline (Danaher & Lichtenstein, 1978; Lemme, Note 1). Certainly, additional changes are required before the individual can stop smoking, and the environmental restructuring must be maintained by appropriate contingencies. Nonetheless, small environmental changes can play an important role in the solution of self-control problems.

Rachlin's research on the commitment response with animals provides more solid experimental evidence for this approach. The focus of analysis is on commitment responses. These responses commit the organism to engaging in a response that is incompatible with the problem response. In the standard situation, the consequences for the two available responses will result in the organism emitting the problem response. But in the commitment response approach at an earlier time, the organism has an opportunity to emit the commitment response before the onset of the situation in which the problem response typically occurs. The commitment response is followed by a different set of stimuli in the presence of which only the alternative (desired) response can occur. The key to this interpretation is that preferences vary over time. The alcoholic, while sober, is more likely to make a commitment to abstain from drinking if the next opportunity to drink is sometime in the future than if the opportunity is immediately at hand. Thus, if the environment can be arranged appropriately, the organism will emit the commitment response and the desired response in turn. Rachlin and Green (1972) demonstrated these relations in an experiment in which pigeons, when given the choice of responding for immediate 2-second access or delayed 4-second access, preferred the immediate consequence. From an analysis of the combined gradients of delay and magnitude, it was predicted that if the pigeons were forced to make the choice 10 seconds in advance of the opportunity to earn an immediate or delayed reward, they would choose the larger but delayed reward. In general this prediction was confirmed. Rachlin and Green suggest that *when invented by an individual*, the commitment-response paradigm may be a viable self-management technique.

Finally, the psychological ecology literature provides a rich body of research bearing directly on how to effect behavior by structuring the environment, research that is largely ignored by behaviorists. Although the position and research are too extensive to cover here, the essence can be summarized as follows: More accurate prediction of behavior in a particular situation can be made from knowledge of the behavior setting (physical/psychological structure) than is possible from knowledge of the individual characteristics of the person entering that setting. Specifically, as Barker (1968) has argued,

> While it is possible to smoke at a Worship Service, to dance during a Court Session, and to recite a Latin lesson in a Machine Shop, such matchings of behavior and behavior settings almost never occur in Midwest (Oskaloosa), although they would not be infrequent if these kinds of behavior were distributed among behavior settings by chance.

In short, the physical/psychological environment plays a major role in determining behavior, and behavior change can be facilitated by environmental restructuring.

Returning to the self-control problem of the student who was having difficulty studying, how might the environment be modified to deal with the problem? First, applying the environmental restructuring principle, the student would not set some contrived self-reinforcement contingency. Rather, the effort would be directed at increasing the likelihood that he or she would enter a setting such as the library where studying is a high-probability response. Such a change in behavior could be accomplished by identifying a friend who regularly studies in the library and asking to study with that person. Next the student should attempt to reinforce the friend for being a study partner. Such reinforcement will in turn increase the likelihood that the friend will reinforce our student's studying behavior. The outcome of the suggested steps would be for our student to regularly study in the library with his or her friend. These proposed steps do not represent a piecemeal approach to the problem; rather, each step can be derived from the principles outlined in the analysis of self-management skills and self-control problems. Although different problems and environmental situations will require different sets of responses to change the behavior/environmental contingencies, those responses will also follow from a similar process.

TEACHING SELF-MANAGEMENT SKILLS[5]

If one accepts the arguments concerning the analysis of self-reinforcement (and, by implication, self-punishment) and private events, then self-management training should not focus on those topics, but rather on how to analyze and restructure the personal environment. Studies by individuals at the Self-Control Research and Training Unit, Washington State University (Niemann & Brigham, Note 2; Gross, Brigham, Hopper, & Bologna, 1980; Brigham, Hill, Hopper, & Adams, 1980; and Contreras, Brigham, Handel, & Castillo, Note 3) have explored this approach. To date, most of the work has been programmatic or developmental in nature, concerned with the production and testing of materials and procedures. The evolving program does not emphasize self-management techniques such as self-recording per se, but rather how self-recording can be used to analyze and understand behavior/environment interactions. First and foremost, students are taught that behavior is lawful and orderly. Further, the student learns that by manipulating aspects of the environment, it becomes possible to change behavior, both their own and that of others. The program begins with a section on defining and measuring behavior/environment interactions. Discussions and demonstrations are then followed by an exercise similar to the example below.

A frequent source of friction between teenagers and parents is the use of the telephone. It is suggested to the students that they could use these new skills to examine this problem. The idea that they can actually collect information (data) relevant to this problem and then use the information to help solve the problem comes as a considerable surprise to most of them. And that, of course, is one of the the major functions of the exercise—the demonstration that the techniques they are learning are of practical value.

Definitions and recording procedures are developed, and the students proceed to collect data. After several observations are collected, the students analyze them and try to draw some conclusions. The data may then be used to design an informal behavior-change plan or they may form the basis for systematically negotiating a contract with the student's parents concerning the use of the telephone. Other sections of the course are treated in a similar manner. First there is a reading with discussion, followed by demonstrations and practice, and finally the student engages in some form of exercise related to the main procedures of the section. Thus a primary objective of the program is to give the student actual experience in both analyzing and manipulating behavior/environment interactions. It is expected that skills acquired in this manner are more likely to be utilized by the students in their "real" environment.

Using this approach, juvenile delinquents have learned to reduce or eliminate their delinquent behavior, chronically unemployed youth have successfully acquired jobs, and students regularly in trouble at school have reduced the frequency of responses which in the past had led to detentions and suspensions. Maintenance of treatment effects, of course, is of major concern in any program and constitutes part of the rationale for developing self-management training programs (i.e., the individual so trained should be able to independently deal with the specific target behaviors and related ones). A 1-year follow-up of the behavior-problem students involved in the Brigham et al. (1980) study showed that 14 of 19 students were no longer considered behavior problems by their teachers, and as a group, the reduction in detentions received in the 1980/1981 academic year compared to 1979/1980 was significant at the .001 level. Recently, Gross (Note 4) used a similar set of techniques. In short, a wide variety of self-control problems have been successfully dealt with using self-management training.

To reiterate, the strategy in each case was not to exclusively teach techniques directly related to the problem behaviors, but instead to teach the full range of self-management skills outlined in the preceding section. Training takes place in small groups and involves didactic instruction based on *Managing everyday problems: A manual of applied psychology for youth*, modeling and practicing of specific skills, and conducting one to three personally designed behavior modification and/or self-management projects. The student attempts to analyze and modify the personal behavior problem(s) only after having mastered the prerequisite skills. While the student is learning all of the various techniques, there is a continuing focus on behavior/environment interactions. As argued earlier, no matter what skills are taught, they must interface with the larger environment beyond the training setting to be useful and to be maintained.

The model of self-management skills presented here is a straight-forward one. It emphasizes the individual's ability to discriminate and modify behavior/environment contingencies and interactions, rather than focusing on complex and elegant cognitive processes or hypothetical constructs. The positive results obtained with the self-management model and the procedures described here do not, of course, demonstrate that this analysis of self-management is correct. It will be necessary to test the procedures derived from a fully elaborated behavioral model of self-management against alternative models and procedures. Further, it must be demonstrated that the behavioral model can generate unique analyses and treatments for self-management problems before it can be asserted that it is both a logical and empirical treatment of the phenomenon of the self-management area. Such convincing evidence must await the theoretical analysis of the research reported in the remainder of this volume and future research inspired by the volume.

NOTES

1. The term "ultimate" has been used here to parallel Skinner's (1953) usage. Recently, however, "momentary and distal" or "long-term" have been used to make the same functional distinction between "day-to-day" and "ultimate."
2. I recognize that few people who are judged to display self-management skills would discuss their skills in terms of the model proposed here. However, it is unlikely they would correctly use the language of more cognitive models either. In general, people are not well trained in describing their own or another person's behavior. But that is not the point here. The argument concerns the processes controlling the development and maintenance of these behaviors, not whether the individual can correctly identify them. It is argued that the proposed model is a parsimonious way of interpreting self-management skills.
3. Other authors have treated the issues related to motivation and the distinction between knowing and doing in similar but sufficiently different ways that the reader may wish to examine (e.g., Goldiamond, 1965; Karoly, 1981).
4. Although the anecdote is presented to illustrate environmental restructuring per se, it is appropriate to ask whose self-control problem was it? From the perspective of this paper, it was both mine and my children's. Their inability to meet the requirements of my "reasonable" contingencies and ride without the various forms of fighting frequently lead to my making loud threats of bodily harm and occasionally carrying them out. Since I prefer to characterize my behavior as calm, logical, and reasoned, such responses on my part were personally aversive. Thus, the patterns of responding to the immediate situation by all of us represented personal self-control problems.
5. Rather than presenting much detail here on the actual materials and procedures used in the research on teaching self-management, the reader is referred to the papers cited. Also, copies of *Managing Everyday Problems: A Manual of Applied Psychology for Youth* are available from the Self-Control Research and Training Unit, Department of Psychology, Washington State University, Pullman, Washington 99164

REFERENCE NOTES

1. Lemme, I. *An Analysis of Smoking Behavior.* Unpublished Masters Thesis, Washington State University, Pullman, Washington 99164.

2. Niemann, J., & Brigham, T. A. *The development and experimental validation of a course in self-management for sixth graders.* Paper presented at the Meeting of the Association for Behavior analysis, Chicago, 1976.
3. Contreras, J., Brigham, T. A., Handel, G., & Castillo, A. *A comparison of two approaches for improving social and job placement skills.* Paper submitted for publication.
4. Gross, A. *Self-Management training and medication compliance in adolescent diabetics.* Paper submitted for publication.

REFERENCES

Baer, D. M. On relation between basic and applied research. In A. C. Catania & T. A. Brigham (Eds.), *Handbook of applied behavior analysis.* New York: Irvington, Inc., 1978.
Bandura, A. Vicarious and self-reinforcement processes. In R. Glaser (Ed.), *The nature of reinforcement.* New York: Academic Press, 1971.
Bandura, A. Self-reinforcement: Theoretical and methodological considerations. *Behaviorism,* 1975, *4,* 135–155.
Bandura, A. *Social learning theory.* Englewood Cliffs, N. J.: Prentice-Hall, 1977.
Bandura, A., & Mahoney, M. J. Maintenance and transfer of self-reinforcement functions. *Behavior Research and Therapy,* 1974, *12,* 89–97.
Barker, R. G. *Ecological psychology.* Stanford, Calif.: Stanford University Press, 1968.
Brigham, T. A. Self-control. In A. C. Catania & T. A. Brigham (Eds.), *Handbook of applied behavior analysis.* New York: Irvington, 1978.
Brigham, T. A., Hill, B., Hopper, C., & Adams, J. Self-management training as an alternative to expulsion. Progress report ESEA Title IV C., 1980.
Catania, A. C. The myth of self-reinforcement. In T. A. Brigham, R. Hawkins, J. Scott, & T. F. McLaughlin (Eds.), *Behavior analysis in education: Self-control and reading.* Dubuque, Iowa: Kendal/Hunt, 1976.
Danaher, B. and Lichtenstein, E. *Become an ex-smoker.* Englewood Cliffs, N.J.: Prentice-Hall, Inc., 1978.
Dethier, V. G. *To know a fly.* San Francisco, Calif.: Holden-Day, Inc., 1962.
Fixsen, D., Phillips, E., & Wolf, M. Mission-orientation behavior research: The teaching family model. In A. C. Catania & T. A. Brigham (Eds.), *Handbook of applied behavior analysis.* New York: Irvington, 1978.
Goldiamond, I. Self-control procedures in personal behavior problems. *Psychological Record,* 1965, *17,* 851–868.
Goldiamond, I. Self-reinforcement. *Journal of Applied Behavior Analysis,* 1976, *9,* 509–514.
Goldiamond, I. Fables, armadyliccs, and self-reinforcement. *Journal of Applied Behavior Analysis,* 1976, *9,* 521–525.
Goldstein, A. P., & Kanfer, F. H. *Maximizing Treatment gains.* New York: Academic Press, 1979.
Graubard, P., Rosenberg, H., & Miller, M. Student applications of behavior modification to teachers and environments or ecological approaches to social deviancy. In R. Ulrich, T. Stachnick, & J. Mabry (Eds.), *Control of human behavior* (Vol. 3). Glenview, Ill.: Scott Foresman, 1974.
Gross, A., Brigham, T. A., Hopper, C., & Bologna, N. Self-management and social skills training: A study with predelinquent and delinquent youth, *Criminal justice and behavior,* 1980, *7,* 161–184.
Hartig, M., & Kanfer, F. H. The role of verbal self-instructions in children's resistance to temptation. *Journal of Personality and Social Psychology,* 1973, *25,* 259–267.

Jaynes, J. *The origins of consciousness in the breakdown of the bicameral mind.* Boston: Houghton Mifflin, 1977.

Kanfer, F. H., Karoly, P., & Newman, A. Reduction of children's fear of the dark by competence-related and situational threat-related verbal cues. *Journal of Consulting and Clinical Psychology,* 1975, *43,* 251–258.

Kanfer, F. H., & Phillips, J. S. *Learning foundations of behavior therapy.* New York: Wiley, 1970.

Karoly, P. Self-management problems in children. In E. J. Mash & L. G. Terdal (Eds.), *Behavioral assessment of childhood disorders.* New York: Guilford Press, 1981.

Karoly, P., & Briggs, N. Z. Effects of rules and directed delays on components of children's inhibitory self-control. *Journal of Experimental Child Psychology,* 1978, *26,* 267–279.

Karoly, P., & Steffen, J. J. (Eds.), *Improving the long-term effects of psychotherapy.* New York: Gardner Press, 1980.

Lovaas, O. I. *Behavioral treatment of autistic children.* Morristown, N.J.: General Learning Press, 1973.

Mahoney, M. J. *Cognition and behavior modification.* Cambridge, Mass.: Ballinger, 1974.

Mahoney, M. J. Terminal terminology: A self-regulated response to Goldiamond. *Journal of Applied Behavior Analysis,* 1976, *9,* 515–517.

Meichenbaum, D. *Cognitive-behavior modification.* New York: Plenum Press, 1977.

O'Leary, S. G., & Dubey, D. R. Applications of self-control procedures by children: A review. *Journal of Applied Behavior Analysis,* 1979, *12,* 449–466.

Rapoport, A. *Operational philosophy.* New York: John Wiley & Sons, 1953.

Rachlin, H., & Green, L. Commitment, choice and self-control. *Journal of the Experimental analysis of Behavior,* 1972, *17,* 15–22.

Rachlin, H. Reinforcing and punishing thoughts. *Behavior Therapy,* 1977, *8,* 659–665.

Rehm, L. P., & Marston, A. R. Reduction of social anxiety through modification of self-reinforcement. *Journal of Consulting and Clinical Psychology,* 1968, *32,* 565–574.

Reppuci, N., & Saunders, J. Social psychology of behavior modification: Problems of implementation in natural settings. *American Psychologist,* 1974, *29,* 649–660.

Sidman, M. *Tactics of scientific research.* New York: Basic Books, 1960.

Skinner, B. F. *Walden two.* New York: Macmillan, 1948.

Skinner, B. F. *Science and human behavior.* New York: Macmillan, 1953.

Skinner, B. F. A case history in scientific method. *American Psychologist,* 1956, *11,* 221–233.

Skinner, B. F. *About behaviorism.* New York: Knopf, 1974.

Snyder, J., & White, M. The use of cognitive self-instruction in the treatment of behaviorally disturbed adolescents. *Behavior Therapy,* 1979, *10,* 227–235.

Stokes, T., & Baer, D. M. An implicit technology of generalization. *Journal of Applied Behavior Analysis,* 1977, *10,* 349–358.

Watson, D. L., & Tharp, R. G. *Self-directed behavior: Self-modification for personal adjustment.* Monterey, Calif.: Brooks/Cole, 1972.

3
Biopsychosocial Aspects of Self-Management
Judith Rodin

A major focus of modern intellectual history, especially in philosophy and science, has centered around the issues of determinism and free will. This is hardly surprising, since control over one's destiny, knowledge of the laws of nature, the privilege of choice, and freedom are among the higher values of most of mankind. Theoretical concerns with the process of self-regulation have evolved, in part, from this tradition. Averill (1973) and White (1959), recognizing the general adaptive significance of control over the environment, have argued that the need for control is a deep-seated motivational process of phylogenetic as well as ontogenetic origin.

Self-regulation implies the ability to produce and/or maintain a given behavior or, more broadly, any state in general, especially when there is a perceived discrepancy between actual and optimal states. Consistent with Mahoney and Arnkoff (1978), I believe that the issue of self-control takes on its most important dimensions if approached from the perspective of the labeler instead of that of the labeled behavior. For the most part, self-control lies in the eyes of the beholder. In other words, it is an attribution of the observer more than a characteristic of the behavior itself, and therefore the context and the history of the given behavior are major factors that determine whether or not the behavior is labeled self-control. For example, if two people at a party decline a drink, one of them a nondrinker and the other an alcoholic who has been trying to stop drinking, we would only describe the latter as showing self-control. Thus, self-control is not an intrinsic property of the behavior itself. Emphasis on the environment or the context in which the behavior occurs also highlights another crucial feature of self-control: labeling a behavior as self-control usually requires a situation where something that is valued is available, and yet the individual fails to consume it although there are no discernible external controls preventing him from doing so (cf. Kanfer, 1970). In other words, if a person declines the offer of a rich dessert when there are several available and his host is urging consumption, we would label his refusal as an indication of self-control. However, if the physician he was seeing for weight control was his dinner partner, we would not impute the exercise of self-control in explaining the same behavior.

This paper takes a biopsychosocial perspective on the processes of self-regulation. Fundamentally, I assume that survival depends on reflexive and instrumentally learned self-regulatory processes commonly called *homeostasis*. I shall present the integrated system involved in homeostasis as the conceptual model through which to understand and teach self-regulatory mechanisms at the behavioral level as well. I shall attempt to show that this is especially useful for two reasons. First, it implies that there is a reference or comparison level against which the person compares current inputs. Second, it suggests that this level may be accessible via both internal and external cues. This view implies, quite correctly, that there is a strong and reciprocal relationship between behavioral and biological effects, a theme that will be developed and reiterated throughout this chapter. Interestingly, this poses both advantages and dilemmas for teaching self-regulatory skills, which I will discuss.

In developing a general model of self-regulation, one needs to consider motivation and/or goal setting, specific responses (learned or reflexive skills), cues to elicit both the motivation and the responses (especially cues signaling a discrepancy from optimal conditions), reinforcement, and feedback. Without all of these variables, self-regulatory processes will be non-systematic, irregular, and relatively weak. Because of the biological focus of this chapter, some of these will be given more attention than others; however, such uneven treatment only derives from the task of this chapter. Ultimately, all elements must be given careful theoretical scrutiny so that practical questions of clinical significance regarding the effectiveness of self-regulation can be answered (see the chapters in Parts II and III of this volume).

The concept of feedback is crucial for understanding the biological basis of self-regulation, and is considered in the present chapter. The identification of internal and external cues for self-regulation is also discussed, especially to debate the precise cue function possible for physiological stimuli. The issue of how people come to identify and label their internal physiological states is of crucial theoretical and practical concern for self-regulation. Two examples of how physiological variables affect cues for self-regulation are described. The first deals with the role of symptoms in taking medication for hypertension. The second concerns the role of weight gain as a cue for self-regulation following smoking cessation. The implications of these issues for clinical procedures are then considered.

It is crucial, however, before beginning this exercise, to discuss the goals of developing technologies with regard to self-control of behavior. If self-control processes are merely of interest as a collection of technologies that are to be applied to specific practical problems, and which ignore underlying explanatory mechanisms, they will fail both as a science and as a problem-solving technology. Many have argued, as I do, that good theory is the basis for the most effective practice. The theory is the analytic vehicle by which the practitioner analyzes the client's problems, plans a treatment, evaluates the outcome, and revises (if necessary) the intervention. Thus, the goal must be not only to work out the specific techniques for teaching self-regulation skills, but to develop a theoretical perspective regarding the processes of self-regulation. It is essential to point out that even if a technique works, it may not have any theoretical import. Thus, even if specification of a particular class of variables is effective in practice, this does not provide face-valid evidence that it is theoretically meaningful. The benefit of theory is that it allows us to know how and why a particular technique works so that we can develop general principles that will ensure more effective technologies. If an explanatory model is powerful, it can help us to understand a variety of behaviors in a variety of settings. While we may need different technologies for different problems, we do not need different theories. An explanatory model can also direct us toward effective interventions by pinpointing causal processes that are amenable to change and those that are not. However, we cannot expect an explanatory model to account for all of the variance observed in an applied problem. After all, there are many reasons why a person may fail to engage in self-regulatory behavior at any given time.

The biopsychosocial model presented in this paper assumes that cues from multiple levels of information interact in the self-regulation of behavior. These levels include physiological cues, social stimuli, thoughts, and feelings. An interaction model such as this assumes that these levels are not simply additive and therefore interchangeable. Rather, several levels may be required for effective self-regulation, including both the biological and the psychosocial. This view further implies that erroneous or maladaptive processes at one level may make the operation of cues in the service of self-control from other levels more difficult, perhaps even impossible under certain circumstances. One cannot hope to develop self-regulation effectively, according to this theory, without understanding the *multiple processes* and *multiple levels* that participate in self-regulatory behavior.

To summarize, the scope of this chapter is a broad consideration of what a general model of self-regulation should include and a specific focus on the effects of biological factors on behavior and behavioral factors on the biology of the individual. Three main themes can be noted. First, the general model of self-regulation is one which requires a firm biological as well as social base. Processes at the biological and social/environmental levels not only interact, but can reciprocally cause changes in one another. Second, the clinician must not confuse the technology with the "science" of self-management. Once a theoretical model of self-regulation is specified, it must be subjected to empirical scrutiny to be confirmed or disconfirmed by the data. Obvious as this may sound, theory-driven work in this area is surprisingly absent, although there are some notable exceptions. If practice were to be based on theory, present theory would require that the end result of a self-management process would be one that is continuously planned for, sustained, and managed by a complex of responses at various levels.

A third major theme of this paper is the view of a homeostatic process inherent in self-regulation. The individual refers a current state to some comparison level, and based on internal and/or external cues, readjusts his or her behaviors or physiological responses in order to bring them closer to that comparison point. The importance of an implicit or explicit referent, even at the biological level, is often missing in discussions of self-regulation.

While noting that a full theory of self-regulation must include the biological as well as behavioral levels, this chapter is also limited by its mandate to consider the biological aspects of self-management in particular. Its overly one-sided emphasis is meant to complement other chapters in this volume, whose task was to focus particularly on other domains (e.g., cognitive). In the long run, all these elements must be considered together.

HOMEOSTASIS AS A METAPHOR FOR ALL SELF-REGULATION

Reflexive, Auto-Regulatory Homeostasis

One theoretical approach to the issue of self-regulation is to understand its biological significance for the organism. At the most primitive level of analysis, most of our life-maintaining biological processes depend on auto-regulatory, homeostatic processes. Breathing, the flow of blood, the beat of the heart—all depend on an exquisite, biologically programmed system of feedback and feed-forward controls. In some ways, this precise reflex system may serve as a metaphor and conceptual model for self-regulation at the behavioral level as well. The need to survive provides the fundamental motivation and primary goal for these biological activities. Various organs in the body, especially the brain, have the ability to monitor and modify specific visceral responses. The nervous system represents the feedback mechanism that actively and continuously assures that the goal of life maintenance is being met adequately and adaptively for the organism. The outcome of survival serves as the primary reinforcer for these responses.

Homeostatic Self-Regulation Based on Instrumental Responses

If we move from reflexive regulation or autoregulation to the next level of analysis, the homeostatic regulation of many different functions also depends on instrumentally learned skeletal responses in addition to reflexive ones. Fish have been shown to swim to waters whose temperatures are optimal for their growth. This is not merely reflexive, since Rozin and Mayer (1961) have shown that fish can learn an arbitrary response of pressing a lever to regulate their water temperature to within a few degrees of what is optimal. People, too, have learned to regulate their body temperature optimally through the use of heaters, air conditioning, and clothing. In these examples, the response acts on the external environment which, in turn, changes the internal state back to its optimal point. What triggered the response was some internal cue of discrepancy from optimum (Miller & Dworkin 1980). It is also possible for the skeletal response to effect some change in a visceral response, instead of in the external environment. The rest of the feedback process would remain the same as just described. For example, Pickering and Miller (1977) treated a patient whose heart would suddenly start contracting between normal heartbeats, called premature ventricular contractions, which made him feel faint. He was taught responses (small exercise techniques) that stimulated reflexes that, in turn, speeded up the heart. This interrupted the problematic alteration of normal beats and the premature contractions and returned his heart to a normal sinus rhythm.

The data are less clear about the likelihood that a visceral response that corrects an internal, homeostatic imbalance could be instrumentally learned as a *direct* response (without a prior skeletal response) to the cues indicating the discrepancy. Can people change their blood pressure, for example, without using skeletal responses to produce these voluntary changes? When the pioneering work of Miller and his colleagues (Miller, 1969) suggested that autonomic responses could be controlled through operant conditioning without peripheral mediation, it appeared that even autonomic responses were potentially open to self-regulation.

Striking in this conception of plasticity was the notion that large and physiologically significant changes in autonomic responding could be shaped by operant conditioning and that the progress of such conditioning could occur unconstrained by intrinsic homeostatic processes. There is little question that early applications of biofeedback training to the treatment of visceral pathology derived considerable impetus from the conception of autonomic plasticity that was implicit in the promise of this achievement. Surprisingly, some investigators (e.g., Lynch & Shuri, 1978) avoided the term "self-regulation" in discussing these processes, however. They did so in order to avoid the connotation that control could emanate solely from within the organisms. They chose instead to emphasize that responses are regulated by their association with certain external consequences (e.g., feedback, reward, or unconditioned stimuli). This appears to be a fundamental misunderstanding of the operation of self-regulatory processes.

To extend the homeostasis metaphor to a general principle of self-regulation, all such processes begin with motivation and commitment toward self-maintenance, which includes the establishment of essential goals. There must also be specific skills for monitoring and modifying relevant events on the basis of cues from multiple levels of information, including the internal and external environment. Also necessary is reinforcement for making these responses and a feedback process that actively checks for progress toward the goals. Whether we are talking about a visceral organ or the individual as a whole, self-regulation involves carrying out specific plans of action and using specific skills. In this way, the individual copes effectively with environmental and internally produced events. As a result, the effect of self-regulation may be an action on the external environment or an action on a visceral organ or some other element of the internal milieu.

The homeostasis metaphor has heuristic value for another reason. It stimulates us to view the metagoal of self-regulation as the maintenance of behavior at an optimal level for the organism (cf. Berlyne, 1960). Others have considered self-regulation in the service of danger reduction (Leventhal, Meyer, & Nerenz, 1980) or distress elimination (Miller & Dworkin, 1980), but seeing all of these events as part of a more general process provides a theoretical continuity among all processes that involve the maintenance of the individual at the most optimal level possible. However, interventions in self-regulation may always be limited because homeostatic "controlled quantities" continue to act at various other levels besides the one being changed. This may occur in contradistinction to those which the person is trying to manage.

PHYSIOLOGICAL CONSEQUENCES OF SELF-REGULATION

Given the biological basis of self-regulation as a process, it may be expected that physiological mechanisms would be especially primed to be responsive to all self-regulatory acts, even those occurring at the behavioral level. If striving for control and choice are emergent properties of basic biological processes, we might consider the physiologically pathological consequences for the organism of a lack of adequate self-regulatory events. It is instructive at this point to consider the animal literature with regard to control and feedback in order to explicate this point. In the animal literature, control is defined as the ability to make active responses, typically during the occurrence of an aversive stimulus.

Control

Control appears to be a factor that can reduce an organism's physiological response to a stimulus such as shock. For example, it has been observed that rats able to press a lever to avoid shock show less severe physiological disturbance, as measured by weight loss and gastric lesions, than yoked controls which cannot respond, even though both groups receive the same amount of shock (Weiss, 1968). Similarly, animals able to escape from shock show less elevation of plasma corticosterone over the course of testing than animals receiving the same amount of inescapable shock (Davis, Porter, Livingstone, Herrmann, MacFadden, & Levine, 1977). Control over high-intensity noise can also reduce plasma cortisol levels. Hanson, Larson, and Snowden (1976) observed that rhesus monkeys that had control over noise showed plasma cortisol levels similar to animals that were not exposed to noise, and that both of these groups were significantly less elevated than animals with no control over the aversive stimulus. When animals in the group with control suddenly lost control (the lever no longer terminated noise), cortisol levels rose to those of the no-control group. Thus, having control reduces the physiological effects of stressors in the environment. And previous experience with control can significantly alter the ability to cope with subsequent aversive stimuli.

Loss of Control

Mandler (1964) has persuasively argued that the withdrawal of effective coping responses is physiologically, emotionally, and behaviorally significant. Consistent with this view, Mason, Brady, and Tolson (1966) showed that while exposure of monkeys to shocks alone or to temporally paced avoidance resulted in only modest increases in plasma norepinephrine and corticosterone levels, the presentation of unavoidable shocks to monkeys *after* they had already learned the avoidance response produced dramatic increases in both of these endocrines. That such signs of increased stress cannot be attributed to the increased number of shocks or to the frustration experience when animals are deprived of control over aversive events can be demonstrated by removing the manipulandum with which the organism exerts control, but *without* delivering further shock. Animals which experience this sort of loss of control still show dramatic increases in steroids (Mason et al., 1966; Coover, Ursin, & Levine, 1973). Comparable experiments have shown increases in ulceration (Weiss, 1971a, b) and cortisol levels (Hanson et al., 1976).

Feedback

Feedback can be defined as stimuli occurring after a response, not associated with the stressor (Weiss, 1971a). These stimuli provide input or information to an organism indicating that it has done the right thing and/or that the aversive stimulus is over. In a number of studies, it has been shown that relevant information or feedback can have a pronounced effect on the response to an aversive stimulus. In Weiss' studies (1971a, 1971b), for example, shock did not produce ulceration under all conditions; the psychological variables of control and feedback primarily determined the response to shock.

In one experiment (1971b), animals in a signaled-shock condition received a brief pulse of shock whenever they performed a well-learned avoidance response. These animals developed more severe ulcers and exhibited higher corticosterone levels than yoked animals which received exactly the same shocks, but could not perform the avoidance-escape response. It is unlikely that the additional shocks received increased the ulceration or the plasma corticosteroid levels in the avoidance group, since both avoidance and yoked subjects received extra shocks. Yet, only animals who actively made avoidance responses showed increased ulceration. Instead, it appears that reducing the feedback information is what increased the ulceration in this situation. For avoidance-escape animals, the additional shocks dramatically altered relevant feedback. Whereas in the normal-signal condition, responding produced stimuli that were not associated with shock (e.g., signal offset, shock offset), when punishment shocks were added, responses now produced stimuli associated with shock; in fact, responding produced the shock itself. Thus, it appears that feedback is an important variable in determining an organism's physiological response. Lack of feedback can increase stress responses such as ulceration, and increased feedback can reduce these same "symptomatic" responses. The degree of somatic stress produced is the product of an interaction between the number of coping attempts the animal makes and the amount of relevant feedback received for those responses (Weiss, 1971a).

Levine and his colleagues (Hennessey, King, McClure, & Levine, 1977; Levine, Goldman, & Coover, 1972) have demonstrated that the pituitary adrenal system, in particular, responds to changes in environmental contingencies and feedback. They reasoned that effective coping requires contingent feedback and that feedback, in turn, should lower corticosteroid levels. According to Ursin, Baade, and Levine (1978), the pituitary adrenal system does not simply habituate with experience as the autonomic system does. Rather, it is actively suppressed by informational feedback and control. This is a significant point because we are not dealing with a reduction of a physiological response to baseline via habituation, but rather with an active suppression of this system as a result of manipulations involving feedback and active coping. This is important for our consideration of self-regulatory processes because physiological changes in this system derive from response-produced contingencies.

The pituitary adrenal system also is responsive to changes in expectancies. Changes from predictable to unpredictable events are a sufficient condition to cause increases in pituitary adrenal activity (Levine & Coover, 1976). Such expectancies regarding environmental contingencies are important features of the process of self-regulation. We may assume that self-regulation, as opposed to external regulation, has the additional advantage of reducing unpredictability in the environment, at least to the extent that individuals can control the termination of undesirable events and control the onset of continuation of desirable events.

Human Studies

To the extent that analogous processes are operative in animals and people, a clear danger to biological integrity and health is presented by excessive exposure to uncontrollable events and/or the absence of a repertoire of self-controlling behaviors. It has been clearly demonstrated in humans that lack of control-relevant behaviors will generally activate both the pituitary adrenal system (e.g., Sachar, 1975) and the sympathetic-adrenal system (e.g., Frankenhaeuser, 1975a; 1975b). In a typical study, Lundberg and Frankenhaeuser (1978) tested subjects who performed mental arithmetic problems while exposed to aversive noise. Randomly selected subjects were able to choose among noise intensities and a yoked partner was exposed to the same noise. The group that was unable to choose its own intensities secreted significantly more cortisol.

When explicit skills for self-regulation are taught, coping with all varieties of aversive stressors improves substantially and has profound physiological consequences (Rodin, 1980, in press(a); Ursin et al., 1978). Ursin et al. tested novice parachute jumpers in the Norwegian Army as they learned to jump. They were tested in the week before training began, immediately before and after jumps from the mock training tower, and 2 hours post-jump. All hormones showed a significant and dramatic rise at the first jump in the mock tower training apparatus, then a clear and consistent decrease that was correlated with skill at mastering this particular task, not with repeated exposure per se.

Rodin (in press, a) taught elderly nursing home residents explicit behavioral self-regulation skills. Skills for memory and control over interpersonal interactions were the major foci of this particular intervention. Compared to no-treatment controls and groups given equal attention but no skills training, subjects in the skills group reported experiencing significantly more control, fewer and less disturbing daily "hassles," and less stress, in addition to showing improved performance on a variety of behavioral measures. Most important, urinary free cortisol levels were not only significantly lowered following the intervention, but, unlike levels of the other groups, remained lower at a 1-year follow-up.

In another study (Rodin, 1980), we confirmed the relationship between explicit contingency training and suppression of corticosteroids in elderly persons. We reasoned that the requirements for a strong test were, first, that the person would have repeated exposures to the same stressor and, second, that the characteristics of the stressor would remain constant such that if physiological changes did occur, they would be a function of the subject's reaction to the stressor and not to a change in the stressor itself. We decided to focus on the nurse-patient interaction as the stress-provoking stimulus, since it was one of the most high-frequency, high-intensity problems that patients reported. The study varied the amount of control with the amount of informational feedback in an orthogonal design. There was also a no-treatment control group.

The data showed that the group with the greatest suppression in corticosteroid level was the group with control and informational feedback. The next best group was given feedback but no control, and the third best group had control but no feedback. Thus, we may conclude that two components of the process of self-regulation—active coping responses and feedback regarding the efficacy of one's responses—seem to be important variables in suppressing pituitary adrenal activity for elderly nursing home residents.

The significance of these data rests on the repeated demonstration that sustained activation of these physiological variables produces somatic pathology in humans just as it does in animals. Persistent high levels of the tonic activation system may be related to pathology in a variety of ways. For example, high norepinephrine levels have been related to high blood pressure (Glass, 1977); high cortisol levels may be related to a failure of immune mechanisms, since corticosteroids have immunosuppressive properties (Gabrielson & Good, 1967), and free-fatty-acid levels are related to increased risk of cardiovascular disease (Goldbourt, Medalie, & Neufeld, 1975). Interestingly, however, there is also evidence that in some individuals, excessive efforts to assert control can have negative effects on many of these same physiological processes. The work of Glass and his colleagues (Glass, 1977), for example, considers Type A individuals who are so hard driven that they exert continued effort to exercise control even in the face of maladaptive outcomes of uncontrollable situations. Glass postulates that this repeated and frustrated desire for control whenever other people have ceased to make such efforts may be related to increased catecholamine output which, in turn, contributes to atherosclerosis. Thus, the effects of control-relevant self-regulation on biological processes are not totally simple and straightforward. We have yet to understand fully the conditions under which exercising control is maladaptive for the health and illness of people in general.

Thus far, I have considered how several features of the process of self-regulation — in particular, control (or active coping) and feedback — directly affect the physiological status of the individual via central-nervous-system-mediated pathways. It is also the case that behaviors used in the service of self-regulation may, themselves, influence the biological integrity of the body. For example, cutting down on food consumption or increased exercise may directly reduce the likelihood of cardiovascular disease. Once more, however, not all self-regulatory behaviors are equally adaptive for health. For example, smoking or drinking may be self-regulated techniques for reducing high levels of job-related or personal stress; yet they may have grave cumulative physiological effects on the individual, leading to increased incidence of a variety of diseases, including cancer, heart disease, and liver disorders.

The previous example, and that of the Type A person who appears over-driven for control, point out that the adaptive nature of self-regulatory responses must be measured, in part, by their overall biological consequences for the individual. The stressed business executive may feel less tension after a five-martini lunch, but may also be slowly killing himself with alcohol. Thus, the goals of self-regulatory behaviors are not always clear-cut and may even be contradictory, involving multiple short-term gains and long-term costs. It is not even the case that decisions about what is adaptive are straightforward when the self-regulatory process is directed toward rectifying a presumably maladaptive behavior (for one's health and physical status) such as overeating or drug use. The psychological stresses associated with deprivation of these "addictive" substances have, for some, more severe biological consequences than the behaviors themselves. Proponents of self-regulation suggest that the perceived control and increased efficacy that result from successful self-regulation have an effect on reducing these psychological stresses (e.g., Bandura, 1977), but this remains a major issue for future research.

One further essential point is that physiological status, in large part, determines the chronic level at which all behavior, including self-regulation, occurs. For example, overweight people are more physically primed to be tempted by tasty food and to store more of it as fat, simply as a consequence of being overweight (due to the metabolic and endocrine changes associated with obesity). Any successful self-regulatory strategy must take account of these chronic physiological states. In some ways, the external context is easier to manage. One can reorganize the environment, avoid certain classes of stimuli, shut out or distract one's self from others, and develop a set of cues that serve to facilitate self-control. But physiology can still have a major and sometimes uncontrollable effect. This is especially, but not exclusively, true for behaviors with biological consequences such as smoking, drinking, eating, anxiety, anger, sleep disturbances, or the like. Certainly, the physiological effects of substances themselves make self-control difficult, but in more ways than a simplistic addiction notion would convey. While many substances have pharmacological properties that make self-control problematic, it may also be that the long-term compulsive use of a substance may change the body in ways that make any form of control more difficult.

EXTERNAL AND INTERNAL CUES SIGNALING DISCREPANCY FROM GOAL (OPTIMAL LEVEL)

Above, I suggested that the homeostatic life-maintenance processes may be seen as the most basic form of biological self-regulation, and I have tried to show how biological systems are affected by the presence and absence of self-regulatory processes at the behavioral level as well. Physiological factors also play a major role in self-regulation by serving as cues for self-controlling responses. As such, they are part of the category of internal or self-generated stimuli that may function to elicit and maintain self-regulated behavior. The second major category is external events, which by their natural occurrence or by explicit manipulation support the control of a particular behavior or class of behaviors or provide cues for the expression of those behaviors (Rodin, Maloff, & Becker, in press).

External Cues for Self-Regulation

As an example of this second category, the external factors that facilitate the regulation of one's own behavior generally range from sociocultural processes (such as norms and value systems), at one end, to elements in one's own environment that signal a discrepancy from one's goals, at the other end. I am excluding from this group formal external cues for the control of behavior such as explicit laws and sanctions. Although the ability to incarcerate or fire, for example, greatly enhances coercive power, it may not enhance the likelihood that self-control will occur. For example, people typically drive slowly on the highway when a police car is in sight, but they generally speed up after it passes. Thus, the legal symbol with ability to exercise coercive power is not enhancing generalized self-regulation at all. In an even more extreme argument, Zinberg and Fraser (1978) suggest that formal control can often be shown to work against the processes operating to promote self-regulation and the internal control of behavior. For example, they argue that the formal controls of the prohibition era in the United States actually acted to encourage uncontrolled drinking. People went to speakeasies to get drunk rather than to drink.

In using the term "informal social controls," I am referring to the informal rules and other guides to behavior created in microenvironments by groups that have no formal code or mechanisms for enforcement. Examples of these are families, friendship groups, teenage cliques, and the like. These controls have their effects on behavior by salient, external symbols, such as the executive lunchroom or living in a halfway house for recovered alcoholics or addicts, and by more subtle symbols of the relevant norms and values, such as wearing the pin of a weight control club or passing a highway sign that says "speed kills." Both settings per se and the learned practices associated with a particular informal control may also come to have powerful cue functions for self-control behaviors. These are presumed to function as external cues for the exercise of self-control rather than being external controls per se (e.g., being watched by a policeman). In addition, the possibility for internal cues to participate in the self-regulation of behavior also arises, since through learning and acceptance of certain informal sanctions, the process of internalization takes place.

The immediate context, encompassing set and setting, also provides important external cues for self-control. Often, self-regulation involves choosing whether or not to be exposed to stimulating environmental cues (e.g., a former alcoholic who does not go to cocktail parties or a dieter who does not bring fattening foods into the house). The avoidance of cues associated with temptation may not always be possible, however, and other cues in the environment must be learned as signals for self-regulatory behaviors if they are to be effective in the long-run. Several behavioral self-management programs incorporate such procedures (e.g., Mahoney & Mahoney, 1976).

In contrast, one set of elements that impedes internalization is the overly strong imposition of external control per se. That is why it is so important to distinguish between external cues for self-control and actual external controls themselves. The negative effect of external controls on the internalization of cues for control appears true even when rewarding rather than negative incentives are used. In fact, in many instances, overly sufficient rewards for avoiding a behavior can undermine the processes facilitating self-control. In such cases, people resume the behavior when the rewards are removed. For example, if people are paid a large bonus to stop smoking, they may be more likely to resume smoking when the rewards are withdrawn than are people given a smaller inducement or no reward at all. This occurs because with strong rewards, people often correctly or incorrectly attribute the desirable behavior change to the reward rather than to their own motivation, or to their own choice and commitment (Lepper, Green, & Nisbett, 1973). In either case, they are more likely to relapse following the removal of the reward because of this attribution. As the example implies, self-control processes are strengthened when people can perceive *themselves* as the agents of change.

Internal Cues for Self-Regulation

The second class of self-control cues involves the internal stimuli which signal a discrepancy between current and optimal state. These include internal standards, affect, private verbal commands, and physiological signals, for example. People relying on internal cues need, therefore, to have a repertoire of techniques for monitoring and evaluating these internal events. Even the absence of internal physiological cues may have signal value, such as when a dieter uses the absence of hunger pangs as a cue to refrain from eating.

While the ability to use internal cues in the self-regulation of behavior depends on being able to monitor one's internal physical states, thoughts, and feelings, self-observation and awareness are only the first step, since these cues must then be used to elicit and guide appropriate behaviors. Again, to take weight control as an example, dieters must learn to notice and evaluate their responses to the taste of food, using their assessment as a cue for self-control processes. If the food is not very good, which they often find to be the case, that must be used as a signal to stop eating. Similarly, if it is too good, they must also learn to introduce other self-limiting control behaviors.

The relevance of internal cues for self-regulation, of course, varies for different problems. Once again, the specific focus on biological levels represents the task of this chapter rather than a failure to recognize that there are often other possiblities or that there are problems for which physiological cues are less relevant.

The precise cue function of physiological variables has been widely debated in some circles. Motivated in part by Cannon's critique of the James-Lange theory of emotions, which argues that physiological responses are often too slow and undifferentiated to serve as cues for the labeling of emotions, Schachter and Singer (1962) proposed a two-part theory of emotion. Physiological arousal was presumed to motivate a search for a label for the stirred-up state, but was itself not assumed to provide that label. Although the experimental procedures used to test this theory have come under recent attack (Maslach, 1979; Marshall & Zimbardo, 1979), the notion that physiological cues alone provide insufficient information in and of themselves to guide labeling and behavior has been widely accepted.

People also appear especially vulnerable to attributional errors regarding their physiological states, providing further evidence for the view that they are not able to derive precise cues on the basis of physiological signals alone. In part, this position may be valid. When everything is working smoothly, feedback from physiological processes may not be accessed at the conscious level. Even when something feels wrong, the discomfort may be hard to identify. Not only are most bodily signals ambiguous, but many are unfamiliar. When these physical sensations are difficult to evaluate objectively, they lead to even more speculative inferences than occur normally, which may make for possibly erroneous perceptions. These perceptions and causal inferences may dramatically effect the processes of self-regulation by creating a set of incorrect or dysfunctional cues. This diagnostic error may also prevent realistic appraisal of potential action that could be taken by the individual.

We have preliminary data suggesting that some of the emotional reactivity often reported in overweight people may be a consequence of obesity-caused irregularity in the circadian rhythm of certain hormones such as cortisol and in triglycerides. The ambiguity of arousal produced by disturbances in these rhythms could generate anxiety and lead the person to search the external environment for an explanation for his arousal (Schachter & Singer, 1962). Similar attributional processes may occur in response to other ambiguous arousal states produced by shifts in the many metabolic and endocrine processes that are associated with overeating (Horton, Danforth, Sims, & Salans, 1975). Consequently, overweight people may mislabel their ambiguous and variable symptoms, which are actually caused by internal physiological changes, and attribute them to family quarrels, for example, or to other events occurring in the environment, again challenging self-regulatory processes by providing inappropriate cues for behavior.

We also conducted a series of studies where blood samples were drawn continuously from hungry subjects. During this period, a steak was grilled in front of them, providing a rich array of visual, auditory, and olfactory cues (Rodin, 1978). Some individuals, regardless of their current level of body weight, actually secreted insulin simply upon seeing, hearing, and smelling this palatable food. These data suggest that some people are literally turned on by the sight and thought of food, with their anabolic processes begun before the food even enters the mouth. Further work by our group suggests that the more palatable the food is, the more likely people are to trigger this kind of an insulin response. These metabolic and physiological responses challenge self-regulatory processes because they are unobservable to the individual and are only experienced as an increased feeling of hunger or an increased desire to eat, even when the individual is not in a state of energy deficit. While the experience can perhaps become the cue for self-regulatory behaviors, it is clearly a more demanding task against the background of a physiological substrate that is pressing the individual toward consumption. Furthermore, sometimes experienced hunger *is* a signal of energy needs and thus, at such times, is an appropriate cue for eating. Yet, we lack ways to teach the individual to distinguish between these two types of hunger experience.

The whole issue, then, of how people come to identify and label their internal physiological states is of crucial theoretical concern for self-regulation. Unfortunately, the observation and detection of biological cues is neither simple nor straightforward. Many of the biological events that motivate behavior are not subject to conscious awareness; others can be cues, but require environmental circumstances to provide the labels, and often there is great room for attributional error. It has been suggested that greater self-awareness derives from focusing one's attention inward (Duval & Wickland, 1972). The implication of this line of reasoning is that individuals who learned to focus their attention on their physiological responses, rather than on environmental cues, could come to identify and use their internal states in the service of self-regulation, and with diminished error. Griggs and Stunkard (1964) successfully taught overweight subjects to identify when their stomachs were contracting and to focus on these and other internal sensations to determine whether or not they were truly hungry. Earlier work (Stunkard & Koch, 1964) had indicated that overweight people did not have greater (or fewer) stomach contractions than people of normal weight. Yet, subjects could not regulate their eating even though they came to be able to identify quite readily their internal cues for hunger. In fact, some subjects actually gained weight. Much more work is needed in conjunction with the other critical processes involved in self-regulation (e.g., motivation, feedback) before we can determine how effective teaching attention to internal cues can be for clinical self-regulation.

Conscious Awareness

Another theoretical issue, related to the one just discussed, is whether self-regulation can occur in the absence of explicit, consciously available cues. This is an especially interesting problem when one considers biological processes as the behaviors to be regulated as well as the cues for self-regulation. Consider, for example, control of visceral processes such as blood pressure, which has been thought to occur without conscious cues. I would maintain that control of biological state, like control of behavior, cannot occur in the absence of an explicit set of cues, and that whether the individuals are identifying the *correct* cues or not, they are using *some* cues with which feedback from their behavior seems to covary. Clearly, when they are informed about the changes, as in the case of biofeedback, self-regulation learning is more effective than when they are simply asked to change certain physiological responses or conditions and are given no feedback with regard to the efficacy of their attempts. But in both cases, subjects would be seen as hypothesis testing, focusing inward, and trying to identify a set of cues by which *they* are regulating their visceral states.

Consider the case of the stimulation of visceral receptors, for example, which in the range of physiological intensities does not spontaneously invoke any subjective sensations. Yet these unconscious visceral stimuli can be rendered conscious, which is essential if self-regulatory behaviors are to be systematic and nonrandom. For example, by means of verbal feedback, Adám (1978) taught a group of subjects to perceive duodenal stimuli that, prior to conditioning, had not been conscious. He was also able, using verbal conditioning, to teach women to perceive unconscious uterine impulses. Starting from the level of the subjective sensation of discomfort, the voltage of the successive train of uterine impulses was lowered step by step. Each visceral stimulation was accompanied by verbal feedback—"The uterine stimulus is now applied" or "You now feel vibration in your abdomen." After 10 to 50 such associative trials, the subjects became aware of the stimulus at a voltage much lower than the initial subjective threshold. These studies suggest that by using feedback, it is possible to teach subjects to notice and perceive visceral stimuli that were not in conscious awareness prior to conditioning. Thereafter, self-regulatory behaviors may be taught. Interestingly, these investigators were unable to explain the mechanism of the results of the feedback experiment. But it is obvious that the feedback (in this case, verbal control) was the essential factor in bringing the subsensory, visceral impulses into consciousness.

In discussing these data, Adám (1978) questioned whether this technique has any theoretical importance or whether it is merely an attractive laboratory artifact. I would maintain that it has considerable theoretical import, since it confirms feedback as a crucial process in the self-regulatory cycle and points to a mechanism by which physiological stimuli may become available to cue self-regulating behaviors.

BIOLOGICAL VARIABLES AFFECTING SELF-REGULATION

In this section, I will consider two very different examples of how self-regulation processes may operate, with special emphasis on biological aspects of cues for self-regulation. The first comes from the work of Leventhal and his co-workers (Leventhal et al., 1980; Meyer, Leventhal, & Gutman, in press) and has to do with self-regulation of medication taken for hypertension. The second comes from my own work and has to do with self-regulation in the area of weight control and smoking cessation. In considering the more general implications of these studies, it may be emphasized that the *onset* of self-regulation is always occasioned by cues indicating a need for change or redirection. Thus, magnifying or enhancing the distinctiveness of these cues can be extremely useful to activate self-regulation. These examples show, however, that self-regulation may also be undermined by highly distinctive but inappropriate cues.

The Role of Symptoms in Medication Taking

Leventhal and his co-workers began their investigation of the determinants of taking hypertension medication by assuming that patients are motivated to protect themselves against threats such as those posed by high blood pressure. But motivation or the desire to act is not the sole determinant of behavior. The individual's behavior is also determined by the available cues that must be brought forth in the service of self-regulation and all of the competing cues and pressures that oppose self-regulation. One set of pro-self-regulation cues involves information from providers of health care. This information allows the individual to understand the consequences of the elevated pressure and the risks attendant to it. And yet, often patients do not appear to regulate their behavior on the basis of this information at all, as a very large literature on noncompliance attests. The reasons, Leventhal and his co-workers argue, is that patients have a second, highly salient, and continuously available source of information that participates in self-regulatory processes. These are the sensations and symptoms arising from the body, which are seen by patients as consequences of high blood pressure. Certainly, there may be a variety of concrete sensations that are present at the time that the patient is told that his blood pressure is elevated, or associated with events that he views as causes of his high blood pressure. These sensory cues come to represent hypertension. This occurs despite the fact that health care providers tell patients that the disorder is asymptomatic and a "silent killer."

This tendency to focus on bodily cues when one is ill develops because, from one's earliest childhood, illness has meant symptoms and getting well has meant the disappearance of symptoms. So there is a powerful, concrete representation of illness as a symptom, and the patient begins to focus on and become increasingly aware of his internal state. I would argue that there is always a whole constellation of physical sensations potentially accessible for people to experience, and that the reason why we do or do not attend to them has to do with the way information is processed. For example, one's focus of attention at any given time depends on what is most salient or where the weight of the cues are in terms of their demandingness. Usually, these are in the external environment. As discussed in the preceding section, most people, unless specifically motivated or instructed to do so, do not spontaneously focus attention inward. However, when it does occur, attention to various bodily states may increase the perceived intensity of the symptom. For example, many sports contestants agree that at the very height of the competition they are unaware of the aches and pains. By contrast, instructions requiring subjects to attend to cold pressor pain usually increase self-reports of pain (e.g., Kanfer & Goldfoot, 1966).

In addition, the experience of symptoms relies on the interpretive set of the subject at the time that his attention is focusing on one set of symptoms or another. The interpretive set established by instructions to adopt a particular attitude toward a sensory experience can have a profound impact (Pennebaker & Skelton, 1978). For pain-related symptoms, the interpretive component actually defines the sensory experience as painful. For nonpainful symptoms, however, the interpretive context determines whether the experienced sensations are defined as symptomatic at all.

Moods may also function as interpretive sets and undoubtedly can therefore affect interpretation of bodily states as well. Pennebaker and Skelton (1978) report correlational evidence showing that negative moods are directly related to symptom reports. It seems likely that experiencing a loss or lack of control also changes the focus of attention inward in a way that heightens the level of symptom experience. This is an especially significant notion since it builds still another feedback structure between attention to bodily conditions and self-regulatory processes. Thus, a greater sense of control might lead to a decreased focus on bodily signals and symptoms than might otherwise be expected. If we carry this intriguing speculation to the extreme, we might expect that individuals with a greater sense of control actually experience fewer symptoms or recover faster from the illnesses that they develop. Support for such a notion comes from our own work (Langer & Rodin, 1976; Rodin & Langer, 1977; Rodin, 1980), as well as from the work of Glass (1977) and Schmale and Iker (1966, 1971). The physiological consequences of efficacy expectations and self-produced outcomes may turn out to be their most profound effect.

In summary, when a person is told he has a particular illness (in Leventhal's examples, high blood pressure), he may focus his attention inward and begin to define this abstraction in concrete, symptomatic terms such as heart beating, stress, face flushing, headache, and so on. Once the patient selects the concrete symptom or set of symptoms to represent blood pressure elevations, he is likely to monitor these symptoms to determine the correlates or causes of blood pressure elevation and declines. This means that self-regulated behavior (in this instance, taking the medication) will be affected by the extent to which the behavior or treatment is seen as reducing the severity of the symptoms. Indeed, degree of adherence to a medically prescribed regimen will depend on the overlap between it and the self-generated prescription generated by this analysis, according to Leventhal and his co-workers.

This line of reasoning is especially interesting because there is actually no way of establishing whether the symptoms Leventhal's subjects report are valid signs of blood pressure elevations or not. Thus, while perceived symptomatic changes with treatment influence adherence to treatment, and therefore blood pressure outcomes, these effects appear to be independent of the actual validity of the symptoms as indicators of blood pressure elevations. Thus, a symptom can regulate adherence and, in turn, regulate blood pressure, regardless of its link to objective blood pressure levels.

Although medical authorities deny that bodily sensations are reliably associated with blood pressure elevations, Leventhal and his co-workers found that the great majority of respondents thought otherwise. Most patients found a simple way to avoid conflict between their own and the physician's view of the value of sensations as indications of pressure changes. Especially interesting for our theoretical concerns was the fact that sensation monitoring appeared to develop even more extensively over time. Eighty-eight percent of a group that was actively being treated believed in symptoms, whereas only 52 percent of newly discovered hypertensives did. Moreover, longitudinally, the percentage reporting symptoms of high blood pressure increased over time. There was also a change in the symptoms reported over time. As people progressed in treatment, they appeared to discount heart rate, for example, as a sign of high blood pressure.

Because patients believed that they were able to monitor the symptoms of high blood pressure, it is clear that they would expect treatment to modify these symptoms. Thus, we assume that a large proportion of patients who were actively taking medication perceived beneficial effects of treatment on alleviating the symptoms they believed were associated with high blood pressure. This is strongly supported in the Leventhal data. Thus, the symptoms served as cues and the removal of symptoms as positive feedback in the self-regulation of drug-taking behavior. The disconfirming feedback that developed from the failure for symptoms to be reduced was associated with decisions not to remain in treatment.

If we assume that patients are motivated to attempt to understand and regulate their own behavior, symptoms are important cues that participate in the regulation of behavior in the domain of illness. Symptoms are highly available cues that can be experienced directly and that can give instant and continuous feedback about the progress of one's illness. They are extremely convenient devices for determining the causes of disease and for evaluating effectiveness of treatments. Representing the illness as palpable and highly available symptoms allows for ongoing analysis, selection, and evaluation of specific coping efforts. According to Leventhal and his co-workers, it may be that patients, who can generate a detailed representation of the hypertensive process, will be those who will show a greater use of self-regulation because they would be those who could generate a detailed and specific plan for dealing with the illness on the basis of specifiable cues. The less concrete the representation and the cues, the more abstract the goals may be, and therefore the more inefficient and weak the self-regulatory processes. The patient's representation of illness thus provides a focus for self-regulating behaviors that may expand into a greater sense of self-determination and control over both emotional experiences and the quality of life in general. Again, we must raise the question, however, of the short-term versus long-term gains of these self-regulatory behaviors, if stopping or starting treatment is what is at issue.

In this example, the adaptive consequence of the self-regulation of behavior, based on symptoms and physiological factors as cues, depended on the happenstance of which cues the person had identified as symptoms and their association with medication taking or its termination. But some patients may stop taking their medication when the symptoms cease, assuming that they are now better. These people may not resume treatment with the medication until a recurrence of these or other symptoms. On the other hand, different patients may continue taking their medication when their symptoms disappear, attributing the lack of symptoms to the continued medication taking. For them, a resumption of symptoms would lead to discontinuing usage.

The Role of Weight Gain as a Cue After Smoking Cessation

Now, consider a radically different example of the way that biological processes may influence self-regulatory behaviors, the case of smoking cessation and weight gain that usually occurs as a consequence. Several studies have suggested that most people gain some weight following smoking cessation, with the average weight gain in each study ranging between 7 and 21 pounds. Here, the problem is that there is an observable cue for self-regulation, one's change in body weight, which signals discrepancy from optimal level, so the person's attention is now drawn inward. But, unlike the hypertensive example discussed above, this cue is not the most useful for self-regulatory behaviors. What is intriguing, and represents a challenge to the development and utilization of self-regulation skills, is the possibility that these people could have gained weight without changing a single aspect of their eating behavior. Moreover, using weight gain as the cue to initiate and maintain self-regulatory behaviors, and the very behaviors themselves, could exacerbate the condition they are seeking to control.

Despite the conventional wisdom, the empirical data suggesting that people overeat when they stop smoking are very weak. There are a variety of reasons why increased consumption has been expected to occur following smoking cessation. Psychodynamic theories most often hypothesize oral gratification as the underlying cause of smoking behavior; persons with oral tendencies might eat more to substitute for the absence of cigarettes. A second line of reasoning, which focuses on commonalities among substance use, argues for the interchangeability of food for cigarettes at some level. Both theories would predict increased frequency of consumption after smoking cessation. At present, support for these assertions is largely anecdotal. Several other possible factors affecting the relationship between food intake and smoking have received empirical consideration, however.

Since the amount one consumes is strongly affected by the perceived palatability of food, several investigators have considered whether smoking affects the senses of taste and olfaction. Although former smokers often report that they experience an improvement in their sense of smell and taste upon quitting (Elgerot, 1978), experimental evidence as to whether smoking or nicotine actually alters the smoker's sense of taste or smell is inconclusive (Pangborn & Trabue, 1973).

After smoking cessation, factors affecting meal termination might also be altered. Many smokers report that they crave a cigarette upon completion of a meal; casual observations tend to confirm the immediacy with which many smokers light up after eating. It may be that for the smoker, this cigarette is an unambiguous marker of the termination of the meal. Upon cessation of smoking, the individual loses this marker and may be more inclined to proceed to take second helpings or the high-calorie desserts that are often consumed at the end of the meal.

Studies investigating changes in eating habits following the cessation of smoking have primarily relied upon retrospective interviews. Wynder, Kaufman, and Lesser (1967) found that among 224 subjects, all of whom had quit smoking from 3 months to 10 years earlier, 70 percent reported having gained weight and 67 percent reported that their actual food intake, especially the consumption of sweets, had increased when they stopped smoking. However, Goudet and Hugli (1969), in a similar study, found no significant changes in the consumption of kinds of sweet foods, leading them to conclude that the commonly accepted belief that the cessation of smoking leads to increased consumption of sweets does not appear true. Retrospective studies are problematic because considerably increased or different patterns of food intake may not have actually occurred, but rather may have been invoked by the subjects as a post hoc explanation of the weight gain they knew they had experienced (cf. Nisbett & Wilson, 1977).

Clearly, increases in the frequency and duration of meals, the amount of food consumed at a meal, or changes in the types of food eaten (e.g., the proportions of protein, carbohydrate, and fat) could account for the weight gain persons experience upon stopping smoking. Few studies have compared the eating habits of smokers and nonsmokers, and none has attempted the longitudinal studies that would be necessary to assess systematically changes in these parameters that would reflect differential calorie intake.

While the requisite longitudinal data are lacking, several studies have compared the food intake of current smokers to current nonsmokers in cross-sectional studies. If it were found that smokers consumed fewer calories than nonsmokers, the data would help to explain why smokers weigh less than nonsmokers and would lend support to the assertion that the weight gain that followed cessation was due to increased consumption. Despite this highly plausible line of reasoning, however, most of these studies have shown that smokers actually consume *more* rather than fewer calories per day than nonsmokers. For example, Lincoln (1969) evaluated a national sample of 885 middle-aged men who completed questionnaires concerning their food and beverage consumption over a period of 24 hours. Analyses revealed that smokers reported consuming an average of about 250 calories more than the nonsmokers, with the heaviest smokers consuming about 575 calories more than nonsmokers. Nonetheless, these smokers weighed about 6.5 pounds less than the nonsmokers. Data for a few recent abstainers were also available and indicated that within a few months of stopping smoking, these ex-smokers had gained an average of about 8 pounds, despite a reported decrease in daily food intake of 200 calories.

Additional evidence, suggesting that smoking is associated with consumption of more rather than less calories, comes from data regarding the food intake of smokers and nonsmokers during pregnancy. Admittedly, in view of the wide-ranging endocrinological changes that accompany a pregnancy, inferences from the pregnant to the nonpregnant state must be made with caution. Picone et al. (Note 1) monitored the weight gains of a matched group of smokers and nonsmokers over the course of their pregnancies. At each clinic visit, a dietary assessment by a 24-hour recall was obtained, resulting in the collection of 2 to 6 recalls for each of the 60 subjects. Overall, despite lower weight gains during the pregnancy, smoking mothers reported consuming significantly more (310) calories per day than did the nonsmoking mothers. These results are highly consistent with those of another study (Higgins, Note 2) in which it was found that the average daily intake of expectant mothers who smoked was 294 calories and 10 grams of protein per day greater than for pregnant nonsmokers.

These paradoxical findings — that smokers weigh less and eat more than nonsmokers — suggest that physiological, especially metabolic, factors may be of major importance in determining the body weight of cigarette smokers. To consider the direct physiological effects of nicotine, Schnecter and Cook (1976) administered .4 or .8 mg/kg of nicotine intra-peritoneally 2 or 3 times per day for 5 weeks in rats. During this period, the animals lost weight, compared to saline-injected controls, but without a decrease in food consumption or change in activity levels. This finding is consistent with other evidence from dogs (Kerschbaum, Beller, & Khorsandrian, 1965), guinea pigs (Evans, Hughes, & Jones, 1967; Hughes, Jones, & Nicholas, 1970), hamsters (Passey, 1957; 1958), mice (Passey, 1957; 1958) showing a depression of body weight or growth induced by cigarette smoke or nicotine, despite there being no decrease in food consumption.

The observation of weight loss without parallel decreases in food consumption suggests two possible effects of smoking: The nicotine ingested by habitual smokers may result in less efficient storage of calories by changing the physiology of the gut, thereby disrupting absorption, or by biasing particular metabolic processes away from storage. A second effect of nicotine may be that of altering the processes of metabolism in a manner that facilitates calorie expenditure. Activation of either or both of these mechanisms could account for body weight being lower among smokers than nonsmokers, if calorie ingestion were equal or even greater among smokers. On the basis of the studies I will review next, both of these seem to be true.

Schnedorf and Ivy (1938) conducted the only study in which the effect of smoking on clearance through the entire alimentary tract was compared between smokers and nonsmokers. The dietary histories of one group of 10 habitual smokers and a second group of 10 nonsmokers were obtained, and a two-week dietary regime was prescribed so as to keep quantity and quality of food intake constant. With the noon meal on each day of the two weeks, subjects consumed knotted, colored strings to serve as markers. In the first week, both groups continued smoking or not smoking; in the second week, the habitual smokers stopped smoking, whereas the nonsmokers smoked a minimum of six cigarettes per day. The time at which the colored strings were passed in the stools was the measure and tended to confirm the impression currently accepted that smoking tends to increase the propulsive activity of the colon. If foodstuffs consumed are moved through the alimentary tract faster in the smoker than the nonsmoker, then the gut of the smoker may be wasting more of those calories that are consumed, thereby permitting increased caloric consumption and equal or lowered body weight.

The lower body weights observed among smokers may also be explained by alterations in metabolic pathways caused by smoking, resulting in fewer of these calories being stored, or their being stored via less energy-conserving enzymatic pathways (Stirling & Stock, 1973). A major effect of smoking appears to be that of biasing metabolic pathways such that more calories, either ingested or mobilized from fat stores, remain in the bloodstream longer where they are more readily available for utilization. The calorie storage that does occur may favor more energy-expending pathways such as protein synthesis over fat storage.

This bias away from storage of calories in adipose tissue among those who smoke provides a key for explaining why smokers may actually weigh less than nonsmokers. The lipostatic hypothesis of body weight regulation has a long tradition in physiology. Apparently, some mechanism exists for signaling the need for food intake when a depletion of an optimal energy reserve in adipose tissue is sensed. Nicotine's effect on metabolic pathways may be that a desired level of adipose reserve is not attained, and one hunger "signal" in the smoker is "left on" more often.

The effect of smoking on body weight has, to this point, focused primarily on the mechanisms of calorie intake and storage that may be altered and may return to normal upon cessation, along with consequent weight gain. There may also be a general reduction in thermogenic efficiency upon stopping smoking, an effect that would be reflected in lower resting metabolic rates and body temperatures and a reduction in respiratory quotients (Goldman, Haisman, Bynum, Salans, Danforth, Horton, & Sims, 1976). At least in the short-term, the evidence is quite clear that for most subjects, smoking results in a detectable increase in metabolic rate. Dill, Edwards, and Forbes (1934) had eight smokers rest for a period of 90 minutes prior to smoking one cigarette over a period of 5 to 10 minutes. Oxygen consumption was observed to increase on the average of about 10 percent in the 45 minutes after smoking.

All these lines of evidence suggest that an increase in body weight, following smoking cessation, would be possible even without increased consumption, given an hypothesized combination of mechanisms influenced by the physiological effects of nicotine. The decelerating rate of metabolism that would follow cessation provides a way in which former smokers could gain weight. If the newly abstinent smoker notices his weight gain and somewhat increased taste acuity, he may impose self-regulatory activity on his food consumption, using hunger, good taste, and the scale as cues for suppressing his desire to eat. Against the background of a newly sluggish metabolism, however, greatly reduced food consumption may be exactly what he does not need, since too few calories may make his metabolic processes slow down even more (Rodin, in press b). Self-regulation of food consumption immediately after smoking cessation may, therefore, be extremely maladaptive.

Here we have a condition that is just the opposite of the illness example. These individuals should be looking for inner signals and states as cues to adjust their behavior, but they have had no prior experience that enables them to identify these cues. So they look to personal shortcoming or to the environment. Cues from these domains can undermine self-regulation because they promote the development of incorrect or only partially effective behavioral strategies. This leads to negative feedback and decreased efficacy, which may be especially demoralizing when coupled with weight gain. It is likely that aerobic exercise, which speeds up metabolism, rather than greatly reduced food consumption, should be the self-regulation strategy of choice under these circumstances. But weight change may not be the appropriate feedback cue, since the metabolic changes induced by exercise may have a greater effect on the time taken to achieve a new weight plateau than on weight loss per se. People used to viewing daily or even weekly weight changes as the cue for self-regulation may have difficulty developing an appropriate set of behavioral skills in this domain. Indeed, in some cases, the best self-regulatory strategy may be to do nothing at all.

THERAPEUTIC IMPLICATIONS

At present, there are no published studies describing the development of a self-regulation therapy based on the full conceptual model described in this chapter, although many vary a few or even several of the crucial components. It would not be useful, however, to attempt a comparative outcome analysis of these studies as a function of which components or how many components they have considered, since I am presuming that effective self-regulation depends on these all functioning in mutually interdependent ways. The development of this model into a therapeutic technology is the concern of much of my present research in weight control.

There has been considerable interest in teaching systematic self-regulatory behaviors for weight control since the mid 1960s. Unfortunately, the magnitude of weight loss has not been clinically significant in many instances, and there are poor long-term maintenance data on many of these behavioral treatments. Regardless of the specific type of treatment being used, better and more comprehensive assessment of the type of obesity and the nature of the specific behavioral deficit is essential prior to self-management training in order to obtain good treatment and maintenance results. Unfortunately, such assessment procedures have often been omitted from weight-loss programs.

In addition, it is already clear that some erroneous assumptions formed the initial foundation on which self-regulated treatment of obesity was developed. For example, all obesity is not the result of overeating due to a learning disorder. Physiology directly influences eating behavior, in conjunction with specific conditioning history and current environmental stimuli. For example, if, through surgery, fat cells are removed from animals, thereby altering their fat-storage capability, results show that these animals *decrease* their desire for rich-tasting, high-calorie foods (Faust, Johnson, & Hirsch, 1977). Thus, the ability to store fat may directly affect eating behavior and influence consumption. Self-regulation strategies must be sensitive to the complex interaction between these physiological and behavioral variables, and must be based on a theoretical model regarding the process of self-regulation. Without this, a fair test of whether effective self-regulation can be taught is not possible.

To effect long-term behavior change, all features of the self-regulation process must be dealt with during the therapeutic intervention, and each of these has a biological component to which attention must be given. To return to the general model developed earlier, the individual must have learned skills that will allow him to monitor and modify his own behavior. This depends, in part, on his ability to produce or utilize cues from multiple levels of information, which then serve as eliciting stimuli for self-regulatory behaviors. Cognitive, internal-physiological, and external-environmental cues are all essential in this regard. In general, the individual who has multiple sources of cues and highly differentiated behavioral strategies in response to different patterns of cues will show the most effective self-regulation. The response repertoire is a crucial component and must include not only overt behavior, but cognitive, skeletal, and visceral responses.

Second, there must be motivation which is continuous throughout the instruction phase and maintainable beyond. The homeostatic model developed here assumes a built-in motive to restore balance, to return to the ideal comparison level. But sometimes this fundamental motive is subverted by other motives that push and pull the person to engage in behaviors that oppose self-regulation. The more salient the cues for self-regulation, the more weight may be given to this built-in motive to restore balance. Individuals must learn especially to identify cues that signal a discrepancy between their actual and optimal states. The sources of motivation may be diverse for a single individual, but even the best-learned self-regulation skills will not be used if the individual loses the motivation to employ them. Motivation has cognitive (memories, expectations, plans), emotional (feelings, hopes), and physiological (drive states) components that can be called upon in the service of self-regulation. The individual must develop and have the ability to keep developing a series of short- and long-term goals; without specifiable goals, motivation will surely wane.

There must also be reinforcement for making self-regulatory responses, which comes from meeting self-determined goals. Unfortunately, many attempts to maximize self-regulation seem to have faltered because these reinforcers are either inadequate, ineffectively administered, or too weak to compete with the reinforcement derived from the behaviors the individual is trying to change. The ability of self-administered reward and punishment to sustain long-term self-regulation has thus far failed to be demonstrated. More research is needed to determine how this can occur, but therapists must recognize that this weak link in the chain of techniques currently available can undermine self-regulation.

Finally, individuals must have firmly in place a feedback process that informs them about progress toward their goals. Again, multiple sources of feedback including information regarding biological, cognitive, emotional, and environmental changes may all be important, although to different degrees for different behaviors. The most effective feedback not only confirms that something changed, but also tells how and why. It is through this process that individuals begin to develop efficacy expectations, which increase the likelihood of self-regulation. But the "how and why" components are influenced by the attributions people make for the effects they have had on the environment or on their own internal states. Unless they attribute the changes to their own self-determined acts, the feedback will have little consequence for promoting self-regulatory ability. Such attributional processes are important for all types of self-regulation, but may be especially important for those behaviors that have physiological consequences or rely on physiological discriminative stimuli.

There are a variety of techniques for accomplishing these prescriptions. However, some of these have taken on a certain ritualistically important quality (for example, self-monitoring), and we have begun to lose sight of the processes that they are presumed to affect. One goal of a *theory* of self-regulation is to guide us to select from and develop further a whole armamentarium of techniques that are motivated by this theoretical view. The *magic is not in the technique* per se, but in the process that it is presumably tapping into. Thus, techniques for cue identification, goal setting, self-generated feedback, internal self-awareness, cognitive restructuring, plan/expectancy elaboration, coping skills training, relapse rehearsal, and, above all, techniques for self-sustenance of motivation to use all these skills and techniques are the technology but not the science of self-regulation. The latter depends on good theory. Only good theories will tell us which techniques to develop, for whom they should work, and in what situations, because they allow us to know how and why things work.

Let us consider one of the therapeutic implications of this line of reasoning, again sampling from my own research on óbesity. The biopsychosocial model leads to the prediction that the external cues which have internal physiological consequences will have the strongest effect on eating behavior. Research confirmed this proposition, and the theoretical model allowed us to predict which individuals would trigger insulin and other gastrointestinal secretions to the sight and thought of food (Rodin, 1978). Based on this theoretical model, different kinds of skills for self-regulation seem mandated for this group of individuals. Techniques like preplanning or consciously focusing on food in order to regulate one's intake would be maladaptive for such people. Instead, strategies such as avoiding food thoughts, distraction, and the like are more useful, and we have shown this to be true in our clinical work. But there are also the strategies that people hit upon spontaneously.

We observed that the externally responsive individuals who, in our studies, showed the greatest insulin release at the sight and thought of food, and yet had been able to keep their weight off for longer than one year without learning self-regulation skills from a clinician, were those whose behaviors were the very antithesis of continuous choice and decision making. These individuals had built a very rigid lifestyle for themselves (for example, one had not deviated at all from eating the same lunch at the same restaurant for years), thus avoiding choices and decision making. At the metalevel, perhaps this can be conceived of as self-regulation, since unpredictability was reduced and the individual displayed total self-control; but it was inflexible coping, at best, and was maladaptive for other domains of the person's life. However, they had independently evolved a practice that was consistent with theory-based research. Specifically, some individuals may be so turned on metabolically by certain foods that it is better to have none at all. Note that this line of reasoning is inconsistent with much of our current practice in weight control, with its emphasis on teaching persons how to eat everything they like, but in a controlled fashion.

My most memorable therapeutic failure, a few years ago, was a case where I did not follow this particular mandate. The client swore that seeing and thinking about food turned him on beyond control. I knew that he was at least two standard deviations away from anyone in his weight-loss group in the amount he salivated and released insulin in response to seeing and thinking about palatable, sweet foods. Since he was the most motivated member of the group, and without my current wisdom of hindsight, I continued to press upon him the skills required for moderate, controlled ingestion—one cookie instead of none or the whole box. He did well during treatment, albeit his weight loss was not consistent, but he continued to lament the extraordinary effort that it took. I assured him it would get easier, feeling certain that with practice and the increased efficacy he was experiencing in this domain, it would. As soon as the program was over, he often ate uncontrollably and regained much of his weight.

While no program is entirely successful for everyone, this story highlights the fact that for most of the dysfunctional behaviors we are treating, there is an unavoidable baseline of biological status. All the skills and new habits in the world will not override that fact. It is not that such clients are incapable of self-regulation, but rather that our theoretical models should be used to provide guidance regarding what kinds of cues, skills, and feedback are appropriate for which individuals.

SUMMARY

In this chapter, I have tried to present a general model of self-regulation, based on the biological process of homeostasis, which I think has potentially great heuristic value for theory-building and clinical practice. In my discussion of the overall model, I focused primarily on the causes and effects of physiological variables within this general process of self-regulation, as was my assigned task for this chapter. Many of the problems we treat deal with substance use or are states, such as anxiety or phobias, that provoke intense physiological reactions. For these, especially, a model of self-regulation which takes biological variables into account is essential. Good basic research and theory building in this area will inform clinical practice, but the influence must also work in reverse. Good clinical practice is a form of theory construction and hypothesis testing about each individual client, but should also be used to construct testable, general principles that may be scrutinized by basic research. At present, self-regulation therapy is more a promise than an accomplishment; the real work remains to be done.

REFERENCE NOTES

1. Picone, T. A., Allen, L. H., Schramm, M., & Ferris, M. *Maternal pregnancy weight gain and smoking: Effects on human placental development and neonatal behavior.* Paper presented at Federation of American Societies for Experimental Biology. Anaheim, California, April 17, 1980.
2. Higgins, A. C. Nutritional supplements and the outcome of pregnancy (p. 93). Proceedings of a workshop, November 3–5, 1971, Sagamere Beach, Mass.

REFERENCES

Adám, G. Visceroception, awareness, and behavior. In G. E. Schwartz & D. Shapiro (Eds.), *Consciousness and self-regulation* (Vol. 2). New York: Plenum Press, 1978.

Averill, J. R. Personal control over aversive stimuli and its relationship to stress. *Psychological Bulletin*, 1973, *80*, 286.

Bandura, A. Self-efficacy: Toward a unifying theory of behavioral change. *Psychological Review*, 1977, *84*, 191–215.

Berlyne, D. *Conflict, arousal and curiosity.* New York: McGraw-Hill, 1960.

Coover, G. D., Ursin, H., & Levine, S. Plasma-corticosterone levels during active-avoidance learning in rats. *Journal of Comparative and Physiological Psychology*, 1973, *82*, 170.

Davis, H., Porter, J. W., Livingstone, J., Hermann, T., MacFadden, L., & Levine, S. Pituitary-adrenal activity and leverpress shock escape behavior. *Physiological Psychology*, 1977, *5*, 280–284.

Dill, D. B., Edwards, H. T., & Forbes, W. H. Tobacco smoking in relation to blood sugar, blood lactic acid and metabolism. *American Journal of Physiology*, 1934, *109*, 118–122.

Duval, S., & Wickland, R. A. *A theory of objective self-awareness.* New York: Academic Press, 1972.

Elgerot, A. Psychological and physiological changes during tobacco abstinence in habitual smokers. *Journal of Clinical Psychology*, 1978, *34*, 759–764.

Evans, J. R., Hughes, R. E., & Jones, P. R. Some effects of cigarette smoking in guinea pigs. *Proceedings of the Nutrition Society*, 1967, *26*, xxxvi.

Faust, M., Johnson, P. R., & Hirsch, J. Surgical removal of adipose tissue alters feeding behavior and the development of obesity in rats. *Science*, 1977, *197*, 393.

Frankenhaeuser, M. Experimental approaches to the study of catecholamines and emotion. In L. Levi (Ed.), *Emotions: Their parameters and measurement*. New York: Raven Press, 1975. (a)

Frankenhaeuser, M. Sympathetic adrenomedullary activity, behavior and the psychosocial environment. In P. H. Venables & M. J. Christie (Eds.), *Research in psychophysiology*. New York: Wiley, 1975. (b)

Gabrielson, A. E., & Good, R. A. Chemical suppression of adaptive immunity. *Advances in Immunology*, 1967, *6*, 91.

Glass, D. C. *Behavior patterns, stress, and coronary disease*. Hillsdale, N.J.: Erlbaum, 1977.

Goldman, R. D., Haisman, M. F., Bynum, G., Salans, L. B., Danforth, E., Jr., Horton, E. S., & Sims, E. A. H. Experimental obesity in man: VIII. Metabolic rate in relation to dietary intake. In G. A. Bray (Ed.), *Obesity in perspective*. Washington, D.C.: U.S. Government Printing Office, 1976.

Goudet, F. J., & Hugli, W. C., Jr. Concomitant habit changes associated with changes in smoking habits. *Medical Times*, 1969, *97*, 195–205.

Gouldbourt, U., Medalie, J. H., & Neufeld, H. N. Clinical myocardial infarctions over a five-year period. III. A multivariate analysis of incidence, the Israel eschemic heart disease study. *Journal of Chronic Disease*, 1975, *28*, 217.

Griggs, R. C., & Stunkard, A. J. The interpretation of gastric motility. II. Sensitivity and bias in the preception of gastric motility. *Archives of General Psychiatry*, 1964, *11*, 82–89.

Hanson, J. D., Larson, M. E., & Snowden, C. T. The effects of control over high-intensity noise or plasma cortisol levels in rhesus monkeys. *Behavioral Biology*, 1976, *16*, 333.

Hennessy, J. W., King, M. G., McClure, T. A., & Levine, S. Uncertainty as defined by the contingency between environmental events, and the adrenocortical response of the rat to electric shock. *Journal of Comparative and Physiological Psychology*. 1977, *91*, 1447–1453.

Horton, E., Danforth, E., Sims, E., & Salans, L. Endocrine and metabolic alterations in spontaneous and experimental obesity. In G. A. Bray (Ed.), *Obesity in perspective*. Washington, D.C.: U.S. Governmenting Printing Office, 1975.

Hughes, R. E., Jones, P. R., & Nicholas, P. Some effects of experimentally produced cigarette smoke on the growth, vitamin C metabolism, and organ weights of guinea pigs. *Journal of Pharmacy and Pharmacology*, 1970, *22*, 823–827.

Kanfer, F. H. Self-regulation: Research, issues, and speculations. In C. Neuringer & J. L. Michael (Eds.), *Behavior modification in clinical psychology*. New York: Appleton-Century-Crofts, 1970.

Kanfer, F. H., & Goldfoot, D. A. Self-control and tolerance of noxious stimulation. *Psychological Reports*, 1966, *18*, 79–85.

Kerschbaum, A., Bellet, S., & Khorsandrian, R. Elevation of serum cholesterol after administration of nicotine. *American Heart Journal*, 1965, *69*, 206–210.

Langer, E., & Rodin, J. The effects of choice and enhanced personal responsibility for the aged: A field experiment in an institutional setting. *Journal of Personality and Social Psychology*, 1976, *34*, 191–198.

Lepper, M. R., Greene, D., & Nisbett, R. E. Undermining children's intrinsic interest with extrinsic rewards: A test of the "overjustification hypothesis." *Journal of Personality and Social Psychology*, 1973, *28*, 129–137.

Leventhal, H., Meyer, D., & Nerenz, D. The common sense representation of illness danger. In S. Rachman (Ed.), *Contributions to medical psychology*. Vol. 2. London: Pergamon Press, 1980.

Levine, S., & Coover, G. D. Environmental control of suppression of the pituitary-adrenal system. *Physiology and Behavior*, 1976, *17*, 35–37.

Levine, S., Goldman, L., & Coover, G. D. Expectancy and the pituitary-adrenal system. In R. Poerter & J. Knight (Eds.), *Physiology, emotion and psychosomatic illness* (Ciba Foundation Symposium 8). Amsterdam: Elsevier, 1972.

Lincoln, J. E. Weight gain after cessation of smoking. *Journal of the American Medical Association*, 1969, *210*, 1965.

Lundberg, U., & Frankenhaeuser, M. Psychophysiological reactions to noise as modified by personal control over stimulus intensity. *Biological Psychology*, 1978, *6*, 51.

Lynch, W. C., & Schuri, U. Acquired control of peripheral vascular responses. In G. E. Schwartz & D. Shapiro (Eds.), *Consciousness and self-regulation.* Vol. 2. New York: Plenum Press, 1978.

Mahoney, M. J., & Arnkoff, D. B. Cognitive and self-control therapies. In S. L. Garfield & A. E. Bergin (Eds.), *Handbook of psychotherapy and behavior change* (2nd ed.). New York: Wiley, 1978.

Mahoney, M. J., & Mahoney, K. *Permanent weight control.* New York: W. W. Norton, 1976.

Mandler, G. The interruption of behavior. In P. Levine (Ed.), *Nebraska symposium on motivation*, 1964, *12*, 163.

Marshall, G. D., & Zimbardo, P. G. Affective consequences of inadequately explained physiological arousal. *Journal of Personality and Social Psychology*, 1979, *37*, 970–988.

Maslach, C. Negative emotional biasing of unexplained arousal. *Journal of Personality and Social Psychology*, 1979, *37*, 953–969.

Mason, J. W., Brady, J. V., & Tolson, W. W. Behavioral adaptations and endocrine activity: Psychoendocrine differentiation of emotional states. In R. Levine (Ed.), *Endocrines and the central nervous system.* Baltimore, Md: Williams & Wilkins, 1966.

Meyer, D., Leventhal, H., & Gutmann, M. Symptoms in hypertension: How patients evaluate and treat them. *New England Journal of Medicine*, in press.

Miller, N. E. Learning of visceral and glandular respoonses. *Science*, 1969, *163*, 434–445.

Miller, N. E., & Dworkin, B. R. Different ways in which learning is involved in homeostasis. In R. F. Thompson, L. H. Hicks, & V. B. Shvyrkov (Eds.), *Neural mechanisms of goal-directed behavior and learning.* New York: Academic Press, 1980.

Nisbett, R. E., & Wilson, T. Telling more than we can know: Verbal reports on mental processes. *Psychological Review*, 1977, *84*, 231–259.

Pangborn, R. M., & Trabue, I. M. Gustatory responses during periods of controlled and ad lib cigarette smoking. *Perception and Psychophysics*, 1973, *1*, 139–144.

Passey, R. D. Cavedrogenity of cigarette tars. *British Empire Cancer Campaign Annual Report*, 1957, *35*, 65–66.

Passey, R. D. Cigarette smoke and cancer of the lung. *British Empire Cancer Annual Report*, 1958, *36*, 48–49.

Pennebaker, J. W., & Skelton, J. A. Psychological parameters of physical symptoms. *Personality and Social Psychology Bulletin*, 1978, *4*, 524–530.

Pickering, T. G., & Miller, N. E. Learned voluntary control of heart rate and rhythm in two subjects with premature ventricular contractions. *British Heart Journal*, 1977, *39*, 152–159.

Rodin, J. Has the distinction between internal versus external control of feeding outlived its usefulness? In G. A. Bray (Ed.), *Recent advances in obesity research.* Vol. 2. London: Newman Publishing, 1978.

Rodin, J. Managing the stress of aging: The role of control and coping. In S. Levine & H. Ursin (Eds.), *Coping and health.* New York: Academic Press, 1980.

Rodin, J. Effects of self-control training on health and behavior in aging. *Revue Internationale de Psychologie Appliquee*, in press. (a)

Rodin, J. *Exploding the weight myths.* London: Multimedia Publications, in press. (b)

Rodin, J., & Langer, E. Long-term effects of a control-relevant intervention with the institutionalized aged. *Journal of Personality and Social Psychology*, 1977, *35*, 897–902.

Rodin, J., Maloff, D., & Becker, H. Self-control: The role of environmental and self-generated cues. In P. Levison (Ed.), *Substance abuse: Habitual behavior and self-control.*
Boulder, Colo.: Westview/Praeger Press, in press.

Rozin, P. N., & Mayer, J. Thermoreinforcement and thermoregulatory behavior in the gold-
fish, *Carassius auratus. Science,* 1961, *134,* 942–943.

Sachar, E. J. Neuroendocrine abnormalities in depressive illness. In E. J. Sachar (Ed.), *Topics
in psychoendocrinology.* New York: Grune & Stratton, 1975.

Schachter, S., & Singer, J. E. Cognitive, social, and physiological determinants of emotional
state. *Psychological Review,* 1962, *69,* 379–399.

Schmale, A., & Iker, H. The psychological setting of uterine cervical cancer. *Annals of the
New York Academy of Sciences,* 1966, *125,* 807–813.

Schmale, A. H., & Iker, H. Hopelessness as a predictor of cervical cancer. *Social Science and
Medicine,* 1971, *5,* 95–100.

Schnecter, M. D., & Cook, P. Nicotine induced weight loss in rats without an effect on appe-
tite. *European Journal of Pharmacology,* 1976, *38,* 63–69.

Schnedorf, J. C., & Ivy, A. C. The effect of tobacco smoking on the alimentary canal. *Journal
of American Medical Association,* 1938, *112,* 898–903.

Stirling, J. L., & Stock, M. J. Non-conservative mechanisms of energy metabolism in thermo-
genesis. In M. Apfelbaum (Ed.), *Energy balance in man.* Paris: Mason, 1973.

Stunkard, A. J., & Koch, C. The interpretation of gastric motility: I. Apparent bias in the
reports of hunger by obese persons. *Archives of General Psychiatry,* 1964, *11,* 74–82.

Ursin, H., Baade, E., & Levine, S. *Psychobiology of stress.* New York: Academic Press,
1978.

Weiss, J. M. Effects of coping responses on stress. *Journal of Comparative and Physiological
Psychology,* 1968, *65,* 251–260.

Weiss, J. M. Effects of coping behavior with and without a feedback signal on stress pathology
in rats. *Journal of Comparative and Physiological Psychology,* 1971, *77,* 22. (a)

Weiss, J. M. Effects of punishing the coping response (conflict) on stress pathology in rats.
Journal of Comparative and Physiological Psychology, 1971, *77,* 14. (b)

White, R. W. Motivation reconsidered: The concept of competence. *Psychological Review,*
1959, *66,* 297–323.

Wynder, E. L., Kaufman, P. L., & Lesser, R. L. A short-term follow-up study on ex-cigarette
smokers with special emphasis on persistent cough and weight gain. *American Review of
Respiratory Diseases,* 1967, *96,* 645–655.

Zinberg, N., & Fraser, K. The role of the social setting in the prevention and treatment of
alcoholism. In J. H. Mendelson (Ed.), *Diagnosis and treatment of alcoholism.*

4

An Information-Processing Perspective on Self-Management*

Charles S. Carver and Michael F. Scheier

Human behavior is not random. Nor, for the most part, do people simply ricochet around their environments, propelled by whatever force has last impinged upon them. To the contrary, human behavior is usually goal directed, though we are not always successful in attaining our goals. Said differently, behavior is self-regulated or self-managed. This assertion, in a sense, defines the subject matter of this chapter. In the following pages we are going to be discussing the ways in which we believe people go about regulating their behavior, deciding how to act, and translating those intentions into actions.

There are, of course, many different ways of looking at the process of self-regulation, as is witnessed by the diverse points of view represented in Part I of this book. We are not going to attempt here a survey of all the perspectives that have been influential over the years. Rather, we will focus on a single viewpoint: a perspective that is usually identified with the terms *information processing*, *cybernetic*, and *control theory* (terms that we will use interchangeably here). We will attempt to make a persuasive case that such an approach provides a very useful tool for the analysis of human behavior. Though our focus is on the information-processing approach, we

*Preparation of this chapter was facilitated by NSF grants BNS 8021859 and BNS 8107236.

will not entirely disregard other points of view. Later in the chapter, we argue that without their necessarily having been aware of it, proponents of social learning theory have been moving steadily in the direction of cybernetic models of self-regulation for several years.

Before beginning our examination of control theory as a model of self-management, we should point out two additional limitations on the scope of our undertaking. First, we have not addressed issues of development. We are personality and social psychologists. Our descriptions throughout the chapter have implicitly assumed a more or less fully functioning adult, as is characteristic of the writings of most researchers in our field. This does not mean that control-theoretic concepts are not potentially useful to developmental psychologists (cf. Ozer, 1979). But we do not feel competent ourselves to wade into that area.

Finally, we should point out that this chapter presents a conceptual approach to self-management *in general*. Accordingly, we have focused on normal behavior and its regulation, rather than on deviant behavior and its therapeutic alteration. We do make some suggestions about the implications that our general approach may have for inefficient self-management. And we do point to some similarities between this model and other current theories that bear on such phenomena as anxiety and depression. But for the most part, our discussion is limited to "normal" processes of self-regulation.

We begin with a discussion of the central ideas of control theory as an approach to understanding self-regulating systems. Then we turn more explicity to the domain of living systems and consider how the self-regulatory processes central to control theory might be realized in human thought and action. The latter part of that discussion heavily emphasizes recent research findings from cognitive, personality, and social psychology. It is of course true that any model of self-regulation also suggests ways in which self-regulation is prevented or interrupted. That possibility is taken up next. Having by that point presented our model in its entirety, we then turn to a discussion of the relationships between these ideas and several other theories bearing on both normal and abnormal behavior. We close the chapter with an examination of the relationship between the cybernetic approach and the learning approach to self-regulation, and with a brief outline of several implications of our model for inefficient self-management.

CYBERNETICS AND CONTROL

Cybernetics was defined by Wiener (1948) as the science of communication and control. Its principles are self-regulatory principles. They are applicable to virtually any kind of self-regulating system (e.g., electronic, electro-mechanical, or biological systems). Most illustrations of the logic of control theory make use of devices like thermostats or computer programs. But this logic is also implicit in the functioning of the homeostatic systems that regulate body temperature, levels of nutrients in the blood, and so on (cf. Cannon, 1932). We suggest, moreover, that it is also implicit in *behavioral* self-regulation.

The Feedback Loop

The basic unit of cybernetic control is the negative feedback loop (figure 4.1). It is termed a "negative," or discrepancy-reducing, loop because its overall function is to reduce or eliminate any perceptible discrepancy between a sensed value and some standard of comparison. The feedback loop has several component processes. As will be clear in a moment, where to begin in describing the component processes must be decided somewhat arbitrarily. It is perhaps most intuitive, however, to begin with the input function (the left box of figure 4.1). The input function is the sensing or perception of some existing state of affairs. As we describe these component processes, we will also provide a running account of how they take place in a simple electromechanical control device: a thermostat. To begin, the input function of a thermostat is the sensing of the current room temperature.

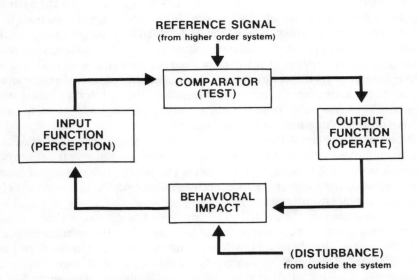

Fig. 4.1. The component functions of a feedback loop, the basic unit of cybernetic control. From C. S. Carver & M. F. Scheier, *Attention and self-regulation: A control-theory approach to human behavior* (New York: Springer-Verlag, 1981) page 168.

The value that is sensed via the input function is transferred to the next component of the loop, called a "comparator." The comparator is so named because it compares the sensed present state against a "reference value" which is provided from outside the loop—a point that will be clarified shortly. (For a thermostat, the reference value is the temperature at which the device has been set.) This comparison process, which Miller, Galanter, and Pribram (1960) referred to as a "test," has only two potential outcomes: either the two values are the same, or they are discriminably different. If they are the same, no further action is called for. If they are different, control is transferred to an output function (which Miller et al. referred to as "operate").

Though it is not always obvious and not always overt, the output function is *behavior*. If a comparison reveals a discrepancy between the sensed value and the reference value (or standard of comparison), a change in present behavior is authorized, the purpose of which is to counter the sensed discrepancy. Thus the reference value can easily be conceptualized as providing a *goal* for behavior (cf. Powers, 1973b). To continue with our example, if the comparison taking place within the thermostat reveals that the room temperature has become discriminably higher than the reference value, an air conditioning unit may be activated.

The mere emission of the behavioral output per se does not counter the discrepancy, however. The output has an influence only by making an impact on the system's "environment" (i.e., anything external to the system itself). When the output function has an impact on the environment, the result is a different state of affairs than had existed before the behavior took place. The existence of this different state of affairs, in turn, causes a change in the *perception* of the present situation (see figure 4.1). This new perception goes to the comparator, which checks it against the reference value. If the action has countered the deviation, the action may be discontinued. (Thus, once the room has cooled to the thermostat's set point, the air conditioner's compressor is deactivated.)

Note that a system of this configuration forms a *closed loop of control*. As we indicated earlier, saying where it "begins" is somewhat arbitrary, because successful self-regulation requires the proper functioning of each component of the loop. If the loop becomes disconnected at any point, effective self-regulation ceases.

As is indicated in figure 4.1, there are two places where external influences enter the loop. These external influences are the reference signal (which we have already mentioned), and what is referred to in the figure as "disturbance." This latter influence reflects the existence of what may be a continually changing environment. Unpredictable and often uncontrollable influences impinge on the system. We commonly think of such influences as creating discrepancies between present state and the reference value (e.g., a blazing midday sun raises the room's temperature). But interestingly enough, external disturbances sometimes act to *reduce* discrepancies (e.g., a sudden thunderstorm may cool the room). The essence of "disturbance" as an influence is that it changes the existing state, and does so completely apart from the behavior of the system.

It is critically important to recognize, in this regard, that what is controlled in a cybernetic system—what is conceptually at the heart of the feedback loop—is not the behavioral output per se. It is the *perceived discrepancy between the present state and the comparison value*. It does not matter how the discrepancy was created or how it is reduced (i.e., through the system's behavioral output or through an environmental disturbance). The system has only one goal: to keep the discrepancy minimized (see Powers, 1973a; 1973b; 1979, for further elaboration and illustrations of this point).

We have followed the traditional path of least resistance by using the thermostat as our beginning example. But the component functions that we have just described are as easily observed in human behavior as in a thermostat. Let's consider next a very simple behavioral example and map it onto the components of figure 4.1. Most people have a mental representation of how they ought to look in the morning as they leave for work. This representation reflects both cultural norms and our memories of what we typically look like. It is not at all unusual to check on one's appearance before leaving by looking in a mirror. In so doing, the person observes a reflected image (perceptual input function) and compares it to the stored representation. If there is a discrepancy substantial enough to be noticed (e.g., one's hair is out of place, one is still in pajamas), a rearrangement is undertaken (i.e., an output function) to counter the sensed deviation.

Relationships Among Feedback Loops. Now that we have established at least the plausibility of construing human behavior in terms of control-theoretic constructs, let us elaborate upon the basic construct. Though the feedback loop is of considerable interest in its own right, *a single loop is not an adequate model of much of anything*. Indeed, as we point out below, it will not even really account for the behavior of a room thermostat. The limited scope of the single feedback loop does not pose a problem for control theory, however, because of the fact that feedback loops can be interconnected. Two facets of this potential interconnection deserve some mention.

Branching chains. The first of these facets is illustrated most easily by using Miller and associates' (1960) TOTE sequence as a vehicle. This construct is a linear sequence that describes the behavior of a single feedback loop (see figure 4.2). The "test" (comparison) process in this sequence is a binary, yes-or-no decision. Based on the outcome of this decision, control is transferred

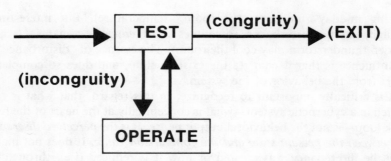

Fig. 4.2   The TOTE unit, a linear description of the behavior of a feedback system. From G. A. Miller, E. Galanter, & K. H. Pribram, *Plans and the structure of behavior* (New York: Holt, Rinehart, & Winston, 1960). Page 26.

either to an "operate" function (similar to the output function of figure 4.1) or to "exit." Exit transfers control out of this loop altogether. But in systems which have a branching organization, exit transfers control *to another loop.* This loop in turn makes another binary decision. Indeed, the operate (which we have been treating as if it were a simple unitary process) may also have subcomponents, each of which consists of a feedback loop, involving separate tests and operates.

The result of having a large number of loops linked together in this fashion is a repeatedly branching chain — a "decision tree." Moreover, the chain is not limited to simply branching continually outward. It is perfectly feasible for one of the paths of control stemming from a TOTE unit that is very deep into the chain to lead back to a much *earlier* part of the chain. This possibility further compounds the potential complexity offered by such an organization, though the complexity derives from what are extremely simple elements.

This type of organization is, for example, the basis for high-speed digital computers. The functioning of a computer consists of enormously complex chains of what are essentially no more than binary decisions. But just as the single feedback loop can be seen in behavior, a branching organization of activity is also perceptible in a great many human behaviors. Consider, for example, the use of "troubleshooting" heuristics, the kind of thing that an amateur mechanic might use in evaluating and resolving problems with a car. An illustration of this sort of heuristic is shown as a flow diagram in figure 4.3. At several points in the behavioral sequence there are "tests." The outcome of each test is a binary decision. Which outcome occurs at any point determines the person's next behavior.

Hierarchies of feedback loops. A second important consideration is that feedback loops can be organized hierarchically (see, for example, Powers,

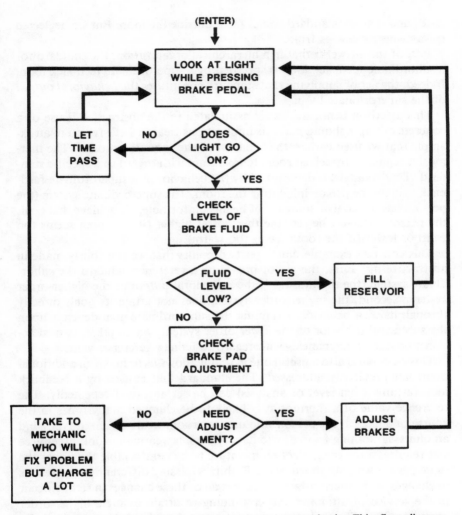

Fig. 4.3. A troubleshooting heuristic for an amateur mechanic. This flow diagram describes the decision-making and behavioral sequence that is followed by a person who notices that the brake warning signal on a car's dashboard has begun to light up when the brake pedal is pressed. From C. S. Carver & M. F. Scheier, *Attention and Self-regulation: A control-theory approach to human behavior* (New York: Springer-Verlag, 1981) page 19.

1973b, 1979). Given such an organization, the overall system would have both *super*ordinate goals and *sub*ordinate goals. By introducing the possibility of a hierarchical organization, we can now address more fully a point that we glossed over earlier. Specifically, we pointed out that a given feedback loop regulates its activity with respect to some reference value, or standard, and that the standard comes from outside the loop. But we neglected to say where it comes from.

Part of the answer is that in a hierarchical organization, the standard for a subordinate feedback loop is specified by a superordinate feedback loop. Indeed, the act of supplying that standard constitutes the *behavioral output* of the superordinate loop.

This assertion is not too easily assimilated in the abstract. But use of a concrete example should make its implications clearer. Let's return to an example that we used earlier: the behavior of the room thermostat. The thermostat regulates perceived room temperature with regard to a specific standard. That standard is determined by the behavior of a superordinate feedback system: the person inhabiting the room. The superordinate system (the person) has the goal or standard of being comfortable. To achieve that goal, the person behaves: he sets the thermostat higher (if the room seems too cold) or lower (if the room seems too warm).

This concrete example illustrates two points that we previously made in abstract terms. First, the act of providing a reference value to the subordinate system (the thermostat) is the behavioral *output* of the higher-order system. Second, the higher-order system does not attain its goals directly through its own behavior. Attaining the superordinate goal depends upon the successful behavior of the lower-order system, which takes its own action to reduce discrepancies with regard to its new reference value.

This example is also a useful one in that it allows us to make an additional point not previously addressed. The standard that is used by a feedback loop (at any given level of analysis) can be set and reset repeatedly. The reference value of a thermostat is likely to be changed many times in the course of a week if the person who uses the room wears different types and amounts of clothing from day to day. A person wearing a wool three-piece suit requires a lower ambient temperature to be comfortable than does the same person wearing shorts and a T-shirt. Dressing differently thus results in changes in the thermostat setting. Yet all of these changes in setting occur in the service of attaining and continuing to attain a single higher-order goal: comfort. The fact that standards at a given level of control can be changed repeatedly by a higher-order system gives a hierarchically organized control system a very high degree of flexibility in behavior.

There is implicit in this discussion an assumption concerning time, a dimension that we have carefully ignored until now. The assumption is that in a hierarchy of control structures, subordinate systems operate on a faster time scale than do superordinate systems. This is not really surprising, because a low-level feedback loop executes its matching-to-standard activity as a *component* of the matching-to-standard sequence at a higher level. Thus, a lower-level system may match several different standards sequentially in the course of a single discrepancy reduction at a higher level. The fact that the time scale of self-regulation becomes slower at higher and higher levels of control is important, as we shall illustrate in a moment when we turn to human behavior.

Hierarchical organization and behavior. The concept of hierarchical organization allows us to address a truth that is self-evident but is often ignored. In particular, people are plainly capable of executing very abstract behavioral acts (e.g., writing a book chapter) by means of subsidiary actions that are so concrete that they appear to have no connection whatever to the abstract goal (e.g., grasping a pen, holding it at an appropriate angle and with appropriate pressure, and moving it across paper to form patterns). Evidence of this general capability is everywhere. This makes it quite remarkable how completely the capability is ignored by most theories of behavior. It has not gone unnoticed by control theorists, however.

The most explicit statement on the matter that we are aware of has been made by Powers (1973a; 1979). He has argued for the existence of a hierarchy of control in behavioral self-regulation, in which each successive superordinate level of feedback systems "behaves" by specifying reference values for the next lower level of control (see figure 4.4). At the lowest level of control, the behavioral output is *literally* behavior, the only overt behavior there actually ever is: changes in muscle tensions.

For our purposes here, a full description of the Powers model is unnecessary. The levels of control that are of the greatest relevance to personality, social, and clinical psychologists are the relatively superordinate levels that Powers termed "Sequence control," "Program control" (the next higher), "Principle control" (the next higher yet), and "control of System Concepts" (the highest that Powers postulated). It is these levels upon which we will focus.[1]

To illustrate the nature of these three levels of control, and to simultaneously show how the hierarchical analysis could be applied to very abstract kinds of behavior, consider the following case. A young man (a high school student) has an image of himself as a good and thoughtful person. That self-image is an example of what Powers (1973a) termed a system concept — a high-level, overriding reference value. The young man often takes pains to try to act in such a way that his behavior closely approximates that ideal. Doing this represents self-regulation at the level of System Concepts.

But exactly what does it mean to be a good and thoughtful person? What behaviors define such personal attributes? A partial answer to this question is that a person who is thoughtful chooses his actions in accordance with certain guiding *principles*, principles that revolve around anticipating the needs of others and taking care of those needs unbidden. For example, this particular young man ascribes to the principle that he should go out of his

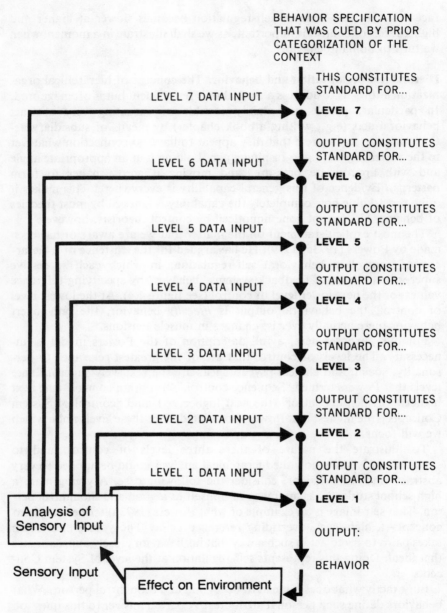

Fig. 4.4. Diagram of a seven-level hierarchy of feedback systems. The behavioral output for each superordinate system consists of resetting the reference value for the next lower system. The output of the lowest-level system is overt behavior. Goal attainment is monitored at each level by perceptual input appropriate to that level. From C. S. Carver & M. F. Scheier, *Attention and self-regulation: A control-theory approach to human behavior* (New York: Springer-Verlag, 1981) page 130.

way to help his parents around the house. He uses this principle (from time to time) to guide his behavior. Doing this represents self-regulation at the Principle level of control (the level that is directly subordinate to control of System Concepts).

Even specifying this sort of guiding principle does not provide a complete answer to our question, however. What does it really mean to go out of your way to be helpful? How is that principle put into action? Helpfulness is, in fact, a very general quality of behavior, which could be realized in any number of different ways. Helpfulness might be expressed as taking out the garbage without being asked, shoveling snow off the front walk before anyone else has done so, or picking up the wreckage of the Sunday paper from around the living room. Having decided to express the quality of helpfulness in his behavior, how would our young man translate that intention into action?

Translating a principle into overt activity requires control at the next subordinate level, the Program level (roughly equivalent to what may be more familiar to some readers as a "script"; cf., Schank & Abelson, 1977). A program is a partial specification of behavior, but it is more than simply a list of actions. That is, not all of the acts in a program are specified. In a program, one goes through a series of implicit "if-then" decisions. What actually is done at any given point in the program depends upon what action has come before, and what specific conditions exist at the decision point. (The flow diagram in figure 4.3, for example, represents a program.) To be more concrete about it, the young man in our illustration looks around the living room, sees that it is already tidy, and decides that picking up the living room is not the way in which he will be helpful. Going to the kitchen, he finds that the garbage bag holds only an empty coffee can (and decides not to bother emptying it) and he sees that there are no dirty dishes in the sink. Looking out the window, however, he notices that it snowed that afternoon, and he decides to shovel the walks. The principle of helpfulness, then, is to be matched in terms of shoveling snow.

Though we are now getting considerably closer to overt behavior, we are not quite there yet. Shoveling snow is the summary label for an activity that takes place over a somewhat extended period of time. It requires that component acts be executed in a given *sequence* (e.g., pointing the shovel downward, moving it forward in a scooping motion, picking it up, and turning it to release the snow). Seeing that these various events occur in the right order represents control at the Sequence level, the next level below Program control. But even those component acts are more complicated than they look. They require the creation of appropriate configurations (e.g., hands placed properly on the shovel, the shovel placed at the desired angle to the snow). And creating these configurations (and the transitions between configurations, as the person moves the shovel) requires the creation (and adjustment and readjustment) of patterns of muscle tensions.

Regulation of muscle tensions is the most basic level of control. It is at that level that physical behavior occurs.

Now, in order to establish a feel for the hierarchical organization more completely in your mind, ask yourself some questions. As we see the young man plunging his shovel into the fresh snow, exactly what goal is he trying to attain? What standard is he trying to match? Is he creating appropriate muscle tensions? Creating the desired angle between the shovel and the snow? Scooping into the snow? Shoveling the walks? Being helpful to his parents? Or is he trying to maintain his self-image as a good and thoughtful person?

The answer, of course, is that (given our construction of the situation) he is in the process of attaining *all* of these goals. Note that the goals are being attained faster at lower levels than at higher levels. Specific muscle tensions are created faster than a single stroke of the shovel is executed; it takes more than one stroke to get the walk shoveled, and it takes more than one instance of shoveling the walks to establish and maintain one's self-image as a thoughtful person. Note also that each level of control except the lowest "behaves" not overtly, but by specifying a value to be matched at the next lower level (figure 4.4). At the lowest level, the value to be matched is a muscle tension. This value is matched by means of a physical action.

Two additional questions. There are two additional questions that we should address briefly before we go further. What level of control is superordinate at any given time? And where does the reference value at that superordinate level come from?

A partial answer to the first question is provided by the assumption that whatever level is being *attended to* is superordinate at that moment. All of the levels lower than the one to which attention is directed presumably continue to self-regulate, because their activity is necessary for self-regulation at the higher level. We suggest, however (though this suggestion is clearly speculative), that self-regulation at any level *higher* than the one being focused on ceases until attention is redirected to that higher level (see Carver & Scheier, 1981, for greater detail). Thus, once the young man in our example begins to shovel snow, he may continue to self-regulate at the Program and Sequence levels (and below), but might temporarily be distracted from the fact that the behavioral program he has entered is also consistent with higher order goals.

Considering the question from a different light, we would assume that, for the most part in adult self-regulation, the Program level is usually superordinate, though occasionally something makes a reference value salient at the Principle level, or (less frequently) at the level of System Concepts. Precisely what causes attention to focus on such higher order concerns is quite difficult to specify. On the other hand, it is easier to point out circumstances in which attention is drawn to lower levels. This commonly happens whenever a problem is encountered in creating a match between input and reference value at those levels (cf. Kimble & Perlmuter, 1970). Should such a problem occur, the level at which the match is being prevented will temporarily become superordinate. It is possible, in theory, for any level of the hierarchy to be the focus of attention, and thus to be temporarily superordinate. We assume, however, that most social behavior occurs at the Program and Principle levels.

And where does the behavioral standard come from at whatever level is superordinate? This question is a bit trickier. But a partial answer to it comes from the following argument: that perceiving one's behavioral context (whether social or nonsocial) involves the comparison of raw sensory input to stored records of prior perceptions; that those records are catalogued according to some organizational scheme; and that information regarding *behavior* is stored along with some of those records of perceptions. When such a categorizational structure is accessed in recognizing perceptual input, the behavioral information is also accessed. This information — provided by a recognition and classification of one's contextion — becomes the superordinate reference value. This description was considerably condensed. But just below we address in greater detail a body of theory and research bearing on this line of argument.

SELF-REGULATION OF BEHAVIOR

The above account of control theory and its applicability to behavior is far from being the first attempt to make such an application. The possibility of using cybernetic concept in the analysis of human functioning aroused interest in some quarters as early as the 1960s (e.g., Guilford, 1965; Hunt, 1965; Miller et al., 1960; Taylor, 1960). There was also a somewhat independent interest in information-processing ideas among a few personality and clinical psychologists a few years later (see, e.g., Bieri, Atkins, Briar, Leaman, Miller, & Tripodi, 1966; Loehlin, 1968; Mancuso, 1970; Schroder & Suedfeld, 1970). Nevertheless, cybernetic principles of self-regulation never really caught the imagination of theorists in personality and social psychology. There were probably many reasons for this. But we think that one important reason may have been the fact that it was somewhat difficult to point to links between the components of cybernetic control, on the one hand, and either psychological states or experimental manipulations, on the other. Thus, to the hard-headed experimentalist, the cybernetic approach may have been regarded as vaguely interesting conceptually, but not very useful empirically.

We believe, however, that we can point to a set of research findings that suggests a way around this obstacle. That is, an empirical literature concerning human behavior has begun to develop which seems especially well suited to interpretation in control-theory terms. There appears, in fact, to be a clear conceptual link between the experimental manipulations used in this area (and the psychological states postulated to be caused by those manipulations) and a specific component process of cybernetic control. The literature in question derives from Duval and Wicklund's (1972) theory of objective self-awareness, though we have suggested an interpretation of that literature which differs from the Duval-Wicklund interpretation (see Carver, 1979; Carver & Scheier, 1981). The recent development of this research area leads us to suggest that there is now an opportunity to more carefully examine the utility of control theory in analyzing human behavior. This examination can be conducted not merely with regard to general notions about the nature of self-regulatory processes, but also with regard to empirical support for those notions. In the sections that follow, we present a brief description of what we see as a reasonable first approximation of a control-theory approach to behavioral self-regulation.

Evoking a Behavioral Standard

As we noted just above, a cybernetic approach to motivation requires that there be some reference value to use as a behavioral standard at whatever level of control is superordinate. We suggested there that in adult behavior, this standard typically derives from an analysis of the behavioral context. (We should also note, however, that standards can be suggested by an examination of the self as well.) The first stage of an information-processing model of behavior thus must be an information-processing model of the processes by which a standard becomes salient.

Cognitive psychologists have developed a variety of theories to account for the fact that perceptual experiences are eventually organized into implicit or explicit categories (see, e.g., Anderson, 1980). The knowledge structures comprising these categories are typically referred to as perceptual or recognitory schemas. Some theorists have argued that a schema is best viewed as having two components: a representation of a hypothetical "best member" of the category (called a prototype), and information regarding how far from that "best" member a given perceptual event can deviate and still belong to the category (e.g., Posner, 1969; Posner & Keele, 1968; Franks & Bransford, 1971; Rosch, 1973). Others have argued that a schema is best conceptualized in terms of the past frequencies with which particular stimulus attributes have been encoded as being relevant to the schema (Reitman & Bower, 1973; Neumann, 1977).

Despite these theoretical disagreements, however, there is a general consensus that such knowledge structures are built up in memory and that they are used to identify new perceptions, while simultaneously undergoing a continued evolution themselves (cf. Ginsburg & Opper, 1969; Piaget, 1971). That is, some salient attribute or attributes of the new perception apparently are used to access or call up one or more schemas (in a preliminary way). The schema (derived from past experiences) then suggests the presence of additional attributes, which can be confirmed, resulting ultimately in a recognition or classification of the perception. The result is that the perception is defined partly in terms of the sensory input, and partly in terms of the knowledge structure through which the input is interpreted (cf. Neisser, 1976). Indeed, the process of categorizing may also be followed by a tendency to assume the existence of schema-consistent attributes even when those attributes have *not* yet been verified.

Many social psychologists have come to view the process of person perception as involving much the same functions. Knowledge about people—both perceptual and conceptual knowledge—appears to be organized in a schematic fashion (see, e.g., Cantor & Mischel, 1977; Taylor & Crocker, 1979). Attributes of persons are not simply stored in memory in a disorganized fashion. We also store information concerning co-occurence of attributes, resulting in an elaborate network of knowledge. Morever, if we access a schema on the basis of one salient attribute of a new stimulus, it appears to evoke other aspects of the associated knowledge structure. Based on this preliminary categorization, the perceiver tends to assume the presence of attributes not yet observed. This tendency has long since been characterized as the use of an "implicit personality theory" (e.g., Hastorf, Schneider, & Polefka, 1970). When given a limited amount of information about someone, we flesh it out with other information provided by our stored knowledge of what characteristics commonly occur together.

Similar processes have been postulated in the perception of behavior settings (e.g., Barker, 1968; Wicker, 1972; Stokols, 1978). Data bearing on the behavior setting as a perceptual unit come mostly from trained observers, rather than naive subjects. But there is evidence that physical settings form recognizable categories and that those categories are defined partly on the basis of "structural" or nonbehavioral cues.

The argument is also made that knowledge structures are used to organize one's perceptual and conceptual knowledge about oneself (e.g., Markus, 1977; Rogers, 1977; Rogers, Rogers, & Kuiper, 1979). For example, people have self-concepts, which can be viewed as implicit theories of what our *own* personalities are like (cf. Epstein, 1973). As with the implicit theories we have regarding the personalities of others, these self-concepts presumably reflect long histories of perceiving and encoding our own characteristics. Considerable evidence has recently been reported that over the years this conceptual self-knowledge creates an elaborate structure that is used for interpreting and encoding information (cf. Rogers, 1977; Rogers et al., 1979). In addition to conceptual schemas, there are also perceptual schemas concerning the self. Such schemas are used to interpret and recognize the sensory information that is delivered from internal sensory receptors. What schema is accessed by a stimulus may determine, for example, whether the experience is perceived as benign or as stress-inducing (see, e.g., Leventhal, 1980).

In all three of these cases—persons, settings, and self—information appears to be stored in organized knowledge structures.[2] The information presumably is accessed when a current perception is being recognized by reference to one of those structures. So far we have dealt only with recognition and categorization. But this general line of reasoning also suggests a way of conceptualizing how a behavioral standard is evoked at whatever level of control is superordinate. Specifically, it seems reasonable to suggest that many knowledge structures incorporate behavioral information, as well as strictly perceptual or conceptual information. If a schema which includes behavior-specifying information is accessed, the behavioral information is evoked, in the same manner as is any other schema-related information. For example, just as accessing the category "cup" promotes the inference of a round top, accessing the category "church" evokes the behavioral specifications of walking softly and keeping one's voice low.

This assumption is consistent with theoretical positions taken by many cognitive psychologists (see, e.g., Rosch, 1978). It also fits well with findings from at least one study of environment perception and from several studies of person perception. Let us consider these research areas in turn.

Price (1974) asked subjects to examine a list of behaviors (e.g., run, talk, write, eat), each of which was portrayed as taking place in a list of different settings (e.g., in class, in an elevator, in a dorm lounge). Subjects were asked to rate the appropriateness of each behavior in each setting (in random order). Price's findings indicated that classes of settings "demanded" or "pulled for" classes of behaviors. This study must be regarded as preliminary, in that it involved only a limited range of behaviors and settings, but the results do suggest that behavior-specifying information is closely linked in people's minds with specifications of settings.

Evidence also exists that categorizing a *person* has an important impact on how the perceiver subsequently behaves toward that person. Relatively arbitrary group assignments (i.e., the target person either is or is not a member of the subject's group) have been found to lead to reliable biases in behaviors such as allocation of money (e.g., Allen & Wilder, 1975; Billig & Tajfel, 1973) and seeking of information about the person (Wilder & Allen, 1978). Variations in racial categorization lead to variations in perceivers' behavioral tendencies (Rubovits & Maehr, 1973), as do variations in perceived physical attractiveness (Snyder, Tanke, & Berscheid, 1977). It is important to note that these effects do not simply represent secondary inferences about what the person is like. They represent acts of *behavior* stemming from the categorization. Again, this evidence appears to indicate that behavioral specification is closely linked to certain kinds of category-membership judgments.

Self-Directed Attention and Self-Regulation

The evoking of a behavioral standard is the first necessary process in a control-theory approach to behavioral self-management. The second process is the operation of the feedback loop that creates behavioral conformity to that standard. Our position is that when a standard has already become salient, the matching-to-standard sequence (at whatever level of control is superordinate) is partially governed by one's attentional focus (Carver, 1979; Carver & Scheier, 1981; Wicklund, 1979). More specifically, behavioral conformity to the reference value is induced when attention is *self*-directed. We construe self-focus in this context as leading to the "test" component of the feedback loop—that is, the comparison between one's present state and the standard. The more likely this test is to occur, the more likely the person is to attempt to conform to the standard.[3]

There are two rather separate aspects to this characterization of the effects of self-focus. The first is that when attention is self-focused and a standard is salient, the tendency to compare oneself to the standard increases. The second is that this comparison is followed by behavioral output intended to reduce any discrepancy that is perceived between the two. Let us consider these points separately.

Comparison with Standards. *Does* self-attention lead to a comparison between one's present state and the salient standard? Recent research suggests that it does. In a series of studies (Scheier & Carver, Note 1) we attempted to create situations in which covert, internal comparisons between self and standard (which we assume are of primary importance) would be facilitated by the obtaining of external, standard-relevant information. It was reasoned that if self-focus leads to comparisons between present state and the salient standard, self-focus should also lead more reliably to seeking of the relevant information.

The series of studies that tested this reasoning utilized both experimental manipulations of self-attention (i.e., a mirrored surface or an observer facing the subject) and individual differences in the disposition to be self-attentive. In one paradigm, subjects were asked to copy complex geometric figures that were projected onto a screen, as accurately as they could. The figures were projected for only a few seconds at a time (during which the subject could not draw), but subjects could view each figure as often as they desired. In each of two studies, highly self-focused subjects consulted the figures more frequently than did less self-focused subjects. Presumably this occurred in the service of comparing their behavior (copying) to the situationally salient standard (accuracy).

Additional research was based on the assumption that performance norms constitute information that is relevant to the self-versus-standard comparison in test settings (cf. Trope, 1975). Subjects in one study were allowed to choose items from two sets: those for which norms were available, and those for which norms were not available. Subjects in another study were given an opportunity to examine norms for test items after having worked on the items. In both cases, high levels of self-focus were associated with enhanced norm-seeking behavior. Taken as a group, the four studies appear to converge upon the conclusion that self-focus induces a comparison between one's present behavior and salient standards.

Discrepancy Reduction. If the comparison between present state and standard reveals a discrepancy, the result is a behavioral attempt to reduce the discrepancy. Consistent with this picture of the self-regulatory process, a wide variety of research has shown that self-focusing manipulations increase the degree to which subjects' behavior conforms to salient behavioral standards. For example, Wicklund and Duval (1971) put subjects into a situation where they were to copy prose and to do so rapidly. Subjects copied more in a given period of time when working in front of a mirror than with no mirror. Similarly, a series of studies of instrumental aggression (Scheier, Fenigstein, & Buss, 1974; Carver, 1974, 1975) found that subjects utilized experimentally induced standards about how much aggression was suitable (standards that varied from study to study) to a greater degree when self-focus was high than when it was lower. These illustrations do not by any means exhaust the range of matching-to-standard effects that have been induced by manipulations of self-attention. A longer description of such effects may be found elsewhere (Carver & Scheier, 1981).

We might note in passing that most of the effects concerning self-attention and discrepancy reduction involve self-regulation at either the Program level or Principle level of control. These are the levels that we suggested earlier are normally superordinate in adult behavior. On the other hand, results of at least one research project suggest that self-directed attention can enhance self-regulation even in systems that are usually thought to be inaccessible to conscious control. That is, Schwartz (Note 2) has reported the finding that having subjects attend to their breathing and to their heart rates resulted in decreased variability in such behavior. Decreased variability may be seen as greater "regulation" of the behavior.

Absence of Self-Regulation and Misregulation

We have argued above that increases in self-focus result in enhanced behavioral self-regulation. It is the self-focus-induced checking and adjusting of behavior that we believe underlies effective functioning. We see this process as the normal state of affairs. It also follows from this argument, however, that decreased self-focus leads to a relative *absence* of self-regulation (at least at the superordinate Program or Principle level, where self-focus is most commonly involved in self-regulation). Recall from our earlier discussion of control theory that effective self-regulation requires that all components of the loop be functioning. If self-focus is decreased, less attention is directed to the self-versus-standard comparison at (for example) the Program level of control. The result is that regulation at that level is discontinued and the next lower level temporarily becomes superordinate. Note that our use of the phrase "absence of regulation" thus applies strictly to absence of regulation *at a given level of analysis*.

It is arguable that precisely this chain of events underlies the psychological and behavioral phenomena known as deindividuation. Diener (1980) has suggested that involvement in group activities results in a reduction in self-awareness. People then fail to compare their behavior to the personal and social standards that usually govern it. Behavior subsequently becomes more spontaneous and impulsive. Thus *behavior* continues to occur, but there is an absence of regulation at higher levels of abstraction. Support for this analysis has come from at least two studies (Diener, 1979; Prentice-Dunn & Rogers, 1980).

This approach to deindividuation suggests that it is a state in which the comparator which normally functions at the Program level or higher has ceased to compare perceptual input with the standard that is available to it. But the feedback loop can also be disrupted in other ways. For example, in some circumstances, the perceptual input is unavailable, for one reason or another. One is therefore unable to tell how one compares to the standard. With no way to determine how to adjust one's behavior, effective self-regulation ceases.

Sometimes people do continue their attempts to self-regulate, however, *despite* the fact that there is no standard-relevant input available. Such a condition is one reflection of what we have termed "misregulation" (Carver & Scheier, 1981). Misregulation occurs when the person either is utilizing irrelevant perceptual input or is using a standard that is inappropriate to effective self-regulation at higher levels of control.

An easy illustration of the first case is the experience of a person who is being taken in by flattery or ingratiation. The person is utilizing the reactions of someone else as perceptual input to determine what his or her own present state is. (Am I competent? Am I witty?) But the information conveyed in that reaction is actually meaningless, with regard to the standard in question. Another example of this sort of disjunction is what happens when a person attends to verbal cues from another person in an interaction, but fails to pick up the nonverbal cues that are being delivered simultaneously. And it may be those nonverbal cues that are actually most informative concerning the person's present situation. Thus the person is regulating his or her behavior on the basis of faulty perceptions.

Another interesting illustration of the second case—the use of an inappropriate standard—comes from the field of behavioral medicine. Hypertension is a disorder which has no perceptible symptoms. Yet many hypertensives eventually choose some particular symptom and use it as an index to their present condition (Leventhal, Meyer, & Nerenz, 1980). If the symptom in question goes away, they feel that their blood pressure has gone down, and they may stop taking their medication. Their standard of comparison has become the absence of that symptom. But recall that the symptom bears no relation to the progress of the disease. Thus they are regulating their behavior with regard to an inappropriate standard. Matching that standard will do nothing to promote goal attainment at the higher level of abstraction (i.e., keeping blood pressure low).

Though there are many ways in which the self-regulating feedback can be disconnected, probably the most common cause of disrupted self-regulation is the inability to produce a behavior that will reduce the sensed discrepancy. If no behavior is available that can reduce the discrepancy, or if the appropriate behavior cannot be executed, self-regulation is interrupted and ceases temporarily. This state of affairs is quite common in behavior. It is no surprise, therefore, that it has received a good deal of attention in theory and research.

Interruption of Behavior

Impediments encountered in the execution of some behavior can come from many sources and can come in many forms. Such impediments may be external (i.e., some environmental, temporal, or social constraint frustrates the behavior) or they may be internal (i.e., some deficiency within the self makes the behavior difficult to do, or rising fear may cause one to stop the attempt momentarily). The interruptions to which these stimuli lead may be momentary or prolonged, depending on the situation. The interruption is presumed to lead to an assessment of outcome expectancy. This is a subjective judgment of the likelihood of attaining the goal, given the situation and one's present resources. If the behavior in question is aimed at attaining a subcomponent of a larger-scale goal, the assessment process may be restricted to the attainment of the component goal, or it may apply to the larger-scale goal. The outcome expectancy that results from the assessment process is reflected both in behavior and in affect. These will be considered in turn.

Outcome Expectancy and the Approach-Withdrawal Decision. We regard the expectancy judgment as a binary decision. That is, we believe that there is a sort of psychological "watershed" in people's responses to this judgment (see figure 4.5). If expectancies are favorable, the person returns to the discrepancy-reduction attempt. If expectancies are *un*favorable, the person experiences an impetus to withdraw from further attempts.[4] When the precise subjective probability at which these two probabilities diverge is difficult to say. Indeed, the point at which attempts cease and withdrawal begins doubtlessly varies with a number of factors, including the importance of the behavioral dimension in question. Yet it would seem to be the case that all behavioral responses fall ultimately into one or the other of these categories: renewed efforts, or withdrawal. Both of these responses are presumed to be enhanced by further self-focus.

We should note that this withdrawal impulse can potentially lead to several quite different effects, again depending upon the circumstances that are encountered. If the situation incorporates no constraints against executing the impulse behaviorally, the person may literally withdraw from the setting. But there are many situations in which social pressures exist which make that difficult. In such situations, the withdrawal impulse may be executed mentally rather than physically. The person may simply attempt to ignore the psychological dimension in question (if possible), or may distract himself or herself with standard-irrelevant rumination. If the situation is one in which the salient behavioral dimension concerns task performance, this mental withdrawal may be reflected in a performance decrement, as the person ignores solution-relevant cues.

Finally, we should note that withdrawal sometimes is followed by the setting of a less stringent goal than had been taken up originally. In this case, the person withdraws from the attempt to match a particular *standard* of behavior, but does not withdraw completely from consideration of the behavioral *dimension*.

Research on Reassertion-Withdrawal. Some of these processes have been investigated in recent studies, addressing several different behavioral domains. The first study (Carver, Blaney, & Scheier, 1979a) examined the model's applicability to fear-related behavior. Subjects were selected as being moderately fearful of snakes, but as varying in their chronic expectancies of being able to cope successfully with their fear. It was predicted that mirror-enhanced self-focus during the attempt to approach and hold a snake would lead uniformly to increased awareness of rising fear, resulting (again uniformly) in interruption of behavior. Consistent with this reasoning, greater anxiety was reported among both subject groups when self-focus was higher than when it was lower. The pretest groups did not differ from each other, in this regard, which was also as predicted.

How subjects would *respond* to this interruption was expected to depend upon their chronic expectancies that they held of being able to cope with the fear. This also proved to be the case. Self-focus led to significantly earlier

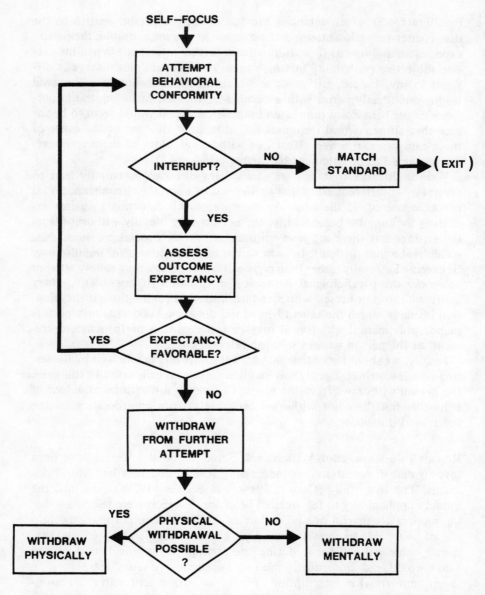

Fig. 4.5. Flow chart description of the reassertion-withdrawal decision that takes place when an ongoing behavioral attempt is interrupted by conditions such as a task frustration or rising fear. Adapted from C. S. Carver, A cybernetic model of self-attention processes, *Journal of Personality and Social Psychology*, 1979, *37*, 1251–1281. From C. S. Carver & M. F. Scheier, *Attention and self-regulation* (New York: Springer-Verlag, 1981) page 194.

withdrawal among subjects who doubted their ability to cope. But the same stimulus tended to facilitate approach among the more confident subjects.

Subsequent research applied this theoretical model to persistence at an insoluble problem (Carver, Blaney, & Scheier, 1979b). A large discrepancy between present state and standard was created among all subjects in this research by means of an initial failure. Some subjects then were led to have favorable expectancies of making up for that failure on a second task; others were led to have unfavorable expectancies. Once again, mirror-enhanced self-focus interacted with expectancies. Persistence among subjects with favorable expectancies was greater when attention was self-directed than when it was not. And there was less persistence among subjects with unfavorable expectancies when attention was self-directed than when it was not.

As we indicated above, physical execution of the withdrawal impulse is sometimes prevented by social or other constraints. In such cases, the withdrawal impetus leads to psychological or mental withdrawal from the standard or the behavioral dimension. This would be reflected in performance decrements, as the person failed to make use of available goal-relevant information. Support for this portion of the model comes from a study by Brockner (1979). Brockner was interested in the interactive effects of low self-esteem and self-directed attention upon performance. He predicted that either manipulated or dispositional self-focus would impair performance among persons low in self-esteem following an initial failure, but would not do so following an initial success. His data supported this reasoning, and also supported the position that this performance difference was mediated by differences in outcome expectancies.

This theoretical analysis also accounts well for the findings of several earlier studies conducted by other researchers in the self-awareness area (e.g., Duval, Wicklund, & Fine, 1972; Gibbons & Wicklund, 1976; Steenbarger & Aderman, 1979). And it has received additional support in other recently conducted research (see Carver & Scheier, 1981, for greater detail).

Affective Consequences: The Role of Attributions. In the preceding sections we focused on the behavioral consequences of the outcome expectancy judgment. But this judgment process is also believed to have affective consequences. It is not clear whether the affective response is best construed as being independent of and parallel to the behavioral response; as precipitating the behavioral response; or as comprising an alternative to the behavioral response (cf. Leventhal, 1980). It seems likely, however, that there will tend to be an inverse (if imperfect) relationship between the occurrence of the two.

We regard the person's *outcome* expectancy as the primary determinant of the general tone of whatever affect is experienced at this stage, positive or negative. We have taken the position (Carver, 1979; Carver & Scheier, 1981) that the primary role of attributions regarding the expectancy is to influence the more precise nature of the affect (though *not* to influence behavior). That is, an unfavorable outcome expectancy produces negative affect. But whether that affect is experienced as shame and lowered self-esteem or as anger and resentment depends upon whether the unfavorable expectancy is attributable to personal deficiencies or to external constraints. Similarly, a favorable outcome expectancy produces positive affect. But whether the experience is one of pride or of gratitude depends upon whether the expectancy is attributable to one's own efforts and abilities or to a beneficent environment.

This position on our part is quite comparable to that taken recently by Weiner and his colleagues (Weiner, Russell, & Lerman, 1978, 1979), though the two positions were derived independently. Weiner et al. presented data from two studies which appear to give considerable support for this general line of reasoning. Subjects were asked to examine a series of successful and unsuccessful outcomes (Weiner et al., 1978), or to recall a series of their own past outcomes (Weiner et al., 1979), the outcome in each case being attributed to some specific causal factor. Subjects were then to indicate what emotions the person experiencing the outcome had felt.

The findings from these studies indicated that a general affective tone was associated with type of outcome. Success was associated with positive feelings, failure with negative feelings. But specific emotions were uniquely associated with specific attributions for outcomes. For example, successes that were self-attributed were associated with pride, whereas successes that were attributed to another person were associated with gratitude.

We should point out that these findings provide only indirect support for our reasoning, being two steps removed from our theoretical position. First, the judgments were made on the basis of outcomes rather than expectancies. Though the two are clearly related to each other, they are just as clearly distinct. Second, in neither of those studies did subjects actually experience their outcomes immediately prior to making their affect ratings. Thus it is possible that the findings reflect opinions about what people would experience rather than reflecting veridical experiences. Nevertheless, the findings are suggestive and intriguing.

THEORETICAL IMPLICATIONS

The theoretical model outlined in the preceding pages has some interesting similarities to other theories that have been advanced independently by persons both within and outside personality/social psychology. These similarities suggest the potential of successfully integrating diverse lines of thought and areas of research within a single coherent framework. In several cases, however, the present analysis appears to contribute elements that the other theories do not. In the following sections we briefly address several of the theories and the relationships between them and our own model. We begin with a theory from social psychology and move gradually in the direction of what could be regarded as maladaptive behaviors.

Comparisons with Other Theories

Helplessness theory. An area of theorizing to which aspects of our model bear more than a passing resemblance concerns learned helplessness in humans. The basic findings to which helplessness theories apply are that exposure to uncontrollable outcomes sometimes leads to giving-up responses, at other times to reassertion responses. Recent approaches to human helplessness have emphasized the role played in these effects by cognitive variables, particularly subjects' expectancies (e.g., Abramson, Seligman, & Teasdale, 1978; Wortman & Brehm, 1975). That is, the occurrence of either giving up or reassertion appears to depend upon whether or not subjects expect to be able to produce the desired outcome when attempting the task that constitutes the dependent measure.

Our reasoning is quite consistent with this sort of model of helplessness. However, the fact that our ideas originated in a broader context suggests that helplessness effects are simply a *specific reflection of more general principles* of behavioral self-regulation. We find this rather simple statement to be quite important in its implications.

Moreover, our approach to helplessness phenomena adds to other theories in several respects. First, we have pointed out that both reassertion and giving-up behaviors are influenced by self-directed attention (e.g., Carver et al., 1979b). Second, we suggest the possibility that the various performance impairments that are associated with helplessness have their roots in a withdrawal impulse, which is often executed mentally rather than physically. Finally, our position on the affective consequences of various combinations of outcome expectancies and attributions appears to cover more ground than has been done by helplessness theories (cf. Abramson et al., 1978). Though our statement in this regard does not *conflict* with the alternative statements, we have explicitly considered cases that others have not.

Test Anxiety. As a final example, consider the body of research and theory bearing on test anxiety. Though early theorists in this area emphasized the function of physiological reactivity, more recent theorists have focused instead on cognitive variables. The statement with the greatest similarity to our own model comes from Wine (1971, 1980). Wine has characterized the test anxious as being hampered in their efforts during evaluative exams by high levels of self-focus. This high degree of self-attention presumably causes poor performance by distracting attention away from the task.

Though we would not disagree with Wine in her assertion that self-attention is disruptive to the test anxious, we would interpret those effects somewhat differently than she does. We assume that persons high in test anxiety commonly gravitate to having unfavorable expectancies in evaluative testing situations. They may be more likely than the non-test-anxious to interrupt their behavior, and an unfavorable expectancy would thereupon lead to a withdrawal impulse. The exam setting is not physically escapable, however. Thus the withdrawal impulse is executed mentally rather than behaviorally. The result is poor task performance and the phenomenological experience of a protracted state of self-focus.

Both our model and Wine's can account for performance impairments among the test anxious. But our model seems more general than hers in two respects. First, Wine's model offers no basis for predicting that self-focus can *facilitate* behavior among the non-test-anxious, to which a wide variety of research evidence attests. Second, only our model would predict that self-focus can facilitate performances even among those high in test anxiety, under the appropriate circumstances. It is interesting, in that regard, that Slapion and Carver (1981) have found such an effect, in a nonevaluative situation that was conducive to favorable expectancies.

Alternative Models of Motivation

We would now like to turn to an issue that concerns our attempt to apply control-theoretic concepts to the analysis of behavioral self-management. The learning paradigm has had an enormous impact on motivational constructs in human psychology. Probably the most pervasive motivational assumption in social psychology today is that behavior (or even attitude change) is impelled by aversive drive states. This assumption, deriving from Hull (e.g., 1952) is deeply ingrained in the field. It is part of social comparison theory and dissonance theory, and it provides the basis for the most commonly accepted interpretation of social-facilitation effects. Indeed, the drive assumption is also part of Duval and Wicklund's (1972; Wicklund, 1979) analysis of self-awareness effects. That is, they assume that the awareness of a discrepancy between one's present state and a salient standard creates an aversive drive state which has the goal of eliminating the awareness of the discrepancy.

By implication, we have taken the position in this chapter that a control-theory approach to motivation should be considered as a viable successor to drive models (among others). But how shall the determination be made as to whether one approach is more useful or more "correct" than the other? It will not help in this case to compare behavioral predictions, because the two classes of theory make similar predictions regarding overt behavior. Where they differ is in the assumptions that are made regarding mediating states. Motivational theories in the older tradition incorporate a drive assumption. We do not.

Drive theory and social facilitation. Though the drive assumption has been made in many behavioral domains, perhaps nowhere has it been more prominent than in the literature of social facilitation. Zajonc (1965; 1966) argued that the facilitating effect of coactors or observers could best be accounted for by assuming that such stimuli increased the subject's drive level. Though other theorists have since raised questions about the *basis* for such a drive state (e.g., Cottrell, 1968, 1972; Henchy & Glass, 1968; Sanders & Baron, 1975; Sanders, Baron, & Moore, 1978), they have almost invariably agreed about the *existence* of such a state.

The drive assumption appears also to have received empirical support (Martens, 1969a, 1969b; Cohen & Davis, 1973). Most researchers have assumed that drive would be reflected in arousal (cf. Malmo, 1958). Using a measure called the Palmar Sweat Index (PSI), Martens (1969a, 1969b), among others, has demonstrated that the presence of an audience in a facilitation setting led to increased fingertip sweating, a pattern that had previously been characterized as reflecting arousal (Dabbs, Johnson, & Leventhal, 1968).

There are two bases for concern about how those findings should be interpreted, however. First, Martens took his PSI measures between trials of a task, during a period in which, as he acknowledged (1969a), subjects were sitting idly viewing the audience. Thus we cannot tell whether the arousal state generalized to the period of performing the task. Second, though Dabbs et al. (1968) had suggested that increased PSI reflects arousal, they also suggested at the same time quite a separate possibility—that it reflected a readiness to engage the environment. Perhaps while facing the audience Martens' subjects were not "aroused," but rather were simply directing their attention outward—engaging the environment—in an attempt to gain information about the audience's reaction to their performances.

What, then, would have been their states while attempting the task? We, of course, would assume that task concentration involves self-focus, as part of the engagement of the discrepancy-reducing feedback loop. Interestingly enough, Dabbs et al. (1968) used phrases such as "inward focus" and an "attempt to concentrate" to characterize *decreases* in PSI. There thus seems to be a plausible basis for the prediction that PSI values should decrease while the task is actually being attempted.

We should point out that such a prediction does not seem readily derivable from any version of drive theory. We should also note that, although the validity of the PSI as a measure of drive may be questioned on a wide variety of grounds, most of the evidence of the existence of drive as a mediator of facilitation has come from studies using the PSI (cf. Geen & Gange, 1977).

We recently conducted a study of the PSI patterns associated with performance facilitation (Carver & Scheier, in press), in which subjects performed a continuous task before an audience, a mirror, or with no manipulation. PSI measures were taken at several points in the course of the session, including two times when the subject was working. We found — consistent with the reasoning outlined above — that PSI levels among all subject groups decreased significantly during the periods of task performance (see Carver & Scheier, in press, or Carver & Scheier, 1981, for greater detail). Thus the "arousal" found by Martens apparently does not generalize to periods of task performance. This has the further implication that prior evidence of the existence of drive must be viewed as quite equivocal.

How are these findings to be interpreted? They do not appear to be compatible with drive theory. But what relevance do they have for cybernetic theory?

Response patterning. A tentative answer is suggested by an emerging alternative approach to the understanding of physiological activity, which emphasizes qualitative differences in the patterning of responses rather than simply response magnitude. Deriving from positions taken by Sokolov (1963) and the Laceys (Lacey, 1967; Lacey & Lacey, 1970), this perspective holds that specific patterns of physiological activity are associated with different modes of perceptual-cognitive functioning (e.g., Williams, Bittker, Buchsbaum, & Wynne, 1975; Williams, 1978). According to this view, what is observed in physiological activity is not simply "arousal." Instead, one pattern of change may reflect "sensory intake" as a processing mode, and another pattern may reflect "sensory rejection." Indeed, descriptions of these processing modes (Williams et al., 1975) seem not too different from Dabbs and associates' (1968) characterization of the psychological states associated with increases and decreases in PSI, respectively.

The response-patterning conceptualization of physiological activity is perfectly compatible with cybernetic thinking. That is, it is quite obvious that changes in bodily state are required in order to do work. But, given that the work done in the body is complex and involved, such changes must necessarily be complex and subtle. Treating all such changes as "arousal" must ultimately be misleading. Research has really just begun concerning the possibility that shifts in response patterns provide information about what sorts of information-processing events are momentarily dominating behavior. But it is research that clearly warrants further attention.

Implications for Maladaptive Self-Management

We would like to close this chapter with a brief exploration of several of the implications that the sort of model we have been discussing may have for the understanding of inefficient or maladaptive self-management. (By implication, of course, these points also bear on issues relating to the therapy process as well.) It is likely that none of these insights is unique to our approach. Because we offer them as theoretical speculations, however, rather than as insights from clinical practice, all are grounded in a single theoretical perspective.

We have alluded in previous parts of our discussion to several potential points of difficulty in self-management. That is, we described earlier how the logic of the feedback loop requires that all components of the loop be operational if self-regulation is to proceed. We also noted in that context that there are several points at which that operation can go awry.

Consider, for example, the perceptual input function. It is important that the person utilize veridical and relevant input information for his or her self-regulation. If the person attends to channels of input that are irrelevant, misleading, or distorted in some fashion with respect to the goal that is guiding self-regulation, the perception of discrepancies between present state and standard of comparison can be grossly inaccurate. This can result in either of two problems. Discrepancies may actually exist but be unrecognized; or substantial discrepancies may be perceived where none actually exists. Either of these cases would create a difficulty for self-management. Similarly, if *no* attention is paid to the effects of one's behavior, behavior ceases to be guided by whatever standard might otherwise be utilized.

More common, perhaps, are problems on the output side of the loop.[5] The most obvious instance of such a problem is the development of an inability (or a perceived inability) to execute a known behavior in a case where doing the behavior would allow one to conform successfully to the salient standard. This is what happens, for example, when fear becomes debilitating because the person has developed an unfavorable expectancy of being able to cope with the fear. When efforts at the fear-provoking behavior are interrupted by the perception of rising anxiety, the result is withdrawal from the attempt. We would apply the same sort of reasoning to the behavior of the person who feels depressed and upset over perceived inadequacies in domains that do not involve anxiety. These perceived inadequacies are associated with unfavorable expectancies for goal attainment. When frustrations are encountered in the course of behavior, the result is a cessation of effort. This, of course, results in further evidence of inadequacy, which may further lower expectancies of successful outcomes in the future. Thus, the person with low self-esteem inadvertently helps to create conditions that maintain self-esteem at a low level.

Let us also point to two somewhat more subtle facets of the giving-up response that follows from unfavorable expectancies. Both of these points stem from the fact that many behavioral goals are sufficiently involved that they entail the attainment of several (often many) subordinate goals. The first point involves the expectancy judgment process. When behavior is interrupted — for example, by frustration or fear — the person's outcome assessment may be directed either toward the specific subgoal that is presently being attempted or toward the overall goal. It seems likely that the expectancy which derives from the assessment process will differ as a function of which of these goals is salient. More specifically, it seems likely that expectancies will be more favorable when examining the component goal than when examining the larger goal. It thus seems reasonable to suggest that continued efforts (the consequence of a favorable expectancy) are more likely to occur if people can be induced to focus on smaller steps, one at a time, than if they are allowed to become paralyzed by the magnitude of a large-scale undertaking.

The second point derives from the assumption that subordinate goals may be viewed in terms of a hierarchy of control. Recall that "behavior" at a superordinate level of the hierarchy can be viewed as comprising the resetting of goal values at the next lower level. Living up to a principle, for example, means specifying a program of action which, if followed, would cause the principle to be expressed in behavior. There is an assumption hidden in that characterization: that self-regulation will occur smoothly only if goals are easily specified all down the line.

Behavior is occasionally disrupted by poor goal specifications at relatively low levels of the hierarchy (for example, a novice golfer may have trouble creating the appropriate relationship between his hands and the club). But usually the lower-level reference values are specified pretty automatically. It seems likely, on the other hand, that a good deal of the disruption of successful self-management stems from the inability to specify subordinate goals at higher levels of control. In particular, we would speculate that difficulties are most often encountered in specifying programs of action which are suitable for the attainment of goals at the principle level, or the level of system concepts. For example, many people want to behave in ways that will make them "successful" or "likable." But what program of overt behavior will move the person toward such a goal is often less clear. It seems likely that this is the level at which the control process is most often interrupted, and it is here where people are most likely to need assistance — that is, in prescribing particular concrete courses of action for attaining higher-level goals.[6]

Finally, we should note that the expectancy construct is applicable at many different levels of analysis. In the preceding paragraphs we emphasized the person's expectancy of being able to successfully produce a given behavior or outcome in the course of normal activity. But the same logic is also applicable to the therapeutic attempt to alter a maladaptive behavioral tendency. People who are convinced that there will be no change no matter what they do will make little effort to create changes. Only if the person has gained some confidence that change is possible will the interruptions caused by fear or frustration lead to renewed efforts rather than to giving up. This general line of reasoning, of course, has been articulated many times before in discussions of the therapy process (see, e.g., Bandura, 1977; Kanfer & Hagerman, 1981; Murray & Jacobson, 1978).

In closing, we repeat that most of the points made in this section represent speculations derived from a theoretical model of normal behavior. We think that they are potentially useful speculations. We find it encouraging, in that regard, that our ideas seem generally consistent with the viewpoints of those clinicians who have recently emphasized the importance of cognitive variables in maladaptive behavior and its alteration (e.g., Beck, 1976; Meichenbaum, 1977). Nevertheless, our ideas on the subject remain to be tested empirically. Conducting such tests comprises a goal for the future.

NOTES

1. We should note that our account of the applicability of this model to social behavior is considerably abbreviated in this chapter. Readers with an interest in a more complete account may wish to consult our longer discussion (Carver & Scheier, 1981).
2. This is not to say that these knowledge structures inevitably provide accurate reflections of reality, however. There is considerable evidence that biases exist in such processes as the seeking out and encoding of information and the use of available information to make decisions. For example, there is a tendency to differentially seek out information that would confirm a previously encoded association, and to ignore potentially disconfirming information (e.g., Einhorn, 1980; Einhorn & Hogarth, 1978; Jenkins & Ward, 1965). This often results in the firmly held conviction that an association exists where in fact it does not (cf. Chapman & Chapman, 1967, 1969). Though tangential to present concerns, these processing biases have obvious implications for the stability of such mental structures as prejudices and unfavorable self-concepts.
3. Our use of terms such as "self-attention," "self-focus," and "self-awareness" (terms that we use interchangeably) is not intended to convey any deep, thorough, prolonged, or profound analysis or examination of the "self." Such terms are intended to refer simply to the momentary direction of one's attention to salient aspects of the self. In the present context, we assume that what is salient is one's present behavior and the salient behavioral standard.
4. See Carver and Scheier (1981) for a discussion of several of the bases of expectancies, including prior outcomes, attributions of the causes of those outcomes, performance norms, etc.
5. The distinction between this and the previous case is similar to that made by Kanfer (1961) between problems that require cognitive restructuring versus those that require the building in of some behavioral skill.
6. Indeed, the fact that consciousness so typically resides at these levels of control may reflect

an ongoing attempt to automate the specification of goals at these levels. Though we find this speculation intriguing, further pursuit of it is beyond the scope of this chapter.

REFERENCE NOTES

1. Scheier, M. F., & Carver, C. S. *Self-directed attention and the comparison of self with standards.* Manuscript submitted for publication, 1981.
2. Schwartz, G. E. *Self-attention and automatic psychophysiological self-regulation: A cybernetic analysis.* Paper presented at the annual meeting of the American Psychological Association, Montreal, 1980.

REFERENCES

Abramson, L. Y., Seligman, M. E. P., & Teasdale, J. D. Learned helplessness in humans: Critique and reformulation. *Journal of Abnormal Psychology*, 1978, *87*, 49–74.

Allen, V. L., & Wilder, D. A. Categorization, belief similarity, and intergroup discrimination. *Journal of Personality and Social Psychology*, 1975, *32*, 971–977.

Anderson, J. R. *Cognitive psychology and its implications.* San Francisco: Freeman, 1980.

Bandura, A. Self-efficacy: Toward a unifying theory of behavioral change. *Psychological Review*, 1977, *84*, 191–215.

Barker, R. G. *Ecological psychology: Concepts and methods for studying the environment of human behavior.* Stanford, Calif.: Stanford University Press, 1968.

Beck, A. T. *Cognitive therapy and the emotional disorders.* New York: International Universities Press, 1976.

Bieri, J., Atkins, A. L., Briar, S., Leaman, R. L., Miller, H., & Tripodi, T. *Clinical and social judgment: The discrimination of behavioral information.* New York: Wiley, 1966.

Billig, M., & Tajfel, H. Social categorization and similarity in intergroup behavior. *European Journal of Social Psychology*, 1973, *3*, 27–52.

Brockner, J. The effects of self esteem, success-failure, and self-consciousness on task performance. *Journal of Personality and Social Psychology*, 1979, *37*, 1732–1741.

Cannon, W. B. *The wisdom of the body.* New York: W. W. Norton, 1932.

Cantor, N., & Mischel, W. Traits as prototypes: Effects on recognition memory. *Journal of Personality and Social Psychology*, 1977, *35*, 38–48.

Carver, C. S. Facilitation of physical agression through objective self-awareness. *Journal of Experimental Social Psychology*, 1974, *10*, 365–370.

Carver, C. S. Physical aggression as a function of objective self-awareness and attitudes toward punishment. *Journal of Experimental Social Psychology*, 1975, *11*, 510–519.

Carver, C. S. A cybernetic model of self-attention processes. *Journal of Personality and Social Psychology*, 1979, *37*, 1251–1281.

Carver, C. S., Blaney, P. H., & Scheier, M. F. Focus of attention, chronic expectancy, and responses to a feared stimulus. *Journal of Personality and Social Psychology*, 1979, *37*, 1186–1195. (a)

Carver, C. S., Blaney, P. H., & Scheier, M. F. Reassertion and giving up: The interactive role of self-directed attention and outcome expectancy. *Journal of Personality and Social Psychology*, 1979, *37*, 1859–1870. (b)

Carver, C. S., & Scheier, M. F. *Attention and self-regulation: A control-theory approach to human behavior.* New York: Springer-Verlag, 1981.

Carver, C. S., & Scheier, M. F. The self-attention-induced feedback loop and social facilitation. *Journal of Experimental Social Psychology*, in press.

Chapman, L. J., & Chapman, J. P. Genesis of popular but erroneous psychodiagnostic observations. *Journal of Abnormal Psychology*, 1967, *72*, 193–204.

Chapman, L. J., & Chapman, J. P. Illusory correlation as an obstacle to the use of valid psychodiagnostic signs. *Journal of Abnormal Psychology*, 1969, *74*, 271–280.

Cohen, J. L., & Davis, J. H. Effects of audience status, evaluation, and time of action on performance with hidden word problems. *Journal of Personality and Social Psychology*, 1973, *27*, 74–85.

Cottrell, N. B. Performance in the presence of other human beings: Mere presence, audience, and affiliation effects. In E. C. Simmel, R. A. Hoppe, & G. A. Milton (Eds.), *Social facilitation and imitative behavior*. Boston: Allyn & Bacon, 1968.

Cottrell, N. B. Social facilitation. In C. G. McClintock (Ed.), *Experimental social psychology*. New York: Holt, Rinehart, & Winston, 1972.

Dabbs, J. M., Jr., Johnson, J. E., & Leventhal, H. Palmar sweating: A quick and simple measure. *Journal of Experimental Psychology*, 1968, *78*, 347–350.

Diener, E. Deindividuation, self-awareness, and disinhibition. *Journal of Personality and Social Psychology*, 1979, *37*, 1160–1171.

Diener, E. Deindividuation: The absence of self-awareness and self-regulation in group members. In P. B. Paulus (Ed.), *The psychology of group influence*. Hillsdale, N.J.: Erlbaum, 1980.

Duval, S., & Wicklund, R. A. *A theory of objective self-awareness*. New York: Academic Press, 1972.

Duval, S., Wicklund, R. A., & Fine, R. L. Avoidance of objective self-awareness under conditions of high and low intra-self discrepancy. In S. Duval & R. A. Wicklund, *A theory of objective self-awareness*. New York: Academic Press, 1972.

Einhorn, H. J. Learning from experience and suboptimal rules in decision making. In T. Wallsten (Ed.), *Cognitive processes in choice and decision behavior*. Hillsdale, N.J.: Erlbaum, 1980.

Einhorn, H. J., & Hogarth, R. M. Confidence in judgment: Persistence of the illusion of validity. *Psychological Review*, 1978, *85*, 395–416.

Epstein, S. The self-concept revisited: Or a theory of a theory. *American Psychologist*, 1973, *28*, 404–416.

Franks, J. J., & Bransford, J. D. Abstraction of visual patterns. *Journal of Experimental Psychology*, 1971, *90*, 65–74.

Geen, R. G., & Gange, J. J. Drive theory of social facilitation: Twelve years of theory and research. *Psychological Bulletin*, 1977, *84*, 1267–1288.

Gibbons, F. X., & Wicklund, R. A. Selective exposure to the self. *Journal of Research in Personality*, 1976, *10*, 98–106.

Ginsburg, H., & Opper, S. *Piaget's theory of intellectual development: An introduction*. Englewood Cliffs, N.J.: Prentice-Hall, 1969.

Guilford, J. P. Motivation in an informational psychology. In D. Levine (Ed.), *Nebraska symposium on motivation* (Vol. 20). Lincoln: University of Nebraska Press, 1965.

Hastorf, A. H., Schneider, D., & Polefka, J. *Person perception*. Menlo Park, Calif.: Addison-Wesley, 1970.

Henchy, T., & Glass, D. C. Evaluation apprehension and the social facilitation of dominant and subordinate responses. *Journal of Personality and Social Psychology*, 1968, *10*, 446–454.

Hull, C. L. *A behavior system*. New Haven, Conn.: Yale University Press, 1952.

Hunt, J. McV. Intrinsic motivation and its role in psychological development. In D. Levine (Ed.), *Nebraska symposium on motivation* (Vol. 20). Lincoln: University of Nebraska Press, 1965.

Jenkins, H. M., & Ward, W. C. Judgment of contingency between responses and outcomes. *Psychological Monographs: General and Applied*, 1965, *79*, (1, Whole No. 594).

Kanfer, F. H. Comments on learning and psychotherapy. *Psychological Reports*, 1961, *9*, 681.

Kanfer, F. H., & Hagerman, S. The role of self-regulation. In L. P. Rehm (Ed.), *Behavior therapy for depression: Present status and future directions*. New York: Academic Press, 1981.

Kimble, G. A., & Perlmuter, L. C. The problem of volition. *Psychological Review*, 1970, *77*, 361–384.

Lacey, J. I. Somantic response patterning and stress: Some revisions of activation theory. In M. H. Appley & R. Trumbull (Eds.), *Psychological stress*. New York: Appleton-Century-Crofts, 1967.

Lacey, J. I., & Lacey, B. C. Some autonomic-central nervous system relationships. In P. Black (Ed.), *Physiological correlates of emotion*. New York: Academic Press, 1970.

Leventhal, H. Toward a comprehensive theory of emotion. In L. Berkowitz (Ed.), *Advances in experimental social psychology*. Vol. 13. New York: Academic Press, 1980.

Leventhal, H., Meyer, D., & Nerenz, D. The common sense representation of illness danger. In S. Rachman (Ed.), *Medical Psychology*. Vol. 2. New York: Pergamon, 1980.

Loehlin, J. C. *Computer models of personality*. New York: Random House, 1968.

Malmo, R. B. Measurement of drive: An unsolved problem in psychology. In M. R. Jones (Ed.), *Nebraska symposium on motivation* Vol. 6. Lincoln: University of Nebraska Press, 1958.

Mancuso, J. C. (Ed.) *Readings for a cognitive theory of personality*. New York: Holt, Rinehart, & Winston, 1970.

Markus, H. Self-schemata and processing information about the self. *Journal of Personality and Social Psychology*, 1977, *35*, 63–78.

Martens, R. Palmar sweating and the presence of an audience. *Journal of Experimental Social Psychology*, 1969, *5*, 371–374. (a)

Martens, R. Audience effects on learning and performance. *Journal of Personality and Social Psychology*, 1969, *12*, 252–260. (b)

Meichenbaum, D. *Cognitive-behavior modification: An integrative approach*. New York: Plenum, 1977.

Miller, G. A., Galanter, E., & Pribram, K. H. *Plans and the structure of behavior*. New York: Holt, Rinehart, & Winston, 1960.

Murray, E. J., & Jacobson, L. I. Cognition and learning in traditional and behavioral therapy. In S. L. Garfield & A. E. Bergin (Eds.), *Handbook of psychotherapy and behavior change* (2nd ed.). New York: Wiley, 1978.

Neisser, U. *Cognition and reality*. San Francisco: Freeman, 1976.

Neumann, P. G. Visual prototype formation with discontinuous representation of dimensions of variability. *Memory and Cognition*, 1977, *5*, 187–197.

Ozer, M. (Ed.) *A cybernetic approach to the assessment of children*. Boulder, Colo.: Westview Press, 1979.

Piaget, J. *Biology and knowledge: An essay on the relations between organic regulations and cognitive processes*. Chicago: University of Chicago Press, 1971.

Posner, M. I. Abstraction and the process of recognition. In G. H. Bower & J. T. Spence (Eds.), *The psychology of learning and motivation*. Vol. 3. New York: Academic Press, 1969.

Posner, M. I., & Keele, S. W. On the genesis of abstract ideas. *Journal of Experimental Psychology*, 1968, *77*, 353–363.

Powers, W. T. *Behavior: The control of perception*. Chicago: Aldine, 1973. (a)

Powers, W. T. Feedback: Beyond behaviorism. *Science*, 1973, *179*, 351–356. (b)

Powers, W. T. A cybernetic model for research in human development. In M. Ozer (Ed.), *A cybernetic approach to the assessment of children*. Boulder, Colo.: Westview Press, 1979.

Prentice-Dunn, S., & Rogers, R. W. Effects of deindividuating situational cues and aggressive models on subjective deindividuation and agression. *Journal of Personality and Social*

Psychology, 1980, *39*, 104–113.

Price, R. H. The taxonomic classification of behaviors and situations and the problem of behavior-environment congruence. *Human Relations*, 1974, *27*, 567–585.

Reitman, J. S., & Bower, G. H. Storage and later recognition of exemplars of concepts. *Cognitive Psychology*, 1973, *4*, 194–206.

Rogers, T. B. Self-reference in memory: Recognition of personality items. *Journal of Research in Personality*, 1977, *11*, 295–305.

Rogers, T. B., Rogers, P. J., & Kuiper, N. A. Evidence for the self as a cognitive prototype: The "false alarms effect." *Personality and Social Psychology Bulletin*, 1979, *5*, 53–56.

Rosch, E. On the internal structure of perceptual and semantic categories. In T. E. Moore (Ed.), *Cognitive development and the acquisition of language.* New York: Academic Press, 1973.

Rosch, E. Principles of categorization. In E. Rosch & B. B. Lloyd (Eds.) *Cognition and categorization.* Hillsdale, N.J.: Erlbaum, 1978.

Rubovits, P. C., & Maehr, M. L. Pygmalion black and white. *Journal of Personality and social Psychology*, 1973, *25*, 210–218.

Sanders, G. S., & Baron, R. S. The motivating effects of distraction on task performance. *Journal of Personality and Social Psychology* 1975, *32*, 956–963.

Sanders, G. S., Baron, R. S., & Moore, D. L. Distraction and social comparison as mediators of social facilitation effects. *Journal of Experimental Social Psychology*, 1978, *14*, 291–303.

Schank, R. C., & Abelson, R. P. *Scripts, plans, goals, and understanding.* Hillsdale, N.J.: Erlbaum, 1977.

Scheier, M. F., Fenigstein, A., & Buss, A. H. Self-awareness and physical agression. *Journal of Experimental Social Psychology*, 1974, *10*, 264–273.

Schroder, H. M., & Suedfeld, P. (Eds.), *Personality theory and information processing.* New York: Ronald Press, 1970.

Schwartz, G. E. The brain as a health care system. In G. C. Stone, F. Cohen, & N. E. Adler (Eds.), *Health Psychology—A handbook.* San Francisco: Jossey-Bass, 1979.

Slapion, M. J., & Carver, C. S. Self-directed attention and facilitation of intellectual performance among persons high in test anxiety. *Cognitive Therapy and Research*, 1981, *5*, 115–121.

Snyder, M., Tanke, E. D., & Berscheid, E. Social perception and interpersonal behavior: On the self-fulfilling nature of social stereotypes. *Journal of Personality and Social Psychology*, 1977, *35*, 656–666.

Sokolov, Y. N. *Perception and the conditioned reflex.* New York: Macmillan, 1963.

Steenbarger, B. N., & Aderman, D. Objective self-awareness as a nonaversive state: Effect of anticipating discrepancy reduction. *Journal of Personality*, 1979, *47*, 330–339.

Stokols, D. Environmental psychology. In M. R. Rosenzweig & L. W. Porter (Eds.), *Annual review of psychology.* Vol. 29. Palo Alto, Calif.: Annual Reviews, 1978.

Taylor, D. W. Toward an information-processing theory of motivation. In M. R. Jones (Ed.), *Nebraska symposium on motivation.* Vol. 8. Lincoln: University of Nebraska Press, 1960.

Taylor, S. E., & Crocker, J. Schematic bases of social information processing. In E. T. Higgins, P. Herman, & M. P. Zanna (Eds.), *The Ontario symposium on personality and social psychology.* Vol. 1. Hillsdale, N.J.: Erlbaum, 1979.

Trope, Y. Seeking information about one's own ability as a determinant of choice among tasks. *Journal of Personality and Social Psychology*, 1975, *32*, 1004–1013.

Weiner, B., Russell, D., & Lerman, D. Affective consequences of causal ascriptions. In J. H. Harvey, W. Ickes, & R. F. Kidd (Eds.), *New directions in attribution research* (Vol. 2). Hillsdale, N.J.: Erlbaum, 1978.

Weiner, B., Russell, D., & Lerman, D. The cognition-emotion process in achievement-related contexts. *Journal of Personality and Social Psychology*, 1979, *37*, 1211–1220.

Wicker, A. W. Processes which mediate behavior-environment congruence. *Behavioral Sci-*

ence, 1972, *17*, 265–277.

Wicklund, R. A. The influence of self on human behavior. *American Scientist*, 1979, *67*, 187–193.

Wicklund, R. A., & Duval, S. Opinion change and performance facilitation as a result of objective self-awareness. *Journal of Experimental Social Psychology*, 1971, *7*, 319–342.

Wiener, N. *Cybernetics: Control and communication in the animal and the machine.* Cambridge, Mass.: M.I.T. Press, 1948.

Wilder, D. A., & Allen, V. L. Group membership and preference for information about others. *Personality and Social Psychology Bulletin*, 1978, *4*, 106–110.

Williams, R. B., Jr. Psychophysiological processes, the coronary-prone behavior pattern, and coronary heart disease. In T. M. Dembroski et al. (Eds.), *Coronary-prone behavior.* New York: Springer-Verlag, 1978.

Williams, R. B., Jr., Bittker, T. E., Buchsbaum, M. S., & Wynne, L. C. Cardiovascular and neurophysiologic correlates of sensory intake and rejection: I. Effect of cognitive tasks. *Psychophysiology*, 1975, *12*, 427–433.

Wine, J. D. Test anxiety and direction of attention. *Psychological Bulletin*, 1971, *76*, 92–104.

Wine, J. D. Cognitive-attentional theory of test anxiety. In G. Saroson (Ed.), *Test anxiety: Theory, research, and application.* Hillsdale, N.J.: Erlbaum, 1980.

Wortman, C. B., & Brehm, J. W. Responses to uncontrollable outcomes: An integration of reactance theory and the learned helplessness model. In L. Berkowitz (Ed.), *Advances in experimental social psychology.* Vol. 8. New York: Academic Press, 1975.

Zajonc, R. B. Social facilitation. *Science*, 1965, *149*, 269–274.

Zajonc, R. B. *Social psychology: An experimental approach.* Belmont, Calif.: Wadsworth, 1966.

5

On the Self-Management of Mood, Affect, and Attention
Eric Klinger

Every reader is likely to have a working sense of what is meant by the words *mood*, *affect*, and *attention*. When it comes to defining them, psychological science has, in fact, not progressed very far beyond the common wisdom; but a good many facts about these phenomena have become reasonably well established, a good many myths have been dispelled, and some genuine discoveries have been made. The result is that we know enough to start suggesting ways of applying our knowledge clinically. This chapter tries to outline our basic knowledge in these areas in a way that will facilitate application, the details of which are left to later chapters.

OVERVIEW

Emotions, under various names, have been a source of wonder and concern to philosophers, physicians, administrators, teachers, spouses, parents, children, lovers, and friends since the beginning of human records. Disordered emotions and moods are prominent features of almost every major form of psychopathology. The unpredictable affects of hebephrenia, the rages associated with paranoid and manic disorders, the apathy of depressives and many schizophrenics, the fears and anxieties of neurotics (and of people in many other diagnostic groups), the reduced fear levels of psychopaths, the emotional liability of various personality disorders—these attributes are generally considered among the most central features of the respective classifications.

Attention as such has not played as prominent a role in our conceptions of psychopathology. Nevertheless, disorders of attention occur quite clearly in the form of attentional withdrawal by many schizophrenics and depressives from the things or events people are ordinarily expected to attend to, and in the form of distractibility. Even a prominent behavioral theory of schizophrenia (Ullman & Krasner, 1969) placed attentional dysfunction at the etiologic heart of the disorder.

Outside of clinical settings, both emotions and attention are matters of strong concern to people. Parents and teachers spend a considerable amount of time dealing with fear, anger, and depression in children. They often hope to inculcate "appropriate" shame and guilt reactions. Furthermore, a major part of socialization and education consists of training children to pay attention to people, objects, and processes toward which the society considers it suitable and productive to attend.

Definitions

It is probably best not to try to define "emotion" and "mood" too stringently. The reason for this is that the words refer to a group of global reactions that vary considerably among themselves and are not very different from other global reactions that are often not included in the emotion category, such as the phenomena often referred to as "drives." Thus, there is general agreement that fear and joy are emotions, whereas hunger and thirst are drives; but there is little agreement on how to classify love. Are fear and joy more alike than, say, fear and hunger? The semantic debate is, at this point in our science, not worth the energy. Among the people who have researched emotion most intensively, however, there is a growing consensus on a list of reactions (or states) that ought to be considered emotions. The list tends to include joy, interest, fear, anger, sadness (distress or depression), surprise, disgust, shame, and contempt. The basic list is Silvan Tomkins' (1962, 1980). Izard (1977, Izard & Buechler, 1980) adds guilt to the list, whereas Plutchik (1962, 1980) adds acceptance as a basic reaction and deletes contempt and shame. What is a "primary" emotion to one investigator may be a mixture of other primaries to another investigator; but there is a fair amount of agreement on primaries, even so. This list constitutes the working definition of emotion for purposes of this chapter, but the focus will be on the emotions that have been the most problematical and about which we know the most: fear, anger, and depression.

What do these reactions have in common? First, all of them are total-organismic reactions. They are central nervous system reactions that involve humoral changes such as adrenal flow and brain catecholamine changes, motor changes affecting facial expression and posture, and changes in the quality of our inner experience—the direct affective qualities that provide the subjective "feel" of fear, anger, and the rest. All of them are more or less easily conditionable to formerly neutral stimuli. Insofar as they differ from basic drives such as hunger, it may be in their greater conditionability. It is likely, but not yet by any means certain, that each emotion has its own particular patterning of these subjective, behavioral, and psychophysiological components.

By "mood" this chapter simply means a disposition to react with a certain emotion during a period of time greater than a few moments but less than a lifetime. That is, mood refers to the central tendency of emotional states over any given time period. When the trend of emotional reactivity changes, we speak of a change of mood. Thus, after losing a loved one, we may be inclined to react to more stimuli than usual with the kind of sadness, distress, or apathy that are characteristic of depression. We can then speak of a depressed mood.

This chapter defines attention as the enhancement of cognitive processing that goes with keeping a set of stimuli, whether external or internal, at the focus of consciousness. When the stimuli are external, attention usually entails focusing some of our receptors (eyes, ears, etc.) on the source of the stimuli. When the "stimuli" are internal, such as our own thoughts, we may deliberately try to reduce all sense-mediated information.

It might appear from these definitions that emotion and attention are quite separate, but they have many links. Attention to something is ordinarily a prerequisite for emotional reaction to the thing, and emotion theorists commonly identify one basic emotion, such as "interest" or "excitement" (Tomkins and Izard) or "anticipation" (Plutchik), as accompanying intense attention.

An Emerging Contemporary View of Emotion in Capsule Form

In the remainder of the chapter I will sketch out one contemporary view of emotion. But it may be useful here to summarize the main outlines of emotional theory as it seems to be emerging in the minds of many investigators. Emotional reactions are seen as first of all built on a biological base, as aspects of species-specific reaction tendencies to specified classes of stimuli. Different emotions constitute discrete basic reactions (primary emotions, in Plutchik's sense) or mixtures of primary reactions, though there is still some disagreement concerning the identity of the primary reactions. Emotions are regarded as readily conditionable or at least detachable from the contexts in which they originally appear. Because they amplify drives (in Tomkin's sense), they constitute the most powerful immediate motivators of behavior. However, emotional reactions are highly interdependent with cognitive processes, which then become an important mediating and moderating influence on emotional response.

Chapter Objectives

The plan of the chapter is to first elaborate one version of the general model described above and related conceptions of attention, placing emotion and attention in the context of psychological functioning in general. Next, I shall examine the determinants of emotion and attention in greater detail. The chapter then examines the principles involved in these determinants to draw out their implications for helping people gain control over their own emotional and attentional processes. The identification of such variables as arousal, incentive disengagement, adaption level, attribution, competence, and the management of current concerns provide tools for both the clinician and the researcher.

EMOTION AND ATTENTION IN THE CONTEXT OF THE FUNCTIONING ORGANISM

To understand the roles that emotion and attention play, we must first understand the nature of the organisms of which they are a part. These organisms are themselves parts of a larger system. Living organisms evolved as stable species presumably because they were able to hold together over time a stable set of attributes—attributes that enabled the individuals to grow through standard sequences of change and to generate new individuals to replace the older individuals who would inevitably succumb to the accidents of nature. Within the larger system, organisms can remain stable only through a constant battle against the forces of entropy—against the tendency for complex systems to fly apart into simpler forms, as we all do in death. The battle against entropy takes the form of replenishment and self-protection. Given an organism with an internal structure capable of orderly existence, survival means replacing lost substances with new ones. It also means guiding those replacement substances to the places in the organism that need them; and since the chemical processes involved in all this often produce substances inimical to the survival of the organismic system, there must be provisions for eliminating these. Finally, survival means locating hospitable environmental conditions.

In short, organisms are primarily homeostatic, substance-processing systems. Whatever else may be true of them and of us is secondary to these basic imperatives. To be sure, the homeostasis may be a changing one. Individuals who have already procreated or who have reached a stage of development in which procreation or protection of offspring has declined may be designed to die, thus improving the survivability of the species. But, at least up to the point at which organisms have successfully generated other individuals to replace them, their biological design must give priority to substance processing.

It follows that species survive insofar as they are designed to locate the substances and the other necessary environmental conditons that they need. There are two major kinds of plans for achieving this. The *sessile* plan is to station organisms in ways largely beyond their own control in settings that can, on the average, be expected to provide the requisite substances and circumstances. In this plan there is a gain in organismic simplicity and energy expenditure at the cost of exposing the organism to the uncontrollable hazards of remaining in that place. The *motile* plan is to provide the organism with the capacity to move toward the things it needs and away from the things that imperil its existence. Under this plan, the organism achieves greatly enhanced flexibility and resourcefulness at the cost of greater organismic complexity and energy expenditure. Both plans can prove highly successful. At higher phyletic levels, the sessile and motile plans correspond with few exceptions to the plant and animal kingdoms, respectively. Humans are clearly motile organisms.

Both sessile and motile organisms are necessarily designed to the specifications imposed by their environments. After all, they and their environments are interacting parts of the same larger system. Motile organisms are accordingly designed to locate the conditions and substances they need and to process the substances. Most of the substance processing is nonbehavioral and need not concern us, but the locating is predominantly behavioral. Humans are, like other organisms, designed to locate substances and conditions that foster individual life and procreation. To put this in somewhat more psychological language, humans, like other organisms, are inherently designed around goal striving. Goal striving is in this sense an organizational cornerstone of zoological functioning.

Orientation and Evaluation in Goal Striving

In order for goal striving to succeed, it is necessary for an organism to *detect* objects in its environment that hold opportunities or constitute threats and to *evaluate* each object to determine which response to it would be most adaptive. When the initial detection is insufficiently informative for evaluation to take place, the organism must acquire additional information, which it normally does by *orienting* toward the information source in such a way as to focus its receptors on the source. Once the organism has gained the necessary information and begun to respond, it must *monitor* progress with respect to the goal and to assess this progress with a view to optimizing behavior. In other words, the organism must receive sensory feedback regarding its changing relationship to the goal object and must *evaluate* that feedback.

It may now already be apparent how these basic organismic functions of detection, orientation, monitoring, and evaluation relate to attention and emotion. At the human level, detection appears initially to occur through

what Neisser (1967) has called *preattentive processes* that, by definition, go
on outside the realm of conscious awareness; but orientation and monitoring correspond to attention as defined in this chapter. I have argued
elsewhere (Klinger, 1977), and will argue briefly in the next section, that the
evaluative activity described above involves emotion. If so, then it is clear
that attention and emotion are biologically indispensable components of
human functioning.

Affect as Evaluative Response

Emotion, as we have seen, is a complex reaction involving humoral, motor,
and experiential features. This chapter employs the term "affect" to refer to
the experiential facet of emotion. Affect, in the argument of this section,
constitutes the central representation of evaluative feedback. That is, people are, like other organisms, programmed biologically to respond in
species-typical (i.e., instinctive) ways to specific classes of stimuli. Each instinctive type of response consists of a complex of components that includes
emotion. The response classes to which instinctive reactions occur can be
enlarged through learning, and the particular form of the overt motor
response changes with learning and can be inhibited almost entirely. Even if
inhibited, however, most of the emotional component remains. Thus, even
when there are no overt signs of response, emotion constitutes a kind of *incipient response*. It is likely that there are relatively few varieties of species-
typical responses at the human level, such as joy-and-approach, anger-and-
attack-or-assert, fear-and-avoid, disgust-and-disgorge, distress, and
perhaps a few more. Thus, each emotion is linked to a primitive response
type in a class of response types that, taken together, constitute most of the
possible general directions that the behavior of a primitive organism can
take, relative to the objects it encounters. As individuals learn that new
stimulus situations hold consequences that are partly similar to previous
ones, they tag them with the appropriate emotional response. Thus, emotions act as behavioral codes and the affective components represent the
coded values of any given situation centrally.

There are a number of aspects of this system that may seem unnecessary.
For instance, what is the point of coding situations emotionally? It seems
likely that a coding process of this kind represents a highly efficient way of
funneling the tremendous number of situations an individual may face into
a limited number of basic adaptive response channels. This funneling process not only constitutes a *de facto* categorization of situations, but also
mobilizes the organism to respond with the response class most likely to
promote survival in that situation. This obviates the need to develop
through evolution or learning a completely different response pattern for
every possible kind of situation. It equips the organism with a base of adap-

tive stimulus-response patterns on which to build through learned elaboration. It reduces the time required in a given situation for deciding the basic character of the situation and mobilizing to meet its opportunities or challenges.

One might also wonder about the adaptive significance of positive emotional responses. It is easy enough to accept the idea that fear might help mobilize someone to run away or anger to strengthen an attack, but what about joy and hope? Lazarus (1980) makes an interesting suggestion here: "Positively toned emotions serve three basic psychological functions in coping, namely, as breathers from stress, as sustainers of coping effort and commitment, and as restorers" (p. 208). That is, positive emotion, like negative, normally carries a degree of arousal, thus supporting endurance and resolve while steering behavior toward the object of the goal pursuit, rather than away or against as in fear and anger.

Some investigators have suggested that people's emotional experiences can be described in terms of only two dimensions, usually labeled something like pleasant versus unpleasant and aroused versus unaroused, and therefore the categorization of emotions into an array of primaries is unnecessary and probably artificial. The two-dimensional factor structure of emotion has been obtained repeatedly (e.g., Plutchik, 1980; Zevon & Tellegen, Note 1), although not universally (e.g., Bush, 1973). A strong case can be made that the two dimensions can be profitably rotated so that they become redefined as a dimension of positive affect and a second dimension of negative affect (Zevon & Tellegen, Note 1). Thus, all affects communicate fundamentally the extent to which things are "good for me" and "bad for me." However, this need not signify that finer distinctions among emotions do not exist. It is plain that at least negative emotions carry information about the nature of the negativity and some general outlines for how to respond. In any case, analyses of affect within subjects demonstrate the existence of additional factors that correspond roughly to Tomkin's and Izard's categories as described above (Zevon & Tellegen, Note 1). In Zevon and Tellegen's words, "the two dimensions . . . represent a structure that is complementary rather than incompatible with a multidimensional view of mood variation" (p. 14).

Within the framework of this chapter, then, affect serves an evaluative function in two related ways. First, it serves to evaluate situations and their objects. Second, it serves to evaluate situational trends, especially how well or poorly a goal pursuit is going. In this latter form it functions as evaluative feedback to supplement the sensory feedback.

What is the evidence that emotion in fact functions in the way described? The evidence that primary emotions exist as components of instinctive response patterns has been reviewed elsewhere (Klinger, 1977) and will be briefly summarized here. First, several kinds of emotional expression are recognized across cultural boundaries, even when the cultures have always been essentially out of communication with one another (Ekman, 1972; Ekman, Sorenson, & Friesen, 1969). Not only do New Guinea tribesman and California university students recognize each other's facial expressions; they also agree on the general types of situations that give rise to them. Ekman et al. found general agreement with respect to joy, sadness, anger, and disgust. Their subjects tended to confuse the meaning of facial expressions that registered fear with those that registered surprise. When facial expressions are so similar across enormous geographic and cultural distances, and especially when the meanings of those expressions — the kinds of human situations giving rise to them — are so similar cross-culturally, it is hard not to conclude that emotional expressions and the larger emotional patterns of which these are part constitute species-typical responses to certain stock kinds of situations.

A second class of evidence brings brain research to bear on the question. A number of investigators (Heath, 1963; 1964; Mark & Ervin, 1970) have shown that the human brain can be stimulated electrically so as to produce some discrete emotions, such as pleasure and anger. There is in these situations no change in the environment that can account for the changed emotions produced by stimulation. Since the brain registers no sensations when stimulated in these locations — no pain, for instance — the subject apparently has no conscious way of knowing that stimulation has started or stopped other than by the change in affect itself. Investigators who have worked with animal brains have known since Olds and Milner's (1954) pioneering work that brain stimulation can be rewarding or punishing (presumably, pleasant or unpleasant), from the finding that animals can be induced to work to turn such stimulation on or off. Interestingly, they have also found (e.g., Glickman, 1973; Valenstein et al., 1970) that when stimulation of brain sites is rewarding or punishing, stimulation of those same locations also seems to instigate corresponding action, such as looking for food, attacking prey, copulating, exploring, and so on. Thus, there is reason to believe that the brain mechanisms that subserve affective response are structurally linked with those involved in the instigation of species-typical behavior.

The notion that affect serves as evaluative feedback has also received support. This evidence primarily takes the form of finding that when an investigator interferes with an emotion pharmacologically, this intervention changes behavior. For instance, Schachter and Ono (in Schachter & Latané, 1964) found that tranquilized students were more likely to cheat in scoring their own examinations, presumably because the chlorpromazine reduced the students' level of fear, which is one of the factors that restrains people from cheating. Psychopaths hypothetically suffer naturally from reduced fear responding. Schachter and Latané (1964) found that administering adrenaline helped psychopathic subjects learn to avoid electric shocks. When hungry rats are placed in conflict by placing food in a spot where they had previously received electric shocks, the rats are more "reckless" about approaching food if they are under the influence of alcohol, which reduces fear (Barry & Miller, 1962; Freed, 1968). The upshot of these studies seems to be that emotion is not just an energizer, much less an epiphenomenon, but is rather a process with a very direct role in the guidance of behavior. The role shown in these studies is completely consistent with the notion that affect serves as evaluative feedback.

From Homeostasis to Information and Mastery

The discussion so far has regarded affect as an internal signal that evaluates the import of events and objects. Specific affects constitute species-typical responses to specific classes of stimuli. The most basic classes of stimuli bear directly on homeostasis—ingestion, elimination, temperature regulation, and pain—as well as on reproduction. On the next level, affects seem to be geared to social stimuli, through imprinting in many species and probably through simpler mechanisms in others. Thus, even without the benefit of learning, imprinted ducklings emit high rates of alarm calls in the absence of the object they are imprinted on or in the presence of strange objects (Hoffman & DePaulo, 1977). Similarly, human infants become attached to care-givers and develop fears of strangers, probably without specifically learning to be afraid (Bowlby, 1973). Social stimuli obviously bear on the survival of individuals and species.

Beyond social stimuli, however, some species also seem to have evolved positive affective responses to certain kinds of new information and to mastery. Thus, Harlow and his colleagues were able to show that Rhesus monkeys are willing to work for the opportunity to watch interesting stimuli such as an electric train and for the opportunity to manipulate and disassemble latch mechanisms (Butler, 1953; Harlow, Harlow, & Meyer, 1950). The investigations largely ruled out the possibility that the behavior could be attributed to rewards other than the stimulation or the manipulative behavior. Many species besides humans manifest curiosity. Humans seem particularly drawn to opportunities for mastery of problems just beyond their previous levels of accomplishments. Sroufe and Waters (1976) have shown that the most powerful generalization to be made about the elicitors of smiling behavior in infants is that infants smile when they experience a rise in tension followed by a drop in tension. At the earliest ages, the tension is produced by sheer stimulation and drops after the stimulation ends. At older ages, the tension occurs because someone does something slightly novel or arousing and the tension drops when the infant recognizes the something as benign. The older the infant, the more complex or challenging the stimulation must be to elicit smiling. In adulthood, we find a similar pattern in the often carefully crafted form of humor (Koestler, 1964). Tension rises as the listener is led into a vicarious dilemma or danger, or a riddle. The tension drops with an unexpected resolution (the "punch line") that throws the events of the joke into an unforeseen frame of reference. That is, things suddenly "fall into place" as the listener cognitively masters the joke. Most people are also familiar with the relief and grin of victory over a difficult puzzle, problem, or opponent. It appears that people smile or laugh when they master a challenge.

In short, the affective evaluative function appears to have expanded with evolution from one that is substance-specific (able to recognize the substances and physical conditions that foster survival) to one that is also function-specific and information-specific, in the sense of being keyed to mastery, insight, certainty, and cognitive consistency. If there are, in fact, species-typical affective responses to epistemic events and to mastery, they reflect, of course, the fact that these kinds of outcomes have become species-typical goals. Humans are very much information-striving and mastery-striving organisms (cf., also Harter's discussion of developmental factors in mastery, in this volume).

Current Concerns: Evolution of Time-Binding Goal Pursuits

Part of the significance of social, informational, and mastery goals is that these are to a large degree independent of drives that arise from tissue deficits or hormonal levels. Both sated and hungry persons can enjoy circuses and achievement. But there is another way in which evolution appears to have transcended immediate physiological and situational determinants of behavior: organisms at the human level have evolved the capacity to become committed to goals that they cannot directly sense at the time of commitment and whose attainment lies well in the future. Many mammals are capable of detour behavior—figuring out ways to get around obstacles to a goal object they have reason to believe is there. Some primate species appear able to form somewhat longer-term plans. Humans, clearly, can envision future goals and strive hard, sometimes for decades, to realize them. A Ph.D., the Nobel Prize, a person romantically loved, and a million dollars are all in this category. The significant point for present purposes is that people remain oriented toward such goals while periodically living in situations unrelated to this goal but related to other goals; and the person may become deeply involved in other goals and strive for them during the same time period, without the person losing commitment to or necessarily "forgetting" the first goal. Thus, graduate students may fall in love, marry, have children, hold jobs unrelated to their degree work, and go on interesting vacations, all while remaining committed to their doctoral degree.

This kind of persistence must reflect continuing brain activity that keeps the goal psychologically alive between the time of commitment and the time at which the goal is attained or relinquished. I have called this kind of continuing state a *current concern*. Research has shown that while people are in a state of current concern about some goal they are more responsive than they would otherwise be to cues related to the concern (Hoelscher, Klinger, & Barta, 1981; Klinger, 1977; 1978). Thus, presenting people with words related to their current concerns (as contrasted with nonconcern-related cues) is more likely to shift their thoughts and dreams in the direction of the concern represented by the cue.

For affect theory, the significant point is that this evolution of a capacity for current concerns has been accompanied by the evolution of affective responses that reflect the degree of progress the person is making in pursuit of the goal. Many species, even some birds, respond with grief-like behavior upon loss of a mate, territory, or position in a dominance hierarchy. Humans, however, can respond with arousal, anger, and depression when thwarted in their pursuit of a goal they have never experienced directly — one they may have experienced vicariously or perhaps solely in their imagination. The power of current concerns (as defined here) is clearly depicted by the fact that people can experience such trenchant emotions over the outcome of a pursuit so far removed from homeostatic considerations and with such a tenuous reality in the striver's life. It is nevertheless apparently the case that disruption of goal pursuits leads to a lawful sequence of emotional reaction (an incentive-disengagement cycle): first, those emotions associated with invigoration and arousal, then anger, and finally depression, with anger persisting during the depression at least in the form of irritability. This sequence is followed in most instances by gradual recovery (Klinger, 1977).

Most people live with many concerns current at the same time. They nevertheless appear to remain more or less responsive to cues related to each of them. The flow of attention and thought content seems to be steered from moment to moment by the mental and environmental flow of concern-related cues. Thus, as each new cue is sensed, it appears nonconsciously to be accorded a kind of priority that determines the likelihood of its being processed further. When a person is focusing deliberately and operantly on a particular mental task, only very high priority cues break through the inhibitory activity that protects ongoing behavior from disruption. When the person is in a relaxed, nonoperant (*respondent*) state, the likelihood of lower-priority cues intruding on consciousness is much increased. It seems very likely that what determines the priority accorded a concern-related cue is its capacity to elicit an affective response. This capacity is in turn enhanced if the goal pursuit that the cue reflects has become threatened or disrupted in some way (Klinger, Barta, & Maxeiner, 1980). Thus, it appears that attentional mechanisms are themselves steered in part by emotional response, which is in turn anchored in goal striving. In this way, people are able to pick their way through the welter of stimulation around them, responding to the cues most likely to bear on the attainment of their most important goals.

PSYCHOLOGICAL DETERMINANTS
OF AFFECT AND MOOD

To gain the power to control affect, or to help other people control it, one must understand the factors that determine it. This section will examine five classes of determinants: biological factors (such as inheritance), developmental factors, arousal, the portents of the situations in which people find themselves or that they expect, and mental imagery.

Major General Determinants

Constitution. Since emotional response is, like everything else human, a biological process, part of what determines it is the character of the biological apparatus that participates in it. Individuals of a species vary along all biological dimensions; the dimensions governing emotional response are not exceptions. Constitutional differences probably do not offer a handy tool for the self-management of emotions. However, knowing that they exist and what are their principal dimensions helps to provide perspective on the emotional reactions of particular clients. For instance, it keeps therapists from forgetting that nonexperiential and nonpathological sources of strong emotional response tendencies exist, thus alerting them to variations in the biological baselines around which a therapeutic regimen must work.

There is substantial evidence for believing that human emotionality varies among individuals partly for reasons of genetic inheritance (Buss & Plomin, 1975). In childhood, identical twins are emotionally somewhat more alike than are fraternal twins. Research on emotion generally has tended to focus on negative emotions such as fear and anger, and the evidence for inheritability of emotional dispositions must also be regarded as limited to this dimension of emotional reactivity. We may thus conclude tentatively that different people are born with the tendency to respond with different amplitudes of joy, fear, and anger to substantially similar circumstances. Emotionally very reactive individuals are also probably more prone to form conditioned emotional reactions and are therefore more likely to develop neurotic symptoms, but the evidence on this deduction is still quite weak. Apart from general levels of emotionality, the argument of this chapter would suggest that specific kinds of emotional response to innately prescribed sets of stimuli are also subject to genetic variation, but research has not yet progressed to the point that this hypothesis can be adequately evaluated.

Developmental factors. Given a particular constitution, developmental factors probably help determine the general amplitude of emotional response and certainly help determine the objects to which particular responses occur. In regard to general emotionality, early work with animals appeared to arrive at an important conclusion: the amount of stimulation an infant receives determines the level of its emotionality as an adult. Most of this work was done with rats. The stimulation tended to consist of human handling of the rat pups or electrically shocking them. The measures of emotionality were often the adult rats' level of activity in an "open field" box (fear suppresses activity), the animal's tendency to dispense with crouching (a fear response) after clicks, higher rates of drinking by thirsty rats, and others. In general, the more highly stimulated rat pups grew up to be less emotional (that is, less fearful) adults (Denenberg, 1964). There is just the slightest indication (Solkoff, Yaffe, Weintraub, & Blase, 1969) that handling has somewhat similar effects on human infants. Thus, the level of stimulation and perhaps of trauma early in life may codetermine the level of emotional reactivity of the adult.

The effects described above relate to the overall level of emotionality, or at least of fear responding. Another class of developmental factors, conditioning, determines the level and variety of emotional response to most of the objects and events in the person's life beyond early infancy. That is, given that people are born to respond with particular affect to certain species-specific stimuli, conditioning broadens the classes of stimuli that elicit affect to include the enormous variety of things that adults have feelings about. This is a processs that probably characterizes most species in the animal kingdom and seems well established, despite questions about its generality at the human level (Brewer, 1974). Thus, octopi can be conditioned to fear (display defensive behavior toward) shrimp extract when it is paired with electric shock (Walters, Carew, & Kandel, 1981) and rat pups can acquire a preference for (a tendency to spend time with) orange-scented pine chips when their odor is paired with nursing (Brake, 1981). In each case, a formerly neutral stimulus acquires positive or negative value through association with a stimulus that innately already carries such value and affect.

Arousal. Under natural conditions, the strength with which people experience emotion is highly correlated with the level of their autonomic arousal. People who are terrified are likely to have rapidly beating hearts, sweaty palms, and strong adrenal flow. People who have just received extreme good news probably also experience increased autonomic activity, given that they often "feel like jumping with joy."

Just what role arousal plays in emotion is, however, still unclear (Leventhal, 1980). It does, at this time, seem clear that the lack of arousal may somewhat alter the emotional experience. For instance, paraplegics with lesions high in their spinal column lack the innervation necessary for autonomic arousal (in the strictly neural sense) to become translated into glandular and effector activity. They nevertheless experience at least certain emotions, such as fear and anger, although they often describe them as "cold" emotions, presumably since they lack the heart-rate and other autonomic changes that render emotions "hot" (Hohmann, 1966). If it is true that subtracting arousal from emotion still leaves a form of emotion, it is also true that creating arousal through adrenalin injection fails to create emotion (Maranon, 1924), although such imposed arousal probably is experienced as somewhat unpleasant (Maslach, 1979). Thus, arousal by itself, although probably not entirely "neutral" in an affective sense, is neither necessary nor sufficient to produce various emotional experiences.

On the other hand, there is considerable indication that arousal may serve to amplify ongoing emotional experiences. That is, when arousal is raised through some method prior to a certain situation, emotional responses to the subsequent situation are likely to be experienced more strongly. The usefulness of a "warm-up" comedy act preceding the main act is well known, as is the cumulative, escalating effect of successive frustrations, closely spaced in time, on anger. When people are given opportunities to shock another person repeatedly without provocation, the shock intensities increase over sessions (Goldstein, Davis, & Herman, 1975), which indicates either a process of progressive disinhibition or that aggressive arousal increases subsequent aggression. When people are insulted, they respond with greater retaliative aggression if the insult was preceded by physiologically arousing physical exercise—biking—than if they had been involved in a more sedentary activity—threading discs (Zillmann & Bryant, 1974). In general, the evidence indicates that general arousal aggravates irritable aggression unless the individual can attribute the arousal to something other than his or her own anger (Rule & Nesdale, 1976).

Outside of anger and aggression, arousal also amplifies other kinds of states. People who are still aroused physiologically by exercise are more sexually responsive to sexual stimuli (Cantor, Zillman, & Bryant, 1975). Additionally, recently frightened men express greater attraction to newly met women, and men who have received a denigrating report on their personalities express greater affective response to a subsequently introduced woman—greater liking if the latter signals acceptance, and greater disliking if the latter signals rejection (Walster, 1971). When psychopaths, whose fear responses tend to be weaker than those of other people, are injected with adrenaline, their specific inability to learn to avoid shock is reversed, presumably because their anticipatory fear responses have been amplified; and conversely, when college students are given the tranquilizer chlorpromazine, they cheat more often, presumably because their fear responses have been attenuated (Schachter & Latané, 1964).

Whether all of these effects can be attributed to changes in raw arousal is at this point an unresolved question. Perhaps even more centrally, whether arousal can be considered in any sense a unitary variable is at this point rather doubtful, since different ways of measuring arousal — measurements of different component systems — are not very well correlated. It is therefore too early to draw final conclusions, but the data would seem to support a preliminary conclusion: Arousal of one kind or another serves to amplify ongoing emotional experiences, but does not constitute emotion, and it is neither necessary nor sufficient for the occurrence of emotional response.

The portents of situations. Given a certain emotional apparatus endowed biologically and developmentally, the most important determinant of the emotions a person will feel at any given moment is the person's perception of what the future holds for him or her, both the immediate future within a present situation and the longer-range future. The emphasis here is on perception (in the broadest sense). Presumably, a normally functioning person will perceive situations in ways not usually at great variance from their reality, but insofar as the perception shows some deviation from objective reality, it is still the perception, not the reality, that determines emotion. This point is crucial for the treatment of most disorders in which "troubled" emotion plays a part.

Furthermore, what counts is not some abstract perception of where the person's situation is heading, but perception *in relation to* the person's goals and expectations. All deliberate action is launched with some objective and some idea, however imperfectly specified, of how to reach it. Often, people strive for a goal with the realization that any of numerous possible things might go amiss and that they may have to fall back on any of numerous corresponding contingency plans for dealing with such problems. People might assign varying probabilities to these contingencies, and some may be perceived as more costly in energy, time, and substance than others; but all are in some sense expected, at least as possibilities. Emotion shifts regularly according to the events that transpire. As long as the action and the feedback progress within expectable limits, affect is likely to remain at least modestly positive. If events dictate shifting to a more costly but anticipated procedure, affect is likely to turn angrier. But if progress stops and becomes irretrievably thwarted, the responses are, at perhaps different times, likely to be anger and depression; and if the person feels helpless to defend against some threatened harm, the response is likely to be fear. Thus, affect is a function of the changing relationship of the individual to his or her goal-related situations. One theorist suggests that all emotion depends on "interruption (blocking, inhibition) of ongoing, organized thought and behavior" (Mandler, 1980, p. 225). This generalization may be too restricted, but certainly interruption is a major instigator of negatively toned emotion.

Of course, events also give rise to positive emotions. People are generally pleased with success in their strivings and pleased with unexpected gains. But the strength of their feeling depends not only on the objective value of their success and not even just on the person's realistic appraisal of the success. It depends also, at least in part, on the extent to which the outcome departed from what the person was used to. In fact, judgments of size, weight, brightness, and probably all other quantitative dimensions are made in relation to what Helson (e.g., 1964) has called the person's *adaption level*. This level corresponds to the average (the geometric mean, in this instance) of the experience the judge has had with events of the same kind as those being judged, especially the more recent experiences. For instance, to a person used to seeing automobiles that are mostly 5-meters long or longer, a 4½-meter car looks small. To a person used to seeing mostly 4-meter or shorter cars on the street, the 4½-meter car looks large. As this is written, American cars are being downsized year by year. The older cars that once looked "normal" now look like wallowing behemoths, and the newer cars that now look "normal" are of the size that Americans once ridiculed as "toys." In much the same way, the rewards we receive become ordinary and lose much of their ability to evoke joy if we experience them repeatedly. Thus, to people who are accustomed to receiving a regular salary check, the arrival of the check evokes only modest joy as long as the amount does no better than to keep pace with inflation. A better-than-expected raise, even if the percentage increase is not especially large, may however evoke considerably greater-than-ordinary joy. A raise below the rate of inflation will give rise to resentment and perhaps depression. Thus, perceptions of situations and emotional responses to them depend on the frame of reference provided by adaption levels, which depend on tacit expectation based on past experiences.

As indicated earlier, however, emotional responses are determined less by situational perceptions as such than by the perceptions in relation to goals. In other words, one of the mediators between perception and emotion is ordinarily a process of *cognitive appraisal* (Arnold, 1960; Lazarus, 1966). Since, within the argument of this chapter, certain basic emotional responses are unlearned responses to particular kinds of stimuli, not all emotional responses require cognitive appraisal to take place. For instance, startle and fear responses to sudden loud noises are likely to be virtually immediate. However, most emotional responses beyond earliest infancy occur to stimuli not specified by the innate "wiring" of the person's brain.

Presumably, the reason that the person responds emotionally anyway is that cognitive appraisal, developed through learning, transforms the raw perception of the situation to a form that links up with the emotional response mechanism. Thus, the sudden announcement that your job will be eliminated—meaningless to the infant—comes to have some of the same initial effects on emotional response as the sudden loud noise. It is this transformational process, which links up new stimuli to archaic emotional response systems, that is the function of cognitive appraisal.

The learned-appraisal process need not involve elaborate cognitive activity and need not be conscious. People can acquire a liking for polygons presented repeatedly for only one millisecond at a time, even though they show no signs of recognizing the polygons later (Zajonc, 1980). Affective learning here actually precedes cognitive learning. Nevertheless, the appraisal process can also become rather complicated. Lazarus (e.g., 1980), who has contributed important research findings in this area, distinguishes among primary appraisal, secondary appraisal, and reappraisal. Primary appraisal in this framework "is the evaluation of every transaction or encounter for its significance for well-being" (p. 193). The event being appraised may be irrelevant, "benign-positive," or "stressful" in the sense of signifying harm, loss, threat, or challenge. Secondary appraisal consists of "evaluating coping resources and options" (p. 193) that might be brought to bear on the source of the stress. Secondary appraisal forms an integral part of the basis for emotional response, since, for instance, a potentially dangerous threat (such as a car speeding toward one) for which there is a ready remedy (such as stepping back onto the sidewalk) is likely to evoke only very slight fear and perhaps a bit of annoyance. Nightmares sometimes consist of the threat along with disabling of the coping response (for instance, finding oneself rooted to the street), thereby unleashing terror. Reappraisal in Lazarus' scheme may take the form of taking in and evaluating information about the person's "changing relationship with the environment" (p. 194); and the "intrapsychic effort of coping with stress" such as "denial of danger and avoiding thinking about it" (p. 124). The latter is aimed at reducing emotional distress without directly affecting the environment.

One consideration that becomes plain in this view of appraisal is that the process is a continuous one that reflects and participates in the continuing interaction of the individual with his or her environment. As the appraisal leads to emotions that mobilize the person for action, as emotional distress comes under control or coping responses begin to get the situation under control, appraisal reflects these changes and leads to corresponding modifications in emotional response.

One might ask, from an emotion-theory standpoint, what it is that motivates and steers the cognitive appraisal process. No research yet performed is adequate as a basis for answering this question, but the theoretical lineage set in motion most clearly by Tomkins (1962) suggests an answer: Stimuli that have not been fully understood and coped with give rise to the action-plus-emotion of interest, which includes orientation toward the thing along with continuing information processing in regard to it — continuing exploration of its possible significance for the individual.

Research focused on the relation of appraisal and emotion is still somewhat scarce. In some sense, the entire enormous attribution literature is relevant to the question, but some more direct evidence is also available. For instance, Lazarus (1966) has shown that experimentally inducing people to employ the "intrapsychic coping" responses of intellectualization or denial before they see a stress-inducing film of bloodshed reduces their emotional responding as measured by skin conductance. Work on fear of failure indicates that those with the greatest fear appraise failure as reflecting on the relatively less controllable aspect of their functioning, their ability, whereas people low in fear of failure attribute failure to more easily remediable aspects, such as not putting forth enough effort or succumbing to bad luck (e.g., Heckhausen, 1975). The ability attribution reflects more gravely on the person's worth because ability is less changeable and hence makes failure more threatening, more unpleasant, and more fear-inspiring. In a somewhat different vein, students who have been led to attribute the symptoms of their own fear to a placebo pill they received were more likely to cheat, presumably because they then underestimated the danger signals contained in their own fear of cheating (Dienstbier & Munter, 1971). Conversely, when people are led to expect that a placebo will relax them and they are then provoked to anger by a confederate of the experimenter, they respond with greater aggression to the confererate than do people who were told that the placebo would produce arousal symptoms (Younger & Doob, 1978). Presumably, the group that expected to be aroused by the pill interpreted their arousal level as respresenting less anger than would have been the case had they not expected to feel aroused. Thus, a variety of kinds of appraisals affects the direction, amplitude, and behavioral consequences of emotion.

Much of the value of Lazarus' scheme for analyzing appraisal processes lies in its identification of the various sources of cognitive influence on emotion. Each of these sources offers a focus for clinical scrutiny and a point of leverage for therapeutic intervention in altering emotional response.

Mental imagery. It is not only actual situations that affect emotion. There is ample clinical and experimental evidence that mental imagery carries with it much of the affect that would have been induced had the imagined sequences been real. When people are asked to imagine scenes that are happy or enraging or sad, they are left *feeling* happier, angrier, sadder (Schwartz,

Fair, Salt, Mandel, & Klerman, 1976; Strickland, Hale, & Anderson, 1975). Students who have learned lists of words rich in aggressive imagery ("fist," "punch," and so on) deliver more intense electric shocks to other students (Turner & Layton, 1976). People asked to imagine frightening scenes experience increased fear, especially if they are induced to imagine not only the exteroceptive data of vision and audition but also the interoceptive, somesthetic, cognitive, and other kinds of data regarding their own imaginary responses in the imaginary situation around them (Lang, 1977). When subjects are asked to imagine being shocked electrically every time they hear a certain tone, their skin conductance responses to the tone habituate more slowly for the vivid imagers than for nonvivid imagers (Drummond, White, & Ashton, 1978), indicating that the imaginary shocks have set up an element of real fear conditioning to the tone.

It may seem strange that something as apparently ethereal as imagery should have such potent effects. In fact, the experimental methods probably do not come close to unleashing the powerful emotions normally released in frightening dreams, which are, after all, also mental imagery. However, the power of mental imagery is not so strange when one considers what it really represents—a conscious facet of much of the individual's total psychological apparatus, excluding principally receptor and effector activity, and not even these completely (Klinger, 1981). Although emotional arousal certainly affects imagery, imagery in turn can be used to control emotion.

DETERMINANTS OF ATTENTION

Loosely speaking, attention is the label given to an individual's selection of stimulus inputs for perceptual or cognitive processing. The individual may select the direction from which to receive inputs or the modality of the input. In either instance, attention is a matter of focusing. From the large amount of information that could or does impinge on the individual's sense organs, he or she chooses a very small subset for special *attention* (see Carver and Scheier in this volume).

Beyond this general statement, attention can be regarded in at least three ways. First, it can be thought of phenomenologically in terms of consciousness. Second, it can be thought of as a respondent orienting behavior. Finally, it can be thought of as active operant activity integrated into larger operant behavior sequences. We shall consider each of these perspectives in turn.

Attention and Consciousness

Of all the stimuli that leave their impressions on our receptors, very few enter consciousness. We "see" many things that we do not notice and "hear" many things to which we do not listen. Most of the time, we do not notice our chairs pressing against our backsides or our shoes squeezing our feet. We become conscious of them, if we so choose, by "redirecting our attention." This may entail actually adjusting our receptors by, for instance, turning our heads slightly in order to get the object of interest into the center of our foveae, or we may do so by turning out one sense modality and turning in another — for instance, ending our examination of a slide to listen more closely to the speaker who has projected it. We may even redirect attention within a modality without changing our receptors, as when we tune out a party conversation we are engaged in to eavesdrop on another conversation going on next to us. Redirection of this kind can be hard work, but it can go on with a minimum of changes at the overt behavioral level.

It is intuitively obvious that where we direct our attention greatly affects our ability to function. Thus, a generation of experimentation with dichotic listening (listening to two different streams of simultaneous auditory stimulation, one to each ear) has shown that when people are asked to listen to one channel and ignore the other, they are able to perform very little cognitive processing on the information carried by the ignored channel. Mischel and his collaborators (e.g., Mischel, Ebbesen, & Zeiss, 1972) have shown that keeping the consummatory aspects of a goal object in consciousness reduces children's resistance to the temptation to consummate it. Conscious images, as we have seen, also affect mood. These are merely illustrations of the finding that, notwithstanding the power that has been ascribed to unconscious processes, conscious focusing plays a paramount role in effective functioning.

Attention as Respondent Orienting Behavior

It is possible to control attention in the sense of deliberately maintaining a specific focus or of deliberately shifting focus to search for something or to process better something that had already entered awareness. Nevertheless attention, which is so intimately bound up with consciousness, is steered much of the time by nonconscious processes. If we grant that attention is an active focusing process that excludes much available stimulation from consciousness, then we must be able to explain how it is that some unexpected events can intrude on consciousness, can break through the inhibitions that keep others out. This kind of phenomenon can be explained only if we assume that we come equipped with a nonconscious gatekeeper of our consciousness, some process that performs a preliminary evaluation of the significance of nonconscious stimulation and admits to consciousness only those stimuli that meet certain criteria. "Admitting to consciousness" here means turning one's attention to the stimuli in question. No one knows in detail what this gatekeeping process is like. Neisser (1967) has dubbed it the *preattentive* process (but has cautioned that the term *not* be overused and that, often, preattention involves *skill* and *choice*; cf. 1976).

Psychologists interested in classical conditioning have, since Pavlov, studied "orienting reflexes," response complexes that include skin conductance increases, constriction of peripheral blood vessels in the hand, and other vascular and motor changes, often associated with overt changes in receptor orientation. The pattern of behavior when someone knocks on our door is very likely to include an orienting reflex. Orienting responses almost certainly involved shifts in attention and probably overlap heavily the class of instances in which preattentive processes are responsible for the shift. Thus, the study of orienting reactions is likely to constitute study of a behavioral index of attentional shifts produced by preattentive processes. It is worth noting at this point that orienting reactions can also be regarded as in part emotional responses, involving the affects of interest and surprise.

There is little doubt that preattentive processes exist in something like the form indicated. Apart from their logical necessity and various kinds of indirect evidence, the best evidence may come from studies of dichotic listening in which the experimenter asks subjects to "shadow" (repeat continuously) the content of one channel while embedding emotionally arousing stimuli into the channel the subject is instructed to ignore. Assays of what information subjects can recall from the unattended channel in such an experiment generally support the assumption that subjects indeed ignore it. However, embedding the subject's name nevertheless tends to attract the subject's attention (Moray, 1959); and if electric shocks are first paired with several names of cities, names of other cities played on an unattended channel elicit orienting reactions, but no recall of the stimuli that produced them (Corteen & Wood, 1972). Playing stimuli on an unattended channel increases subjects' liking for them, despite their being still unable to recognize them (Wilson, 1979).

One important class of evidence regarding preattentive processes comes from studies of habituation. In a sizeable literature, the data show that if stimuli that arouse orienting reactions are repeated in regular fashion, the orienting responses to them gradually lose strength and disappear. It appears very much as if repetition of stimuli that lead to no special consequences for the subject demonstrates the innocuousness and irrelevance of the stimuli for the subject, with the result that these stimuli are henceforth excluded from consciousness.

Preattentive determinants of attention. To what stimuli do preattentive processes direct attention? The stimuli are most likely those which are most emotionally arousing. These are likely to be novel stimuli, species typically arousing stimuli, conditioned to produce emotional responses, or stimuli associated with current concerns.

Evidence to support this generalization comes from a variety of sources. The dichotic listening studies described above showed orienting responses to cues on unattended channels when the cues were associated with the person's own name or had been conditioned to shock. Sleeping subjects can execute simple actions in response to a variety of stimuli in accordance with instructions provided before going to sleep. They have also been shown to incorporate into their dreams the soundtrack of a frightening film they had seen before going to sleep (Dekoninck & Koulack, 1975) and words associated with their current concerns if played during their sleep (Hoelscher, Klinger, & Barta, 1981).

Since it could be argued that emotionally conditioned stimuli are *ipso facto* related to a current concern, and that novel and species-typically arousing stimuli innately instate current concerns, however short-lived, the evidence described above could be subsumed under the generalization that *preattentive processes admit to consciousness unattended stimuli that are related to current concerns.*

Although people tend to notice stimuli related to their current concerns, they notice some stimuli much more readily than others. Some of this difference is probably attributable to the physical properties of the stimuli, but another part is probably attributable to the nature of the current concerns to which the stimuli are related. Unfortunately, there is little direct evidence regarding the properties of current concerns (concern influence variables) that affect attention. However, it is known that the frequency with which people think about various concerns, according to people's later reports, is correlated with certain specific variables: the person's strength of commitment to pursuing the goal of the concern, the value of the goal and the probability of attaining it, the imminence of having to do something about the goal, and various kinds of disruptions of goal striving, such as personal relationships that are threatened in some way and unexpected difficulties that impede reaching goals (Klinger, Barta, & Maxeiner, 1980). Fairly routine kinds of pursuits are reportedly thought about less than others. Perhaps some of these concern-influence variables also govern the tendency for preattentive processes to direct attention.

Attention as Operant Activity

The skilled-response sequences that make up much of behavior beyond early infancy are built up out of simpler response elements. Whether the behavior is tying shoe laces, brushing teeth, typing, driving, or playing the piano, there was a time in the person's life when learning the behavior meant approximating some model of the behavior with bits and pieces of one's own repertory, which were then gradually molded, rearranged, and chained together. With enough practice, the new behavior sequence becomes smooth and skilled. This process is called *response integration.* Well-integrated behavior is characterized by smooth flow and by sharply reduced need for conscious attention to the segments of the behavior. In fact, after behavior has been integrated, focusing attention on its parts can disorganize it, as people who try to teach others to drive or to play an instrument sometimes find out to their embarrassment.

Although the need for effortful conscious attention is reduced in integrated behavior, this does not mean that the role of attention is attenuated. Rather, as with the rest of the sequence, attentional acts have become integrated into the sequence and have become automatized so that they occur without conscious direction. Their role has also become somewhat simplified. To a large extent, attention within an integrated behavior sequence is one of monitoring stimulus input within certain expectable limits and along certain expected variables. If the stimulus flux falls inside those limits on those variables, behavior accommodates to it more or less automatically. If the stimulus flux exceeds the limits, it is likely to trigger fully conscious focusing. For example, people can drive long distances in normal traffic while thinking about other matters, listening to the radio, or conversing with a passenger. They may later have almost no recollection of their driving behavior or the traffic conditions. If, however, they suddenly see a car approaching them in their own lane, they are likely to quickly "come to" with a start. It is likely that as a result of not having paid full attention, their reaction to an emergency will be slower than it might have been. Nevertheless, the frequent repetition of behavior, leading to its integration and automatization, positively disposes the person to move focal attention away from the behavior.

Integrated behavior does not manifest the same level of integration under all conditions. It is, of course, subject to interruption by the kinds of emotionally arousing stimuli described in the previous section. Furthermore, the quality of the integration seems to suffer when the person is fatigued, sleepy, asleep, under the influence of some psychoactive drugs, or psychotic (Klinger, 1971). Under these conditions, the "seams" of the behavior seem to weaken and there is a greater tendency for competing response segments to intrude at the points in the sequences that require the greatest degree of decision making or use of stimulus feedback, thus producing "errors." It follows that under such conditions, extraneous current-concern-related stimuli are more likely to intrude at vulnerable points in the sequence, resulting in increased distraction and mind wandering.

Although the previous paragraphs have referred to "stimuli," some of the most prominent cues to which we respond are our own mental events. Thus, thoughts (including images) may themselves arouse emotions and bear on current concerns other than those involved in ongoing activity. Correspondingly, people preoccupied with pressing current concerns often continually interrupt and disrupt their own activity as their thoughts cue off mental activity that interferes with what they are trying to do.

Control of attention in operant thought and action. One of the principal dimensions that differentiates types of thoughts is the degree to which a thought is deliberate and directed — a "working" thought — versus thoughts that are spontaneous, undirected, and involuntary, as in mind wandering, dreaming, and much daydreaming (Klinger, 1978; 1978/79). The first extreme might be called *operant* and the second *respondent*. Respondent thoughts are inherently uncontrolled in any deliberate way, but, of course, they obey certain specific laws that may be subsumed under what I have called the *Induction Principle* (Klinger, 1977). This principle simply states that new thoughts are elicited (*induced*) by attention moving to a cue associated with one of the person's current concerns, the content of the thought being one that in some way incorporates or "bridges" the content of both the cue and the concern. Thus, thought content shifts from one focus to another according to the appearance of external cues and of cues generated internally by a person's own thought stream that are concern-related and emotionally evocative enough to pass the criteria of the preattentive processes.

Operant thought probably obeys the same general laws as respondent thought, with the exception that the operant thinker imposes some additional behaviors on the spontaneous flow of thought. These "operant elements" include, among others, evaluating the extent to which the operant thoughts or acts have advanced the person toward the goals at which the operant sequence is directed, and deliberately controlling attention. Research that required subjects to think aloud while working on mental or manual problems or while letting their minds wander has shown these two operant elements to occur much more frequently in operant than in respondent thought (Klinger, 1974).

Work using thought sampling (Klinger, Note 2; Klinger, Barta, & Glas, 1981) has shown that people who are doing well on examinations or whose teams are scoring well in basketball are significantly better focused on the activity at hand than those doing less well. A major source of distraction under these intense task conditions is evaluative thought — evaluations of one's own performance as it unfolds, or the performance of others. Nevertheless, even under examination conditions, students still spend a significant proportion of their time thinking thoughts that are not focused on the operations of answering the examination questions.

The issue of attentional control has become of paramount importance in the understanding and treatment of evaluation anxiety, such as anxiety about taking tests. This attentional approach to test anxiety enjoys a long tradition, having originated in 1952 with George Mandler and S. B. Sarason and having been nurtured along by I. B. Sarason (e.g., 1972; 1980). There is now a large and convincing accumulation of evidence that one of the principal factors that disrupts the performance of text-anxious individuals is their failure to focus their attention efficiently under stress. Thus, close analysis of the correlation between measures of test anxiety and performance shows that the items in such measures that tap "worry"—that is, preoccupation with the threatening aspects of the test rather than with problem solving itself—are well correlated (inversely) with performance on tests, but items that assess emotionality are largely uncorrelated with performance (Deffenbacher, 1980). (Interestingly, emotionality items are also uncorrelated with physiological measures of emotional arousal.) Observations of children indicate that the more anxious children let their attention wander more often to things irrelevant to their tasks (Dusek, 1980) and focus less often on information that might help them in their tasks (Wine, 1980) than is true of the less anxious. Heart-rate studies indicate that anxious individuals show less heart-rate deceleration than nonanxious people in response to a signal warning of an upcoming task, which suggests that they attune themselves less to receive the coming task information (Holroyd & Appel, 1980). Finally, attempts to help test-anxious individuals control their attention by exposing them to coping models, by guiding their attention during tasks, or by training them to control their attention improves their task performance relative to that of less anxious individuals (Dusek, 1980; Geen, 1980; Sarason, 1975; Wine 1971, 1980). Wine (1980) in particular suggests that high-test-anxious individuals attend to tasks less efficiently than do low-test-anxious individuals because their current concerns are more inclined toward avoiding other people's negative evaluations of them. As a result, high-test-anxious individuals are more preoccupied with themselves and their plight and busier anticipating negative evaluations, all of which distracts them from simply attending to the specific steps of performing effectively.

A considerable literature also implicates attentional deficiencies in schizophrenics' ability to perform well on various kinds of tasks (e.g., McGhie & Chapman, 1961; Shakow, 1962). Indeed, even clinically normal children who are at risk by virtue of having schizophrenic mothers manifest reaction-time deficits that are presumably attributable to attentional problems (Marcus, Note 3). The pattern of behavior in schizophrenia in general suggests strongly that psychotic episodes may be characterized by a reduced capacity to exert operant control over the respondent stream of thought and action. The attentional deficit in schizophrenia is presumably hard to control through voluntary efforts by the affected individual, but there are indications that it can be reduced by special practice with a task (Shakow, 1962) and by raising the amplitude of the simulus feedback (Lang & Buss, 1965).

GAINING SELF-CONTROL OVER AFFECT, MOOD, AND ATTENTION

The chapter up to this point has provided concepts and specific empirical relationships for understanding the factors that determine affect and attention. It is not the purpose of this chapter to review the literature on self-management practices themselves. That will be done in the parts of the book that follow. This section, however, presents an overview to indicate the applications of the principles already described.

Managing Arousal Directly

We have seen that physiological arousal acts to amplify the experience of emotion, at least if the individual has no reason to attribute the arousal to something nonemotional. This function is established especially well for anxiety and anger. Attempts to control these emotions have, therefore, focused heavily on reducing arousal directly. Little need be said about the popularity of anxiety-reducing medication since the mid-1950s. The 1960s, in turn, building on Schultze's autogenic training and Jacobson's progressive relation as well as on ancient meditative disciplines saw the burgeoning of relaxation and meditative practices. There is no question that these methods are effective in countering physiological arousal and, in that sense, in reducing emotionality. There is also reason to believe that regular practices of these methods confers certain general health benefits (e.g., Benson, 1976) and possibly some psychological benefits as well that are not restricted to the duration of the relaxation sessions alone. Nevertheless, it is also becoming clear that these practices do not by themselves improve anxiety-based disorders such as phobias and compulsions (Marks, 1976), or at least they are an inefficient way to treat these disorders. However, the usefulness of relaxation is considerably improved when it is taught as a self-control procedure (Goldfried & Trier, 1974) — that is, as a tool to be applied voluntarily whenever arousal becomes a problem. Relaxation then becomes a skill and a tactic that enables clients to continue their improvement after the end of therapy.

Managing Emotional Response Directly

Emotional response can be modified by direct conditioning. This is probably the process involved in changing one's liking of something through subliminal exposure to it (Zajonc, 1980), and could in principle be applied to any affect, but in practice research has focused almost exclusively on fear. Apart from the myth-shrouded impact of Little Albert, the first influential clinical attempt to apply an affective conditioning procedure (at least in the English-speaking literature) seems to have been Wolpe's (1958).

The effective ingredient in this and subsequent methods seems to have been to expose clients to representation of the thing feared in such a way as to block avoidance and escape. In this way the client can fully experience the innocuousness of exposure. In the form of systematic desensitization, which is the most common variant of the method, the exposure takes place in the client's imagery. The more direct, *in vivo* methods are more effective (Marks, 1976), but so are self-control variants that teach clients the principles of desensitization and encourage them to develop desensitization skills for application whenever it seems appropriate (e.g., Barrios & Shigetomi, 1979; Deffenbacher & Parks, 1979; Denney & Rupert, 1977; Goldfried, 1971). Here, as in relaxation, the advantage goes to the client who can use the method as a tool specifically targeted at the kinds of situations that can create problems. Suinn's anxiety management training program also incorporates this feature, but adds some further ones as well (see Deffenbacher & Suinn's chapter in this volume).

Managing Emotion by Controlling Attention and Imagery

One of the features that sets off anxiety management training (AMT) from older desensitization methods is its training component for learning to control attention voluntarily. As in desensitization, clients learn relaxation. They also learn to distinguish the early signs of growing anxiety—they become sensitized to their own emotional states. They are also trained in vivid imaging for use in the key part of the program, which consists of teaching subjects to shift easily among images of situations that provoke anxiety, induce relaxation, or evoke competency. Thus, by controlling their imagery, clients gain the power to control their emotional states. This method is about equal to self-control desensitization in effectiveness, including the power to reduce anxiety to nontargeted areas (Deffenbacher, Michaels, Michaels, & Daly, 1980).

Attention appears to play a significant role in depression as well. One of the components in Kanfer's model of depression is the increased rate of the depressed person's self-monitoring, arising presumably from heightened current concerns about his or her own worth and competency. When people are induced to attend closely to their own failures in an experimental task, they subsequently evaluate themselves more unfavorably and reward themselves less than in alternative conditions (Kirschenbaum & Karoly, 1977); and when subjects low in self-esteem are encouraged to concentrate on the task at hand, they improve their performance more than do subjects high in self-esteem, presumably because they reduce attending self-consciously to themselves (Brockner & Hulton, 1978). Consequently, the Kanfer model has led to a self-control treatment model for depression (Kanfer & Hagerman, 1981; Rehm, 1977) that focuses on shifting the person's monitoring away from self and away from failures and shortcomings, as well as seeking to change the bases (such as rigid inappropriate standards) for low self-evaluations. The program has shown itself to be significantly better in relieving depression than nonspecific group therapy (Fuchs & Rehm, 1977) and an assertion skills treatment (Rehm, 1979).

Managing Emotion by Controlling Perceptions, Attributions, and Expectancies

Albert Ellis was one of the first psychologists to perform therapy by modifying directly the beliefs of his clients. Using methods that shocked the therapeutic community of his time, he flayed away verbally at clients' flawed cognitive assumptions that maintained their psychological disturbance. His Rational Emotive Therapy was transformed by Goldfried to a more behavioristic, self-statement-based form and renamed "rational restructuring" (Goldfried, Decenteceo, & Weinberg, 1974). In this form, it has been found somewhat superior to self-control desensitization in reducing self-reported anxiety (Kanter & Goldfried, 1979). Training clients to say things to themselves is, of course, a behavioral form of altering cognitive beliefs. Self-statements form components of effective treatment programs for reducing nighttime fears in children (Graziano & Mooney, 1980), for controlling anger (Novaco, 1976), for reducing depression (as in the Kanfer and Rehm approaches), and as part of test-anxiety approaches described previously, especially in Meichenbaum's (Meichenbaum, Turk, & Burstein, 1975) stress-inoculation procedure.

The role of the self-statement varies somewhat, of course, according to the emotion and the target situation. Thus, the point of self-statements in anxiety and depression is to avert catastrophic thinking by reminding clients of the control they in fact retain over their own behavior, by limiting the scope of anticipated loss in the event of failure, and by continually refocusing attention away from self-centered thoughts and into the work of problem solving. In dealing with depression, self-statements also serve to counter the kinds of beliefs about self and the situation that lead to despair and surrender. In effect, clients are helped to avoid the plunge into depression by strengthening the beliefs and expectancies necessary to maintain invigoration. In relation to anger, similarly, self-statements remind the individual of alternative, constructive responses that prevent incentive-disengagement from proceeding beyond invigoration.

Skill Training

Not infrequently, the beliefs that lead to anxiety or depression are based in actual experience. Although they have become outdated, the client has not yet discovered that fact. Sometimes the client's present limitations are also real, but the client is unaware of his or her potentiality for acquiring new skills. When subjects have learned that they are helpless in a situation, experience with successfully solving new problems overcomes the sense of helplessness (Klein & Seligman, 1976). Thus, teaching study skills to test-anxious students improves their academic performance, especially in combination with other treatment components aimed at controlling anxiety (Harris & Johnson, 1980; Lent & Russell, 1978), although study skills training by itself is less effective in modifying anxiety.

Managing Adaptation Levels

I have seen no research that has tried to harness knowledge of the adaptation level for clinical purposes. It seems clear, however, that the potentiality for its use exists. People who understand the psychological aftereffects of powerful, protracted euphoria might choose to space their rewards and dole them out in moderate doses. Parents may reduce depression and hostility in children by applying this principle to holidays and birthdays.

Imagery Methods

We have already seen some of the many uses of imagery in behavior-therapy-based methods for self-management. In addition to these, guided imagery techniques have developed to the point of great promise, and the optimistic clinical reports are being joined by controlled investigations demonstrating their effectiveness (e.g., Leuner, 1978, 1980). One of the major approaches to imagery therapy, Shorr's "psycho-imagination therapy," has given rise to a self-help book (Shorr, 1977) that encourages readers to explore and interpret their imagery in response to a wide variety of more or less standard imaginal starting points. There is as yet no evidence regarding the effectiveness of such self-help, but it seems likely that people who have some rudimentary understanding of interpretive principles would benefit from using their imagery as a resource for self-understanding and personal growth. Techniques of finishing waking fantasies or dreams that were interrupted, perhaps defensively, or of continuing fantasies and dreams beyond their natural termination points, may shed light on assumptions underlying emotions and behavior. For instance, discovering what it is one fears if one does *not* avoid or escape something in fantasy can provide a reading of the assumptions or expectations underlying the fear. Furthermore, the cases reported in the clinical literature suggest strongly that under suitable circumstances, psychological problems can be not only illuminated, but also resolved purely within the arena of fantasy, without interpretation by a therapist or intellectual insight by the client. Given an appropriate theoretical view of the nature of imagery (e.g., Klinger, 1981), this need not seem as surprising or improbable as it does from the perspective of conventional viewpoints on imagery. The circumstances under which such imagery procedures work well as self-management methods remain to be delineated.

Self-Management of Current Concerns and Thought Flow

Among the problems that require clinical attention are distraction from work, work blocks, and an inability to think creatively enough. Current-concerns theory has a number of hypotheses to offer (as yet, unfortunately, untried in clinical contexts) regarding the management of such problems.

Distraction is often a matter of current concerns unrelated to the person's immediate tasks exercising a prepotent influence on preattentive processes and thought flow. In this event, it may be more efficient to stop trying to work at the lower priority goal and give full attention to solving the other problem. Often, of course, it is impossible to solve the other problem right away. In that case, one can use the finding that concerns gain influence over thought processes when the person is unsettled as to next steps toward the goal—that is, when goal striving is disrupted and there is no integrated program for proceeding (Klinger, Barta, & Maxeiner, 1980). We would then predict from current-concerns that distraction would be reduced if the person focused on the distracting problem long enough to decide on next steps or to make contingency plans, thus reducing uncertainty about the goal pursuit.

Distraction also often results from not wishing to forget to do certain things at a later time or a reluctance to lose one's present grasp of the distracting situation by turning attention to something else, even though the something else is what the person is supposedly trying to do now. The content-cycling nature of fantasy normally serves as a reminder mechanism and as a medium for mental rehearsal, at the price of periodic distraction. This functon of fantasy can, however, probably be made a smaller source of distraction from other activity by noting down the things to be remembered later or the emergent understanding one has of the situation for the purpose of later retrieval. That is, the "external memory" removes some of the burden that rests on fantasy and enables the individual to focus more easily on something else.

The current-concerns theory of fantasy gives rise to a partial theory of creativity (Klinger, 1971). This theory states that creativity requires, among other things, regnant current concerns about the problem one wishes to be creative about, periods of deep immersion in the subject matter of the problem, and ample opportunities to engage in respondent thinking.

SUMMARY

Animal organisms, if motile, survive by goal striving, around which they are completely organized. Affect and attention constitute indispensable components of their goal-striving organization. Affect serves as an aspect of instinctive behavior that codes objects and situations as boding well or ill for the organism, provides schematic directions for the response to the situation, and serves as evaluative feedback regarding the progress of the organism's goal pursuits. Attention refers to processes that enhance information processing. It is in part steered by preattentive processes that detect and funnel to consciousness emotionally arousing stimuli that may have a significant bearing on survival or procreation.

At higher-animal levels, and certainly at the human level, organisms have evolved the capacity to strive for particular goals over long time periods despite numerous interruptions, but this persistence in goal striving requires a continuing brain state called a *current concern*. Affect has evolved in relation to the capacity for current concerns, and goals have evolved from purely substance processing, or self-protective ones, to include information processing and effective functioning. Human affect is determined by constitution, developmental factors (including learning), arousal, mental imagery, and the perceived portents of situations for goal striving. The perception of portents is itself dependent on adaptation-level effects, conditioned affects, and cognitive appraisal processes. Each of these determinants provides means for controlling affect.

Attention was examined from the perspective of consciousness, respondent orienting behavior, and operant activity. The chapter explored the role of attention in maintaining inappropriate affective responses such as anxiety and depression, explored the implications of the factors that govern affect and attention for self-management, and described the application of the principles of affect and attention in methods for control of arousal, emotional responsivity, attention and imagery, perceptions, attributions, expectancies, skill training, adaptation levels, imagery, and control of current concerns.

REFERENCE NOTES

1 . Zevon, M. A., & Tellegen, A. *The structure of mood change: An idiographic/nomothetic analysis.* Unpublished manuscript, 1981.
2 . Klinger, E. *Thought content, anxiety, and test performance.* Unpublished manuscript, 1979.
3 . Marcus, L. M. *Studies of attention in children vulnerable to psychopathology.* Unpublished Ph.D. dissertation, University of Minnesota, 1972.

REFERENCES

Arnold, M. B. *Emotion and personality.* New York: Columbia University Press, 1960. 2 vols.
Barrios, B. A., & Shigetomi, C. C. Coping skills training for the management of anxiety: A critical review. *Behavior Therapy*, 1979, *10*, 491–522.
Barry, H., III, & Miller, N. E. Effects of drugs on approach-avoidance conflict tested re-

peatedly by means of a "telescope alley." *Journal of Comparative and Physiological Psychology*, 1962, *55*, 201–210.

Benson, H. *The relaxation response.* New York: Morrow, 1976.

Bowlby, J. *Attachment and loss.* Vol. 2. *Separation.* New York: Basic Books, 1973.

Brake, S. C. Suckling infant rats learn a preference for a novel olfactory stimulus paired with milk delivery. *Science*, 1981, *211*, 506–508.

Brewer, W. F. There is no convincing evidence for operant or classical conditioning in adult humans. In W. B. Weimer & D. S. Palermo (Eds.), *Cognition and the symbolic processes.* Hillsdale, N.J.: Erlbaum 1974.

Brockner, J., & Hulton, A. B. How to reverse the vicious cycle of low self-esteem: The importance of attentional focus. *Journal of Experimental Social Psychology*, 1978, *14*, 564–578.

Bush, L. E., II. Individual differences multidimensional scaling of adjectives denoting feelings. *Journal of Personality and Social Psychology*, 1973, *25*, 50–57.

Buss, A. H., & Plomin, R. *A temperament theory of personality development.* New York: Wiley, 1975.

Butler, R. A. Discrimination learning by rhesus monkeys to visual-exploration motivation. *Journal of Comparative and Physiological Psychology*, 1953, *46*, 95–98.

Cantor, J. R., Zillman, D., & Bryant, J. Enhancement of experienced sexual arousal in response to erotic stimuli through misattribution of unrelated residual excitation. *Journal of Personality and Social Psychology*, 1975, *32*, 69–75.

Corteen, R. S., & Wood, B. Autonomic responses to shock-associated words in an unattended channel. *Journal of Experimental Psychology*, 1972, *94*, 308–313.

Deffenbacher, J. L. Worry and emotionality in text anxiety. In I. G. Sarason (Ed.), *Test anxiety: Theory, research and applications.* Hillsdale, N.J.: Erlbaum, 1980.

Deffenbacher, J. L., Michaels, A. C., Michaels, T., & Daley, P. C. Comparison of anxiety management training and self-control desensitization. *Journal of Counseling Psychology*, 1980, *27*, 232–239.

Deffenbacher, J. L., & Parks, D. H. A comparison of traditional and self-control desensitization. *Journal of Counseling Psychology*, 1979, *26*, 93–97.

DeKoninck, J. M., & Koulack, D. Dream content and adaptation to a stressful situation. *Journal of Abnormal Psychology*, 1975, *84*, 250–260.

Denenberg, V. H. Critical periods, stimulus input and emotional reactivity: A theory of infantile stimulation. *Psychological Review*, 1964, *71*, 335–351.

Denney, D. R., & Rupert, P. A. Desensitization and self-control in the treatment of test anxiety. *Journal of Counseling Psychology*, 1977, *24*, 272–280.

Dienstbier, R. A., & Munter, P. O. Cheating as a function of the labeling of natural arousal. *Journal of Personality and Social Psychology*, 1971, *17*, 208–213.

Drummond, P., White, K., & Ashton, R. Imagery vividness affects habituation rate. *Psychophysiology*, 1978, *15*, 193–195.

Dusek, J. B. The development of test anxiety in children. In I. G. Sarason (Ed.), *Test anxiety: Theory, research, and applications.* Hillsdale, N.J.: Erlbaum, 1980.

Ekman, P. Universals and cultural differences in facial expressions of emotion. In J. Cole (Ed.), *Nebraska Symposium on Motivation*, 1971. Lincoln: University of Nebraska Press, 1972.

Ekman, P., Sorenson, E. R., & Friesen, W. V. Pan-cultural elements in facial displays of emotion. *Science*, 1969, *164*, 86–88.

Freed, E. X. Effect of alcohol on conflict behaviors. *Psychological Reports*, 1968, *23*, 151–159.

Fuchs, C. Z., & Rehm, L. P. A self-control behavior therapy program for depression. *Journal of Consulting and Clinical Psychology*, 1977, *45*, 206–215.

Geen, R. G. Test anxiety and cue utilization. In I. G. Sarason (Ed.), *Test anxiety: Theory, research, and applications.* Hillsdale, N.J.: Erlbaum, 1980.

Glickman, S. E. Responses and reinforcement. In R. A. Hinde & J. Stevenson-Hinde (Eds.), *Constraints on learning: Limitations and predispositions*. New York: Academic Press, 1973.

Goldfried, M. R. Systematic desensitization as training in self-control. *Journal of Consulting and Clinical Psychology*, 1971, *37*, 228–234.

Goldfried, M. R., Decenteceo, E. T., & Weinberg, L. Systematic rational restructuring as a self-control technique. *Behavior Therapy*, 1974, *5*, 247–254.

Goldfried, M. R., & Trier, C. S. Effectiveness of relaxation as an active coping skill. *Journal of Abnormal Psychology*, 1974, *83*, 348–355.

Goldstein, J. H., Davis, R. W., & Herman, D. Escalation of aggression: Experimental studies. *Journal of Personality and Social Psychology*, 1975, *31*, 162–170.

Graziano, A. M., & Mooney, K. C. Family self-control instruction for children's night-time fear reduction. *Journal of Consulting and Clinical Psychology*, 1980, *48*, 206–213.

Harlow, H. F., Harlow, M. K., & Meyer, D. R. Learning motivated by a manipulation drive. *Journal of Experimental Psychology*, 1950, *40*, 228–234.

Harris, G., & Johnson, S. B. Comparison of individualized covert modeling, self-control desensitization, and study skills training for alleviation of test anxiety. *Journal of Consulting and Clinical Psychology*, 1980, *48*, 186–194.

Heath, E. G. Electrical self-stimulation of the brain in man. *American Journal of Psychiatry*, 1963, *120*, 571–577.

Heath, R. G. (Ed.) *The role of pleasure in behavior*. New York: Hoeber, 1964.

Heckhausen, H. Fear of a failure as a self-reinforcing motive system. In I. G. Sarason & C. Spielberger (Eds.), *Stress and anxiety*. Vol. 2. Washington, D.C.: Hemisphere, 1975.

Helson, H. *Adaptation-level theory: An experimental and systematic approach to behavior*. New York: Harper & Row, 1964.

Hoelscher, T. J., Klinger, E., & Barta, S. G. Incorporation of conern- and nonconcern-related verbal stimuli into dream content. *Journal of Abnormal Psychology*, 1981, *49*, 88–91.

Hoffman, H. S., & DePaolo, P. Behavioral control by an imprinting stimulus. *American Scientist*, 1977, *65*, 58–66.

Hohmann, G. W. Some effects of spinal cord lesions on experienced emotional feelings. *Psychophysiology*, 1966, *3*, 143–156.

Holroyd, K. A., & Appel, M. A. Test anxiety and physiological responding. In I. G. Sarason (Ed.), *Test anxiety: Theory, research, and applications*. Hillsdale, N.J.: Erlbaum, 1980.

Izard, C. E. *Human emotions*. New York: Plenum, 1977.

Izard, C. E., & Buechler, S. Aspects of consciousness and personality in terms of differential emotions theory. In R. Plutchik & H. Kellerman (Eds.), *Emotion: Theory, research, and experience:* Vol. 1: *Theories of emotion*. New York: Academic Press, 1980.

Kanfer, F. H., & Hagerman, S. The role of self-regulation. In L. P. Rehm (Ed.), *Behavior therapy for depression*. New York: Academic Press, 1981.

Kanter, N. J., & Goldfried, M. R. Relative effectiveness of rational restructuring and self-control desensitization in the reduction of interpersonal anxiety. *Behavior Therapy*, 1979, *10*, 472–490.

Kirschenbaum, D. S., & Karoly, P. When self-regulation fails: Tests of some preliminary hypotheses. *Journal of Consulting and Clinical Psychology*, 1977, *45*, 1116–1125.

Klein, D. C., & Seligman, M. E. Reversal of performance deficits and perceptual deficits in learned helplessness and depression. *Journal of Abnormal Psychology*, 1976, *85*, 11–26.

Klinger, E. *Structure and functions of fantasy*. New York: Wiley, 1971.

Klinger, E. Utterances to evaluate steps and control attention distinguish operant from respondent thought while thinking out loud. *Bulletin of the Psychonomic Society*, 1974, *4*, 44–45.

Klinger, E. *Meaning and Void: Inner experience and the incentives in people's lives*. Minneapolis: University of Minnesota Press, 1977.

Klinger, E. Modes of normal conscious flow. In K. S. Pope & J. L. Singer (Eds.), *The stream of consciousness: Scientific investigations into the flow of human experience*. New York: Plenum, 1978.

Klinger, E. Dimensions of thought and imagery in normal waking states. *Journal of Altered States of Consciousness*, 1978/79, *4*, 97–113.

Klinger, E. The central place of imagery in human functioning. In E. Klinger (Ed.), *Imagery: Concepts, results, and applications*. New York: Plenum, 1981.

Klinger, E., Barta, S. G., & Maxeiner, M. E. Motivational correlates of thought content frequency and commitment. *Journal of Personality and Social Psychology*, 1980, *39*, 1222–1237.

Klinger, E., Barta, S. G., & Glas, R. Thought content and gap time in basketball. *Cognitive Therapy and Research*, 1981, *5*, 109–114.

Koestler, A. *The act of creation*. New York: Macmillan, 1964.

Lang, P. J. Imagery in therapy: An information processing analysis of fear. *Behavior Therapy*, 1977, *8*, 862–886.

Lang, P. J., & Buss, A. H. Psychological deficit in schizophrenia: II. Interference and activation. *Journal of Abnormal Psychology*, 1965, *70*, 77–106.

Lazarus, R. S. Psychological stress and the coping process. New York: McGraw-Hill, 1966.

Lazarus, R. S., Kanner, A. D., & Folkman, S. Emotions: A cognitive-phenomenological analysis. In R. Plutchik & H. Kellerman (Eds.), *Emotion: Theory, research, and experience*. Vol. 1. *Theories of emotion*. New York: Academic Press, 1980.

Lent, R. W., & Russell, R. K. Treatment of test anxiety by cue-controlled desensitization and study-skills training. *Journal of Counseling Psychology*, 1978, *25*, 217–224.

Leuner, H. Basic principles and therapeutic efficacy of guided affective imagery (GAI). In J. L. Singer & K. S. Pope (Eds.), *The power of human imagination: New methods in psychotherapy*. New York: Plenum, 1978.

Leuner, H. *Katathymes Bilderleben: Ergebnisse in Theorie und Praxis*. Bern: Huber, 1980.

Leventhal, H. Toward a comprehensive theory of emotion. In L. Berkowitz (Ed.), *Advances in experimental social psychology* Vol. 13. New York: Academic Press, 1980.

Mandler, G. The generation of emotion: A psychological theory. In R. Plutchik & H. Kellerman (Eds.), *Emotion: Theory, research, and experience*. Vol. 1. *Theories of emotion*. New York: Academic Press, 1980.

Mandler, G., & Sarason, S. B. A study of anxiety and learning. *Journal of Abnormal and Social Psychology*, 1952, *47*, 166–173.

Marañon, G. Contribution à l'étude de l'action émotive de l'adrénaline. *Revue francaise d' Endocrinologie*, 1942, *2*, 301–325.

Mark, V. H., & Ervin, F. R. *Violence and the brain*. New York: Harper & Row, 1970.

Marks, I. Advances in the healing of psychopathology: Exposure treatment. In G. Serban (Ed.), *Psychopathology of human adaptation*. New York: Plenum, 1976.

Maslach, C. Negative emotional biasing of unexplained arousal. *Journal of Personality and Social Psychology*, 1979, *37*, 953–969.

McGhie, A., & Chapman, J. Disorders of attention and perception in early schizophrenia. *British Journal of Medical Psychology*, 1961, *34*, 103–116.

Meichenbaum, D., Turk, D., & Burstein, S. The nature of coping with stress. In I. G. Sarason & C. D. Spielberger (Eds.), *Stress and anxiety*. Vol. 2. Washington, D.C.: Hemisphere, 1975.

Mischel, W., Ebbesen, E. B., & Zeiss, A. R. Cognitive and attentional mechanisms in delay of gratification. *Journal of Personality and Social Psychology*, 1972, *21*, 204–218.

Moray, N. Attention in dichotic listening: Affective cues and the influence of instructions. *Quarterly Journal of Experimental Psychology*, 1959, *11*, 56–60.

Mowrer, O. H. *Learning theory and behavior*. New York: Wiley, 1960. (a)

Mowrer, O. H. *Learning theory and symbolic behavior*. New York: 1960. (b)

Neisser, U. *Cognitive psychology.* New York: Appleton-Century-Crofts, 1967.

Neisser, U. *Cognition and reality.* San Francisco: W. H. Freeman, 1976.

Novaco, R. W. Treatment of chronic anger through cognitive and relaxation controls. *Journal of Consulting and Clinical Psychology,* 1976, *44,* 681.

Olds, J., & Milner, P. Positive reinforcement produced by electrical stimulation of septal area and other regions of the rat brain. *Journal of Comparative and Physiological Psychology,* 1954, *47,* 419–427.

Plutchik, R. *The emotions: Facts, theories, and a new model.* New York: Random House, 1962.

Plutchik, R. A general psychoevolutionary theory of emotion. In R. Plutchik & H. Kellerman (Eds.), *Emotion: Theory, research, and experience.* Vol. 1. *Theories of emotion.* New York: Academic Press, 1980.

Rehm, L. P. A comparison of self-control and assertion skills treatments of depression. *Behavior Therapy,* 1979, *10,* 429–442.

Rule, B. B., & Nesdale, A. R. Emotional arousal and aggressive behavior. *Psychological Bulletin,* 1976, *83,* 851–863.

Sarason, I. G. Experimental approaches to test anxiety: Attention and the uses of information. In C. D. Spielberger (Ed.), *Anxiety: Current trends in theory and research.* Vol. 2. New York: Academic Press, 1972.

Sarason, I. G. Test anxiety and the self-disclosing coping model. *Journal of Consulting and Clinical Psychology,* 1975, *443,* 148–153.

Sarason, I. G. Introduction to the study of test anxiety. In I. G. Sarason (Ed.), *Test anxiety: Theory, research, and applications.* Hillsdale, N.J.: Erlbaum, 1980.

Schachter, S., & Latané, B. Crime, cognition, and the autonomic nervous system. In D. Levine (Ed.), *Nebraska symposium on motivation,* 1964. Lincoln, Nebraska: University of Nebraska Press, 1964.

Schwartz, G. E., Fair, P. L., Salt, P., Mandel, M. R., & Klerman, G. L. Facial muscle patterning to affective imagery in depressed and non-depressed subjects. *Science,* 1976, *192,* 489–491.

Shakow, D. Segmental set: A theory of the formal psychological deficit in schizophrenia. *Archives of General Psychiatry,* 1962, *6,* 17–33.

Shoor, J. E. *Go see the movie in your head.* New York: Popular Library, 1977.

Solkoff, N., Yaffe, S., Weintraub, D., & Blase, B. Effects of handling on the subsequent developments of premature infants. *Developmental Psychology,* 1969, *1,* 765–768.

Sroufe, L. A., & Waters, E. The ontogenesis of smiling and laughter: A perspective on the organization of developmental infancy. *Psychological Review,* 1976, *83,* 173–189.

Strickland, B. R., Hale, W. D., & Anderson, L. K. Effect of induced mood states on activity and self-reported affect. *Journal of Consulting and Clinical Psychology,* 1975, *43,* 587.

Tomkins, S. S. *Affect, imagery, consciousness.* Vol. 1. *The positive affects.* New York: Springer, 1962.

Tomkins, S. S. Affect as amplification: Some modifications in theory. In R. Plutchik & H. Kellerman (Eds.), *Emotion: Theory, research, and experience.* Vol. 1. *Theories of emotion.* New York; Academic Press, 1980.

Turner, C. W., & Layton, J. F. Verbal imagery and connotation as memory-induced mediators of aggressive behavior. *Journal of Personality and Social Psychology,* 1976, *33,* 755–763.

Ullman, L. P., & Krasner, L. *A psychological approach to abnormal behavior.* Englewood Cliffs, N.J.: Prentice-Hall, 1969.

Valenstein, E. S., Cox, V. C., & Kakolewski, J. W. Reexamination of the role of the hypothalamus in motivation. *Psychological Review,* 1970, *77,* 16–31.

Walster, E. Passionate love. In B. I. Murstein (Ed.), *Theories of attraction and love.* New York: Springer, 1971.

Walters, E. T., Carew, T. J., & Kandel, E. R. Associative learning in *Aplysia:* Evidence for conditioned fear in an invertebrate. *Science*, 1981, *211*, 504–506.

Wilson, W. R. Feeling more than we can know: Exposure effects without learning. *Journal of Personality and Social Psychology*, 1979, *37*, 811–821.

Wine, J. D. Test anxiety and direction of attention. *Psychological Bulletin*, 1971, *76*, 92–104.

Wine, J. D. Cognitive-attentional theory of test anxiety. In I. G. Sarason (Ed.), *Test anxiety: Theory, research, and applications*. Hillsdale, N.J.: Erlbaum, 1980.

Wolpe, J. *Psychotherapy by reciprocal inhibition*. Stanford, Calif.: Stanford University Press, 1958.

Younger, J. C., & Doob, A. N. Attribution and aggression: The misattribution of anger. *Journal of Research in Personality*, 1978, *12*, 164–171.

Zajonc, R. B. Feeling and thinking: Preferences need no inferences. *American Psychologist*, 1980, *35*, 151–175.

Zillman, D., & Bryant, J. Effect of residual excitement on the emotional response to provocation and delayed aggressive behavior. *Journal of Personality and Social Psychology*, 1974, *30*, 782–791.

6

A Developmental Perspective on Some Parameters of Self-Regulation in Children

Susan Harter*

SETTING THE STAGE: WHAT THIS DEVELOPMENTAL DRAMA IS AND ISN'T

As one unaccustomed to "writer's block," my difficulty in beginning this chapter was puzzling, indeed. Self-monitoring, self-evaluation, and self-reward were each conceptual friends with whom I thought I felt quite comfortable, and each has received my empirical attention in some form. To the extent that these represented critical component skills in the self-regulation process, I should therefore have something to say. But what? The source of my expressive aphasia eventually surfaced in the realization that as a developmentalist, my frame of reference was very different from the majority of those who have tackled the issues of self-regulation, self-management, and self-control within the behavior modification tradition.

My own synopsis of this latter perspective is as follows: the context for self-control is a temporal conflict involving either a socially prohibited behavior which the child would prefer to perform (e.g., aggression) or a socially desirable behavior which the child does not particularly wish to perform (e.g., sharing). The former involves a short-term gain, but long-range loss; while the latter involves a short-term loss, but long-run gain. The initial impetus for controlling such behaviors lies with adults who hope to enlist the child's aid so as to free them from the burden of continual

*The research summarized in this chapter was supported by Research Grant, HD-09613 from the National Institute of Child Health and Human Development, National Institute of Health, U.S.P.H.S.

surveillance. Presumably this is undertaken for the greater good of society as well as the individual child, not to mention the sanity of parents and educators. In the bulk of this literature, intervention strategies are directed toward modifying an established behavior pattern which the child has no obvious desire to alter, at least in the short run. To effect such a change, to facilitate self-control, recent theoretical models have focused on a variety of component skills including goal setting, self-monitoring, self-verbalization, self-evaluation, and self-reinforcement. There has been an increasing recognition that cognitive process variables are important in mediating behavioral change, an emphasis which has caused many to adopt the term "cognitive-behavior modification."

How did this perspective contrast with my own, as an avowed developmentalist? First and foremost, the starting point was very different, framing a very different set of questions. I have been primarily interested in the ontogenetic change of a variety of *competencies* which were observable in the child's naturalistic environment. The focus has been on three skill domains: cognitive competence, social relationships with peers, and physical abilities.

Within the *cognitive* realm, we observe the young child learning the names of colors, attempting to solve puzzles, learning how to count, attempting to write. With increasing age, attention shifts to an interest in reading, to the learning of arithmetic skills, and to the acquisition of knowledge in a variety of areas, including traditional academic subjects. With regard to *peer relationships*, one observes the increasing importance of developing and maintaining friendships as the child matures. In the sphere of *physical* abilities, the young child struggles to climb jungle gyms, hop, skip, run, and to throw and catch a ball. In the older child we see energy focused on the further development of physical skills within the context of individual and team sports, where athletic prowess is the measure of one's success.

Specifically, I have been concerned with the following questions: (a) What *motivates* these mastery attempts in the developing child, and what are the *rewards* for such behaviors? To what extent are these rewards *external* and how do rewards which are initially extrinsic become internalized in the form of *self-reward*? (b) What do we (as socializing agents) do to foster or discourage these mastery behaviors, and through what *cognitive* filters do children at different developmental levels process these messages? (c) What *attributions* do children make concerning who or what is responsible for their successes and failures, and who or what do they view as in control? (d) How does the child *evaluate* his or her competence? (e) What accounts for the extensive *individual differences* we observe in these constructs, namely, motivational orientation and the use of self-reward, the self-evaluation of one's competence, and the attributions concerning the source of control over the outcomes in one's life? (f) Finally what or where is the *self* in this developmental saga?

The point of this contrast is not to fabricate a bout between Hobbes in the black trunks and Rousseau in the white. The intent was to clarify for myself, and hopefully for the reader, the differing contexts in which terms such as "self-evaluation," "self-reward," and "control" can be and have been employed. Having done this, two options for structuring this chapter became apparent. As a starting point, I could take the constructs as conceptually and operationally defined by those of the cognitive-behavior modification persuasion and attempt to analyze them from a developmental perspective, a strategy which Bandura (1977a, 1977b) has urged. Or alternatively, I could treat such constructs as self-observation, self-evaluation, and self-reward, within a developmental frame of reference, within the context of my own theoretical model, and hopefully point to some implications for self-regulation and self-control. The aphasic curtain was lifted when it became clear that I really had no choice but to do the latter.

TO WHAT DOES THE "SELF" REFER?

It would seem that any comprehensive understanding of self-observation, self-evaluation, and self-reward must attend to the self as an active agent engaging in these processes, as well as to the self as an object, or as the cognitive construction to which these processes are applied. While obviously these two selves are housed within the same psychological skin, there are heuristic reasons for considering them separately. For the developmentalist, such a framework raises a number of intriguing questions.

We do not find infants and very young children engaging in the process of self-observation, self-evaluation, and self-reward. That is, while infants are able to attend to the consequences of many of their actions, they cannot yet mentally represent or construct a picture of the self as an object which they themselves can observe, evaluate, or reward. Thus, we can begin to ask what cognitive abilities might be involved and what factors govern the emergence of these processes? What skills are required of the child to engage in self-reward, for example? For some, an answer to this question may necessitate a descriptive account of the cognitive-developmental capacities required to perform a self-rewarding act. Others may extend their analysis to an account of some "internalization" process whereby rewarding messages, initially uttered by external socializing agents, become incorporated into the child's psychological vocabulary in the form of covert self-approving evaluations. The larger question here would appear to be: How do developmental changes in the self as subject, as knower, and as actor (which in this example is the potential self-rewarder) conspire with the events in one's socialization history to produce ontogenetic differences in the nature of the self-rewarding process itself?

Another set of developmental questions concerns changes in the self as the *rewardee*, as the object of self-evaluation and the self-rewarding process. What particular behaviors or cognitions are rewarded, and how do these change with age or vary across individuals? Does Jack Horner think he is a good boy merely because he performed the specific behavioral act of pulling out a plum? Or is he acknowledging a broader sense of competence? If so, is his focus on the fine-motor skills involved, or is he pleased with the cognitive accomplishment of thinking through how he could achieve this goal? Alternatively, is the object of the self-reward the "morality" of the act or the boy, invoking some maxim to the effect that good boys pull plums out of pies? If so, is the target of his evaluation simply the behavior of plum-pulling, or is the object of this reward some sense of self as a person, as an individual who possesses admirable qualities (cf., Carver and Scheier's multilevel information processing model, in Chapter 4 of this volume).

A developmental approach to this second set of questions will require a careful look at ontogenetic changes in the cognitive construction, which we have labeled the self as object. For example, evidence (see Harter, in press d; Rosenberg, 1979) suggests that the young child initially describes himself or herself in terms of specific behaviors, achievements, and physical characteristics, whereas with development, trait-like characteristics, particularly interpersonal traits, take on more salience. During adolescence, one also observes that a predominance of emotions, attitudes, wishes, and dreams come to define the self; there is a focus on one's "psychological interior" (Rosenberg, 1979). On the basis of these trends, Rosenberg describes the metamorphosis of the self, concluding that the child functions initially as a radical behaviorist, then appears in the guise of a trait theorist, and ultimately dons the mantle of a Freudian in his or her self-descriptions. It would seem that if the psychological "seat" of the self as an object of evaluation shifts in such a manner, these changes would have important implications for our attempts to intervene and to bring about changes in the regulation of the "self." In particular, such an analysis suggests that we first identify the dimensions of the self which are relevant to the child's self-definition, and tailor our intervention strategies accordingly. We will consider the implications of this suggestion in a subsequent section (see also Copeland's chapter in this volume).

Admittedly, these are issues which have been sketched in broad outline and provide only a very general framework. I have singled out self-reward for special emphasis since, developmentally, it can be observed in a rudimentary form at relatively young ages, if we accept "good boy" or "good girl" utterances as the earliest manifestation of self-reward. In contrast, the processes of self-observation and self-evaluation, *as they appear* in models of *adult* functioning (e.g., Kanfer, 1977, 1980; Bandura, 1978; Wicklund, 1975), would appear to require skills that the young child does not yet possess. Thus, we will first turn to an examination of how the earliest forms of self-reward might be established.

I would first like to emphasize that the points of view expressed in this chapter are those of but one developmentalist. I was invited to present an overview of my own theorizing and research and to explore the implications which this approach might have for the processes involved in self-regulation. There now exists a rich and burgeoning developmental literature outside my own research area which can also be brought to bear on this topic. However, a treatment of the broader developmental perspective was beyond the scope of this chapter.

SELF-REWARD AS A PROCESS OF INTERNALIZATION

Since we do not observe the self-rewarding process in infants, how does this capacity come to be acquired? The model proposed begins with an analysis of the *external* rewards which are dispensed to the child by child-rearing agents, and suggests how they become internalized. In naturalistic child-rearing situations, we frequently observe that behavior initially under the control of external rewards such as parental praise eventually come to be controlled by the child, the self. Thus our task is to explain how the praise and approval of parents become incorporated into a self-approving voice which can come to control the child's behavior?

Let us take as a behavioral domain the earliest mastery attempts on the part of the child to dress herself. We will highlight the implications of *positive* reinforcement. Initially, these mastery attempts are rewarded by a hug, perhaps something tangible such as a favorite food, a toy, or some primary reinforcer which is accompanied by verbal praise, "good girl." The child experiences positive effect in response to the tangible reward which is paired with the potential secondary reward, verbal approval. Through these pairings, verbal approval takes on secondary reinforcing properties and is sufficient to maintain the behavior in the absence of continual primary reinforcement. Approval alone produces positive affect, which in turn mediates the behavior. Here, I am in agreement with Aronfreed (1969) in that these processes must occur within a general atmosphere of nurturance. In such an atmosphere, the power of parental praise is established very early, and the child's desire to please the parents, to maintain their approval, contributes to the effectiveness of such praise as an external reward controlling the child's behavior.

What next happens in the absence of external verbal approval, given such a history? Typically, we observe the young child attempting to dress herself alone, uttering "good girl" to herself. Or we may see this displaced onto play where the girl praises her doll as the doll is made to dress herself. A general modeling analysis can handle this occurrence nicely. In the parlance of my own framework, the child has observed herself as the object of parental reward, as the rewardee. She not only engages in the rewarded behavior, dressing herself, but can now also imitate the rewarding process itself; she can be her own rewarder as well. The child's own utterances now function as a tertiary reinforcer for dressing behavior. According to this formulation, these self-approving utterances are accompanied by positive affect which acts as the mediator and maintains the behavior.

This particular analysis is based on a number of assumptions which at this point are speculative in nature. It is assumed that parental models in question are perceived as powerful as well as nurturant, and that they are figures upon whom the child is dependent and wishes to please. In addition, the contingencies between the child's behavior and the initial external reward must be clear and consistent. These assumptions have received some support in previous research (see Aronfreed, 1969; Bandura, 1969, 1971).

Product versus Process and Personal Control

In most such analyses, the focus is typically on the behavioral *product* which is rewarded. Within the domain of mastery behaviors, the emphasis on achievement has prevailed. I would like to suggest here that it is equally important to reward the mastery *process* itself, the *attempts* at learning, and the child's sense of control over the outcome. This suggestion goes beyond the notion of rewarding successive approximations, in that these approximations are usually miniproducts, components of the larger product which in our example above would be the "properly dressed child." Rather, I am referring to a parental message which communicates that it's wonderful that the child wants to learn how to get dressed and can do so. Such a reinforcing message would seem to collaborate with the child's own intrinsic desire to master and to control the environment, as well as one's self within that environment. Here I am using the term "intrinsic" in the sense of White's (1959) effectance motivation construct. It's value, I believe, lies in its use as a descriptive label for those mastery efforts we see on the part of the infant and young child which are very adaptive from an evolutionary point of view.

In my opinion, we have devoted too little attention to the responses which care-givers make to the mastery attempt itself as a worthwhile endeavor, to the child's joy in the mastery process, and to the child's role in producing environmental effects. Rather, we have tended to focus on the adult's evaluation of the success or failure of the child's response, on the accuracy, the correctness of the product (see Harter, 1981). In part, this undoubtedly reflects a societal value in that tangible products and achievements are held up as a desirable goal and appropriately rewarded. From a developmental perspective, however, it behooves us to recognize that the earliest mastery behaviors of the infant and young child are not directed toward a manifest product, as such. Rather, they reflect the exercising, the demonstration, and the control of newly developed skills and schemas. The young child may well produce a tangible effect, for example, move the mobile, fasten a button, make crayon scribbles, or build a block tower. However, the joy appears to be derived from the mastery *process*, and we observe little desire on the part of the child to preserve the product of those efforts, to put them on display. (The *parents* are the ones who bedeck the showcase with junior's creations, for all to see.) It is only later in development that the presentation as well as preservation of the product take on meaning for the child.

To the extent, then, that we attend primarily to the *product* during the earliest years, and ignore those behavioral attempts which constitute the process of "production," we may ultimately attenuate the child's desire to engage in the mastery process itself, and may weaken the child's sense of control over such efforts. We will return to some data which suggest that this is precisely what we are doing in much of our educational system today.

For the *young* child, it has been suggested that we could do more to reward the behavioral components of the mastery *process*. For the *older* child and the adult, the picture becomes more complex. Two developments are noteworthy. Products become accepted, if not required, symbols of mastery and accomplishment by the socializing environment. Secondly, the elementary school child develops a concept of one's own personness in the sense that one can take the self as an object of observation. Whereas the younger child could appreciate the specific behavioral acts which defined both the mastery process and product, he or she did not yet have a stable sense of self as a person who is defined in terms of various trait labels and psychological attributes—for example, I am a nice person, a popular person, an intelligent person. (See Harter, in press d, for a review of evidence bearing on this point).

What, then, are the implications for our reward analysis? What is to be rewarded, ideally, during the years of middle childhood and beyond? I would speculate that the message that older children and adults would like to hear is that one is a skillful and worthwhile *person* who is responsible for performing competently. When we praise a child for a product—the all-A report card, the merit badge, the clean room—it should not simply be the *product* which is admirable, but the *child herself* who is wonderful for having demonstrated the skills or engaged in the activity that resulted in the product. The message should be "*You* are great," not just "That is great." That is, we want to reward *characteristics* of the *person* and emphasize their role in the process. This strategy would appear to become increasingly critical during middle childhood and beyond, when the child's self-concept and self-description shifts to personal traits and attributes. Such traits come to define the rewardee.

In our attempts to modify children's behavior, it is all well and good to pinpoint behavioral goals and objectives and to specify reinforcement contingencies. However, I would hypothesize that to be most effective, it is not just the behavioral product which we want to reinforce, but the characteristics of the behaving child as a person, particularly their responsibility and control in producing the behavioral effect. Our own findings based on self-report data from third through sixth grades indirectly support such a claim, in that the best predictor of children's intrinsic mastery motivation in the classroom is the combination of their perceived cognitive competence, perceived control over classroom outcomes, and their feelings of general self-worth, namely, how much they like themselves as persons (Harter & Engstrom, Note 1). Our speculation is that children high on this constellation of variables may have received a multiple message for their mastery efforts: not only was the product successful, but they, as worthwhile persons, were responsible for making it happen.

THE ROLE OF AFFECT AND A PROPOSED DEVELOPMENTAL SEQUENCE

I have suggested that positive affect is an important mediator in the internalization process. Positive affect associated with the initial primary rewards becomes attached to the secondary reinforcer — parental approval — and to the child's eventual imitation of this verbal praise. Here I am making an assumption which has recently come back into vogue in the developmental literature, namely, that the motivation to seek pleasure and to avoid pain is the initial prime mover. In the present analysis, positive affect has been emphasized, in part for illustrative purposes. Aronfreed (1968, 1969, 1976) has also underscored the role of affect in the internalization process, although he has highlighted *punishment* in the self-control process. A variety of aversive states may be experienced (e.g., fear, shame, guilt), although the common denominator appears to be anxiety and its motivational properties. While Aronfreed does not deny the role of cognitive representations in the control of one's behavior, he draws attention to the role of affect partly in reaction to the seeming overemphasis on observational learning and cognitive-verbal mediation in the recent behavioral literature.

If one accepts the assumption that affect is a critical mediator of the behavioral effects observed in the internalization process, then the first manifestations of self-reward can be explained in a rather straightforward fashion, based on the principles of operant learning, higher-order conditioning, and modeling. In accounting for the two- or three-year-old's first self-reinforcing verbalizations, there is no need to invoke the type of self-evaluation and self-monitoring processes which are seemingly observed with older children and adults. I am contending that the very young child cannot engage in a comparison between her present performance and internalized performance standards, since these standards have not yet been crystallized; nor could she control two such cognitions simultaneously. Nor does she yet have the cognitive skills and necessary socialization experiences which would allow her to engage in social comparison for the purposes of evaluating her own performance positvely or negatively. (We will return to this issue in a later section.) Relatedly, she cannot effectively engage in self-monitoring.

This discussion is leading toward the following hypotheses: Developmentally, the *order* in which the critical component processes of self-regulation are initially *acquired* is just the *reverse* of the order in which they are postulated to operate in adulthood, namely, self-monitoring, self-evaluation, and self-reinforcement. That is, I am arguing that children first learn to imitate verbal approval and apply it to their own behavior before they are capable of self-evaluation, and that the processes of self-evaluation must be acquired before they can fully appreciate those situations in which they should monitor their behavior.

Take, as an example, the young child whose mother is attempting to teach her to pick up her clothes. She has previously learned to imitate mommy's approval in the form of "good girl," which leads to an experience of positive affect. However, she next must learn to discriminate between those actions which are good and those which are bad; she must learn how to evaluate her behavior. Mommy initially serves as the evaluator, telling her that she is a good girl when she puts her dirty clothes in the hamper, and that she is not a good girl when she doesn't. The child internalizes these standards for self-evaluation. As a next step in the process, Mommy begins to set the stage for self-monitoring, by initially monitoring the child's behavior. Mommy, as monitor, says things like "Now *you* know what you are supposed to do with your dirty shirt," setting the conditions for the child.* Eventually, this component of the process becomes internalized, such that the child can monitor her own behavior. The developmental acquisition sequence, then, is self-reward, self-evaluation, and then self-monitoring.

---

*I am grateful to Sybillyn Jennings for suggesting this analysis of Mommy as Monitor, and to Lucia Wainwright for supplying the example from her experience with her own child.

There is no necessary contradiction here between this analysis of how such processes are developmentally acquired and how they operate in adulthood. In Kanfer's model (1977, 1980), for example, particular conditions trigger the chain of self-regulatory processes, beginning with the self-monitoring component. This is followed by the self-evaluative component which in turn leads to self-reward, if such reinforcement is appropriate. This is the logical *operating* sequence for adults. However, the sequence can only operate in this manner if each of the component processes is present or available in one's repertoire. I have suggested above that the availability of these components is itself a developmental question of interest, and have postulated that the actual *acquisition* sequence may occur in the reverse order. Once all of the requisite components have been established, then the self-regulatory chain of events occurs in the order which Kanfer has postulated.

In our cognitive-behavior-modification efforts with children, potential problems might arise, therefore, if we attempt to apply the adult models inappropriately to the behavior of children at developmental levels where the component skills have not yet been acquired. For example, we may encounter difficulty if we attempt to teach isolated component skills, particularly if we begin with those components occurring at the beginning of the sequence in the adult models (e.g., self-monitoring). One may well coerce a first-grader to keep track of his arithmetic errors. However, if this behavior is not performed in the service of self-evaluation, which in turn will lead to an anticipated self-reward with its affective concomitants, it is unlikely that this procedure will be effective, especially from the standpoint of maintenance. If there is no affective light at the end of the tunnel, as it were, no internalized motivation to engage in the behavior, why should it reoccur in the absence of surveillance, punishment, or extrinsic reward?

This analysis implies that in our intervention strategies to foster self-regulation, we begin at the beginning, as defined by the *developmental* sequence postulated. Such a procedure would first identify an appropriate primary reward and attempt to establish the secondary reinforcing properties of verbal approval, as described in the developmental paradigm. While this first step may, on the surface, appear unnecessary, clinicians working with certain deviant populations will be quick to acknowledge that praise is not necessarily reinforcing; nor can all children engage in self-reward. In keeping with the earlier discussion, the target for such reinforcement should not only be the behavioral product in question, but the child should be rewarded for her own role in bringing about such an effect, highlighting this mastery effort as a worthwhile characteristic of her as a person.

While the earliest manifestation of self-reward, so acquired, may well have a parrot-like quality, the child should gradually internalize a variety of reward functions which will make self-evaluation possible. We now turn to a discussion of the functions of reward within the internalization process and their implications for self-evaluation and self-reward.

THE FUNCTIONS OF REWARD

In the preceding section, the internalization process was described in general terms. It seems fruitful now to examine the more specific functions of external rewards and to explore their implications for self-reward. As a framework, it appears reasonable to distinguish between two general functions of external reward, a motivational-emotional function and an informational function, a distinction which others (e.g., Aronfreed, 1969; Bandura, 1971) have also suggested. Rewards not only provide the motivation for subsequent engagement in the behavior, but provide information, feedback, performance criteria. However, further distinctions within each of these categories might also be meaningful. With regard to the motivational-emotional dimension, reward functions as an *incentive* to engage in the behavior in anticipation of future rewards, and it also results in the experience of positive *affect*. In considering the informational functions, two subcategories also suggest themselves. At one level, rewards provide information about what behaviors are *important* to perform, defining a set of *mastery goals*. At a more specific level, reward provides the *evaluative criteria* for the success or failure of a given behavior or response. Thus the child receives information about what she *should* be doing as well as whether she is doing it *correctly*.

It seems likely, furthermore, that socialization agents vary with regard to which reward functions their praise or approval may emphasize. The message "That's good, I'll bet you can do it again" may highlight the *incentive* function, encouraging the child to engage in the behavior. Approval in the form of "That's good, and you seem really happy that you can do that" may call attention to the *affective* properties of reward and the pleasure derived from mastery attempts. The parent who tells her child "I'm really glad that you did your homework because its important for you to learn as much as you can" places emphasis on the *importance* of learning as a mastery goal. The parental utterance "I'm pleased that you got every one of your spelling words right except one" is highlighting the *correctness* of the rewarded response and the *criteria* for making such a determination.

Although a given reinforcer may serve more than one or even all of these functions simultaneously, it seems fruitful to make these conceptual distinctions and to examine their implications for the internalization process. If the child internalizes the external rewarding message and develops the capacity to reward herself, perhaps these same functions can now be examined as they apply to *self*-reward. How do these functions operate within a motivational and informational reward system which has become "intrinsic," in which the child appears "self-motivated"?

An Interlude on the Use of the Term "Intrinsic"

It is essential first to clarify the meaning of the term "intrinsic" in this context. Here, it does *not* refer to the type of basic biological property of the organism which White attempted to capture in his postulation of an effectance motive. Rather, I am now using the term "intrinsic" to refer to an experiential process whereby motivational and informational functions once extrinsic to the child are modeled, incorporated, such that they become internal to the child. Thus, this second source might best be labeled "internalized" motivation, in contrast to the more basic effectance-like motivation for which the term "intrinsic" is more appropriate.

I am in no way denying the importance of White's postulate, but merely am trying to suggest that it may be fruitful to think about two separate sources for what appears to be self-motivated behavior. They very basic physiological urge toward mastery, competence, and control over the environment can certainly be seen in the behavior of infants in a form that is difficult to account for in terms of a particular reinforcement history. This effectance urge represents *one* source. However, the expression of that drive obviously becomes channeled and shaped (i.e., learned) through the reward processes described in the previous section. Thus, the internalization of the external reward functions can be conceptualized as a second source of "intrinsic" motivation, that is, internalized motivation. Both sources may be simultaneously operative, although the contribution of each source may vary from behavior to behavior. Climbing a jungle gym may satisfy one's effectance urge and not reflect much cultural shaping. To the extent that cleaning one's room or sharing appear to be self-motivated, it is highly likely that the processes responsible reflect the second source, the internalization of rewards which were initially extrinsic or external.

In much of the behavioral and social psychological literature, the term "intrinsic motivation" is operationally defined in terms of time on task or professed liking for an activity in the *absence* of *current extrinsic* rewards, controls, or surveillance. Thus, activities such as drawing, doing puzzles, or playing baseball are considered to be "intrinsically motivated." I am suggesting that we might do well to analyze such behaviors in terms of the contribution of each source of intrinsicality. Such an analysis may help to clarify some of the confusion regarding the extent to which extrinsic reinforcers are claimed to "undermine intrinsic motivation."

If the primary source of motivation is an effectance-like process in which the exercise of skills is inherently pleasurable, one would anticipate that the unexpected appearance of extrinsic reinforcement would have some disruptive effect on the behavior. If, however, the behavior was initially learned through the application of extrinsic rewards whose functions were subsequently incorporated into the child's self-reward system, it is much less likely that extrinsic rewards will disrupt such an apparently self-motivated behavior. In fact, it may serve to support the self-reward system and thereby to maintain the behavior. Determining the initial source or, in all likelihood, the relative contribution of "intrinsic" and "internalized" sources for a given behavior may require considerable ingenuity as well as sensitivity to the reinforcement history of a particular child. We are facing this challenge in the research efforts to be discussed where we have only begun to appreciate the need to make such distinctions and to operationalize them accordingly.

FUNCTION AND SOURCE: A POSSIBLE FRAMEWORK

In discussing the process by which external rewards might become internalized, two general reward functions were highlighted: those which can be viewed as *motivational*, impelling the child to engage in the behavior, and those which can be considered to be *informational*, leading to the acquisition of knowledge, rules, and contingencies. Traditionally, we have identified these functions as characteristics of *external* rewards. The previous discussion has suggested that they can also be considered to be characteristics of one's *self-reward* system, in that the child comes to internalize these functions. Conceptually, these distinctions lead to four combinations depicted in the two-by-two section on the left in table 6.1.

The discussion also attempted to clarify the different meanings of the term "intrinsic" in the literature. In table 6.1, to the right, it is suggested that the child's initial mastery urge also has both motivational and informational components. It not only impels the child to engage in mastery behaviors, but also allows the child to acquire information about the impact of his behavior on the world; it allows one to learn rules and contingencies. It was further suggested that when a particular behavior does not appear to be under the direct control of external rewards, such seemingly self-motivated behavior may be under the control of internalized reward functions, one's intrinsic mastery urge, or some combination of these two sources. Thus, table 6.1 provides a framework for conceptualizing the particular sources of motivation and information and serves as a guide for one's empirical efforts to operationalize these constructs.

In a sense, I am putting the conceptual cart before the empirical horse in arguing for such a framework. These dimensions did *not guide* our own research initially, but emerged from the findings themselves. The particular

Table 6.1. Function and Source: A Possible Framework

	Source		
Function, to provide:	External Reward	Internalized (self) Reward	Intrinsic Mastery Urge
Motivation to perform.	Behavior under direct control of external reward.	Self-motivated behavior, which was *formerly* under control of external reward.	Self-motivated behavior, impelled by pleasure from mastery; enjoyment of the learning process.
Information about rules, contingencies.	External rewards provide information needed to understand rules, contingencies.	Contingencies, rules have been learned, no longer dependent upon external reward	Contingencies discoveries through one's own experimentation, observation.

empirical context involved an attempt to examine what motivates children's classroom learning. At the outset, we identified a single general dimension along which we could characterize a child's orientation toward learning, an intrinsic-extrinsic dimension. This empirical saga, and how it led to the more differentiated framework just presented, is described in the following section.

INTRINSIC VERSUS EXTRINSIC ORIENTATION IN THE CLASSROOM

Our initial intent was to focus on intrinsic versus extrinsic *motivation* as it applied to classroom learning, and to develop a self-report measure to assess the child's orientation. The overarching question was as follows: To what degree is a child's motivation for classroom learning determined by his or her intrinsic interest in learning and mastery, in contrast to an extrinsic orientation in which the child is motivated to obtain teacher approval and grades? We first sought to identify certain qualitative dimensions which would be relevant to classroom learning. Considerable pilot work revealed that five dimensions or factors could be reliably assessed, each defined by an intrinsic and an extrinsic pole. Each of these dimensions defined a separate subscale, the poles of which can be described as follows:

- *Preference for challenge versus preference for easy work assigned.* Is the child intrinsically motivated to perform hard, challenging work, or does he or she prefer to do the easier work assigned by the teacher?

- *Incentive to work to satisfy one's own interest and curiosity versus working to please the teacher and obtain good grades.* Here, as the subscale title indicates, we were interested in the relative strength of the child's intrinsic interest in learning compared to a more extrinsic orientation to obtain teacher approval and grades.
- *Independent mastery attempts versus dependence on the teacher.* This subscale taps the degree to which a child prefers to figure out problems on his or her own in contrast to a dependence on the teacher for help and guidance, particularly when it comes to figuring out problems and assignments.
- *Independent judgment versus reliance on teacher's judgment.* This subscale assesses whether the child feels that he or she is capable of making certain judgments about what to do in the classroom, in contrast to a dependence on the teacher's opinion or judgment about what to do.
- *Internal criteria for success/failure versus external criteria for success/failure.* Does the child have some internal sense of whether he or she has succeeded or done poorly on a test or on a school assignment, or is the child dependent upon external sources of evaluation such as teacher feedback, grades, and marks?

The question format is one which we have designed for use with this scale as well as our Perceived Competence Scale, and the rationale can be found in the detailed descriptions of these instruments (see Harter, in press b, in press c). A major purpose was to devise a format which would offset the tendency to give socially desirable responses, which we have found to be a problem with a typical true-false as well as other two-choice formats. In our new "structured alternative format" the child is presented with the following type of question:

Really True for Me	Sort of True for Me				Sort of True for Me	Really True for Me
☐	☐	Some kids know when they've made a mistake without checking with the teacher	but	Other kids need to check with the teacher to know if they've made a mistake.	☐	☐

The child is first asked to decide which kind of kid is most like him or her, and then asked whether this is only sort of true or really true for him or her. Each item is scored on an ordinal scale from 1 to 4, where a score of 1 indicated the maximum extrinsic orientation and a score of 4 indicated the maximum intrinsic orientation.

The effectiveness of this question format lies in the implication that half of the kids in the world (or in one's reference group) view themselves in one way, whereas the other half view themselves in the opposite manner. That is, this type of question legitimizes either choice. The option of checking sort of true for me or really true for me broadens the range of choices over the typical two-choice format. Additionally, none of the choices involve the response "false." Rather, the child must decide which of the options is most true for him or her.

Our samples to date have been cross-sectional, from third to ninth grades. The findings reveal very striking but unpredicted developmental trends. Two of the subscales, Independent Judgment versus Reliance on Teacher's Judgment and Internal Criteria versus External Criteria, show the same linear trend across these grades. Scores for third-graders are relatively extrinsic, crossing the midpoint in the later elementary school grades into the intrinsic range for the junior high pupils. The *opposite* linear trend is found for the three remaining subscales, Preference for Challenge versus Preference for Easy Work, Curiosity/Interest versus Teacher Approval/Grades, and Independent Mastery versus Dependence on the Teacher. For each of these dimensions, children begin with relatively intrinsic scores in the younger grades and shift toward a more extrinsic orientation (see fig. 6.1).

Initially, these findings were rather puzzling. Since one cluster of subscales showed a dramatic developmental increase, whereas a second cluster revealed an equally dramatic developmental decrease, we were obviously not measuring a unitary intrinsic-extrinsic dimension. Thus, we needed to consider the possibility that our clusters were tapping content which was qualitatively quite different. Upon closer examination of the subscale content, it appeared that the three subscales in one cluster, Preference for Challenge versus Preference for Easy Work, Working to Satisfy One's Interest and Curiosity versus Working to Please the Teacher and Obtain Good Grades, and Independent Mastery Attempts versus Dependence on the Teacher, each had a distinctive *motivational* flavor in that each tapped issues involving what the child *wants* to do, *likes* to do, or *prefers*.

A child high on this first cluster is telling us that she enjoys challenging or difficult schoolwork; she prefers to explore new material and to ask questions, and she likes figuring out problems and assignments on her own. A child low on this cluster prefers to do the easier assignments, would rather get the teacher's approval for work accomplished than delve into new material, and prefers to enlist the teacher's aid when confronted with difficult problems or assignments. Thus, we interpreted the *high* scorer as a child who is *intrinsically motivated* to engage in the *mastery process*, who chooses to learn for the sake of learning. The low scorer on this cluster, in

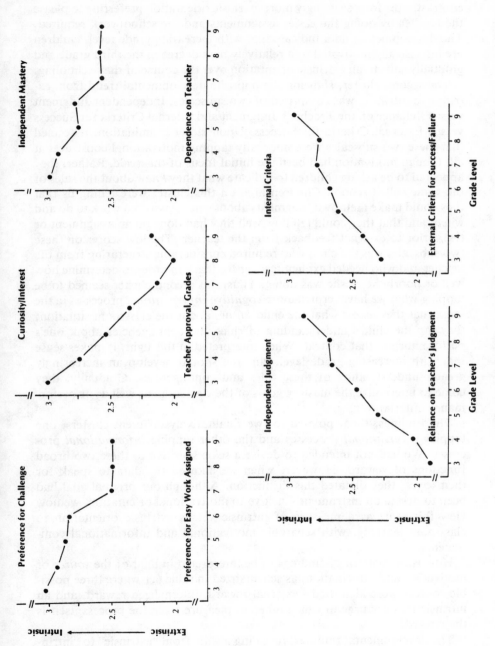

Fig. 6.1. Subscale means for each grade.

contrast, opts for a seemingly more extrinsic orientation preferring to please the teacher by doing the easier assignments and the schoolwork required. The developmental data indicate that with increasing grade level, children are intrinsically motivated to a relatively high degree in the third grade and gradually shift to an extrinsic orientation over the course of their schooling.

The second cluster, showing the opposite developmental trend from extrinsic to intrinsic, was comprised of two subscales, Independent Judgment versus Reliance on the Teacher's Judgment and Internal Criteria for Success versus External Criteria for Success. Upon closer examination, it seemed that these two subscales were not really tapping motivational constructs at all, though motivation had been the initial focus of this scale. Rather, they appeared to be asking children to indicate what they *knew* about the rules of the game called school. Children high on this cluster were telling us that they could make their own judgments about what classroom work to do and when, and that they could tell how well they had done on an assignment or test, prior to external feedback from the teacher. The low scorer on these two subscales was the child who required considerable structuring from the teacher and who needed explicit teacher feedback in order to determine how well or poorly he or she was doing. Thus, this second cluster seemed to be tapping what we have termed more *cognitive-informational* processes in the sense that they assess what the child *knows* about the classroom situation; they tap the child's understanding of rules and contingencies about one's performance in that context. When interpreted in this light, it makes sense that with increasing grade level, children should develop an increasingly greater understanding of these rules and contingencies. Gradually, they come to internalize the mastery goals of the classroom as well as its performance criteria.

The findings, then, pointed to two qualitatively different clusters, one tapping *motivational* processes and the other tapping *informational* processes. We had not intended to devise a scale sensitive to these two broad functions of reward. However, when we allowed the data to speak for themselves, they dictated this distinction. Although our original goal had been to design an instrument sensitive to motivational orientation, we now view this scale as a measure of intrinsic versus extrinsic orientation to classroom learning, with separable motivational and informational components.

How is the pattern of findings to be interpreted in light of the *source* of motivation and information, as schematized in table 6.1 where three possible sources were identified—external reward, internalized reward, and an intrinsic mastery urge in which inherent pleasure from the process itself is the reward?

The developmental findings, revealing a shift from "extrinsic" to "intrinsic" classroom orientation on the second cluster labeled "cognitive-informational processes" can best be interpreted as the shift from reliance on external reward to internalized (self) reward. For the youngest children, external reward, fee iback, is needed to define classroom rules, goals, and performance criteria. These come to be internalized as a function of length of time in school, such that the child develops his or her own self-reward system. Thus, the developmental change can be described in terms of an expected and interpretable shift from the lower left-hand cell in table 6.1, Informational Function, *External* Reward, to the lower middle cell, *Internalized* (self) reward.

The interpretation of the developmental shift from "intrinsic" to "extrinsic" for the motivational cluster is more troublesome, at first glance. In part, this results from the fact that we had not yet conceptualized the *three* sources of motivation outlined in table 6.1. Thus, we needed to take a closer look at both the intrinsic and extrinsic poles defining these particular motivational subscales. When one examines the *intrinsic* poles, they all appear to tap enjoyment in the basic mastery process itself—being curious, seeking challenge, and figuring things out on one's own. They tap one's desire to engage in mastery attempts, to exercise one's cognitive skills, and to be in control of these events. As such, they are more akin to intrinsic motivation in the sense of the effectance-like process identified, the basic mastery urge depicted in the upper right-hand cell in table 6.1.

Viewed in this light, we can offer an interpretation for why such motivation should decline over the course of schooling. I would submit that we are not reinforcing such an orientation in the majority of our classrooms, and that to a large degree, our external rewards are dispensed for products which involve completing the assigned work in response to the teacher's bidding. The behaviors actually rewarded may be incompatible with the basic mastery process as I have defined it, in which case extrinsic rewards will serve to undermine children's more natural intrinsic motivation.

Do the data for these subscales tapping motivational orientation really suggest, however, that with increasing grade level, children are actually becoming more *extrinsic*? (Doesn't this run counter to our developmental theorizing?) Previously, I have offered such an interpretation (Harter, in press a, in press c), although, upon further reflection, there is a more subtle interpretation that can be advanced. Responses to the "extrinsic" pole could be viewed as an internalization of the messages of a school culture which reinforces an orientation toward simply doing what the teacher assigns, merely getting grades, and requesting help with assignments in order to achieve this goal. The "extrinsic" pole on each of these subscales defines an extremely conservative approach to obtaining a product, an acceptable level of achievement, which may well be reinforced by the system. I am reminded here of one bright sixth-grader who scored very low (i.e., in the "extrinsic" direction) on the curiosity subscale. When we later asked him why he wasn't very curious, he said "Well, if you ask too many questions, then it's not good because you get the teacher off the track!" Another such child told us "You're just supposed to do the straight work."

What I am suggesting is that children who have *internalized* these particular motivations and goals would be expected to score in the "extrinsic" direction as operationally defined on these subscales. That is, the scale, in its present form, does not allow one to determine whether the extrinsically scoring child is presently performing to obtain external rewards (upper *left* cell) or whether he or she has already internalized these reward functions (upper *middle* cell). A different scale structure is necessary to tease apart these two possible interpretations of an extrinsic score on the motivational subscales.

If the data from the three motivational subscales are interpreted as a demonstration of how children internalize the motivational reward functions dispensed by the school culture, then these trends are perfectly compatible with the developmental shift toward more "intrinsic" scores on the two *informational* subscales, which are seen to reflect an internalization of the mastery goals and criteria for success put forth by the school culture.

What we need, then, is a more differentiated scale structure in order to test the relative strength of *both* potential sources of self-motivation, the effectance-like mastery urge and self-reward based on the internalization process, in addition to the strength of one's reliance on *extrinsic* rewards. This is a focus of our current research. We feel that information on the relative strength of each source of motivation would in turn have implications for the potential use of extrinsic reinforcers in various intervention programs. If the earlier analysis has merit, then one would only want to employ extrinsic reinforcers in situations where the behavior was initially established or shaped in such a manner; one would not choose to employ extrinsic rewards if the behavior was largely fueled by the more basic effectance-like mastery urge, since such a practice would seemingly prove disruptive to the child in the long run.

INTRINSIC VERSUS EXTRINSIC ORIENTATION, PERCEIVED CONTROL, AND PERCEIVED COMPETENCE

In addition to exploring the complexities of one's motivational and informational orientation, we have also been interested in the relationship which these constructs bear to the child's perceived competence and perceived control. While these constructs, broadly defined, were thought to relate to reward orientation, we have been interested in developing a more precise predictive model of how the components of these constructs influence one another.

The conceptual and psychometric history of the perceived competence and perceived control constructs has been described in detail elsewhere (see Harter, in press a, in press b; Connell, Note 2). Briefly, we adopted a situation-specific framework where "situation" was defined in terms of competence domain. We focused on three domains: cognitive competence, primarily in school; social competence, defined in terms of peer friendships; and physical competence, largely tapping athletic prowess. We initially assumed that children do not feel equally competent, or in control to the same degree, in all domains. In constructing self-report scales to assess both perceived competence (Harter, in press d) and perceived control (Connell, Note 2), we found clear support for such an assumption.

Initially, the perceived competence scale provided a single score for each competence domain. When we subsequently turned our attention to some of the subtleties of the cognitive subscale, Connell and I discovered that there were actually two subsets of items, one tapping a rather straightforward evaluative appraisal, such as "I am good at school work," in contrast to items which were more affectively laden, such as "I worry about whether I can do my schoolwork" or "I feel happy because I do well at schoolwork." Thus, for this subscale, separate scores reflecting *evaluative* and *affective* reaction can be obtained.

The perceived control scale is considerably more complicated in structure. Connell's initial intent was to devise a measure in which each source of control could be assessed independently. This constitutes a conceptual departure from the existing locus-of-control scales for both children and adults where it is assumed that there is a single dimension (internal-external) which can be tapped by one score. I have described elsewhere (Harter, in press a) how Connell initially adopted three potential sources of control which had been reported in the adult literature: Internal, Powerful Others, and Chance. His empirical efforts eventually led him to the conclusion that children do not make systematic attributions based on chance or luck. What he did discover, however, is that children will acknowledge that they simply don't *know* who or what is responsible for a success or failure outcome in a particular competence domain. Thus a separate subscale, labeled *Unknown* source of control, was created and can be compared to the two sources of known control: Internal — I am responsible; and Powerful Others — someone else is responsible. For each source of control, separate subscales tap perceived control over successes and failures, for each of the three competence domains: cognitive, social, and physical.

We have been interested in how these attributions are related to both the motivational and informational components on our intrinsic-extrinsic scale and to perceived as well as actual competence. *Actual* competence for this domain was defined in terms of achievement test scores. Connell and I began with the cognitive domain, and have tested several alternative models of the relationships among these variables, using structural equation techniques (Connell & Harter, Note 3).

We sought to test four plausible models, each of which postulated a different variable as the "prime mover" in the predictive chain. One such model begins with effectance-like intrinsic mastery motivation as the variable which in turn affects the other variables in the network. A second model postulates *achievement* as the all-important factor which in turn affects perceived competence, control, and reward orientation. In a third model, we sought to give a fair hearing to those who view *self-evaluation*, or perceived competence in our system, as the critical variable which best predicts the others in this network. Given the increasing emphasis on cognitive variables as determinants and mediators of behavior, the fourth model placed the perceived control variable at the beginning of the predictive chain. (The entire set of specific predictions for each model can be found in Connell & Harter, Note 3.)

We tested these models employing data from a sample of 730 pupils spanning the grade range from third to ninth. While there are some differences between elementary and junior high pupils, the model which best fits both groups is one in which perceived control is the primary predictive variable (See figure 6.2). More specifically, it is the *Unknown* source of control score which best predicts other variables in this particular network. The Unknown score predicts two other variables in what appears to be a cognitive cluster: (1) perceived *internality* as a source of control and (2) the *informational* subscales from the intrinsic-extrinsic orientation scale. Thus, (1) the *lower* the child's Unknown score (the less she says she doesn't know what is responsible for the outcomes in her life), the more likely is that child to acknowledge that *she* is responsible, and the less likely she is to see powerful others in control. In addition, (2) the *lower* the *Unknown* score, the *higher* the scores on independent judgment (versus reliance on teacher) and on internal criteria for success/failure (versus external criteria); that is, the less a child acknowledges that she *doesn't* know who or what is responsible, the less dependent she is on external guidance and feedback.

Interestingly, the Unknown source of control score also predicts achievement. The more the child acknowledges that she doesn't know who or what is in control, the lower her level of actual achievement in the classroom. This achievement score, in turn, predicts the child's perceived competence as would be expected. However, it influences the *evaluative* component most directly. The higher the child's actual competence or achievement, the more that child is likely to evaluate herself as being competent. This evaluative component, in turn, predicts the *affective* component. The more

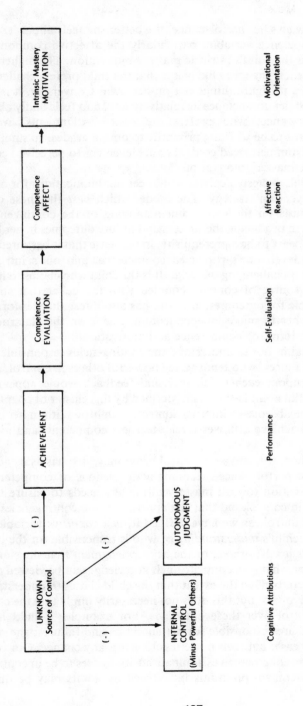

Fig. 6.2. Major Pathways among variables for the Cognitive Competence domain.

UNKNOWN
Source of Control

ACHIEVEMENT

Competence
EVALUATION

Competence
AFFECT

Intrinsic Mastery
MOTIVATION

AUTONOMOUS
JUDGMENT

INTERNAL
CONTROL
(Minus Powerful Others)

Cognitive Attributions

Performance

Self-Evaluation

Affective
Reaction

Motivational
Orientation

(-) designates negative relationship

competent a child views her performance, the better she feels about it. It is the perceived competence variable, particularly the affective component, which then predicts the child's intrinsic mastery motivation. The higher the feelings of competence, the more likely it is that the child prefers challenge, is curious, and likes to figure things out on her own. Conversely, it is the child who perceived her competence as relatively low, and feels badly about her school performance, who prefers the easier assignments, wants assistance, and seems to be working primarily to obtain grades. In sum, the major chain goes from perceived control to achievement to perceived competence to intrinsic mastery motivation.

Each of the models we tested carries with it certain implications for one's choice of an intervention strategy. The model which *best* fits these data would place emphasis on the child's understanding of the contingencies which are involved in producing the success and failure outcomes in her life. This knowledge appears to be a prerequisite, in the sense that it best predicts one's achievement level, one's perceived competence, and one's intrinsic motivation to master challenging material. It is the child who claims to have knowledge of the source of control, coupled with the belief that she is primarily responsible for outcomes, and who has also internalized information which allows her to make independent judgments in the classroom, who fares better in terms of competence and motivation.

The child who claims not to understand the contingencies responsible for her successes and failures, who tends to see powerful others in control, and who is dependent upon teacher guidance and feedback would appear to need help at the initial point in the chain, defined by this cluster of cognitive variables. For in the absence of internal control, with little faith in her own judgment, she will achieve at lower levels, feel less competent, and avoid further challenge.

It would seem, then, that any self-control program which has as its goals improved academic performance, accompanying feelings of competence, and increased motivation toward mastery ultimately needs to ensure that the child herself is in control and that she appreciates the contingencies involved. Perceived control, as we have defined it, is a *cognitive* variable in that it refers to the child's *understanding* of who is responsible for the outcomes in her life. Is it self, others, or the acknowledgment that she simply doesn't know who or what is in control? Such knowledge can be viewed as a form of "cognitive control" to the extent that the child claims to understand the contingencies involved; but this does not necessarily imply that the child has *behavioral* control over these outcomes. For example, a child may perceive that others are responsible for her successes and failures; she may *know* this to be the case, but feels powerless to effect any change. Our own data imply that if the child perceives adult authority figures to be in control, the efficacy of self-control programs introduced by adults may be questionable, since such a child does not believe that she herself is responsible for behavioral outcomes.

On the surface, it would seem that these suggestions are consistent with recent trends toward *cognitive*-behavior modification. However, this depends upon which cognitions we are discussing. Consider the cognitive processes involved in self-monitoring. If the child is encouraged to set a particular goal and then taught to monitor the discrete successes and failures which are relevant to obtaining that goal, it is unlikely that these particular cognitions alone will have much of an influence unless the child also feels that she is truly responsible for bringing about the particular outcomes.

The cognitive-behavioral program instituted by Meichenbaum and his colleagues (Meichenbaum, 1976, 1977, 1979) would appear to influence the child's sense of control, although perceived control per se is not the target variable. In order to facilitate problem solving, young children go through a training sequence in which overt self instruction that is designed to guide behavior gradually becomes more covert. From the perspective of control, the training procedure appears to be designed such that the child takes over increasing responsibility for her performance. I would hypothesize that it is not just the actual ability to make use of covert self-instruction in the form of private speech that is the critical factor, but the acccompanying knowledge that one can have an effect and that one is responsible for the ensuing successes or failures. I am suggesting that it is not merely the skill in using covert speech to guide behavior, but also the particular *content* of the message, namely, the implied attribution that "I am responsible."

If this were the case, then one would expect that scores on the perceived control scale would predict individual differences in the efficacy of such programs. Two more specific predictions follow from this analysis. Children who are both relatively high in internality and low on the Unknown subscale would make the best use of such a training program in the sense that they would acquire the skills most readily. Secondly, children who are relatively low in internality and high on the Unknown scale at the beginning of such a program should shift toward greater internality and lower Unknown scores as a result of the training (cf. Copeland's chapter in this volume).

However directly or indirectly one attempts to influence this cognitive cluster of variables, the implication from our data is that changes in the other variables, achievement, perceived competence, and intrinsic mastery motivation should follow. To the extent that this represents a causal chain, one would predict that they would be affected in that order. However, this hypothesis has yet to be tested in the type of longitudinal design which would be required.

There is a seduction in these suggestions, however; namely, that all we need to do is to shape or shift attributions, to alter cognitions. In fact, such an "ultracognitive" approach has been suggested by Weiner (1981). For example, a child who attributes her poor achievement to the lack of native ability (a relatively *stable* attribution in Weiner's formulation) should be encouraged to adopt an attribution based on effort—an "unstable" attribution in the sense that it is something she can presumably alter. There is the implication, in such a suggestion, that the child's attributions are not only maladaptive, but somehow "wrong." Maybe yes, maybe no. For the retarded child, the learning disabled child, or the child whose lack of ability seems genuinely related to lack of endowment, we may be doing a great psychological disservice to somehow try to convince her otherwise. However, for the child performing well on tests of fluid intelligence, or "g", who is nevertheless convinced she is not smart, channelling attributions toward effort may well be appropriate. In our zeal for *cognitive*-behavior modification, we need to guard against an overemphasis on the cognitive. Hopefully the cognitions we wish to instill bear a direct relationship to behavioral reality, a link which we need to emphasize in demonstrating to children that they are indeed responsible and in control.

The cognitive emphasis should also not distract our attention from the *affective* variables which may mediate certain behavioral effects. Our data suggest that the cognitive evaluative component of one's perceived competence had a direct impact on the child's affective reaction to such an appraisal, and it is largely this *affective* response which predicts the child's intrinsic motivation to engage in challenging schoolwork. Such an affective reaction may well be an important defining feature of *self-reward*, as it naturally occurs in children. The self-approving voice makes one *feel* good, which is the real reward that provides the incentive to engage in the behavior again. One may operationally define self-reward as the administration of a token to one's self contingent on a certain level of performance. However, without the affective component, it would seem that such manipulations will not produce the desired motivational and behavioral effects.

THEORIES IN THE MIND OF THE DEVELOPING CHILD: IMPLICATIONS FOR BEHAVIORAL CHANGE

At the outset of this chapter, it was suggested that a developmental perspective must take into account potential changes in the self as an active agent engaged in the self-regulation process. One such change involves cognitive-developmental differences in the theories which children hold with regard to attributions and motivations for their own behavior. As Karoly (1977), among others, has noted, however, there has been relatively little attention paid to developmental variables in the cognitive-behavior modification literature. While our own data do not bear on the issue of how developmental differences directly affect the effectiveness of intervention strategies designed to promote self-control, they point to number of implications.

In discussing the perceived control construct, the importance of ensuring that the child understands the contingencies between behavior and outcomes was stressed. Our data indicate, however, that there are definite developmental trends which may interact with strategies designed to effect such a goal. Grade differences in the Unknown score represent the most dramatic example (Connell, Note 2). Across grades three through six, this score gradually decreases, indicating that with increasing age during the elementary school years, children are less likely to acknowledge that they don't know who or what is responsible for outcomes. Then there is an abrupt rise in this score in the seventh grade, indicating that these first-year junior high pupils no longer seem to understand the contingencies governing their successes and failures. The score gradually drops over the eighth and ninth grades, suggesting that they come to learn what are undoubtedly new rules and contigencies which are appropriate in junior high school. To the extent that this score may be a reflection of a cognitive set toward understanding the contingencies in one's environment, more attention to establishing clear contingencies may be needed during the earlier elementary school years as well as the first year of junior high.

There is another dimension in Connell's scale which reveals an interesting developmental trend. Half of the items refer to events in the child's personal life (e.g., "The reason *I* succeed at school is because I work hard"), whereas the other half are worded as maxims (e.g., "The reason that *kids* succeed at school is because they work hard"). The data indicate that during the elementary school years, children claim that they know more about the contingencies governing other kid's behavior than they do about their own, and this descrepancy becomes smaller with increasing grade level into junior high. This finding suggests that peer-modeling techniques might be particularly effective during earlier elementary school years, if care is taken to highlight the fact that the contingencies which govern other kid's behavior also apply to one's own behavior.

The discussion of children's changing *motivations* for performing in the classroom also revealed developmental differences, reflecting a gradual decrease in one's intrinsic mastery motivation, as children seem to shift to the values of the school culture. In that discussion, it was suggested that we distinguish between three sources of motivation: effectance-like intrinsic motivation, extrinsic motivation, and internalized self-reward functions for which extrinsic approval was the initial model. The identification of which sources of motivation are operative at a particular developmental level, or for any given child, would seem to be paramount in constructing an effective cognitive-behavioral change program.

A recent dissertation (Chandler, Note 4) suggests that the picture is more

complex than these three general sources of motivation. Chandler inter-
viewed children between the ages of 5 and 12 concerning why they performed a range of behaviors. Two types of behavior categories were identified: *mastery* behaviors such as building something, playing a ball game,
reading books; and "*socialized*" behaviors initially required by parents, such
as picking up one's room, going to bed on time, and doing what mom asks
without talking back or arguing. Chandler found that the children's
responses could be coded according to the following types of reasons offered for why they performed these activities:

a. *Anticipation of external reward or approval, avoidance of disapproval.*
   These included gaining or maintaining adult approval, avoiding adult
   approval or punishment, gaining or maintaining peer approval, avoiding
   peer approval, and the anticipation of a specific tangible reward.
b. *Following an explicit rule*; for example, "I'm supposed to clean my
   room."
c. *Invoking either a positive or negative maxim*; for example, "Your body
   needs a good night's beauty sleep." "If you don't brush your teeth, the
   yellow sets in."
d. *Achievement of goals set by and for the self*; for example, "I want to
   know the facts so I read a lot." "I like to play so I won't have flabby
   muscles."
e. *Pursuit of challenge and/or mastery of the skill*; for example, "I play because I want to learn to hit better."
f. *Pleasure or interest in the activity itself*; for example, "Building is fun."
   "Reading is interesting."

The identification of these categories provides a much richer picture of
the general sources of motivation identified. While the first category provides clear examples of an extrinsic reward orientation, the categories which
make mention of rules, maxims, and achievement of goals for the self seem
to reflect several possible dimensions, perhaps even a sequence, defining the
internalization process. The last two categories, challenge and mastery, as
well as pleasure or interest in the activity itself, make direct reference to the
effectance source of intrinsic motivation, the mastery urge.

Chandler is now pursuing a number of lines of empirical inquiry including an examination of the relationship between type of motivation and
type of behavior; developmental differences in the use of these categories;
and the relationship between type of child-rearing technique reported by
parents and the child's motivation for performing the behavior.

With regard to the relationship between type of motivation and type of
behavior, Chandler's data clearly indicate that when one considers the
category of *mastery* behaviors, the predominate motivations are of the ef-

fectance type, responses *e* and *f*. When one examines the category of "*socialized*" behaviors, reasons *a* through *d* are given as the primary motivations for engaging in these acts. Chandler has now examined two of these four motivations for engaging in socialized behaviors developmentally, (*a*) external reward and (*d*) goals set by and for the self. Over the age range sampled, 5 to 12, motivations based on external reward show a dramatic developmental decline, whereas motivations involving the achievement of goals set by and for the self show an age-related increase. These developmental shifts bolster our hypothesis that reliance on external rewards as a course of motivation declines developmentally, whereas internalized goals become increasingly more important as motivators of the child's behavior.

Of particular interest to those concerned with the issue of self-control will be a determination of which child-rearing techniques lead to those categories reflecting varying degrees of internalized control over those behaviors which must be "socialized." At another level, these findings suggest that the efficacy of a given behavioral change program will in part depend upon a match between the motivational orientation of the child and the particular incentive system embedded in the program. A relatively straightforward diagnostic procedure, based on Chandler's categories, may represent one strategy for obtaining information in this regard.

For example, in designing a program to enhance reading skills, one may first want to determine the child's perception of what motivates her to read. Is it to gain approval? Avoid punishment? Is she following a rule or maxim which dictates that children are supposed to know how to read? Is she reading to fulfill some goal she has set for herself, for example, because she wants to "know the facts"? One strategy would be to match the program incentive to the child's expressed motivation for engaging in the behavior. For those explicitly interested in developing self-control over the behavior, the more difficult task of changing a child's motivational orientation may be the training task. How does one shift the child's orientation toward the achievement of goals set by and for the self? Chandler is in the process of analyzing her data on parental child-rearing techniques, and these findings may bear on this question. In the meantime, her developmental data should serve as a caution against the overly enthusiastic who would attempt to establish self-goals in the young child at an age when a different orientation, external rewards or rules, is developmentally more apropriate.

Children's Theories of Change

In the quest for theories of behavioral change, many voices have been heard; however, we may have overlooked one rather large group of potential theorists—the children themselves. What do *they* think is responsible for alterations in their behavior, and how might such information enhance our understanding of development and be potentially useful in applied contexts as well? We have embarked on these questions within the framework of the three competence domains we initially targeted; cognitive, social, and physical competence.

We first became interested in this topic when we attempted to design a downward extension of the perceived competence scale for young children ages 4 and 5 (Harter & Pike, 1981). Although we designed items to tap cognitive, social, and physical skills, the data did not bear witness to such a threefold division, in contrast to our findings with older children. Rather, a two-factor solution seemed to capture the essence of the judgments of our young subjects. One factor was defined by competence items from both the cognitive and physical subscales, whereas the second factor was comprised of peer popularity items (as well as an additional set of items we added to tap the child's perception of the degree to which her mother liked or accepted her). We speculated that while the cognitive and physical domains may well be perceived as involving mastery and the competent performance of skills, perhaps content tapping social acceptance represented a very different dimension which was not perceived in terms of competence at all.

This was one of the hypotheses that Chris Chao (Note 5) has pursued in her dissertation; in order to test it, we became involved in an analysis of children's theories of behavioral change. Briefly, we designed a procedure where we presented the child subject with two pictures at a time from a given domain; one depicting a child who excelled (e.g., could perform the cognitive or physical activity well, or for the social domain, had a lot of friends), and one depicting a child who was doing poorly. We then asked the subject "what would have to happen" for the child who was doing poorly to be like the child who was doing well. The findings first revealed that the explanations for how behavior could be changed in the cognitive and physical domains were very different from those in the social domain. The route to perfecting one's cognitive and physical abilities was paved with practice, learning, and the need to master skills. There was no such competence or skill orientation in their descriptions of how one procures friends: one simply finds them, asks them to be friends, or is fortunate in having other people supply them.

This gave us our first clue that perhaps children, young children at least, do not think of the social arena as a "skill domain" at all, and that our use of the term social "competence" may well have been a misnomer. What we seem to be tapping is *perceived popularity* or acceptance. While children clearly have a desire to have a lot of friends, their theories of how to become popular make no mention of acquiring social *skills*. We think this finding has obvious implications, given the proliferating number of programs designed to enhance social skills and social competence. If children are operating under an entirely different theory, then it is highly unlikely that these programs will have much of an impact, particularly from the standpoint of maintenance.

We are currently extending this study into the elementary school grades in order to determine whether, developmentally, children's theories of how friendships are formed shift to a more skill orientation. If so, what skills do they see as relevant, and to what degree do these overlap with the competencies which are the focus of existing programs? Given the high correlation which we find between perceived *physical* competence and perceived *popularity* for the elementary school grades, we anticipate the attributes such as athletic ability may be viewed as more relevant to social success than the concept of social skills. This is not an argument against social skills training. However, for such training to be effective, we may need to convince children that such skills can have positive benefits, and alter their theories accordingly.

Chao's findings with preschool and kindergarten children also reveal that within the *cognitive* and *physical* domains, there are six minitheories suggested for how to achieve competence and improve one's skills. These can be ordered along a dimension from passive dependence on others and/or external assistance to increasing autonomy and personal control over the change process:

a. *Passive dependence on others* who basically perform the competent behavior for the child who acts as a "puppet." For example, the parent puts the child on jungle gym, or the adult hands the puzzle piece to the child who merely places it in the designated spot.
b. The child is the "*passive recipient of maturation*" in that she acknowledges that she will be able to perform the skill competently "when I am five" or "when I'm bigger."
c. The child merely needs *external aids* or accoutrements, and a related prescription, such as "If I get new jogging shoes I'll be able to run fast" or "I'll have to eat the cereal which doesn't have any sugar in it and then I'll be able to do it."
d. *Direct Instruction*: someone needs to teach the child the skill. For example, "You could go to puzzle school," or "You could get someone to teach you."
e. *Observational Learning*, where the child observes a competent model engage in the skill and then imitates these actions. For example, "I could watch someone else do it and then try it by myself."
f. *Self-initiated activity and personal effort*, where competence is within the child's own grasp, through her own efforts and control. For example, "I would have to practice running every day to be good."

Depending on one's outlook, it can be either comforting or disconcerting to realize that much of the entire history of the psychology of learning and education is alive and well in the minds of our 4- and 5-year-olds. We have begun to extend our inquiry into the elementary school years, where we find more sophisticated versions of many of these same strategies for learning. One new theory to emerge might be labeled "social engineering" in that the child expresses the need to make some adjustments in her social environment in order to better master a particular skill. For example, one child indicated that she could do her schoolwork better if she spent less time with her friends.

We would also like to determine what factors influence the child's choice of a particular theory for change. It does *not* appear that these mechanisms for change represent a developmental sequence in the sense that they are *age*-related. To some extent, it represents an *experiential* sequence, a progression of steps for learning a new skill, particularly the latter steps. The more competent the child is at the skill, the more autonomously she can function in performing that skill. To the extent that competence at a particular skill is age related, one might expect to find some correlations between age and preference for a particular learning style. However, it is likely that individual differences in competence will be a more powerful predictor than developmental level. We are currently testing that hypothesis.

There are undoubtedly many other individual difference factors which might also affect a child's preferred theory of mastery, including the variables we have studied in older children, that is, intrinsic versus extrinsic orientation and perceived source of control. The major implication for programs of behavioral change and/or self-regulation is that there be some convergence between the child's theory and the principles of change upon which the program is based. In certain instances, it may seem advisable to alter the child's theory, if it seem less than adaptive. The main point to be underscored is that the child brings with her considerable theoretical baggage, excess or otherwise, and it is important to identify these particular cognitions before attempting to instill those dictated by the program.

CHARACTERISTICS OF THE SELF AS AN OBJECT OF EVALUATION

The previous discussion highlighted the self as an active agent who cognitively constructs theories about her interactions with the world. However, we also need to consider the self as an object of evaluation and examine the picture of the self which is constructed. We raised this question in an earlier section using Jack Horner's utterance, "What a good boy am

I," as a statement which requires further analysis with regard to its referent. For the developmentalist, the task is to identify which defining features of the self are salient at a given age or level.

It was noted, in introducing this issue, that data from Rosenberg (1979) indicate that the features most salient for his youngest subjects, age 8, were largely physical and behavioral characteristics. During the later elementary school years, there is an increasing mention of trait-like characteristics, especially interpersonal traits such as nice, friendly, mean, honest, and helpful. Adolescence, bringing with it the ability to introspect, marks a shift toward "psychological constructs" which define the self, one's thoughts, emotions, attitudes, and the degree to which they are perceived as fragmented versus unified. While these developmental shifts are interesting, we do not yet have any compelling framework for systematically assessing the salience of the defining features of the self developmentally.

Building upon the notions of Epstein (1973) and Coopersmith (1967), I have recently suggested that we move toward a hierarchical model in which we identify the potential dimensions of self-evaluation (Harter, in press d). Four were suggested: competence, control or power, morality, and social acceptability. Underneath each of these dimensions would be particular content domains which would undoubtedly change with age. For example, under social acceptability, concern with parental and adult acceptance would be prominent during the earlier years, and the issue of peer acceptance, particularly same-gender peers, would take on more salience during the elementary school period. Opposite-gender acceptance would then follow in adolescence. The relevance of such an analysis to those interested in strategies for behavioral change would be to pinpoint how the child defines herself with regard to these dimensions and domains and to identify the salience of each. Consider the issue of self-control as an evaluative dimension itself. Data by Minton (Note 6) indicate that this is a domain which emerges during the middle elementary school years as a basis for evaluating one's moral worth. That is, concern over controlling one's anger or aggression is spontaneously mentioned as a basis for the evaluation of oneself as a good or bad person. Rosenberg (1979) reports a similar finding, namely, that issues involving self-control take on increasing salience in children's self-definitions toward the end of the elementary school years.

Given that many programs are specifically directed toward control of socially undesirable behavior, the salience of this self-evaluative dimension would greatly facilitate such efforts. The developmental findings have less happy implications for those who are attempting to institute such self-control programs for younger children. One could certainly demonstrate that younger children know, for example, that "hitting other kids is bad behavior," if you ask them. The point is that if they do not carry this judgment around as a salient self-evaluative dimension, they will have considerably less motivation to alter their behavior. There will be little personal commitment to bring about any behavioral change.

There is another sense in which a developmental analysis does not offer much promise to those attempting to institute self-control programs with young children, particularly if self-awareness is a critical component. Several lines of thought now point to the conclusion that young children either do not have the ability or do not have the interest in focusing on themselves as an object of evaluation (see Harter, in press d). This suggestion has its historical roots in Cooley's (1902) notion of the "looking-glass self" and Mead's (1934) concept of the "generalized other." Basically, these analyses contend that one's picture of the self, as an object of evaluation, emerges as the reflected appraisals of significant others, a process which must await the emergence of the ability to take the perspective of another person. Developmentally, this typically occurs somewhere between the ages of 6 to 8. Prior to this, we do not see children engaged in self-observation, particularly self-criticism, nor do they seem to make use of social comparison information for the purpose of *self-evaluation*. There is recent evidence (reviewed in Harter, in press d) that until the young child can take the perspective of another and recognize the significance of others' evaluations in shaping one's own self-definition, social comparison information will not dramatically or systematically affect one's performance estimates. We may well be able to teach young children to mechanically monitor correct and incorrect responses, or to attend to the performance of another child. However, until the child is cognitively capable of observing the self as an object of internalized evaluations, both positive *and* negative, it is unlikely that such procedures will have the desired effect.

BIPOLAR EVALUATIVE DIMENSIONS IN A UNI-DIMENSIONAL MIND

The manner in which evaluative labels are first applied by children is the topic of another cognitive-developmental story which for me began in the play-therapy room. My clients have been young children of at least normal intelligence, in the 6- to 9-year-old range. Their presenting problems have included a variety of school learning difficulties as well as problems in handling their aggression. Independent of the particular problem or symptom, I came to observe a common occurrence in these young clients: when they described their emotions or evaluated themselves in terms of attributes, they were unable to acknowledge both positive and negative poles of a given dimension simultaneously.

The smart-dumb dichotomy was one such evaluative arena. My young clients with school learning problems could only view themselves as "all dumb," even though each had obvious intellectual strengths. Those young children with problems in handling aggression would typically view themselves as "all bad," despite my attempts to point out other commendable aspects of their behavior. In describing emotions, this phenomenon manifested itself in their assertions of being "all happy" in situations where sadness or anger was also warranted. Conversely, they would claim to be "all mad" in situations where positive feelings were also appropriate. I have documented other clinical examples elsewhere (Harter, 1977), and have described a drawing technique which has been effective in helping children realize that they can have more than one feeling in a situation and can possess two seemingly incompatible evaluative attributes.

In interpreting this phenomenon, I initially relied heavily on Piagetian theory, linking this mode of thinking to preoperational thought (see Harter, 1977; Harter, Note 7). We know from many Piagetian tasks—for example, conservation and multiplication of classes—that one cognitive limitation of the preoperational period is the fact that the young child can only attend to one perceptual dimension at a time. In the conservation task, when the young child insists that there is more water in the taller and narrower glass, her judgment is dominated by her perception of the single most salient physical dimension—in this case, height.

Thus, I initially extrapolated these principles to the child's understanding of affect and trait labels. It seemed reasonable that when a child was faced with judgments involving such opposites as smart versus dumb or good versus bad, her cognitive limitations make it difficult to view both as simultaneously operative. Our normative-developmental research (see Harter, Note 7) has now documented these effects systematically, particularly with regard to children's understanding of affect labels, where the developmental sequence involves a number of steps.

The relevance of these findings for the self-regulation process lies in their implications for the self-evaluative component in particular. What should be the defining characteristics of the self as an object of evaluation? Young children, in the 4- to 6-year range are likely to make all-or-none judgments; for example, they are all smart or all dumb, independent of the "evidence." This phenomenon is also likely to be observed in older children with psychological problems for whom this tendency is exacerbated. Thus, when one employs objectively defined monitoring procedures for tracking correct and incorrect responses or positive and negative behaviors, these will not necessarily be processed into an evaluative judgment which corresponds to the actual tally on the recording form. In all likelihood, performance feedback for the young child, or for the older child with adjustment problems, will be interpreted in an all-or-none fashion, leading the child to a conclusion which is very different from the inference of the onlooking adult. The result may well be failure to observe self-reward, behavioral change in the short run, or maintenance in the longer run.

This propensity to think in either-or dichotomies would appear to be particularly intractible at younger ages. Although I have suggested some potential techniques for use with children which may help to facilitate a differentiated picture of one's attributes and emotions, the child must be at the appropriate cognitive-developmental level; this appears to be well into concrete operational thought. However, the ability to demonstrate concrete operational thought on tasks requiring judgments about *physical* attributes in the inanimate world does not necessarily dictate that the child can apply such thinking to attributes of the self as an object of evaluation. I would hypothesize that the process of thinking about the self is considerably more complex and requires extensive experience in processing the evaluations of others in the service of forming one's self-definition. There is no pessimism intended here. Rather, the intent is to highlight a cognitive-developmental process which should illuminate our understanding of self-evaluation. To the extent that we can appreciate and assess it, we will be in a better position to prescribe experiences and treatment plans which can help children evaluate themselves more realistically.

CONCLUDING HOPES AND FEARS

A major theme has been the hope that we not lose the "self" in our attempts to objectify the components of the self-regulatory process, and that we attend to how the self changes with development. If we take seriously the framework that views the child as a cognitive theorist herself, then we must deal with her ontogenetic fickleness, since her theories will change as she develops (which is perhaps not a bad model for adult theorists). Many of these theories involve her understanding of what causes her own behavior as well as the very features which define the self.

A developmental perspective does not simply mean that one accepts the notion of broadly defined cognitive stages à la Piaget. It is unlikely that an appreciation of such developmental levels alone will enhance our understanding of the components in the process of self-regulation and control. A more fruitful approach would be to take such components as self-evaluation and self-reward and ask not only how they might be age-related, but what age-related *experiences* contribute to such developmental change. However, I would quickly urge that we not take, as a starting point in such an analysis, the operational definitions of these constructs as they are applied to *adults* and then ask how children at different developmental levels perform these component skills, so defined.

Rather, we should first ask what constructs such as self-evaluation and self-reward actually mean *within the context of development itself*. Such an approach may dictate very different definitions of the constructs. Or, alternatively, it may result in the need for different definitions of the same construct label for different developmental levels as well as different procedures for operationalizing these constructs.

Once the components have been identified in terms of their relevance to the developmental process, we can then address issues of sequence. I have suggested here that a developmental acquisition sequence of the components as identified in adult models may be just the reverse of how those processes operate in adulthood. However, this is not the most ideal approach, in that I took those components as a starting point in that particular analysis. Further thought needs to be given to what are the naturally occurring components at different levels of development and how these might be ordered.

It would also appear that we need to bring motivation and affect back into the fold of constructs. We have strayed from our learning theory origins, in that our earlier theoretical models placed heavy emphasis on behavior that was motivated by affective consequences. Somehow, in the proliferation of bigger and better cognitive models, we seem to have lost these roots. In the design of our cognitively oriented procedures, perhaps we have forgotten to ask why the child would want to monitor or control her behavior in the first place. For what purpose? For the child, what's at the end of the new mental maze we've constructed with its cognitive twists and turns? It was suggested that the child's *affective* response to her evaluation of her competence may represent a critical component of *self-reward*, in the naturalistic environment. This component may well be missing in our cognitive-behavioral attempts to operationally define self-reward as the administration to the self of a prize or symbolic token for achieving particular performance standards. If there is no affective light at the end of the tunnel, such procedures may well be ineffective. Within this same context, we need to think more about the child's level of *commitment*, an important factor in the successful use of self-regulatory paradigms with adults.

It has also been urged that we clarify our use of the term "intrinsic." If we consider it as an inference from behavior which does not seem to be performed to obtain obvious external rewards, we run into trouble. I have suggested a three-fold distinction: between behavior which is motivated by an effectance-like pleasure from mastery, behavior which is motivated by external rewards, and behavior which is motivated by a self-reward system based on an internalization of the functions of extrinsic reward. Within these categories, there will be further subdivisions: a few were mentioned, based on interview data in which children generated responses to questions concerning why they perform the behaviors they do. This led to an emphasis on the importance of determining the child's perceived source of motivation and the use of this information in designing programs for self-change. This framework may also help to clarify some of the confusion regarding the effects of extrinsic rewards on seemingly "intrinsic" motivation. It was hypothesized that extrinsic rewards may well undermine the more effectance-like intrinsic motivation, but would not disrupt behavior governed largely by an internalized reward structure, and may even enhance the latter.

The importance of a cognitive variable which was labeled "perceived control" was also discussed. Children's understanding of the contingencies which govern the successes and failures in their lives has emerged as a powerful predictor in our own research. Our data indicate that knowledge of these contingencies, coupled with the attribution of internal control or personal responsibility, is critical. Moreover, it functions as the primary predictor in the following chain: perceived control, actual achievement level, evaluation of one's cognitive competence, affective reaction to one's competence appraisal, and motivation to engage in further mastery attempts. We need to attend to each of these links in the chain and to consider affective and motivational variables as well as cognitive and behavioral factors.

In our own research efforts, it is fair to say that we have not devoted sufficient attention to overt behavior. Nor have we yet addressed the critical issue of the antecedents of the parameters we have isolated. As I indicated at the outset of this chapter, our starting point was very different from those interested in behavioral change. Clearly, we now need to extend our analyses into the behavioral realm. Fortunately, the field as a whole has emerged from the previous era where we hotly disputed which particular theoretical orientation was "correct." There is growing appreciation for how different approaches might converge to provide a more comprehensive picture of the developing child. However, we each have some distance to go to meet that challenge.

REFERENCE NOTES

1. Harter, S., & Engstrom, R. *Perceived competence and self-esteem as predictors of the child's mastery motivation.* Unpublished manuscript, University of Denver, 1981.
2. Connell, J. P. *A multidimensional measure of children's perceptions of control: A comprehensive assessment of the development of children's perceptions of control.* Unpublished manuscript, 1980.
3. Connell, J. P., & Harter, S. *The relationship between children's motivational orientation, perceived competence, and perceptions of control: A test of alternative models.* Unpublished manuscript, University of Denver, 1981.
4. Chandler, C. *The effects of parenting techniques and attitudes on developmental changes in children's motivational orientations.* Unpublished doctoral dissertation, University of Denver, 1981.

5. Chao, C. *Perceived and actual competence in children with and without imaginary friends.* Unpublished doctoral dissertation, University of Denver, 1981.
6. Minton, B. *Dimensions of information underlying children's judgments of their competence.* Unpublished masters thesis, University of Denver, 1979.
7. Harter, S. *Children's understanding of multiple emotions: A cognitive-developmental approach.* Invited address to the Piaget Society, June, 1979.

REFERENCES

Aronfreed, J. *Conduct and conscience.* New York: Academic Press, 1968.

Aronfreed, J. The concept of internalization. In D. A. Goslin (Ed.), *Handbook of socialization theory and research.* New York: Rand-McNally, 1969.

Aronfreed, J. Moral development from the standpoint of a general psychological theory. In T. Lickona (Ed.), *Moral development and behavior.* New York: Holt, Rinehart & Winston, 1976.

Bandura, A. Social learning theory of identificatory processes. In D. A. Goslin (Ed.), *Handbook of socialization theory and research.* New York: Rand-McNally, 1969.

Bandura, A. Analysis of modeling processes. In A. Bandura (Ed.), *Psychological modeling: Conflicting theories.* Chicago: Aldine-Atherton, 1971.

Bandura, A. Self-efficacy: Toward a unifying theory of behavioral change, *Psychological Review,* 1977, *84,* 191–215. (a)

Bandura, A. *Social learning theory.* Englewood Cliffs, N.J.: Prentice-Hall, 1977. (b)

Bandura, A. The self system in reciprocal determinism. *American Psychologist,* 1978, *33,* 344–358.

Cooley, C. H. *Human nature and the social order.* New York: Scribners, 1902.

Coopersmith, S. *The antecedents of self-esteem.* San Francisco: W. H. Freeman 1967.

Epstein, S. The self-concept revisited or a theory of a theory. *American Psychologist,* 1973, *28,* 405–416.

Harter, S. A cognitive-developmental approach to children's expression of conflicting feelings and a technique to facilitate such expression in play therapy. *Journal of Consulting and Clinical Psychology,* 1977, *45,* 417–432.

Harter, S. Effectance motivation reconsidered: Toward a developmental model. *Human Development,* 1978, *1,* 34–64.

Harter, S. The development of competence motivation in the mastery of cognitive and physical skills: Is there still a place for joy? In G. C. Roberts and D. M. Landers (Eds.), *Psychology of motor behavior and sport, 1980.* Champaign, Ill.: Human Kinetics Publishers, 1981.

Harter, S. A model of intrinsic mastery motivation in children: Individual differences and developmental change. In *Minnesota symposium on child psychology* (Vol. 14). Hillsdale, New Jersey: Lawrence Erlbaum, in press (a).

Harter, S. The perceived competence scale for children. *Child Development,* in press (b).

Harter, S. A new self-report scale of intrinsic versus extrinsic orientation in the classroom: Motivational and informational components. *Developmental Psychology,* in press (c).

Harter, S. Developmental perspectives on the self-system. In M. Hetherington (Ed.), *Social Development: Carmichael's manual on child psychology.* New York: Wiley, in press (d).

Harter, S. & Pike R. *The pictorial perceived competence scale for young children.* Test manual, University of Denver, 1981.

Kanfer, F. The many faces of self-control or behavior modifications changes its focus. In R. Stuart (Ed.), *Behavioral self-management.* New York: Bruner/Mazel, 1977.

Kanfer, F. H. Self-management methods. In F. H. Kanfer & A. P. Goldstein (Eds.), *Helping people change: A textbook of methods*. (2nd ed.) New York: Pergamon Press, 1980.

Karoly, P. Behavioral self-management in children: Concepts, methods, issues, and directions. In M. Hersen, R. Eisler, & P. Miller (Eds.), *Progress in behavior modification*. Vol. 5. New York: Academic Press, 1977.

Mead, G. H. *Mind, self, and society*. Chicago: University of Chicago Press, 1934.

Meichenbaum, D. Toward a cognitive theory of self-control. In G. Schwartz & D. Shapiro (Eds.), *Consciousness and self-regulation*. New York: Plenum Press, 1976.

Meichenbaum, D. *Cognitive-behavior modification*. New York: Plenum, 1977.

Meichenbaum, D. Teaching children self-control. In B. Lahey & A. Kazdin (Eds.), *Advances in child clinical psychology*. Vol. 2. New York: Plenum, 1979.

Rosenberg, M. *Conceiving the self*. New York: Basic Books, 1979.

Weiner, B. The role of affect in sports psychology. In G. C. Roberts and D. M. Landers (Eds.), *Psychology of Motor Behavior and Sport, 1980*. Champaign, Ill.: Human Kinetics Publishers, 1981.

White, R. W. Motivation reconsidered: The concept of competence. *Psychological Review*, 1959, *66*, 297–333.

Wicklund, R. A. Objective self-awareness. In L. Berkowitz (Ed.), *Advances in experimental social psychology*. Vol. 8. New York: Academic Press, 1975.

Part II:

Assessment and Treatment of Children's Self-Management Problems

Part II.

7

Individual Difference Factors in Children's Self-Management: Toward Individualized Treatments

Anne P. Copeland

Self-management training has grown rapidly as a successful and appealing approach to helping children. Through a systematic combination of such treatment components as modeling, self-evaluation and praise, and self-awareness, the problems of impulsivity, aggression, and anxiety have been particularly well addressed with component skills training (Craighead, Wilcoxon-Craighead, & Meyers, 1978; Kanfer, 1975; Karoly, 1977) and cognitive self-instruction (Meichenbaum, 1977). The enthusiasm which self-management training for children has engendered is striking.

To date, attention has been focused on improving the self-management treatment package. Dimensions such as type of self-verbalization (Kendall & Wilcox, 1980), inclusion of modeling (Meichenbaum & Goodman, 1971), and use of reinforcers (Masters & Mokros, 1974) have been systematically examined in an attempt to develop optimum treatments.

When positive training findings are published, however, it is not always clear just how universally beneficial the approach has been. The publication of group data may camouflage the improvement variability which may exist within treatments. Publications of single- or few-case studies, for their part, reveal little about which children respond most favorably. And last, the general policy of not publishing negative results prevents the dissemination of valuable information about what variations in treatment or in subject populations are to be avoided. Self-management training probably "works better" for some children than for others, even with identical treatment instructions, therapists, and therapy situations. As has been previously pointed out (Karoly, 1977; Kendall, 1977; Meichenbaum, 1977), there is a need to attend to the characteristics of "responders" versus "nonresponders." Consider, for example, two children referred because of impulsivity and/or hyperactivity. Jason and Jennifer appear to present very similar problems. They both have been labeled "hyperactive" by their pediatrician, both of their teachers have rated them as far above the mean on teacher rating scales of hyperactivity, they both get into fights with their peers, and both are doing poorly in school. A psychologist, well-trained and enthusiastic about new self-management techniques, accepts them both in a self-control group she is starting. Using the latest informaton from the research literature, she allows the children to define their own criteria for success, she emphasizes pride and feelings of acomplishment as feedback, and she teaches generalized rather than specific approach strategies. After many weeks of modeling, teaching self-evaluation, coping with errors, and self-praise, Jason is remarkably "improved," according to all sources, while Jennifer is, if anything, worse. Yet the children got identical instruction from the same therapist in the same setting.

What accounts for this difference in responsiveness to treatment, a phenomenon surely known by every clinician, is the topic of this chapter. We will return to Jennifer and Jason throughout, learning more about them and discovering how their individual characteristics might have influenced their response to treatment. Until we understand how individual differences interact with different types of intervention, we will not be able to prescribe treatments differentially, and we will thus be inefficient in our case management of children. It is the intent here to highlight the importance of considering individual-difference factors, to present indications from the current literature about which characteristics of children seem to affect treatment success, and to suggest directions for future research in the area.

That person variables and situation variables may interact in determining an individual's response repertoire or behavior has been a much-discussed topic in personality theory for the past several years (Bowers, 1973; Mischel, 1973; Ekehammar, 1974). Convincing, though not always heeded, arguments for attending to individual differences in applied educational and psychological research have been offered repeatedly by Cronbach (1957, 1975; Cronbach & Snow, 1977). Experimental psychology, in particular, has become dominated by between-treatment studies, relegating individual differences to the ranks of "an annoyance rather than a challenge to the experimenter" (Cronbach, 1957). Cronbach suggests that, instead of trying to find the one treatment that would be best for all people (the applied experimental psychology approach), the field might profit from treating different people differently (the applied correlational psychology approach). It may be, for example, that Treatment A is more successful with people low on characteristic X, while people high on characteristic X profit more from Treatment B. One illustration of this possibility is in the apparent differential responsiveness to educational approaches by children of differing social classes — with lower-class children tending to respond better to structured and concrete teaching methods and with middle-class children often profiting more from a less structured, problem-oriented approach (Cronbach, 1975; Brophy & Evertson, 1973). Thus, it is not surprising that therapists concerned with teaching children self-control are now facing the necessity of sorting through an array of treatment paradigms and trying to choose the best alternative for each child.

SELF-MANAGEMENT PARADIGMS

Evidence for the importance of individual differences will be drawn here from three self-managment research areas: cognitive self-instructional (CSI) training; component skills training based on Kanfer's three-phase model (Kanfer, 1975); and delay-of-gratification/resistance-to-temptation training. In each area, studies are reviewed which sought to help children perform a low-probability behavior (e.g., performing a task slowly, playing nonaggressively, waiting a long time before playing with an attractive toy) by teaching them, through modeling, self-verbalization, or some type of self-awareness, how to successfully manage their own behavior.

The CSI studies, based on the work of Luria (1961) and Vygotsky (1962) and on the later applications by Bem (1967), Palkes, Stewart, and Kahana (1968), and Meichenbaum and Goodman (1971), focus on teaching children to talk to themselves. Initially, an adult performs some task (usually one which requires planning and careful execution, such as mazes or copying designs) while reciting aloud an effective strategy. Then the child performs the same or a similar task while the adult verbalizes the strategy. At this point, the child takes over, performing the task and speaking the instructions as well. These he speaks at first aloud, then by whispering, and finally silently. The effective strategy which is taught typically focuses on reiterating the directions (i.e., the goal of the task) in a question-and-answer format (e.g., "What am I supposed to do now? I am supposed to make a design just like that one over there."); on self-guiding and planning statements (e.g., "I'd better be careful and go slowly. Here's a line this way, then up, now an X.");

on coping with errors (e.g., "Oops, that line went the wrong way. Well, I'll just fix it, and try to be more careful next time."); and on self-evaluation and self-reinforcement (e.g., "Good! I did it! It looks just right!"). The child's cognitive style, academic performance, classroom behavior, and/or parent reports are assessed before and after treatment, and sometimes at a follow-up session. In the prototypical group research study, the performance after treatment of a group of children receiving this CSI training is compared with the performance of children in attention control and/or no-treatment control groups. The length and number of sessions, the training and assessment materials, and the exact instructions have varied considerably, though not systematically, across studies.

Other types of behavioral self-management packages which exclude the specific focus on teaching children to instruct themselves have been extensively reviewed (Karoly, 1977; Craighead, Wilcoxon-Craighead, & Meyers, 1978). The common denominator among these studies is their use of a self-management model (Kanfer, 1975) based on modeling, self-observation and evaluation, and self-reinforcement. Self-evaluation for behavioral, cognitive, and/or social task standards are typically set and modeled by an adult and later matched by the children. Accurate self-assessment of the quality of performance is emphasized, with subsequent notice being given to externally awarded and finally self-awarded reinforcement. A goal is to have the child spontaneously use the self-guidance techniques without prompting from adults.

Finally, variables which influence a child's ability or willingness to control his or her own behavior have also been studied within the paradigms of delay of gratification and resistance to temptation. The research on these topics typically has not been of a clinical or therapeutic nature, but rather has focused on normal children's ability to prevent themselves from doing something desirable or to postpone rewards. For example, a child may be given a choice between having a small toy immediately or receiving a larger, more attractive toy the next day. Or, a child may be allowed to play in a room but be instructed not to play with or touch one particularly attractive object. In each case, the children's ultimate behavior and decision time are relevant dependent measures. Although the original work in this area emphasized a developmental description of normal children's behavior in tempting situations, (e.g., Mischel & Metzner, 1962), later work which examined the effects of modeling (e.g., Mischel & Patterson, 1976) has obvious clinical significance to the field of self-management.

It is not clear exactly how self-control tasks interrelate (Toner, Holstein, & Hetherington, 1977; Meichenbaum, 1979) or that similar processes determine the degree of self-control in the different tasks (Masters & Binger, 1978). Nevertheless, the major paradigms for studying how to effect children's self-management share many components and all have relevance for us as we begin to understand different children's responsiveness to different treatments.

SUBJECT CHARACTERISTICS AFFECTING SELF-MANAGEMENT TRAINING

Following is a list of subject characteristics which have been found in at least one study from one of the major research areas to affect self-management training. These characteristics include demographic variables, indications of cognitive ability and style, and aspects of training which appear to alter the attitudes of the subjects in some way. This latter category is not strictly a subject characteristic, but it is included in an attempt not to overlook any dimension that might significantly influence children's responses to intervention. For the sake of organization, discussion of each category of characteristics will first center on those from CSI projects, then those from the component skills training projects, and finally on those from the temptation developmental studies. A summary of the findings for each type of variable is found in table 7.1.

It should also be made clear that there are many research reports and case studies which, while providing useful information about treatment components and situational variables, did not examine any subject characteristics and, thus, will not be mentioned here. Few of the studies to be cited in the following sections, in fact, had subject characteristics as a main, or even less-than-offhand, focus. Fewer still would meet the stringent methodological requirements for studying Aptitude X Treatment Interactions prescribed by Cronbach and Snow (1977). General laws are not yet apparent in most case, so the emphasis remains on preliminary examination of subject effects.

Demographic Variables

Age. Self-management training has been used successfully with children of many ages, ranging from preschoolers (Bornstein & Quevillon, 1976; Karoly & Dirks, 1977) to adolescents (Anderson, Fodor, & Alpert, 1976; Williams & Akamatsu, 1978), although the majority of studies have focused on elementary-school-aged children. This is logical, as this is often the time when demands for structure and compliance first become strong in a child's life. It is important to remember, however, that the range of abilities, introspection, and adult-centeredness varies enormously from younger to older children; it seems likely, therefore, that different treatment modalities would be appropriate for children of different ages. In our case study example, for instance, Jennifer is 6 years old and Jason is 9. How this age dif-

Table 7.1 Summary of Conclusions about Individual Differences

Subject Variable	Conclusions
1. Age and Cognitive Level	1a. Older/more mature children are more able to invent their own self-management strategies than are younger or less mature children. 1b. Strategies taught to older children should be more abstract and general; younger children need more structured and concrete strategies.
2. Race, Residence, or SES	2a. Children improve more when trained by models or adults of their own race. 2b. Perhaps because of a more external locus of control, lower SES children seem to respond more to external rewards while middle-class children profit more under intrinsic rewards.
3. Gender	3a. Most self-management studies show no clear gender differences in response to treatment. Support for needing to match sex of model/adult to sex of child comes only from related modeling literature.
4. Medication Status	4a. Long-term studies are limited by lack of random assignment to drug and placebo groups. 4b. It may be that medicated children, with this history of external control, profit more from other-controlled rather than self-controlled management, at least initially.
5. Cognitive Tempo	5a. Both impulsive and reflective children can benefit from self-management training. 5b. Impulsive children may need more structured and tangible feedback than reflective children.
6. Attributional Style	6a. "Internal" attributers benefit more from self-determined feedback and internalized rewards. The opposite is true for "external" attributers. 6b. Internality, as a goal itself or as a setting condition for self-management training, can be taught to children.
7. Verbalization Rates	7a. In self-instructional treatment studies, there has been a surprising lack of a relationship between use of instructions and positive outcome, although use of instructions is difficult to assess. 7b. In other paradigms, "high verbalizers" do show more self-control, although this may merely indicate general compliance. 7c. Rate of use of spontaneous verbalizations are directly related to self-control or improved performance on difficult tasks.

Table 7.1. (Cont.)

Subject Variable	Conclusions
8. Training Variables	8a. The quality and type of previous experience with adults influences children's later self-control or compliance. 8b. Children who are rated as more interested and involved respond best to self-control training. 8c. Perceived high similarity between model and child can improve treatment effectiveness. 8d. Positive training settings are conducive to performance improvement and responsiveness to treatment.

ference might influence treatment outcome becomes clear as we examine the literature.

There are a fair number of self-management studies which do report that children of different ages responded differently to various conditions. In each of the following cases, younger and older children differed in whether they were able to produce their own management strategies, and/or in how relevant the actual content of the instructions was to their performance. For example, kindergartern and first-grade children were asked to control their finger-tapping response by saying "faster" or "slower" either overtly or covertly (Meichenbaum & Goodman, 1969; Meichenbaum, 1975). Covert self-instructions had little effect on kindergartners (perhaps because they failed to use them), while overt instructions helped children of both ages. Denney (1975) examined the responses of 6-, 8-, and 10-year-olds to three treatments designed to encourage the use of constraint-seeking questions in a 20-questions game. Children were exposed to an exemplary model only, to a model who also verbalized a strategy (cognitive modeling), or to this cognitive modeling plus self-rehearsal training in which the children were taught to repeat the strategy statements. Although cognitive modeling was the most successful condition for all ages, the difference between the cognitive and the exemplary model was the greatest for the youngest group. The 6-year-olds appeared to need the help of the cognitive model's explanations more than did the older children. A similar conclusion was reached by Wolf (1972) who found that, compared to 2-year-old children, 9-year-old children were not differentially sensitive to the additional information provided in an elaborated verbalization condition. In addition, Mischel, Mischel, and Hood (Note 1) found that as children got older they became more cognizant of what self-control treatments would be most effective for themselves. Toner and Smith (1977) found that preschool girls showed greater delays when they had been given a relevant rule verbalization to rehearse, whereas the older, second- and third-grade girls apparently did not need such a rule suggested to them. Similarly, Miller, Weinstein, and Karniol (1978) found that the only condition in which third-graders delayed gratification longer than kindergartners was when the children had been given no instructions about what to say to themselves during the waiting period. The authors concluded that kindergarten children may not produce effective self-verbalizations without specific instructions to do so. Third-graders did appear to spontaneously produce moderately effective mediating self-verbalizations. Task-oriented verbalizations, however, were helpful in increasing the length of delay for both age groups. These studies all seem to suggest that, when left to their own devices, older children tend to produce their own, fairly effective verbalization strategies.

The effect of the actual content of controlling verbalizations on children of different ages, however, warrants close inspection. Hartig and Kanfer (1973) compared the effectiveness of verbalizing positive consequences for nontransgression, negative consequences for transgressions, instructions not to transgress, task-irrelevant instructions, and no instructions on the self-control of 3- to 7-year-old children. Of those who actually repeated the self-instructions, younger children in all the instruction conditions performed similarly. Older children, however, transgressed more in the task-irrelevant condition. The content of the instructions, then, was not irrelevant for the older children. Similary, Birch (1966) instructed 2- to 7-year-old children to push a lever down and to keep holding it down. He repeated this instruction after 3 and 6 minutes, then the children were given one of four instructions. Reminders to keep the lever held down were given either periodically (every 15 seconds) or contingent upon the child's release, *and* either verbally (specific instructions) or in the form of a buzzer (which the child had to translate to mean a reminder). Age X group interactions suggested that the youngest children in the somewhat abstract, buzzer conditions kept the lever pressed down the least, and that they got worse over time. These youngest children were able, on the other hand, to maintain their performance over time when the instructions were presented verbally, and thus more concretely. An interesting developmental progression of content differences was demonstrated by Jensen and Buhanan (1974). In a resistance to temptation task, 4-year-olds deviated less under fear or punitive instructions, 6-year-olds under promised reward conditions, and 8-year-olds under intrinsic-empathy instructions.

In summary, it seems that young (even preschool) children like Jennifer can profit from self-management training, but the instructions that are used need to be more specific and structured than they do for older children. At this point in our understanding, no specific age guidelines can be given about when to use which type of training; age differences are only grossly understood. In addition, inasmuch as age and cognitive level are intertwined, we probably can never be specific about age limits, but rather we will learn more about how cognitive maturity (described either by age or IQ) influences responsiveness to treatment. The relative effectiveness of concrete (e.g. "I should look at the clock") versus conceptual (e.g. "I should think about what I'm supposed to do") self-instructions was examined by Kendall and Wilcox (1980), who found greater improvement on teacher ratings of self-control and hyperactivity for the conceptual labeling groups. The subjects in this study, however, were 8- to 12-years old, older than the younger groups cited above. It would be interesting to investigate whether concerete labeling is actually *more* effective than conceptual labeling with *younger* children. A second conclusion is that, for older (or more mature) children like Jason, self-management training should include a new, developmentally appropriate strategy, as a redundant one appears to be either useless or even detrimental (Carter, Patterson, & Quasebarth, 1979; Hagen, Meacham & Mesibov, 1970). By treating Jason and Jennifer in an identical manner, the psychologist ignored the importance of these factors. As their training was fairly abstract and self-generated, Jason, the older child, improved, but Jennifer did not.

Race, residence, and SES. Because of the confounding in our culture among race, urban versus non-urban residence, and socioeconomic status (SES), the influence of these factors on treatment outcome will be examined together. It is particularly unclear in this case whether differences which occur across these types of children are due to the direct effect of the condition (e.g., living in the city versus living in a suburb) or to the wide range of correlated factors (e.g., education level of parents, quality of past schooling). Nevertheless, because in the reviewed literature it is the three factors of race, residence, and SES that are typically reported, our conclusions must initially be based on them. As shown below, too few studies exist to make many prescriptive conclusions, but it does seem clear that treatment outcome is modulated by these three factors. We can keep in mind that in our example, Jennifer is a white child living in an urban setting whereas Jason is a suburban black child. The psychologist is black.

Genshaft and Hirt (1979) trained 40 7-year-old impulsive children in the use of CSI methods of self-control. All children were of comparable IQ, SES, and geographic residence, and groups were matched on sex. Half the children were white and half were black. Each child was trained by a white peer, black peer, or no peer model; there were equal numbers of race-matched and race-crossed model-subject pairs. The results of this study highlight the importance of race, even though there was not clear support for the use of CSI training. Subjects trained by white models increased their MFF latency across time more than subjects trained by black or no models.

However, improvements on Wechsler Intelligence Scale for Children (WISC) Picture Arrangement scores occurred only when children had been trained by models of their own race.

In terms of residence and SES, several studies have shown a treatment to "work" for one group and not the other. Murray (1979) found differences between city and suburban children in performance on a delay task depending on whether the children spoke aloud or not. The groups differed in IQ as well as residence, however, so a clear interpretation of the findings is made difficult. Monohan and O'Leary (1971) report two studies which examined the effects of self-instructional training and the length of delay between training and opportunity to break a rule. In the first experiment with rural, white children, self-instructional training was effective in preventing rule breaking. Training appeared to be unsuccessful, however, in the second experiment with urban, northern, black children. And, Toner, Moore, and Kidder (Note 2) increased middle-class children's resistance to deviation by having them think they were serving as models for other children. When they tried to replicate the study with same-aged "disadvantaged" children, the act of serving as a model for other children had no impact. Both of these studies suggest only SES/race/residence main effects, of course, rather than interactions with a particular treatment. In contrast, it should be noted that Robertson, Kendall, and Urbain (Note 3) found children of different SES groups to respond similarly to cognitive behavioral treatments.

Zigler and Child (1969) have suggested that lower-class children respond more favorably to extrinsic incentives, while middle-class children profit more under conditions of intrinsic reward. While it is not clear that SES really accounts for these differences (Baron & Ganz, 1972; Baron, Cowan, & McDonald, 1974), it does appear that SES, race, and/or residential location may be important factors in the prescription of types of reinforcement.

Unfortunately, most CSI studies do not report the racial or SES makeup of their samples. We can sometimes infer SES, as when Bornstein and Quevillon (1976) reported the successful CSI training of three Head Start Children. And occasionally (Nelson & Birkimer, 1978) the sample is identified by race. Although not all studies which examine SES effects find differences (Shure & Spivack, 1972), based on the sum of the available evidence, we should probably, at this point, be careful to match the races of therapist and child and to investigate further the demands, content, and types of self-control we teach children of different backgrounds. Jason and the psychologist are both black, and Jason, being from a middle-class suburb, brought optimal conditions to the training sessions. His success may have been due in part to these factors.

Gender. If differences in how boys and girls respond to treatments exist, they would be important to understand in planning self-control programs. There is, of course, little theoretical basis for predicting many gender differences; in fact, most self-management studies which report on analyses for sex differences have found no significant effects (Brodzinsky, Feuer, & Owens, 1977; Egeland, 1974; Genshaft & Hirt, 1979; Hartig & Kanfer, 1973; Kanfer, Karoly, & Newman, 1975; Malamuth, 1979; Mischel & Patterson, 1976; Patterson & Mischel, 1975; Sagotsky, Patterson, & Lepper, 1978). Many other studies do not report on sex difference analyses, although both boys and girls were studied; the assumption can be made that no gender effects were found.

A few exceptions in which boys responded to treatment conditions differently from girls do appear in the literature. Casey (Note 4) had first- and fourth-graders either self-instruct or listen to adult instructions about not cheating. Instructions focused either on a simple "do this, don't do that" command, on cheating, or on honesty. Although several main treatment effects were also reported, girls who had been taught to self-instruct about honesty were the ones who cheated least. In a study of subject variables' ability to predict verbal control of nonverbal behavior, Van Duyne (1974) found that Wechsler Preschool and Primary Scale of Intelligence (WPPSI) Performance IQ scores accounted for twice as much variance in predicting verbal control in boys as girls. Age accounted for five times more variance for girls than boys. Finally, several other reports of sex differences exist, but the interactions tend to be so complex and apparently contradictory that few useful generalizations can be made (e.g., LaVoie, 1974; Masters & Santrock, 1976). It appears, then, that if sex differences are going to prove to be at all relevant in planning self-control programs, higher-order rather than two-way interactions or main effects will have to be explored, with special attention paid to the generalizability of such interactions from one project to the next. From the general modeling literature, we might expect perceived similarity between adult and child to be important in affecting success (Akamatsu & Thelen, 1974), and so, would recommend matching the gender of the therapist and the child. There is no direct confirmation of the importance of this from the self-management literature, however. Jennifer and Jason's difference in outcome is probably not due to their gender difference.

Medication status. Very little information exists about the effects of psychostimulant drugs on children's response to various forms of self-management training. As Whalen and Henker (1976) have pointed out, this is a potentially critical area to a child's overall success in school. That is, the long-term psychological effect of having one's behavior controlled by such an external agent as a medication may be to teach, subtly, that self-control is a useless enterprise to attempt. Further, it is possible that stimulants themselves directly influence (either positively or negatively) children's ability to complete a self-management program. For these reasons, understanding the interaction between medication status and treatment responsiveness is important. (Jennifer, in our example, has been medicated for several years, whereas Jason's problems have, to date, been addressed with behavior modification techniques.) An unfortunate methodological obstacle keeps research in this area from being easily done. It is clear that drug versus nondrug comparison groups should be randomly constituted; this is not so much a problem for short-term studies as for the studies of long-term psychological effects. It is perhaps for this reason that we know so little about this important area.

Some initial guidelines exist, however. In one double-blind investigation of the interactive effects of medication with other treatments or situations with hyperactive children, Whalen, Henker, Collins, Finck, and Dotemoto (1979) examined the interplay between several classroom variables (noise level and source of pace regulation) and medication status. Interactions were complex and varied, depending on the situation and dependent measure. In general, hyperactive boys taking a placebo were observably different (e.g., emitting more negative verbalizations, more unexpected behavior) from their medicated hyperactive and control peers in some, but not all, classroom conditions. Bugental, Whalen, and Henker (1977) studied the interaction of medication status and attributional style on the response of hyperactive boys to CSI versus external reinforcement treatment. They reported the potentially interesting finding that nonmedicated children (like Jason) improved significantly more under CSI than reinforcement training and medicated children (like Jennifer) improved under the opposite conditions. Conclusions from these research or case studies about the interaction between treatment and medication status are severely limited, however, by the lack of random assignment to the medication groups and consequently the probable difference in the initial severity of symptoms and/or family attitudinal patterns of the two groups. A study of this type and focus which includes random assignment would be enlightening and timely.

To summarize, several clearly specifiable demographic variables have been shown to influence self-management treatment outcome. Had the psychologist in our example been aware of these factors, she would have altered the training sessions to fit the individual needs of Jennifer and Jason. Jennifer, being younger, living in the city and having a history of being controlled with medication, might have been more responsive to a more concrete and structured training program, a white (i.e., same-race) adult model, and more tangible feedback. In many cases, the variables discussed in this section may be mediated by some cognitive ability or style variable which would more basically and directly explain the influence of the demographic characteristics. These are described below.

Cognitive Ability and Style Variables

Underlying the variables of age, residence, and socioeconomic status are probably such factors as cognitive and/or verbal maturity, expectations about where control is centered (with self or with others), and general compliance. Some research studies have reported directly on the impact of these variables on treatment outcome.

Intelligence. As noted above, self-management training can successfully alter the problem-solving style of children as young as preschool aged. A related question is whether children's level of cognitive ability in part determines what type of treatment is optimal for them. Might it be true that brighter children would more readily incorporate self-management strategies into their repertoire and thus respond better to that kind of treatment, while less bright children need and use beneficially more external contingencies? In addition to some as-yet-unspecified minimum amount of intelligence, self-management training requires that children be able to remember the training techniques, to be able to decide when to use them, and to be flexible/fluent in their utilization. Age and intelligence are both indicators of cognitive level; because Jennifer was younger than Jason, for example, it is hard to determine whether her lower IQ (in the normal range) was relevant in interfering with treatment success, as compared to Jason's higher IQ (in the above-average range). The use of self-control training with retarded children is a downward extension of this issue (Bender, 1977; Guralnick, 1976; Kendall, 1977; Norton & Lester, 1979; Leon & Pepe, Note 5; Watson & Hall, Note 6). The importance of intelligence on performance under treatment, then, is relevant to discussion of individual differences (see also Litrownik, in this volume).

In many cases, children with higher IQs have responded better to self-management training than have less cognitively mature children. Although only individual subjects' data were presented, Barkley, Copeland, and Sivage (1980) suggested, in their discussion of the results of an extended CSI training program, that the lower-mental-age boys (who, in some cases, had higher chronological ages) exhibited greater deterioration after a self-monitoring and reinforcement schedule was thinned out than did boys with higher mental ages. Similarly, Leon and Pepe (Note 5) taught CSI techniques to learning disabled (LD) and retarded children who had arithmetic skill deficits. Although both groups benefited more from CSI than traditional arithmetic training, LD children (presumably of higher IQ than the retarded children) in the CSI group showed the greatest improvement. In contrast, however, in a study examining the interaction of cognitive level (as assessed by Piagetian tasks) with response to CSI training (Schleser, Meyers, & Cohen, Note 7), preoperational (cognitively less mature) children benefited more from CSI training than concrete operational (more mature) children. The children in the latter group were noted to use their own strategies spontaneously. Differences in procedures and self-statements probably account for the inconsistency across studies.

Differences in the *type* of management training which is optimal also appear to be modulated by IQ differences. Ridberg, Parke, and Hetherington (1971) compared 50 impulsive and 50 reflective fourth-grade boys' responses to models. Each boy was shown a model exhibiting a cognitive tempo opposite to his own tempo. The models verbalized a strategy, demonstrated planning, or did both or neither of these. In the more clinically relevant condition in which impulsive children watched a reflective model, lower-IQ boys increased their latency in responding on a cognitive tempo task when the model both verbalized and showed a scanning technique. In contrast, higher IQ boys' latency scores increased more when the model *either* verbalized *or* scanned, but not both. Errors were similarly decreased for high IQ boys when they were given only one cue; all treatment groups resulted in similar decreases in errors, however, for low-IQ boys. In other words, if the cues were extremely varied, as when both the verbalization and scanning strategies were presented, the higher-IQ boys, who may have already been employing successful strategies, but tried to use the extra information anyway, performed more poorly. Lower-IQ boys, on the other hand, benefited from having more cues. As was found with the age variable, then, higher-functioning children appear to be more able to invent and use their own self-control strategies. Lower-IQ children may need structured, explicit, and programmed assistance (see Pressley, 1979, for further discussion of this point).

Cognitive tempo. Self-management training has been often used with children who show attention or impulsivity problems. Were it known what type of treatment leads to the most improvement for severely versus mildly impulsive children, we could design more accurate and individualized treatment plans based upon diagnostic material. For example, Jason shows some areas (e.g., coloring, board games) in which he uses a reflective style, whereas Jennifer's mother and teacher could not think of any reflective or passive behaviors which Jennifer enjoys. This difference in what styles and behaviors the children bring to treatment is bound to influence their responsiveness to intervention. Just how the effects are manifested is not clear, but there are some indicators from the literature. One problem plaguing researchers and clinicians who define "impulsivity" via a median-split technique from scores on a cognitive tempo task like the Matching Familiar Figures (MFF) test (Kagan, 1965) is that there is no assurance that their "impulsive" group is comparable to others' "impulsive" groups (Egeland & Weinberg, 1976; Salkind, Note 8). Sinclair (Note 9) actually includes this as a possible explanation for negative results found in a CSI evaluation project. This lack of comparability across studies limits the generalizations drawn below about the importance of the degree of impulsivity initially exhibited by the children. It is not clear where one study's "impulsivity" overlaps with another study's "reflectivity," because the two labels often refer to different scores in different studies. Therefore, even though it is clinically more relevant to determine how impulsive children respond to treatment, studies of both "reflective" and "impulsive" children will be mentioned (see Chapter 8, for a further description of the MFF).

Differences in responsiveness to treatment by reflective and impulsive children have been reported in several studies, although generalizations about self-control training are hard to glean from them. Nelson, Finch, and Hooke (1975) found response cost to be more effective in changing impulsive children's styles, whereas reflective children improved under reinforcement. Brodzinsky, Feuer, and Owens (1977) divided fourth- and seventh-grade children into one of four tempo groups: reflective, impulsive, fast-accurate, and slow-inaccurate. Reflective children were better able than impulsive or slow-inaccurate children to paraphrase multiple meanings of sentences and to detect the ambiguities in the sentences. However, when the experimenter prompted the subjects to find alternative meanings, tempo group differences disappeared, even though the reflective group was not apparently near ceiling level. The prompts, then, facilitated the performance of the impulsive and slow-inaccurate children more than the reflective children. In a self-paced program designed to improve problem-solving skills, Greer and Blank (1977) compared trained and untrained children on MFF tempo scores, conceptual style analytic thinking scores, and problem-solving skills. Children who made either few or an intermediate number of MFF errors (i.e., the more reflective children) who received training were later willing to spend more time solving problems than the comparable untrained subjects. In contrast, the trained children who had made many pretest MFF errors were *less* willing to spend time at problem solving than their untrained high-error peers. The more impulsive (and parenthetically, the low-analytic) children appeared to benefit less from the training program. Because the self-paced program did not control for the amount of time spent with the training materials, one explanation of these findings must remain that the impulsive children did not have comparable exposure to the treatment. In fact, it is unclear whether, in general, reflectives and impulsives differ in their cognitive maturity or in their preferred perceptual processing strategy (Zelniker, Renan, Sorer, & Shavit, 1977). The results of these studies suggest, however, that while impulsive children like Jennifer may require more tangible and structured treatment programs than reflective (or perhaps, less impulsive, as in the case of Jason) children, they can benefit from self-control training of many types. For example, Kendall and Wilcox (1980) recommended combining response-cost contingencies with

CSI treatment. Given the prevalence of impulsivity in the groups of children taught self-management, it is surprising how little is to be concluded from the literature about the importance of this variable as a subject characteristic.

In a study about a related cognitive variable, Malamuth (1979) found no differences in response to CSI training between children who were high versus those who were low on measures of sustained attention or distractibility. It is encouraging to think, then, that self-control training is appropriate for children with a wide range of cognitive styles, although more research clearly is needed before putting confidence in such a conclusion.

Attributional style. A promising style characteristic which may influence a child's response to self-management treatment is that of attributions of personal causation. Whether or not children feel they have control over events in their lives should logically be related more specifically to their responsiveness to being taught self-control (Kopel & Arkowitz, 1975). In our case study examples, for instance, Jason, the child who responded favorably to the Self-Control group, was assessed as having an "internal locus of control"; that is, he attributed successes on his part to his own positive qualities, and failures to such factors as lack of effort and ability. In contrast, Jennifer, perhaps because of her schooling and at-home experiences, attributed events to external causes such as good and bad luck. It is not surprising that the message to "control your own behavior" would be easier to incorporate for Jason than Jennifer. The bulk of the literature relevant to this topic has addressed the issue of whether internally controlled children respond better to internally administered treatment (as in self-management training) and externally controlled children perform preferentially to external feedback. In several cases, perceived control has been used as a dependent variable, the underlying assumption apparently being that an internal locus of control is optimal.

In general, the hypothesis that internal and external perceptions of control or responsibility interact in the expected direction (as stated above) has been supported. Bugental et al. (1977) found that a CSI intervention produced greater improvement than a social reinforcement program for children who were nonmedicated and/or were high scorers (internal attributions) on the perceived personal causality measure (a quantification of structured interview results based on children's perceptions of the importance of potential causal agents for school success and failure). The reinforcement program was more effective in reducing errors for the medicated and low-scoring (external) children. As noted above, however, this study is limited by the lack of random assignment into the medication group. In investigating the suggestion mentioned above that lower-class children prefer extrinsic and middle-class children prefer intrinsic rewards (Zigler & Child,

1969), Baron and Ganz (1972) administered to fifth-grade lower-class black males the Intellectual Achievement Responsibility (IAR) scale (Crandall, Katkovsky, & Crandall, 1965). Children scoring in the Internal or External direction were asked to perform a simple discrimination task under one of three conditions: the experimenter gave correctness feedback (Extrinsic), the child checked his own correctness (Intrinsic), or the child received both types of feedback (Combined). As expected, the Internal group made more correct responses under Intrinsic feedback than did the External group. The External group showed greater improvement under Extrinsic feedback than did the Internals. The Combined feedback was equally effective for both locus-of-control groups. The generality of this finding was illustrated by its replication with lower-class white children and college students (Baron et al., 1974). In a college self-paced course, Blumenfeld, Newman, Johnson, and Taylor (Note 10) found that when students were in control of the pace of the course, the resources, and the amount of information to be studied, the locus-of-control construct was useful in determining the course outcome. In a replication of this study, however, the authors noted no such relationship. In investigating more closely Bandura and Perloff's (1967) finding that self-monitored and externally controlled reinforcers were equally effective, Switzky and Haywood (1974) found that intrinsically motivated children (as selected on Haywood's 1968 Choice Motivator Scale) persisted longer at a task under self-reinforcement whereas extrinsically motivated subjects performed longer under externally controlled rewards. Similar results were noted for older (M age = 134.87 months) but not younger (M = 89.75 months) children by Barling and Patz (1980). Dweck and Repucci (1973) demonstrated the impact of perceived personal responsibility on fifth-grader's response to soluble and insoluble puzzles. With one adult (A1), block design puzzles were always soluble; with another adult (A2) they were always insoluble. After pretraining with these two adults, A2 then presented soluble puzzles. Even though they had been able to solve the puzzles with A1, children who took less personal responsibility for their actions were likely to be unable to solve these new designs given by A2. A parallel though nonsignificant relationship between locus of control and resisting distraction was reported by Patterson and Mischel (1975). Thus, there is quite a bit of compelling evidence that internalized perceptions of control are conducive to responding well to treatments which involve some degree of self-regulation. In contrast, perceived external control appears to interact more favorably with treatments controlled by other people. Both of these methods are possible even within the framework of "self-management," but a clinician needs to be aware of how directive he or she must be in setting up the program for the child, especially at the beginning.

Given the apparent importance of attributional style, it is encouraging to note that internality has been taught to children with some success (Dweck,

1975; Miller, Brickman, & Bolen, 1975; Hanel, Note 11). Blackwood (1970), for example, used mediation training (i.e., rehearsing consequences to misdeeds) to maximize the effects of a traditional behavior modification program. We do *not* have to conclude, therefore, that only "internal" children can profit from self-control interventions. Through reattribution training, children like Jennifer could be brought to the point where they take more responsibility for their own behavior, thus setting the stage for specific self-management training. Crandall and associates' IAR Scale (1965), Nowicki and Strickland's Locus of Control Scale for Children (1973), Haywood's (1968) Choice Motivator Scale, and the Stanford Preschool Internal-External Scale (Mischel, Zeiss, & Zeiss, 1974) seem to be good, validated tools which can be used as we begin to investigate further the impact of attributional style on self-management training methods and effects.

In a few instances, attributional style has been used as a dependent measure of the effectiveness of training programs. In a 6-month follow-up of the Bugental et al. (1977) study, Bugental, Collins, Collins, and Chaney (1978) found that the CSI training group as a whole seemed to show longer-standing increases in perceived control than the reinforcement group who, in turn, showed longer-standing improved teacher ratings. Both groups showed similar decreases in Porteus Maze errors. In another CSI training study, Watson and Hall (Note 6) found that perceived academic responsibility increased for some, but not all, CSI conditions. When CSI was accompanied by relaxation training only, students showed more increased responsibility than when CSI was accompanied by biofeedback and relaxation. No interactions between training type and responsibility were reported. Given the concerns mentioned by Whalen and Henker (1976) about the long-term psychological effects of external types of treatment (e.g., stimulant drugs) on hyperactive children, it is encouraging that self-management training can, indeed, alter children's self-perceptions in a positive direction.

Spontaneous verbalizations. In CSI training in particular, children are taught to manage their own behavior and cognitive approach by verbalizing instructions to themselves. The issue of whether the children actually consistently use the self-instructions, then, would seem to influence their responsiveness to treatment. Unfortunately (given the importance of this issue), it is very difficult to assess whether children are, in fact, using the instructions. An integral part of the CSI training, in fact, involves getting the children to use self-instructions covertly so that, by definition, their use is unobservable. Generally, implementation is assumed when there are actual audible vocalizations, lip movements, or reports of use. While limited, these are probably useful measures, at least at the beginning when the strategies being taught are new to the children. (Compliance to component skills training programs is somewhat easier to assess; self-feedback and evaluation records can be made tangible, at least temporarily. While compliance here is an important issue, it is a general one, and is not related to the use of verbalizations per se).

Only a few CSI programs have reported on the relationship between the use of self-instructions and subsequent performance on criterion tasks. In general, the relationship has been nonsignificant. Higa (Note 12), in a study in which no differences in improvement between a CSI group and a non-CSI direct training group were found, also found no correlation between children's actual use of self-instructions and their task performance. Similarly, in a quasi-CSI intervention, children with writing deficiencies who were taught self-instructions did improve more than children who received direct or no training, but there was a nonsignificant negative relationship between the number of self-instructions the children emitted and the quality of their writing (Robin, Armel, & O'Leary, 1975). Meacham (1978) also found children's motor activity not to be influenced by their use of verbal self-instructions.

In contrast to these rather disheartening findings, several investigators who taught children to instruct themselves in order to increase their self-control in temptation resistance studies have found that higher rates of verbalization correlate positively with better control. When Monahan and O'Leary (1971) attempted to teach self-instruction to decrease rule breaking among urban, northern, black children, they did not find positive effects for the training group as a whole, but there was a strong and significant correlation between the frequency of use of self-instructions and the absence of rule breaking. Fry (1978) taught 7- to 8-year-old children to verbalize overtly, covertly, or both overtly and covertly in order to help them resist playing with a forbidden toy. He watched the children during the task and, according to how much they said and/or the frequency of their lip movements, divided them into "high verbalizers" or "low verbalizers." High verbalizers who had been taught to self-instruct both overtly and covertly were the children who resisted the tempting toy the longest. As described above, Hartig and Kanfer (1973) compared the effect of self-instructions with several different contents on children's resistance to temptation. In the meaningful-content conditions (i.e., positive consequences for nontransgressing, negative consequences for transgressing, and instructions not to transgress), those children who actually did verbalize the coping strategy showed significantly better self-control than nonverbalizers. Finally, preschoolers and kindergarteners were found by Carter et al. (1979) to persist longer when they used the suggested verbalization strategy than when they did not. Thus it appears that, at least in CSI analogue studies, children who obey the directions of the experimenter and actually use the self-instructions do exhibit more self-control than children who do not, audibly or visibly, self-instruct. Whether this is due to an absolute value of internal, regulatory speech or rather to generalized obedience (children who comply with directions to self-instruct also complying with directions to resist temptation) is unclear from these studies. One would hope to find that use of self-instructions correlates with behaviors which are less obviously under simple voluntary control, for example, cognitive skills or problem solving.

This problem of interpretation is partially addressed by studies which record children's spontaneous private speech during task performance. Here, compliance to demands of an adult is not an issue, as the child has not been directed to self-instruct. This approach is limited by there being at least two reasons for a child not exhibiting private speech; these two reasons yield very different conclusions about a child's self-control. Either a child has not yet learned to use private speech to control his behavior, or he has learned to use it so effectively that control occurs through covert speech. In both cases, the child does not speak, but the implications about the degree of self-control expected are obviously opposite. Nevertheless, where performance is found to vary with use of private speech, we can learn something about children's natural development of control. Asarnow and Meichenbaum (1979) assessed whether kindergarteners rehearsed spontaneously while performing a serial recall task. Later they were given CSI training, a rehearsal instruction, or mere practice. Those children who initially showed some use of rehearsal improved at recall regardless of their training condition. Of the nonproducers of rehearsal, CSI training resulted in greater improvement at post-test than the other conditions. Apparently then, for children this age, self-verbalization (either spontaneously-occurring or taught) is related to performance improvement. Kendall and Finch (in press) used amount of verbalization as a dependent measure in a CSI training study. Impulsive children who received CSI training showed greater pretest to post-test gains in verbalization while doing the MFF than did untreated children. Interestingly, although their greater MFF performance improvements were maintained at follow-up, these differences in verbalization rates were still not found, suggesting that the treated children had internalized the self-statements. Martin (Note 13) reported a similar positive relationship between the number of spontaneous vocalizations and delay time in a resistance to temptation situation. The quantity of the vocalizations appeared to be more relevant than the content. Beaudichon (1973) found a relationship between the nature of utterances and a child's performance level on difficult tasks. Children who did better on these difficult tasks tended to use more immediately regulatory private speech. Long-term regulatory utterances did not significantly affect performance. In spite of the limitation noted above about the interpretation of the absence of private speech, the literature on private speech supports its use as an indication of developmental maturity (Kohlberg, Yaeger, & Hjertholm, 1968; Beaudichon, 1973; Fuson, Note 14), impulsivity (Meichenbaum, 1975; Copeland, 1979; Kleiman, Note 15), independence (Kleiman, Note 15), and verbal ability (Kleiman, Note 15), all of which may be more directly relevant factors in predicting a child's response to self-control training (see also Zivin, 1979).

In summary, the cognitive abilities and sets that children bring to self-management training can be widely divergent and require individual attention. More mature, reflective, verbal, and intelligent children, like older children, can benefit from training which is more abstract, self-initiated, and general. Impulsive and less mature children, like younger children, would profit from more structured input. Attributions of causality also may be relevant, in that "internalizers" seem to perform better with internal systems and feedback, while tangible and external programs seem to help "externalizers" more.

Aspects of Training

In this final group of variables are those which describe the previous experience or the current treatment settings which face the child. Inasmuch as these variables describe differences in how children approach the training, they are relevant to our understanding of individual differences.

Pretraining experience. It would be useful to know which pretraining experiences have an impact on a child's responsiveness to treatment, especially where these experiences are modifiable. This is potentially a critical area in self-management research because so many of the hyperactive/aggressive/impulsive children typically treated have a history of many different interventions, some of which may influence the effectiveness of the self-management training. Examples of the most clinically relevant questions would be: "What is the child's motivation to change, and has it been altered by previous repeated failure?" "What is the effect of having taken stimulant drugs for a number of years on the effectiveness of self-management training?" "Are children who have taken drugs for many years more resistant to training than those who have just begun a drug regimen?" "Does a history of being in a strictly externally based behavior modification program over a period of time set up a child to expect failure in self-management training?"

We find, for example, that Jennifer's history of taking medication to control hyperactivity may have taught her, implicitly, that she has no control over her behavior. Some forms of behavior modification, those involving purely external control, could teach a child the same "lesson." The impact of this history obviously is felt when self-management is taught, and thus is important to understand for each child. Unfortunately, no training studies have reported systematically on these variables. Helpful pretraining experiences have been suggested by Meichenbaum (1979) and Kendall (1977), but parametric studies of their utility have not been reported.

At a more "micro-behavior" level, several studies have reported on the impact of various pretraining experiences. Burron and Bucher (1978) reinforced half their sample of 7- to 8-year-olds for self-instructing and then responding in accordance to their self-instructions (Contingent group). The other half were reinforced for instructing themselves to do one thing then actually doing the opposite (Noncontingent group). In a subsequent temptation situation where the children were told not to press a key, subjects in the Noncontingent group broke the rule more often than those in the Contingent condition. While not a very surprising finding, this study highlights the importance of reinforcement contingencies as they accompany self-instructions. Karoly and Kanfer (1974) demonstrated a similar reliance on previous experience by children who were asked to play "The Scarecrow Game" (a measure of tolerance that involves holding one's arms out to the side for as long as possible). Before this game, however, children had experiences in the experimental setting in which contracts with the experimenter had been kept, were kept but were accompanied by a reprimand, were not made at all, or were broken either to the benefit or detriment of the child. For example, in the beneficial broken contract group, a contract promised that one piece of candy would be given for a boring task, but two were actually given. Children having no contract experience played the Scarecrow Game least long, while children in the beneficial broken contract condition played it significantly longer than any other group. Thus, different experiences with adults influence children in their later self-control performance.

Prior experience in the form of specific pretraining has, in addition, been found to improve self-control. Zelniker and Oppenheimer (1973) initially trained children to discern distinctive features of drawings by having them choose from a group of pictures the one which was different from the others. These children showed performance superior to that of children trained on the MFF (in which only one picture of a group matches a sample exactly) on a subsequent transfer task. The former group apparently learned to process the features of the task more accurately, thus improving their later performance. Bem (1967) found that 3-year-olds had trouble following instructions to press a lever the same number of times as the number of lights that were switched on a board. Four-year-olds were able to follow these directions. The 3-year-olds were then taught first with feedback and then with self-instructions, and were subsequently able to perform the task. As stated above, perhaps many of the subject characteristics which prove to be relevant in predicting the success of CSI training can be, themselves, taught initially.

Therapist variables. The type of model, or therapist, used in conducting self-management training would seemingly be a treatment, not a subject, characteristic. As the model and child interact, however, changes in the approach of the child to the task may develop. Certainly, the quality of the relationship would logically be related to improvement. Therapists' ratings of the quality of their relationships with the children during CSI training, for example, were found to be positively related to the classroom teachers' ratings of the children's self-control and to MFF error and latency improvement (Kendall & Wilcox, 1980). In addition, the children's ratings of their relationships with the therapists correlated positively with the therapists' ratings of the child's improvement. The importance of the different kinds of model-child relationships was also suggested by a CSI training program with natural change agents (Glenwick & Barocas, 1979). Impulsive fifth-and sixth-graders were taught CSI techniques by the experimenter, their parents, their teachers, both parents and teachers, or were not taught to them at all. Academic achievement improved for all children in CSI groups, but there were a few differential responses to treatments which depended on who served as the model. If parents were involved in the training, they rated out-of-school behavior as improved; possibly a placebo effect. When teachers were the only models, children improved on block design and on Porteus Maze performance. Some of the teacher ratings of behavior dropped for those children who received no CSI training or training only by their parents. The long-standing and dominant relationships that the child has with the model, then, may be influential in determining the quality of the approach the child takes to training.

Besides the model-child relationship, the similarity perceived by the subjects between the model and themselves has been found to affect the success of other types of treatments (Jakibchuk & Smeriglio, 1976) as well. Socially nonresponsive preschoolers were shown a videotape of a child moving from solitary to group play. The narrator of the film (always a child's voice) spoke in the first person or the third person as he described the child's actions. Comparison groups observed a control or no videotape. The first-person-narrated videotape was clearly superior to the other conditions in affecting the subjects' social responsiveness both at an immediate post-test and at a 3-week follow-up assessment. The authors suggest that the differential success of this condition might be due to a greater perceived similarity to the model, higher levels of attention to a first-person narrator, or greater ease in remembering the self-instructions when they are already in the first person. Regardless of which of these explanations is or are correct, they suggest the desirability of peer therapists/tutors for CSI training. A more definitive statement would require a study in which the effects of an adult and a child model were compared. Finally, Masters and Binger (1978) found that inhibition of activity among 4-year-old boys *and* girls was much less with a female experimenter than with a male experimenter.

Therapist/model characteristics, as they interact with subject variables, then, clearly deserve closer attention. Akamatsu and Thelen (1974) have reviewed the importance of observer characteristics in the general modeling literature; further discussion of this topic is available there.

Affect of the situation. Inasmuch as the affect of a therapy situation influences the affect, the approach, and thus potentially the behavior, of the child (Pressley, 1979), we should consider those variables which impinge on a child during treatment. Santrock (1976) observed the effect on task persistence of happy versus sad versus neutral self-statements, happy versus sad versus neutral experimenter affect, and a "happy" versus "sad" versus "neutral" room. Children who heard happy self-statements persisted longer than those who heard sad or neutral statements, but only when the experimenter appeared happy and had told a happy story. There was a trend for the effects to be additive, such that the greatest persistence was shown by children in a happy room with a happy experimenter, hearing happy self-statements. The second least persistence was shown by the group exposed to a sad setting, sad experimenter, and sad self-statements. Similarly, in varying the affective and cognitive content of the statements children were instructed to say, Masters and Santrock (1976) were able to influence task persistence. Evaluations of the enjoyment, difficulty, and success of the game, the affective tone of the statements, and pleasantness of an accompanying thought were all varied in separate experiments. In each case, positive affect tended to result in greater task persistence. Moore, Clyburn, and Underwood (1976) had preschoolers think "happy," "sad," or neutral thoughts while they attempted to delay gratification. Delays tended to be longest for children, especially girls, who thought "happy" thoughts and shortest for those thinking "sad" thoughts. What the experimenter provides for the child, then, in terms of affective atmosphere clearly influences the self-control exhibited.

CLINICAL AND RESEARCH IMPLICATIONS

Many studies of how to teach children self-control have been reviewed here, with an emphasis on deriving information about what kinds of children are most responsive to the many treatment variations. Despite extensive examination, only a few firm conclusions can be made about what characteristics of children are important to consider when planning self-control treatments for them. Few of the studies examined individual differences per se, and fewer still reported on how individual differences interacted with different types of treatment. Hopefully, however, many ideas can be generated by this search to guide clinical and research endeavors.

Figure 7.1 illustrates the sorts of variables which indicate different types of training and feedback.

A brief summary of the characteristics which appear to be most related to responsiveness to treatment can be outlined here. It is at this point, as much from a theoretical rationale as an empirical one, that these guidelines for future work are proposed. Future investigations are needed to confirm or disconfirm the accuracy and usefulness of each of the following suggestions:

1. It appears that cognitive maturity (as a function either of age or intellectual ability) influences response to treatment. Specifically, younger children may respond better to the more concrete and structured self-control instructions, needing a fuller description of what to do to help themselves. In contrast, older children seem to be able to generate their own ideas and preferences, and may transfer the training effects more readily if they have been taught general, more abstract rules.

2. Attribution of personal causality, while not yet firmly linked to responsiveness to specific self-management training per se, is a variable which deserves our close attention. Internality apparently is related to success with self-modulated feedback and externality with other-controlled feedback.

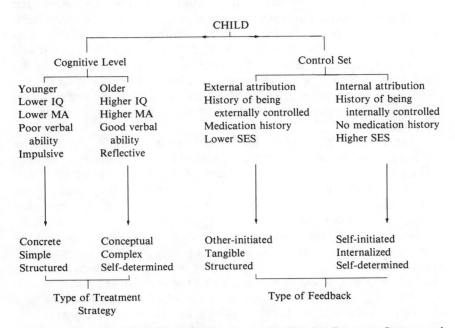

Fig. 7.1. Flow Chart of Decision-Making Process in Choosing Treatment Strategy and Feedback

Conversely, there appears in the literature a real value put on having internal perceptions of control, in the absolute sense (i.e., regardless of how it interacts with treatment). Successfully learning self-control may, in fact, teach internality to children. Thus, the interaction of attribution and self-control is a potentially fruitful area for further investigation.

3. Cognitive tempo is obviously a relevant variable in this area, given the emphasis on altering impulsivity. As might be expected, however, reflective children are generally more responsive to self-control training than are the children who need it more, the impulsive ones. Most likely is the explanation that self-management fits more easily with the existing behavior of reflective children; impulsive children are being asked to alter their behavior in a more profound way. Nevertheless, self-control training has been successful with both groups, given the proper structure. How the treatment needs to be altered to maximize its effectiveness for impulsive children is still not clear. Probably increased structures and more tangible and frequent feedback will be conducive to treatment success for them.

4. Theoretically it would make sense to recommend being very careful to ensure that children who are being taught verbal self-instructions actually verbalize to themselves. Naturalistic observations of spontaneous vocalization and research on resistance to temptation support the notion that (appropriate) verbalization improves self-control. Surprisingly, several self-management studies have found no relationship between use of self-instructions and improvement in self-control. Thus, it is only tentatively that the suggestion can be made to stress the importance of making sure the children actually use our verbal instructions. It would be interesting and important to know whether (and for whom) the act of deriving one's own instructions rather than being urged to use the therapist's leads to greater compliance.

5. Finally, there is a group of individual difference variables about which we have only initial information concerning their relevance to self-management training. In each case, main effects or interactions with treatment outcome have been noted, but inconsistently or inconclusively so. These variables include social class, race, residential location, medication status, and conditions in the treatment setting. Their impact on individual children's learning of self-management needs to be examined closely.

In short, some guideposts exist, and we should start exploring systematically each of the pathways before us. Until we can delineate the optimal recipients of self-management training, we will be prescribing and administering it ineffectively. Until we know which treatment is best for a given type of child, some children will be helped in an inefficient way. Two directions are available to researchers who wish to clarify how to maximize the effectiveness of self-management training: parametric analysis of the interaction of the individual difference variables with several types of self-control training; and examination of the modifiability of the variables which prove to be relevant. These directions, described more fully below, are clearly interlinked and can be pursued simultaneously.

First, and most basically, a need exists to understand how to match children and treatments. This, of course, has been the premise of this entire review. Specifically, these questions should be asked: Which subject variables are important to consider in self-management training, and which are not? What level of a relevant subject variable is associated with maximum responsiveness to a given treatment? What are the treatment variables which can be manipulated to fit various types of children? How do the treatment variants interact with the different levels of the relevant subject variable factors? Finally, can we learn about the importance of any individual difference variables as they influence theory-specific components separately (e.g., self-monitoring, self-reinforcement)? This requires a rather fine-grained analysis which is far from accessible from the current literature, but would be helpful in the future.

Methodologically, several options exist for the researcher interested in these questions. Given a large enough sample, a multiple regression analysis of the impact of several variables on different treatment outcomes is the soundest approach (Cronbach & Snow, 1977). Smaller, more applied research studies will probably need to rely on factorial analyses. Splitting subjects into two (e.g., internal versus external; high IQ versus low IQ) or more (e.g., young and intermediate versus old; upper and middle versus lower class) groups even when the variables are continuous is a common practice. Unfortunately, much information is lost this way; subjects very similar to each other but who fall on different sides of the dividing line are compared to each other in a test for group differences. A conservative estimate of the importance of a subject characteristic is the result of such an approach. Thus, where possible, programmatic exploration of the importance of related individual difference characteristics should include enough subjects and an appropriate design to permit multiple regression analyses. In this way, the impact of the various subject characteristics on two or more treatments can be determined by examining differences in regression lines.

The second major direction for researchers interested in matching children and treatments concerns the possibility of modifying the children to optimize their responsiveness to treatment. Actually, this is the converse of the position advocated throughout most of this paper; but both positions may have merit. Specifically, instead of choosing different treatments for different children, can we change the child so he or she will respond better to a given treatment? Lest this sound rather Orwellian, it should first be pointed out that only a few variables are probably alterable (e.g., personal attribution, motivation to change, pretraining experience), while many are not (e.g., age, race, residence, SES). An independent decision would have to be made about the ethics of modifying a child's characteristics in a direction associated with more responsiveness to CSI treatment. For example, would we be willing to "make" children more internally controlled if it would improve the success of self-management training? Would we take him or her off a prescribed drug? Would we put him or her *on* drugs? Are there any helpful pretraining practices which would be objectionable to the overall welfare of the child? Although these questions are extremely important, they may well be answered in a way that will allow us one more avenue for helping impulsive children.

REFERENCE NOTES

1. Mischel, W., Mischel, H. N., & Hood, S. W. *The development of knowledge of effective ideation to delay gratification.* Unpublished manuscript, Stanford University, 1978.
2. Toner, I. J., Moore, L. P., & Kidder, P. J. *The effect of serving as a model of self-control on subsequent resistance to deviation in children.* Paper presented at the meeting of the Society for Research in Child Development, 1977.
3. Robertson, L. B., Kendall, P. C., & Urbain, E. S. *Cognitive-behavioral treatments with children: A multistudy analysis of the function of socioeconomic status (SES) in treatment outcome and generalization.* Paper presented at the meeting of the Association for Advancement of Behavior Therapy, 1979.
4. Casey, W. M. *Teaching children to be honest through verbal self-instructions.* Paper presented at the meeting of the Eastern Psychological Association, 1978.
5. Leon, J. A., & Pepe, H. J. *Self-instructional training: Cognitive behavior modification as a resource room strategy.* Unpublished manuscript, 1978.
6. Watson, D. L., & Hall, D. L. *Self-control of hyperactivity.* Unpublished manuscript, La Mesa–Spring Valley School District, San Diego, 1977.
7. Schleser, R., Meyers, A., & Cohen, R. *Cross-task consistency as a function of cognitive level and instructional package.* Unpublished manuscript, Memphis State University, 1978.
8. Salkind, N. J. *Norms for the Matching Familiar Figures Test.* Unpublished manuscript, University of Kansas, 1977.
9. Sinclair, C. *Cognitive versus social-behavioral training in the generalization of a self-instructional program for impulsive children.* Unpublished masters thesis, University of Calgary, 1976.
10. Blumenfeld, G. J., Newman, I., Johnson, A., & Taylor, T. *Relationships of student characteristics and achievement in a self-paced CMI application.* Paper presented at the meeting of the American Psychological Association, 1979.
11. Hanel, J. *Der Einfluss eines Motivänder—ungsprogramms auf schulleistung-sschwache misserfolgsmotivierte grandschüler der 4 Klasse.* Unpublished diploma thesis, Psychologisches Institut der Ruhr-Universität, 1975. Cited in H. Heckhausen, Fear of failure as a self-reinforcement and motive system. In I. Sarason, & C. Spielberge (Eds.), *Stress and anxiety* (Vol. 2). Washington, D. C.: Hemisphere, 1975.
12. Higa, W. *Self-instructional versus direct training in modifying children's impulsive behavior.* Unpublished doctoral dissertation, University of Hawaii, 1973.
13. Martin, R. *Spontaneous private speech and the mediation of behavior in a resistance-to-temptation paradigm.* Unpublished manuscript, Ball State University, 1978.
14. Fuson, K. C. *Developmental patterns on speech-for-self.* Paper presented at the meeting of the Society for Research in Child Development, 1979.

15. Kleiman, A. *The use of private speech in young children and its relation to social speech.* Unpublished doctoral dissertation. University of Chicago, 1974.

REFERENCES

Akamatsu, T. J., & Thelen, M. H. Review of the literature on observer characteristics and imitation. *Developmental Psychology,* 1974, *10,* 38–47.

Anderson, L., Fodor, I., & Alpert, M. A comparison of methods for training self-control. *Behavior Therapy,* 1976, *7,* 649–658.

Asarnow, J. R., & Meichenbaum, D. Verbal rehearsal and serial recall. The mediational training of kindergarten children. *Child Development,* 1979, *50,* 1173–1177.

Bandura, A., & Perloff, B. Relative efficacy of self-monitored and externally imposed reinforcement systems. *Journal of Personality and Social Psychology,* 1976, *7,* 111–116.

Barkley, R. A., Copeland, A. P., & Sivage, C. A self-control classroom for hyperactive children. *Journal of Autism and Developmental Disorders,* 1980, *10,* 75–89.

Barling, J., & Patz, M. Differences following self and external reinforcement as a function of locus of control and age: A social learning analysis. *Personality and Individual Differences,* 1980, *1,* 79–85.

Baron, R. M., Cowan, G., Ganz, R. L., & McDonald, M. Interaction of locus of control and type of performance feedback: Considerations of external validity. *Journal of Personality and Social Psychology,* 1974, *21,* 124–130.

Baron, R. M., & Ganz, R. L. Effects of locus control and type of feedback on the task performance of lower-class black children. *Journal of Personality and Social Psychology,* 1972, *21,* 124–130.

Beaudichon, J. Nature and instrumental function of private speech in problem-solving situations. *Merrill-Palmer Quarterly,* 1973, *19,* 117–135.

Bem, S. Verbal self-control: The establishment of effective self-instruction. *Journal of Experimental Psychology,* 1967, *74,* 485–491.

Bender, N. N. Verbal mediation as an instructional technique with young trainable mentally retarded children. *Journal of Special Education,* 1977, *11,* 449–455.

Birch, D. Verbal control of nonverbal behavior. *Journal of Experimental Child Psychology,* 1966, *4,* 266–275.

Blackwood, R. The operant conditioning of verbally mediated self-control in the classroom. *Journal of School Psychology,* 1970, *8,* 251–258.

Bornstein, P. H., & Quevillon, R. P. The effects of a self-instructional package on overactive preschool boys. *Journal of Applied Behavioral Analysis,* 1976, *9,* 179–188.

Bowers, K. S. Situationism in psychology: An analysis and a critique. *Psychological Review,* 1973, *80,* 307–336.

Brodzinsky, D., Feuer, V., & Owens, J. Detection of linguistic ambiguity by reflective, impulsive, fast accurate, and slow inaccurate children. *Journal of Educational Psychology,* 1977, *69,* 237–243.

Brophy, J. E., & Evertson, C. M. *Low-inference observational coding measures and teacher effectiveness.* Austin: University of Texas, 1973. (ERIC Document Reproduction Service No. ED 077879).

Bugental, D. B., Collins, S., Collins, L., & Chaney, L. A. Attributional and behavioral changes following two behavioral management interventions with hyperactive boys: A follow-up study. *Child Development,* 1978, *49,* 247–250.

Bugental, D. B., Whalen, C. K., & Henker, B. Causal attributions of hyperactive children and motivational assumptions of two behavior-change approaches: Evidence for an interactionist position. *Child Development,* 1977, *48,* 874–884.

Burron, D., & Bucher, B. Self-instructions as discriminative cues for rule breaking or rule following. *Journal of Experimental Child Psychology*, 1978, *26*, 46–57.

Carter, D. B., Patterson, C. J., & Quasebarth, S. J. Development of children's use of plans for self-control. *Cognitive Therapy and Research*, 1979, *3*, 407–413.

Copeland, A. P. Types of private speech produced by hyperactive and nonhyperactive boys. *Journal of Abnormal Child Psychology*, 1979, *7*, 169–177.

Craighead, W. E., Wilcoxon-Craighead, L., & Meyers, A. W. New directions in behavior modification with children. In M. Hersen, R. M. Eisler, & P. M. Miller (Eds.), *Progress in behavior modification* Vol. 6. New York: Academic Press, 1978.

Crandall, V. C., Katkovsky, W., & Crandall, V. G. Children's belief in their own control of reinforcements in intellectual-academic achievement situations. *Child Development*, 1965, *36*, 91–109.

Cronbach, I. J. The two disciplines of scientific psychology. *American Psychologist*, 1957, *12*, 671–684.

Cronbach, L. J. Beyond the two disciplines of scientific psychology. *American Psychologist*, 1975, *30*, 116–127.

Cronbach, L. J., & Snow, R. E. *Aptitudes and instructional methods.* New York: Irvington, 1977.

Denney, D. R. The effects of exemplary and cognitive models and self-rehearsal on children's interrogative strategies. *Journal of Experimental Child Psychology*, 1975, *19*, 476–488.

Dweck, C. S. The role of expectations and attributions in the alleviation of learned helplessness. *Journal of Personality and Social Psychology*, 1975, *31*, 674–685.

Dweck, C. S., & Repucci, D. Learned helplessness and reinforcement responsibility in children. *Journal of Personality and Social Psychology*, 1973, *25*, 109–116.

Egeland, B. Training impulsive children in the use of more efficient scanning techniques. *Child Development*, 1974, *45*, 165–171.

Egeland, B., & Weinberg, R. A. The Matching Familiar Figures Test: A look at its psychometric credibility. *Child Development*, 1976, *47*, 483–491.

Ekehammar, B. Interactionism in personality from a historical perspective. *Psychological Bulletin*, 1974, *81*, 1026–1048.

Fry, P. S. Resistance to temptation as a function of the duration of self-verbalization. *British Journal of Social and Clinical Psychology*, 1978, *17*, 111–116.

Genshaft, J. L., & Hirt, M. Race effects in modifying cognitive impulsivity through self-instruction and modeling. *Journal of Experimental Child Psychology*, 1979, *27*, 185–194.

Glenwick, D. S., & Barocas, R. Training impulsive children in verbal self-control by use of natural change agents. *Journal of Special Education*, 1979, *13*, 387–398.

Greer, R. N., & Blank, S. S. Cognitive style, conceptual tempo, and problem solving: Modification through programmed instruction. *American Educational Research Journal*, 1977, *14*, 295–315.

Guralnick, M. J. Solving complex perceptual discrimination problems: Techniques for the development of problem-solving strategies. *American Journal of Mental Deficiency*, 1976, *81*, 18–25.

Hagen, J. W., Meacham, J. A., & Mesibov, G. Verbal learning, rehearsal and short-term memory. *Cognitive Psychology*, 1970, *1*, 47–58.

Hartig, M., & Kanfer, F. H. The role of verbal self-instructions in children's resistance to temptation. *Journal of Personality and Social Psychology*, 1973, *25*, 259–267.

Haywood, H. C. Motivational orientation of over-achieving and under-achieving elementary school children. *American Journal of Mental Deficiency*, 1968, *72*, 662–667.

Jakibchuk, A., & Smeriglio, V. L. The influence of symbolic modeling on the social behavior of preschool children with low levels of social responsiveness. *Child Development*, 1976, *47*, 838–841.

Jensen, L., & Buhanan, K. Resistance to temptation following three types of motivational instructions among four-, six-, and eight-year old female children. *Journal of Genetic Psychology*, 1974, *125*, 51–59.

Kagan, J. Impulsive and reflective children: Significance of conceptual tempo. In J. D. Krumbolz (Ed.), *Learning and the Educational Process*. Chicago: Rand-McNally, 1965.

Kanfer, F. H. Self-management methods. In F. H. Kanfer & A. P. Goldstein (Eds.), *Helping people change*. New York: Pergamon, 1975.

Kanfer, F. H., Karoly, P., & Newman, A. Reduction of children's fear of the dark by competence-related and situational threat-related verbal cues. *Journal of Consulting and Clinical Psychology*, 1975, *43*, 251–258.

Karoly, P. Behavioral self-management in children: Concepts, methods, issues, and directions. In M. Hersen, R. M. Eisler, & P. M. Miller, Eds., *Progress in behavior modification*. Vol. 5. New York: Academic Press, 1977.

Karoly, P., & Dirks, M. J. Developing self-control in preschool children through correspondence training. *Behavior Therapy*, 1977, *8*, 398–405.

Karoly, P., & Kanfer, F. H. Effects of prior contractual experiences on self-control in children. *Developmental Psychology*, 1974, *10*, 459–460.

Kendall, P. C. On the efficacious use of verbal self-instructional procedures with children. *Cognitive Therapy and Research*, 1977, *1*, 331–341.

Kendall, P.C., & Finch, A. J. Analyses of changes in verbal behavior following a cognitive-behavioral treatment for impulsivity. *Journal of Abnormal Child Psychology*, in press.

Kendall, P. C., & Wilcox, L. E. Cognitive-behavioral treatment for impulsivity: Concrete versus conceptual training in non-self-controlled problem children. *Journal of Consulting and Clinical Psychology*, 1980, *48*, 80–91.

Kohlberg, L., Yaeger, J., & Hjertholm, E. Private speech: Four studies and a review of theories. *Child Development*, 1968, *39*, 691–736.

Kopel, S., & Arkowitz, H. The role of attribution and self-perception in behavior change: Implications for behavior therapy. *Genetic Psychology Monographs*, 1975, *92*, 175–212.

La Voie, J. C. Cognitive determinants of resistance to deviation in seven-, nine-, and eleven-year-old children of low and high maturity of moral judgment. *Developmental Psychology*, 1974, *10*, 393–403.

Luria, A. R. *The role of speech in the regulation of normal and abnormal behavior*. New York: Liveright, 1961.

Malamuth, Z. N. Self-management training for children with reading problems. Effects on reading performance and sustained attention. *Cognitive Therapy and Research*, 1979, *3*, 279–289.

Masters, J. C., & Binger, C. G. Interrupting the flow of behavior: The stability and development of children's initiation and maintenance of compliant response inhibition. *Merrill-Palmer Quarterly*, 1978, *24*, 229–242.

Masters, J. C., & Mokros, J. R. Self-reinforcement processes in children. In H. W. Reese (Ed.), *Advances in child development and behavior*. Vol. 9. New York: Academic Press, 1974.

Masters, J. C., & Santrock J. W. Studies in the self-regulation of behavior. Effects of contingent cognitive and effective events. *Developmental Psychology*, 1976, *12*, 334–348.

Meacham, J. A. Verbal guidance through remembering the goals of actions. *Child Development*, 1978, *49*, 188–193.

Meichenbaum, D. Theoretical and treatment implications of developmental research on verbal control of behavior. *Canadian Psychological Record*, 1975, *16*, 22–27.

Meichenbaum, D. *Cognitive-behavior modification*. New York: Plenum, 1977.

Meichenbaum, D. *Cognitive Behavior Modification Newsletter*, 1979, *4*.

Meichenbaum, D., & Goodman, J. The developmental control of operant motor responding by verbal operants. *Journal of Experimental Child Psychology*, 1969, *7*, 553–565.

Meichenbaum, D., & Goodman, J. Training impulsive children to talk to themselves: A means of developing self-control. *Journal of Abnormal Psychology*, 1971, *77*, 115–126.

Miller, R., Brickman, P., & Bolen, D. Attribution versus persuasion as a means for modifying behavior. *Journal of Personality and Social Psychology*, 1975, *31*, 430–441.

Miller, D. T., Weinstein, S. M., & Karniol, R. Effects of age and self-verbalization on children's ability to delay gratification. *Developmental Psychology*, 1978, *14*, 569–570.

Mischel, W. Toward a cognitive social learning reconceptualization of personality. *Psychological Review*, 1973, *80*, 252–283.

Mischel, W. & Metzner, R. Preference for delayed reward as a function of age, intelligence, and length of delay interval. *Journal of Abnormal and Social Psychology*, 1962, *64*, 425–431.

Mischel, W. & Patterson, C. Substantive and structural elements of effective plans for self-control. *Journal of Personality and Social Psychology*, 1976, 34, 942–950.

Mischel, W., Zeiss, R., & Zeiss, A. Internal-external control and persistence: Validation and implications of the Stanford Preschool Internal-External Scale. *Journal of Personality and Social Psychology*, 1974, *29*, 265–278.

Monahan, J., & O'Leary, K. D. Effects of self-instruction on rule-breaking behavior. *Psychological Reports*, 1971, *29*, 1059–1066.

Moore, B. S., Clyburn, A., & Underwood, B. The role of affect in delay of gratification. *Child Development*, 1976, *47*, 273–276.

Murray, J. D. Spontaneous private speech and performance on a delayed match-to-sample task. *Journal of Experimental Child Psychology*, 1979, *27*, 286–302.

Nelson, W. J. Jr., & Birkimer, J. C. Role of self-instruction and self-reinforcement in the modification of impulsivity. *Journal of Consulting and Clinical Psychology*, 1978, *46*, 183.

Nelson, W. M., Finch, A. J., & Hooke, J. F. Effects of reinforcement and response cost on cognitive style in emotionally disturbed boys. *Journal of Abnormal Psychology*, 1975, *84*, 426–428.

Norton, G. R., & Lester, C. J. The effects of modeling and verbal cues on concept acquisition of moderate retardates. *Cognitive Therapy and Research*, 1979, *3*, 87–90.

Nowicki, S., & Strickland, B. A locus of control scale for children. *Journal of Consulting and Clinical Psychology*, 1973, *40*, 148–155.

Palkes, H., Stewart, M., & Kahana, B. Porteus maze performance after training in self-directed verbal commands. *Child Development*, 1968, *39*, 817–826.

Patterson, C., & Mischel, W. Plans to resist distraction. *Developmental Psychology*, 1975, *11*, 369–378.

Pressley, M. Increasing children's self-control through cognitive interventions. *Review of Educational Research*, 1979, *49*, 319–370.

Ridberg, E. H., Parke, R. D., & Hetherington, E. M. Modification of impulsive and reflective cognitive styles through observation of film-mediated models. *Developmental Psychology*, 1971, *5*, 369–377.

Robin, A. L., Armel, S., & O'Leary, K. D. The effects of self-instructions on writing deficiencies. *Behavior Therapy*, 1975, *6*, 178–187.

Sagotsky, G., Patterson, C. J., & Lepper, M. R. Training children's self-control: A field experiment in self-monitoring and goal-setting in the classroom. *Journal of Experimental Child Psychology*, 1978, *25*, 242–253.

Santrock, J. W. Affect and facilitative self-control: Influence of ecological setting, cognition, and social agent. *Journal of Educational Psychology*, 1976, *68*, 529–535.

Shure, M., & Spivack, G. Means-ends thinking, adjustment and social class among elementary school-aged children. *Journal of Consulting and Clinical Psychology*, 1972, *38*, 348–353.

Switzky, H. N., & Haywood, H. C. Motivational orientation and the relative efficacy of self-monitored and externally imposed reinforcement systems for children. *Journal of Personality and Social Psychology*, 1974, *30*, 360–366.

Toner, I. J., Holstein, R. B., & Hetherington, E. M. Reflection-impulsivity and self-control in preschool children. *Child Development*, 1977, *48*, 239–245.

Toner, I. J., & Smith, R. A. Age and overt verbalization in delay-maintenance behavior in children. *Journal of Experimental Child Psychology*, 1977, *24*, 123–128.

Van Duyne, H. J. Age and intelligence factors as predictors of the development of verbal control of nonverbal behavior. *The Journal of Genetic Psychology*, 1974, *124*, 321–331.

Vygotsky, L. S. *Thought and language*. New York: Wiley, 1962.

Whalen, C. K., & Henker, B. Psychostimulants and children: A review and analysis. *Psychological Bulletin*, 1976, *83*, 1113–1130.

Whalen, C. K., Henker, B., Collins, B. E., Finck, D., & Dotemoto, S. A social ecology of hyperactive boys: Medication effects in structured classroom environments. *Journal of Applied Behavior Analysis*, 1979, *12*, 65–81.

Williams, D. Y., & Akamatsu, T. J. Cognitive self-guidance training with juvenile delinquents: Applicability and generalization. *Cognitive Therapy and Research*, 1978, *2*, 285–288.

Wolf, T. M. A developmental investigation of televised modeled verbalization on resistance to temptation. *Developmental Psychology*, 1972, *6*, 537.

Wolf, T. M. Effects of televised modeled verbalizations and behavior on resistance to deviation. *Developmental Psychology*, 1973, *8*, 51–56.

Zelniker, T., & Oppenheimer, L. Modification of information processing of impulsive children. *Child Development*, 1973, *44*, 445–450.

Zelniker, T., Renan, A., Sorer, I., & Shavit, Y. Effect of perceptual processing strategies on problem solving of reflective and impulsive children. *Child Development*, 1977, *48*, 1436–1442.

Zigler, E., & Child, I. L. Socialization. In G. Lindzey & E. Aronson (Eds.), *The handbook of social psychology*. Vol. 3. Reading, Mass.: Addison-Wesley, 1969.

Zivin, G. (Ed.), *The development of self-regulation through private speech*. New York: Wiley, 1979.

8

Assessing the Cognitive and Behavioral Components of Children's Self-Management*
Philip C. Kendall
and
Carolyn L. Williams

The emergence of self-management as an acceptable topic for scientific inquiry did not occur without challenges. Those who espoused a radical behavioral position emphasizing that patterns of human action are functionally related to environmental factors were not eager to accept the "self" or "person" as a component of behavior (see Chapter 2, this volume). The Skinnerian perspective (Skinner, 1971) continues to present the argument that an individual's behavioral repertoire, self-concept, and even life-purpose are modifiable by environmental manipulation. While the demonstrations that environmental manipulations can alter these and other targets are continuing to be produced by researchers, such data do not imply that the same behaviors cannot be controlled through self-management. In fact,

*This chapter was completed while the first author was at the Center for Advanced Study in the Behavioral Sciences. We are grateful for financial support provided by the National Institute of Mental Health (#5-T32-MH14581-05) and the MacArthur Foundation. We are also grateful to the University of Minnesota Graduate School for grants in support of research related to children's self-control (#441-0749-5236-02; #440-0160-4909-02).

a literature has emerged which indicates the powerful influence of self-management skills on behavior.

Efforts to appraise the process of self-management from a behavioral perspective have been enlightening, but a less than complete explanatory system has led to the recent efforts to better understand the "self" component of self-management. As is becoming evident in both the theoretical and research literatures, the self-component is loaded heavily with cognitive processing variables. Complete knowledge about self-management requires that both behavioral and cognitive factors be considered.

ASSESSMENT METHODS

Psychological assessment methods for the measurement of children's self-control include behavioral observations, analogue tasks, rating scales, self-assessments, psychological tests, and less-employed methods such as archival records and interviews. Observational assessment procedures provide a methodology for assessing the frequency of certain behaviors; for example, attention to a task, or record keeping during self-monitoring. Children have been asked to solve picture problems and to complete verbal scenarios. While these tasks are not projective in the sense that responders project unconscious material onto ambivalent or formless content, they often require the child to describe an event or tell a story so the examiner can evaluate a cognitive processing skill. Rating scales, completed by parents and/or teachers, offer data that represent how the child is seen by other adults, while sociometric procedures provide the perspective of other children. Since the child is in the best position to report thoughts, feelings, or beliefs, self-report inventories have also been seen as appropriate. However, the use of self-reports requires the child's ability to read and understand the items and to reflect on personal history (though brief) to be able to answer accurately. Archival records, such as the incidences of disruptive classroom behavior, can be included in an assessment of self-control, though such records often show extreme variation in quality over time. Finally, interviews often result in a high completion rate (but it may at times be more important to interview parents or teachers than the children themselves).

Behavioral Observations

Two major contributions of behavioral assessment have been its emphasis upon systematic use and evaluation of observational procedures and its emphasis on situational specificity. As a result, psychologists recognize that they can no longer rely solely on information available in their offices, but must observe their client's behavior directly in naturalistic settings. Although once proclaimed to be the panacea for all the problems associated with the more traditional assessment methods, behavioral observations are now considered in a more balanced fashion. That is, before the late 1960s, behavioral observations were believed to give an accurate, reliable, valid, and objective presentation of the client's behavior, even though these characteristics often were not directly studied. However, current behavioral assessors are studying the reliability (see papers in *Journal of Applied Behavior Analysis*, 1979, *12*, No. 4), validity (e.g., Abikoff, Gittelman-Klein, & Klein, 1977; see also comments by Haynes & Kerns, 1979), and reactivity (e.g., Nelson, Kapust, & Dorsey, 1978) of their observational procedures.

A wealth of information derived from empirical studies is being accumulated, describing some of the limitations of observational procedures and how to control for the problems inherent in their use. Kent and Foster (1977) and Cone and Foster (in press) provide excellent summaries of these studies. For instance, behaviorists designing observation systems are considering the expectation biases of the observers, reactivity of the procedures, biases in the methods of estimating reliability, differences in the various types of observational procedures (e.g., *in vivo* versus one-way mirrors), and training of the observers. More confidence can be placed in the data obtained from observations when these issues are resolved.

Although much of children's self-management and self-control relies on cognitive processes not directly observable by outsiders, behavioral observations have a role in the assessment of self-management and self-control. For instance, the ultimate goal of any therapeutic program is the control of the behavior that led to the child's being referred. Can a treatment be considered completely successful if only changes in cognitive processes are demonstrated, with no demonstrable changes in overt behavior? After all, children are referred for fighting, not for thinking aggressive thoughts! Since the goal of cognitive-behavioral training is improved thinking *and* behaving (Kendall & Hollon, 1979), behavioral observations can play an important part in treatment evaluation.

Before treatment is initiated, behavioral observation can be used to delineate the problem behavior(s) and the conditions(s) under which the problems are exacerbated. It is at this point that the clinician considers treatment possibilities and decides whether self-management or self-control training is indicated. Karoly (1981) points out that *no problem is a self-management problem by definition*. For example, we cannot assume that a child's obesity or school failure is due to a lack of self-management skills. Both can be accurately attributed to a variety of other things. Obesity can be the result of parental feeding practices (e.g., a parent feeding the child high-caloric foods), and school failure can be associated with a physical deficit (e.g., a hearing or vision problem). Comprehensive behavioral observations help to specify the problem behaviors by describing the antecedents and consequences of the behavior. In addition, Evans and Nelson (1977) suggest an ecological assessment. Features of the environment, such as where the child sits in class, may be contributing to the behavior problem.

Unfortunately, behavioral observations are not suited for all types of target behaviors. Asher, Renshaw, Geraci, and Dor (Note 1) described some of the problems inherent in the use of naturalistic observations in the classroom to assess peer acceptance. Among the problems are the low frequency of relevant behaviors (e.g., sharing, aggression), increasing diversity of relevant behaviors with increasing age, lack of opportunity to emit relevant behaviors in the classroom, and relevant behaviors that are too difficult to code reliably (e.g., sense of humor, conceit). Karoly (1981) also suggested that many of the target behaviors for self-management training are difficult to observe. Among the behaviors he lists are stealing, lying, self-critical thoughts, daydreaming, between-meal eating, and covert self-instruction. On the other hand, behaviors that are observed in self-regulation research include, for example, talking out or making inappropriate noise without the permission of the teacher, hitting or physically annoying other students, and leaving desks to go to unassigned or inappropriate activities (Bolstad & Johnson, 1972).

Despite the many problems in the use of behavioral observations, several procedures are available to the clinician and/or researcher. Two examples of home observations are the codes developed by Patterson, Ray, Shaw, and Cobb (Note 2) and Forehand, Peed, and Roberts (Note 3). Patterson and associates' observational system focuses on family interactions, with trained observers recording 29 behavioral categories in an interval recording procedure. The family is observed one hour before their dinner, while remaining in two adjoining rooms (to ease the observers' task) and without watching television (to facilitate interactions). Each family member is observed for two 5-minute intervals. Behaviors of both the target family member and those interacting with him or her are recorded. Frequency data on the variety of behaviors can be examined to isolate self-control deficits and to assess therapeutic changes.

Forehand and associates' (Note 3) system focuses on the mother-child interaction of children between the ages of 2 and 8 years in either the home or the clinic. Forehand et al. also require restrictions, such as no television during the observation period. Their interval system, described in Forehand, Sturgis, McMahon, Aguar, Green, Wells, and Breiner (1979), permits the recording of both parent behaviors and sequential child-parent behaviors. The recorded parent behaviors are (1) rewards, (2) alpha commands — orders, rules, suggestions, or questions to which a motoric response is appropriate and feasible, (3) beta commands — those to which a child has no immediate opportunity to demonstrate compliance, and (4) use of a time-out procedure. The recorded sequential child-parent behaviors are (1) child compliance to a parental alpha command within 5 seconds, (2) child noncompliance to a parental alpha command within 5 seconds, and (3) contingent attention of the parent to the child following child compliance. Again, frequency data provide a basis for identifying self-control deficits and evaluating self-produced behavior change. Both systems, Patterson et al. (Note 2) and Forehand et al. (Note 3), have been used in empirical studies (e.g., Forehand et al., 1979; Patterson, Cobb, & Ray, 1973; Patterson, 1974; Peed, Roberts, and Forehand, 1977).

Classroom observations are more common than are home observation procedures, and a number of classroom observational systems, as well as instances when only one or two behaviors of interest to a particular investigator are coded, are described in the literature. Behaviors thought to be incompatible with academic learning are often observed. Cobb (1972, 1973) developed a system used for observing attentional focusing in the classroom. Trained observers recorded children's behavior during structured academic tasks, such as group discussions and individual academic work. The behavioral categories in Cobb's system are: attending, talking to the teacher (positive and negative), interacting with peers (positive and negative), volunteering, initiating to the teacher, complying, self-stimulation, inappropriate locale, playing noisy, not complying, looking around, and not attending. Cobb (1972) reported that observers can use this system reliably after 4 hours of training and that, for example, observations of attending taking during arithmetic lessons correlated in the .65 range with standardized arithmetic test scores. An observation system developed by O'Leary, Romanczyk, Kass, Dietz, and Santogrossi (Note 4) allows for observations of both child and teacher behaviors. Trained observers code 9 categories of disruptive child behavior and 11 categories of teacher behavior in 20-second intervals. The system does not, however, allow for recording student-teacher interaction. Forehand et al. (1979) present a school coding system used to examine whether the results of a parent training program generalize to the classroom. Two categories of child behavior (compliance and inappropriate behavior) and two categories of teacher behavior (commands and attention) are coded.

Classroom observations also are used to assess children's interpersonal or social behaviors, although the problems associated with observations are particularly troublesome in these cases. Nevertheless, several promising observation systems have been employed (e.g., Hymel & Asher, Note 5; Gottman, Gonzo, & Rasmussen, 1975; Wahler, 1975). The work of Gottman and his colleagues led them to the conclusion that the measure of *frequency* of peer interactions is insensitive to treatment outcome and is a questionable criterion for identifying socially isolated or rejected children (Gottman, 1977a, 1977b; Gottman, Gonzo, & Schuler, 1976). Therefore, their system goes beyond mere frequency count and includes qualitative measure of social interactions such as dispensing positive reinforcers verbally, peer interaction neutral, and alone and off task (Gottman et al., 1975). Measures of the qualitative aspects of children's self-controlled behavior should also be developed.

Kendall and his colleagues used behavioral observations to provide validational support for the Self-Control Rating Scale (Kendall & Wilcox, 1979; Kendall, Zupan, & Robertson, Note 6). In the first study, the subjects' behavior was observed during an individual testing session with an examiner (Kendall & Wilcox, 1979). An independent observer recorded the following child behaviors: off-task verbal behavior; off-task physical behavior; off-task attention; out of seat; and interruptions. Kendall et al. (Note 6) adapted this code for classroom observations by retaining the first four measures, eliminating the fifth, and adding "bugging others verbally and physically."

The observation systems described thus far require trained nonparticipant observers. While such observers are important in basic research and in an empirical demonstration of treatment efficacy, practicing clinicians seldom have the time or resources to employ them. Often, clinicians resort to participant observers (e.g., parents, teachers, even peers). Participant observers are useful for low-frequency target behaviors: when the amount of time required for the observation of even a few instances of the behavior might prohibit the use of nonparticipant observers. Teachers (e.g., Osborne, 1969) and parents (e.g., Friedman, 1980; Graziano & Mooney, 1980; Hall, Axelrod, Tyler, Grief, Jones & Robertson, 1972) have been trained to provide the data. Reliability checks can be made by the clinician, or as in the case of the Hall et al. (1972) study, by a spouse, a neighbor, a sibling, or an aunt. As is true for all observation systems, observer training and systematic reliability checks are important considerations with participant observers.

Karoly (1981) suggests two potential problems with using parents as observers: their intimate relationship with the child may interfere with their producing reliable, valid data; and the clinician may not have the required time to provide the extensive training necessary to ensure "objective" home observations. Karoly's solution, which he reports using in his clinical work, requires parents to unobtrusively turn on a tape recorder whenever the problem behavior occurs. Tape recorders can be used automatically at critical points during the day (e.g., getting up in the morning, dinner time, bedtime) or switched on when the problem behavior occurs (e.g., a fight with a sibling). The tape provides a permanent record of the child's and other's behaviors, which the clinician can review in his or her office.

Analogue Tasks

Common among the methods for assessing children's self-control are analogue tasks. "Analogues" provide situations in which self-management responses are possible and desirable. Whereas a child may not have the opportunity to emit self-management responses during a naturalistic observation period, analogue tasks are designed to ensure the possibility of these responses occurring when unobtrusive observers are present to record the child's behavior. Thus, analogue tasks are more cost-efficient than naturalistic observations (see Nay, 1977, for a consideration of the larger domain of analogue assessments). However, analogue procedures are useful only to the extent to which they produce data which are generalizable to real world behaviors.

Resistance to temptation procedures. Perhaps the most common of the analogue tasks are resistance-to-temptation procedures. Like other analogues, resistance-to-temptation tasks vary and do not consist of a standad method used by all researchers and clinicians. Individuals often adopt the procedures to their particular setting and for their own purposes. Nevertheless, there is consistency in that resistance-to-temptation analogues place the child in a conflict situation where there is free access to some but not all desirable objects or rewards. The child's behavior in the tempting conflict is observed. These analogues typically seek to produce situations where one can observe a child's ability to inhibit undesirable behavior.

Forbidden toy procedure. In the forbidden toy procedure, the child typically is placed in a room equipped for unobtrusive observation (e.g., with microphones and a one-way mirror) and is told that he or she can play with one toy (usually a less attractive one) but not with another (a more attractive one). The child is left alone in the room, and his or her behavior is observed (e.g., latency to first transgression; number of transgressions). Karoly and Briggs (1978) and LaVoie (1974) provide examples of this procedure.

Several investigators modified different aspects of the forbidden-toy procedure to obtain additional or different information about children's self-control responses. Fry (1978) added a component to the procedure which assessed the duration of a child's self-verbalization after various training sessions and before the forbidden toy procedure. Children were taken individually to the room with the forbidden toy and explained the rules. In a second room the child received one of three types of self-instruction training about the rules (overt speech, covert speech, and a combination of the two). At this point, the child was left alone in the second room for 15 minutes. The child was encouraged to practice the self-instructions by talking to a puppet, which was equipped with a hidden microphone. An observer timed the duration of the child's self-verbalizations. The results indicated that this duration measure was related to the child's subsequent performance in the room with the forbidden toy. Children who were high self-verbalizers had higher latency scores (time in seconds to first transgression) than did the low self-verbalizers.

Sawin and Parke (1979) examined the relative effectiveness of the content of self-instructions for first and second grade boys in a forbidden toy procedure. In the experimental task, the boy was left alone with a toy crane and a toy tank for 10 minutes. He was instructed that he could play with the tank, but not the crane. The boys were assigned to one of the following groups: self-instruction training with a prohibitive rule *and* a redirective instruction (i.e., "I'm not allowed to play with the crane, but I am allowed to play with the tank."), self-instruction training with the prohibitive rule only (i.e., "I'm not allowed to play with the crane."); self-instruction training with the redirective instruction only (i.e., "I'm allowed to play with the tank."); and no self-instruction training. During the task, an observer recorded the frequency and duration of touching the prohibited toy, the number of times the subject verbalized the instructions aloud, and the number of audible irrelevant verbalizations. The results showed that for first- and second-grade boys, training in the prohibitive self-instruction produced less deviant behavior. However, training in the redirective self-instruction resulted in reduced deviant behavior only among the second-graders, and increased deviant behavior for the first-graders. We are reminded here of Luria's (1961) description of the impellent function of language for younger children and its more controlling functions for older children.

Another version of the forbidden toy procedure does not give the child the option of playing with the less attractive toy. Instead, the child is forbidden to play with or touch any of the toys in the room. Toner, Parke, and Yussen (1978) illustrate the procedure. Children in their study were left in a room by themselves with five forbidden toys. The child's behavior was observed during the 6 minutes of isolation for the total number of times he or she touched the toys, the total duration of transgression, and the total number of imitations of a model's behavior (shown to the child prior to the procedure). Their measures of the number of transgressions and the duration of transgression were sensitive to their treatment conditions, whereas the number of imitations was not.

Grusec, Kuczynski, Rushton, and Simutis (1979) added a work component and a tempter (either a "talking table" or a young woman) to the procedure. Children in their first experiment were asked to sort a collection of approximately 300 cards into neat, same-colored piles. Also in the room with the child was "Charlie the friendly table" who had several attractive toys on and around him. Charlie was equipped with a tape-recorder speaker which enabled him to attempt to distract the child every 1.5 minutes by asking the child to leave the cards and play with Charlie. Several variables were studied in their first experiment. In one group the child was told by the experimenter and Charlie that most children yielded and played with Charlie, whereas the other group was told that most children ignored Charlie and completed their work. The children were also exposed to one of three modeling conditions: a yielding model who played with Charlie, a resisting model who ignored Charlie, or a no-model control. The child was left alone in the room with Charlie and instructed to sort the cards. Unobtrusive observers recorded the latency to first approaching Charlie's table, the total duration of transgression throughout the temptation phase, and the length of time spent sorting the cards. On both immediate and delayed tests, children exposed to the yielding model deviated more quickly and longer than the control group. Children who saw the resisting model deviated less quickly and worked longer than the control group. The expectancy manipulation yielded no significant results. In the second experiment reported in Grusec et al. (1979), a similar procedure was used, except Charlie was replaced by a real woman, and the models offered rationales for their choices. On several of the measures, only resisting models or resisting models who offered rationales were effective. The desire to gather certain types of clinical data may require that assessments involve an alteration in procedures. Variations such as those used in Grusec et al. (1979) are examples for adaptive use of the forbidden toy analogue.

Although the forbidden-toy procedures have been used with preschool children, Peele and Routh (1978) noted that 3-year-old and younger children often become very upset when left in a room by themselves. As a result, Peele and Routh (1978) studied the mother and child together. In their modification of the forbidden-toy procedure, a mother and her 3-year-old child were placed in a room divided into four quarters by masking tape on the floor. Each quadrant contained a table and chair. In the three forbidden quadrants, identical toys were on each table. The fourth quadrant, where the mother and child were instructed to stay, contained two chairs, the table, a magazine, and the same toys as the other quadrant (toys-present condition) *or* no toys at all (toys-absent condition). Mothers were instructed to keep their children in the one quadrant by whatever method they chose. Mothers and children were tested in each condition for 15 minutes. Observers recorded the presence of three child behaviors (time spent touching any forbidden toy, time spent in any type of vocalization, and quadrant changes) and seven maternal behaviors (time in instruction and command, time praising child, time in vocal disapproval or criticism, time in other conversation, time in physical contact, time in engaging child in appropriate activity, and time reading magazine). Peele and Routh (1978) found that children who entered off-limit areas most often had mothers who issued instructions and commands. Children who spent the most time self-vocalizing spent the least time playing with forbidden toys, thus seeming to have the best self-control. Also, since the child's vocalizations were not related meaningfully to any of the maternal behaviors, Peele and Routh

(1978) suggested that children's self-vocalizations may be related to the degree of self-control of which the child is capable. This issue merits further study.

Delay of gratification tasks. The second type of resistance to temptation procedure, the delay of gratification tasks, gives the child a choice between having an immediate, less-desirable reward or waiting some designated period of time for a more desirable reward. In some studies, the child is left alone in a room to wait with some type of device (e.g., a bell) enabling him or her to signal the experimenter to return. The child is told that if he or she signals the experimenter, he or she will recieve the less preferred reward. If the child waits a preset period of time (e.g., 20 minutes) for the experimenter to return, without signaling, he or she receives the preferred reward. The child's behavior, usually how long he or she waits, is recorded. Again, as with the forbidden toy tasks, a number of variations in these and related procedures exist.

Mischel (1974) gives a very complete description of his and his colleagues' work with delay-of-gratification tasks. One of the variations he has used with the procedure is "Mr. Talk Box," a method for determining what the children actually are doing during the waiting period. Mr. Talk Box (essentially a tape recorder and a microphone) speaks to the child and tells him or her that he loves for children to fill his "big ears . . . with all the things they think and feel, no matter what." From then on, Mr. Talk Box is very nondirective and a good Rogerian, reinforcing the child's speech with "ahems" and "ahas." Mischel (1974) reports that Mr. Talk box is effective with many children who engage in long and lively discussions with him and thus unknowingly reveal their waiting strategies to psychologists.

A significant variation in the delay-of-gratification procedure described by Mischel (1974) is whether the child is left to wait with the actual rewards present, with a symbolic representation of them, or with no rewards present. Mischel (1974) reports studies which demonstrate that children wait longer when the rewards are *not* present than when they are present. However, children waited even longer when the rewards were symbolically present compared to the rewards-not-present condition. Symbolic presentation of the rewards has been accomplished by showing slides of them to the child during the waiting periods (Mischel & Moore, 1973).

Mischel (1974) suggested another feature of the delay-of-gratification tasks which might influence the child's responses: whether the child is left with nothing to do during the waiting period or whether he or she has "work" to do. Although the Mischel and Moore (1973) study found no main effects for their waiting-working variable, Mischel (1974) pointed out that no firm conclusions could be drawn at that time regarding working and waiting tasks, since their working task (tapping a key) was dull and repetitive and might not have been substantially different than the waiting period for the subjects.

A recent study (Patterson & Carter, 1979) demonstrated differences in working and waiting conditions within delay-of-gratification procedures. In their working task, children were asked to help feed "Baby Bird," a quart jar altered to resemble a hungry yellow bird. The child was instructed to feed Baby Bird marbles until they reached a bright yellow line painted at the top of the jar. Children in the waiting condition were asked to wait in the room with Baby Bird. Patterson and Carter (1979) also varied the presence of the rewards: half the children in each condition had the rewards present; for the other half, the rewards were absent. Their results revealed that children in the working condition waited significantly longer when the rewards were present than when they were absent. However, children in the waiting condition waited significantly longer when the rewards were absent. These results suggest that the cognitive dimensions of children's effective self-control in working situations may differ substantially from those in waiting conditions.

Lewittes and Israel (1978) demonstrated that children who believe their behavior leads to consequences for other children will delay longer. A marshmallow and a pretzel were used as rewards. Children were assigned to one of four groups: (1) knowing that their behavior would lead to same consequences for other children they did not know; (2) knowing that their behavior would lead to the same consequences for their classmates who knew the subject's responsibility; (3) same as 2, but the classmates did not know of the subjects' responsibility; and (4) a no-other-person consequence. The authors suggested that the children probably viewed the longer delay as a more mature, prosocial behavior, and delayed more when others would be affected by their behavior.

Considerable variation exists in the types of rewards used by different investigators and clinicians. Some are consumable (e.g., pretzels and marshmallows) and some have acquired secondary reinforcement value (e.g., money and tokens). Patterson and Carter (1979) used award certificates (Good Player Awards) and obtained similar voluntary behavior as with the seemingly more salient reinforcers. As Mischel (1974) pointed out, selection of the rewards is important. They must provide a high-conflict situation. That is, they must be sufficiently different that one is preferable to the other, yet the difference must also be small enough that the immediately available reward is tempting throughout the waiting period. A pretesting of the rewards seems indicated.

Delay of gratification tasks involve a trade-off of value and time. The reward value is either high or low and the delivery time is either now or at some point in the future. For example, Kendall and Wilcox (1979) offered each child as a reward for cooperation the choice between a pencil that he or she could have "right now" (at the end of testing) or a felt-tipped Flair pen for which he or she would have to wait until tomorrow. Children's delay of gratification, as assessed by their choice, was not meaningfully related to other tests and observations of self-controlled behavior (Kendall & Wilcox, 1979). It is possible that the delay of gratification task used by Kendall and Wilcox (1979) was insensitive, since there was only one item, limited choices, and a pretesting of the child's actual preference was not conducted. In a subsequent study, Kendall et al. (Note 6) offered children a more elaborate delay-of-gratification option. In this study, four rewards were offered, with children's specific reward preferences determined prior to the task. That is, each child was given the choice between their first-preferred reward tomorrow or their least-preferred reward right now. As in the Kendall and Wilcox (1979) study, this delay of gratification assessment was not meaningfully related to other self-controlled behaviors or to teachers' self-control ratings.

Although resistance-to-temptation analogue tasks are usually fun for the children and relatively easy for the psychologist to implement, there are several factors to consider when designing a resistance to temptation analogue task. Minimal requirements include a suitable room with observation equipment and trained observers. In the forbidden-toy procedure, the child has to be assured of privacy and unobtrusive observation is crucial. Important also are the selection of appropriate toys for the forbidden-toy task and appropriate rewards for the delay-of-gratification task. Consider, for example, what it would mean if a child did not touch the forbidden toy because he or she had the same one at home or if another child waited for the pretzel because he or she was allergic to marshmallows. In the delay-of-gratification procedure, the child also has to be sure that he or she will actually receive the delayed reward if he or she waits. The child's trust in the experimenter needs to be established, or in the least, assessed, before confidence is placed on the findings from the task. A recent study's report that procedural variations other than the prohibitive rule can influence a child's valuation of the entire toy set underlines the importance of methodological considerations (Hom & Maxwell, 1979).

Ethical issues need to be considered when using resistance-to-temptation tasks. Sawin and Parke (1979) described two ethical problems: the procedures require that the subjects' behavior be observed without their knowledge, thus necessitating a cover story, and the subjects who engage in deviant behavior may experience guilt. In order to alleviate these problems, Sawin and Parke (1979) included a pleasant play period for the child with an accepting and nurturant experimenter immediately after their resistance-to-temptation task. They also decided against a formal debriefing for their first- and second-grade subjects because they felt some of the children would have difficulty understanding the reasons for the study and might experience an exacerbation of any guilt feelings with such an explanation.

A final consideration in the use of delay of gratification procedures is the findings of the Kendall and Wilcox (1979) and Kendall et al. (Note 6) studies. In these two separate studies providing a matrix of correlations representing the interrelationships of multimethod self-control assessments, a delay-of-gratification task was not found to be significantly correlated with almost all of the other assessments (see data presented later in table 8.2). One must question, therefore, whether the brief delay-of-gratification assessment provides clinically meaningful data or whether the findings are limited to other narrowly defined value/time trade-off situations.

Scarecrow game. A different type of self-control from that which is assessed by the resistance to temptation procedures is the self-control that is required to allow a child to endure an unpleasant, immediate situation for longer–term goals. Studying in order to earn a good grade is often offered as an example of this type of situation. The self-control necessary in these situations is much less studied, probably due to the hesitancy of researchers to place children in "aversive" situations (Karoly, 1977). Karoly and his colleagues (Karoly & Dirks, 1977; Karoly & Kanfer, 1974) have offered the "scarecrow game" as a solution to this dilemma. Preschool and elementary school children are challenged to see if they can imitate a scarecrow by extending their arms at shoulder level for as long as possible. The duration of their arm extension is taken as a measure of the children's tolerance to aversive stimulation. Karoly (1977) reports that the scarecrow game is reliable when the children are given practice trials, sensitive to various treatments, and can be used to assess the effectiveness of different socialization agents in the child's environment (e.g., does the child perform longer for his or her teacher or mother?).

The scarecrow task was also administered as part of the multimethod assessment of self–control (Kendall et al., Note 6). Correlations between the child's tolerance for aversive stimulation and other measures (e.g., ratings, tests) of self-control were not meaningful. These data underscore the specificity of any single operationalization of aversive tolerance within the broad construct of self-control.

Self-reinforcement tasks. A number of analogue tasks designed to assess children's self-reinforcement have been described in the literature. These tasks usually involve giving the child some type of work to do and access to tangible rewards (e.g., money, tokens, and candy). The child is instructed to use the rewards for self-reinforcement of performance on the task. Bandura and Perloff (1967) introduced one of the first of these analogues, a wheel-turning task. Children aged 7 to 10 were asked to help the experimenter test some game equipment. The children were presented with a rectangular box with an attached wheel and indicator lights signifying the performance levels. Different number of complete turns of the wheel would illuminate different lights. The apparatus also contained an automatic chip dispenser which delivered plastic tokens at the press of a button. The children were told the tokens were redeemable for toys at the conclusion of the session.

Winston, Torrey, and Labbee (1978) varied the wheel-turning task of Bandura and Perloff (1967) in order to allow the child more freedom to shift his or her performance standards. Children in their study worked on the wheel-turning task in sessions on four consecutive days. The children were allowed to set their own criteria for how many wheel turns would earn a token. Tokens were exchanged immediately for either 2 or 10 seconds of cartoon viewing time. Children could follow one of two strategies to increase their cartoon viewing time: lower their standards for self-reinforcement, or turn the wheel faster to maintain high standards for self-reinforcement. The results showed that the children lowered their standards to gain more tokens and decreased their rate of wheel-turning across the sessions. This result was even more apparent for children in the 2-second exchange condition. The presence or absence of an adult in the room did not have a significant effect on the children's performance.

Tasks more ecologically meaningful than wheel turning are also used in analogue assessment of self-reinforcement. Felixbrod and O'Leary (1973, 1974) used 300 arithmetic problems (15 sheets with 20 problems per sheet) in their analogue. Jones adopted this task in group (Jones & Evans, 1980) and multiple baseline (Jones & Ollendick, 1979) design studies of the external influences on children's self-reinforcement. Jones' work is important for he demonstrates that variables in addition to self-reinforcement may be operating in these analogue situations. Jones, Nelson, and Kazdin (1977) reviewed the literature on self-reinforcement and concluded that events preceding the self-reinforcement procedure (history), whether a behavioral goal was specified to the subject (criterion-setting), whether the subject observed and recorded his behavior (self-monitoring), whether an external agent monitored the subject's behavior and/or delivery of reinforcement (surveillance), what the explicit instructions to the subjects were (instructional sets), whether the subjects were free of external contingencies under which self-reinforcement was administered (external contingencies on the self-reinforcing response), and whether there was external control or demand characteristics on the target behavior (external contingencies on the target behavior) were all potentially important influences on self-reinforcement. Psychologists wishing to assess children's self-reinforcement need to be aware of the issues affecting self-reinforcement and aware that self-reinforcing behaviors are only a small part of self-control and self-management.

Attribution tasks. Assessments of children's attributional styles appears to be a promising area for research on the effectiveness of self-control/self-management therapies. This is the case for two reasons. First, to the extent that a child attributes outcomes to his or her own behavior, the greater the likelihood that a self-control treatment will *match* the child's personal understanding of behavior. In contrast, self-control treatments might experience "philosophical rejection" from children with external attributional preferences. The first step in treating a child with an external preference might be to remediate this attributional style. The second reason relates to internalization of treatment outcome. Here, it would be desirable to find changes in self-control-treated children's attributions. The greater the success of self-control procedures, the greater the child's acceptance of personal responsibility for response outcomes. Analogue conditions which require a child to make causal attributions about the reasons for behavior provide samples of the child's perception of personal responsibility for those behaviors.

Whereas self-report inventories are frequently used to assess children's attributions, analogue tasks have also been used (see also Metalsky & Abramson, 1981, for a discussion of the assessment of attributions). Typically, attributional assessments with children require the child to work on a task programmed by the experimenter (unbeknownst to the child) to be either a success or failure experience for the child. The child is then asked to explain his or her performance. Causal attributions are the individuals' own explanation for the causes of their behavior — they disambiguate from many possible causes the person's perceived cause for the behavior in question. While adults may generate various causal explanations, children are often provided with a list of possibilities from which to choose.

Diener and Dweck (1978) used a procedure similar to that just described to study "learned helplessness" in children. Their task consisted of a three-dimension, two-choice discrimination problem in which the child searched for the one solution that was correct. The children were given extensive training on hypothesis testing before they were exposed to the failure condition. After the eight training problems, the child continued with the four test problems, always being told that his or her answer was "wrong." After the fourth problem, the child was asked, "Why do you think you had trouble with these problems?"

In the second study reported in Diener and Dweck (1978), the same procedure was used with the added component of asking the child to "think out loud." All verbalizations were transcribed verbatim. The child was asked to think out loud on the last two of the training problems and all four of the failure problems so that changes following failure could be noted. An important aspect of their procedure was that the experimenter tried to ensure that the child was proud of his or her performance before he or she left the experiment by telling each child that he or she did so well that the experimenter gave four harder problems intended for older children. Diener and Dweck (1978) divided the children into helpless and mastery-oriented groups (using the Intellectual Achievement Responsibility Scale: Crandall, Katkovsky, & Crandall, 1965). Their results showed that helpless children attributed failure to lack of ability; whereas mastery-oriented children made few attributions, but instead engaged in self-monitoring and self-instructions. Using the same task, Diener and Dweck (1980) reported that, compared to mastery-oriented children, helpless children underestimated the number of successes, overestimated the number of failures, did not attribute success to ability, and did not expect success to continue. To the extent that children who can engage in self-control are mastery oriented, these findings suggest that a child with a deficit in self-control might make less satisfactory attributions than a mastery child. Perhaps a child who learns to engage in self-controlled behaviors (a mastery experience) would come to make attributions consistent with a sense of personal control. More importantly, for present purposes, these studies offer useful methodology for the time-efficient and potentially fruitful measurement of children's attributions (cf., also Harter's chapter in this volume).

Ames and Felker (1979) provide another example of a task used to assess attributions. Children in their study were required to trace over all the lines of a puzzle, without retracing any line. There were solvable and insolvable versions of the puzzles. The puzzles were placed in six different stacks of 10 puzzles each in front of the child. The child was instructed to select one puzzle from each stack and solve them. In the success condition, five of the stacks had solvable puzzles and one stack contained insolvable puzzles; in the failure condition, five stacks had insolvable puzzles and one stack had solvable puzzles. Several dependent measures were used after the puzzle-solving tasks. Children were shown a pie graph consisting of two colors, one representing skill and the other representing luck. Children were to use the graph to indicate how much of their performance was attributable to skill and how much was attributable to luck. A score was obtained by taking the number of exposed degrees of each color and dividing by 10. Measures of self-reinforcement and self-punishment were also taken. Subjects were asked to estimate the number of stars (1 to 10) they deserved for their performance. Finally, measures of self-congratulations for the success condition and measures of self-criticism for the failure condition were taken by reading five statements to the subjects. Examples of self-congratulations are "I'm a good worker, I feel smart" and examples of self-criticisms are "I feel bad, I really did a lousy job." Children circled yes or no for the statement indicating if it described what they felt like saying.

Rating Scales

Characteristic of the rating scale method of assessment is the fact that an observer (rater) places the person being rated at a point along a continuum to which a numerical value has been assigned. Rating scales consist of a series of items each of which requires the rater to make a specific assessment. There are numerous methodologies for developing rating scales and there are numerous uses for them.

Within the domain of children's self-management, parents and teachers are valuable sources of data about the target children. These significant members of the child's environment are not typically trained observers of specific target behaviors; however, they do observe children for extended periods of time and potentially are providers of useful data. Rating scales can provide an appropriate and valuable assessment methodology. For example, examination of the generalization of treatment effects requires assessment in extra-therapy settings. In the case of self-control training, parents' and teachers' ratings of children in the home and/or classroom can provide valuable information. Adult ratings of target children's behavior are also important, since the adult is often the source of the referral and correspondingly the one whose evaluation of and satisfaction with the effects of treatment is sought.

An early attempt to use the rating scale methodology to assess self-controlled behaviors in children was the Impulsive Classroom Behavior Scale (Weinrich, Note 7). A brief nine-item rating scale, the ICBS, has been used for an indication of treatment-produced changes in the classroom (Kendall & Finch, 1978). However, psychometric properties of the ICBS have not been investigated very much.

More recently, Kendall and Wilcox (1979) developed a rating scale specifically for the assessment of children's self-control. The Self-Control Rating Scale (SCRS) was developed for use by teachers and parents in the study of (a) the generalization of self-controlled behavior to extra-therapy settings following therapeutic intervention and (b) the nomological network of relationships associated with self-control in children. The SCRS consists of 33 items, each of which is rated on a 7-point scale. Descriptive anchor words are provided at the end of the continuum for each item (see table 8.1). The Number 4 at the center of the 7-point scale is underlined to designate it as characteristic of the average child. The positions along the rating scale are expressly defined on the basis of the characteristics of the given population of children. Deviations below and above the 4 are indications of greater than average or less than average degrees of self-control, respectively. Table 8.1 presents the instructions, items, and rating format of the SCRS.

Of the 33 items, 10 are descriptive of self-controlled action (e.g., item 8).

Table 8.1.   Kendall-Wilcox Self-Control Rating Scale

Please rate this child according to the descriptions below by circling the appropriate number. The underlined 4 in the center of each row represents where the average child would fall on this item. Please do not hesitate to use the entire range of possible ratings.

1. When the child promises to do something, can you count on him or her to do it?

   1 2 3 <u>4</u> 5 6 7
   always   never

2. Does the child butt into games or activities even when he or she hasn't been invited?

   1 2 3 <u>4</u> 5 6 7
   never   often

3. Can the child deliberately calm down when he or she is excited or all wound up?

   1 2 3 <u>4</u> 5 6 7
   yes   no

4. Is the quality of the child's work all about the same or does it vary a lot?

   1 2 3 <u>4</u> 5 6 7
   same   varies

5. Does the child work for long-range goals?

   1 2 3 <u>4</u> 5 6 7
   yes   no

6. When the child asks a question, does he or she wait for an answer, or jump to something else (e.g., a new question) before waiting for an answer?

   1 2 3 <u>4</u> 5 6 7
   waits   jumps

7. Does the child interrupt inappropriately in conversations with peers, or wait his or her turn to speak?

   1 2 3 <u>4</u> 5 6 7
   waits   interrupt

8. Does the child stick to what he or she is doing until he or she is finished with it?

   1 2 3 <u>4</u> 5 6 7
   yes   no

9. Does the child follow the instructions of responsible adults?

   1 2 3 <u>4</u> 5 6 7
   no   yes

10. Does the child have to have everything right away?

   1 2 3 <u>4</u> 5 6 7
   yes   no

11. When the child has to wait in line, does he or she do so patiently?

   1 2 3 <u>4</u> 5 6 7
   yes   no

12. Does the child sit still?

   1 2 3 <u>4</u> 5 6 7
   yes   no

13. Can the child follow suggestions of others in group projects, or does he or she insist on imposing his or her own ideas?

   1 2 3 <u>4</u> 5 6 7
   able to follow   imposes

14. Does the child have to be reminded several times to do something before he or she does it?

   1 2 3 <u>4</u> 5 6 7
   never   always

Table 8.1. (Cont.)

15. When reprimanded, does the child answer back
inappropriately?

1 2 3 <u>4</u> 5 6 7
never   always

16. Is the child accident prone?

1 2 3 <u>4</u> 5 6 7
no   yes

17. Does the child neglect or forget regular chores
or tasks?

1 2 3 <u>4</u> 5 6 7
never   always

18. Are there days when the child seems incapable
of settling down to work?

1 2 3 <u>4</u> 5 6 7
never   often

19. Would the child more likely grab a smaller toy
today or wait for a larger toy tomorrow, if
given the choice?

1 2 3 <u>4</u> 5 6 7
wait   grab

20. Does the child grab for the belongings of
others?

1 2 3 <u>4</u> 5 6 7
never   often

21. Does the child bother others when they're trying to do things?

1 2 3 <u>4</u> 5 6 7
no   yes

22. Does the child break basic rules?

1 2 3 <u>4</u> 5 6 7
never   always

23. Does the child watch where he or she is going?

1 2 3 <u>4</u> 5 6 7
always   never

24. In answering questions, does the child give one
thoughtful answer, or blurt out several answers
all at once?

1 2 3 <u>4</u> 5 6 7
one answer   several

25. Is the child easily distracted from his or her
work or chores?

1 2 3 <u>4</u> 5 6 7
no   yes

26. Would you describe this child more as careful
or careless?

1 2 3 <u>4</u> 5 6 7
careful   careless

27. Does the child play well with peers (follows
rules, waits turn, cooperates)?

1 2 3 <u>4</u> 5 6 7
yes   no

28. Does the child jump or switch from activity to
activity rather than sticking to one thing at a
time?

1 2 3 <u>4</u> 5 6 7
sticks to one   switches

29. If a task is at first too difficult for the child,
will he or she get frustrated and quit, or first
seek help with the problem?

1 2 3 <u>4</u> 5 6 7
seek help   quit

30. Does the child disrupt games?

1 2 3 <u>4</u> 5 6 7
never   often

Table 8.1. (Cont.)

31. Does the child think before he or she acts?

    1 2 3 <u>4</u> 5 6 7
    always   never

32. If the child paid more attention to his or her work, do you think he or she would do much better than at present?

    1 2 3 <u>4</u> 5 6 7
    no   yes

33. Does the child do too many things at once, or does he or she concentrate on one thing at a time?

    1 2 3 <u>4</u> 5 6 7
    one thing   too many

Source: From P. C. Kendall & L. E. Wilcox. Self-control in children: Development of a rating scale. *Jounal of Consulting and Clinical Psychology*, 1979, *47*, 1020–1029. SCRS copyright Philip C. Kendall, 1979.

Another 13 items are indicative of impulsivity (e.g., item 20) and the last 10 are worded to denote both possibilities (e.g., item 7). The anchor words are arranged such that scoring the SCRS is accomplished by totaling the ratings for each individual item. The higher the SCRS score, the greater the child's lack of self-control. Lower SCRS scores indicate more self-control.

In an initial investigation of the SCRS, Kendall and Wilcox (1979) had teachers provide self-control ratings of 110 randomly selected third- to sixth-grade children and assessed the childrens' IQ, chronological and mental age, Matching Familiar Figures (MFF) test, Porteus Maze performance, delay of gratification choice, and classroom behavior using behavioral observations. The intercorrelations are provided in table 8.2.

The SCRS was found to be significantly correlated with latency and error scores from the MFF test (shorter latencies and more errors related to a lack of self-control), the Q score from the Porteus Maze, and behavioral observations taken in a testing situation. Only the SCRS shows convergence (significant correlations) with the majority of other data. The absence of significant correlations with IQ and MA provides discriminant validity, in that differences in SCRS scores are not associated with intellective differences among the children. Because of the developmental factors associated with self-control, it is important to note that the significant correlations remained significant when both mental age and chronological age were partialled out. Kendall and Wilcox (1979) also compared children referred for self-control training with matched nonreferred children. The referred children scored in the less self-controlled direction, and significantly so, on the teachers' SCRS ratings, MFF latencies, and behavioral observations taken during testing.

Further analyses of the SCRS provided some additional support for the validity of the SCRS (Kendall et al., Note 6). In a randomly selected sample

Table 8.2. Intercorrelations of the various tests and observations.

Measure	2	3	4	5	6	7	8	9
1 Age	-.02	.09	-.17*	-.12	-.33**	-.24*	-.08	-.19*
2 PPVT IQ		-.48**	-.07	.04	-.02	-.05	-.08	-.07
3 PPVT MA			.03	-.15*	-.09	-.06	-.03	-.05
4 MFF errors				-.43**	.27**	.01	-.15*	.28**
5 MFF latency					.20*	.15*	.12	-.19*
6 Porteus Q						.14	.07	.35**
7 Behavioral observations total score							.08	.28**
8 Delay of gratification								-.05
9 Self-control Rating Scale								

PPVT = Peabody Picture Vocabulary Test; MA = mental age; MFF = Matching Familiar Figures.

*P < .05

**P < .005

Source: Adapted from P. C. Kendall and L. E. Wilcox, Self-control in children: Development of a rating scale, *Journal of Consulting and Clinical Psychology*, 1979, 47, 1020–1029. Copyright 1979 American Psychological Association. Reproduced by permission.

of 98 second- to fifth-graders, the teachers' ratings indicated that children lacking in self-control were considered more maladjusted and that their maladjustment was expressed as externalization of conflict (Achenbach, 1966). That is, children lacking self-control tend to discharge their conflicts onto the environment rather than turning them inward against themselves. In addition, children demonstrating social perspective-taking abilities, as measured by Chandler's bystander cartoons (1973; see page 270), were rated as having more self-control. Moreover, naturalistic observation of six categories of non-self-controlled classroom behavior also produced some significant relationships (e.g., off-task attention; out of seat) with teacher's SCRS ratings. The analogue assessment procedures that were employed (scarecrow, delay of gratification) were not, however, significantly correlated with self-control. Another comparison of children referred for self-control training and matched nonreferred children evidenced significantly higher SCRS ratings, significantly higher rates of off-task-physical, out-of-seat, and bugging-others-verbally behaviors.

Reliability data on the SCRS were quite acceptable. A test-retest correlation for a sample of 24 randomly selected children was .84. Internal consistency was .98 according to Cronbach's (1951) alpha (Kendall & Wilcox, 1979). Data are also available that indicate the sensitivity of the SCRS to changes in behavior such as that produced by treatment (e.g., Kendall & Wilcox, 1980; Kendall & Zupan, in press). Both the psychometric qualities of the SCRS and the evidence for convergent and discriminant validity appear sufficient to warrant its continued use in research. For instance, additional research is needed on parents and teachers as raters of self-control, the family and school experiences associated with self-control, and the influences of cognitive development and environmental alterations of the self-controlled behavior of children.

Self-Assessments

The distinction between assessment and treatment is less clear for certain of the self-assessment methods. In fact, self-monitoring is postulated as the necessary first component of self-management skills (e.g., Kanfer, 1980). An individual must have an accurate picture of his or her behavior before he or she can use self-management techniques to change it. Self-assessment techniques, by their nature, require people to examine their behavior. This may be particularly important in the treatment of children, since children rarely seek treatment on their own. It is their parents, teachers, or other care-givers who perceive a problem and bring the child to the attention of mental health professionals. It is not unreasonable to assume that many children who enter treatment in this manner may not even be aware of their problem behavior, making their cooperation difficult to obtain. Therefore, getting them to be aware of the behaviors that are causing difficulties is one of the first major treatment goals. Self-monitoring, or getting the child to observe his or her behavior, is one way to accomplish this.

Self-report inventories may also accomplish this, but in a much less direct fashion and to a lesser degree. A child filling out a self-report inventory focuses on his or her behavior and might compare it to the behavior of others. He or she may get a different perspective on his or her behavior by answering the questions on the inventory. However, this requires some form of reflective processing of the information about the self and others, and it may not be until a later stage of development or after treatment that such reflection proves beneficial.

Self-monitoring. Self-monitoring is similar to direct observation, except that the individual is observing his or her *own* behavior. An advantage of self-monitoring over direct observation is that many more behaviors are accessible to self-monitoring than are to direct observations. For example, the domain of cognitive variables (e.g., private events, thoughts) is open to self-monitoring (Hollon & Kendall, 1981). Self-monitoring is also considerably less expensive than direct observations, and many of the procedures used in direct observation (e.g., event sampling, time-sampling) can be adopted for self-monitoring.

A number of devices exist to assist a child in the self-recording stage of self-monitoring. The most widely used and readily available are the paper-and-pencil techniques, where the child is requested to keep a behavior diary in a notebook or on cards. In a more elaborate fashion, Kunzelman (1970) developed a "countoon" to assist children's self-monitoring. The countoon allows the child to record the antecedents, incidence, and consequences of the target behavior in a pictorial sequence. Various mechanical counters, timing devices, and electronic equipment can be used to assist in self-monitoring (see Ciminero, Nelson, & Lipinski, 1977 for a more complete description).

Reactivity, or changes in behavior that occur merely as a result of being observed, effects self-monitoring as it does direct observation. Reactivity is an asset when self-monitoring is intended more as a treatment procedure. Ciminero et al. (1977) described a number of variables that influence the reactivity of self-monitoring: valence of the target behavior, subjects' motivation to change the target behavior, the setting of performance goals, performance feedback and reinforcement, the nature of the target behavior, the number of target behaviors being self-recorded, the schedule of self-recording, and the timing of self-recording. Apparently, a complex of factors affect self-monitoring and clinicians and researchers need to attend to these issues.

The accuracy of self-monitoring cannot be implicitly assumed. Children do not automatically produce accurate records of their behavior. Fortunately, studies demonstrate that accurate self-monitoring can be trained and reinforced (see also Gross and Drabman's chapter in this volume). Peacock, Lyman, and Rickard (1978), for instance, demonstrated that disturbed boys exaggerated their cabin-cleaning behavior when a no-accuracy contingency was in effect. However, when an accuracy contingency was employed, the children's ratings of their cabin-cleaning behavior matched the observer's ratings. Children improved the accuracy of their ratings by changing their *behavior* for the easy items (e.g., pillow in place) and by changing their *ratings* for the hard items (e.g., floor around bed mopped).

Self-report inventories. Very few self-report inventories have been developed to assess children's self-management. One is tempted to call this state of affairs "unfortunate," because reliable and valid inventories might well be useful in research and application of self-control principles. However, given the difficulties with children's self-report on trait-type tests, the state of affairs may be best considered desirable.

The literature contains two self-report inventories for use with children that are designed to assess their impulsivity (i.e., non-self-controlled behavior). The Impulse Control Categorization Instrument (ICCI), developed by Matsushima (1964), contains 24 sentence situations to which children state their degrees of choice between spontaneously impulsive-aggressive behavior and behavior requiring impulse control. A four-point continuum is employed. For example, "If a boy stepped on my foot, I would sock him. YES yes no NO." As part of the instructions, the child is told that the large "YES" indicates definitely yes while the small "yes" stands for probably yes. This is also true for the large and small "no's." The child is specifically instructed to work as fast as he or she can, since the questions are not "think" questions.

The ICCI is said to assess self-control over immediate action when aroused. Although the odd-even reliability of .93 is acceptable, limited validation of the scale has been provided beyond the data reported by Matsushima (1964). A lack of support for the ICCI as an instrument sensitive to change was provided by Kendall and Finch (1978). In this study, performance measures and teacher ratings evidence positive changes while the children's self-report showed no meaningful variations due to treatment.

A second instrument, the Impulsivity Scale (IS), is a 25-item, true-false, self-report scale designed to assess a child's tendency to be restless, to indulge in horseplay, to lose control, and to enter activities with excessive vigor (Sutton-Smith & Rosenberg, 1959; Hirschfield, 1965, revision). Test-retest reliability was .85 (Sutton-Smith & Rosenberg, 1959), and significant relationships with teacher rankings and classroom observations (Hirschfield, 1965) were acceptable. As with the ICCI, sensitivity to treatment effects has not been reported for the IS. On the contrary, Kendall and Finch (1978) reported that despite task performance and classroom behavior changes, the self-report inventories did not evidence improvements.

Several additional shortcomings render self-report inventories for assessing children's self-control as a less than adequate methodology. Some of the items on the ICCI and the IS are laughable and silly and create a difficult atmosphere for the child to respond seriously. More importantly, self-controlled and non-self-controlled children were found not to differ in their responses to a self-report questionnaire designed to assess knowledge of appropriate self-controlled behavior (Lumsden, Note 8). These data suggest that even impulsive, non-self-controlled children have information about the inappropriateness of certain behavior and that they can report it; this knowledge does not, however, translate into their behavior. The lack of a meaningful connection between what children "say" and what they "do" in terms of self-control suggests that children, when examined by adults, may readily provide socially desirable responses. They can state the appropriate answer in spite of the fact that they behave in an entirely different manner. Perhaps also, since there is a lack of correspondence between "saying" and "doing," verbal control of behavior should be a part of self-management training (e.g., Karoly & Dirks, 1977).

Some children's self-report inventories have had some research success assessing generalized expectancies (e.g., locus of control). The Nowicki-Strickland Internal-External Scale for Children (Nowicki & Strickland, 1973), perhaps the most widely used measure of locus of control, consists of 40 yes-no items, keyed such that a high score indicates an externally oriented locus of control. Another self-report measure of locus of control was developed by Crandall et al (1965) to assess children's locus of responsibility for academic performance. Feder (Note 9) used a self-report scale to assess the intrinsic versus extrinsic reward orientation of subjects. Recently, Cohen, Gelfand, Dodd, Jensen, and Turner (1980) combined information from a child questionnaire about weight control with a parent questionnaire in their evaluation of maintenance of weight loss in children and adolescents. To the extent that an internal locus of control indicates the child's tendency to hold an expectancy that he or she affects his or her environment, these self-report scales reflect an aspect of self-control.

Children's attributions have also been assessed via the self-report of choices of response alternatives for a series of brief vignettes. For example, Leon, Kendall, and Garber (1980) used such a procedure to examine the attributional preferences associated with depression in children. Among other findings, depressed children evidenced a tendency to attribute positive events to external causes and negative events to internal causes.

When using self-report inventories, examiners have sometimes read each of the items to the children. Although this practice is not universal, it should be employed, since children often show marked differences in reading level, vocabulary, and reading speed. Even when the inventory items are read to the children, the children do not always make the distinction between what is typically the case for them and what might be the case at the present time. For example, a children's self-report inventory has been developed to assess state and trait anxiety (Spielberger, 1973). State anxiety refers to how the children feel "right now," whereas trait anxiety refers to how the children typically or "generally" feel. In studies of anxiety in children, it has been found that not only a child's current emotional state will change due to stress, but also the child's self-reported trait level of anxiety (Finch & Kendall, 1979; Finch, Kendall, Montgomery, & Morris, 1975). Essentially, the potency and vividness of the current situation prevails over prior experiences. Although this example refers to the assessment of an emotional response, the potential dilemma of children's current conditions overriding what is typical exists for all children's self-report assessments.

Psychologic Tests

The use of standard psychological tests for the diagnosis of children's disorders has been the subject of criticism. Indeed, many behaviorists maintain that traditional tests have little to offer the clinician (e.g., Nelson & Hayes, 1979). While we do not encourage an uncritical return to the use of a standard battery of psychological tests, we do wish to emphasize that children's performances on certain tests can be useful in designing and evaluating children's self-management programs. However, with the enormous array of tests available, what tests would be most productive in the assessment of what functions? Two areas that merit consideration include problem solving and interpersonal cognition.

A child's cognitive and behavioral skills and his or her ability to make adaptive use of both cognitive processing and behavioral inhibition skills to solve personal problems will affect the child's appropriateness for self-management training (and the likelihood of program success). The child's ability can be assessed either by performance on nonsocial, impersonal tasks, or by storytelling procedures, in which the emphasis is on interpersonal problem solving and social cognition. In addition to these skills, one must also consider the child's motivation to employ the skills in appropriate contexts. Motivational factors are essential to the success of self-management programs (Karoly, 1981).

Impersonal problem-solving. Among the assortment of tasks that children have been required to solve, two procedures have been used extensively in research and appear to be useful in implementing and evaluating self-management programs: the Porteus mazes and the Matching Familiar

Figures test. The Porteus mazes, originally designed as an adjunct to measures of intelligence (Porteus, 1933), have proved particularly sensitive, for example, in the identification of delinquency (Riddle & Roberts, 1977).

The test consists of a series of mazes of graded difficulty (Porteus, 1955) that produce two distinct scores: a test quotient (TQ) and a qualitative (Q) score. The Q score consists of a number of qualitative errors such as the rate of lifting the pencil contrary to instructions, cutting corners in the mazes, and touching or crossing the sides of the alleyways in the maze. The TQ is based on the highest level of maze successfully completed and the number of trials required to solve each maze. Riddle and Roberts (1977) concluded that considerable data indicate that the Q score discriminates between delinquent and normal reference groups and also between recidivist and non-recidivist delinquent groups. The TQ did not discriminate, but was associated with visual ability and spatial memory. The Q score appears most sensitive to levels of social adjustment; as a measure of foresight, planning ability, and a lack of impulsivity, it may contribute to decisions about children's self-management programs. For example, early research on the effects of self-instructions (e.g., Palkes, Stewart, & Freedman, 1972; Palkes, Stewart, & Kahana, 1968) and more recent research on the effectiveness of cognitive-behavioral interventions (e.g., Douglas, Parry, Marton, & Garson, 1976; Kendall & Wilcox, 1980) have employed the Porteus mazes for treatment evaluation. Alternate forms of the Porteus mazes are available when repeated assessments are anticipated (as in treatment outcome evaluations).

Kagan and his colleagues (Kagan, Rossman, Day, Albert, & Phillips, 1964), while interested in the development of conceptual tempo, introduced a 12-item matching-to-sample task called the Matching Familiar Figures (MFF) test. Researchers have employed the MFF to study numerous factors associated with conceptual tempo such as problem-solving strategies, persistance, age-related changes, and reading ability (see Kendall & Finch, 1979; Messer, 1976). Some recent evidence (Messer & Brodzinsky, 1979) indicates that impulsive children, especially boys, exercise less self-control over their aggressive thoughts than nonimpulsives and that fantasy aggressions predicted overt aggression among the impulsives.

In each of the MFF items the child is shown a single picture of an object and is instructed to select from an array of six variants the one picture that is identical to the stimulus figure. A preschool version of the MFF requires the subject to choose from four variants. There is also available the Kansas Reflection-Impulsivity Scale for Preschoolers (KRISP) (Wright, Note 10). The examiner records the child's latency to first response and total response errors. Impulsives are identified as having scores above the median on errors and below the median on latency. Thus, the impulsive child is *fast* and inaccurate. Reflective children are those whose performance is below the median in errors and above the median in latency.

This double-median-split procedure can be appropriate when testing large numbers of children, but is not useful when assessing an individual child for a self-management program. In a specific case, a child's MFF test scores would have to be examined in relation to other children's performance as reported in the published literature (see Messer, 1976) or in unpublished form (Salkind, Note 11). Also, since changes in MFF performance after treatment can be said to indicate an increased thoughtfulness in problem solving, a specific child's posttreatment MFF performance can be examined in relation to pretreatment performance.

Caution should be exercised in interpreting MFF latency and error scores. For instance, Ault, Mitchell, and Hartmann (1976) described the low reliability of the error scores as problematic. Egeland and Weinberg (1976) reported that the MFF was more successful at classifying reflective children consistently than impulsive children, but concluded that while the MFF reliability data are not ideal, it compared favorably with other measures of cognitive style. Some questions have also been raised about defining the conceptual tempo dimension on the basis of both latency and error scores. For example, Block, Block and Harrington (1974) present data which indicate that the error scores alone are more useful than errors and latencies in differentiating among behavioral patterns (see also Block, Block, & Harrington, 1975; Kagan & Messer, 1975; Egeland, Bielke, & Kendall, in press). Alternate forms of the MFF, with eight items in each, were developed by Egeland and Weinberg (1976) and have been used in evaluations of self-control treatment (e.g., Kendall & Wilcox, 1980; Kendall & Zupan, in press).

One must also be cautious when interpreting changes in MFF latencies and errors. Although it is generally agreed that fast-inaccurate (impulsive) responding is least desirable, it does not automatically dictate that slow-accurate (reflective) responding is most desirable. Typically, in studies examining changes in MFF latencies and errors, changes in each variable are examined and improvements on both seen as supportive. Such an interpretation is erroneous. For example, while it is advantageous for a child to slow down and make fewer errors, a far superior performance is one in which the child eventually makes fewer errors but takes only a short interval of time to respond. Essentially, fast and accurate responding can be more desirable than slow and accurate performance. Thus, significant reductions in error rates without changing latencies are to be interpreted positively (see, for example, Kendall & Zupan, in press).

Both impersonal problem-solving tasks—the Porteus mazes and the MFF—offer the clinician a sample of the child's behavior in response to standard materials. From this behavior sample, the clinician can make a judgment about the degree to which the child was self-controlled in the task performance. A child lacking self-management skills such as forethought and self-monitoring will fail to provide the necessary self-pacing and self-generated organization necessary to perform well on the tasks. For example, one of the rules of the Porteus mazes is that the child must not lift his or her pencil while working on the maze. At predetermined instances, the examiner can remind the child, but each pencil lift is counted and contributes to the childs' pencil-lift score and subsequently to the Q score. In order to earn a low Q score, the child must self-monitor and inhibit the tendency to lift the pencil, perhaps by self-instructing to keep the pencil on the maze. The child lacking self-management strategies will accrue a high Q score. Such deficits in self-induced cognitive problem-solving are evident in impulsive MFF performance.

These tests provide a behavioral sample from which inferences can be drawn about the child's use of foresight, planning, self-guidance, and related cognitive and behavioral factors within self-management. In conjunction with other data, they provide useful information for treatment planning and evaluation. Since the requirements of these tests correspond to those of many classroom tasks, the tests may be viewed as typical of the child's daily academic assignments.

Measures of interpersonal cognition. In contrast to the *impersonal* nature of the mazes and matching tests, other assessment procedures require the child to solve social *interpersonal* problems. Children's performance on measures of social cognition (see Shantz, 1975) and interpersonal cognitive problem solving (ICPS) tasks (e.g., Spivack, Platt, & Shure, 1976) are examples of this approach (see also Kendall, Pellegrini, & Urbain, 1981).

Perspective-taking. Working on the assumption that problem recognition plays an important role in children's self-management, the centrality of social-cognitive skills is readily apparent. Social cognition here refers to a child's ability to know and understand the perspective of others. When a child possesses social cognitive skills and can assess another child's perspective, the likelihood of the child recognizing an interpersonal dilemma is greatly enhanced.

Assessment of social cognition has focused largely on the perspective-taking (or role-taking) ability of the child and has been based on storytelling behavior. Different assessment procedures are employed depending on the type of perspective taking involved. One can assess how well a child perceives what another person is feeling (i.e., affective perspective taking), what another person is seeing (i.e., spatial/perceptual perspective taking), or what another person is thinking (i.e., cognitive perspective taking).

Affective role taking has been assessed by Borke (1971, 1973) using a picture-selection method. First the examiner shows the child different faces that represent various emotions, and determines that the child can tell the emotions apart from one another. Then the child is told a series of stories in which the main character's experiences are likely to arouse a particular emotion, and particular peer interaction takes place.

Children's affective understanding, a concept akin to empathy, has been assessed by Feshbach and Feshbach (1969) and Feshbach and Roe (1968) using a series of slide sequences depicting affect-arousing situations. Four different emotions are portrayed with slides of either male or female characters. After a narrative describing the situation, the child is asked how he or she feels. Affective matching, where the child feels the same as the child in the story, is considered empathic.

The Borke and Feshbach assessments focus solely on the affective component of perspective taking or social cognition. Whether the affective role-taking skill of a particular child is predictive for success on self-management programs is unknown. However, a large number of the intervention programs that are labeled as one or another type of cognitive-behavioral (Kendall, in press) or social-cognitive (Urbain & Kendall, 1980) treatment for children include training sessions that focus on "affective education." Although deficits in affective knowledge in the target children have not always been examined, it is thought that increased understanding of the feelings of others will facilitate, or is a prerequisite for, learning self-management skills. The assessment procedures of Borke and Feshbach may be most useful in determining whether or not children in need of self-management training do in fact show deficits in the affective domain. This important research question may be thwarted, however, by developmental considerations that reduce the utility of the assessment procedures. For example, while children as young as 3 years have performed the Borke task (e.g., Urberg & Docherty, 1976), by the age of 5 years, most children have completely mastered the task — thus precluding its use with older children. In contrast, while the Feshbach's measure can be used with older children, one might question whether simple affect matching in a mature 10-year-old is an empathic response (cf., also Copeland's discussion in Chapter 7).

Unlike affective perspective taking, cognitive perspective-taking assessments have shown deficits in non-self-controlled problem groups (e.g., Chandler, 1973; Kendall et al., Note 6; Platt, Spivack, Altman, Altman, & Peizer, 1974; Urbain & Kendall, Note 12). Consistently, children supposedly lacking in self-control (e.g., delinquents, impulsives, children identified as lacking self-control based on the SCRS) perform less well on tasks requiring their taking the perspective of another individual. Cognitive perspective-taking assessments have also been employed in therapy-outcome evaluations (e.g., Chandler, Greenspan, & Barenboim, 1974; Kendall & Zupan, in press; Ahammer & Murray, 1979) with improvements in performance suggesting therapeutic benefit. Neale (1966) reported on spatial/perceptual perspective-taking differences between institutionalized and noninstitutionalized children showing perceptual perspective-taking deficits.

Although a wide variety of methods for assessing children's cognitive perspective taking have been discussed elsewhere in relation to cognitive-behavioral interventions (see Kendall et al., 1981), we shall describe briefly two of these procedures: Chandler's bystander cartoons (1973) and Feffer's role-taking task (1959). Both require the child to tell a story and to subsequently retell a story from the perspective of a different story character. Cognitive perspective-taking abilities are evident when the stories remain consistent while the perspectives of both characters are differentiated.

Surprisingly, researchers have reported an absence of meaningful correlations between the Chandler and Feffer tasks (e.g., Kurdek, 1977; Piche, Michlin, Rubin, & Johnson, 1975). Also, although age differences were reported, Paulauskas and Campbell (1979) did not find significant differences in cognitive perspective taking between hyperactive and matched control children. These data should not be taken as evidence of equal cognitive perspective-taking skills, but perhaps as data contraindicative of test validity, since both peer and teacher ratings of hyperactive children's behavior indicate that they behave in a manner evidencing an absence of perspective-taking abilities (e.g., Klein & Young, 1979).

Assessments of perspective-taking abilities can document certain cognitive-developmental deficits which are associated with a deficit in self-controlled behavior. Clinically, it is therefore valuable to assess such abilities and to provide therapeutic experiences designed to enhance perspective taking.

Interpersonal cognitive problem solving. Numerous approaches to the assessment of interpersonal problem solving have appeared in the recent literature. Essentially, the various assessments are intended to measure a series of discrete yet interrelated cognitive problem-solving skills. Unlike the skills needed to solve impersonal puzzles or anagrams, these skills are said to function in social, interpersonal contexts and might best be seen as the application of problem solving and social understanding to interpersonal conflicts.

Spivack and Shure (1974) and Spivack, Platt, and Shure (1976) have reported on the development of a series of interpersonal cognitive problem-solving (ICPS) skills said to be associated with impaired behavioral adjustment. These ICPS skills include sensitivity to interpersonal problems, causal thinking (i.e., spontaneously linking cause and effect), readiness to consider the consequences of behavior, ability to generate a list of possible solutions, and the ability to generate step-by-step means for reaching specific goals.

Among these various measures, means-ends thinking (assessed via the Means-Ends Problem-Solving task, MEPS) has received a good deal of research attention and has demonstrated some discriminant validity by separating disturbed from normal groups (Shure & Spivack, 1972; Platt & Spivack, Note 13). For young children (preschoolers), there is the Preschool Interpersonal Problem-Solving (PIPS) Test. The assessment of means-ends problem solving involves presenting the child with a series of stories (typically six) describing hypothetical problems of an interpersonal nature. In each instance, the examiner presents the initial situation and the final outcome while it is the child's task to fill in the middle of the story. Story responses are scored for the total number of means, elaborations of specific means, perception of potential obstacles to carrying out the means, and use of a time sequence. MEPS protocols have been scored reliably, and changes in MEPS scores have been found as a result of treatment. There exists, however, some variability among researchers in the administration and scoring of the MEPS.

Some concern exists regarding the MEPS and related ICPS tests and their ecological validity (Butler & Meichenbaum, 1981; Kendall & Fischler, Note 14). To what extent do MEPS scores reflect children's actual ability to solve real-life interpersonal problems? Some efforts toward developing more ecologically valid assessments have been reported. For example, Larcen (reported in Allen, Chinsky, Larcen, Lochman, & Selinger, 1976) describes the construction of a simulated real-life problem-solving situation. As the child approached the testing room, he or she was told that the room was occupied and that it could not be used; the child was asked to help solve the problem. This interaction was taped, and later scored for the number of alternative solutions proposed by the subject.

Another innovative measure of problem solving was developed by McClure and colleagues (McClure, Chinsky, & Larcen, 1978) and involved peer group interaction. Children participated in a Friendship Club contest with the following rules: all six children must agree on the best answers to the contest questions, all members must help answer the questions, and all members had to be club officers. In addition, a number of real problems were embedded in the Friendship Club contest situation. For instance, there were only five chairs for the six children, five officer cards for the six members, and the problem of how to distribute the different offices. The entire procedure was taped and later scored for problem-solving responses. Importantly, McClure et al. (1978) report that children who received problem-solving training scored higher than nontreated children.

Children's capacities to generate problem solutions, on tests such as the MEPS and/or in real-life problem situations, are said to mediate adjustment. One important concern pertaining to this proposed relationship is the independence of the ICPS skills from intellectual development. Spivack, Shure, Platt, and their colleagues have conducted analyses in which they have controlled for IQ, suggesting that the mediating function of the ICPS skills is independent of IQ. However, the IQ measure typically used is an index of receptive vocabulary (Peabody Picture Vocabulary Test; Dunn, 1965). Support for the mediational role of ICPS skills would be more convincing if the IQ assessments included various types of intellectual capacities in addition to vocabulary. Additional research, perhaps covarying WISC-R IQ (and separate subtests), will clarify this important question. Also, while PPVT IQ failed to be a significant problem-solving predictor for city children, PPVT IQ was the most significant predictor of problem-solving behavior for suburban children (M. E. Chandler, Note 15). Moreover, Enright and Sutterfield (1980) found that an ecological validation of social problem solving did not hold when a vocabulary index was partialled out.

A second important issue involves the manner of scoring the MEPS protocols. While the total number of means generated indicates the range of possibilities, MEPS scores calculated in this manner may not be the best predictor if children who provide only one or two responses provided the most adaptive response first or second. Well-adjusted children may provide *one* very adaptive, very appropriate, and very likely to be successful means to an end. Therefore, qualitative analysis of MEPS protocols may prove exceedingly valuable.

CLINICAL SUGGESTIONS

The present chapter was designed to provide a description of the procedures that have been or could be used to assess self-management skills and deficits in children. Although a wide variety of procedures, as well as problems inherent in their use, have been described, clinicians who wish to apply the information may still be wondering which of the procedures to use in their practices. The following section is designed to provide some suggestions.

Consider the Shortcomings of the Assessment Procedures

A primary consideration of any type of psychological assessment is method variance, or the sources of variation that are associated with a given assessment procedure, rather than the behavior of interest (Campbell & Fiske, 1959). Moreover, different assessment procedures are more or less susceptible to the various sources of assessment inaccuracy, and some assessment procedures are more costly to implement than are others (e.g., behavioral observations are more costly than rating scales). Decisions related to the clinical use of the assessments should be made with an awareness of the shortcomings associated with the various procedures.

None of the assessment procedures described in this chapter is error-free or nonproblematic. Some of the sources of inaccuracy and problems associated with the procedures described include:

- Generalizability (particularly problematic with some observation systems, analogue tasks, and psychological tests)
- Cost (problematic with observational systems and some self-monitoring procedures that require mechanical devices)
- Rater biases (problematic with observation systems, rating scales)
- The child's limited verbal skills (problematic with all the self-assessments)
- Instruments that are not appropriate for repeated measurement (problematic with psychological tests and analogue tasks without alternate forms)
- Nonobservable responses or private events (problematic with observation systems, analogue tasks, psychological tests, and rating scales)
- Variations in data collection or task administration (problematic with observation systems, analogue tasks, and psychological tests)

Several problems and sources of inaccuracy can be present in all the procedures:

- Lack of clarity. The subject, be it the target child, a rater, or another child, is not given sufficient information to provide accurate data. Since many of the assessment methods entail the child's responding to adult instructions, these instructions must be *clear* for the child.
- Instrument breakdown. The tasks or mechanical aspects of the assessment falter. Tasks are worn-out, stop watches are not wound, tape recorders are dysfunctional.
- The "state" of the child. Specific unusual instances prior to the assessment alter the child's current emotional state and affect the child's performance.
- The "state" of the environment. Specific unusual environmental conditions surrounding the assessment alter the child's performance.
- Response sets. The child brings to the assessment situation a pattern of responding that does not reflect the concept of interest, but rather reflects another, less interesting, construct (e.g., compliance to adult requests, but a lack of self-control).
- Reactivity. The data are the result of observer or examiner interference. The assessment reflects less what is typically the case and is more an indication of what occurs when an observer/examiner is present.

It is our contention that by being aware of these potential shortcomings, clinicians can exert some control over them. For example, for the problem of lack of clarity, the clinician can take care that the individual understands the instructions (e.g., asking child to repeat the instructions back to the assessor to assure comprehension, or reading self-report items to the child). It is only through awareness of the problems that steps can be taken to alleviate them. However, each assessment procedure will still contain some method variance, and it is for this and other reasons that we do not endorse a single procedure. Instead, we suggest that by use of multimethod assessment, the likelihood of assessment inaccuracy is reduced maximally.

Consider the Types of Self-Management Deficits

Assessment for diagnosis of a child's disorder typically relies on a standard battery of tests and a classification system (e.g., DSM III, 1980). Unfortunately, there is no standard battery of "self-control" tests and there are no specific "self-management disorders of childhood" in common classification. A key issue for clinicians concerns the assessment of the type of self-management deficit for each specific child.

Self-management problems can be an issue in many different types of disorders (e.g., hyperactivity, enuresis, delinquency, poor school performance) and, moreover, problems with self-management are not themselves a unitary concept; there are multiple sources of the observed deficit. Three types of self-management deficits illustrate this point: behavioral-skill deficiency, cognitive-developmental deficit, and emotional interference.

In a behavioral-skill deficiency, the child is seen as lacking specific behaviors in his or her repertoire, and these skill deficits result in the self-control problem. Behavioral skills presumed to be absent include the ability to perform specific actions, to engage in self-monitoring and/or self-reinforcement, and to recognize the cues for engaging in self-management. Treatment strategies built on a behavioral-skill deficiency model rely on active practice (rehearsal) of the needed skills, with reinforcement contingent upon performance.

Deficits in cognitive development influence the acquisition, performance, and understanding of self-management problems. A child's difficulty in respecting the property of others may represent a perspective-taking deficiency. Peer/interpersonal conflicts may reflect a lack of social problem solving. Delayed cognitive development may leave a child unable to comprehend his or her personal responsibilities in a self-control problem. Remedial efforts focus on the enhancement of thinking processes to control behavior.

An alternate model for problems in self-management would highlight the child's emotional arousal in specific situations. Behavioral skills may be present in the child's repertoire, and his or her cognitive capacities may be sufficient; yet, when the emotional arousal reaches a certain level, it interferes and short circuits the self-management process. Enough goading can ruffle even the most self-controlled. Affective education and the control of emotional arousal deserve central roles in treatment based on this model.

The apparent increased interest in identifying and assessing the cognitive variables associated with behavioral self-control should prove worthwhile. However, clinical applications of self-management programs would also benefit from an increased focus on the emotional factors (Urbain & Kendall, 1980). A child's ability to engage in the cognitive processing and behavioral actions associated with self-control may be blocked by heightened negative emotional arousal. Excessive arousal may preclude a child's capacity to be self-controlled. On the other hand, emotional states may serve as the ultimate cues for engaging in self-controlled thought and action (e.g., teaching a child that when he or she "sees red" or feels like fighting, to count to ten instead). As emotional factors are assessed and incorporated into self-management programs, we may ultimately come to understand the complete process of self-management.

Each of the three models accounts for some of the self-management problems seen in children. Identifying the major deficit will foster treatment planning, and careful assessments will prove valuable in deficit identification—behavioral, cognitive, and affective assessments must be involved.

Consider Multimethod Assessments: Case Examples

Since there is no single error-free and easily implemented assessment device capable of providing information on the behavioral, cognitive, and affective components of children's self-management capabilities, we endorse a multimethod-assessment approach. Unfortunately, although there has been some interest expressed in a standard assessment battery (Rosenbaum & Drabman, 1979) and there is merit in such a suggestion, a standard battery for all children being considered for self-management training is not yet feasible. Therefore, part of the decision about which assessment procedures to use depends on the clinician's initial judgment about the child's problem. The following two cases illustrate the use of several of the assessment procedures described in this chapter.

Case A: 8-year-old girl with school problems. Cindy was referred to a mental health center by her classroom teacher who was concerned by her poor academic performance and peer relationships. Cindy was a transfer student and was not adapting to the new school environment, even though she had been there three months. Her previous school records indicated that she was an above-average student and had never been referred for psychological evaluation or treatment. Cindy's mother was very receptive to the teacher's request, and arranged an appointment at the local mental health center.

Cindy and her mother were present for the initial intake interview. A detailed history and description of her current behavior revealed that her mother considered her to be a happy child until their recent move across the country. She described Cindy as having to have lots of friends in their old town and not having made any new ones. Her mother indicated that they lived in a neighborhood with no children her age and that she also seemed to have lost interest in her schoolwork, whereas before she had liked to show her mother her work. The mother reported no other problems at home, including Cindy's siblings and the marital relationship. She had no specific information from the teacher about Cindy's classroom behavior.

A brief interview was conducted with Cindy while she and the therapist were playing with a doll house. Cindy indicated that she missed her friends and found her new school work hard and boring. During the doll play, Cindy took the role of the mother, and the therapist played a child who was failing in school. Each of several times the therapist (as the child) asked Cindy (the mother) why he was failing. Cindy gave an internal explanation (e.g., "You're not trying hard enough," "You're being lazy.") When asked if she actually believed that, Cindy replied that most of the time she did, although the work seemed harder at her new school.

After these interviews, the therapist formulated an assessment plan. He obtained permission to interview the school personnel. An initial telephone interview with the teacher was conducted to gain a more clear description of Cindy's classroom behavior. The teacher was also asked to fill out the Self-Control Rating Scale. The therapist asked if the school psychologist could conduct some behavioral observations. The observed behaviors were: time-off task, time interacting with peers, and time working appropriately. The school psychologist was asked to observe Cindy and another peer who the teacher identified as being a good student, same sex, and as with no peer relationship problems. Since there were no recent test data, the therapist arranged for Cindy to take intelligence and achievement tests to determine if she was at the proper grade placement. In addition, the therapist gave the Matching Familiar Figures Test to help ascertain whether or not a hasty performance style was involved in the poor academic performance. Cindy's mother was asked to complete a Self-Control Rating Scale and to keep a diary of Cindy's activities after school.

The assessment plan was intended to provide the therapist with information about Cindy's behavior from several sources, and will allow the therapist to implement and evaluate a treatment that focuses on environmental manipulations (e.g., a different placement; mother enrolling Cindy in "Y" activities or scouting), a self-management program (e.g., self-instruction training for academic work, peer interactions, or both), or some combination of the two.

Case B: 13-year-old boy referred for fire-setting. A probation officer accompanied Johnny and his mother to a psychology clinic as part of the requirements of his probation. Johnny was on probation for setting a fire in a large vacant lot near his affluent neighborhood. The probation officer reported that there had been at least two other incidents during the year in which Johnny was implicated. Johnny and his mother were present during the interview with the probation officer. The officer was asked to specify what was required of the therapist (e.g., whether a report was to be submitted about the treatment outcome). The only request was that the probation officer be notified if Johnny terminated treatment prematurely. It was agreed that the content of Johnny's treatment sessions would be confidential. Johnny and his mother agreed that the court records would be sent to the therapist, and the probation officer agreed to report any further incidents to the therapist.

The therapist then began interviewing Johnny and his mother. His mother began a lengthy monologue about the amount of time she had to spend away from her job because of Johnny's problem. She indicated that neither she nor her husband could afford to spend much more time away from their careers, and left Johnny and his sisters in the care of a housekeeper. Johnny was very quiet when his mother was present, and allowed her to answer the questions directed at him. In an attempt to assess how much cooperation the therapist could expect from his parents, the therapist asked the mother if she and her husband would come to an evening session. The mother doubted it, but agreed to talk with her husband. She also agreed that the therapist could talk to the housekeeper, if necessary.

When Johnny was seen alone, he was quiet and tended to answer with one-word responses. The therapist decided to spend the rest of this session attempting to establish a relationship, and took Johnny for a walk to a park. Later sessions would be used for more extensive information-gathering.

Based on the initial session, the therapist decided that family therapy might be desirable, but difficult. In addition to the mother's seeming disinterest in treatment, Johnny's problem behavior only occurred when he was alone. Johnny's age was another factor, in that he was old enough to have some thoughts about the cause of his problems. Although the therapist planned to continue to try to involve the parents and contact the school to see if there were any problems there, she decided to rely on Johnny for further assessment data. While subsequent sessions continued to focus on relationship building, the therapist began to question Johnny about his problem behavior. She asked him how often he thought about fire-setting, where he got his matches, what he thought about before, during, and after fire-setting. This questioning was done in a nonjudgmental manner. Johnny agreed that he would like help with his problem, and agreed when the therapist asked him to keep an activities diary and to note any impulses for fire-setting. The therapist planned to use the diary to get information about his peer interactions as well as a description of the fire-setting behaviors.

Johnny was also given the Porteus Mazes to examine his foresight and planning abilities and to see if his Q scores were in the range of scores obtained by delinquents. A measure of perspective taking would also be useful, though children at Johnny's age have often captured the skills necessary for the Chandler's bystander cartoons. Further psychological testing was temporarily deferred.

The approach to Johnny's case was different from that to Cindy's for several reasons: his parent's seeming lack of cooperation; the fact that the problem behavior only occurred when he was alone; and his older age. All those reasons contributed to the decision to focus on him for assessment data and probable treatment. However, it is also important to recognize that the therapist again used multiple methods of assessment (i.e., interview, self-monitoring, psychological tasks).

As these cases illustrate (through their incompleteness), there is not as yet a formal set of recommendations to guide self-management assessment. The best guide at present is an awareness of the available methods, of their respective strengths and weaknesses, and of their potential uses. We hope that our efforts have moved our readers in this direction.

REFERENCE NOTES

1. Asher, S. R., Renshaw, P. D., Geraci, R. L., & Dor, A. K. Peer acceptance and social skill training: The selection of program content. In *Promoting social development*. Symposium presented at the meeting of the Society for Research in Child Development, San Francisco, March 1979.
2. Patterson, G. R., Ray, R. S., Shaw, D. A., & Cobb, J. A. *Manual for coding family interactions*. Document No. 01234, 6th revision, 1969. (Available from ASIS National Auxiliary Publications Service, c/o CCM Information Service, Inc., 909 Third Avenue, New York, NY 10011.)
3. Forehand, R., Peed, S., & Roberts, M. *Coding manual for scoring mother-child interaction*. Unpublished manuscript, 1975. (Available from Rex Forehand, Department of Psychology, University of Georgia, Athens, GA 30602.)
4. O'Leary, K. D., Romanczyk, R. G., Kass, R. E., Dietz, A., & Santogrossi, D. *Procedures for classroom observation of teachers and children*. Unpublished manuscript, 1971. (Available from Point-of-Woods Laboratory School, State University of New York at Stony Brook, Stony Brook, NY 11790.)
5. Hymel, S., & Asher, S. R. *Assessment and training of isolated children's social skills*. Paper presented at the meeting of the Society of Research in Child Development, New Orleans, 1977. (ERIC Document Reproduction Service No. EO 136 930.)
6. Kendall, P. C., Zupan, B. A., & Robertson, L. *Self-control in children: Further analyses of the Self-Control Rating Scale*. Manuscript submitted for publication, University of Minnesota, 1980.
7. Weinrich, R. J. *Inducing reflective thinking in impulsive, emotionally disturbed children*. Unpublished master's thesis, Virginia Commonwealth University, 1975.
8. Lumsden, P. *The role of knowledge of socially appropriate behavior in impulsive children*. Unpublished manuscript, University of Minnesota, 1979.
9. Feder, J. L. *A developmental study of the effects of external and self reinforcement of*

cooperative models on the social interaction of dyads. Unpublished doctoral dissertation, University of Denver, 1978.
10. Wright, J. C. *The KRISP: A technical report.* Unpublished manuscript, 1973.
11. Salkind, N. J. *The development of norms for the Matching Familiar Figures test.* Manuscript available from the author, University of Kansas, 1979.
12. Urbain, E. S., & Kendall, P. C. *Interpersonal problem-solving, social perspective-taking and behavioral contingencies: A comparison of group approaches with children.* Manuscript submitted for publication. University of Minnesota, 1980.
13. Platt, J. J., & Spivack, G. *Manual for the means-ends-problem-solving procedure.* Philadelphia: Department of Mental Health Sciences, Hahnemann Community Mental Health/Mental Retardation Center, 1975.
14. Kendall, P. C., & Fischler, G. L. *Interpersonal cognition and behavior.* Research in progress, University of Minnesota, 1980.
15. Chandler, M. E. *Interpersonal control styles and problem solving strategies in self-regulation.* Unpublished doctoral dissertation, University of Rochester, 1977.

REFERENCES

Abikoff, H., Gittelman-Klein, R., & Klein, D. F. Validation of a classroom observation code for hyperactive children. *Journal of Consulting and Clinical Psychology*, 1977, *45*, 772–783.
Achenbach, T. M. The classification of children's psychiatric symptoms: A factor analytic study. *Psychological Monographs*, 1966, *80*. (Whole No. 615.)
Ahammer, S. M., & Murray, J. P. Kindness in the kindergarten: The relative influence of role playing and prosocial television in facilitating altruism. *International Journal of Behavioral Development*, 1979, *2*, 133–157.
Allen, G., Chinsky, J., Larcen, S., Lochman, J. E., & Selinger, H. *Community psychology and the schools: A behaviorally oriented multilevel preventive approach.* Hillsdale, N.J.: Earlbaum, 1976.
Ames, C., & Felker, D. W. Effects of self-concept on children's causal attributions and self-reinforcement. *Journal of Educational Psychology*, 1979, *71*, 613–619.
Ault, R. L., Mitchell, C., & Hartmann, D. P. Some methodological problems in reflection-impulsivity research. *Child Development*, 1976, *47*, 227–231.
Bandura, A., & Perloff, B. Relative efficacy of self-monitored and externally imposed reinforcement systems. *Journal of Personality and Social Psychology*, 1962, *7*, 111–116.
Block, J., Block, J. H., & Harrington, D. M. Some misgivings about the Matching Familiar Figures test as a measure of reflection-impulsivity. *Developmental Psychology*, 1974, *10*, 611–632.
Block, J., Block, J. H., & Harrington, D. M. Comment on the Kagan-Messer reply. *Developmental Psychology*, 1975, *11*, 249–252.
Bolstad, O. D., & Johnson, S. M. Self-regulation in the modification of disruptive classroom behavior. *Journal of Applied Behavior Analysis*, 1972, *5*, 443–454.
Borke, H. Interpersonal perception of young children: Egocentrism or empathy? *Developmental Psychology*, 1971, *5*, 263–269.
Borke, H. The development of empathy in Chinese and American children between three and six years of age: A cross-culture study. *Developmental Psychology*, 1973, *9*, 102–108.
Butler, L., & Meichenbaum, D. Assessing interpersonal problem-solving. In P. C. Kendall & S. D. Hollon (Eds.), *Assessment strategies for cognitive-behavioral interventions.* New York: Academic Press, 1981.
Campbell, D. T., & Fiske, D. W. Convergent and discriminant validation by the multitrait-multimethod matrix. *Psychological Bulletin*, 1959, *56*, 81–105.

Chandler, M. J. Egocentricism and antisocial behavior: The assessment and training of social perspective-taking skills. *Developmental Psychology*, 1973, *9*, 326–332.

Chandler, M. J., Greenspan, S., & Barenboim, C. Assessment and training of role-taking and referential communication skills in institutionalized emotionally disturbed children. *Developmental Psychology*, 1974, *10*, 546–553.

Ciminero, A. R., Nelson, R. O., Lipinski, D. P. Self-monitoring procedures. In A. R. Ciminero, K. S. Calhoun, & H. E. Adams (Eds.), *Handbook of behavioral assessment.* New York: John Wiley & Sons, 1977.

Cobb, J. A. Relationship of discrete classroom behaviors to fourth-grade academic achievement. *Journal of Educational Psychology*, 1972, *63*, 74–80.

Cobb, J. A. Effects of academic survival skill training on low-achieving first graders. *Journal of Education Research*, 1973, *67*, 108–113.

Cohen, E. A., Gelfand, D. M., Dodd, D. K., Jensen, J., & Turner, C. Self-control practices associated with weight loss maintenance in children and adolescents. *Behavior Therapy*, 1980, *11*, 26–37.

Cone, J., & Foster, S. L. Naturalistic observational methods. In P. C. Kendall & J. N. Butcher (Eds.), *Handbook of research methods in clinical psychology.* New York: Wiley, in press.

Crandall, V. C., Katkovsky, W., & Crandall, V. S. Children's beliefs in their control of reinforcements in intellectual-academic achievement situations. *Child Development*, 1965, *36*, 91–109.

Cronbach, L. J. Coefficient alpha and the internal structure of tests. *Psychometrika*, 1951, *16*, 297–334.

Diagnostic and Statistical Manual of Mental Disorders (DSM III). Washington, D.C.: American Psychiatric Association, 1980.

Diener, C. I., & Dweck, C. S. An analysis of learned helplessness: Continuous changes in performance, strategy, and achievement cognitions following failure. *Journal of Personality and Social Psychology*, 1978, *5*, 451–462.

Douglas, V. I., Parry, P., Marton, P., & Garson, C. Assessment of a cognitive training program for hyperactive children. *Journal of Abnormal Child Psychology*, 1976, *4*, 389–410.

Dunn, L. M. *Expanded manual for the Peabody Picture Vocabulary Test.* Minneapolis: American Guidance Series, 1965.

Egeland, B., Bielke, P., & Kendall, P. C. Achievement and adjustment correlates of the Matching Familiar Figures test. *Journal of School Psychology*, in press.

Egeland, B., Weinberg, R. A. The Matching Familiar Figures test: A look at its psychometric credibility. *Child Development*, 1976, *47*, 483–491.

Enright, R. D., & Sutterfield, S. J. An ecological validation of social cognitive development. *Child Development*, 1980, *51*, 156–161.

Evans, I. M., & Nelson, R. O. Assessment of child behavior problems. In A. R. Ciminero, K. S. Calhoun, & H. E. Adams (Eds.), *Handbook of behavioral assessment.* New York: John Wiley & Sons, 1977.

Feffer, M. H. The cognitive implications of role-taking behavior. *Journal of Personality*, 1959, *27*, 152–168.

Felixbrod, J. J., & O'Leary, K. D. Effects of reinforcement on children's academic behavior as a function of self-determined and externally imposed contingencies. *Journal of Applied Behavior Analyses*, 1973, *6*, 241–250.

Felixbrod, J. J., & O'Leary, K. D. Self-determination of academic standards by children: Toward freedom from external control. *Journal of Educational Psychology*, 1974, *66*, 845–850.

Feshbach, N., & Feshbach, S. The relationship between empathy and aggression in two age groups. *Developmental Psychology*, 1969, *1*, 102–107.

Feshbach, N., & Roe, K. Empathy in six- and seven-year-olds. *Child Development*, 1968, *39*, 133–145.

Finch, A. J., & Kendall, P. C. The measurement of anxiety in children: Research findings and methodological problems. In A. J. Finch & P. C. Kendall (Eds.), *Clinical treatment and research in child psychopathology*. New York: Spectrum, 1979.

Finch, A. J., Kendall, P. C., Montgomery, L. E., & Morris, J. Effects of two types of failure on anxiety in emotionally disturbed children. *Journal of Abnormal Psychology*, 1975, *84*, 583-585.

Forehand, R., Sturgis, E. T., McMahon, R. J., Aguar, D., Green, K., Wells, K. C., & Breiner, J. Parent behavioral training to modify child noncompliance. *Behavior Modification*, 1979, *3*, 3-25.

Friedman, S. Self-control in the treatment of Gilles de la Tourette's syndrome: Case study with 18-month follow up. *Journal of Consulting and Clinical Psychology*, 1980, *48*, 400-402.

Fry, P. S. Resistance to temptation as a function of the duration of self-verbalization. *British Journal of Social and Clinical Psychology*, 1978, *17*, 111-116.

Gottman, J. The effects of a modeling film on social isolation in preschool children: A methodological investigation. *Journal of Abnormal Child Psychology*, 1977, *5*, 59-78. (a)

Gottman, J. M. Toward a definition of social isolation in children. *Child Development*, 1977, *48*, 513-517. (b)

Gottman, J., Gonso, J., & Rasmussen, B. Social interaction, social competence, and friendship in children. *Child Development*, 1975, *46*, 709-718.

Gottman, J. M., Gonzo, J., & Schuler, P. Teaching social skills to isolated children. *Journal of Abnormal Child Psychology*, 1976, *4*, 179-197.

Graziano, A. M., & Mooney, K. C. Family self-control instruction for children's nighttime fear reduction. *Journal of Consulting and Clinical Psychology*, 1980, *48*, 206-213.

Grusec, J. E., Kuczynski, L., Rushton, J. P., & Simutis, Z. Learning resistance to temptation through observation. *Developmental Psychology*, 1979, *15*, 233-240.

Hall, R. V., Axelrod, S., Tyler, L., Grief, E., Jones, F. C., & Robertson, R. Modification of behavior problems in the home with a parent as observer and experimenter. *Journal of Applied Behavior Analysis*, 1972, *5*, 53-64.

Haynes, S. N., & Kerns, R. D. Validation of a behavioral observation system. *Journal of Consulting and Clinical Psychology*, 1979, *47*, 397-400.

Hirschfield, P. P. Response set in impulsive children. *Journal of Genetic Psychology*, 1965, *107*, 117-126.

Hollon, S. D., & Kendall, P. C. *In vivo* assessment techniques for cognitive-behavioral processes. In P. C. Kendall & S. D. Hollon (Eds.), *Assessment strategies for cognitive-behavioral interventions*. New York: Academic Press, 1981.

Hom, H. L., & Maxwell, F. R. Methodological considerations in the forbidden toy paradigm. *Developmental Psychology*, 1979, *15*, 654-655.

Jones, R. T., & Evans, H. L. Self-reinforcement: A continuum of external cues. *Journal of Educational Psychology*, 1980, *72*, 625-635.

Jones, R. T., Nelson, R. E., & Kazdin, A. E. The role of external variables in self-reinforcement: A review. *Behavior Modification*, 1977, *1*, 147-177.

Jones, R. T., & Ollendick, T. H. Self-reinforcement: An assessment of external influences. *Journal of Behavioral Assessment*, 1979, *1*, 289-303.

Kagan, J., & Messer, S. B. A reply to "Some misgivings about the Matching Familiar Figures Test as a Measure of Reflection-Impulsivity." *Developmental Psychology*, 1975, *11*, 244-248.

Kagan, J., Rosman, B. L., Day, D., Albert, J., & Phillips, W. Information processing in the child: Significance of analytic and reflective attitudes. *Psychological Monographs*, 1964, *78*, (1, Whole No. 578).

Kanfer, F. H. Self-management methods. In F. H. Kanfer & A. P. Goldstein (Eds.), *Helping people change*. (2nd ed.). New York: Pergamon Press, 1980.

Karoly, P. Behavioral self-management in children: Concepts, methods, issues, and directions. In M. Hersen, R. M. Eisler, & P. M. Miller (Eds.), *Progress in behavior modification.* (Vol. 5). New York: Academic Press, 1977.

Karoly, P. Self-management problems in children. In E. J. Mash & L. G. Terdal (Eds.), *Behavioral assessment of childhood disorders.* New York: Guilford Press, 1981.

Karoly, P., & Briggs, N. Z. Effects of rules and directed delays on components of children's inhibitory self-control. *Journal of Experimental Child Psychology*, 1978, *26*, 267–279.

Karoly, P., & Dirks, M. J. Developing self-control in pre-school children through correspondence training. *Behavior Therapy*, 1977, *8*, 398–405.

Karoly, P., & Kanfer, F. H. Effects of prior contractual experiences on self-control in children. *Developmental Psychology*, 1974, *10*, 459–460.

Kendall, P. C. Cognitive-behavioral interventions with children. In B. B. Lahey & A. E. Kazdin (Eds.), *Advances in clinical child psychology.* (Vol. 4). New York: Plenum Press, in press.

Kendall, P. C., & Finch, A. J. A cognitive-behavioral treatment for impulsivity: A group comparison study. *Journal of Consulting and Clinical Psychology*, 1978, *46*, 110–118.

Kendall, P. C., & Finch, A. J. Developing non-impulsive behavior in children: Cognitive-behavioral strategies for self-control. In P. C. Kendall & S. D. Hollon (Eds.), *Cognitive-behavioral interventions: Theory, research, and problems.* New York: Academic Press, 1979.

Kendall, P. C., & Hollon, S. D. (Eds.) *Cognitive-behavioral interventions: Theory, research, and procedures.* New York: Academic Press, 1979.

Kendall, P. C., Pellegrini, D. S., & Urbain, E. S. Approaches to assessment for cognitive-behavioral interventions with children. In P. C. Kendall & S. D. Hollon (Eds.), *Assessment strategies for cognitive-behavioral interventions.* New York: Academic Press, 1981.

Kendall, P. C., & Wilcox, L. E. Self-control in children: The development of a rating scale. *Journal of Consulting and Clinical Psychology*, 1979, *47*, 1020–1030.

Kendall, P. C., & Wilcox, L. E. A cognitive-behavioral treatment for impulsivity: Concrete versus conceptual training in non-self-controlled problem children. *Journal of Consulting and Clinical Psychology*, 1980, *48*, 80–91.

Kendall, P. C., & Zupan, B. A. Individual versus group application of cognitive-behavioral self-control procedures with children. *Behavior Therapy*, in press.

Kent, R. N., & Foster, S. L. Direct observational procedures: Methodological issues in naturalistic settings. In A. R. Ciminero, K. S. Calhoun, & H. E. Adams (Eds.), *Handbook of behavioral assessment.* New York: John Wiley & Sons, 1977.

Klein, A. R., & Young, R. D. Hyperactive boys in their classroom: Assessment of teacher and peer perceptions, interactions, and classroom behaviors. *Journal of Abnormal Child Psychology*, 1979, *7*, 425–442.

Kunzelmann, H. D. (Ed.) *Precision teaching.* Seattle: Special Child Publications, 1970.

Kurdek, L. A. Structural components and intellectual correlates of cognitive prespective taking in first through fourth grade children. *Child Development*, 1977, *48*, 1503–1511.

LaVoie, J. C. Cognitive determinants of resistance to deviation in seven, nine, and eleven year old children of low and high maturity of moral judgment. *Developmental Psychology*, 1974, *10*, 393–402.

Leon, G. R., Kendall, P. C., & Garber, J. Depression in children: Parent, teacher, and child perspectives. *Journal of Abnormal Child Psychology*, 1980, *8*, 221–236.

Lewittes, D. J., & Israel, A. C. Maintaining children's ongoing delay of gratification through other-oriented consequences. *Developmental Psychology*, 1978, *14*, 181–182.

Luria, A. R. *The role of speech in the regulation of normal and abnormal behavior.* New York: Liveright, 1961.

Mahoney, M. J., & Thoresen, C. E. *Self-control: Power to the person*. Belmont, Calif.: Brooks Cole, 1974.

Matsushima, J. An instrument for classifying impulse control among boys. *Journal of Consulting Psychology*, 1964, *28*, 87–90.

McClure, L., Chinsky, J., & Larcen, S. Enhancing social problem-solving performance in an elementary school setting. *Journal of Educational Psychology*, 1978, *70*, 504–513.

Messer, S. B. Reflection-impulsivity: A review. *Psychological Bulletin*, 1976, *83*, 1026–1052.

Messer, S. B., & Brodzinsky, D. M. The relation of conceptual tempo to aggression and its control. *Child Development*, 1979, *50*, 758–766.

Metalsky, G. I., & Abramson, L. Y. Attributional styles: Toward a framework for conceptualization and assessment. In P. C. Kendall and S. D. Hollon (Eds.), *Assessment strategies for cognitive-behavioral interventions*. New York: Academic Press, 1981.

Mischel, W. Processes in delay of gratification. In L. Berkowitz (Ed.), *Advances in experimental social psychology*. (Vol. 7). New York: Academic Press, 1974.

Mischel, W., & Moore, B. Effects of attention to symbolically presented rewards upon self-control. *Journal of Personality and Social Psychology*, 1973, *28*, 172–179.

Nay, W. R. Analogue measures. In A. R. Ciminero, K. S. Calhoun, & H. E. Adams (Eds.), *Handbook of behavioral assessment*. New York: Wiley, 1977.

Neale, J. M. Egocentrism in institutionalized and non-institutionalized children. *Child Development*, 1966, *37*, 97–101.

Nelson, R. O., & Hayes, S. C. The nature of behavioral assessment: A commentary. *Journal of Applied Behavior Analysis*, 1979, *12*, 491–500.

Nelson, R. O., Kapust, J. A., & Dorsey, B. L. Minimal reactivity of overt classroom observations on student and teacher behaviors. *Behavior Therapy*, 1978, *9*, 695–702.

Nowicki, S., Jr., & Strickland, B. R. A locus of control scale for children. *Journal of Consulting and Clinical Psychology*, 1973, *40*, 148–154.

Osborne, J. G. Free-time as a reinforcer in the management of a classroom behavior. *Journal of Applied Behavior Analysis*, 1969, *2*, 113–118.

Palkes, H., Stewart, M., & Freedman, J. Improvement in maze performance of hyperactive boys as a function of verbal-training procedures. *Journal of Special Education*, 1972, *5*, 337–342.

Palkes, H., Stewart, M., & Kahana, B. Porteus maze performance of hyperactive boys after training in self-directed verbal commands. *Child Development*, 1968, *39*, 817–826.

Patterson, C. J., & Carter, D. B. Attentional determinants of children's self-control in waiting and working situations. *Child Development*, 1979, *50*, 272–275.

Patterson, G. R. Interventions for boys with conduct problems: Multiple settings, treatments, and criteria. *Journal of Consulting and Clinical Psychology*, 1974, *42*, 471–481.

Patterson, G. R., Cobb, J. A., & Ray, R. S. A social engineering technology for retraining the families of aggressive boys. In H. E. Adams & I. P. Unikel (Eds.), *Issues and trends in behavior therapy*. Springfield, Ill.: Thomas, 1973.

Paulauskas, S. L., & Campbell, S. B. G. Social perspective-taking and teacher ratings of peer interaction in hyperactive boys. *Journal of Abnormal Child Psychology*, 1979, *7*, 483–493.

Peacock, R., Lyman, R. D., & Rickard, H. C. Correspondence between self-report and observer report as a function of task difficulty. *Behavior Therapy*, 1978, *9*, 578–583.

Peed, S., Roberts, M., & Forehand, R. Evaluation of the effectiveness of a standardized parent training program in altering the interaction of mothers and their noncompliant children. *Behavior Modification*, 1977, *1*, 323–350.

Peele, R. A., & Routh, D. K. Maternal control and self-control in the 3-year-old child. *Bulletin of the Psychonomic Society*, 1978, *11*, 349–352.

Piche, G., Michlin, M., Rubin, D., & Johnson, F. Relationships between fourth graders' performances on selected role-taking tasks and referential communication accuracy. *Child Development*, 1975, *46*, 965–969.

Platt, J., Spivack, G., Altman, N., Altman, D., & Peizer, S. B. Adolescent problem-solving thinking. *Journal of Consulting and Clinical Psychology*, 1974, *42*, 787–793.

Porteus, S. D. *The maze test and mental differences.* Vineland, N.J.: Smith, 1933.

Porteus, S. D. *The maze test: Recent advances.* Palo Alto, Calif.: Pacific Books, 1955.

Riddle, M., & Robert, A. H. Delinquency, delay of gratification, recidivism, and the Porteus Maze Tests. *Psychological Bulletin*, 1977, *84*, 417–425.

Rosenbaum, M. S., & Drabman, R. S. Self-control training in the classroom. A review and critique. *Journal of Applied Behavior Analysis*, 1979, *12*, 467–486.

Sawin, D. B., & Parke, R. D. Development of self-verbalized control of resistance to deviation. *Developmental Psychology*, 1979, *15*, 120–127.

Shantz, C. V. The development of social cognition. In E. M. Hetherington (Ed.), *Review of child development research.* (Vol. 5). Chicago: University of Chicago Press, 1975.

Shure, M. B., & Spivack, G. Means-ends thinking, adjustment and social class among elementary age children. *Journal of Consulting and Clinical Psychology*, 1972, *38*, 348–353.

Skinner, B. F. *Beyond freedom and dignity.* New York: Knopf, 1971.

Spielberger, C. D. *Preliminary manual for the State-Trait Anxiety Inventory for Children ("How I Feel Questionnaire").* Palo Alto, Calif.: Consulting Psychologists Press, 1973.

Spivack, G., Platt, J., & Shure, M. B. *The problem-solving approach to adjustment.* San Francisco: Jossey-Bass, 1976.

Spivack, G., & Shure, M. B. *Social adjustment of young children: A cognitive approach to solving real-life problems.* San Francisco: Jossey-Bass, 1974.

Sutton-Smith, B., & Rosenberg, B. G. A scale to identify impulsive behavior in children. *Journal of Genetic Psychology*, 1959, *95*, 211–216.

Toner, I. J., Parke, R. D., & Yussen, S. R. The effect of observation of model behavior on the establishment and stability of resistance to deviation in children. *Journal of Genetic Psychology*, 1978, *132*, 283–290.

Urbain, E. S., & Kendall, P. C. Review of social-cognitive problem-solving interventions with children. *Psychological Bulletin*, 1980, *88*, 109–143.

Urberg, K., & Docherty, E. Development of role-taking skills in young children. *Developmental Psychology*, 1976, *12*, 198–203.

Wahler, R. G. Some structural aspects of deviant child behavior. *Journal of Applied Behavioral Analysis*, 1975, *8*, 27–42.

Winston, A. S., Torrey, D., & Labbee, P. Children's self-reinforcement: Some evidence for maximization of payoff and minimization of effort. *Child Development*, 1978, *49*, 882–884.

9

Teaching Self-Recording, Self-Evaluation, and Self-Reward to Nonclinic Children and Adolescents*

Alan M. Gross
and
Ronald S. Drabman

When confronted with a case involving a child, the behavioral clinician usually teaches the relevant adult how to manage the contingencies governing the child's behavior. However, recently there has been increasing interest in teaching children methods to alter their own behavior. This shift in focus seems to have occurred for a number of reasons. When parents, teachers, and other agents control the treatment contingencies they often miss a great deal of behavior. As such, the desired response may not be consistently reinforced (Kazdin, 1975). Those who administer the contingencies may also become discriminative stimuli. The child may learn to perform the target behavior only in the presence of the individual who delivers reinforcers (Redd & Birnbrauer, 1969). Moreover, when children control their own behavior, this allows adults to spend more time teaching other impor-

*The authors thank M. Jeffrey Farrar for his assistance in gathering some of the materials that were used in the preparation of this chapter.

tant skills (O'Leary & Dubey, 1979). Finally, it is hoped that by teaching children to control their own behavior, stronger maintenance effects will result than those obtained under external control (O'Leary & Dubey, 1979).

While many techniques have been incorporated into self management training with children, the three procedures that have received the most attention are self-recording, self-evaluation, and self-reinforcement. Self-recording refers to individuals observing and recording occurrences of their own target behaviors (Nelson, 1977). This procedure is used both to assess responding and as a treatment technique. In self-evaluation, target behavior is monitored by the individual and evaluated on a subjective basis, against a specific criterion. The contingent delivery of rewarding consequences to oneself is often called self-reinforcement.

The purpose of the present chapter is to provide a detailed discussion on the use of these three self-management methods with children and adolescents. We will attempt to go beyond summarizing research and theory and emphasize "how-to" aspects. Our aim is to point out the practical factors involved in applying these methods in the clinical setting. It is hoped that by describing the relevant variables affecting these procedures, we will stimulate further research and enhance the clinical utility or teaching self-management to children.

SELF-RECORDING

Self-recording (or self-monitoring), the observing of one's own behavior, is a two-step procedure. Individuals first must learn to discriminate specific aspects of their behavior in order to determine if the target response has occurred. Upon observing the particular behavior, he or she must then make the self-record response. Here the individual notes the occurrence of the behavior using some predetermined procedure.

Self-recording can be used as an assessment tool and as a behavior-change technique. When employed during assessment, the individual is asked to note problematic events and the circumstances surrounding them. These data allow the therapist to identify behavior-environment relationships, target responses, as well as to suggest behavior change strategies. Once a treatment is selected, subsequent self-recording serves to monitor the frequency of the target behavior, providing data for program evaluation.

When self-recording is used as a treatment technique, the method employed does not differ from that seen when it is implemented for assessment. The act of observing and recording one's own behavior is commonly associated with a change in the frequency of the target response. These reactive effects are generally considered therapeutic, because desirable target behaviors often increase while undesirable target responses decrease in frequency (Broden, Hall, & Mitts, 1971; Kazdin, 1974; Nelson, 1977). Hence, the use of self-recording as a treatment strategy simply attempts to capitalize on this reactivity.

It should be noted, however, that although reactivity at times may be therapeutically useful, it can create problems during assessment. Reactivity to self-recording makes it difficult to obtain stable baseline data. Additionally, evaluating a specific treatment technique can be problematic when the data collection procedure (self-recording) may be contributing to the behavior change. As such, it is necessary at times to have another individual observe the patient's behavior prior to the use of self-monitoring. This provides baseline data to compare with the self-recorded data.

A variety of self-recording techniques have been developed. A very popular method during the early stages of assessment is the *behavioral diary*. This procedure is designed to help the therapist identify relevant variables associated with the problem behavior. The therapist and patient first discuss and define the problem area. The patient is then instructed to carry a small note pad at all times. When the individual is in the problem setting or emits the target behavior, he or she records the circumstances surrounding the response; that is, describing antecedent event, the behavior emitted, and the consequences of the response. For example, a bright 10-year-old boy, referred because he has trouble controlling his temper, might be asked to write down what he was doing just before a temper outburst, giving particular attention to who he was involved with and the nature of the activity. He would also be asked to note what he did when he was upset and what occurred following the outburst. From this information the therapist would attempt to identify the controlling variables and suggest a treatment.

When the target response of a self-management program is a discrete behavior, a frequency count is an appropriate self-recording technique. Here, the individual is instructed to note each occurrence of the particular behavior. To facilitate this procedure, the individual is often provided with specific recording sheets or mechanical counters (e.g., golfer's wrist counter). For example, Ollendick (1981) had a young boy use a wrist counter to monitor the occurrence of his facial tics. He was taught to wear the counter every day and press the button on the instrument whenever he observed himself emitting a facial tic. It is important to note that when frequency counts are used, the individual must be instructed to monitor his or her behavior over a specific daily time interval. Failure to do this makes daily data comparisons invalid.

When the behavior to be monitored is not discrete, duration and time sampling measures are common self-recording techniques. In particular, if the target response varies in length of occurrence (e.g., studying), duration measures may provide the most sensitive estimate of the response. Stop-watches, wristwatches with built in stopwatch accessories, or standard wall clocks can be used to time responding. Choice of a specific instrument will vary depending on the informational needs of the therapist. The patient is simply instructed to activate and stop the device concurrent with starting and completion of the target behavior. If the target behavior was studying, for example, the therapist might ask the student to write down when he or she began and finished studying each day.

Time sampling is also used to record nondiscrete behaviors. Furthermore, at times it is employed with discrete responses that occur at such a high fre-quency that continuous monitoring would become aversive. In time sampl-ing, a large period of time is divided into smaller units. A day, for example, might be divided into 2-hour blocks. At the end of each block, the in-dividual would observe his or her behavior for a 10-minute interval and note whether the behavior occurred during the interval. A variation of this pro-cedure involves having a timer set for different time intervals throughout a large block of time. When the timer sounds, the individual notes whether he or she was engaged in the target behavior at that moment. This is a par-ticularly common technique when teaching children to monitor their on-task classroom behavior. The teacher sets a kitchen timer and asks the children to mark on a specific recording sheet whether they were doing their school work when the timer sounded (Glynn & Thomas, 1974).

Time sampling is a convenient method of data collection. It should be noted, however, that the rates of behavior across time blocks may vary and that this will not be reflected on the data sheet. A child may be on task for the entire 15-minute period prior to the sounding of the cue to record his or her behavior. If the child is not engaged in the response at the moment of the record cue, "off task" will be scored. At the same time, however, a child who was off task for almost the entire interval, but started to work a mo-ment prior to the self-record cue, would score his or her behavior as on task. Extended baseline observations are often conducted to reduce this effect and obtain accurate measures.

In summary, self-recording can be a useful tool during both the assess-ment and treatment stages of a behavioral intervention. During assessment, a behavioral diary may result in information that leads to the identification of target behaviors and the environmental arrangements maintaining these responses. Self-recording throughout treatment also provides data against which an intervention can be evaluated. Finally, the reactive effects of the procedure may contribute to behavior change.

Examples—Clinical and Classroom

The effectiveness of self-recording as a treatment technique with children and adolescents has been demonstrated in several studies. Anthony (1978) treated a 9-year-old boy for trichotillomania using self-monitoring. The youngster was instructed to wear a wrist counter and record urges to pull and instances of hair-pulling. A baseball cap worn by the boy served to cue recording because he had to remove the cap to pull his hair. It was reported that hair-pulling was eliminated following 6 days of treatment and the effects were maintained at the 6-month follow-up. Ollendick (1981) has reported successfully treating facial tics using self-monitoring.

McKenzie and Rushall (1974) used self-monitoring to increase attendance and decrease tardiness to practice sessions with an adolescent swim team. Following 55 days of baseline observations conducted by the experimenters, the youths were given an attendance sheet to record their practice arrival and departure times. The procedure resulted in a dramatic improvement in attendance, which was maintained over a 2-week follow-up.

Self-recording has also been successfully used with children and adolescents in classroom settings. In an early study, Broden, Hall, and Mitts (1971) used self-recording to increase attending in an eighth-grade girl and to decrease talking out in class in an eighth-grade boy. The girl was given a recording sheet with three rows of 10 squares and told to mark whether she was studying during history class "whenever she thought of it." Record sheets were turned into the school counselor, who provided praise for studying. Following a reversal to baseline phase, the teacher was asked to praise the girl for appropriate in-class behavior. Conditions were then altered, and only teacher praise was delivered. In-class study behavior doubled during self-recording and maintained across a 3-week follow-up. Self-recording initially produced a desired decrease in the other student's talking-out-in-class behavior. This effect, however, did not maintain.

Gottman and McFall (1972) used self-recording to increase classroom participation with a group of potential high school dropouts. One half of the class was told to record instances of speaking during class discussions and the remaining youngsters noted instances when they wanted to speak but didn't. The conditions were subsequently reversed. Comparisons with experimenter-collected baseline data revealed that self-recording increased speaking in class. Self-recording of instances where the youth did not participate, but wanted to, resulted in a decrease in the response. The authors concluded that the reactive effects of self-recording at times may be therapeutic.

In an institutional setting for delinquent girls, Seymour and Stokes (1976) added self-recording to an ongoing token program. The youths were given 3-by-5 index cards and told to record whether they performed their chores during specific work sessions. Additionally, the girls were instructed in how to cue the staff to praise them for a job well done. They were then asked to self-record instances of stimulating praise from staff. Results indicated that self-recording increased work performance and frequency of staff praise. More importantly, these behavior changes occurred in the absence of increased token reinforcement.

Affecting Variables

The studies described suggest self-recording to be an effective behavior-change technique. There are instances, however, where behavior change resulting from self-recording has been transient and responding quickly returned to baseline levels (Kazdin, 1974). Other investigators have also reported occasions where no reactive effects were observed following the implementation of self-recording (Mahoney, Moura, & Wade, 1973; Spates & Kanfer, 1977; Stollack, 1967). These inconsistent findings have led to attempts to identify variables influencing the reactivity of the procedure.

Kanfer (1970) hypothesizes that self-recording is part of a feedback loop. People discriminate aspects of their behavior for comparison with their personal behavioral standards. This information then cues self-reinforcement or self-punishment processes to adjust responding accordingly. This suggests that the desirability, or valence, of a behavior would be an important factor affecting self-monitoring.

Kazdin (1974) examined this hypothesis in an experiment with undergraduate college students. Subjects were instructed to construct 40 sentences. They were then divided into three groups and given the following instructions prior to constructing an additional 40 sentences: One group of subjects was told to self-record the use of the words "I" and "we." The other subjects were also instructed to self-record; however, one group was told that intelligent, creative, and sensitive individuals were known to use these words frequently in their writing. The remaining group was given the opposite message. It was reported that self-recording alone had little effect on the use of "I" and "we." Positive valence plus self-recording, however, resulted in an increase, and negative valence plus self-recording resulted in a decline in the frequency with which the subjects used these words in their sentences. Similar findings in a laboratory setting have been reported by Cavior and Marabotto (1976) and Sieck and McFall (1976).

Motivation to alter one's behavior also appears to be an important factor contributing to the therapeutic success of self-recording. Lipinski, Black, Nelson, and Ciminero (1975) asked smokers who wanted or did not want to stop smoking to self-record their rate of cigarette comsumption. They observed a decrease in smoking only among subjects who reported wanting to stop smoking. Similarly, Broden et al. (1971) reported altering the classroom behavior of two eighth-graders using self-recording. The behavior change observed with one student, however, was short-lived. This student did not request assistance in changing his behavior, as did the other youth; the intervention was implemented on the initiative of his teacher.

Kazdin (1974) has observed that goal setting and performance feedback may positively affect the reactivity of self-recording. In the sentence-construction task described above, he observed that subjects given a performance criterion showed greater reactive effects to self-recording than did self-recording subjects who did not have this criterion. Additionally, he found that subjects who were given feedback on their performance of the target behavior in addition to self-recording showed greater reactivity than self-record alone or feedback-only subjects.

Task difficulty also may be an important factor influencing the reactivity of self-recording. Peacock, Layman, and Rickard (1978) monitored the cabin-cleaning behavior of a group of boys at a summer camp. The cleaning chores were divided into easy and difficult tasks. Following an experimenter-gathered baseline, the youths were asked to self-record their performance of the 10 cleaning tasks. This was followed by the adoption of an accuracy contingency that required a specific level of reliability of reporting in order for a boy to gain access to breakfast. Initially, the youngsters reported performing the tasks at a higher level than they were actually performing them. When the accuracy contingency was implemented it was observed that the boys increased their performance on the five easy tasks, but altered their reporting on difficult tasks. Reactivity occurred only with the easy chores.

Reinforcement contingent on behavior change also appears to enhance the reactivity of self-recording (Nelson, 1977). Lipinski et al. (1975) found that college students who were reinforced for face touching when self-recording exhibited greater decrements in this behavior than those who only self-recorded. Nelson, Lipinski, and Black (1976) observed that face touching among retarded subjects showed greater reactivity to self-recording when subjects expected edible reinforcers contingent on behavior change. A difficulty with evaluating the effect of reinforcement on reactivity to self-recording, however, is determining how much of the behavior change is due to the contingent reinforcement. It may be that reinforcement alone would foster this behavior change, rendering self-recording an unnecessary treatment component.

Accuracy of Self-recording

An interesting finding regarding reactivity of self-recording pertains to the accuracy of self-recorded data. Although accurate observation is of crucial importance when self-recording is used during assessment, it appears to be relatively unimportant when self-recording is used as a treatment (Kazdin, 1974). Broden et al. (1971) noted large behavior change in two eighth-grade students using self-recording. It was reported, however, that there was little correlation between the subjects' and experimenter's daily observations. Similarly, Fixen, Phillips, and Wolf (1972) reported that self-recording pro-

duced reactive effects for room-cleaning behavior in adolescent predelinquents, even though poor reliability of observation was observed. Lipinski
and Nelson (1974) have also found reactive effects to self-recording in the
absence of accurate observation.

As previously noted, accuracy may not be important when a clinician is
primarily interested in producing reactive effects with self-monitoring.
When this procedure is used as an assessment technique, however, the ex-
actness of the data becomes crucial. A number of variables have been
shown to influence the accuracy of self-recording. Training individuals in
self-recording appears to positively effect performance. Nelson, Lipinski,
and Boykin (1978) improved accuracy of self-recording in retarded
adolescents by providing definitions of the target behavior, videotape scoring, and in vivo practice. Fixen et al. (1972) used modeling and instructions
to improve self-recording accuracy in adolescent predelinquents. Bornstein,
Mungas, Quevillon, Knivila, Miller, and Holombo (1978) have also improved self-recording accuracy using feedback and verbal praise.

The awareness of a reliability observation also has been shown to improve the accuracy of self-recorded data. Layne, Rickard, Jones, and
Lyman (1976) monitored the cabin-cleaning behavior of male adolescents in
a summer camp setting. The youngsters were given training in self-recording
and asked to record their behavior every morning prior to breakfast.
Following the display of poor accuracy, daily reliability checks were implemented. This procedure resulted in a dramatic improvement in the accuracy of the youths' data. More importantly, accuracy was maintained
when the experimenters altered surveillance to a variable ratio schedule.
Lipinski et al. (1975) have also demonstrated that obtrusive reliability
assessments can improve the accuracy of self-recorded data.

Finally, reinforcement for accurate self-recording has been shown to improve data reporting. Risley and Hart (1968) rewarded children for correspondence between verbal reports of their play behavior and actual
observed play. They found that this resulted in a large increase in self-report
accuracy. Similarly, in the Fixen et al. (1972) study described earlier, token
reinforcement improved self-recording accuracy in predelinquents.

Maximizing Effectiveness of Self-Recording

Although much of the research on self-recording has been conducted with
adults, a number of conclusions can be made regarding variables to consider when using the procedure with children and adolescents. The effectiveness of self-recording during assessment appears to depend on training,
motivation, performance feedback, surveillance, and reinforcement for accurate data reporting. Instructions, role playing, and scoring videotapes of
ones' own behavior may be the most effective training techniques. Using

verbal reinforcement to raise the accuracy of self-recording may be successful in some cases, but tangible reinforcers are generally more powerful. Additionally, once a subject has begun to self-record reliably, surveillance appears to be useful in maintaining this performance. Obtrusive daily checks can be subsequently thinned to a variable-ratio schedule of occurrence. Most importantly, however, the success of self-recording as an assessment technique will depend on the subject's cooperativeness. For this reason, it may be helpful to initially select a simple-to-record target behavior and maximize reinforcement for compliance with instructions. Once the child is reliably self-recording, the procedures described can be used to shape and maintain accuracy. Just like any response, self-recording is an operant and is subject to modification through environmental manipulation.

To increase the likelihood of producing reactive effects with self-recording, the clinician should consider a number of variables. The target behavior chosen should be one that the youth desires to change. This behavior also should be a simple rather than complex task. At times, to accomplish this, a response may need to be broken into components and shaped individually. Providing youngsters with performance goals and feedback regarding their movement toward these goals may also enhance reactivity. Reinforcement for behavior change has also been associated with reactivity to self-recording. Since contingent reinforcement modifies children's behavior in the absence of self-recording, the clinician should weigh the advantages of using these procedures together.

A final point regarding the use of self-recording relates to the child's level of motivation. Clearly, attempting to alter a youngster's behavior which he or she has no desire to change will be difficult, if not impossible, using a procedure that requires a large amount of personal responsibility. Although motivation levels can be altered using operant procedures, this requires a great deal of involvement from external agents. If this problem arises, the clinician must weigh the costs and benefits involved in initially using others to shape compliance so that a self-change program can be implemented. Self-conducted behavior-change programs are not appropriate for all youngsters. Often it may be just as expedient, if not more expedient, to modify a child's responses using external agents.

SELF-EVALUATION

Self-evaluation consists of an individual monitoring his or her behavior and evaluating it, on a subjective basis, against a specific criterion. It is hypothesized that people attempt to behave in a manner consistent with an internal code of behavior and that self-evaluation serves as a feedback mechanism to guide responding. Cautela (1971) asserts that behavior change results from self-evaluation because it elicits covert self-reinforcing or self-punishing statements. Other theorists do not limit these rewards solely to covert events. Many researchers, however, do consider self-evaluation to be a necessary component of any self-management program (e.g., Kanfer).

Training adolescents and children in self-evaluation involves providing the youngsters with a specific criterion with which to compare their behavior. For example, in a math class, Klein and Schuler (Note 1) gave children specific answer sheets and asked them to evaluate their math work by comparing their answers to those on the answer page. Similarly, Ballard and Glynn (1975) wrote the rules of good grammar on the class bulletin board and had students compare their short stories with these rules.

Examples — Clinical and Classroom

It would be expected that if self-evaluation leads to evaluative statements on the part of the child, it would have the potential (depending on the motivation of the youth) to increase or decrease response rates. When used by itself, however, self-evaluation has not been a consistently effective behavior-change technique. Klein and Gory (1976) had third-graders self-evaluate their math work. The children were given an answer sheet with which to compare their workbook assignment answers. The children demonstrated a *decrease* in mean percent correct relative to baseline during self-evaluation. Klein and Schuler (Note 1), however, found that self-evaluation led to an increase in academic performance when children were required to earn the privilege of self-evaluating their math work. The youngsters had to demonstrate a specific percent correct on workbook pages in order to self-score the assignments. Failure to meet this criterion resulted in teacher evaluation. It is not clear, however, whether the increase in math performance was due to self-evaluation. The contingent use of self-evaluation makes this procedure a privilege, and the children may have found it reinforcing to earn new privileges.

Santogrossi, O'Leary, Romanczyk, and Kaufman (1973) investigated the effect of self-evaluation on the classroom behavior of disruptive adolescents. Following baseline, the youngsters were told to self-evaluate their classroom behavior and contingently award themselves points. There were no backup reinforcers associated with the points. Self-evaluation alone had no effect on the youths' disruptive behavior. Teacher-determined points with backup reinforcers were then implemented, and there was a dramatic decline in disruptiveness. Similarly, Turkowitz, O'Leary, and Ironsmith (1975) found that self-evaluation had no effect on the level of disruptive behavior in children manifesting academic and social problems. Teacher-delivered reinforcement, however, produced a sharp decline in disruptive behavior relative to baseline levels. Additionally, it was reported that during self-evaluation, the youngsters' ratings were very inaccurate.

Finally, Ballard and Glynn (1975) used self-evaluation in a self-management program to improve writing skills in third-graders. The children were asked to compare their writing against a chart describing the target behaviors and to record occurrences of the targeted responses. Self-evaluation had no effect on the target behaviors. When reinforcement was made contingent on the occurrence of the target responses, however, there were large increases in the frequency of these behaviors.

Self-evaluation has also been included as a component in programs designed to teach self-management skills to children (e.g., Bolstad & Johnson, 1972; Drabman, Spitalnik, & O'Leary, 1973; Robertson, Simon, Pachman, & Drabman, 1979). In these programs, however, reinforcement is always paired with self-evaluation. As such, it is not possible to determine the effect of self-evaluation alone on the target behavior.

Problems With the Procedure

In addition to the question of efficacy of self-evaluation as a behavior-change strategy, other problems with the procedure have been reported. Gross and Brigham (Note 2) taught seventh-graders to self-evaluate their performance on reading comprehension assignments. Self-evaluation initially resulted in a large decrease in both content and grammatical errors. After the procedure was in effect for a short while, however, the youngsters vehemently complained about the extra work that self-evaluation involved. At this time, a return to baseline performance levels was also noted. The experimenter then told the youngsters that if they performed at a specific accuracy level, they could avoid self-evaluation. The avoidance contingency resulted in an immediate and dramatic decline in assignment errors. Santogrossi et al. (1973) also reported that the adolescents in their study rebelled as the work associated with self-evaluation was increased. These findings suggest that when employing self-evaluation, it may be important to select a relatively simple and easy-to-use evaluation technique.

Summary and Suggestions

The results of the studies discussed raise serious questions regarding the effectiveness of self-evaluation as a behavior-change technique. Evaluating one's behavior according to an external criterion can not be performed without self-monitoring of that behavior. As such, it is very likely that instructing a youngster to self-record acts as a discriminative stimulus for self-evaluation (Rosenbaum & Drabman, 1979). If this is the case, it would not be predicted that using self-evaluation in a self-management program would have any further impact on behavior than what would be expected as a result of the self-recording process. Self-evaluation may have its largest impact when used to teach children to contingently self-deliver rewards.

SELF-REWARD

Numerous questions have been raised regarding the definition of self-reinforcement. The complexities of conceptualizing the process, as well as those involved in deciding on an acceptable terminology to communicate constructs and operations, are illustrated in various theoretical discussions (Bandura, 1975; Brigham, 1978; Catania, 1976). In the applied setting, when an individual self-delivers a reward contingent on the occurrence of a response, it is most often labeled self-reinforcement. This usage does not pay attention to whether there is an increase in frequency of the behavior preceding the reward (Gross & Brigham, 1978). Reinforcement, by definition, however, necessitates such a change. Therefore, it seems more appropriate to refer to this procedure as the delivery of self-reward.

Teaching children to self-reward involves two steps. Because it is necessary to discriminate the occurrence of the target response prior to the self-delivery of a reward, teaching self-reward generally begins with instruction in self-monitoring. Once the child learns to monitor his or her behavior, he or she is instructed to contingently self-deliver rewards.

The rules governing the choice of a reward for a child's self-reward program are the same as those used to guide the selection of any reinforcing stimulus. The stimulus should be a proven motivator for the youngster, and it must meet the practical requirements of the intervention situation.

The most commonly used reward system in children's self-management programs is the token system. Token reinforcers reduce many practical problems that may be encountered by the therapist. Youths can easily award themselves reinforcers with minimal disruption. The therapist can also establish numerous backup reinforcers to reduce the likelihood of satiation. Moreover, varying exchange rates allows for frequent delivery of reinforcers without necessitating an increase in consumption of backups. The programming maintenance of behavior change may also be facilitated by fading tokens over time.

Examples—Clinical and Classroom

The effectiveness of self-reward as a behavior-change strategy has been demonstrated in numerous classroom investigations. Glynn (1970) monitored the daily math test performance of four classes of ninth-grade girls. Every day, the teacher read aloud the test answers, and the girls noted on the top of their papers the number of problems they scored correct. Following this phase, one group of youths received token reinforcers at the rate of one for every four correct answers (total of 5 tokens possible per test). A second group of subjects awarded themselves one to five tokens based on what they thought their test performance merited. The third class of girls was yoked to the teacher-determined token group and was given tokens based on that group's performance. The remaining subjects did not receive any tokens. It was reported that the students in the teacher–and self-delivered token groups exhibited the largest improvements in academic performance. Additionally, there was no significant difference in performance between the self-delivered and externally delivered token subjects. Bolstad and Johnson (1972), Felixbrod and O'Leary (1973, 1974), and Frederiksen and Frederiksen (1975) also have reported self-reward to be equally effective as externally delivered rewards in altering behavior.

Ballard and Glynn (1975) improved story writing in elementary school children by using self-reward. In a muliple baseline design, the number of sentences, number of action words, and number of describing words used in the children's daily story-writing exercise were monitored. The children were then instructed to self-record the occurrence of these specific target behaviors. This was followed by the sequential introduction of self-delivered rewards across target behaviors. Token points were used as rewards. It was reported that self-recording had little effect on the youngsters' writing behavior. The addition of self-reward, however, resulted in substantial increases in the number of sentences written as well as in the usage of action and describing words. Additionally, independent ratings of the children's essays reflected a large improvement.

Self-reward has also been shown to be more effective than self-imposed response cost in altering the reading behavior of second-graders (Humphrey, Karoly, & Kirschenbaum, 1978). In a counterbalanced ABAC design, the children either self-delivered tokens for correct responses or fined themselves tokens for errors on reading workbook assignments. Although both self-management procedures produced increases in work accuracy, the children performed best during the self-reward condition. In a similar study, however, Kaufman and O'Leary (1972) found self-imposed response cost and self-reward to be equally effective in decreasing disruptive behavior in adolescents in a psychiatric hospital school.

In addition to the modification of academic responding, self-reward has been used to alter children's disruptive behavior. Bolstad and Johnson (1972) monitored "on-task" behavior in a second-grade classroom. Following baseline, the youngsters received training in self-recording, self-evaluation, and self-reward. At various intervals while the children worked, a tape recorder sounded a tone. The children were told, upon hearing this tone, to note on specific data sheets whether they were on task. They subsequently awarded themselves rewards based on the number of intervals that they were on task. The procedure resulted in a large decrease in disruptive behavior. Glynn and Thomas (1974) and Glynn, Thomas, and Shee (1976) have reported similar findings.

Affecting Variables

Although a review of applied studies indicates that children can alter their behavior simply by being trained to contingently self-deliver preselected rewards, research in developmental psychology suggests a number of variables that may be important to consider when implementing a self-reward program. Masters (1968, 1972, 1973) and Masters and Peskay (1972) have shown that social comparison can influence a child's use of self-reward. In one study, Masters (1973) had two children simultaneously perform matching-to-sample tasks. One child was considered the subject, and he received the same, more, or less reward than his partner. The subject was then asked to play a game by himself and award himself tokens. He found that children who received less rewards than a peer showed greater levels of subsequent self-reward than children who were more equitably treated.

Models displaying self-reward responses have been shown to profoundly effect a child's standard for self-reward. Hildebrandt, Feldman, and Ditrichs (1973) presented children with specific strict rules for self-reward. The youngsters then played a game with an experimenter who modeled either the strict or a lenient self-reward standard. The children were then told to continue to play this game alone and reward themselves for their performance. When the behavior of the model corresponded with the rules presented, the youths adopted this reward standard. When the model was inconsistent with the rule, however, the children tended to adopt the lenient reward standard. The authors concluded that in attempting to teach children standards of self-reward, it is important to have concordance between rules and the behavior of training models. Mischel and Liebert (1966) have reported similar findings.

Race and sociometric status also appear to affect the children's self-reward standards. Masters and Peskay (1972) had black and white children of various socioeconomic backgrounds work on mazes. After completing each maze, the child pressed a button and received predetermined performance feedback. Some of the children were instructed at this time to take as many tokens as their performance deserved (contingent group). The other youngsters were simply told that after completing each maze, they should take as many tokens as they desired. All the children awarded themselves more rewards following success feedback than following failure feedback. The youngsters also took more rewards in the noncontingent than contingent conditions. However, it was also noted that under all self-reward phases, regardless of their SES status, black children awarded themselves significantly more tokens than white children. This effect was only noted for the white children from lower SES levels.

Children also display various rates of self-reward depending on length and difficulty of task. Masters and Christy (1974) had 7- and 8-year-old children complete card sorting, form-discrimination, and arithmetic tasks in various combinations of length and difficulty. After completing their work session, the youngsters were given the opportunity to award themselves from 1 to 10 tokens based on what they believed they deserved. The longer it took a child to complete a task, the more tokens the child awarded himself or herself. Contrary to predictions, however, a consistent relationship between amount of self-reward and task difficulty was not observed. Further research is necessary to determine the relationship of task difficulty to rates of self-reward.

Achievement standards may also affect self-reward in children. Masters, Furman, and Barden (1977) had 4- and 5-year-olds perform discrimination tasks in which they were given cumulative feedback across trials. Every correct response emitted illuminated a light on a small tower. The children were given either low, medium, high, or accelerating performance standards. Additionally, the youngsters received tokens depending on whether they reached their performance criteria. The youngsters in the high- and accelerating-standard conditions performed best, followed by the medium- and low-standard children. Similar performances were observed when self-delivered praise was substituted for tokens. Although their performances differed, the low- and accelerating-standard groups were awarded the same amount of rewards. This indicates that the performance standards and not rewards accounted for differences in responding (Masters et al., 1977). It was hypothesized that accelerating standards provides incentive to work to earn reinforcers. With low standards, there is little reason to increase performance beyond the criteria, because there are no additional rewards. These findings suggest that in applied settings, self-reward would be more effective if the target behavior was gradually shaped or if the behavior-frequency to reward ratio was continuously increased.

The importance of children having previous experience with externally controlled reinforcement prior to exposure to self-reward has received little attention. Glynn and Thomas (1974) found that third-graders were capable of using self-reward to increase their rate of on-task behavior without previous experience with externally delivered reinforcement. Thomas (1976) has reported similar results. Additionally, Rosenbaum and Drabman (1979), in a recent review, concluded that normal children in a regular classroom could initiate behavior change using self-reward in the absence of previous experience with externally controlled reinforcement. Most studies using self-reward in applied settings, however, have exposed the children to externally delivered reinforcers prior to self-reward training (e.g., Bolstad & Johnson, 1972, Fredericksen & Fredericksen, 1975; Wood & Flynn, 1978). This practice may provide benefits that have not been fully explored. In particular, performance standards may be affected by experience with externally imposed reinforcement contingencies. As noted earlier, children have been shown to adopt performance standards from models (Bandura, Grusec, & Menlove, 1967; Hildebrandt et al., 1966, 1967). Until further research addresses these questions, it may be best to precede self-reward training with externally delivered reinforcement.

Problems with the Procedure

When children are allowed to deliver their own rewards, it is often observed that they choose very lenient performance criteria. Felixbrod and O'Leary (1973) had second-graders complete math problems for points that were exchangeable for prizes. One group of youths was given the opportunity to select their own performance criteria. Each youngster in the second group was yoked to a self-reward-group subject and received the same amount of rewards as that child. Although there were no differences in performance between self- and externally determined reward subjects, over the course of the study, the "self-determined" youngsters tended to choose progressively more lenient performance standards. Brownell, Colletti, Ersner-Herschfield, Herschfield, and Wilson (1977) and Felixbrod and O'Leary (1974) have also reported similar findings.

Brownell et al. (1977) demonstrated that leniency in self-reward performance criteria could be altered using instructions. Using the procedure developed by Felixbrod and O'Leary (1973, 1974), every day prior to math, the children were given a sheet with response-to-reward exchange rates and they were told they could select the exchange rate they desired. The experimenters told some of the children that they wanted them to choose stringent standards, and subsequently provided praise and attention for such selections. The remaining subjects did not receive any prompt when selecting performance contingencies. Children exposed to the prompts tended to select the more stringent criteria, while those not receiving any prompt chose lenient standards. These findings are in agreement with the developmental psychology literature showing that instructions can alter achievement standards (Mischel & Liebert, 1966, 1967).

Related to the issue of leniency is the occurrence of children's self-reward in the absence of the target behavior. In the Santogrossi et al. (1973) study, described earlier, when disruptive adolescents were allowed to award themselves points (exchangeable for backup reinforcers) based on their own evaluation of their behavior, they emitted baseline rates of disruptive responding while awarding themselves high levels of reward. It appears that when youngsters learn there are no aversive contingencies for noncontingent self-reward, they often rate their behavior as appropriate and self-deliver rewards regardless of whether they are behaving appropriately. This is a serious problem because, in essence, it results in contingent reward for inappropriate behavior. Fortunately, this difficulty can be prevented by using an accuracy contingency.

Hundert and Batstone (1978) monitored the math performance of four boys in a special education classroom. The youths were taught to monitor their workbook performance. The boys received points exchangeable for free time, based on their reported accuracy. After determining that the youths were exaggerating their performance, they were told that their workbooks would be collected and checked by the experimenter. Additionally, the boys were informed that inaccurate scoring would result in significant point fines. This contingency greatly reduced the boys' scoring errors. Furthermore, it was reported that accurate scoring and self-reward was maintained when surveillance was performed on a variable-ratio schedule.

Drabman, Spitalnik, and O'Leary (1973) developed a procedure to teach and maintain accurate self-reward. In a classroom of young children, "on-task" behavior was monitored. Following baseline, the teacher evaluated and reinforced (with tokens) each child for appropriate classroom responding. The youngsters were then asked to rate their own behavior and to self-reward at the end of specific time intervals. They were told that if their evaluation matched the teacher's, they would earn bonus tokens. Over time, the matching of teacher and student ratings was faded by gradually selecting fewer children each day for matching. When matching was discontinued, the children independently rated their responding and rewarded themselves tokens based on these evaluations. The procedures resulted in accurate self-reward which was maintained over 12 days. Additionally, there was an increase in "on-task" behavior in control periods in which reinforcement was not available. Robertson, Simon, Pachman, and Drabman (1979), Turkowitz et al. (1975), and Epstein and Goss (1978) have replicated these findings.

Maintenance

Despite the difficulties that have been noted regarding self-reward, there is some evidence to indicate that it may profoundly affect maintenance of behavior change. Wood and Flynn (1978) taught a number of room-cleaning responses to predelinquent youths in a group home. Following baseline and cleaning instructions, a token system based on experimenter evaluation of behavior was implemented. Half of the youngsters were then taught to monitor the occurrence of the target behavior and self-reward contingent on appropriate performance. The others continued to receive tokens from the experimenter based on his evaluation of their performance. When the contingencies on room cleaning were removed, the youths who had experienced training to self-administer rewards maintained high levels of "on-task" performance over a 60-day period. On the other hand, youngsters who only experienced the externally administered tokens showed a substantial decline in room-cleaning behavior. Studies by Drabman et al. (1973), Robertson et al. (1973), and Turkowitz et al. (1975) also indicate that training youngsters to contingently self-reward may facilitate short-term maintenance and generalization of behavior change.

Summary and Suggestions

Self-reward appears to be one of the most powerful components of children's self-management programs. Training youngsters to contingently reward themselves for emitting target behaviors has been repeatedly demonstrated as an effective behavior-change technique. A number of variables have been shown to influence various aspects of self-reward training. Models, instructions, and rules appear to be important to the development of standards for self-reward. This indicates that prior exposure of children to externally controlled reinforcement or to other children involved in self-reward programs may enhance the effectiveness and ease with which children are taught the self-reward procedure. Additionally, exposing youngsters to externally controlled reinforcement offers the opportunity to incorporate the matching procedure into the training method. The matching procedure has been demonstrated as an important tool in preventing lenient and noncontingent self-delivery of rewards. Furthermore, programs that have included a matching component during self-reward training have reported impressive generalization and maintenance-of-treatment effects. Research also indicates that the effect of rewards on behavior may be enhanced by establishing achievement standards of increasing difficulty. This suggests that when teaching children self-reward skills, target behaviors should be broken into component parts and gradually shaped. Alternatively, this same effect could be achieved by altering response-to-reinforcer ratios.

SELF-DETERMINED CONTINGENCIES

In our discussion of self-reward, virtually all the studies described involved children self-delivering rewards according to experimenter- or therapist-determined contingencies. A number of investigations, however, have examined the effect on behavior of allowing children to determine their own reinforcement schedules. Lovitt and Curtiss (1969) had a student self-deliver token points contingent on math performance. Following a phase in which the contingencies were teacher determined, the boy was allowed to determine his own reinforcement schedule. It was observed that the boy performed best when under the self-determination condition. This was noted even when reinforcement rates were held constant across teacher and self-determined phases.

Brownell et al. (1977) had elementary school children do math problems under self-determined and externally determined reinforcement schedules. The youngsters in the self-determined condition were given a set of reinforcement rates and allowed to pick the contingency to which they preferred to respond. The externally determined group was yoked to the self-determined reinforcement group and received the same rate of reward as these subjects. The youngsters responded equally well under both reinforcement conditions. Felixbrod and O'Leary (1973, 1974) have obtained similar findings.

The evidence indicates that self-determined and externally determined contingencies are equally effective in maintaining responding. A problem encountered with self-determined contingencies, however, is that children often choose lenient performance standards. Felixbrod and O'Leary (1973, 1974) have reported that even children who initially select stringent performance criteria change to lenient standards over time. Brownell et al. (1977) also noted that children rapidly learn to maximize their rewards by establishing high reinforcement rates.

The tendency of youths to choose lenient reinforcement contingencies has been controlled using prompts and instructions. In one phase of the Brownell et al. (1977) study, described earlier, some children were told to select whichever contingency they wished. The remaining youths were informed that, although they could select any of the various ccontingencies, the experimenters preferred that they select a stringent one. The selection of a strict contingency resulted in the delivery of praise and attention. It was observed that the youngsters who did not receive the prompt selected a lenient contingency. Subjects in the prompt condition, however, selected a stringent schedule.

Before drawing any conclusion regarding the impact on behavior of allowing children to self-determine their reinforcement contingencies, it is important to note that the investigations in this area have failed to allow the youngsters complete freedom when establishing contingencies. Typically, the child is given a list of alternative reinforcement schedules and told to pick the one to which he or she prefers to respond (e.g., Felixbrod & O'Leary 1973, 1974). Even with these limitations, problems have occurred. The youths tend to select the most lenient reinforcement criteria, which means, in an applied setting, that the child will maximize reinforcement while minimizing performance. Additionally, the likelihood of satiation is increased if the child is able to set a high reinforcement rate. Furthermore, by establishing a lenient reinforcement contingency, children may learn to emit a few appropriate behaviors in a short time period to earn the desired reward, and then stop working and begin to emit inappropriate behavior(s).

Giving children total freedom in determining reinforcement contingencies is unlikely in applied settings. Yet the privilege of choice may be a reinforcer for some youngsters. Brigham and Stoerzinger (1976) found that 7-to 10-year-olds worked harder for a self-selected reward than for the same reward when it was chosen by the experimenter. This suggests that the clinicians might enhance the interest as well as performance of children in self-management programs by allowing them to self-determine (choose) their reinforcement contingencies. In doing this, however, the clinician will likely have to provide limited contingencies from which to select. Given adequate controls, self-determination may be an asset to self-management training. Further research is required before any firm conclusions can be made. In particular, it is important to determine if the positive effect of self-determination (choice) is due to the novelty of the procedure and if it will only have short lived impact.

SELF-INSTRUCTION

Self-instructional training is another potentially important method of developing self-management skills in children (Rosenbaum & Drabman, 1979). The procedure involves teaching youngsters to make verbal statements to themselves in order to guide, direct, or maintain their behavior. In laboratory settings this technique has been shown to have beneficial effects on a variety of behavioral tasks (Bem, 1967; Hartig & Kanfer, 1973; Meichenbaum & Goodman, 1969).

The clinical application of self-instruction training, however, has produced mixed results. Meichenbaum and Goodman (1971) taught self-instruction to second-graders who manifested problems of hyperactive and impulsive behavior. Self-instruction training involved several steps. The youths watched a model perform a task while guiding his behavior by talking aloud. The child then performed the same task while receiving instructions from the experimenter. This was followed by the child performing the task and verbally guiding his or her own responding. Subsequently, the youth performed the task while whispering self-instructions, and finally via covert self-instruction. In the initial stage of training, the experimenter modeled task-relevant skills such as problem definition, planning strategies, guidance, self-evaluation, and self-reward. The children were taught to use self-instruction with a variety of motor tasks of various levels of difficulty. On measures of behavioral and cognitive impulsivity, youngsters who received self-instruction training showed significant improvements in performance relative to control subjects. There were no significant differences between groups, however, on measures of in-class behavior.

Working directly with classroom-related behaviors, Bornstein and Quevillon (1976) taught self-instruction to three overactive 4-year-old boys. The investigators used a training procedure similar to that of Meichenbaum and Goodman (1971), with the modification that the reinforcement was presented contingent on completion of each training step sequence. Relative to baseline, an increase of 65 percent in "on task" behavior was noted following self-instruction training. This improved performance was also observed at follow-up. Robin, Schneider, and Dolnick (1976) also reported reducing in-class aggressive behavior of emotionally disturbed children by using self-instruction training.

Friedling and O'Leary (1979) conducted a systematic replication of the Bornstein and Quevillon (1976) study. Working with hyperactive second- and third-graders, they failed to observe any systematic changes in "on-task" behavior following self-instruction training. They did, however, note increased "on-task" behavior subsequent to the application of a token-reinforcement system.

The mixed results found with the use of self-instruction training with children suggests the need for further research demonstrating its applied significance (Rosenbaum & Drabman, 1979). Additionally, investigation of variables which account for the methods differential success rates in applied situations is also appropriate. Some laboratory experimentation has shown that being reinforced for using self-instructions (Mischel & Patterson, 1976), facility at performing the target behavior (Higa, Tharp, & Calkins, 1978), and the actual use of self-instruction by the child (Monahan & O'Leary, 1971) are directly related to the effectiveness of self-instruction training. Yet, no attempts have been made to evaluate the impact of these variables on clinical applications of the procedure.

CONCLUSIONS & FUTURE DIRECTIONS

Investigations of the effectiveness of self-management with children have shown that youngsters can be taught to observe and record their own behavior and administer their own reinforcement contingencies. To increase the likelihood of successful self-management training, several steps should be followed. Children should begin their training by learning to observe their behavior. Instruction in self-observation should include having the youths compare and match their observations with the ratings of adult observers. Reinforcement should be delivered contingent on accurate self-monitoring. This matching procedure (Drabman et al., 1973) should be faded out after accurate self-recording is established. Additionally, during the matching procedure, the youngsters should experience externally administered reinforcement, contingent on the occurrence of the desired behavior. Control over delivery of reinforcers should be gradually transferred to the children when they can reliably discriminate their behavior. Following the consistent display of appropriate responding, the explicit contingencies should be slowly withdrawn.

In addition to the suggestions regarding *general* procedures to use when teaching children self-management skills, there are a number of factors particular to the *specific* program that will also affect the success of training. Children referred for treatment because of behavior problems will vary in terms of number of disruptive responses exhibited. As such, the clinician will be faced with the decision of whether to treat one problem at a time or to treat them all simultaneously. In these situations, treatment may be more successful if it initially concentrates on the most problematic response. Once improvement has been obtained, treatment should then be gradually altered to include the child's additional inappropriate responses (Drabman & Tucker, 1974).

Similarly, deciding on what portion of each day a treatment should be in effect also must be considered (Drabman & Tucker, 1974). Although it will vary with the severity of the problem, it will often be difficult to obtain immediately behavior change across an entire day. Using a successive-approximation approach, and starting with the time period where the problem is most pronounced, may increase the likelihood the child will be initially successful in his or her use of self-management skills. After an initial success, the program can be expanded to incorporate other relevant times. For example, the poor academic performer may do best if self-management is introduced sequentially across academic subjects.

The selection of rewards is also crucial to the success of a self-management program. This is often simply done by asking the child what he or she desires or by observing the youngster and determining highly preferred events. As noted earlier, however, because it is not always feasible to deliver immediately the preferred rewards, token systems are used in self-management programs. Clinicians should be cautious in the selection of tokens. For example, the young child may respond better to a tangible token (penny, poker chip) than to points. The ability to count and display accumulated wealth may be important to the child. Consideration of the age and preferences of the youngster must be given when selecting tokens.

Deciding on the reinforcement rate is an important factor in the success of the self-reward system. Generally, an attempt is made to maximize responding while minimizing reinforcement. However, too few rewards at the onset of a program may result in the child failing to respond to the contingencies. Starting with a relatively large reinforcement schedule and then gradually increasing the response-to-reward ratio may avoid this potential problem.

If tokens are used in a self-management program, an exchange rate for backup reinforcers must be selected. Frequently clinicians base the exchange rate on the actual cost of a rewarding stimulus or activity. However, problems will be encountered if one fails to attend to the psychological value of a stimulus. Children may be willing to spend more tokens on a 25-cent candy bar than on a 50-cent notebook. Monitoring a child's preference for backup rewards will be helpful in the creation of a successful exchange system.

Although this discussion has focused on self-management training for children, it is clear that these programs initially require a large amount of adult participation. The adult will assist in teaching the child self-management skills, monitoring the child's performance, and collecting data in order to make knowledgeable decisions regarding alterations in the program (e.g., expansion to new times and additional responses; token exchange rate). As such, this person's behavior will have major impact on treatment effectiveness. The treatment mediator must be consistent in his or her interactions with the child and must not change the program without consulting the data. Additionally, the mediator must be patient and willing to help the child alter his or her behavior through successive approximations. Finally, the mediator who frequently praises a child for displaying self-management skills is likely to enhance the effectiveness of a self-management program.

Self-Management Via Behavior Modification Training

The self-management training approaches that have been discussed thus far are those which are most commonly employed in applied settings. Typically, children are taught to administer to themselves the same procedures that therapists would apply if they chose to assume the role of primary treatment mediators. In particular, interventions have focused on teaching youths how to self-deliver a specific technique for a particular problem. The explicit goal of self-management training, however, is to train children to be effective managers of their behavior. Yet few attempts have been made to provide a systematic program of instruction designed to facilitate the acquisition and utilization of behavioral procedures in situations beyond the one initially targeted for treatment.

Gross, Brigham, Hopper, and Bologna (1980) taught predelinquent youths, aged 11 to 15, a course in behavior modification. The youngsters were required to read 10 lessons on the principles and procedures of behavior analysis and to complete study guides and quizzes on each unit. Additionally, the youngsters were required to conduct a self-change project and a behavior modification project to alter another person's behavior. It was reported that the youths were able to learn the fundamentals of behavior technology and successfully alter their own as well as another person's behavior. Additionally, learning these behavior-change skills was associated with a reduction in delinquent behavior.

Gross et al. (1980) suggested that teaching the fundamentals of behavior analysis, in combination with practical experience in the application of the associated techniques, may provide youngsters with a set of readily generalizable management skills. Providing this general working knowledge will not only allow children to manage their own behavior, but it will also enable them to alter the behavior of others who serve as cues for inappropriate responding.

The Gross et al. (1980) study represents a departure from traditional children's self-management training. A number of potential benefits associated with this approach have been suggested. This study, however, is an exploratory first attempt and leaves many questions unanswered regarding the applied significance of this method. It may prove fruitful for clinicians to direct their future self-management research efforts toward determining the full range of applicability of this intervention strategy.

Self-Management for WHOM?

The appropriateness of a behavior-change technique for a specific problem is greatly influenced by the nature of the disorder and patient characteristics. A method that is successful with one child may not be the best procedure to employ with another. To date, the majority of research in children's self-management has been directed toward identifying the critical components of effective training. There is a need, however, for research designed to determine the characteristics of children who are best suited for this type of intervention. Age, clinical status, previous experience with reinforcement programs, and locus of control of reinforcement orientation are just a few variables that need to be explored. Addressing these selection questions may enhance the success of self-management training by identifying those children who are not appropriate for the procedure. Additionally, it may extend the applicability of the method through the development of programs to prepare children for self-management training (cf., Copeland's chapter in this volume).

Generalization

The increased interest in teaching self-management to children has been promoted partially in hopes of enhancing maintenance and generalization of treatment effects (e.g., Stokes & Baer, 1977). Unfortunately, it is difficult to assess the impact that children's self-management has had on these areas, because long term follow-up has been collected so infrequently. Where generalization and maintenance have been assessed, the findings have been mildly encouraging (e.g., Drabman et al., 1973; Robertson et al., 1979; Wood & Flynn, 1978),

In a conceptual analysis of generalization offered by Drabman, Hammer, and Rosenbaum (1979), they suggested that there are 15 classes of generalization. According to this scheme, only three types of generalization have been observed following training children in self-management skills. In particular, investigators have reported the occurrence of time generalization, setting generalization, and time-setting generalization (Rosenbaum & Drabman, 1979). In light of these findings, it is clear that there is a need for further research regarding those factors that can promote generalization across a wide variety of generalization classes.

In Conclusion

In concluding this chapter it seems appropriate to call attention to the relationship of external control to children's self-management. All demonstrations of self-management with children have included external sources of control. This control has been introduced in the form of implementing externally determined contingencies prior to self-determined contingencies (Drabman et al., 1973), requiring children to match their ratings of their behavior with those of an adult observer (Drabman et al., 1973; Robertson et al. 1979), and praising appropriate and ignoring inappropriate behavior displayed when youngsters use self-management skills (Santogrossi et al., 1973, Turkowitz et al., 1975). Additionally, external control has been introduced in the form of limiting the amount of reinforcement youngsters could self-deliver (Felixbrod & O'Leary, 1973, 1974), contingencies governing the delivery of rewards (Brownell et al., 1978), surveillance of self-management behaviors (Layne et al., 1976) and cueing desirable responses (Brownell et al., 1978).

Jones, Nelson, and Kazdin (1977) have suggested that when individuals choose to impose certain contingencies for the self-administration of reinforcing stimuli in the absence of external controlling influences, self-management is evidenced. According to this definition, there have been no demonstrations of theoretical self-management in applied settings.

Skinner (1953) has pointed out, however, that it may not be possible to free behavior from all sources of external control. Simply eliminating obvious, immediate, externally administered reinforcement contingencies does not negate the effects on behavior of a person's learning history. For example, while at first glance it may appear that a person's responding is controlled by the contingent self-delivery of a reward, it can also be argued that such behavior is an avoidance response. That is, the individual has been punished in the past for not completing a behavioral commitment, and therefore emits the response to avoid feelings of shame and guilt.

Rather than viewing self-management as an "either-or" process in which children control their behavior in the absence of external control (a seemingly impossible situation to produce), it may prove more fruitful to view self-management in terms of people learning to control their responding through environmental manipulation. Instead of trying to remove external controlling variables, youngsters should be taught to use these behavior-environment relationships to help guide responding (see Chapters 1 and 16).

The goal of training children in self-management is to help them function more independently and effectively. Teaching children to use procedures that help them to identify and alter response-consequence relationships may be the most practical means of moving toward this goal.

REFERENCE NOTES

1. Klein, R. D., & Schuler, C. F. *Increasing academic performance through the contingent use of self-evaluation.* Paper presented at the meeting of the American Psychological Association, Montreal, August, 1973.
2. Gross, A. M., & Brigham, T. A. *The use of a complex self-evaluation procedure to improve reading comprehension in seventh-grade students.* Paper presented at the meeting of the Western Psychological Association, San Francisco, Calif., 1978.

REFERENCES

Anthony, W. Z. Brief intervention in a case of childhood trichotillomania by self-monitoring. *Journal of Behavior Therapy and Experimental Psychiatry*, 1978, *9*, 173–175.

Ballard, K. D., & Glynn, T. Behavioral self-management in story writing with elementary school children. *Journal of Applied Behavior Analysis*, 1975, *8*, 387–398.

Bandura, A. Self-reinforcement: Theoretical and methodological considerations. *Behaviorism*, 1976, *4*, 135–155.

Bandura, A., Grusec, J. E., & Menlove, F. L. Some social determinants of self-monitoring reinforcement systems. *Journal of Personality and Social Psychology*, 1967, *5*, 449–455.

Bem, S. L. Verbal self-control: The establishment of effective self-instruction. *Journal of Experimental Psychology*, 1967, *74*, 485–491.

Bolstad, O. D., & Johnson, S. M. Self-regulation in the modification of disruptive classroom behavior. *Journal of Applied Behavior Analysis*, 1972, *5*, 443–454.

Bornstein, P. H., & Quevillon, R. P. The effects of a self-instructional package on overactive preschool boys. *Journal of Applied Behavior Analysis*, 1976, *9*, 179–188.

Bornstein, P. H., Mungas, D. M., Quevillon, R. P., Knivila, C. M., Miller, R. K., & Holombo, L. K. Self-monitoring training: Effects of reactivity and accuracy of self-observation. *Behavior Therapy* 1978, *9*, 545–552.

Brigham, T. A. Self-control. In A. C. Catania & T. A. Brigham (Eds.), *The handbook of applied behavior analysis: Social and instructional processes.* New York: Irvington Press, 1978.

Brigham, T. A., & Stoerzinger, A. An experimental analysis of children's preference for self-selected rewards. In T. A. Brigham, R. Hawkins, J. W. Scott, & T. F. McLaughlin (Eds.), *Behavior Analysis in Education*. Dubuque, Iowa: Kendall/Hunt, 1976.

Broden, M., Hall, R. V., and Mitts, B. The effect of self-recording on the classroom behavior of two eighth-grade students. *Journal of Applied Behavior Analysis*, 1971, *4*, 191–199.

Brownell, K. D., Colletti, G., Ersner-Hershfield, R., Hershfield, S. M., & Wilson, G. T. Self-control in school children: Stringency and leniency in self-determined and externally imposed performed standards. *Behavior Therapy*, 1977, *8*, 442–455.

Catania, A. C. The myth of self-reinforcement. *Behaviorism*, 1975, *3*, 192–199.

Cautela, J. R. Covert conditioning. In A. Jacobs & L. B. Sachs (Eds.), *The psychology of private events: Perspectives on covert response systems*. New York: Academic Press, 1971.

Cavior, N., & Marabotto, C. M. Monitoring verbal behaviors in a dyadic interaction: Valence of target behaviors, type, timing, and reactivity to monitoring. *Journal of Consulting and Clinical Psychology*, 1976, *44*, 68–76.

Drabman, R. S., Spitalnik, R., & O'Leary, K. D. Teaching self-control to disruptive children. *Journal of Abnormal Psychology*, 1973, *82*, 10–16.

Drabman, R. S., Hammer, D., & Rosenbaum, M. S. Assessing generalization in behavior modification with children: The generalization map. *Behavioral Assessment*, 1979, *1*, 203–219.

Drabman, R. S., & Tucker, R. D. Why classroom token economies fail. *Journal of School Psychology*, 1974, *12*, 178–188.

Epstein, R., & Goss, C. M. A self-control procedure for the maintenance of nondisruptive behavior in an elementary school child. *Behavior Therapy*, 1978, *9*, 109–117.

Felixbrod, J. J., & O'Leary, K. D. Effects of reinforcement on children's academic behavior as a function of self-determined and externally imposed contingencies. *Journal of Applied Behavior Analysis*, 1973, *6*, 241–250.

Felixbrod, J. J., & O'Leary, K. D. Self-determination of academic standards by children: Toward freedom from external control. *Journal of Educational Psychology*, 1974, *66*, 845–850.

Fixen, D. L., Phillips, E. L., & Wolf, M. M. Achievement Place: The reliability of self-reporting and peer reporting and their effect on behavior. *Journal of Applied Behavior Analysis*, 1972, *5*, 19–33.

Fredericksen, L. W., & Frederiksen, C. B. Teacher determined and self-determined token reinforcement in a special education classroom. *Behavior Therapy*, 1975, *6*, 310–314.

Friedling, C., & O'Leary, S. G. Effects of self-instructional training on second and third-grade hyperactive children: A failure to replicate. *Journal of Applied Behavior Analysis*, 1979, *12*, 211–219.

Glynn, E. L. Classroom applications of self-determined reinforcement. *Journal of Applied Behavior Analysis*, 1970, *3*, 123–132.

Glynn, E. L., & Thomas, J. D. Effect of cueing on self-control of classroom behavior. *Journal of Applied Behavior Analysis*, 1974, *7*, 299–306.

Glynn, E. L., Thomas, J. D., & Shee, S. M. Behavioral self-control of on-task behavior in an elementary classroom. *Journal of Applied Behavior Analysis*, 1973, *6*, 105–113.

Gottman, J. M., & McFall, R. M. Self-monitoring effects in a program for potential high school dropouts: A time series analysis. *Journal of Consulting and Clinical Psychology*, 1972, *39*, 273–281.

Gross, A. M., & Brigham, T. A. Self-delivered consequences versus desensitization in the treatment of fear of rats. *Journal of Clinical Psychology*, 1979, *35*, 384–390.

Gross, A. M., Brigham, T. A., Hopper, C., & Bologna, N. C. Self-management and Social Skills training: A study with predelinquent and delinquent youth. *Criminal Justice and Behavior*, 1980, *7*, 161–184.

Hartig, M., & Kanfer, F. H. The role of verbal self-instructions in children's resistance to temptation. *Journal of Personality and Social Psychology*, 1973, *25*, 259–267.

Higa, W. R., Tharp, R. G., & Calkins, R. P. Developmental verbal control of behavior: Implications for self-instructional training. *Journal of Experimental Child Psychology*, 1978, *26*, 439–497.

Hildebrandt, D. E., Feldman, S. E., & Ditrichs, R. Rules, models, and self-reinforcement in children. *Journal of Personality and Social Psychology*, 1973, *25*, 1–5.

Humphrey, L. L., Karoly, P., & Kirschenbaum, D. S. Self-management in the classroom: Self-imposed response cost versus self-reward. *Behavior Therapy*, 1978, *9*, 592–601.

Hundert, J., & Batstone, D. A practical procedure to maintain pupil's accurate self-rating in a classroom token program. *Behavior Modification*, 1978, *2*, 93–112.

Jones, R. T., Nelson, R. E., & Kazdin, A. E. The role of external variables in self-reinforcement. *Behavior Modification*, 1977, *1*, 147–178.

Kanfer, F. H. Self-regulation: Research, issues, and speculations. In C. Neuringer & J. L. Michael (Eds.), *Behavior modification in clinical psychology*. New York: Appleton-Century-Crofts, 1970.

Kanfer, F. H. The many faces of self-control or behavior modification changes its focus. In R. Stuart (Ed.), *Behavioral self-management*. New York: Brunner/Mazel, 1977.

Kaufman, K. F., & O'Leary, K. D. Reward, cost and self-evaluation procedures for disruptive adolescents in a psychiatric hospital school. *Journal of Applied Behavior Analysis*, 1972, *5*, 292–309.

Kazdin, A. E. Reactive self-monitoring: The effects of response desirability, goal setting, and feedback. *Journal of Consulting and Clinical Psychology*, 1974, *42*, 704–716.

Kazdin, A. E. *Behavior modification in applied settings*. Homewood, Ill.: Dorsey, 1975.

Klein, R. D., & Gory, E. L. The differential effects of noncontingent self-evaluation upon academic performance. In T. A. Brigham, R. Hawkins, J. W. Scott, & T. F. McLaughlin, *Behavior analysis in education*. Dubuque, Iowa: Kendall/Hunt, 1976.

Layne, C. C., Rickard, H. C., Jones, M. T., & Lyman, R. D. Accuracy of self-monitoring on a VR schedule of observer verification. *Behavior Therapy*, 1976, *7*, 481–488.

Lipinski, D. P., & Nelson R. The reactivity and unreliability of self-recording. *Journal of Consulting and Clinical Psychology*, 1974, *42*, 118–123.

Lipinski, D. P., Black, J. L., Nelson, R. O., & Ciminero, A. R. Influences of motivational variables on the reactivity and reliability of self-recording. *Journal of Consulting and Clinical Psychology*, 1975, *43*, 637–646.

Lovitt, T. C., & Curtiss, K. A. Academic response rate as a function of teacher and self-imposed contingencies. *Journal of Applied Behavior Analysis*, 1969, *2*, 49–53.

Mahoney, M. J., Moura, N. G. M., & Wade, T. C. The relative efficacy of self-reward, self-punishment and self-monitoring techniques for weight loss. *Journal of Consulting and Clinical Psychology 1973, 40*, 404–407.

Masters, J. C. Effects of social comparison upon subsequent self-reinforcement behavior in children. *Journal of Personality and Social Psychology*, 1968, *10*, 391–401.

Masters, J. C. Effects of success, failure, and reward-outcome on contingent and non-contingent self-reinforcement. *Developmental Psychology*, 1972, *7*, 110–118.

Masters, J. C. Effects of age and social comparison upon children's nonccontingent self-reinforcement and the value of a reinforcer. *Child Development*, 1973, *44*, 111–116.

Masters, J. C., & Christy, M. D. Achievement standards for contingent self-reinforcement: Effects of task length and task difficulty. *Child Development*, 1974, *45*, 9–13.

Masters, J. C., Furman, W., & Barden, R. C. Effects of achievement standards, tangible rewards and self-dispensed achievement evaluations on children's task mastery. *Child Development*, 1977, *48*, 217–224.

Masters, J. C., & Peskay, J. Effects of race, socioeconomic status, and success or failure upon contingent and non-contingent self-reinforcement in children. *Developmental Psychology*, 1972, *7*, 139–145.

McKenzie, T. L., & Rushall, B. S. Effects of self-recording on attendance and performance in a competitive swimming environment. *Journal of Applied Behavior Analysis*, 1974, *7*, 199–206.

Meichenbaum, D. H., & Goodman, J. The developmental control of operant motor responding by verbal operants. *Journal of Experimental Child Psychology*, 1969, *7*, 553–565.

Meichenbaum, D. H., & Goodman, J. Training impulsive children to talk to themselves: A means of developing self-control. *Journal of Abnormal Psychology*, 1971, *77*, 115–126.

Mischel, W., & Liebert, R. M. Effect of discrepancies between observed and improved reward criteria on their acquisition and transmission. *Journal of Personality and Social Psychology*, 1966, *3*, 45–53.

Mischel, W., & Liebert, R. M. The role of power in the adoption of self-reward patterns. *Child Development*, 1967, *38*, 673–683.

Mischel, W., & Patterson, C. J. Substantive and structural elements of effective plans for self-control. *Journal of Personality and Social Psychology*, 1976, *34*, 942–950.

Monahan, J., & O'Leary, K. D. Effects of self-instruction on rule-breaking behavior. *Psychological Reports*, 1971, *29*, 1059–1066.

Nelson, R. O. Assessment and function of self-monitoring. In M. Hersen, R. M. Eisler, & P. M. Miller (Eds.), *Progress in behavior modification*. (Vol. 5). New York: Pergamon Press, 1977.

Nelson, R. O., Lipinski, D. P., & Black, J. L. The effects of expectancy in the reactivity of self-recording. *Behavior Therapy*, 1975, *6*, 337–349.

Nelson, R. O., Lipinski, D. P., & Boykin, R. A. The effects of self-recording training and the obtrusiveness of the self-recording device on the accuracy and reactivity of self-monitoring. *Behavior Therapy*, 1978, *9*, 200–208.

O'Leary, S. G., & Dubey, D. R. Applications of self-control procedures by children: A review. *Journal of Applied Behavior Analysis*, 1979, *12*, 449–465.

Ollendick, T. Self-monitoring and self-administered overcorrection: The modification of nervous tics in children. *Behavior Modification*, 1981, *5*, 75–84.

Peacock, R., Layman, R. D., Rickard, H. C. Correspondence between self-report and observer report as a function of task difficulty. *Behavior Therapy*, 1978, *9*, 578–583.

Redd, W. H., & Birnbrauer, J. S. Adults as discriminative stimuli for different reinforcement contingencies with retarded children. *Journal of Experimental Child Psychology*, 1969, *7*, 440–447.

Risley, T., & Hart, B. Developing correspondence between nonverbal and verbal behavior of pre-school children. *Journal of Applied Behavior Analysis*, 1968, *1*, 297–301.

Robertson, S. J., Simon, S. J., Pachman, J. S., & Drabman, R. S. Self-control and generalization procedures in a classroom of disruptive retarded children. *Child Behavior Therapy*, 1979, *1*, 347–362.

Robin, A., Schneider, M., & Dolnick, M. The turtle technique: An extended case study of self-control in the classroom. *Psychology in the Schools*, 1976, *13*, 449–453.

Rosenbaum, M. S., & Drabman, R. S. Self-control training in the classroom: A review and critique. *Journal of Applied Behavior Analysis*, 1979, *12*, 467–485.

Santogrossi, D. A., O'Leary, K. D., Romanczyk, R. G., & Kaufman, K. F. Self-evaluation by adolescents in a psychiatric hospital school token program. *Journal of Applied Behavior Analysis*, 1973, *6*, 277–287.

Seymour, F. W., & Stokes, T. F. Self-recording in training girls to increase work and evoke staff praise in an institution for offenders. *Journal of Applied Behavior Analysis*, 1976, *9*, 41–54.

Sieck, W. A., & McFall, R. M. Some determinants of self-monitoring effects. *Journal of Consulting and Clinical Psychology*, 1976, *44*, 958–965.

Skinner, B. F. *Science and human behavior*. New York: Macmillan, 1953.

Spates, C. R., & Kanfer, F. H. Self-monitoring, self-evaluation, and self-reinforcement in children's learning: A test of a multistage self-regulation model. *Behavior Therapy*, 1977, *8*, 9–16.

Stokes, T. F., & Baer, D. M. An implicit technology of generalization. *Journal of Applied Behavior Analysis*, 1977, *10*, 349–367.

Stollack, G. E. Weight loss obtained under different experimental procedures. *Psychotherapy: Theory Research and Practice*, 1967, *4*, 61–64.

Thomas, J. D. Accuracy of self-assessment of on-task behavior by elementary school children. *Journal of Applied Behavior Analysis*, 1976, *9*, 209–210.

Turkowitz, H., O'Leary, K. D., & Ironsmith, M. Generalization and maintenance of appropriate behavior through self-control. *Journal of Consulting and Clinical Psychology*, 1975, *43*, 577–583.

Wood, R., & Flynn, J. M. A self-evaluation token system versus an external evaluation token system alone in a residential setting with predelinquent youths. *Journal of Applied Behavior Analysis*, 1978, *11*, 503–512.

10
Special Considerations in the Self-Management Training of the Developmentally Disabled
Alan J. Litrownik

As suggested by the title of this chapter, I will be considering how self-management skills might be developed in individuals identified as developmentally disabled. These considerations will be "special" because the population is a severely disturbed and/or handicapped one. Such a focus requires specification of what skills can be developed in what kind of individuals.

Thus, the first section of this chapter is devoted to the developmentally disabled, who they are, how they are characterized, intervention strategies, and the need to develop self-management skills. Following this discussion, I will present a model of self-management which I believe not only helps to specify what can be developed, but also suggests how training should progress.

Based on this model and the special population identified, specific suggestions for designing self-management training programs will be offered. These suggestions will then be translated into actual training programs that have been or are currently being applied. After describing these successful programs, I will conclude with an optimistic, but cautious, look to the future.

DEVELOPMENTAL DISABILITIES

The first order of business is the specification of the target population. This is no easy task, as the term "developmental disability" was coined by Congress when it passed the Developmental Disabilities Act of 1970, and its meaning has changed over the last 12 years as a function of political as well as practical considerations (see Akerley, 1979).

Definitions

In singling out developmentally disabled persons, Congress was attempting to identify a subgroup of handicapped individuals who evidenced severe impairments and a lack of normal developmental experience on which they could draw. As a result, intervention with this subgroup of handicapped persons requires training (i.e., habilitation), as opposed to retraining (i.e., rehabilitation). It was assumed that such habilitation necessitated a multitude of coordinated services that had to be applied over a developmentally disabled person's entire lifetime. Once this subgroup was identified, Congress targeted monies to meet their needs.

In order to receive this support, individuals had to have a disability that met the criteria for being (1) developmental, i.e., showing early onset — during the developmental period, (2) chronic, and (3) substantial (i.e., severe delays). Prior to 1978, these criteria were accompanied by a number of specifically identified groups of handicapped persons who were defined as developmentally disabled, such as those with mental retardation, cerebral palsy, epilepsy, autism, and other neurological conditions that were similar to retardation or that required similar treatment. These categorical examples were typically used to define developmental disabilities, since the defining criteria (especially "substantial") were difficult to apply. As a result, much political maneuvering took place in trying to get various disorders included. For example, autism was not initially included (Developmental Disabilities Act of 1970) and persons with the diagnosis of autism did not receive support until it was, in 1975.

Finally, in 1978 these categorical examples (i.e., definitions) were dropped with the renewal of the Developmental Disabilities Act, in favor of a noncategorical functional definition. Thus, labels are no longer the determining factor in defining who is developmentally disabled. Rather, the severity of one's developmental impairment is the determining factor. While some see this as the most appropriate approach, there is still a great deal of disagreement about how substantial a disability must be in order for an individual to qualify as developmentally disabled. Rather than getting involved in the appropriateness of a given decision, I will describe in general and more specific terms the kind of person I will be discussing in the remainder of this chapter.

In general, I will focus on the problems associated with and approaches for developing self-management skills in individuals who are functioning at an impaired level due to cognitive (i.e., moderately, profoundly, or severely retarded) and/or emotional (e.g., pervasive developmental disorder) problems that are most likely a function of biological factors (e.g., neurological, biochemical, chromosomal, genetic, etc.). Since most of my work has focused on moderately to severely retarded and autistic children, I will be describing problems and approaches as they apply to these populations specifically. Though my experience, and necessarily my perspective, is limited to these populations, I *do* believe that the general conceptual and applied approach to working with these groups can be adapted for other developmentally disabled persons.

Characterizations

Retarded persons, in general, have been characterized as dependent and in need of constant supervision (Kurtz & Neisworth, 1976; Mahoney & Mahoney, 1976). In fact, Robinson and Robinson (1976) predicted that those who are moderately retarded "will not achieve any measure of social or economic independence as adults" (p. 374). A similar prognosis has been assumed for autistic children, who are characterized by their lack of social responsiveness and failure to acquire communicative skills. These pervasive deficits are so severe that Ross and Pelham (1981) conclude that only a small proportion of autistic children (less than 5 percent) acquire skills that enable them to function outside an institutional or very structured setting. Treatment approaches and resultant outcomes have necessarily been restricted because of such limited expectations.

Intervention Strategies

For example, when I began working with developmentally disabled children 16 years ago, I believed that these severely impaired individuals could acquire functional skills if programs were appropriately designed and had reasonable objectives. As a trained applied-behavior analyst, and a believer, I programmed each individual's day, determining what was to be done and by whom. Training focused on developing basic self-help, motor, cognitive, and social-personal skills while concurrently eliminating undesirable behaviors (i.e., aggressiveness, tantrums, etc.). Interventions were rigidly applied, controlling the external environment (e.g., situations, contingencies) in order to provide specific experiences necessary for learning to occur.

Though I had some concerns about the children (i.e., how they might "feel"), I accepted the view that they needed to acquire basic skills before I could consult them about what they wanted. It made sense: How could a therapist even consider traditional "talk therapy" if the children could not communicate?

Such training typically involved identification of skills to be acquired, task analyses (breaking these skills down into smaller steps), and specification of techniques (e.g., contingency management, stimulus control) for training responses at each step. Once the necessary skills had been acquired, training continued with the aim of refining these skills, that is, developing proficiency. Finally, external social cues (e.g., the trainer instructing the child to engage in the acquired skills) were gradually withdrawn, so the individual was now initiating the appropriate skill on his or her own. This approach was and continues to be extremely effective in developing specific skills in developmentally disabled persons.

It is unfortunate that some clinicians have been so impressed with the success of these techniques that they see them as the panacea, forgetting that the development of basic skills (e.g., self-help, social, cognitive) was only the first step. For example, as a discussant for a symposium at a recent Association for the Advancement of Behavior Therapy Convention, Koegel (Note 1) made the claim that the developing operant technology was responsible for the current 50 percent "cure rate" and would be responsible for a "total cure" of autism in the next 5 to 10 years. While all applied researchers and operant technicians do recognize the utility of this technology, most are also aware of its limitations, that is, lack of maintenance, transfer, and excessive time demands placed on the trainer (see Hayes, Rincover, & Solnick, 1980).

Operant training leads to the acquisition of specific responses cued by specific situations. There is a lack of generalization, both stimulus and response, leading to mechanical, rote responding. For example, Pamela, one of the stars in Lovaas' 1969 film on language development in autistic children, was shown responding to the question "What did you have for breakfast?" by saying "Toast, eggs. . . ." Quite impressive when comparing this to her initial verbal echolalia, but not so significant when I tell you that whenever I, or anybody else for that matter, asked her this question, she responded with the same list of items. What she actually had for breakfast made no difference, much less whether she had eaten breakfast at all.

Behavior analysts point out that maintenance as well as generalization needs to be programmed (see Stokes & Baer, 1977). But Hayes et al. (1980) warn that one-at-a-time modification of behavior, even when ensuring maintenance and generalization, will not be effective with severely impaired populations of autistic and/or retarded children. Not only are these techniques time consuming and limited in their effectiveness, but they also further the belief that severely impaired persons are dependent and in need of constant supervision. External manipulation of the environment by behavior analysts furthers reliance on external factors, restricts behavioral options, and, in general, results in the development of *reactive* as opposed to *active* response repertoires in these severely disturbed populations. Thus, the limited personal freedom (i.e., the small number of alternative courses of action available and the inability to exercise control) in developmentally disabled individuals is as much, if not more, a function of socially condoned discrimination as it is the result of their personal deficiencies. Operant training approaches do have considerable utility, but at the same time, they are limited. When these inherent limits are reached, a different approach is necessary, since rigid application of operant technology may exacerbate the problems of those who are to be helped.

As pointed out previously (see Litrownik & Steinfeld, 1981), it makes little sense to further restrict the options or choices of such individuals who are already limited as a result of cognitive and/or emotional deficits. With such a change in focus from a concern with *developing appropriate overt responses in an individual* to one that is concerned with the *development of an appropriate individual*, interpretations of typical operant interventions necessarily change.

Several programs aimed at teaching problem-solving skills to normal developing preschool and school-aged children (e.g., Fagen & Long, 1979; Spivack, Platt, & Shure, 1976; Spivack & Shure, 1974) have been described. The objective of these programs is to promote "positive growth" (i.e., independence) and thus prevent problems that would have emerged had these skills not been acquired. Not only has this training been aimed at prevention, but it also has involved remediation in populations of mildly emotionally disturbed (e.g., Camp, 1977; Wilson, Hall, & Watson, 1979) and intellectually handicapped students (e.g., Burgio, Whitman, & Johnson, 1980; Guralnick, 1976; Johnston, Whitman, & Johnson, 1981).

Developmentally disabled individuals evidence severe intellectual and/or emotional deficits that are a function of some assumed organic impairment or dysfunction. Even with these limits and the recognized need to develop some basic skills (e.g., self-help, motor, etc.) first, I do not believe that it is unreasonable to begin focusing on the development of self-management skills in developmentally disabled persons. This assumption is based on the observation that every one of us begins our life with limited skills (i.e., cognitive, motor, social, etc.) that result in our almost total dependence on the external environment (e.g., caretakers). Yet, independent functioning which is one valued goal or outcome of socialization (Kanfer, 1979) develops with the passage of time. For example, I assume that most adaptive adults have progressed to the point where they can get up in the morning, engage in numerous self-help skills, and get out the front door looking appropriate in plenty of time to make it to work or school. Various self-help skills (e.g., dressing, washing, cooking, eating, etc.) that are needed to make it out the door had to be acquired. They developed over time, as did the ability to engage in them with a minimum of external control. I look at my 3-year-old in the morning and know that his clothes have to be put out if he's going to get dressed, his shoes will have to be tied for him, breakfast must be made, and my wife and/or I will have to make sure he gets out the door in time for another day at preschool. He's come a long way, though, from infancy where his every need had to be attended to, but he's still got a ways to go before he can function as independently as my 6-year-old daughter, much less as independently as most adults. My daughter does self-initiate many of these morning-time self-help skills, but does require frequent external prompts. As adults we usually make it out the door without any external prompts. We might check the time, but this monitoring is used to determine how we're doing. From the time we awaken (with or without an alarm set by us) we are periodically monitoring our performance, evaluating the time we have, making decisions about what we will wear and eat, and giving ourselves instructions to hurry or to remember to do something or take something. These behaviors allow us to manage our own lives and to function independently. They develop along with the specific self-help skills (e.g., dressing). My daughter has acquired all of the self-help skills, self-initiates some, and is just beginning to evidence acquisition of these self-managing behaviors, while my son is still working on acquiring some skills (e.g., tying his shoes) and becoming proficient in others (e.g., putting on his shirt, pants, and socks). He will acquire these skills, and he, along with my daughter, will also develop self-management skills (e.g., self-monitoring, self-evaluation, self-instructions) with little formal training.

Developmentally disabled individuals do not acquire these basic self-help skills without formal training. Structured learning experiences take these individuals through stages of skill proficiency, and finally self-initiation. But adaptive, generalized, or independent performance is not observed. The absence of independent functioning is due, I would argue, to the failure of these individuals to develop self-management skills (e.g., self-monitoring, etc.). It is logical to assume that these skills will not develop automatically once basic self-help skills are learned, but require specific training if they are to be acquired. Thus the focus of training needs to change from an exclusive interest in developing skills that are performed independently to one that is also concerned with developing skills that allow an individual to manage his or her own behavior (i.e., developing an independent individual).

SELF-MANAGEMENT

Self-management is any response or combination of responses that an individual performs in order to direct or manipulate his or her own behavior in the relative absence of external incentives. That is, individuals evidence self-managing behavior when they attempt to control one aspect of their life by engaging in other specific or general actions. In the example just described, getting ready to face the day, appropriate and timely performance of the specific skills of, for example, washing and dressing were seen as being determined, to a large extent, by expected long-range effects of making it out the door and self-managing responses which helped guide these activities. Specifically, people talk to themselves, monitor their progress, make decisions about what to wear, and set standards for when they should be ready and how they should look so they can meet the challenges of each new day.

Self-directed, independent, adaptive preparation can result when an individual manages his or her own behaviors. On the other hand, a retarded child may learn to self-initiate washing and dressing when a token is delivered upon completion of these tasks, but performance is not likely to be adaptive unless someone else monitors and cues the child's behavior.

If the intention is to begin developing self-management skills in developmentally disabled persons, then these skills need to be identified. That is, a conceptual model or frame of reference which will help to operationalize the general and specific skills involved in self-management is required. Though these applied efforts necessitate a conceptual model, it should be recognized that the state of our current understanding is such that formalized theories are premature. Rather, a working model of self-management that attempts to integrate a variety of research and applied findings is called for. This is no easy task, as Meichenbaum (1978) noted when he confessed that the more time he spent thinking about this area, the more confused he became. What follows is a working model or conceptualization of self-management that I find helpful in organizing my thinking and applied efforts. My understanding of this area is necessarily based on conceptual models proposed by others to help understand self-regulation (Bandura, 1977; Kanfer, 1978, 1980; Karoly 1977; Thoresen & Mahoney, 1974), cognitive behavior modification (Meichenbaum, 1978; Meichenbaum & Asarnow, 1979), metacognitive development (Brown, 1978; Campione & Brown, 1977; Flavell, 1978), and problem solving (D'Zurilla & Goldfried, 1971). Each of these conceptual models has added to my understanding while also leaving many questions unanswered. The general working model that I present will, I hope, serve the same function for others.

Self-Control versus External Control

Some, it seems (e.g., Castro & Rachlin, 1980; Catania, 1975; Rachlin, 1974), are concerned about whether we can give any explanatory power to constructs that refer to an individual's capacity for controlling his or her own behavior (i.e., self, internal control, etc.). In the tradition of radical behaviorism (see also Chapter 1 of this volume), the ultimate source of control, the external environment, is instead sought; once identified, it is argued, all attempts to control one's own behavior are a function of this external event. Thus the argument is reduced to either-or: behavior is controlled by either external or internal sources, and a search for the unidirectional external determinant follows (Bandura, 1981).

Back in the early stages of our concern for self-management, it was considered to be only one source of possible control (see Kanfer & Karoly, 1972; Mahoney, 1972). That is, self as well as external factors were seen as being responsible for any given outcome. As Bandura (1977, 1981) postulated, all of our responses are a function of *both* environmental and organismic factors, with the relative contribution of each varying along a continuum from complete external to complete internal control.

Thus, when developing self-management skills in severely impaired individuals, it is possible to focus on increasing the relative amount of internal control exerted by an individual, as opposed to the development of an individual who functions independent of any environmental controls. The general goals or objectives can then be broken down into smaller steps where the developmentally disabled person takes more responsibility for managing his or her own behavior with a concurrent decrease in external control. For example, caretakers can take less responsibility for monitoring and manipulating the environment as developmentally disabled individuals begin to do their own monitoring and manipulating.

Outcome/Process/Training

In attempting to understand what is involved in self-management, some basic distinctions need to be made. The first is to differentiate between the targets of self-management efforts and the behaviors or skills that are performed in an attempt to regulate these targets. Skinner (1953) identified the former as controlled responses and the latter as controlling responses. Controlled responses or targeted outcomes vary as a function of controlling responses which are part of the process of self-management. That is, the targeted outcome for a developmentally disabled child might be finishing a page of math problems.

In order to reach this outcome, a trainer could manipulate external cues and/or contingencies. This same outcome could be accomplished via self-management processes if the individual engaged in controlling responses aimed at increasing or decreasing the probability that the target behavior would occur. These controlling responses could include labeling the type of problem, identifying aids such as fingers to count on, checking answers, and positive statements following completed work. Thus, the self-management process includes a series of actions or operations that contribute to the independent and self-directed performance of targeted outcomes.

In addition to this necessary distinction, it should also be recognized that the controlled and/or controlling responses can be developed separately, in sequence, or simultaneously. As I have already mentioned, it is possible to focus on targeted outcomes and to develop them utilizing a variety of external manipulations. These same training methods (e.g., prompting and fading, shaping, imitation, etc.) can be applied in attempting to develop specific controlling responses that are part of the self-management process. In some instances, training of self-management may focus on developing skills that will result in the individual being able to manage his or her own behavior; in others, the focus could include the development of both the outcome and self-management process skills simultaneously. Regardless, a distinction between training procedures or methods and what they are being used to develop must be made.

Outcome

It is important not only to make these distinctions, but also to identify the specific outcome of self-management that is desired, as it will be differentially affected by intervention strategies (see Keogh & Glover, 1980, Lloyd, 1980). Just as different external training approaches are applied as a function of what is to be trained, the appropriateness of a given controlling response or operation is determined, in part, by the targeted outcome. For example, cue-controlled relaxation might be an appropriate operation for a child who has as his or her target getting to sleep at night, but is not appropriate if this same child is attempting to bathe on his or her own.

Outcomes can be categorized along two general dimensions (see figure 10.1). The first involves the strength of the response outcome. This dimension and the distinctions that have been made are responsible, in part, for a great deal of the initial confusion surrounding the use of terms like "self-management" and "self-control" (Mahoney, 1972). Distinctions between these terms have been made based on outcome. That is, self-control is identified as a special case of self-management where an habitual response pattern is inhibited, thus resulting in some short-term negative consequences with a larger later positive outcome (e.g., delay of gratification, resistance to temptation).

More recent distinctions (e.g., Karoly, 1977) are based on whether the targeted response is to be changed or maintained. Expanding on this distinction, it is possible to differentiate between outcomes that require a change in response strength, either increases or decreases, and those that do not. Thus, the objective of self-management could be the acquisition, maintenance, or elimination of some targeted response.

The second categorical dimension refers to the content of the specified

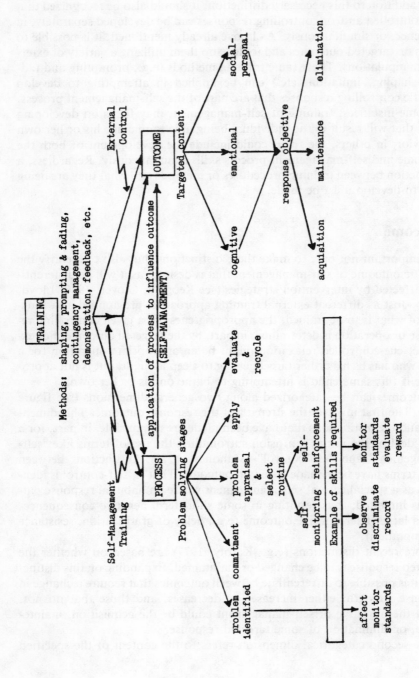

Fig. 10.1. A Working Model of Self-Management.

outcome. That is, the focus of self-management can be on personal-social, cognitive, or emotional responses. Within each of these content domains, behaviors such as dressing, counting, and aggressive outbursts can be targeted for either acquisition, maintenance, or elimination. These distinctions are useful in designing self-management as well as external training programs.

Process

While a variety of specific operations have been identified, I think that the self-management process can best be understood if it is viewed in terms of general problem solving (see also Litrownik and Steinfeld, 1981). Not only can a variety of conceptual approaches be incorporated and integrated, but also the many seemingly unrelated approaches to self-management can be put into perspective. For example, with a general problem-solving conceptualization, it is possible to identify a series of stages, each of which requires a variety of specific skills or operations (see figure 10.1). The first stage includes the identification of a problem and the recognition that something needs to be done to deal with it. According to Kanfer (1978), any disruption in the smooth flow of behavior can serve as a cue for problem solving. Thus unexpected events, those that elicit arousal, and situations, in general, that place adaptive demands on an individual can all serve to identify a problem. Whether or not a problem is identified and the need to solve it is recognized depends, not only on individuals' ability to self-monitor, but also on their labeling of affect, attributions of control, and standards for performance, among others. Thus, individuals in the same situation may begin to deal adaptively with a problem, or fail to initiate the problem-solving process. These failures may be due to different standards or criteria for what constitutes a problem as well as deficiencies in identifying affect, discriminating cues, and making connections between consequences and individual performance. Severely impaired individuals appear to have much difficulty at this first stage, due in part to the fact that caretakers typically identify problems and then externally manipulate the environment in an attempt to solve the problem.

After identifying a problem and recognizing the need to deal with it, a commitment must be made (Karoly, 1977). That is, a decision to spend the effort and energy necessary to solve the problem is made. The ability to make such a commitment is a function of an individual's performance attributions (Henker, Whalen, & Hinshaw, 1980) and anticipation of consequences (Fagen & Long, 1979). For example, an individual who perceives a problem as being under his or her control (internal attribution), with the likelihood that a change will lead to some positive outcome, is more likely to make a commitment. This commitment is typically stated in terms of a general standard or criterion for performance (e.g., "I'm going to clean my room."). Again, developmentally disabled persons have a difficult time making a commitment, as they are not likely to anticipate outcomes or connect outcomes to their own behavior (see Litrownik, Franzini, Geller & Geller, 1977).

In the next stage, the individual begins to focus on the problem and possible solutions. The operations involved at this stage are most closely related to the conceptual framework which has evolved from the area of metacognitive development (see Brown, 1978; Campione & Brown, 1977; Flavell, 1978; Loper, 1980). Specifically, during this third stage, the individual appraises the problem and generates a number of possible solutions. Situational demands, individual capabilities, and available strategies or approaches to cope with the problem are identified. Based on this knowledge, a specific solution or action routine is selected requiring some cognitive evaluation of probable effects. Much of the work conducted in the area of cognitive behavior modification (e.g., Meichenbaum, 1978) has focused on this stage.

As you might imagine, an individual's ability to analyze the problem and generate possible solutions is dependent on cognitive skills as well as one's available repertoire of action routines. Intellectually and/or emotionally impaired individuals have difficulties at this stage due to lagging cognitive awareness (Loper, 1980), an inability to combine component skills (McKinney & Haskins, 1980), and a strategy or action routine deficiency (Litrownik & Steinfeld, 1981).

In the last stage, the selected plan or routine is applied and monitored, and its effectiveness is evaluated. This evaluation is based on the goals established during the commitment stage, with a positive outcome leading to continuance or discontinuance of the routine, and a negative outcome resulting in a return to the previous stage so another possible solution can be identified and implemented.

A number of specific skills and operations are required at each stage, and these need to be identified and operationalized (Kneedler, 1980; Litrownik & Steinfeld, 1981). Much of the focus in self-management training has been on developing specific routines such as self-reinforcement and self-directional statements that can be utilized to deal with an identified problem.

Routines. These routines can be general or specific approaches. That is, the routine may be a general approach to handling any problem or one specific to a class of problems. This is similar to the distinction Baron (1978) made when discussing central and general problem solutions as they related to meta-cognition. General solutions can be applied in any instance, and the result of such an application could be the identification of a central solution, one appropriate for the specific problem encountered. It is with the development of a general problem-solving or self-management routine that generalization will emerge. Of course, limited generalization of specific routines to problems that are similar can be expected if specific training is included. This training could involve programming the application of a routine with a variety of similar problems and gradual reduction of external prompts to utilize the routine. Since most self-management training programs have focused on specific as opposed to general routines, and generalization has not been systematically programmed, the lack of demonstrated general self-management effects is not surprising (see Meichenbaum, 1980; O'Leary, 1980). Such general effects are more likely to be observed when specific routines are developed one at a time and applied to a class of problem situations, with trainees being given the opportunity to discriminate between situations and to select the most appropriate available routine as each new routine is added to the individual's repertoire.

Specific routines that have been identified include: self-instructions, self-monitoring, self-evaluation, self-determined criteria for performance, self-reinforcement, self-punishment, relaxation, and distraction (Drabman & Gross, this volume; O'Leary & Dubey, 1979; Rosenbaum & Drabman, 1979, Thoresen & Mahoney, 1974). Before beginning to develop a given routine, specific skills involved in its operation need to be identified and operationalized. For example, in figure 10.1 specific skills required for self-monitoring and self-reinforcement routines are identified. The former requires the observation of one's own performance, a discrimination between the occurrence or nonoccurrence of a cue for self-recording, and the actual recording response. Self-monitoring can serve as a routine or as one solution to managing a problem while also being one of four component operations involved in self-reinforcement. The other three include setting standards for evaluating and rewarding one's own performance.

Training

In trying to understand what is involved in self-management and how it might be developed, I've attempted to distinguish between the self-management process and outcomes of its application. One last topic needs to be covered if this understanding is to be related to training of self-management. Specifically, methods that can be utilized to develop the self-management processes and/or outcomes need to be identified and differentiated from the specific targeted outcomes and processes to be developed. The methods available for self-management training are any of those typically used to develop new responses and/or discriminations (see figure 10.1). Thus, techniques based on learning principles, such as shaping, prompting and fading, imitation, modeling, feedback, and rehearsal can be apropriately applied in attempting to develop new responses, skill clusters, and/or discriminations as to when, and how to engage in a given response or pattern.

The distinction that needs to be kept in mind is one between these techniques or methods and what responses or skills are to be developed. That is, external training methods can be utilized to develop either specific outcomes, processes, or both. If a training program is aimed at developing behaviors such as putting on a shirt, pants, socks, and shoes with the goal of having a developmentally disabled child getting dressed by himself or herself, the program involves typical external manipulation of the environment or behavior modification. On the other hand, a program could aim at developing specific controlling responses (e.g., self-monitoring, self-instructions), increasing independence while also developing the specific targeted outcomes of, say, putting on a shirt and pants. As indicated in figure 10.1, self-management training occurs when training methods are utilized to develop controlling responses which are part of the self-management process, whereas application of these methods to targeted outcomes results in externally controlled modifications only.

The particular focus of a self-management training program necessarily depends on the repertoire of skills and abilities that an individual initially possesses. This repertoire is important in determining what outcomes might be targeted as well as how training of the self-management process will proceed. If the outcomes specified are already in the individual's repertoire, the focus of training should be on developing the self-management process. That is, specific routines and skills required at each stage of problem solving which allow for independent and adaptive dressing can be developed if an individual already has acquired necessary self-help content skills. On the other hand, if targeted content skills like putting on pants are to be acquired, then training can either focus on developing these first and then developing the self-management process or can attempt to develop the outcome and process simultaneously (O'Leary & Dubey, 1979). The former approach involves developing outcomes via external control (i.e., typical externally controlled intervention) initially, with a gradual relinquishing of control to the individual. Thus, controlling responses that are directly related to the targeted outcome gradually move from the trainer's to the trainee's control. For example, school-aged children can be taught to engage in appropriate task-related behavior via manipulation of the external environment (external monitoring, evaluation, and reward). After performing at some predetermined criterion level, responsibility for these controlling responses can be transferred to the children so they self-monitor, self-evaluate, and self-reward. Such an approach has been successfully applied to populations of special education students (see Polsgrove, 1979; Rosenbaum & Drabman, 1979). The other approach, developing the outcome and process simultaneously, has also been successfully applied in developing task-appropriate behavior along with self-managing skills in hyperactive children (see Meichenbaum, 1978).

While there are a variety of methods that can be utilized to train self-management in individuals, the specific skills to be developed and in what order will depend on a functional assessment of the individual and identification of general outcomes and processes to be acquired. In sum, skills involved in the process of self-management should be training independent of or in combination with targeted outcome skills. This training can focus on acquisition of specific skills required for a given routine; generalization of routine application; and/or developing skills that would lead to problem solving, including the ability to discriminate problem situations, select, and apply already-acquired routines that effectively control outcomes.

SELF-MANAGEMENT TRAINING OF THE DEVELOPMENTALLY DISABLED

In this section I will attempt to apply the conceptual understanding of self-management just presented to the development of training programs for developmentally disabled persons. As indicated earlier, this population evidences severe and numerous deficits in cognitive, emotional, and personal-social functioning. Many of the self-management training programs that have been developed for other populations are not appropriate for this population (see Kendall & Finch, 1979). Specifically, the focus on cognitions, verbalizations, and abstract processes is not likely to lead to improvement in the functioning of developmentally disabled individuals. This is not to say that such a population cannot begin to develop self-management processes, but rather suggests that training must begin at a much more basic level of functioning. That is, specific operations and the skills required need to be identified, developed, and then combined. It is likely that such training will involve small aproximations of general problem solving and will oftentimes require initial development of prerequisite or "readiness" skills (i.e., attention, discriminations, etc.).

General Training Strategies

Not only are there a number of alternatives when considering whether outcomes and/or self-management processes should be developed first or simultaneously, but there are also various strategies for developing self-management processes. One general approach is to identify the necessary component skills or subskills required for self-management and to teach them directly. An example of this approach is found in Fagen and Long's (1976, 1979) curriculum. They identify four clusters of cognitive responses (selection, storage, sequencing and ordering, and anticipating consequences) and four clusters of affective responses (appreciating feelings, managing frustration, inhibition and delay, and relaxation) necessary for self-management. Their curriculum is designed to develop these skill clusters in a variety of situations. Fagen and Long assume that once these skills are acquired they will be applied to problem situations, allowing their regular class students to effectively manage their own behaviors.

There is some question, though, about whether this targeted population of school-aged children will actually benefit from such training (see Haring, 1979; Loper, 1980). That is, young children are extremely concrete in their thinking and may not be able to use these specific skills in combination in order to deal with problem situations that they may encounter. Loper (1980) suggests that regular class students need to be taught various strategies and how to use them, and to be aware of their capacity and of the requirements of a given task or situation. Without this training, the development of specific subskills will not likely lead to general self-management in developmentally normal, much less in exceptional, children.

With proposed lagging cognitive awareness of task demands (Loper, 1980), strategy or problem solution deficiencies (Litrownik & Steinfeld, 1981), and failures to combine component skills that have been acquired (McKinney & Haskins, 1980), a different general approach to developing self-management in the exceptional individual is required. For example, rote subskills need to be developed along with rules for combining them. Rules are required not only for combining these skills, but also in determining when they should be applied. That is, training requires learning to apply these combined subskills to a class of problem situations, and not to others (Haring, 1979; Lloyd, 1980). The general strategy is to: develop specific component skills; demonstrate how these skills can be combined (e.g., into routines) and applied to specific problem situations; develop other routines and identify when they are appropriate to use; and then begin to develop general problem-solving skills which are required for problem identification, commitment, and evaluation. For example, after a couple of effective self-management routines have been developed, an individual can be taught to identify which of the available routines is most appropriate for a given problem situation (i.e., learn to discriminate situations based on task requirements). Other component skills can be taught and then combined to advance performance at each stage of problem solving. These performances would then need to be combined in specific situations and applied to multiple settings, and direct instruction to generalize would need be given in order to develop general problem solving skills (cf., Carver & Scheier's discussion in this volume).

In developing self-management programs for the developmentally disabled, then, the focus should initially be on the development of prerequisite skills (e.g., task orientation), specific component skills involved in a routine, routines which can be applied to specific situations, and finally generalization. Of course, other component skills (such as responding to negative affect by identifying the existence of a problem) may be taught, depending on the individual's needs. But in general, the best strategy is one that builds specific skills and routines before training general problem solving.

Developing a Program

The following six-step process can be followed when designing a program to develop self-management in developmentally disabled persons:

1. *General assessment.* The general level of functioning (e.g., verbal skills, cognitive skills, etc.) should be identified as well as specific problem areas such as behavioral deficits and excesses. Potentially effective training techniques, such as contingency management, modeling, and rehearsal, should also be considered.

2. *Specification of desired outcome.* Following the initial analysis, it is then possible to identify specific problem areas. The problems need to be identified and specific outcomes targeted. If skills are to be acquired, they need to be task analyzed so training can be broken down into small steps. Similar successive approximations or steps to the desired target outcome may also need to be identified when trying to eliminate behaviors. For example, in attempting to eliminate eye-poking, the focus might first be on reducing face touching.

3. *Identification of self-management process.* The specific problem solution or routine that is to be acquired so the individual can manage the behavior identified in step 2 must be specified and broken down into smaller steps. This task analysis should include specification of prerequisite skills and be appropriate for the individual, based on the general assessment (step 1). Thus, the criteria for selecting a routine to develop include the appropriateness of the routine for the identified problem or target (from step 2) as well as the appropriateness of the routine for a given individual who is functioning at a specific level.

4. *Second assessment.* The individual's performance in relationship to the targeted outcome and self-management process to be acquired needs to be assessed. This more specific assessment should be related to the task analyses conducted in steps 2 and 3, and will then lead to the identification of specific training needs.

5. *Design the training program.* Next, the training techniques to be utilized (e.g., demonstrations, contingency management, etc.) and step-by-step procedures for developing targeted self-management processes need to

be specified. If the targeted outcome is also going to be manipulated externally, procedures to increase or decrease it need to be identified.

6. *Evaluation.* Finally, the effectiveness of the program — in terms of whether the self-management process was acquired, applied appropriately, and resulted in the desired outcome — needs to be determined. This evaluation step will serve as an ongoing assessment leading to subsequent training decisions. That is, if the training is effective, plans for developing other routines and/or operations required for, say, problem identification can be made. If the initial intervention was ineffective, additional task analyses and program design will be required.

In order to concretize this general six-step process, I will present some examples of its application in the next sections.

An Example of a Programatic Application

This example is taken from an applied research program that was begun in 1975 with the support of the U.S. Office of Education, Bureau of Education for the Handicapped. This was one of the first, if not the first, programmatic efforts to develop self-regulatory skills in a developmentally disabled population. This initial venture required a great deal of time (4 years), as I and my co-workers did much growing and learning along with the children we were training. Based on what we learned, I am confident that effective self-management training can be accomplished in a much shorter period of time.

The population we chose to work with, moderately retarded (IQ of 25 to 50), has been characterized as dependent, in need of constant supervision, and lacking the potential to achieve any measure of independence as adults. As we and others have pointed out, this dependence may be a result of the limited opportunities provided retarded individuals to develop independent skills (see Litrownik & Steinfeld, 1981; Meichenbaum & Asarnow, 1979). That is, caretakers often limit choices or options and, thus, personal freedom, as it is assumed that the moderately retarded child is limited due to some structural deficit.

In order to begin developing self-management skills, we initially observed 7- to 21-year-old trainable mentally retarded (TMR) students at the Fairhaven schools in San Diego. Not only did we observe the children in a variety of settings (e.g., class, playground, lunch), but we also assessed them on a brief individual intelligence test (Slosson, 1963) and determined whether they could make a number of simple discriminations (e.g., between colors, numbers, quantities, finished work, etc.). We found that most of the students had communication problems (i.e., minimal verbal skills), and many could not make these discriminations. The students that we did target for self-management training ranged in age from 9 to 21, had IQs that ranged from 25 to 50, and had mental ages between 3 and 8 years.

General strategy. When we initiated this program, our long-range objective was to develop general problem-solving or self-management skills that would allow our students to maintain their behavior with a minimum of external control as well as to modify it effectively. These ambitious general goals had to be broken down into more manageable units if we were to get started on the task. After much thought, it was decided to focus on developing one appropriate routine, self-reinforcement, that could be utilized by our students in their classroom. We reasoned that the development of an effective routine such as self-reinforcement was the necessary first step in developing general problem-solving skills and that acquisition of this routine would allow students to begin functioning more independently in some specific situations immediately.

The targeted outcomes or controlled responses that we decided to include in our training were those which the students might be required to perform in their class. In addition, we felt that the development of the self-reinforcement routine and its component operations or skills was of primary importance, and thus decided to minimize the impact that the target responses had on training. So, we attempted to select tasks that required skills that were already in the students' repertoire or would require a minimum of training. The specific objective, then, was to develop a self-reinforcement routine that could be utilized by these developmentally disabled students to maintain their performance on school-related tasks with a minimum of external control.

Component operations. In order to develop this self-reinforcement routine, we needed to specify what it involved. Based on previously proposed conceptual models (e.g., Bandura, 1977; Kanfer, 1977; Thoresen & Mahoney, 1974), we identified four component skills or operations necessary for self-reinforcement: self-monitoring, standard setting, self-evaluation, and self-reward. After identifying these operations, we then attempted to (1) operationalize each, (2) assess our population of TMR students to see if they could perform them or needed to acquire specific skills necessary to engage in these operations, and (3) determine if we could teach these skills and resultant component operations.

Self-monitoring. The first component that we focused on was self-monitoring (see Litrownik, Freitas, & Franzini, 1978). Not only has it been identified as the necessary first step in self-reinforcement (Thoresen & Mahoney, 1974), but there is also some evidence indicating that self-monitoring can affect task performance, that is, serve as a self-management routine itself (see Kanfer, 1977; McFall, 1977; Nelson, 1977).

A previous anecdotal report (Kurtz & Neisworth, 1976) suggested that developmentally disabled persons could be taught a simple self-monitoring skill, namely, adding a pop bead to a string after performing a simple response. Other reports with less severely impaired individuals (e.g., Mahoney & Mahoney, 1976; Nelson, Lipinski, & Black, 1976; Nelson, Lipinski, & Boykin, 1978; Zegiob, Klukas, & Juninger, 1978) indicated that it might be possible to teach retarded persons to monitor their own behavior.

Before attempting to develop this component, we observed that self-monitoring requires the observation of covert and/or overt events, a discrimination cued by these events, and a self-recording response based on the discrimination (Litrownik & Freitas, 1980; Litrownik Freitas, & Franzini, 1978; Litrownik & Steinfeld, 1981). As is the case with external monitoring, self-monitoring can involve a variety of responses to be observed as well as a number of recording responses. The response to be observed can be easily observed and discriminated, or it may be more complex. Similarly, the recording response can vary from the complex (e.g., a detailed description of behavior, its antecedents, and consequences) to the simple (e.g., adding a pop bead after each required response is performed).

So, when designing a self-management training program that includes self-monitoring, one needs to be aware of the various possibilities and be able to specify goals exactly. For our purposes, we decided to assess and then teach, if necessary, a more complex self-monitoring task, one that we believed would lend itself to application in the classroom. Specifically, we wanted to teach our developmentally disabled students to finish a task and then to discriminate between the kind of problem that they had completed and/or to discriminate the various consequences of their performance. These discriminations were then to be utilized in determining whether a self-recording response was to follow. The tasks included seatwork problems where the children were to match a figure on the top of the page with one of two figures below that was the same. All figures could be categorized as either parts of the body (e.g., arm, leg, ear) or simple shapes (e.g., triangle, circle, square). Each time students drew a line between matching parts of the body, they were to self-monitor by placing a red ring over a peg. Following the matching of two shapes, students were to proceed to the next problem without recording.

On the second task, a bowling game, students rolled a small ball down an alley which had 10 pins set up so that the bowling ball traveled below them over marks on the alley. After each roll, a score was shown on a lighted scoreboard directly above the game. Scores were predetermined with all children obtaining scores of 10 on two-thirds of the trials and scores of 1 and 5 on the remaining one-third. Each time a score of 10 was obtained, students were to self-monitor by placing the ring on the peg.

Thirty TMR students were initially pretested on both the bowling (15 trials) and seatwork (24 trials) tasks to determine if they could correctly perform the specified self-monitoring component. At this pretesting and during each subsequent testing (post, retention, and transfer), the children were provided with two practice trials. One required a self-monitoring response, while the other did not. The children were not only instructed to self-monitor appropriately but were also verbally and/or physically prompted to do so on these two practice trials. Even with these instructions and prompted trials, none of the students correctly self-monitored on either task initially. One to two weeks after this pretesting, 20 students (10 training and 10 attention control) were exposed to live and taped demonstrations.

The training group was exposed to two training sessions for first the bowling task and then the seatwork task. The first session for each task involved live demonstrations of appropriate self-monitoring by a female experimenter-model. Training continued either until the child correctly monitored on six consecutive trials without prior demonstrations or until 40 minutes of training time had elapsed. The second session included the showing of a 10-minute color videotape in which Sparky the Clown demonstrated correct self-monitoring behaviors on the same task.

The 10 children in the attention control group were each yoked to a child in the training group, based on a match of gender, CA, MA, and IQ. They were then given an opportunity to perform live bowling trials, seatwork trials, and self-monitoring responses (i.e., putting the ring on the peg) equal in number to those of their yoked partner from the training group. However, no instructions or demonstrations of appropriate self-monitoring responses were provided during this experience. In addition, the attention-control children viewed two control tapes which showed Sparky either bowling or doing seatwork. Following her performance on the bowling trials and seatwork problems, Sparky placed a number of rings on the peg. Thus the yoked attention control group was exposed to a taped model who bowled, completed seatwork problems, and put rings on a peg, just as the training group was. But the self-monitoring response was not associated with a particular score on the bowling game, nor with a particular type of seatwork problem in the control videotape.

Post-testing on the task followed the 10-minute tape (training or control) for the specific task. Retention and transfer of self-monitoring responses were assessed about a week ($\pm$ 2 days) following the post-test. Performances of a no-contract control group (10 students) on the bowling, seatwork, and transfer tasks were assessed at the same intervals as the training and attention control groups. None of the 30 students was able to correctly monitor bowling or seatwork performances initially, even with the detailed instructions and prompted practice trials, but at post, retention, and generalization assessments, the training group significantly outperformed the two control groups while correctly monitoring 90 percent of the time. The control groups, on the other hand, continued to correctly self-monitor at a chance level.

In sum, we found that developmentally disabled students initially could not differentially self-monitor the consequences of their performance (i.e., bowling game) or the problem or activity that they had completed (i.e., seat-work task). Though they could not correctly self-monitor when provided with instructions to do so, we did find that those who were exposed to a 1-hour demonstration training program were able to acquire, retain, and transfer these skills. The skill that these students learned was a complex one relative to those taught mildly retarded populations previously (Mahoney & Mahoney, 1976; Nelson, Lipinski, & Boykin, 1978). Not only did our students have to observe whether they had completed a task or engaged in a single response, but also had to observe and discriminate between the type of task completed and the consequences of their behavior. Based on this result, we assumed that it was possible to teach moderately retarded students differential self-monitoring skills that could be very useful in the classroom, such as monitoring correct versus incorrect performance, high versus low scores, and completion of a task within a specified time.

Standard setting. Our next concern was for the standards or criteria for performance that serve not only as incentives, but also as standards for personal action (Kanfer, 1978). Retarded individuals in general, and developmentally disabled persons specifically, do not set realistic standards for their performance when, and if, they actually do set a standard (Rosen, Diggory, Floor, & Nowakiwska, 1971). In addition, caretakers typically set minimal and/or inconsistent standards for them, rather than teaching them to set their own appropriate standards. If developmentally disabled persons are to function more independently, they must be given an opportunity to set their own standards, as this is a most important component of the self-reinforcement routine (Bandura, 1977; Spates & Kanfer, 1977).

Before we began teaching our TMR students to set their own standards, we had to spend some time trying to determine on what these standards should be based. For example, Bandura (1977) points out that standards can be based on social referents (i.e., observing how others perform and the standards they set), on our own past performances, or on a combination of the two. We decided to try to teach our students to set standards on the same bowling game that were based on others' performance (social referent) as well as their own past performance.

Utilizing modeling techniques, we found that our TMR students could learn to set standards based on observing others perform as well as to acquire a complex concept that would allow them to set standards based on their own past performance (see Litrownik, Cleary, Lecklitner, & Franzini, 1978). Thus, developmentally disabled persons may not set realistic standards for their performance, but they *can learn* to do so.

Self-evaluation and self-reward. In our final preliminary study (Litrownik,

Lecklitner, Cleary, & Franzini, Note 2), we assessed 16 of our TMR students to see if they could evaluate their own performance and then conditionally administer fully accessible rewards. The students were required to perform two tasks, symbol-matching (training) and block design (transfer). For the symbol-matching task, students were presented with one work page at a time. Each page contained a variety of numbers, letters, and shapes in addition to a sample number, letter, or shape at the top of the page. Students were to cross out as many of the numbers, letters, or shapes as they could which matched the sample before a bell rang. The bell was controlled by the experimenter-trainer so that the number of items that were crossed out by each child could be controlled. After each trial, the trainer informed students as to whether they had successfully completed the page (i.e., finished or not finished). In front of both the trainer and the child was a felt scoreboard with their names. In addition, eight felt circular yellow "happy faces" and eight felt green squares were available. If students finished before the bell rang, they were to put a felt "happy face" on the scoreboard (i.e., positive self-evaluation—"I finished"). On the other hand, a green felt square (i.e., negative self-evaluation—"I have to try harder") was to be placed on the scoreboard if the student did not finish. Two clear plastic cups, each containing 20 edibles selected by the student, were placed within reach. Following a positive self-evaluation, students were to reinforce themselves by taking one edible. Students were to abstain from administering a reward following a negative self-evaluation.

On the transfer task, students were required to match a block design (i.e., sequence of colored blocks) that was constructed by the experimenter-trainer before the bell rang. Six 10-block designs of varying difficulty were presented twice to each child in random order. Students were allowed 15 and 30 seconds to complete each design. Each trial was timed by the experimenter-trainer, who signaled the end of the trial by ringing the bell. As with the symbol-matching task, the trainer informed students as to whether they had correctly completed the design. Students were then to self-evaluate and self-reward as they had on the symbol-matching task.

Two practice trials (one success and one failure) on which the experimenter-trainer instructed the child and prompted correct self-evaluative and self-reward responses preceded the 12 symbol-matching assessment trials. On each trial, the trainer rang the bell after the child had crossed out a predetermined number of figures. In this manner, the child was presented with six failure and six success trials in random order.

The block design or transfer task was similarly administered. Following the two practice trials, students were presented with 12 assessment trials (each of six different 10-block designs presented twice, once with a 15- and once with a 30-second time limit). On the transfer task, the success or failure was not directly controlled by the experimenter-trainer, allowing performance to vary as a function of ability and effort. After each trial, students were told whether or not they had correctly completed the design before the bell had rung.

Based on this initial assessment, it was clear that our students could not appropriately evaluate their performance and then conditionally administer rewards. Even though they had been presented with detailed verbal instructions and two prompted practice trials prior to the assessment, none of the 16 students correctly performed these two component skills. We then set out to develop these skills.

Our first task was to break down the training into manageable steps—self-evaluative, self-reward, and combination of the two components. The training at each step was time-limited. For example, 30 minutes were devoted to teaching (i.e., demonstrations, prompting, feedback) the students to discriminate between finish and not finish by putting a happy face or green square on their scoreboard, respectively. This was followed by 10 minutes of training students to take one edible after placing a happy face on the scoreboard. That is, the happy face was now to serve as a cue for self-administering a reward. Finally, 30 minutes were spent attempting to combine these two components—that is, either put a happy face on the scoreboard and self-administer an edible when finishing, or put a green square on the scoreboard and not take an edible when not finishing.

Half of the 16 students received this brief (70-minute) training, and then all were assessed on both tasks again. On this second assessment, the non-trained students continued to evaluate and reward themselves inappropriately, whereas six of the eight students exposed to the training evidenced appropriate self-evaluation and self-reward skills. Not only did these students correctly evaluate and reward their performance on the two tasks, but they also significantly outperformed the nontrained students on the block design task (i.e., outcome or to-be-controlled response). Thus, self-evaluative and self-reward skills could be taught, and if acquired, they did facilitate performance on the targeted outcome.

Summary. With the aim of developing a self-reinforcement routine in our developmentally disabled students, we identified four component skills and translated them into overt responses (i.e., operationalized them). Initial assessment of the students indicated that they could not engage in any of these component skills when specifically instructed to do so. Based on these findings, we designed time-limited training programs to teach these skills. Though the training was brief, we did find that most of the students who were exposed to the programs acquired these component skills. In addition, there was some evidence suggesting that the acquisition and appropriate application of these skills, specifically self-evaluation and self-reward, could facilitate task performance.

Routine: self-monitoring. In our first study (Litrownik, Freitas, & Franzini, 1978), we found that younger TMR students could learn a complex differential self-monitoring skill. This skill, we suggested, could possibly be used as a self-management routine, effectively controlling other targeted outcomes. For example, there is a good deal of evidence suggesting that self-monitoring can lead to changes in the behavior being observed (see Nelson, 1977). Both the degree and direction of these changes, as well as the accuracy of an individual's self-monitoring, appear to be a function of the valence of what is monitored (Kanfer, 1977; Kirschenbaum & Karoly, 1977; McFall, 1977). That is, responses with a negative valence are monitored less accurately, as attention to these responses necessarily leads to negative self-evaluations which can be avoided by inaccurate monitoring. In addition, behaviors with a positive valence that are monitored increase, while responses with a negative valence decrease, as a function of self-monitoring (see Hayes & Cavior, 1977; Sieck & McFall, 1976).

In our next study (Litrownik & Freitas, 1980), we attempted to examine the differential effects of valence on the accuracy and reactivity of self-monitoring in our developmentally disabled students. We had students string as many beads as they could within a limited amount of time and either record positive, negative, or neutral outcomes of their performance or not self-monitor at all.

Forty students were initially trained on three discriminations (red versus blue, large versus small, and work that was finished versus not finished) necessary for participation in this training study. Four groups of 10 students each were established, with one group randomly assigned to monitor each time they finished stringing a tray of beads; monitor each time they did not finish a tray; monitor when they had strung red beads; and string beads without any self-monitoring.

Initially, each student's bead-stringing speed was assessed. Five trials of 25 beads each were presented, and the number of beads strung in 125 seconds was recorded. Following this session and each subsequent training or assessment session, students were given 10 tokens for their participation, which could be traded in for various items such as records, toys, and games. In addition, the necklaces that were strung during the assessment sessions were completed and kept by each student.

The three self-monitoring groups were then exposed to a maximum of 60 minutes of training per day over a total of 5 to 7 days. First, they were taught to record following a trial — when they had strung large as opposed to small beads — by placing a marble in a plastic tube. Training continued until all students were correctly self-recording (i.e., putting a marble in the tube following large-bead trials only) on 10 of 12 consecutive trials. Students who did not self-monitor had an opportunity to string beads on as many trials as the self-monitoring students in order to control for practice effects. Next, the three self-monitoring groups were presented with 12 bead-stringing trials, with one group being told to self-monitor when they finished, one when they did not finish, and one when they had strung red beads. Students who monitored correctly on at least 10 of 12 trials moved on to the next phase, while those that did not were provided with additional demonstration training. This training continued until the student was self-monitoring correctly on at least 10 of 12 consecutive trials. Finally, all 40 students were presented with a 10-trial bead-stringing post-assessment.

The amount of training required for the self-monitoring students to learn to monitor large-bead trials indicated that the three groups were equally capable of acquiring differential self-monitoring skills. That is, all 30 students learned to differentially self-monitor, with each group requiring approximately the same number of training trials. Subsequently, the group that monitored nonfinished trials did not take longer to learn this differential self-monitoring skill; nor were they less accurate in their self-monitoring than the other groups. Thus, valence did not appear to affect self-monitoring accuracy in this instance. On the other hand, analysis of the proportion of beads strung at the two assessments indicated that the group monitoring finished trials significantly outperformed the group that monitored unfinished trials. In addition, examination of performances by the four groups revealed that all the groups improved from pre- to post-assessment, due most likely to practice. Of interest was the observation that the finish and red-bead monitoring groups improved more than the control group, while the group monitoring unfinished trials did not improve as much as the control group. These results suggest that self-monitoring can function as an effective self-management routine. In order to facilitate adaptive performance, developmentally disabled individuals should be taught to monitor positive behaviors or outcomes of their behavior. For example, after discussing this study with a group of parents of developmentally disabled individuals, one parent asked how this would translate to her efforts to deal with her 16-year-old son's bed-wetting problem. She had been keeping a daily chart recording when he had wet his bed. We discussed the implications of the study, and she reasoned that maybe she ought to have him do the recording and that he should record when he had remained dry through the night. A follow-up conversation some 3 weeks later indicated that this approach appeared to be more successful.

Routine: self-reinforcement. The training program that was eventually developed was based on information obtained in the preliminary studies when self-monitoring, standard setting, self-evaluative, and self-reward skills were assessed and trained. For example, we noted that not all of the developmentally disabled students were able to acquire these skills via the brief time-limited training. We observed that students who did acquire these skills were able to sit and attend to a model for a minimum of 10 to 15 minutes. They also possessed certain concepts or were able to make certain discrimination (e.g., numbers, colors, etc.) either initially or after after a few training trials. Based on these observations, we identified a number of "entering behaviors" that seemed to be necessary for effective training to take place.

In addition to identifying these requisite skills, we also broke the self-reinforcement routine into its component skills, requiring mastery on one skill before beginning training on a subsequent skill. Thus, training was criterion based with mastery at each level of training being required. We expected that every student who possessed the requisite entering behaviors could be taught all of the necessary component skills for self-reinforcement.

Training generally began with a videotape demonstration of the skill, followed by an assessment. If students evidenced mastery of a skill following the taped demonstration, they moved on to the next component skill. Students who did not evidence mastery were exposed to more detailed live demonstration procedures until they did reach the criterion for mastery.

In order to operationalize these skills, we designed an apparatus (see figure 10.2) that would allow us to directly observe student performance and also to facilitate training, while being adaptable to a number of situations or tasks to which these students might be exposed in their classroom. The apparatus included manipulanda that corresponded to each self-

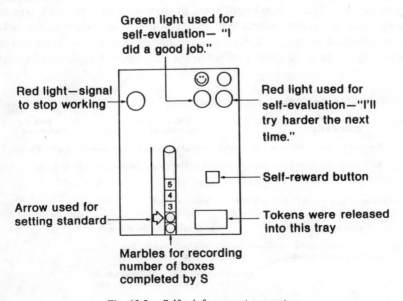

Fig. 10.2. Self-reinforcement apparatus.

reinforcement component skill. Marbles could be placed in the plastic tube to indicate recordings of how many problems had been completed, completed correctly, and so on (self-monitoring component). Performance standards could be set by moving the arrow adjacent to the plastic tube. Self-evaluations based on a visual discrimination (standard set and number of marbles placed in the tube) were indicated by flipping a switch that would light either a green light and green happy face (positive) or a red light (negative). Tokens were self-administered by pressing the reward button and collecting dispensed rewards in the tray. In addition, a red light in the upper left-hand corner of the apparatus which could be controlled by the trainer was utilized to signal that a trial was over (i.e., students were to stop working and begin monitoring, evaluating, and rewarding their performance).

The specific task we selected for our initial training was bead stringing, a task all the students could perform and one which did have some intrinsic value. Our goal was to have students apply a self-reinforcement routine to their performances on this task. Specifically, we wanted them to string as many beads (with a total of 25 possible on a trial — 5 trays of 5 beads each) as they could within a limited time, and then to engage in appropriate self-monitoring, self-evaluation, and self-reward.

In order to develop this routine, we broke our training into five steps (see figure 10.3). At step 1, each trial consisted of a single tray of five beads. Students were to put a marble in the tube only when they finished the single tray of beads before the red light went on signaling that the time was up. The self-evaluation component was added at step 2. If a student finished a tray of beads, then the green light with the happy face was to be turned on. The red light was to be turned on when the tray was not finished. In step 3

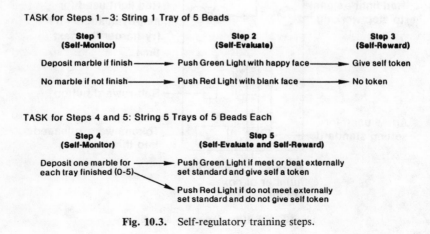

Fig. 10.3. Self-regulatory training steps.

the self-reward component was added to the single-tray trial. If a tray was finished and the green light turned on, then the student was to press the self-reward button and obtain a token. When all the beads in a tray were not strung, the red light was to be turned on, indicating that the student had to try harder next time, and no token was self-administered. At steps 4 and 5, students were presented with five trays of five beads each. They were to drop one marble in the tube for each tray completed during step 4. At step 5 the students were to evaluate their performance after a standard had been set for them, and then to administer rewards contingent on this evaluation.

The criterion-based training procedures that we used at each of these five steps is outlined in figure 10.4. At step 1 students were provided with a series of live demonstrations on how to monitor or record when they had finished a single tray of beads. Following these demonstrations, they were allowed to monitor their bead-stringing performances. They continued until they were correct (i.e., only put a marble in the tube when they finished a tray of beads) on 10 of 12 trials. A 10-minute film was presented to students at step 2 after they had reached criterion on the first step. In this film, a colorful clown model was shown stringing beads, monitoring her performance, and then evaluating her performance on 10 trials. On five of the trials, she finished stringing the single tray of beads, put a marble in the tube, and turned on the green light while saying "I did a good job." For the remaining five trials, our clown model did not finish stringing all the beads in her tray before the red light came on, she did not put a marble in the tube ("not this time, I still have some beads left."), and turned on the red light while indicating that she'd "have to try harder next time." Following this tape, students were presented with 12 single-tray trials. They were instructed to string the beads in the tray until the red light went on signaling them to stop. When they stopped, they were to monitor if they finished and then evaluate their performance, as the clown model had done. The trainers controlled the onset of the "stop light," and on half of the 12 trials, allowed students to finish, and on half, stopped them before they finished. Students who correctly self-monitored and self-evaluated on at least 10 of 12 trials proceeded to step 3. On the other hand, a failure to reach criterion performance resulted in the student being exposed to more detailed live demonstration training procedures. The live training began with three massed demonstrations. That is, the trainer demonstrated appropriate self-monitored and evaluative responses for three trials. These massed demonstrations and subsequent student performances continued until six consecutive correct matches were accomplished by the students or until they made three consecutive errors. If a student was incorrect on three consecutive trials following these massed demonstrations, he or she was exposed to single trial or distributed demonstrations until correct on six consecutive trials. Once they reached this criterion, they were exposed to the massed demonstrations

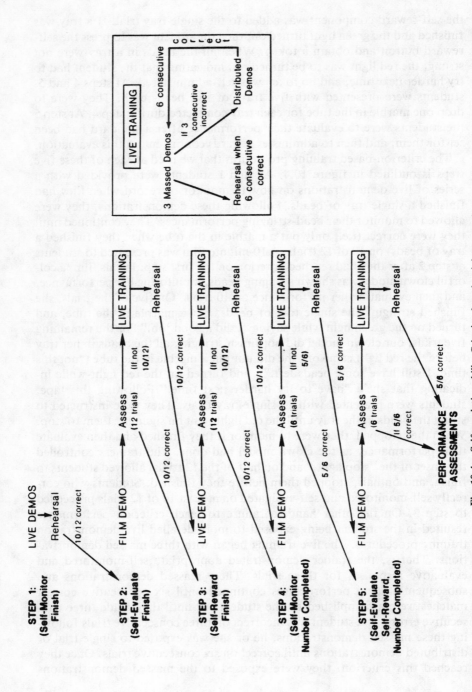

Fig. 10.4. Self-regulating skills: Criterion based training procedures.

again. The same criterion for moving on from the massed demonstrations was in force — six consecutive correct. When students reached this criterion, they moved on to the rehearsal stage of step 2. At this point, students were presented with individual trials without prior demonstrations until correct on 10 of 12 consecutive trials. When this criterion was reached, students proceeded to step 3. Thus, all trainees were performing at the same level (10 out of 12 correct trials or better) when they were introduced to training at step 3.

At steps 3, 4, and 5, the same procedures, with minor modifications, were in effect. For example, at step 3, a live rather than film demonstration preceded initial assessment; at steps 4 and 5, the criterion for moving on (e.g., to step 5 or performance assessments) was five out of six correct.

Throughout the live training, students were provided with prompts to ensure that they engaged in the appropriate component responses. A prompted trial was considered an incorrect trial. During assessments following film demonstrations (i.e., steps 2, 4, and 5), and following the live demonstrations at step 3, students were not provided with corrective prompts so the effects of these demonstrations could be evaluated.

In order to evaluate the training program and the effects of the self-reinforcement routine on targeted responses, we initially assessed the bead-stringing rates of 40 developmentally disabled students (mean IQ = 39, mean MA = 75 months, mean CA = 220 months). Twenty students were then trained to self-monitor, self-evaluate, and self-reward, with 10 of them having an opportunity to set their own standards for performance (the internal group) on post-training assessments and the other 10 having standards set by the trainer (external group). The standard was set at the individual's last performance, with the requirement that the standard could never be lowered, only raised. A third group of 10 students was trained in self-monitoring only, but was allowed to accumulate the same amount of experience stringing beads. The remaining 10 students served as a control group, not receiving training in any of the component skills, but given an opportunity to practice their bead stringing. Following training, bead-stringing performance was assessed again, as was performance on two similar tasks. The first transfer task included four formboards with four forms per board that had to be completed within a limited time, and the second task required students to put five three-piece puzzles together. These two transfer tasks were quite similar to the training task. In addition, when presented with the first transfer task, all students were instructed to self-monitor, evaluate, and reward their performances, but on the second transfer task, no such instructions were provided. Thus, the first transfer task assessed whether students could apply the routine (i.e., component skills) to a similar task, while the second transfer task assessed not only their ability to apply the routine, but also whether they utilized the routine spontaneously.

This design allowed us to evaluate the effectiveness of the live and film demonstrations in developing specific skills at steps 2 through 5, whether the training resulted in the acquisition and transfer of the self-reinforcement routine, and also whether training in this routine affected performance on the training and transfer tasks.

Acquisition of the self-reinforcement routine. Analysis of performances following exposure to the live or film demonstrations indicated that these training procedures were effective, though a number of students (over half) did require additional training. As expected, all 20 students who were exposed to the training reached criterion at step 5. This was accomplished in a minimum of 5 and a maximum of 15 sessions (approximately 1 hour per session). Thus, we were able to develop component skills required for self-reinforcement in all students who had the necessary entering behaviors (i.e., sit for 15 minutes and attend to a task, discriminate between numbers, and work that was or was not completed). In addition, we found that the students continued to engage in the component self-reinforcement skills when presented with the 10 bead-stringing trials at the post-assessment. The students not only completed training and applied it to the training task, but 18 of 20 also applied the process to a similar task when instructed to do so (i.e., formboard) and 12 of 20 spontaneously applied the routine to the puzzle task.

Effects of self-reinforcement routine on task performance. Analyses of performances on the three tasks revealed that the students trained on the self-reinforcement routine significantly outperformed the nontrained students. Specifically, these students strung more beads and put together more puzzles than the control students. In addition, the trained students tended to complete more of the formboards, but this trend was not statistically significant (see Litrownik & Steinfeld, 1981).

The overall effects of training are quite impressive when considering that not all the students trained on the component skills actually applied them to the transfer tasks. We also noted that the majority of the trained students who set their own standards set inappropriate standards, that is, either very high relative to their past performances or very low. In fact, when we defined an "appropriate" standard as equal to or one greater than the students' immediate past performance and then identified those who set appropriate standards on at least 70 percent of the trials, we found that 5, 3, and 3 of the 10 students qualified as appropriate standard setters on the bead stringing, formboard, and puzzle tasks, respectively. These "appropriate standard setters" significantly outperformed the trained students who set inappropriate standards. We also found that the students who utilized the self-reinforcement routine on the puzzle task significantly outperformed the trained students who did not engage in the self-management routine.

This initial evaluation suggested that: (1) we could teach our developmentally disabled students the component skills of self-monitoring, self-evaluation, and self-reward; (2) once these skills were acquired, they were applied by most of the students when instructed to do so, and spontaneously; (3) students trained to utilize this self-reinforcement routine evidenced superior task outcome; (4) students who utilized the routine outperformed students who were trained but did not use the routine; and (5) the setting of standards (i.e., appropriate/inappropriate) appears to be related to task performance.

Based on this evaluation, we (Litrownik & Steinfeld, 1981) decided to try to teach these same students how to set appropriate standards. Fourteen of the 20 students who had been exposed to the self-reinforcement training returned after a summer break. They and 14 returning comparison students participated in this applied study.

The same apparatus (see figure 10.2) was adapted for use with a design-matching task. The task required students to match seven designs (five pieces per design) presented on each trial via a stimulus card. Each design on the stimulus card was drawn to scale and consisted of five component pieces that varied in color (light blue, dark blue, white, green, orange, red, black, or yellow) and shape (square, rectangle, triangle, or parallelogram). These pieces were presented in various positions, with the only requirement being that each piece always touched at least one other piece. A wooden tray, which contained seven small compartments for each design and one large compartment containing 35 foam rubber shapes needed to match all seven designs, was presented to the student on each trial. During performance trials, students were given 2 minutes in which to put as many designs together as possible.

Since the students had previously been trained to self-monitor, self-evaluate, and self-reward on the bead-stringing task, we began by presenting them with a 12-trial assessment (where they did not actually perform on the design task) to see if they had retained these skills, could apply them to the new task, and set their own standards. If students correctly monitored, evaluated and rewarded, and set standards on 10 of 12 trials, they proceeded to the performance assessment (i.e., post-test). Failure to meet this criterion resulted in the student being trained to engage in the appropriate component skills required for self-reinforcement on this task. The training was criterion based and utilized live demonstrations, verbal feedback, and praise, as previously described, but only included the component(s) that the student did not perform during the 12-trial assessment (Steinfeld & Litrownik, Note 3). On the standard-setting component, students were trained to set the arrow (i.e., their standard) at the last score obtained.

The 14 students trained on self-reinforcement had an opportunity to actually work on the design-matching task during the performance assessment, as did the 14 nontrained students. They were presented with 10 trials per day over a 4-day period. A different stimulus card was presented on each trial, so the student never had the opportunity to put together the same design twice. Prior to each day's assessment, the training students had to reach criterion (five out of six correct) on a self-reinforcement accuracy-assessment test. Students who did not reach criterion on this accuracy assessment were provided with additional self-reinforcement training until criterion was reached. Overall, the trained students appropriately applied this routine to their performances (approximately 80 percent of the trials) during the 4-day assessment. Thus, the students did learn to set their own appropriate standards and they utilized the self-reinforcement routine on the design matching task. Analysis of performances on the design task indicated that the trained students who were appropriately applying the self-reinforcement routine significantly outperformed the control students in terms of their output. Specifically, the students who were trained on the self-reinforcement routine put more pieces together in the time allotted than the control students.

CONCLUDING REMARKS

When professional service providers intervene in the lives of developmentally disabled individuals, they typically determine that the focus of their efforts should be on developing specific content skills. This is not unexpected or inappropriate, as these individuals come to us with impoverished behavioral repertoires. Traditionally applied behavior modification techniques can result in the acquisition of specific skills and the development of proficiency in these skills. In some cases, the individuals will initiate acquired skills of their own.

Behavioral technicians recognize that this specific skill acquisition approach may leave us with inflexible, dependent, "nonadaptable" individuals (Stokes & Baer, 1977). And, as Hayes, Rincover, and Solnick (1980) point out, even when generalization of these skills is programmed, our efforts at habilitating developmentally disabled persons will necessarily be limited. There is a push to consider other methods of or targets for our interventions because of these limits, and a recent concern for the "social validity" of our interventions requires careful consideration (see Wolf, 1978). That is, those of us who are involved in providing services need to recognize (especially with children) that we may not always be the best judges of what should be done. Instead, consumers of the service we provide, including the community to which the individual hopes to return, should be involved in determining the appropriateness of our methods and targeted behaviors.

One response to the problem of lack of generalization, limited effects with one-at-a-time behavior modification, and dependent, inflexible, and externally controlled individuals is to begin focusing on the development of self-management. That is, it is possible to begin developing skills that allow an individual to regulate or manage his or her own behavior. These skills develop in most of us, as do content skills (e.g., self-care, social, etc.) without any direct training. This is not the case with developmentally disabled persons; nor is it likely that these self-management skills develop spontaneously after content skills have been trained. If they are to develop, they too must be specifically programmed.

In order to begin such programming in this special population, the skills and operations required need to be identified. In this chapter I have presented a working model of self-management, distinguishing between training, outcome, and process, which, I believe, helps to direct these efforts. In addition, a general six-step process for developing self-management training programs was offered, as were a number of specific applications. These examples suggest that, at a minimum, it is possible to begin to develop basic self-management skills in developmentally disabled persons, and that once acquired, these skills can be utilized effectively by these persons to manage their own behavior.

While the examples presented offer much promise, it should be recognized that the development of a self-management training program is not an easy task. The process I have recommended is very general, and should serve as a guide in developing such programs. For a specific program to be effective, there must be adequate assessment, specification of objectives, task analyses, training, and evaluation. The resultant programs will necessarily move the individual through a number of small steps, such as developing specific skills required for a given routine or problem-solving stage, combining these skills for rote application, applying them to classes of problems, and finally developing discriminations that will lead to appropriate applications of routines to a given problem. Concern for developing adaptive developmentally disabled persons will pay off in the long run. This requires continued efforts to conceptualize and specify what is involved in problem solving along with patient application of techniques to systematically develop identified self-management skills.

REFERENCE NOTES

1. Koegel, R. L. Discussant. In L. Schreibman (Chair), *Current research on the education of autistic children.* Symposium presented at the 13th annual Association for the Advancement of Behavior Therapy Convention, San Francisco, December 1979.
2. Litrownik, A. J., Lecklitner, G. L., Cleary, C. P., & Franzini, L. R. *Acquisition of self-*

evaluation and self-reward skills and their effects on performance. Unpublished manuscript, San Diego State University, 1978.
3. Steinfeld, B. I., & Litrownik, A. J. *The effects of acquired self-regulatory skills on task performance.* Paper presented at the 12th annual Convention for the Association for the Advancement of Behavior Therapy, Chicago, Illinois, 1978.

REFERENCES

Akerley, M. S. The politics of definitions: How autism got included in the Developmental Disabilities Act. *Journal of Autism and Developmental Disorders*, 1979, *9*, 222–231.

Bandura, A. In search of pure unidirectional determinants. *Behavior Therapy*, 1981, *12*, 30–40.

Bandura, A. *Social learning theory.* Englewood Cliffs, N.J.: Prentice-Hall, 1977.

Baron, J. Intelligence and general strategies. In C. Underwood (Ed.), *Strategies in information processing.* London: Academic Press, 1978.

Brown, A. L. Knowing when, where, and how to remember: A problem of metacognition. In R. Glaser (Ed.), *Advances in instructional psychology.* New York: Halsted Press, 1978.

Burgio, L. D., Whitman, T. L., & Johnson, M. R. A self-instructional package for increasing attending behavior in educable mentally retarded children. *Journal of Applied Behavior Analysis*, 1980, *13*, 443–459.

Camp, B. Verbal mediation in young aggressive boys. *Journal of Abnormal Psychology*, 1977, *86*, 145–153.

Campione, J. D., & Brown, A. L. Memory and metamemory development in educable retarded children. In R. V. Kail & J. W. Hagen (Eds.), *Perspectives on the development of memory and cognition.* Hillsdale, N.J.: Lawrence Erlbaum, 1977.

Castro, L., & Rachlin, H. Self-reward, self-monitoring, and self-punishment as feedback in weight control. *Behavior Therapy*, 1980, *11*, 38–48.

Catania, C. A. The myth of self-reinforcement. *Behaviorism*, 1975, *3*, 192–199.

D'Zurilla, T. J., & Goldfried, M. R. Problem solving and behavior modification. *Journal of Abnormal Psychology*, 1971, *78*, 107–126.

Fagen, S. A., & Long, N. J. A psychoeducational curriculum approach to teaching self-control. *Behavioral Disorders*, 1979, *4*, 68–82.

Fagen, S. A., & Long, N. J. Teaching children self-control: A new responsibility for teachers. *Focus on Exceptional Children*, 1976, *7*(8), 1–12.

Flavell, J. H. Metacognitive development. In J. M. Scandura & C. J. Brainerd (Eds.), *Structural/process theories of complex human behavior.* Alphen a.d. Rijn, The Netherlands: Sijthoff & Noordhoff, 1978.

Guralnick, M. J. Solving complex discrimination problems: Techniques for the development of problem-solving strategies. *American Journal of Mental Deficiency*, 1976, *81*, 18–25.

Haring, N. G. Reply to Fagen-Long self-control curriculum. *Behavioral Disorders*, 1979, *4*, 92–96.

Hayes, S. C., & Cavior, N. Multiple tracking and the reactivity of self-monitoring: I. Negative behaviors. *Behavior Therapy*, 1977, *8*, 819–831.

Hayes, S. C., Rincover, A., & Solnick, J. V. The technical drift of applied behavior analysis. *Journal of Applied Behavior Analysis*, 1980, *13*, 275–285.

Henker, B., Whalen, C. K., & Hinshaw, S. P. The attributional contexts of cognitive intervention strategies. *Exceptional Education Quarterly*, 1980, *1*, 17–30.

Johnston, M. B., Whitman, T. L., & Johnson, M. Teaching addition and subtraction to mentally retarded children: A self-instruction program. *Journal of Applied Research in Mental Retardation*, 1981, in press.

Kanfer, F. H. Self-management methods. In F. H. Kanfer & A. P. Goldstein (Eds.), *Helping people change.* New York: Pergamon Press, 1980.

Kanfer, F. H. Self-management: Strategies and tactics. In A. P. Goldstein & F. H. Kanfer (Eds.), *Maximizing treatment gains: Transfer-enhancement in psychotherapy.* New York: Academic Press, 1979.

Kanfer, F. H. The many faces of self-control, or behavior modification changes its focus. In R. B. Stuart (Ed.), *Behavioral self-management: Strategies, techniques, and outcomes.* New York: Brunner/Mazel, 1977.

Kanfer, F. H., & Karoly, P. Self-control: A behavioristic excursion into the lion's den. *Behavior Therapy,* 1972, *3,* 398–416.

Karoly, P. Behavioral self-management in children: Concepts, methods, issues, and directions. In M. Hersen, R. M. Eisler, & P. M. Miller (Eds.), *Progress in behavior modification.* Vol. 5. New York: Academic Press, 1977.

Kendall, P., & Finch. A., Jr. Developing nonimpulsive behavior in children: Cognitive-behavior strategies for self-control. In P. C. Kendall & S. D. Hollon (Eds.), *Cognitive-behavioral interventions: Theory, research and procedures.* New York: Academic Press, 1979.

Keogh, B. K., & Glover, A. T. The generality of cognitive training effects. *Exceptional Education Quarterly,* 1980, *1,* 75–82.

Kirschenbaum, D. S., & Karoly, P. When self-regulation fails: Tests of some preliminary hypotheses. *Journal of Consulting and Clinical Psychology,* 1977, *45,* 1116–1125.

Kneedler, R. D. The use of cognitive training to change social behaviors. *Exceptional Education Quarterly,* 1980, *1,* 65–73.

Kurtz, D. D., & Neisworth, J. T. Self-control possibilities for exceptional children. *Exceptional Children,* 1976, *42,* 212–217.

Litrownik, A. J., Cleary, C. P., Lecklitner, G. L., & Franzini, L. R. Self-regulation in retarded persons: Acquisition of standards for performance. American Journal of Mental Deficiency, 1978, *83,* 86–89.

Litrownik, A. J., Franzini, L. R., Geller, S., & Geller, M. Delay of gratification: Decisional self-control and experience with delay intervals. *American Journal of Mental Deficiency,* 1977, *82,* 149–154.

Litrownik, A. J., & Freitas, J. L. Self-monitoring in moderately retarded adolescents: Reactivity and accuracy as a function of valence. *Behavior Therapy,* 1980, *11,* 245–255.

Litrownik, A. J., Freitas, J. L., & Franzini, L. R. Self-regulation in retarded persons: Assessment and training of self-monitoring skills. *American Journal of Mental Deficiency,* 1978, *82,* 499–506.

Litrownik, A. J., & Steinfeld, B. I. Developing self-regulation in retarded children. In P. Karoly & J. J. Steffen (Eds.), *Advances in child behavior analysis and therapy.* Vol. 2. New York: Gardner Press, 1981.

Lloyd, J. Academic instruction and cognitive behavior modification: The need for attack strategy training. *Exceptional Education Quarterly,* 1980, *1,* 53–63.

Loper, A. B. Metacognitive development: Implications for cognitive training. *Exceptional Education Quarterly,* 1980, *1,* 1–8.

Mahoney, M. J. Research issues in self-management. *Behavior Therapy,* 1972, *3,* 45–63.

Mahoney, M. J., & Mahoney, K. Self-control techniques with the mentally retarded. *Exceptional Children,* 1976, *42,* 338–339.

McFall, R. M. Parameters of self monitoring. In R. B. Stuart (Ed.), *Behavioral self-management: Strategies, techniques, and outcomes.* New York: Brunner/Mazel, 1977.

McKinney, J. D., & Haskins, R. Cognitive training and the development of problem-solving strategies. *Exceptional Education Quarterly,* 1980, *1,* 41–51.

Meichenbaum, D. Cognitive behavior modification with exceptional children: A promise yet unfulfilled. *Exceptional Education Quarterly,* 1980, *1,* 83–88.

352 Self-Management and Behavior Change

Meichenbaum, D. Teaching children self-control. In B. Lahey & A. Kazdin (Eds.), *Advances in clinical child psychology.* Vol. 1. New York: Plenum, 1978.

Meichenbaum, D., & Asarnow, J. Cognitive-behavior modification and metacognitive development: Implications for the classroom. In P. C. Kendall & S. D. Hollon (Eds.), *Cognitive-behavioral interventions: Theory, research and procedures.* New York: Academic Press, 1979.

Nelson, R. O. Assessment and therapeutic functions of self-monitoring. In M. Hersen, R. M. Eisler, & P. M. Miller (Eds.), *Progress in behavior modification.* Vol. 5. New York: Academic Press, 1977.

Nelson, R. O., Lipinski, D. P., & Black, J. L. The reactivity of adult retardates' self-monitoring: A comparison among behaviors of different valences, and a comparison with token reinforcement. *The Psychological Record,* 1976, *26,* 189–201.

Nelson, R. O., Lipinski, D. P., & Boykin, R. A. The effects of self-recorders' training and the obtrusiveness of the self-recording device on the accuracy and reactivity of self-monitoring. *Behavior Therapy,* 1978, *9,* 200–211.

O'Leary, S. A. Response to cognitive training. *Exceptional Education Quarterly,* 1980, *1,* 89–94.

O'Leary, S. G., & Dubey, D. R. Applications of self-control procedures by children: A review. *Journal of Applied Behavior Analysis,* 1979, *12,* 449–465.

Polsgrove, L. Self-control: Methods for child training. *Behavioral Disorders,* 1979, *4,* 116–130.

Rachlin, H. Self-control. *Behaviorism,* 1974, *2,* 94–107.

Robinson, H. B., & Robinson, N. M. *The mentally retarded child: A psychological approach.* New York: McGraw-Hill, 1976.

Rosen, M., Diggory, J. C., Floor, L., & Nowakiwska, M. Self-evaluation, expectancy and performance in the mentally subnormal. *Journal of Mental Deficiency Research,* 1971, *15,* 81–95.

Rosenbaum, M. S., & Drabman, R. S. Self-control training in the classroom: A review and critique. *Journal of Applied Behavior Analysis,* 1979, *12,* 467–485.

Ross, A. O., & Pelham, W. E. Child Psychopathology. *Annual Review of Psychology,* 1981, *32,* 243–278.

Sieck, W. A., & McFall, R. M. Some determinants of self-monitoring effects. *Journal of Consulting and Clinical Psychology,* 1976, *44,* 958–965.

Skinner, B. F. *Science and human behavior.* New York: The Free Press, 1953.

Slosson, R. L. *Slosson Intelligence Test (SIT) for children and adults.* East Aurora, N.Y.: Slosson Educational Publications, 1963.

Spates, C. R., & Kanfer, F. H. Self-monitoring, self-evaluation and self-regulation model. *Behavior Therapy,* 1977, *8,* 9–16.

Spivack, G., Platt, J., & Shure, M. *The problem solving approach to adjustment.* San Francisco: Jossey-Bass, 1976.

Spivack, G., & Shure, M. *Social adjustment of young children: A cognitive approach to solving real life problems.* San Francisco: Jossey-Bass, 1974.

Stokes, T., & Baer, D. An implicit technology of generalization. *Journal of Applied Behavior Analysis,* 1977, *10,* 349–367.

Thoresen, C., & Mahoney, M. J. *Behavioral self-control.* New York: Holt, Rinehart & Winston, 1974.

Wilson, C. F., Hall, D. L., & Watson, D. L. *Teaching children self-control.* San Diego: Office of the San Diego County Superintendent of Schools, 1979.

Wolf, M. M. Social validity: The case of subjective measurement or how applied behavior analysis is finding its heart. *Journal of Applied Behavior Analysis,* 1978, *11,* 203–214.

Zegiob, L., Klukas, N., & Juninger, J. Reactivity of self-monitoring procedures with retarded adolescents. *American Journal of Mental Deficiency,* 1978, *83,* 156–163.

Part III:

Assessment and Treatment of Adult Self-Management Problems

Part III.

11
Self-Management and Interpersonal Skills Learning
Richard M. McFall
and
Kenneth A. Dodge

This chapter critically examines the conceptual and empirical foundations for the assessment and training of interpersonal skills in adults and children. Consistent with the theme of this book, special attention is given to the role of self-management in the acquisition and maintenance of such skills. The chapter is roughly divided into four sections. The first is an overview of the skills concept: the history of skills training is traced; the utility of the construct in predicting psychopathology is evaluated; and specific examples of the construct's application are described. The second is conceptual: the construct of interpersonal skills is considered in detail; a general theoretical model is proposed; and the implications of the model are outlined. The third section is more practical: specific examples of procedures used in the assessment and training of interpersonal skills are presented, and the problems associated with these procedures are discussed. The final section is integrative and prescriptive: the current "state of the art" is summarized; implications for future research and practice are presented; and limitations of the interpersonal skills approach are discussed.

In recent years, the concept of interpersonal or social skills has become increasingly popular among clinical practitioners and researchers. There are sound reasons for this popularity; however, in their enthusiasm, many clinicians have gone far beyond what is logically or empirically warranted. In some cases the excess has been a matter of generalizing from the results of research involving one problem, population, method, or setting, to applications involving a different problem, population, method, or setting. In other cases, it has been a matter of using the social skills approach in circumstances in which there was no evidence concerning its validity. In the worst cases, assessment and intervention procedures that actually are in direct conflict with the available research evidence have been used.

Because we share in the belief that the social skills approach to clinical problems has great promise, we are disturbed to see it being oversold or misapplied. It would be a shame if the approach were discarded prematurely because it failed to live up to unreasonable expectations or failed to succeed when tested inappropriately. For this reason, one of the major overriding goals of this chapter is to encourage practitioners and researchers alike to proceed slowly and to be more critical, cautious, and systematic in their efforts to develop and apply the social skills approach.

RELATIONSHIP BETWEEN INTERPERSONAL SKILLS AND SELF-MANAGEMENT

The concept of interpersonal skills is closely associated with self-management—the general theme of this book. A socially skilled person is someone who demonstrates the ability to operate effectively on his or her environment in a way that maximizes the occurrence of personally desired outcomes. The behavior of socially skilled persons is marked by two important features. First, it is highly adaptive to the specific demands of changing circumstances, often being proactive rather than simply reactive. Second, it seems to be self-regulated—or, to put it another way, under the control of complex behavioral programs brought into the situation by the organism, rather than under the strict control of external stimuli.

The social skills approach to treatment typically emphasizes the use of two general therapy techniques: instigation therapy and replication therapy (Kanfer & Phillips, 1969). Both of these stress the importance of altering the client's responses, as opposed to achieving "insight." They also stress the importance of the client sharing responsibility with the therapist for the planning and conduct of treatment. The client is expected to provide detailed verbal descriptions of problematic life situations, participate in the selection and rehearsal of new ways of dealing with such situations, carry out homework assignments, and monitor and report accurately on the naturalistic consequences of the alternative behavioral strategies. In short, the social skills approach to treatment is aimed specifically at teaching clients new skills that will expand their capacity to self-regulate their behavior.

OVERVIEW OF THE SKILLS CONCEPT

History

Clinicians seem to have discovered the concept of skill only recently, but in reality it is anything but new. In fact, it was implicit in the thinking of Greeks such as Socrates and Demosthenes, who stressed the perfectability of Man. It was a two-step process: first, each imperfection in a person was identified (these tended to be very behavioral in nature); second, methods designed to correct each imperfection were devised (ordinarily these involved exposure to corrective experiences such as logical analysis, modeling, instruction, rehearsal, and testing of alternatives). Demosthenes's method for correcting a speech impediment was an example of such an approach.

In revolutionary America, Benjamin Franklin was an indefatigable proponent of the general notion of skills acquisition, although today he probably would be considered more of a cognitive-behaviorist due to his emphasis on the primary importance of "correct" thinking (cognitive restructuring?) in the self-perfection process.

In the early nineteenth century, during the early days of the mental health movement, the moral model of treatment was most influential (see Caplan, 1969). According to this model, persons who showed evidence of mental disturbance could be cured by being placed in a proper therapeutic environment. Some of the most important elements of this environment included: a peaceful scene, rest, work, religious worship, proper diet, education, humane treatment, and corrective social interaction. In some cases, patients were believed to be suffering from diseases of the brain. In other cases, patients were seen as suffering from negative environmental effects. Regardless of cause, the requisite treatment was aimed at providing patients with a proper and corrective moral education through a structured social milieu. By learning to live a proper life, patient's disorders were expected to be overcome.

With the advent of public mental institutions in the late 1800s, psychiatry and its allied professions lost interest in such seemingly superficial constructs as overt behavior and began a long search for "deeper" biological or intrapsychic causes of mental and behavioral disorders. That search continued essentially uncontested as the central clinical interest until the emergence of the behavioral approaches around 1960. Among non-clinicians, however, interest in a skills and abilities model of behavior was very much alive. For example, early experimental psychologists actively studied the processes involved in the acquisition of perceptual and motor skills. Meanwhile, the group of psychometricians who had forsworn interest in projective assessment techniques was busy developing tests of mental, musical, artistic, and other abilities—the most notable examples being IQ tests. The heyday of nonclinical research into skills and abilities probably came during World War II, when many now-prominent psychologists made brilliant contributions to a diversity of war-related research projects. Personnel screening, selection, and training were the major focus of this work, and many experimental psychologists who were pressed into service on such tasks brought with them a skills-learning perspective and methodology (see *Assessment of Men*, for an example of such work). Other projects focused on man-machine design problems or on increasing the efficiency and productivity of war-related industries. Across these various projects a recurrent strategy was to develop measures of human abilities, to develop ways of assessing task requirements, and to seek ways of achieving the best fit between individual abilities and task demands. Human performance research and industrial-personnel-organizational research was continued and expanded into the private sector in the postwar years, much of it with a continued reliance on the skills-acquisition model.

The movement toward seeing the relevance of learning theories to clinical psychological problems was only beginning in the 1950s. It gathered a full head of steam during the 1960s and became firmly established by the end of the 1970s. The use of the skills concept, however, became prominent only in the last decade of the movement. Possible reasons for this delayed development are fairly easy to surmise. An early atheoretical bias, injected by advocates of the operant approach, encouraged clinicians to focus on discrete, countable units of behavior and to resist temptations to speculate about higher-order organizations in behavior. Advocates of a contrasting perspective, such as the social learning theorists (e.g., Bandura, 1961; Rotter, 1954), concentrated on developing higher-order constructs having to do with the learning process itself (e.g., modeling, expectancies) rather than concerning themselves with the formulation of behavioral taxonomies per se. When general behavioral categories were considered, they tended to suffer in two ways. First, they were units carried over from trait-type personality theories (e.g., aggression, dependency, anxiety). Second, they usually focused on deviant behaviors, thereby implicitly defining normal behavior simply as the absence of such deviance. Meanwhile, psychologists specializing in the area of behavioral assessment offered incisive criticisms of traditional trait and state units of analysis (e.g., Goldfried & Kent, 1972; Mischel, 1968; Peterson, 1968), but failed to supply adequate new conceptual units to take their place. It was against this background that the current clinical use of the skills concept finally began to take shape.

Clinical Precursors of the Skills Concept

A development that helped set the stage for the appearance of the skills concept was the increasing tendency for clinicians to be concerned not only with what their clients were doing *wrong*, but also with what they should be doing *right*. This gradual shift from a proscriptive to a prescriptive emphasis actually represented a risky step for clinicians. That is, it is almost always easier to get people to agree that things are not as they should be than it is to get them to agree on exactly how things should be different. Thus, it was both easier and safer for clinicians to focus on faults than to propose alternatives as solutions. Gradually, however, clinicians realized the necessity of prescribing new behaviors for their clients.

Operant psychologists, of course, had long stressed the necessity of describing goal behaviors in any treatment effort. Their emphasis on shaping desired behaviors through contingent positive reinforcement required that they specify as explicitly as possible the topography of the response to be reinforced. At the same time, operant theory provided no clues that would enable therapists to choose any one behavior as intrinsically more desirable than any other. The theory ostensibly was value free, presumably leaving therapists free to increase or decrease any behavior almost at will. Thus, the operant approach finessed the question of how therapists should select the alternative behaviors for the clients' currently undesirable behaviors.

Looking back, perhaps it is not surprising that the first two major ventures into the risky business of prescriptive behavior therapies dealt with the problems of phobias and learning difficulties in elementary school students. It did not seem presumptuous of Wolpe (1969), for example, to suggest that a person who panics at the image of a nonpoisonous snake should be taught to approach the snake in a relaxed and confident manner. Equally nonprovocative was Wolpe and Lazarus's (1966) suggestion that a person who experiences incapacitating anxiety in interpersonal situations should learn to behave more assertively in such situations. It is interesting to note, however, that these behavioral prescriptions were not put forward simply because they were desirable ends in themselves; rather, they were prescribed because they were seen as incompatible with anxiety responses and thus as means to the end of inhibiting anxiety and fear behavior in the face of snakes or social situations. Nevertheless, the prescription that socially anxious persons learn to behave more assertively served as a catalyst for subsequent developments in assertion training and social skills training.

The problem of learning difficulties in children also provided a naturally fertile and relatively safe ground in which to plant the seeds for the skills approach. Change objectives in an educational context tend to be accepted as "givens"; it is not particularly controversial to assert, for example, that a sixth-grader should be performing certain arithmetic tasks at a specified level of competence. Further, it is not unreasonable to suggest that the student also should demonstrate a certain level of social competence in interactions with peers and teachers. In fact, educators have a legal mandate to do whatever they can, within reason, to identify and correct the academic and interpersonal deficiencies of their students.

The task of specifying desirable behavioral alternatives may seem reasonably straightforward and uncontroversial when dealing with phobias and school problems, but the task is far from simple when dealing with most other types of behavioral disorders. It is not sufficient simply to specify behavioral objectives in terms of the absence of certain undesirable behaviors. One must specify behavioral objectives in terms of positive alternatives, and that task is not always so straightforward or uncontroversial. If a client is reticent in social interactions, for example, exactly how *should* the client behave in such interactions instead? What are the effective or socially skilled responses to each of the myriad interpersonal situations faced by the client? Difficult questions such as these probably contributed to the late emergence of the social skills approach, relative to other learning-based approaches to clinical treatment. As we shall see, the task of specifying desirable behavioral alternatives continues to be problematic.

Competence as a Predictor of Psychopathology

Implicit in our discussion of the social skills model has been the notion that deficits in social skills may be related to, and may often lead to, psychopathological forms of deviant behavior. We have come to an empirical question, one which a number of clinical and longitudinal researchers have addressed. In spite of highly divergent and often woefully inadequate measures of skills and competence, this construct has indeed emerged in the research literature as a correlate of psychopathology, as a prognostic indicator of outcome among psychiatric patients, and as a predictor of later psychopathology.

A number of researchers has taken groups of deviant and nondeviant individuals and demonstrated that the deviant group is relatively socially incompetent. For example, Freedman, Rosenthal, Donahoe, Schlundt, and McFall (1978) used a measure called the Adolescent Problem Inventory to demonstrate that juvenile delinquents are deficient in the social skills of solving everyday problems. Similarly, White (1965) has described the social ineffectiveness of schizophrenic patients as their "enduring liability." Measures of competence have been used successfully to discriminate between essential and reactive alcoholics (Levine & Zigler, 1973), and between process and reactive schizophrenics (Garmezy, 1970). The correlation between incompetence and psychopathology is one found in many domains of pathology and is one that has spanned the entire life cycle, from childhood to old age. A partial list of clinical problems in which competence indicators have been implicated includes the following: aggressive behavior in childhood (Richard & Dodge, Note 1); alcoholism, (Chaney, O'Leary, &

Marlatt, 1978); cardiovascular disease (Meyer, Nash, McAlister, Maccoby, & Sandler, 1980); depression (Lewinsohn, 1974); disorders associated with aging (Eisdorfer & Lawton, 1973); juvenile delinquency (Freedman, Rosenthal, Donahoe, Schlundt, & McFall, 1978); marital distress (Gottman, 1979); mental retardation (Matson, 1980); schizophrenia (Finch & Wallace, 1977); sexual dysfunctions (Lobitz & LoPiccolo, 1972); speech anxiety (Fremouw & Zitter, 1978); test anxiety (Harris & Johnson, 1980); transient situational disorders of wartime (Slater, 1943), ulcers (Brooks & Richardson, 1980); unpopularity in childhood (Gottman, Gonso, & Rasmussen, 1975); and unemployment (Kelly, Laughlin, Claiborne, & Patterson, 1979).

Competence indicators are not merely correlates of psychopathology. The classic work of Zigler and Phillips (1961) represents an example of the utility of competence measures in predicting outcomes among hospitalized psychiatric patients. Using simple and discrete measures of competence, such as intelligence quotients and levels of educational and occupational achievement, these researchers were able to predict successfully which patients would have positive or negative outcomes. Jacobs and his colleagues (1972, 1973) demonstrated that more explicitly social measures of competence, such as evaluations of ones interpersonal relationships, were also predictors of outcome and response to treatment on a psychiatric ward.

Longitudinal research has demonstrated that competence measures taken at one point in life are predictive of psychopathology later. For example, Emory Cowen, the founder of the Rochester Primary Mental Health Project, found that early social competence, as reflected by peer sociometric measures in elementary school, may be a predictor of psychiatric impairment in adult life. Roff (1961) found that these measures could predict which males would receive bad conduct discharges from the military service. Using different measures, Eisdorfer and Lawton (1973) found that competence predicted which adults would later suffer from disorders associated with aging. The range of deviant outcomes that have been predicted from early measures of competence is quite broad, and includes, among others: criminality and sociopathy (Robins, 1966); juvenile delinquency (Roff, Sells, & Golden, 1972); neuroses (Roff, 1963); schizophrenia (Kohn & Clausen, 1955); school dropout (Ullman, 1957); and suicide, along with attempted suicide (Stengel, 1971). The conclusion that one quickly reaches is that incompetence is an undifferentiated and nonspecific predictor of a wide variety of maladaptive outcomes.

A strong implication of this body of literature is that if many of these problems can be predicted from measures of social competence, then they can be prevented as well. This exciting message has two components: by improving the social skills of psychopathological individuals, we may be able to alter their pathological state; by equipping children who are at risk for maladaptive outcomes with an armamentarium of social skills and competence, we may be able to prevent those maladaptive outcomes later in life. Project Head Start, one of the largest and most ambitious social programs initiated by the federal government to date, was conceived with these goals in mind. Unfortunately, these ideas are still being evaluated under the scrutiny of empiricism. Therefore, we must exercise a great deal of caution in proceeding with this kind of work.

Three additional problem areas in which the skills concept has received extensive research attention include problems in assertion, problems in heterosexual relations, and problems in children's peer relations. For reasons of practicality, these three problem areas will be used throughout the remainder of this chapter to illustrate the current status of theory, research, and practice in the general area of social skills.

Current State of the Art

Up to now, most of the researchers in social skills either have focused upon single skills and behavior in a single situation or have conceptualized social competence as a broad, trait-like characteristic of humans that applies uniformly to all situations. The terms "skills" and "competence" have been used in varying ways, sometimes interchangeably and sometimes implying different phenomena. A coherent theory of the skills concept has been lacking and is now sorely needed to bring this field forward. Even with these problems, we have been intrigued by the broad range of clinical areas that have benefited from a focus on social skills. Also, the construct, loose and ill-defined as it has been, appears to show promise as a predictor of later adaptive and maladaptive outcomes. We can only hope that the utility of the concept will be enhanced by a refined theory.

THEORY

Defining Social Skills and Competence

Until recently, the terms "social skills," "interpersonal skills," "social competence," and "personal effectiveness" have been used more or less interchangeably, as though they all referred to the same general aspect of human behavior. Occasionally, however, they have been used as though one term (e.g., social competence) was a function of another term (e.g., social skills). Generally, the meanings of the various terms and the distinctions among them have never been terribly clear; thus, before we begin a theoretical discussion, it would be wise to avoid confusion by defining our terms.

Competence. McFall (1982) has proposed a two-tiered model of social competence and social skills. In that model, competence is considered the more general of the two terms, referring to the value-based, relativistic evaluations made either by the individual or by significant others concerning the adequacy of the person's global performance of a particular task, in a particular setting, at a particular time. In other words, task performance is judged to be competent or incompetent by someone according to certain implicit or explicit criteria. Often the performance evaluation is then extended to the person who emitted the behavior; thus, when a performance is judged to be competent, the performer also may be given the accolade of being a competent person. It should be stressed, however, that this personal attribution is largely gratuitous, since, in fact, the performance, not the performer, provides the basis for the competence judgment. At best, calling the individual competent only amounts to a prediction that the same person's performance is likely to be judged as competent again—at least at other times, if not in other tasks and situations.

McFall's (1982) view of competence has several important implications. First, competence is not seen as an essence of either the person or of the person's performance. Rather, it is an evaluative label given to the person's performance (and by inference to the person) *by* someone. This means that different judges may evaluate the same behavior differently. The same judges may change their evaluations as their criteria change. Evaluations also may be subject to bias from extraneous or contextual influences on the judges. In short, *there can be no absolute definition of a competent response, since competence inherently involves relativistic value judgments.*

Another implication of McFall's view is that in order to assess competence, we need to study the judgment process by which behaviors are evaluated, as well as to study the behaviors themselves. Thus, for example, Donahoe (Note 2) found that most judges tended to use two, or at most three, categories when evaluating the competence of teenage boys' responses to problematic situations in a role-play test by Freedman (see Freedman, Rosenthal, Donahoe, Schlundt, & McFall, 1978). Judges were asked to make subtle discriminations along an 8-point rating scale. While they used values all along the 8-point rating scale, subsequent analyses of the ratings revealed that in most cases, the ratings actually sorted subjects into two discriminable clusters, corresponding to "good" and "not good" judgments. Within each cluster it was possible to rank-order subjects' performances, using mean ratings, but the reliability of these rankings was not adequate to permit confident conclusions about the relative competence of individuals within clusters.

If the meaning of competence is so relativistic and subjective, how is it possible to assess and design treatment programs for competence? Perhaps an analogy can shed light on this point. There are many different languages, dialects, and colloquial forms of communication; thus, language competence can be judged only with reference to a particular set of linguistic criteria. For example, what is considered competent language for an adolescent among a group of peers may not be considered competent when that adolescent is applying for a job, and vice versa. When evaluating the competence of a sample of language, one also would be interested in knowing something about who was performing; a youngster may be evaluated differently than an adult, for example. Furthermore, all of these considerations tend to change over time, thereby requiring the person who is studying language competence to study the changing patterns of language usage.

Judgments about the competence of other types of human behavior also must be made with reference to such contextual factors as the setting, task, participants, cultural expectations, and all other important constraints on performance. Thus far, social scientists have not developed a satisfactory comprehensive model of all these constraints. In lieu of such a model, investigators have tended to rely on the intuitive judgments of persons who are assumed to be knowledgeable about the performance standards for selected tasks within a culture. Eventually, this stopgap method for identifying competency criteria must be replaced by empirically developed theoretical models of the grammatical rules and structure of task-specific competent social behavior (cf., Kanfer & Karoly's discussion of dialectics; in this volume).

Skills. McFall's (1982) two-tiered model distinguishes between competence and social skills, with the latter term referring to the specific underlying component processes that enable a person to perform in a manner that has been identified as competent. In other words, the identification of relevant skills ordinarily will be carried out within the framework of a given conception of what is a competent performance. This can be illustrated with a simple example. Suppose you are confronted on the street by a mugger. What is a competent response in this situation? If fleeing is judged to be competent, then the motor skills required to perform that task would be of primary interest. However, if talking your way out of the situation were considered most competent, then the requisite verbal skills would be most important. In either case, once one has subjectively decided on a competent response, an assessment of the skill components of that performance can be made relatively objectively.

Until recently, this hierarchical relationship between competence and skills has not been clearly outlined. Investigators have tended to treat the two terms either as synonyms or in a vaguely circular manner. Typically, a person whose performance is judged to be competent is said to be skilled. The inferred skills, in turn, are said to be the reason for the person's competent performance. No independent effort is made to specify or assess the inferred skills; rather, the evidence offered for their existence is the very performance from which they were inferred and for which they also were presented as an explanation.

In a later section of this chapter, several problems that have arisen from faulty uses of the skills concept will be illustrated in some detail. For now, the key point is simply that the skills concept, if it is to have utility, must be more than a post hoc and circular explanation for competent performance. Ideally, specific skills should be open to independent identification and assessment. In turn, it should be possible to use the results of an appropriate skills assessment to predict to judgments of performance competence. Returning to our earlier example, an independent assessment of motor skills should be predictive of an individual's success in fleeing from a mugger. Note, however, that a motor-skills assessment should predict less well to an individual's success in talking his or her way out of being mugged; thus, the relevant skills assessment — or the predictive utility of a particular assessment — is tied to the situation-specific conception of competent performance.

Skills are task-specific behavioral programs that are presumably acquired through a learning process. Skills may be based in cognitive structures (such as the skills of reading and interpreting the social cues displayed by another person) or in sensory motor structures (such as the skills of displaying social cues to another individual). Often, skills are acquired in hierarchical fashion. For example, the skill of successfully telling a funny joke assumes a prerequisite cognitive ability to understand the joke's meaning and also the ability to recognize another person's cognitive perspective so that the other person may be "set up" for the joke. These component skills can be combined in the higher order skill of delivering the joke with appropriate timing. An analogy to the concept of social skill hierarchies is found in the development of children's arithmetic skills. In order to understand and perform simple addition of single digit numbers, a child must first understand the concept of number and be able to recognize the various numerical digits. Also, he or she must understand the concept of addition as "putting together." By combining these subskills, the child can master the higher-order skill of additon. The same concepts may apply to the structure and acquisition of other skills.

Social. Throughout this chapter, the skills concept is qualified by two adjectives: "social" and "interpersonal." The purpose of these qualifiers is to remind us of our perspective or frame of reference. They emphasize the fact that our interest in a person's behavior is in terms of its social or interpersonal implications. These qualifiers are not meant to restrict our focus only to behaviors that actually occur in a social context; rather, they direct our attention to the social implications of nearly all behaviors. Since people live in a social world, most behaviors — public or private; verbal, motoric, or autonomic — can be analyzed in terms of their social implications. It is in this broadest sense that the qualifiers are used here. At the same time, however, since a person's performance in explicitly social tasks and contexts has the most direct and important social implications, the following discussion will tend to emphasize interpersonal behavior.

Components of the Social Skills Model

Figure 11.1 presents a schematic representation of the proposed relationship between competence and skills. Most previous models of social skills have focused on the situational (stimulus) and performance (response) components in this diagram, overlooking or minimizing the importance of the intervening organismic component. To the extent that some models have been concerned with the organismic component, they have tended to address it only inferentially. The present model provides a general outline of the types of skills that would be essential for effective or competent social performance. Each skill is considered to be a necessary, but insufficient step toward competent responding. The model proposes that skills can be construed in a manner similar to the component processes in a human-information-processing model. One advantage of this approach is that is takes into consideration the sequential relationships among the skill components. Importantly, the model also makes possible an independent assessment of each individual's specific skills and deficits, with an eye toward using the assessment results to predict the individual's performance on specific tasks. In addition, this conception has straightforward implications for the design and evaluation of programs aimed at enhancing the competence of an individual's performance in given tasks. These implications of the model should become more apparent as the specific skills, or component processes, within the model are described in more detail.

Decoding skills. For an individual to respond appropriately in an interpersonal situation, he or she must accurately receive, perceive, and interpret the incoming stimulus information in that situation. In short, the ability to decode relevant incoming information is a necessary (but not sufficient) condition for competent performance. One can imagine how a person's performance would be negatively affected if, for example, a sensory problem interfered with the reception of information. Similarly, if the person could receive the incoming sensory information, but misperceived it, this would hamper performance. Finally, if the person received and perceived the information, but misinterpreted its meaning or implications, this also would disrupt performance. One important implication of the social skills model is that irrational thoughts and attributions may be conceived of as decoding-skills deficits. A person who misinterprets another's behavior may subsequently perform in ways that would be judged incompetent. For example, if a child misinterprets an accidental behavior by a peer (such as bumping into his back) as a malevolently intended act ("He hit me on purpose"), that child may respond with aggression toward the peer, which could be judged

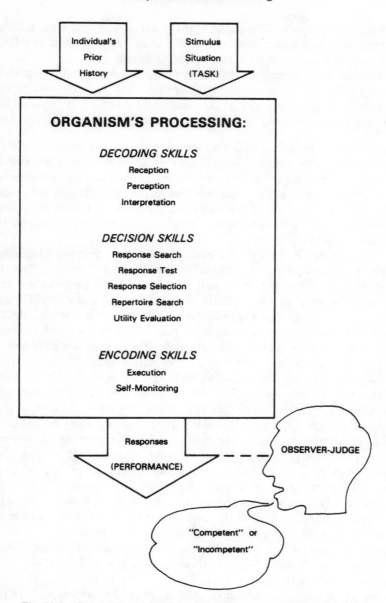

Fig. 11.1. Proposed model of interpersonal competence and social skills.

as inappropriate. In fact, Dodge (1980, 1981) has found that aggressive boys with conduct problems frequently make such misinterpretations and that these misinterpretations lead to inappropriate behavioral responses.

Furthermore, Dodge and Newman (1981) have found that such misinterpretations are most likely to occur when a child fails to attend to relevant
social cues, that is, when he is not skilled in decoding.

Of course, if the person accurately receives, perceives, and interprets the
incoming information, this does not guarantee that he or she will perform
competently. Problems in any of the subsequent stages of the information-
processing sequence could impair the individual's eventual performance.

Decision skills. This phase of the information-processing sequence involves
at least five steps or subcomponents, each representing a necessary (but not
sufficient) condition for competent task performance. The first step consists of a search for possible responses that might meet the task demands of
the immediate situation. If the individual is unable to generate possible
response alternatives of sufficient quality to meet the task demands, then
performance is likely to suffer.

The second step in the decision process involves testing the adequacy of
the match between response alternatives and the task demands. The individual who is unskilled at such matching is likely to perform less competently in the end. As with the case of decoding skills, irrational thoughts
and fears may also disrupt the decision processes of an individual. Because
of prior experiences, a person might misjudge the adequacy of a particular
response in a certain situation. For example, a person who tries to secure a
date by complimenting a potential partner may experience failure. (Then
again, it might work.) It is possible that the person who experiences failure
with this method will not consider this response possibility in future situations. One way to conceive of this step of the process is in terms of probabilities. Past experience may lead this person to assign a low probability of
success in securing a date to the method of complimenting the potential
partner. For other persons, this method may receive a high probability of
success. Of course, persons who inaccurately recall their prior experiences,
or who inappropriately generalize from one situation to another, may
generate grossly inaccurate estimates of the probability of success for a particular method. This could be the case, for example, with the person who
refuses to tell a joke to a partner for fear of being ridiculed.

The third step involves the selection of the response that best fits the particular situation. If this selection process is faulty, it will negatively affect
the person's task performance.

In the fourth step, the individual searches his or her own repertoire for a
response of the type that was selected in the preceding step. It is conceivable
that a person may know what response is called for in a particular situation,
but not have the required response readily available in his or her repertoire.

Assuming that the individual has successfully carried out the preceding
four steps, the final step in the decision process involves an evaluation of

the utility of actually carrying out the selected response. A person may know what response is called for and have the response in his or her repertoire, but decide that the risks associated with performing the response are too high. The person may feel, for example, that the consequences of a possible failure are too aversive to be risked. If the person decides against carrying out the selected response, then the decision process is recycled until an appropriate, available, and acceptable response is found. There are two ways in which this fifth step can have a determined impact on the quality of a person's subsequent task performance. First, if the person is kept from engaging in an otherwise competent response by excessive concerns about facing improbable but negative outcomes, then this will lead to overly constricted response choices. Second, if the person inaccurately assesses the probability or utility of a response's outcome, then this faulty decision process is likely to lead to flawed performances.

Encoding skills. This final phase of the information-processing sequence involves two skills: execution and self-monitoring. First, the behavioral program selected in the preceding phase must be transformed, or encoded, into actual behavior. Verbal, motor, and autonomic activities must be executed in a skilled and coordinated manner if the intended instrumental effect on the environment is to be accomplished. Problems in execution may arise from a number of sources, such as lack of practice, fatigue, or disruptive influences. Whatever the reason, it is possible for a person to decode incoming task-relevant stimuli accurately and to decide on an appropriate course of action, only to fall short of a competent performance because of a faulty execution. The execution of interpersonal behavior involves more than the direct manipulation of the physical environment. Social behavior primarily involves the sending of social information through all expressive channels, verbal and nonverbal. It is this aspect of the execution process that is of primary interest to us, and the one in which individuals encounter most difficulty in their social performance.

Second, self-monitoring skills are critical because behavioral programs are carried out in dynamic environments. This means that the performer must continuously monitor the relationship between the intended and actual impact of the performance, and must continuously make subtle adjustments in the execution of the behavioral program. In other words, to perform competently, the person must monitor and adapt the behaviors as they are being executed. It should be evident that this final step in the proposed information-processing sequence—self-monitoring—actually corresponds to a recycling of the entire process. With this final step, we have described a feedback loop in which the individual's own behavior, in the execution step, alters the environment and thus requires that the entire process be repeated.

The proposed model, of course, is merely a representation of the sequence through which incoming stimuli, or situational tasks, are transformed into responses, or task performances. In reality, the process typically is transacted with amazing speed. While some situational tasks may involve a rather deliberate and time-consuming progression through each of the steps outlined in figure 11.1, some may involve a truncated sequence that is less conscious and more rapid. Task processing of the first type would correspond to what Shiffrin and Schneider (1977) have labeled as "controlled," whle the second type would be called "automatic." Controlled processing is required by novel or complex tasks, while automatic processing is possible with routine, familiar, and well-rehearsed tasks. Automatic processing can be reflexive, organized at the spinal cord level, and without conscious effort or awareness.

We wish to note that several of the component processes that we propose have been studied by previous researchers, usually one process at a time. For example, Spivack and his colleagues (e.g., Spivack, Platt, & Shure, 1976) have studied the importance of the skill of generating alternative solutions to interpersonal problems as a determinant of competent social behavior. This skill is, in some ways, comparable to the first step of the decision process of our model.

The present model has several advantages over previous, simpler conceptualizations of social skills, in addition to those already mentioned. First, the model articulates a *combination* of skills, each of which is necessary but insufficient, that may be required for competent performance. Second, the model goes beyond a simple listing of requisite skills by articulating a *sequence* of processes that are necessary for competent performance. Each of the skills is necessary, but it is also necessary that they be performed in the appropriate sequence. Finally, the model articulates a *path of competent performance through time.* Not only must a combination of skills be performed in a proper sequence, the sequence also must be repeated, through a process of feedback and self-monitoring. Competent social performance is truly a complex phenomenon. This model is but a first step in coming to an appreciation of that complexity.

The Relation between Skills and Deviance

This section articulates an inferential leap from a discussion of social competence to one of psychopathology. It is hypothesized in the present model that individuals who repeatedly display incompetent performances in critical social situations may eventually come to behave in highly deviant ways that may be called psychopathological. The process by which the deviant behavior develops is not clear at this point, although it is easy to conjecture about negative feedback loops between the individual and the social environment that lead the individual down increasingly deviant pathways.

For example, a young man may perform incompetently in job interview situations and fail to secure employment. The negative feedback from the social environment may interact with cognitive errors within the young man—"I can't do anything right." The aberrant cognitions may combine with skill deficiencies to lead the man, literally, to drink. The drinking may lead to further incompetence in job interview situations and, eventually, the combination could turn the man into an alcoholic. Or perhaps the man may become depressed or turn to criminal activities. At this point in theorizing, the outcomes of social incompetence are nonspecific. Any of a number of deviant outcomes are possible. Recalling our discussion of the longitudinal research on the precursors of psychopathology, we note that a theory of nonspecific but deviant consequences of social incompetence is entirely consistent with the presently available data. Further research and theory are required to articulate the pathways by which incompetence in particular situations at particular times may lead to particular psychopathologies. Obviously, other variables must also be involved, but the contribution of social incompetence may be greater than previously thought.

Implications for treatment. The notion that psychopathology may be related to social incompetence presents exciting possibilities for clinicians. First, it makes logical sense (not yet empirically verified, however) to consider that improving the social competence of persons suffering from psychiatric impairment may result in better adaptation for them. Second, it may be possible to prevent some forms of psychopathology by improving the social competence of children who may be at risk. Neither of these ideas is new to clinicians, who may shake their heads skeptically, as if to say "But how do we train social competence?"

The presently formulated model provides a framework for this training. The proposed training is highly complex, for the clinician must consider, simultaneously: the critical situations in which the client displays social incompetence; the tasks that the client attempts to complete in these situations; the skills that are required to complete the critical tasks successfully; the specific skill deficiencies that the client displays; and an appropriate method for training the client to overcome the skill deficiencies. These considerations lead to such a complex matrix of treatment possibilities that we cannot offer a "treatment package." In fact, we will argue that any such "package" could not possibly meet the specific needs of clients. This is not to say that clinicians should abandon their attempts to train social skills in their clients. On the contrary, these attempts, if conducted under the conditions we have articulated, may lead to promising outcomes.

It is important to note, at this point, that a therapist need not remedy every last one of a client's skills deficits in order to resolve the client's major problems. In some cases, the client may be deficient in certain skills that are uninvolved in the client's problem and that seldom, if ever, are required in the client's world. For example, it is of little consequence to most people that they are unskilled at discriminating among the various stages of pregnancy in camels; that skill would be more critical, of course, if the client lived in a nomadic desert culture.

In other cases, it may not be critical to remedy certain of the client's skills deficits as long as it is simpler and satisfactory to design the client's environment in such a way that the deficits are neutralized or circumvented. For example, a salesperson who finds it difficult to meet and influence strangers may decide to change jobs. Often it is better to adapt the task or situation to the person's skills rather than to do it the other way around. The use of prosthetic or orthetic devices to compensate for skills deficits also fits into this category. For example, access to pocket calculators has made it less critical for individuals to know how to compute such things as square roots.

There is another way in which the clinician may not need to assume direct responsibility for remedying all of a client's skills deficits. In some cases, the client who has been taught one new skill will be exposed to new environmental circumstances, and these, in turn, will help teach the client other new skills through the operation of "natural" contingencies.

The bulk of the work for the clinician will come under the rubric of "assessment" with the client; for, the clinician must determine the situations, tasks, skills, and skill deficits that may be implicated in a client's problem. The "treatment," or training of specific skills, follows directly from a thorough assessment and will in most cases involve rehearsal, feedback, reinforcement, and practice. In the next section, we will return to the three problem areas named earlier and will present a discussion of practical issues in skills training for each of the areas. In keeping with the self-management theme of this volume, the emphasis will be placed on training clients in behavioral repertoires that they may carry with them beyond the duration of a treatment program. The skills approach has been formulated with self-management in mind.

PRACTICAL ISSUES

Uniformity Myths and Social Skills Training

Kiesler (1966) coined the term "uniformity assumption myths" to describe several unwarranted but widespread beliefs among psychotherapy researchers that have seriously hampered progress toward the development of effective treatment techniques. Some of the most serious uniformity myths are: that patients tend to be more alike than different; that therapists tend to be interchangeable; and that there is an ideal psychotherapy technique that is likely to be maximally beneficial for all patients.

Uniformity myths similar to these certainly have exerted a negative influence on efforts to develop valid assessment and treatment methods in the area of social skills. For example, assessment efforts have been impeded by the tendency to treat social incompetence as though it were a unitary problem. It is assumed that a person who behaves incompetently in certain situations is likely to be generally incompetent; such a person is expected to show relatively consistent levels of social incompetence across time and across situations. This assumption has led investigators to search for an ideal measure of competence that will assess each individual's "true" level of general competence and predict each individual's performance across a wide range of situations.

Other common uniformity myths in the area of skills assessment are: that all instances of social incompetence in an individual stem from a single cause and, thus, are functionally equivalent; that it is reasonable to add the number of instances of incompetence to yield a single summary score reflecting the person's overall incompetence; that it is reasonable to use a single standard for judging the competence of all responses to one or more situations; and that different measures of competence should yield highly correlated results, despite differences in the specific content or methods used in such measures.

The development of effective treatment techniques also has been hampered by therapists' tendencies to view all social skills problems from a unitary perspective. Therapists have assumed that all patients with social skills deficits require the same treatment, especially when the patients' deficits are topographically similar.

The model proposed in this chapter stands in sharp contrast to such unitary views of interpersonal competence and social skills. For example, the model suggests that faulty performance may stem from deficits in any number of the processing steps outlined in figure 11.1. There is not necessarily a one-to-one relationship between the observable incompetence and the underlying deficits. Thus two persons may show similar deficiencies on a task, but suffer from different patterns of underlying deficits. Conversely, two persons with similar patterns of underlying deficits may manifest them through topographically dissimilar overt behaviors. Moreover, not all performance problems within an individual can be traced to the same skill deficits in every instance. Finally, the model's emphasis on the relativistic and value-based nature of competence judgments is a recognition of the fact that different responses may be considered competent for different persons in similar situations, which means that treatments must take into account individual differences among patients, rather than trying to offer the same treatment or solution to everyone.

With this general introduction to some of the practical complexities and implications of the proposed model, we now turn to a consideratin of three major and representative areas of social skills research—assertion, heterosexual realtions, and children's friendships. The first of these areas will receive more extensive coverage than the others because the general problems encountered in defining, assessing, and treating social skills deficits will be discussed fully there, and then will not be repeated in our coverage of the second and third areas.

Assertion

Definition — what is assertion? Wolpe and Lazarus (1966), who were primarily responsible for stimulating interest in the area of assertion, offered this conceptualization:

> The term "assertive behavior" is used quite broadly to cover all socially acceptable expressions of personal rights and feelings. A polite refusal to accede to an unreasonable request; a genuine expression of praise, endearment, appreciation, or respect; an exclamation of joy, irritation, adulation, or disgust — may all be considered examples of assertive behavior. (p.39)

Their general conceptualization represented, at best, only an idealized definition. It was appealing in the abstract, but rather difficult to use as a practical guide for dealing with the specific problems of clients. The one aspect of their definition that was relatively easy to apply to real-life cases was the part involving the polite refusal of unreasonable requests. Unfortunately, because this was the most accessible part of their conception, therapists, researchers, and authors of self-help books tended to emphasize it almost to the exclusion of the remaining parts. Some of the earliest controlled laboratory studies of assertion training (McFall & Lillesand, 1971; McFall & Twentyman, 1973), for example, used a paradigm that narrowly focused on training subjects to refuse unreasonable requests. This paradigm represented an expedient research strategy, forced by the discovery in a preceding study (McFall & Marston, 1970) that the other aspects of Wolpe and Lazarus's conception could not be defined and measured with satisfactory reliability. The net effect of the general emphasis on refusal responses was to give the assertion concept a negative, self-centered, and socially insensitive connotation — a narrow shade of meaning never intended by Wolpe and Lazarus. This unfortunate negative emphasis has caused investigators to worry about the distinctions between "assertion" and "aggression"; it also has been reflected in the titles of best-selling books such as *Don't say yes when you want to say no* (Fensterheim & Baer, 1975) and *When I say no, I feel guilty* (Smith, 1975).

Not all investigators have conceived of assertion so narrowly. A broader definition, which has received considerable use, is that assertive behavior involves standing up for one's rights without infringing on the rights of others (e.g., Dawley & Wenrich, 1976). Yet another approach to defining assertion more broadly has been to list several descriptive features—for example, assertive behavior is self-enhancing; is expressive; makes one feel good about one's self; helps one achieve desired goals; is when one chooses for one's self; and does not hurt, depreciate, or infringe on others (Alberti & Emmons, 1978).

The problem with such general definitions, of course, is that they contribute little to our ability to identify specific instances of assertive behavior in real life. When dealing with actual clients, it often is extremely difficult to determine what "rights" the client should stand up for. Although some authors have suggested a list of "rights," the actual status of such so-called rights is open to debate. Merely calling something a "right" does not make it so. Adding to the confusion, it usually is not very clear just how the client should behave in order to "stand up" for any claimed rights. And while it may be admirable to espouse the principle of not infringing on the rights of others, it is not a simple matter to determine who has what rights in a given situation. Also, not every interpersonal problem can be resolved without someone losing something. Finally, the use of such terms as "self-enhancing" and "expressive" to define assertion achieves little if such terms are equally vague and difficult to assess.

The most specific approach to defining assertion has been to provide concrete examples of responses which, according to the author of the definition, are intrinsically assertive. For example, Smith (1975) has advocated that an assertive thing to do when you want to get something from someone is to use the "broken record" technique; this involves calmly stating what you want, over and over again, until you get it.

There are obvious problems with treating certain responses as though they were intrinsically assertive. To do so fails to take into consideration many important factors, such as the personal values and objectives of the client, the specific circumstances facing the client, or the probable effects of the prescribed response in the client's situation. No response can be judged as intrinsically assertive independent of its context and consequences. The tendency to label certain responses as good examples of assertion, regardless of their contexts or consequences, probably represents a sociopolitical stance by the therapist. That is, the therapist is promoting certain behaviors—based on the therapist's beliefs about how people *should* behave—without regard for the client's personal goals and values.

In recent years, there has been a conceptual shift away from the search for a general definition of assertion toward a situation-specific analysis of assertive behavior. With this change, assertion is no longer viewed as a personality trait of the individual, but is seen as a quality of the individual's performance in a particular interpersonal situation. The term "assertion," itself, has become less critical in such an analysis; in its place, investigators have begun to think in more general terms, such as "personal effectiveness" or "interpersonal competence." The reader will recognize that these concepts are entirely consistent with the theoretical model of competence and skills which we have presented in this chapter. In effect, the earlier concept of assertion has been subsumed under the more general and more workable concept of interpersonal competence.

Assessment. Efforts to develop standardized measures of assertion have been only marginally successful. The reasons for this follow from the preceding discussion concerning problems in defining the construct. If we have difficulty knowing an assertive response when we see one, then we cannot reasonably hope to measure assertion with much precision. Recent reviews of assessment research (e.g., Bellack, 1979; McFall, in press; Rich & Schroeder, 1976) indicate that most available measures are seriously deficient. For example, the intercorrelations among the measures, all of which purport to be measuring the same construct, typically are lower than one might expect. Correlations between the measures and external criteria also tend to be rather low. Individual measures often suffer from internal problems, such as poor internal consistency and questionable test-retest reliability.

Problems in assessing assertion probably have stemmed in part from the operation in uniformity assumption myths, which were discussed earlier. The best measures of assertion thus far have been those, such as the Conflict Resolution Inventory (McFall & Lillesand, 1971), which have focused on subjects' responses to specific and homogeneous classes of problem situations — such as responses to unreasonable requests among college students — rather than sampling widely from many diverse types of so-called assertion situations. This focused approach to assessment is consistent with a situation-specific conception of assertion. It does not assume the existence of a general response predisposition or personality trait. It simply assumes that the best predictor of an individual's response to a particular situation is that individual's past response to the same situation.

What are the practical implications of all this for the assessment of assertion problems in individual clients? Since there are no satisfactory instruments with which to conduct a general, standardized assessment of clients' assertion problems, clinicians must carry out thorough and systematic individualized assessments of each client's life circumstances, objectives, and resources. This requires that the clinician rely on a sound theoretical framework to guide the individualized assessment. The theoretical model proposed in this chapter is intended as such a guide.

How can the proposed model be used in the assessment of assertion? First, the clinician needs to reconceptualize the client's problems in terms of interpersonal competence and social skills, rather than assertion. Within this framework, the next step is to conduct a functional analysis (see Goldfried & D'Zurilla, 1969; Kanfer & Saslow, 1969) to discover what circumstances in the client's life are associated with increases or decreases in the client's problems. This analysis cannot be carried out in the abstract, but must be tied to the unique settings, persons, values, and objectives of each client.

The next step is based on a key theoretical assumption—namely, that psychological problems involving a social incompetence are the product of a mismatch between the life tasks confronting an individual and the social skills that the individual brings to the tasks. When a functional analysis reveals a link between a situation and a psychological problem, the clinician should look for the presence of a *task-skill mismatch*. In other words, the clinician first looks for an area in which the client is performing incompetently; then the clinician should look for specific skills deficits that might account for the faulty performance. The clinician should not be content simply to infer that a skills deficit exists. Rather, it is important in the design of treatment plans to identify what specific deficits are operating. Our proposed model (see figure 11.1) outlines the sequential series of information-processing skills that the clinician would want to assess.

Finding deficits in the proposed skills is analogous to using troubleshooting procedures to find electrical or mechanical problems in a complex system. The basic idea is to conduct a series of probes of the system in order systematically to rule out plausible sources of difficulty and isolate true problems. In effect, incompetent task performance represents a system failure, and the clinician's troubleshooting task is to trace the stimulus signal through the steps of the skills model to determine where the problems are. It is important to remember that the proposed model involves a sequentially organized system. This means that it is possible to conclude that there are no problems in antecedent stages of the sequence if the incoming stimulus information successfully reaches a given stage in the processing system. However, failures detected at one stage are difficult to interpret, since they could have resulted from problems anywhere in the sequence up to that point. Of course, the system need not be analyzed with troubleshooting strategies. The clinician could choose simply to test each component in the system individually, in the way that an engineer might dismantle a machine and examine each part for signs of trouble. (See Schwartz & Gottman, 1976, for an example of a task analysis of assertive behavior.)

How does the clinician test or probe an individual's skills? The clinician can use self-report methods, such as recollections or systematic self-monitoring; simulation or role-playing methods; or direct observations of actual task performance. One of the first places to look for possible problems is in the client's response repertoire. If the client does not have access to effective responses for a particular task, then incompetent performance is bound to follow. The clinician can assess the availability of responses by simply asking the client to demonstrate such responses.

Another example of a decision skill that can be assessed fairly easily is the client's response search capability. The clinician can present relevant problem situations and ask the client to generate a list of effective responses. The quality (not the quantity) of the client's best alternatives is of primary interest here.

Yet another decision skill—utility evaluation—might be tested by presenting the client with all of the relevant information necessary to make such an evaluation, including a situational task description, and a possible response solution, and asking the client to evaluate the utility of the response.

Treatment. The primary objective of assessing an individual's social skills, of course, is to provide a sound basis for designing intervention plans. The treatment of social incompetence can be approached from two directions: Once task-relevant skills deficits have been identified, significant discrepancies between task demands and current skills can be resolved either by increasing the client's skills (the approach taken in most behavioral therapies) or by changing the environmental task demands to fit the client's available skills (an approach that deserves more frequent consideration).

Research on skill training techniques suggests that a combination of modeling, coaching, rehearsal, homework assignments, and constructive feedback has produced generally beneficial results with a variety of client populations and problems. However, skill training is basically an educational treatment; therefore, the best therapy methods are those that are most efficient and effective at teaching clients the new skills they need in order to manage their own environments competently. Since different individuals learn better with different teaching methods, the best advice, once again, is to individualize treatment plans rather than searching for one method to use with all skill-training clients.

The most difficult aspect of designing a skill-training program is deciding what the *content* should be. Once a client's skills deficits have been pinpointed and the appropriate new skills have been selected, it is not too difficult to select a procedure with which to teach the new skills. At the risk of oversimplification, the critical methodological elements of any skill-training program are: show, tell, do, and evaluate. In the more formal language of psychology, these elements are called, demonstration, instruction, practice, and knowledge of results. Generally it is wise to begin teaching the new skills in a safe environment, where mistakes are of little real consequence and where analysis, rehearsal, and feedback can be carried out freely. Eventually, when the client has achieved a minimal level of proficiency in the new skill, the client must test the skill in naturalistic settings. The selection of such real-life tests can be a delicate matter. Selected tasks should not exceed the client's preparation for them; a client who fails may become reluctant to try out other new skills in the future.

Consequation versus instigation. There is one important respect in which skill training differs from many other behavioral treatment approaches. It stresses the use of instigation procedures and makes minimal use of consequation procedures; in most other behavioral approaches, the emphasis is reversed. Consequation therapies attempt to modify responses indirectly by manipulating their consequences, whereas instigation therapies attempt to modify responses directly through verbal instructions and examples. One advantage of the instigation approach is that it is potentially more efficient because it is more direct; rather than waiting for the desired responses, or their approximations, to occur and then reinforcing them, it seeks to generate the desired responses in the most rapid manner possible. A second advantage stems from the fact that instigation therapies ordinarily do not manipulate the response consequences, but allow them to occur naturally. This is not only more cost-efficient, but it also ensures that clients will be taught only new responses that have genuine social validity. In other words, if the clinician attempts to teach new responses with no utility for a client's actual life situation, then — in the absence of any therapist-controlled reinforcements — the responses will not be supported and will not be acquired and maintained.

Perhaps the greatest advantage of instigation therapies over consequation therapies is that the former are best suited to teaching clients to manage their own lives. The clinician and client collaborate in using a systematic problem-solving procedure, which is similar in many respects to the scientific method; when using this general method, clients are taught to treat the naturally occurring consequences of their experimental problem-solving efforts as the data with which to evaluate the validity or invalidity of various response alternatives. By making clients into independent problem solvers, we have taught them skills with which they can engage in effective self-management.

Heterosexual Relations

Definition. There are fewer definitional problems with the concept of heterosexual relations than there are with the concept of assertion. By its nature, the concept of heterosexual relations directs our attention away from intrapsychic events or personality traits, and toward a specific class of social interactions. The genders of the participants in the interactions are designated explicitly and the general interpersonal objectives of the interactions are implied. In short, we are concerned with the ability of men and women to interact with one another as members of the opposite sex, to develop mutually satisfying dyadic relationships, and to engage in appropriate dating behaviors and other forms of intimate activity.

The area of heterosexual relations has been viewed primarily from a learning perspective. It is generally accepted that males and females learn the social rituals that govern their interactions, and that persons who are awkward or shy about engaging in such rituals probably are that way either because they have not had adequate experience in such situations or because their experiences in such situations have been negative.

Incompetence in heterosexual relations is relatively easy to define, at least in the extreme cases. For example, a college-age male in our culture who wants to date women but rarely does so is easily classified as having problems in his heterosexual relations. Although some may regard such a problem as unimportant, research evidence compels a different view. One of the best single predictors of serious adult psychopathology is the lack of heterosexual relationships in adolescence and early adulthood (e.g., Zigler & Levine, 1981).

Incompetence of a less blatant sort is evident in the inability of some individuals to establish long-term mutually satisfying relationships with members of the opposite sex, despite their expressed interest in doing so. Such persons may suffer isolation and loneliness, or perhaps out of desperation may settle for a permanent but unhappy relationship with an inappropriate partner. Finally, statistics on divorce, spouse abuse, and general marital distress indicate that problems in heterosexual relations are not something to treat lightly.

Assessment. Heterosexual relations typically have not been viewed from the perspective of personality traits. This may account for the relative paucity of standardized measures in the problem area. Most investigators have been satisfied simply to rely on self-reports of heterosexual activities and difficulties. Sometimes such reports involve nothing more than clients' verbalized recollections. Structured interviews or questionnaires asking for similar recall information are slightly better methods. A major improvement in the quality of information is achieved through the use of more systematic concurrent recording procedures, such as diaries or other self-monitoring methods. For example, clients may be asked to record specific details concerning each social interaction with a member of the opposite sex over the course of one or more weeks.

Simulation procedures add a behavioral dimension to the assessment of heterosexual performance. Role-playing is a widely used form of simulation. It offers the advantages of greater efficiency and flexiblity. Clients may be asked to imagine that they are engaged in various scenes with a confederate of the opposite sex. The clinician is able to control some of the most interesting parameters of the interaction, such as setting, task, prior relationship, timing, and other constraints—simply through instructions. Role-played vignettes provide information that self-report methods cannot; most important, the clinician is able to observe actual samples of a client's heterosexual behavior. While it is reasonable to question the degree to which role-played behaviors are representative of naturalistic behaviors in similar situations, there probably is even greater reason to question the representativeness and informational value of data from most self-report methods.

All of the assessment procedures discussed thus far are aimed at providing descriptive information about a client's past or present level of functioning in selected heterosexual situations. Based on the results of such methods, the clinician may be able to identify critical areas or patterns of the client's competent and incompetent performance. However, the methods are not particularly useful if the clinician wants to figure out *why* the client is performing incompetently. To go beyond descriptive assessment, the clinician needs a theoretical model of the processes underlying incompetent heterosexual performance. The model of social skills introduced in this chapter represents an attempt to provide the broad outlines of such a model.

Let's consider the assessment implications of the proposed model for the area of heterosexual relations. Suppose a male client complained that he wanted to have dates with women, but that he had difficulty doing so. Our first assessment step would be to gather the most accurate information possible concerning his current and past pattern of heterosexual interactions. Among other things, we would want to know: Has he ever dated? If so, when, who, under what circumstances, and with what results? Does he currently date at all? If so, when, who, under what circumstances, and with what results? What circumstances make dating most difficult? What circumstances make it easier? If he sometimes has dates, what does he do on the dates? What are the positive and negative experiences he recalls from such dating experiences? In effect, these questions are part of a functional analysis of actual dating behavior.

All of the above information may be obtained through questionnaires or, better yet, structured interviews. In addition, the client may be asked to keep a diary of all interactions with females during one week. This might tell us something about the frequency, duration, and circumstances of any dates, as well as about routine heterosexual interactions.

Based on information from the preceding sources, we next would need to zero in on the specific areas of heterosexual interactions that seem problematic. Our goal would be to gain a better understanding of our client's strengths and weaknesses in performing specific heterosexual tasks. We would want to observe simulated or actual samples of specific task performances to determine what the client could or could not do competently. For this assessment, it would help if we already had developed a list of heterosexual tasks that were known to be important, common aspects of successful heterosexual relations. In other words, at some point we need to conduct a systematic task analysis in order to determine what heterosexual tasks are most critical for our client to handle competently if he is to have satisfactory heterosexual relationships.

A comprehensive task analysis of heterosexual relations has not yet been conducted; but some of the component tasks involved in dating have been studied. The task of initiating dates seems to be a major obstacle for many clients—particularly male clients, since the social rituals in our society typically place the greatest burden for initiation on the male. It is easy to see how a client who was incompetent at initiating dates could develop serious problems in heterosexual relations generally. No matter how competent a male might be in all other aspects of his relations with women, he won't have much opportunity to demonstrate his competence if he doesn't ever initiate a relationship. This example demonstrates how it is possible for a single deficit to have far-reaching negative consequences. By the same token, it is possible that many males might no longer experience serious dating problems if only they could overcome their deficits in initiating dates. In fact, research evidence suggests that the one major and consistent difference between high-frequency daters and low-frequency daters among college-age males is their willingness to take the initiative and ask women for dates (Twentyman, Boland, & McFall, in press). Furthermore, recent research also indicates that dating-initiation issues are a major problem for college-age females (Muehlenhard & McFall, in press). Finally, one of the most successful treatment programs yet developed for nondating college students concentrates on overcoming the initiation problem by arranging *in vivo* practice for the shy men and women clients in initiating actual dates with one another (Christensen & Arkowitz, 1974).

Once an assessment procedure has isolated specific heterosexual tasks in which a client performs incompetently, the next step is to identify the particular skill deficits that are responsible for the client's incompetence. It is at this stage that our proposed model makes its greatest contribution. To illustrate how the model might work, imagine that you are working with a male client who finds it difficult to ask women for dates. Before designing a treatment program for this client, you first would want to determine *why* the client was not initiating dates. Any of the skills outlined in our model (see Figure 11.1) may be involved in the client's problem; only a systematic search through the sequence of processing stages will help to determine which skills are involved.

A logical place to begin this search would be with the *execution* component of encoding skills: can the client execute the initiation task competently if asked to do so in a nonthreatening simulation and if given very explicit instructions for what to do? To assess the *self-monitoring* component, the client might be asked to critique his own performance. The next most logical place to look would be at the *utility evaluation* component of decision skills: What does the client expect to be the outcome of such behavior, and how does he weigh the potential costs and benefits of behaving in this manner with an actual woman whom he finds attractive? It may be that the client is quite proficient at executing an initiation response, but simply is unwilling to accept the relatively remote, but nevertheless real, risk of being rejected. On the other hand, the client may be unrealistically exaggerating the risk of rejection.

Continuing with the skills assessment, you also might examine the client's decision skills in the areas of *response search*, *test*, and *selection*. For example, the client might be given descriptions of several hypothetical heterosexual situations and asked to generate appropriate solutions to each problem situation. By asking the client to engage in this problem solving aloud, you may gain some understanding of which components in this process may need attention. By asking the subject to indicate whether he believes he has the necessary responses to perform each of the problem solutions he generates, you also may get some insight into his *repertoire search*.

Finally, you will want to assess the clients decoding skills, especially as they relate to his competence in initiating dates. You will want to know how accurately he is able to read the social cues by which women indicate that they feel positively or negatively toward a man. If the client feels uncertain about such cue-reading, or if he is prone to misread cues as though they were negative, this will disrupt his performance in initiation situations.

Treatment. The results from a systematic task analysis and skills assessment should have direct implications for treatment. Without a task analysis, clinicians would be forced to guess what the client should learn to do differently in order to become more competent. Actual treatment programs designed without benefit of any task analysis have attempted to train clients in new behaviors that they did not really need. For example, many heterosexual skills training programs have attempted to increase clients' rates of eye contact during heterosexual conversations; however, subsequent research has shown that non-dating college men actually may not differ from high-frequency daters in their rate of eye contact (Twentyman, Boland, & McFall, in press). If based on a systematic task analysis, treatment programs can determine more precisely what situations are most important for clients to handle, and what behaviors are most effective in those situations.

Without a skills assessment, clinicians either would be forced to treat all clients as though they were deficient in all component skills, or would have to limit their treatment to coverage of a few skills and hope that such treatment was appropriate for most clients. In contrast, treatments based on an individualized assessment of each client's skills can be designed to meet the specific needs of each client most efficiently and effectively.

To illustrate how this might work, consider how you would design a treatment program for a male client, such as the one discussed previously, who experiences difficulty initiating dates with women. The task analysis has already focused your attention on the critical task of asking women for dates. It also has informed you of the ways in which a man can initiate dates most successfully or competently. And your skills assessment has uncovered specific skills deficits that contribute to the problem experienced by your client. Suppose, for example, that your assessment had shown that the client could identify appropriate responses when interacting with a potential date, but was uncertain about the availability of such responses in his repertoire, was unpracticed in the execution of such responses, and was unwilling to risk the negative consequences of performing incompetently. The skill training program prescribed for this client would focus on three objectives: (a) increasing the client's awareness of his performance abilities and limits; (b) providing a positive learning environment in which to practice appropriate responses; and (c) examining the realistic costs and benefits of performing the rehearsed responses. Of course, if the skills assessment had uncovered a different pattern of deficits (e.g., faulty decoding skills), a different treatment program would be prescribed (e.g., learning to tell whether a woman is interested in dating you or not).

Thus far, experimental therapy programs in the area of heterosexual relations have tended to treat all clients as though they were alike and as though they all needed the same intervention. Hopefully, the model of heterosexual competencies and skills presented here will lead clinicians to take a more individualized and effective approach. Moreover, by teaching general skills, rather than rote responses to specific situations, the results of assessment and treatment efforts will foster clients' effective self-management of their heterosexual relationships.

Children's Peer Relations

Definition. The study of problems in children's peer relations have been conceptualized according to the same learning perspective that has characterized the study of adult heterosexual relations. That is, it is generally accepted that, over time, children learn the social rules and norms that dictate their interactions with peers, and that they become increasingly skillful at performing various social tasks. Problems in peer relations present the clinician with an additional concern, however. That concern is the child's developmental level. It is assumed that a child learns peer relationship skills over a long period of time. Also, a young child is not expected to perform as skillfully as an older child. Nobody would expect a 4-year-old child to display the same verbal communication skills that the average 14-year-old displays. This concern leads us to reaffirm the relative nature of a judgment of competence. A child's level of social competence must be judged according to the norms of his same-age peer group. A judgment of competence is always made in comparison to some reference group. Of course, this concept also applies to adults, but it is more salient for the clinician working with children.

This concern leads us to a general definition of social competence in children's peer relations. Essentially, we are concerned with a child's ability to interact effectively with his or her peers and to develop and maintain friendships at a level appropriate for and commensurate with his or her same-age peer group. Incompetence in children's peer relations is also defined in reference to a peer group. The child who is incompetent in peer relations may display any of a wide variety of social behavioral difficulties, from isolation and withdrawal to aggression and hyperactivity. Also, he or she may be deficient in any of a number of objectively measured social skills.

Assessment. Assessment of incompetence in children's peer relations follows the same conceptual course as that in adult problems. We can therefore move more quickly through the necessary steps of his process than we did when considering the previous problems. These steps may be summarized as follows: (a) conceptualizations of the child's difficulties in terms of social incompetence; (b) a functional analysis of the circumstances, tasks, and situations in which the problem is displayed; (c) identification of the specific skills that are required to perform in each situation that is a locus of the child's problems; and (d) assessment of the requisite skills for competent performance in the identified situations.

By now, the first step of this process is a given, and need not be discussed in detail. Suffice it to say that the child who displays peer behavioral problems *may* be performing incompetently. The second step is more problematic. The same concerns about a child's developmental level that were present when considering a definition of incompetence in heterosexual relations must be present when the clinician considers the critical social tasks that a child is expected to perform. The task of developing a sexually intimate relationship is, of course, irrelevant to the average 7-year-old, but the task of initiating friendships may be highly relevant. Attention to a child's peer group norms is critical at this step of the assessment process. A functional analysis of the problematic situations for a child is usually made through careful observation of the child in a natural setting, such as the classroom or playground. Given the child's limited self-report skills, direct observation is probably even more critical in the assessment process for a child than it is for an adult. Reports by teachers and parents also can be very helpful, if the clinician is able to ask specific and behaviorally based questions.

Observation of the child's problematic peer behavior often leads directly to the identification of the interpersonal tasks in which the child is incompetent. Consider the 5-year-old boy who consistently bosses peers and threatens them with aggression. He says, for example, "Joey, you sit over here, or I'll hit you." It is possible that he does so as a way of initiating contact with Joey. The coercive behavior serves to minimize the probability of rejection. A functional analysis could verify this possibility. We might identify the problematic situation, then, as the initiation of peer contact in a dyadic situation. The next step of this assessment would be to identify the specific skills that are required to initiate peer contact competently. Again, these skills are often age specific, because of the nature of the dyadic relationship. Verbal conversation skills, including referential communication, may be required for adolescents, whereas simple requests or invitations to play may be required for 5-year-olds. The model proposed in figure 11.1 is offered as a guide for the clinician in conceptualizing the *kinds* of skills (largely information-processing skills) that may be required to perform a task.

The final step of the assessment process is the identification of skill deficits. Once the clinician has an idea of the requisite skills for competent performance in a specific task, the assessment of those skills follows directly, according to the troubleshooting procedures outlined previously. Consider once again the problem of initiating peer contact in a dyadic situation. The clinician could ask the child to describe ways of initiating friendship or contact, as a way of assessing whether or not appropriate alternatives are present in the child's response repertoire. The clinician could also ask the child to act out, or role-play, such responses. Also, cue-reading skills may be critical for the child to be able to determine whether or not initiation is likely to be successful. A particular peer who is busy at work may not accept *any* initiation by the child. Therefore, the child must be able to identify a peer's cues concerning receptivity of contact. These cue-reading skills may be assessed by observation of the timing of a child's initiation attempts.

Treatment. Intervention with children to train social skills follows directly from the assessment process. It should be obvious from our discussion of the highly idiosyncratic nature of children's social behavior that if a clinician hopes to apply a "package" of procedures to *all* socially incompetent children in identical fashion, he or she is doomed to failure. The clinician would be training some children in skills they already possess, and invariably would neglect other skills they lack. Also, since skills must be trained *within* a situation, the matrix of skills to be trained in any package would have to be multiplied by the total number of potentially critical situations. Rather than seek the "ultimate package," we suggest that clinicians focus their interventions on the specific skill deficiencies that they can identify in a child.

The most promising *methods* of social skill training for children that have been identified to date have included coaching, modeling, and reinforcement (Asher, Oden, & Gottman, 1977). These methods are similar to the previously named methods of instruction, demonstration, and feedback. It may be appropriate to apply these methods in private at first. Dyadic or small group training sessions could follow, so that rehearsal and feedback could be conducted freely and with close supervision. Finally, the child could be coached to "try out" the acquired skills in ecologically relevant situations. As always, the need for repeated assessments following the intervention is present, in order to evaluate empirically the success of one's efforts.

IMPLICATIONS FOR FUTURE RESEARCH AND PRACTICE

A Problem-Solving Model for Intervention

In articulating a process of assessment and treatment of problems in social competence, we have followed a general model of clinical practice; one that may have potential for use in other clinical problem areas as well. In fact, we hope that this model will become "standard practice" in clinical training. This model is one of problem solving and is depicted in figure 11.2. The problem-solving approach to clinical practice has been articulated in various forms elsewhere (cf., Gottman, 1974; Haley, 1976; Spivack, Platt, and Shure, 1976). Four specific, clearly identifiable, and sequential steps constitute the problem-solving process. These steps have been articulated previously by McFall (1976). According to this problem-solving model, *both* clinicians and patients are thought to be problem solvers. The clinician solves the patient's problems in therapy by teaching the patient to be an effective problem solver in real life.

The first step is problem identification and definition. How one conceptualizes a client's difficulties will dictate the course of assessment and treatment to be followed. Of course, the major source of data for the clinician is the client's self-report of the problem. However, the clinician's job is to integrate that report with psychological theory and with assessment data that the clinician has collected. The clinician "offers" a problem definition to the client, for mutual agreement.

Once the problem is defined, the clinician must specify behavioral change objectives. These objectives must be attainable; that is, they must take into account the present behavioral, cognitive, and physiological limits of the client. The objectives must also have a behavioral focus. To set as a goal the growth of "ego strength," for example, would not give the client a reasonable understanding of the intervention goals; nor would it provide a

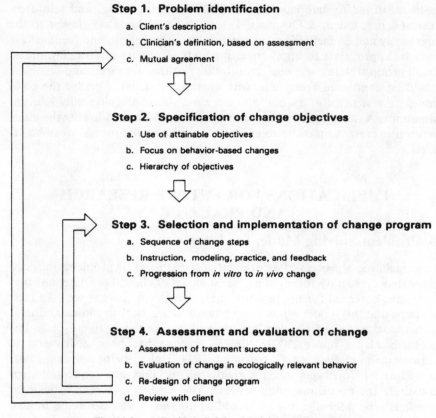

Step 1. Problem identification
  a. Client's description
  b. Clinician's definition, based on assessment
  c. Mutual agreement

Step 2. Specification of change objectives
  a. Use of attainable objectives
  b. Focus on behavior-based changes
  c. Hierarchy of objectives

Step 3. Selection and implementation of change program
  a. Sequence of change steps
  b. Instruction, modeling, practice, and feedback
  c. Progression from *in vitro* to *in vivo* change

Step 4. Assessment and evaluation of change
  a. Assessment of treatment success
  b. Evaluation of change in ecologically relevant behavior
  c. Re-design of change program
  d. Review with client

Fig. 11.2. A Problem-Solving Model for Intervention.

reasonable method of intervention evaluation. Finally, the goals will most likely be arranged in a hierarchical fashion. Consider the client who wishes to become skilled in heterosexual relations. A high-order goal may be to initiate dates. This goal may be divided into smaller tasks, each consisting of a specific skill. These low-order goals might include verbal fluency in asking someone for a date, the ability to recognize willing versus nonwilling partners, and knowledge of appropriate and enjoyable activities. We suggest that an effective change program will be one structured in such an explicitly hierarchical fashion.

Once the change objectives are outlined, the next step is to select and implement the change program. Given a hierarchy of change goals, the clinician and client will come to a mutually agreeable sequence of change steps. These will be ordered according to the hierarchy, according to increased difficulty, and probably according to a progression from *in vitro* (in the therapy session) applications to *in vivo* (in the real world) applications. Of course, the actual procedures of change will vary according to the client and the problem, but most skills training change programs consist of instruction by the clinician, modeling by the clinician or a third person, practice by the client, and feedback.

Feedback is critical both to the client and to the clinician, and leads into the fourth step of the problem-solving model for intervention. This step is assessment and evaluation of change. We suggest that this step follow quite strictly from the objectives laid out by the clinician and client in the second step of the program. The most limited assessment is that of the treatment itself. Has the client followed the change program? Does the client now display skills that were not previously in his or her repertoire? Beyond these questions, the clinician and client must ask, How has the program changed the client's behavior in and satisfaction with ecologically relevant situations? It is quite possible that, at this stage, the clinician will realize that additional changes are required. The problem-solving system would then feed back to step three with the institution of a revised change program. It is also possible that the client will come to a reformulation of the original problem itself. For example, a couple that comes to a clinician in hopes of learning parenting skills may realize in the course of treatment that they are deficient in marital interaction skills. At this point, the system feeds back to the first step of the program and to mutual agreement about problem identification.

The model we have described is a broad one, applicable to many problems. In fact, we hope the reader will see a similarity between this approach and the scientific method itself. Inherent in the steps we have proposed are the steps of observation, hypothesis generation, hypothesis testing through experimentation, and reformulation of theory. These are the steps of scientific inquiry, and are perfectly consistent with the procedures followed by the scientific clinician.

Limitations and Cautions

Several of the models that we have proposed, including the problem-solving model for intervention and the interpersonal skills model of social competence, are based on a combination of research data and scientific reasoning. The work in these areas is barely in its infancy, however. Therefore, we wish to express caution to clinicians proposing to extrapolate from our reasoning. Also, we wish to articulate several of the limitations of the interpersonal skills approach.

Populations. Whereas skills deficits have been identified in a host of psychopathological populations, unfortunately, most successful treatment studies have been conducted with college student populations. Target populations vary in a number of characteristics, including age, gender, ethnicity, cultural background, and type and severity of psychopathology. The degree to which success in a skills training program will generalize from one population to another is an empirical question. In a sense, then, each treatment program becomes an experiment. We propose that each clinician consider himself or herself an experimental researcher. Each treatment program would be based on hypotheses, generated by previous research, which would be proven or disproven. A clear advantage of taking this approach is that, should the "experiment" prove unsuccessful, the clinician would be able to "reject" the hypothesis and move to another perspective.

Since the notion of competence is subjectively based, the clinician must also be aware of the changing norms and frames of reference as he or she applies this approach to new populations. Competence in heterosexual dating performance in New York City may be quite different from competence in the rural Appalachian areas of West Virginia. Each cultural unit may have varying norms concerning competence; therefore, skills training in each cultural unit may have to consist of varying procedures. Cultural norms could also dictate the goals of intervention. Training a Moslem princess in heterosexual dating skills may be inappropriate. Likewise, training a burdened, married mother who lives in a highly restrictive and conservative environment the skills of assertion may present her with a new set of interpersonal problems. This is not to say that the approach we have outlined is inappropriate for this woman; on the contrary, it may be highly appropriate, but the clinician must consider the environment and population of focus.

Contraindications. Given the "infancy stage" of research in this area, we can articulate only two contraindications for the interpersonal skills approach. The first is the limited cognitive, physiological, and behavioral potential of the client. Of course, it is unreasonable to expect a mentally retarded client to learn complex skills of social cue reading, just as it is unreasonable to expect a mute client to learn verbal communication skills. The limits of a client's potential must be considered in the design of any change program. We do not wish to overemphasize this point, however, because the skills approach may offer clients the possibility of reaching levels of performance that are beyond what they thought could be attained. The skills approach assumes that behavioral repertoires are acquired through learning. To assume that a particular skill is beyond the ken of a client may be unnecessarily limiting (cf., Litrownik's chapter, in this volume).

The second contraindication is unwillingness on the part of the client to engage in such a process. This approach assumes a client in need, one who is willing to listen, to try out new behaviors, to self-monitor, and to engage in a dialogue with the clinician. Again, however, we do not wish to overemphasize this point. It is frequently the case that clients who were formerly somewhat unwilling to engage in treatment become active participants once they see the potential fruits of their work.

Training for therapists. Given that each treatment case is an experiment, we suggest that the best clinician will be the one who is trained to think critically, to reason scientifically, and to be familiar with principles of hypothesis testing. We suspect that the clinicians most likely to adopt the skill perspective will be those who reject a "trait" perspective of human behavior, and who are trained in a behavioristic heritage. Training for therapists is actually training of a specified set of skills. Assuming that clinical training begins with a scientific and behavioristic background, we suggest that clinicians learn the "skills" of social skills training in the same manner that their clients learn social skills themselves. That is, clinicians must think of their training as a problem-solving process. Clinical skills can be best learned by didactic presentation, coaching and modeling by supervisors, practice and rehearsal, and feedback on performance. Clinical training does not usually follow these procedures systematically, perhaps because a detailed task analysis of competent clinicial performance has yet to be conducted.

CONCLUSIONS

This chapter has critically examined the conceptual and empirical foundations for the assessment and training of interpersonal skills in adults and children. The history of skills training has been traced, and the utility of the construct in predicting psychopathology has been evaluated. A general theoretical model of interpersonal competence has been offered. This model clarifies the nature of skills versus competence, and describes a sequential set of information processing skills which are necessary but insufficient requisites for competent social behavior. Finally, procedures for assessment and training of interpersonal skills have been outlined within a general problem-solving model for intervention.

We hope that the reader of this chapter has come away with several conclusions. First, the increasing popularity of social skills training is quite justified from a conceptual or theoretical viewpoint. The empirical literature, however, is in an early stage. Therefore, the practicing clinician must view each case as an experiment to be approached with a great deal of caution. Second, the interpersonal skills concept shows promise as a general model of the development of deviant behaviors. Skills deficiencies are associated with a wide variety of clinical problems, and the skills approach to intervention may have merit in a number of areas. Third, social skills are most appropriately conceptualized as rather specific behavioral repertoires that must be assessed within particular situations. Skills can be assessed objectively, whereas competence is a subjectively determined judgment about performance. Finally, intervention according to the interpersonal-skills perspective may be conceived of as a problem-solving process. The clinician is a scientific troubleshooter who must search a complex system for specific deficits. The model of the system's functioning that has been offered provides a framework upon which the search can be conducted. The message, then, is one of guarded optimism. Rather than conclude with a trite statement that "more research is needed," we hope that clinicians will view their clinical practice as field research. We encourage clinicians to test the interpersonal skills model and to report the results back to the field.

REFERENCE NOTES

1. Richard, B. A., & Dodge, K. A. *Social maladjustment and problem solving in school-aged children.* Unpublished manuscript, Indiana University, 1981.
2. Donahoe, C. P., Jr. *Definitions of competence and the assessment of social skills of adolescent boys.* Unpublished Masters Thesis, University of Wisconsin, Madison, 1978.
3. Dodge, K. A. *Social competence and aggressive behavior in children.* Presented as an invited paper to the Midwestern Psychological Association, Detroit, 1981.

REFERENCES

Alberti, R. E., & Emmons, M. L. *Your perfect right.* (3rd ed.) San Luis Obispo, Calif.: Impact, 1978.

Asher, S. R., Oden, S. L., & Gottman, J. M. Children's friendships in school settings. In L. G. Katz (Ed.), *Current topics in early childhood education.* Vol. 1. Hillsdale, N.J.: L. Erlbaum Associates, 1977.

Bandura, A. Psychotherapy as a learning process. *Psychological Bulletin*, 1961, *58*, 143–159.

Bellack, A. S. A critical appraisal of strategies for assessing social skills. *Behavioral Assessment*, 1979, *1*, 157–176.

Brooks, G. R., & Richardson, F. C. Emotional skills training: A treatment program for duodenal ulcer. *Behavior Therapy*, 1980, *11*, 198–207.

Caplan, R. *Psychiatry and the community in nineteenth-century America.* New York: Basic Books, 1969.

Chaney, E. F., O'Leary, M. R., & Marlatt, G. A. Skill training with alcoholics. *Journal of Consulting and Clinical Psychology*, 1978, *46*, 1092–1104.

Christensen, A., & Arkowitz, H. Preliminary report on practice dating and feedback as treatment for college dating problems. *Journal of Counseling Psychology*, 1974, *21*, 92–95.

Dawley, H. H., Jr., & Wenrich, W. W. *Achieving assertive behavior.* Monterey, Calif.: Brooks/Cole, 1976.

Dodge, K. A. Social cognition and children's aggressive behavior. *Child Development*, 1980, *51*, 162–170.

Dodge, K. A., & Newman, J. P. Biased decision-making processes in aggressive boys. *Journal of Abnormal Psychology*, in press.

Eisdorfer, C., & Lawton, M. P. *The psychology of adult development and aging.* Washington, D.C.: American Psychological Association, 1973.

Fensterheim, H., & Baer, J. *Don't say yes when you want to say no.* New York: Dell, 1975.

Finch, B. E., & Wallace, C. J. Successful interpersonal skills training with schizophrenic inpatients. *Journal of Consulting and Clinical Psychology*, 1977, *45*, 885-890.

Freedman, B. J., Rosenthal, L., Donahoe, C. P., Jr., Schlundt, D. G., & McFall, R. M. A social-behavioral analysis of skill deficits in delinquent and nondeliquent adolescent boys. *Journal of Consulting and Clinical Psychology*, 1978, *46*, 1448-1462.

Fremouw, W. F., & Zitter, R. E. A comparison of skills training and cognitive restructuring-relaxation for the treatment of speech anxiety. *Behavior Therapy*, 1978, *9*, 248-259.

Garmezy, N. Process and reactive schizophrenia: Some conceptions and issues. *Schizophrenia Bulletin*, 1970, Issue No. 2, 30-74.

Goldfried, M. R., & D'Zurilla, T. J. A behavioral-analytic model for assessing competence. In C. D. Spielberger (Ed.), *Current topics in clinical and community psychology.* Vol. 1. New York: Academic Press, 1969.

Goldfried, M. R., & Kent, R. N. Traditional versus behavioral assessment: A comparison of methodological and theoretical assumptions. *Psychological Bulletin*, 1972, *77*, 409-420.

Gottman, J. M. *Marital interaction: Experimental investigations.* New York: Academic Press, 1979.

Gottman, J. M., Gonso, J., & Rasmussen, B. Social interaction, social competence, and friendship in children. *Child Development*, 1975, *46*, 709-718.

Gottman, J. M., & Leiblum, S. R. *How to do psychotherapy and how to evaluate it.* New York: Holt, Rinehart, & Winston, 1974.

Haley, J. *Problem solving therapy.* San Francisco: Jossey-Bass, 1976.

Jacobs, M. A., Muller, J. J., Anderson, J., & Skinner, J. R. Therapeutic expectations, premorbid adjustment, and manifest distress levels as predictors of improvement in hospitalized patients. *Journal of Consulting and Clinical Psychology*, 1972, *39*, 455-461.

Jacobs, M. A., Muller, J. J., Anderson, J., & Skinner, J. C. Prediction of improvement in coping pathology in hospitalized psychiatric patients: A replication study. *Journal of Consulting and Clinical Psychology*, 1973, *40*, 343-349.

Kanfer, F. H., & Phillips, J. S. A survey of current behavior therapies and a proposal for classification. In C. Franks (Ed.), *Behavior therapy: Appraisal and status.* New York: McGraw-Hill, 1969.

Kanfer, F. H., & Saslow, G. Behavioral diagnosis. In C. M. Franks (Ed.), *Behavior therapy: Appraisal and status.* New York: McGraw-Hill, 1969.

Kelly, J. A., Laughlin, C., Claiborne, M., & Patterson, J. A group procedure for teaching job interviewing skills to formerly hospitalized psychiatric patients. *Behavior Therapy*, 1979, *10*, 299-310.

Kiesler, D. J. Some myths of psychotherapy research and the search for a paradigm. *Psychological Bulletin*, 1966, *65*, 110-136.

Kohn, M., & Clausen, J. Social isolation and schizophrenia. *American Sociological Review*, 1955, *20*, 265-273.

Levine, J., & Zigler, E. The essential-reactive distinction in alcoholism: A developmental approach. *Journal of Abnormal Psychology*, 1973, *81*, 242-249.

Lewinsohn, P. M. Clinical and theoretical aspects of despression. In K. S. Calhoun, H. E. Adams, & K. M. Mitchell (Eds.), *Innovative treatment methods in psychopathology.* New York: John Wiley & Sons, 1974.

Lobitz, W. C., & LoPiccolo, J. New methods in the behavioral treatment of sexual dysfunction. *Journal of Behavior Therapy and Experimental Psychiatry*, 1972, *3*, 275-281.

Matson, J. L. A controlled group study of pedestrian-skill training for the mentally retarded. *Behavior Research and Therapy*, 1980, *18*, 99-106.

McFall, R. M. *Behavioral Training: A skill-acquisition approach to clinical problems.* Morristown, N.J.: General Learning Press, 1976.

McFall, R. M. A review and reformulation of the concept of social skills. *Behavioral Assessment*, 1982, *4*, 1–33.

McFall, R. M., & Lillesand, D. B. Behavior rehearsal with modeling and coaching in assertion training. *Journal of Abnormal Psychology*, 1971, *77*, 313–323.

McFall, R. M., & Marston, A. R. An experimental investigation of behavior rehearsal in assertive training. *Journal of Abnormal Psychology*, 1970, *76*, 295–303.

McFall, R. M., & Twentyman, C. T. Four experiments on the relative contributions of rehearsal, modeling, and coaching to assertion training. *Journal of Abnormal Psychology*, 1973, *81*, 199–218.

Meyer, A. J., Nash, J. D., McAlister, A. L., Maccoby, N., & Farquhar, J. W. Skills training in a cardiovascular health education campaign. *Journal of Consulting and Clinical Psychology*, 1980, *48*, 129–142.

Mischel, W. *Personality and assessment.* New York: John Wiley & Sons, 1968.

Muehlenhard, C. L., & McFall, R. M. Dating initiation from a woman's perspective. *Behavior Therapy*, in press.

Office of Strategic Services Staff. *Assessment of men.* New York: Rinehart & Co., 1948.

Peterson, D. R. *The clinical study of social behavior.* New York: Appleton-Century-Crofts, 1968.

Rich, A. R., & Schroeder, H. E. Research issues in assertiveness training. *Psychological Bulletin*, 1976, *83*, 1081–1096.

Robins, N. L. *Deviant children grown up.* Baltimore, Md.: Williams & Wilkins, 1966.

Roff, M. Childhood social relations and young adult bad conduct. *Journal of Abnormal and Social Psychology*, 1961, *65*, 333–337.

Roff, M. Childhood social interactions and young psychosis. *Journal of Clinical Psychology*, 1963, *19*, 152–157.

Roff, M., Sells, S. B., & Golden, M. *Social adjustment and personality development in children.* Minneapolis: University of Minnesota Press, 1972.

Rotter, J. B. *Social learning and clinical psychology.* Englewood Cliffs, N.J.: Prentice-Hall, 1954.

Schwartz, R. M., & Gottman, J. M. Towards a task analysis of assertive behavior. *Journal of Consulting and Clinical Psychology*, 1976, *44*, 910–920.

Shiffrin, R. M., & Schneider, W. Controlled and automatic human information processing: II. Perceptual learning, automatic attending, and a general theory. *Psychological Review*, 1977, *84*, 127–190.

Slater, E. The neurotic constitution. *Journal of Neurology and Psychiatry*, 1943, *6*, 1–6.

Smith, M. J. *When I say no, I feel guilty.* New York: Dial Press, 1975.

Spivack, G., Platt, J. J., & Shure, M. B. *The problem solving approach to adjustment.* San Francisco: Jossey-Bass, 1976.

Stengel, E. *Suicide and attempted suicide.* Middlesex, England: Penguin, 1971.

Twentyman, C. T., Boland, T., & McFall, R. M. Four studies exploring the problem of heterosocial avoidance in college males. *Behavior Modification*, in press.

Ullman, C. A. Teachers, peers, and tests as predictors of adjustment. *Journal of Educational Psychology*, 1957, *48*, 257–267.

White, R. W. The experience of efficacy in schizophrenia. *Psychiatry*, 1965, *28*, 199–211.

Wolpe, J. *The practice of behavior therapy.* New York: Pergamon Press, 1969.

Wolpe, J., & Lazarus, A. A. *Behavior therapy techniques.* New York: Pergamon, 1966.

Zigler, E., & Levine, J. Premorbid competence in schizophrenia: What is being measured? *Journal of Consulting and Clinical Psychology.* 1981, *49*, 96–105.

Zigler, E., & Phillips, L. Social competence and outcome in psychiatric disorder. *Journal of Abnormal and Social Psychology*, 1961, *63*, 264–271.

12
The Self-Control of Anxiety
Jerry L. Deffenbacher and
Richard M. Suinn

THE COSTS OF ANXIETY

Unrelieved anxiety in modern life is a significant and pervasive problem. Nearly every individual experiences moments of anxiety or situations in which he or she is tense and uncomfortable. Although anxiety can be stimulating at mild to moderate levels, most persons still find such tension to be distracting and discomforting. At higher levels, the effects of anxiety are more serious experiences with debilitating consequences. For example, individuals with generalized anxiety disorders experience nearly chronic elevations of anxiety, often punctuated with periods of intense panic. Specific anxiety reactions interfere significantly with personal development and satisfaction as well. For example, untreated fear of public speaking has been associated with a 60 percent college dropout rate and lower grades (Paul, 1968), and may decrease the individual's freedom in choosing a vocation (Daly & McCroskey, 1975). Test anxiety interferes with performance on both classroom and aptitude tests (e.g., Deffenbacher, 1977; Sarason, 1972) and may also lower self-esteem and limit educational-vocational development. Agoraphobics have their range of movement and behavioral capacities severely limited by fears of being alone in public places. While these are but a few of many examples that could be cited, they show that for most people anxiety is psychologically noxious and can severely limit personal-social-educational-vocational adjustment.

Anxiety can take a physical toll as well, and may be involved in disease processes in several ways. First, the response of anxiety in itself involves physical symptoms, some of which, such as muscle tension, dry mouth, and shortness of breath, are disquieting and uncomfortable, while others, such as severe diarrhea and nausea, may be severe enough to warrant treatment in their own right. Second, chronic anxiety appears to increase the risk and/or severity of some diseases, such as atherosclerosis (Jenkins, Zyzanski, Ryan, Flessas, & Tannebaum, 1977). Third, anxiety may also exacerbate physical problems already present, as in anxiety worsening a dermatological condition caused by toxic agents or back pain caused by disc damage. Fourth, unrelieved anxiety appears to play a significant role in a number of psychophysiological disorders such as asthma, essential hypertension, and the tension of migraine headaches (Rimm & Somervill, 1977). Fifth, anxiety can influence disease processes to the extent that it motivates avoidance of or interferes with diagnostic and treatment procedures, allowing the disease to worsen because the individual is not receiving proper medical attention. For example, one of the most common reasons given by cancer patients for not seeking early diagnostic procedures is the fear of the possible outcomes (Henderson, 1966). This is true even for forms of cancer like breast cancer where patients have knowledge of and competency in a reliable self-examination procedure (Magerey, Todd, & Blizard, 1977; Neeman & Neeman, 1974). Finally, anxiety may precipitate behaviors which are themselves potentially dangerous. For example, many persons rely upon minor tranquilizers or alcohol to relieve anxiety. While temporarily useful for anxiety, ingesting such drugs represents, for many, a loss of self-control and a decrease in sense of self-efficacy, to say nothing of the negative side effects, such as increased risk of serious accident and chemical dependency or addiction. Thus, the physical effects of anxiety on the human body can range from temporary discomfort to more severe and potentially life-threatening consequences.

THE SELF-CONTROL OF ANXIETY

Anxiety is also costly in that it is often described and experienced by clients as involving a loss of "self-control." It is something that happens to them, something to which they are victim. Moreover, people feel that the presence of uncontrolled anxiety will in turn force them to adopt defensive behaviors that mean a further loss of self-determination.

Traditional two-factor learning theory descriptions of anxiety (e.g., Wolpe, 1973) are similar to client descriptions in that they place a very heavy emphasis on external, environmental or "alpha" (Kanfer, 1971, 1977; Kanfer & Karoly, 1972) control. External stimuli elicit anxiety which in turn prompts escape or avoidance behaviors which lower anxiety. That is, through the continuous pairings with noxious events, previously neutral stimuli acquire the capacity to elicit anxiety (via alpha control), and, through negative reinforcement, individuals learn escape and avoidance behaviors which lower anxiety and its associated noxiousness. With repeated pairings, these behavioral chains become highly reinforced and smooth in execution, extending alpha control over the escape and avoidance behaviors. The behavioral chain can take on a kind of reflexive automaticity such that the presence of the anxiety-arousing stimulus leads rapidly to either escape or avoidance.

Traditional behavioral approaches to anxiety reduction (e.g., systematic desensitization and flooding) have been equally externally or "alpha control-oriented." The therapeutic procedures are designed to alter directly the relationship between the external stimuli and responses to them. For example, in theory at least, desensitization deconditions anxiety as relaxation is paired to previously fear-arousing stimuli in greater response strength than is anxiety. In flooding, anxious individuals are confronted with anxiety arousing stimuli and experience high levels of arousal, but are denied the opportunity to escape. Eventually the anxiety extinguishes. In turn this breaks up the stimulus-escape/avoidance linkage. In such procedures, little or no emphasis is put on developing internal psychological processes which might mitigate the maladaptive stimulus input-response output relationship.

Self-control (Thoresen & Mahoney, 1974) or beta-control (Kanfer, 1971, 1977; Kanfer & Karoly, 1972) approaches to anxiety reduction, on the other hand, shift the emphasis to various internal processes. They involve a focus on changing internal or covert psychological mechanisms which can potentially moderate and lower the probability, intensity and/or duration of the anxiety response pattern. Generally, these procedures teach anxious individuals to discriminate anxiety-related cues (most often the internal, responsed-produced cues of anxiety arousal) and to initiate a new chain of internal coping behaviors to break the old stimulus-anxiety arousal chain. Individuals are trained to initiate these coping behaviors without external prompting. Clients thereby become more active agents, as they develop self-controlled skills with which to manage the experience of anxiety.

This focus on internal cueing and coping responses in the self-control model, in our opinion, gives rise to the possibility of overcoming three problems found in more traditional interventions (such as desensitization and flooding). First, while traditional interventions are effective in reducing circumscribed anxieties (Paul, 1969; Rimm & Masters, 1974), their effects are somewhat limited. Treatment effects generalize only to anxieties elicited by situations similar to the treated anxiety. The effects of self-control interventions need not be so stimulus bound. Since the cueing of the coping responses is internal, individuals can employ the coping skills whenever and wherever they experience anxiety arousal. That is, self-control treatments should result in nontargeted anxiety reduction as the cues for anxiety management come from within the individual. Second, maintenance of effects for more traditional interventions is based on the positive consequences of anxiety reduction continually outweighing whatever aversive conditioning may occur in the future. Otherwise, anxieties are likely to be reconditioned. Maintenance of anxiety reduction within the self-control model should be more consistent, as clients learn coping skills with which they continually manage their affective responses. Furthermore, the anxiety-control repertoire may be continually strengthened by the total or partial reduction of stress which it engenders. Finally, self-control interventions offer the potential of both prevention and remediation, rather than remediation only. Even when traditional interventions are successful, they do not offer clients skills with which to manage dissimilar stressors in the future. When clients experience future anxieties, they are encouraged to return for further treatment. Self-control interventions, on the other hand, systematically teach a set of generalized coping skills with which to handle not only the present, but also future stress (Barrios & Shigetomi, 1979, 1980).

The topic of this chapter is specifically the self-control or self-management of anxiety. First, we will discuss the inferential nature of anxiety and its multichannel assessment. In turn we will relate this multichannel model of anxiety to three general self-control approaches to anxiety reduction: affective coping skills training, cognitive coping skills training, and combined cognitive and affective coping skills training. Specific self-control programs within each of these areas will be reviewed in detail. This review will be followed by two concluding sections; one summarizes key elements in the development of quality self-control interventions, and the other outlines major research issues in the self-control of anxiety.

THE NATURE OF ANXIETY

Arriving at a definition of the nature of anxiety is no easy task. Definitions tend to be somewhat circular, often on the order of anxiety being the "state of the person when he or she is anxious." A most useful approach to the definition of anxiety is to view it not as a "thing" or "state" with singular defining characteristics, but as an inferential construct (Borkovec, Weerts, & Bernstein, 1977; Lang, 1969, 1971; Suinn, 1977a). That is, anxiety is a label and a conclusion (or inference) drawn by an observer with access to data descriptive of another person. The data typically involve one or more response channels. One such response channel is the affective-physiological, in which anxiety is characterized by subjective feelings of apprehension, tension, dread, and accompanying physiological activation (Spielberger, 1966). A second channel is the cognitive channel. Here anxiety is reflected in overt descriptions of one's self as anxious, by various negative covert verbal and imaginal directions of attention, and by interference with normal cognitive-attentional functioning. The third channel is the somatic-behavioral arena, where anxiety is inferred from data such as motor tremor, speech disfluencies, avoidance and escape behavior, and performance deterioration. Thus, within this multichannel model, "anxiety" is an observer's inference drawn from personal characteristics in one or more of three assessment domains.

Furthermore, the same constellation of characteristics need not be present in every case to conclude that anxiety is present. For example, one anxious client may report great worry (cognitive) and avoid anxiety-arousing circumstances consistently (somatic-behavioral), and yet show only modest physiological arousal (affective-physiological). Similarly, another anxious client might show heightened autonomic arousal (affective-physiological) and yet consistently demonstrate approach (somatic-behavioral) toward the feared stimulus (Leitenberg, Agras, Butz, & Wincze, 1971). Indeed, considerable research has supported this conceptualization by showing that response domains are, at best, modestly correlated, and that even within a given domain, elements are not necessarily highly correlated in a consistent manner (Deffenbacher, 1980; Lang, 1969, 1971). In sum, anxiety may refer to different things in different cases.

It is also useful to be aware of the time-or situational-embeddedness of anxiety reactions. The various aspects of anxiety responses may occur at different times relative to the precipitating condition. For example, a cognitive response may be present prior to an event; for example, the situation of a person worrying about a forthcoming musical performance or test a week or two away. On the other hand, the individual may show none of the affective-physiological, cognitive, or somatic-behavioral signs of anxiety during a stressful event, but "shake like a leaf" as soon as the event is over, in a kind of delayed reaction. Finally, anxiety may accumulate over time such that its presence is inferred from reactions far removed from the original stress. A good example of this is the tension headache which may appear several hours after the stressful experience.

These statements imply that it is sometimes possible to identify the exact situation or event which prompts the response patterns from which we infer the presence of anxiety. For convenience, we will refer to such events as stressors; a stressor being defined as a threatening or aversive event. The stressor may acquire its threat value from its own characteristics, such as an event which is physically harmful or life threatening. A stressor may also acquire its value by virtue of its meaning for the person. College students, for example, rate losing a job as significantly more stressful than do non-college-students (Marx, Garrity, & Bowers, 1975). The personal characteristics and history of the individual also influence the stress value of an event. If the person possesses inadequate coping skills, has been faced with a number of stressful circumstances recently, does not believe in his or her ability, or perceives the stressor as beyond personal control, then the event may have more threat value.

Some would deplore the lack of specificity in the definition of anxiety and would push for a cleaner, more specific definition of anxiety. We are suggesting an alternative. We are suggesting that, by its very nature, *anxiety is a human inference, with different referent points in different individuals.* Rather than argue about the "true" nature of anxiety, we are proposing that the inferential nature of anxiety be accepted, and that in assessing and describing a given case, clinicians should specify concretely the defining characteristics of the individual's response and relate these directly to treatment selection and design. With these goals in mind, we will return to the response channels and break each down into subcategories in which anxiety-related data may be found.

THE ASSESSMENT OF ANXIETY

The breakdown of the anxiety response channels is summarized in table 12.1. The subcategories may not be exhaustive and certainly are not mutually exclusive. They are presented, however, as a way of organizing information about a client, of conceptualizing the nature of the presenting concern, and, hopefully, of assisting in the selection and development of a treatment plan, self-control or otherwise. Each subarea will be described briefly along with examples of how therapists may collect data in this area.

The affective-physiological domain may be meaningfully subdivided into three areas. The first of these is *subjective feelings of anxiety and tension.* Anxious clients often report feelings of tension, anxiety, apprehension, dread, and the like. For example, a client may report dreading to go somewhere and feeling like he or she will fall apart. Some of these feelings are connected to specific situations, whereas others are less concretely connected to external stimuli and appear more general or "free floating." Because of their subjective nature the major source of data is likely to be client self-report. Reflective interviewing in which the therapist paraphrases and summarizes the client's expression of anxiety-related affect and then follows up with requests for concrete examples of instances in which such feelings were felt will tend to develop a "picture" of the affect profile and some of the stimuli which elicit it. The interviewer may also notice the client appearing uncomfortable or uneasy while discussing certain topics. Self-monitoring homework is also a useful adjunct in collecting more information about intercurrent life experiences with anxiety.

The second area is *heightened autonomic arousal.* Examples would in-

Table 12.1.   Multichannel Assessment of Anxiety

I. Affective—Physiological Response Channel
  A. Subjective feelings of anxiety and tension
  B. Heightened autonomic arousal
  C. Increase in common anxiety-related psychophysiological disorders

II. Cognitive Response Channel
  A. Memory
    1. Interference with learning and memory storage
    2. Interference with memory retrieval
  B. Performance
    1. Performance deterioration
    2. Stereotypical, inflexible approaches to problem-solving
    3. Spectator role
  C. Attention
    1. Inability to focus attention and concentration
    2. Misdirection of attention to worrisome ruminations
    3. Misdirection of attention to excessively high performance standards
    4. Misdirection of attention to autonomic arousal
    5. Misdirection of attention to catastrophic images

III. Somatic-Behavioral Response Channel
  A. Muscle tension
  B. Behavioral disruption and performance deterioration
  C. Off-task behavior
  D. Behavioral constriction, rigidity, stereotypy and compulsivity
  E. Avoidance
  F. Escape

clude increased heart or respiration rate, elevated blood pressure, sweating, and nauseous sensations. Direct, formal observation using psycho-physiological recording equipment (e.g., EMG readings while the person is imagining an anxiety arousing situation, or pulse rate and blood pressure immediately following a stressful task) are preferred sources of data, where they can possibly be collected. In many cases, the interviewer will have to rely on client descriptions and self-monitoring of these physiological indices of anxiety. In some cases, the interviewer's informal observations during the interview (e.g., noticing beads of sweat on the forehead or a client holding the stomach while discussing certain material) will provide useful supplements to client self-report.

The third aspect is an *increase in common anxiety-related psychophysiological disorders*. Examples of these include tension headaches, ulcerative colitis, sleep onset insomnia, fatigue, asthma, and certain dermatological disorders. This subcategory is separated from indices of autonomic arousal noted above, not because they are unrelated, but because some individuals are relatively unaware of and do not report physiological arousal, but do experience and report one or more psychophysiological problems. Often, clients will report such problems spontaneously or with minimal therapist prompting. Requests for greater detail regarding the problem will generally elicit a full description of the problem. Information may also come as a part of a referral from a physician who has examined or treated the person. In either case, medical consultation and evaluation is important in evaluating this aspect of anxiety.

Data from several different subareas in the cognitive response channel can also lead to an inference of anxiety. The cognitive domain has been divided into the areas of memory, performance, and attention, each of which has been further subdivided.

One of these subdomains of memory is *interference with learning and memory storage.* In the face of anxiety arousal, many people do not appear to code and store information well. For example, test-anxious students often report that they read material but are unable to recall it even a few minutes later. Research has supported this in that individuals who report considerable anxiety show greater problems in learning (e.g.., Sarason, 1972) and a decreased amount of information stored and/or deficiencies in the depth of information processing (e.g., Mueller, 1980). For example, anxious individuals consistently store and recall fewer digits in a digit-span task than less anxious individuals (e.g., Mueller, 1967). Often the interviewer will gather this information from client self-report. Detailed interviewing about the nature and conditions under which this happens will help separate anxiety interferences from skill deficits. Information from others or from records (such as academic testing) may also be helpful in identifying the discrepancy between learning and memory capacities under anxiety-arousing and non-anxiety-arousing circumstances. On occasion the interviewer will see this type of problem within a session. For example, the person will not accurately code information that is anxiety arousing, but will code similar information about a nonstressful topic.

Another aspect of anxiety involvement with memory functions is *interference with memory retrieval.* Here the information has been stored and is available under less stressful conditions, but cannot be recalled in the face of the stressor. A common example is that of the individual who forgets portions of a well-rehearsed speech. In more extreme forms, a panicked individual may appear disoriented and not be able to recall even basic life information, like a home address. Client self-report of things such as "blanking out" or "getting so nervous that I couldn't remember my own name" are common examples of information in this area which an interviewer will encounter. Such client comments should be followed up for specific examples and clarification of such descriptions.

Cognitive performance parameters, too, may reflect or lead to a conclusion that anxiety is present. One very important area is *cognitive performance deterioration.* Evidence for anxiety may be present when cognitive tasks which the person can ordinarily do are either not done or are done poorly. For example, the person may be unable to organize information into a logically sound essay (called writing or test anxiety), yet under other circumstances clearly demonstrates the capacity to do so. The cognitive performance deterioration may be due to factors in many other domains, but is still an important index of anxiety. Clients will often describe examples of this problem, and the interviewer should follow up with requests for specific examples and descriptions. Some cognitive performance deterioration may also be observed through role-play or behavioral sampling assessments (e.g., simulated test conditions). For example, the literature on test anxiety (e.g., Deffenbacher, 1978; Sarason, 1972) shows that highly anxious individuals perform less well on the same task under high evaluative stress conditions (e.g., conditions which stress the difficult, comparative, or time-limited nature of the task) than under low evaluative stress.

Another anxiety-related aspect of cognitive performance is *stereotypical, inflexible approaches to problem solving.* When anxious, individuals often become cognitively "rigid" in their approach to dealing with the stressor and are unable to flexibly think through and solve the problem. In the absence of stress, they may be able to resolve the problem. Some individuals seem to get locked into narrow cognitive sets and compulsively attempt certain solutions, even in the face of feedback that the solutions are not working. That is, under stress, they appear to persevere on irrelevancies of the situation and/or upon ineffective solutions to the problem. For example, test-anxious subjects under evaluative stress tend to have difficulty leaving unsolved problems or ineffective problem-solving strategies (Deffenbacher, 1978; Deffenbacher & Hazaleus, Note 1). Clients demonstrating such tendencies will say things like "You know it was dumb, but I just couldn't let go of thinking about it that way," or "I just got stuck there. It was like I had tunnel vision and couldn't get untracked and move on with it." Interview questions around the topic of how the person approached and tried to solve the problem often will elicit information in this area.

A final element of cognitive performance-related processes potentially indicative of anxiety is the *spectator role.* In this case, individuals describe themselves from the perspective of an external observer. It is as if they are participant observers in the situation, looking on at themselves rather than being inside themselves in touch with their own experiences. The spectator role is not as severe as depersonalization. In the spectator role, individuals are somewhat detached from their experience, but clearly experience it as their own, whereas in depersonalization, the experience is seen as alien to the individuals, not even as their own. The spectator role may reflect a cognitive strategy designed to distance the person from the experience of anxiety, and is often reflected literally in the way clients describe their experience. Some describe the experience as if they were watching themselves on television or in a movie. Others describe it as being there in the situation, but like another person looking on. For example, one of our clients described this aspect as "being there, but being outside looking on at himself." Various researchers have noted this aspect of anxiety. For example, Masters and Johnson (1970) described this role as one of the cardinal features of anxiety in sexual relationships. Mahoney and Avener (1977) reported similar differences between successful and unsuccessful (more often anxious) Olympic athletes. Athletes who are anxious often report being separated from their bodies, usually at a maximally stressful time such as the start of a race. More recently, Wine (1980) has suggested this role to be an important aspect of test anxiety. The interviewer can often get a lead for this type of experience by listening to how the clients describe their experiences and then probing concretely, as needed, about whether they felt on the inside of the experience or outside looking on.

Anxiety may also be reflected in attentional difficulties. One of these is the *inability to focus or concentrate in a sustained way*. The individual is not able to attend to the task at hand with any consistency and is very distracted and distractible. Attention may wander across a number of items, often in rapid succession. Clients will often report this type of state in phrases like "I was so nervous that I couldn't concentrate on a thing"; or "My mind just kept wandering all over the place"; or "I just couldn't focus." The interviewer may also notice this in the flow of the interview as the person cannot seem to focus on or stay with an anxiety-arousing topic. Role-plays and simulations may also reveal a similar pattern.

While anxiety may be inferred from an inability to focus attention in a sustained way, it may also be suggested by several ways in which individuals *inappropriately direct attention*. For example, people may become preoccupied with *worrisome ruminations*. They tend to focus incessantly on possible dangerous or harmful consequences and to think obsessively about these, rather than about objective reality and the probabilities involved. These ruminations often tend to be catastrophic, overgeneralized distortions of reality (Beck, 1976) reflected in interview content such as "I know he doesn't like me; I just know it. I know he is never going to ask me out again, and I just can't stand the thought of that," or "I just know that I'm going to mess up in front of everybody, and they're all going to laugh at me. I'd just die if that happened." If such content is not reported spontaneously such that the interviewer can follow it up, direct inquiries can be made about what the client thinks while being anxious or what goes on in his or her head in reference to the anxiety-arousing experience.

"Anxious" individuals may also have and attend to *excessively high performance standards*. Their expectations for how they should perform or should be are often so high that it would take perfection or near perfection to meet them. They must do or be "right" in order to judge or evaluate themselves adequately. Their thoughts and self-dialogue often tend to be very absolutistic with the personal and/or environmental consequences of failing to meet these standards being catastrophic in an all-or-none way (Beck, 1966; Ellis, 1962); for example, "I've got to do it just 'right', or it will be awful," or "I must get into X (a most prestigious) graduate school. I'll just die if I don't." Such individuals tend to be preoccupied with how they are performing or measuring up, and often deliver severe self-criticism for any feedback indicating they are not meeting the mark. Even when they have done or are doing well, they tend to be preoccupied with the possibility that they will not meet the standard on another occasion. In extreme form, such individuals are anxious a great deal of the time because some aspect of their being or behavior might be evaluated negatively by someone else. Interviewing such clients often reveals a concern about "correct" performance in the interview. More detailed inquiry around the topics of how the person "must" perform and what will happen if the standards are not met will concretize the absolute, catastrophic nature of the self-evaluational processes.

Anxiety may also be inferred from *inappropriate attention to autonomic arousal*. Here individuals focus their attention on their physiological arousal, even if their arousal is not inordinately high or is no higher than nonanxious individuals in the same circumstances (Holroyd & Appel, 1980). That is, they focus internally on their arousal and become preoccupied with it to some extent. Not only do they focus on the arousal, but generally tend to evaluate it negatively and make negative predictions from it: "Oh no, there's the tension in my shoulders again. I'm going to have a headache for sure," or "My stomach is knotting up. My god, here we go again. Jim, you idiot, can't you ever get your act together with women?" In such cases they not only have problems created by the autonomic arousal per se, but also those stemming from focusing on it and directing attention away from the situation at hand. Interviewing around the meaning of and reaction to physiological arousal tends to uncover this tendency, if it is present.

Another misdirection of attention is to *catastrophic images*, either real or fantastic in nature. Some anxious individuals tend to imagine or recall highly negative, traumatic images which in turn become part of the internal stimulus complex prompting anxiety. For example, many of the panic attacks of individuals with generalized anxiety disorders have been found to be prompted by internal images of very negative proportion — for example, of having a heart attack or becoming an alcoholic derelict (Beck, Laude, & Bohnert, 1974). Some phobics focus attention in this way as well, as illustrated in two cases treated by one of the authors. One severely driving phobic recalled and constantly focused upon images of a serious auto accident of several years before (a noncurrent, but real traumatic image) when even thinking about driving. The other, a public speaking phobic, had clear images of the audience all laughing at her (a fantasy image) when confronted with any possibility of public speaking. Both avoided these situations, based in part on the anxiety elicited by the imagery. Even if the external circumstances are relatively innocuous, inclusion of such internal imagery content contributes significantly to experienced anxiety. Careful interviewing about what the client experiences while anxious or what is "going on in their heads" may pick up such imagery processes. While some such imagery may be reported spontaneously or with minimal probing, the presence and influence of such imagery is often subtle and hard to tease out, and may require other procedures (see below) in order to locate and evaluate its importance.

One problem of relying solely on the interview process in assessing the cognitive domain and its subareas is that people are often not aware of the internal or external processes involved. Assessment procedures that create or recreate events may increase the probability that clients will be able to track and report upon the processes involved. Several emerging procedures which require that individuals focus concretely on some real, retrieved, or standardized stimulus can greatly supplement interviewing. For example, individuals may be asked to retrieve, in imagery, a specific anxiety arousing event, become anxious, and then to focus on the kinds of things they are thinking or attending to. A more *in vivo* approach is to have individuals role-play or simulate such an experience and then to discuss with the interviewer the cognitive component while it is still fresh. A supplement to this approach is to videotape the simulation and have the person view the tape and engage in thinking aloud about what he or she was thinking/attending to at the different points in the tape. Self-monitoring may also be a useful adjunct. Clients may be asked to track their thoughts and feelings in anxiety arousing situations. As they become more skilled in the monitoring itself they can tune in more carefully to aspects of their conscious experiencing, (images they experience, internal dialogue, etc.). Recently, Meichenbaum (1977) has also suggested the possibility of developing standardized stimuli, TAT-like stimuli and audio-videotape vignettes, to which individuals could respond in a "think aloud" mode. Cognitively oriented questionnaires like that of Schwartz and Gottman (1976), in assessing cognitive aspects of social anxiety and unassertive behavior, could be developed and further aid the assessment of cognitive subdomains in anxiety reactions.

Aspects of anxiety may also be found in the somatic-behavioral domain and its subareas. Perhaps the least complex of these is that of *muscle tension* and its correlates. This category refers to the direct effects of heightened arousal on the voluntary musculature, and includes indices such as muscle tension, rigidity, and cramping in areas such as the neck and shoulders, hand tremor, shakiness, finger and foot tapping, bruxism, and the like. While there is some overlap with the affective-physiological subareas, this subarea is being presented separately because the voluntary musculature is a different route of anxiety expression and because the effects are much more directly observable to an outsider. Generally, clients will readily report examples of such tension-related effects, and follow-up interviewing for detail will flesh out the picture. Additionally, the interviewer may actually witness some of the somatic effects directly (e.g., see hand tremor or a very tight jaw during the interview) or indirectly (e.g., very shaky handwriting on intake forms where the client was describing major sources of anxiety). The interviewer may also have indirect information from others, such as a referral from a dentist for bruxism. Self-monitoring for the way that the client experiences anxiety will often add additional information.

A second facet of the somatic-behavioral domain is *behavioral disruption and performance deterioration.* Somatic muscle involvement may become so great that it begins to disrupt motor behavior, as in speech disfluencies or hand tremor interfering with smooth writing. Similarly, muscle involvement may significantly lower performance; for example, missed dance steps in a recital or hand cramping which interferes with writing on a test. Some males may become so anxious that they are tongue tied and stuttering and unable to ask for dates, or skilled athletes become so tense that they are unable to smoothly perform those skills that have been well rehearsed. In some cases it is hard to discern whether the performance deterioration is a direct effect of arousal on the somatic musculature or is a function of one or more of the cognitive-attentional deficits noted above. In either case, somatic involvement is another source of information suggesting the presence of anxiety in the individual's life. Clients will often readily report examples of performance disruption and deterioration to the interviewer. In many cases they are the reasons for which the person seeks therapy. Simulation and role-played enactments of anxiety-arousing circumstances may also demonstrate performance disruption.

Anxiety may also be reflected in *off-task behavior*, that is, directing behavior away from the task at hand. In some cases this may indicate attempts at escaping the situation, but in others it reflects ineffective and wasteful attempts at coping with the situation. For example, highly test-anxious children spend more time glancing away from an evaluative task (Nottleman & Hill, 1977), and highly test-anxious college students spend more time off-task, a portion of which was spent looking around the room and looking at the clock (Deffenbacher, 1978). Detailed and concrete interviewing about what individuals were doing and spending their time in anxiety arousing situations may pick up some of this information. However, it may take behavioral observation of real or simulated conditions to track the off-task behavior, as people are often not aware of the behavior unless it is marked or pronounced.

Anxiety may also be inferred from *behavioral constriction, rigidity, stereotypy and compulsivity.* Under stress, many individuals show a much narrower range of behavior than they otherwise possess. The behavior is run off in rigid, sometimes almost superstitious, stereotypical patterns. The behavior is often repeated, even though it may not be effective. Personal or environmental barriers which break up the pattern appear to elicit only more distress. For example, some test-anxious individuals must sit in the same place with their materials arranged just so before every exam in a class, becoming very upset if somehow blocked from doing so. Persistence in the same sexual approach behavior, even though it is meeting with rebuff, is another example of behavioral constriction and rigidity. Detailed interviewing for concrete examples is often necessary to pick up the more rigid, compulsive aspects of behavior. Often, it is the descriptions of observers, such as spouses, parents, and roommates, that reveal this type of information, as the persons themselves may not see the pattern clearly.

Avoidance and *escape* behaviors are very important indices of anxiety. Concerted efforts to keep from coming in contact with a situation, or to leave the field if confronted with it, are commonly taken as evidence of anxiety or arousal in a specific setting. Avoidance and escape behaviors may be active, such as physically moving away from the stimulus, or may be more passive, such as looking away from the stimulus; but they are all directed at removing the person from the noxiousness of the stimulus. Phobias are perhaps the clearest examples involving avoidance and escape behaviors. The speech-anxious student who avoids taking classes where oral presentations are known requirements and who rapidly drops the class or changes sections when such a requirement is made known provides an example of such behaviors. Client descriptions of what they do when they become anxious are often the first source of information about escape/avoidance behaviors, though escape/avoidance behaviors may be the basis of a referral from someone other than the client (e.g., a teacher referral of a student who avoids exams). If the information is first encountered in the interview, clients should be asked to describe in concrete behavioral detail how they attempt to cope with their anxiety in specific situations. Self-monitoring homework will often provide greater detail about the escape/avoidance behaviors as well as uncover other anxiety-arousing situations in which the escape/avoidance patterns are prevalent. Paper and pencil instruments such as the Fear Inventory (Wolpe, 1973) are also helpful in quickly locating stimulus conditions which may elicit escape/avoidance behaviors.

THE DECISION TO TREAT ANXIETY

Anxiety might be inferred from client data and yet still not be treated. For treatment to be designed, the anxiety should be a *severe, exaggerated response which the individual desires to change.* Desire to change is usually an easy judgment since clients often present themselves voluntarily for change. The exaggerated or overreactive component too is usually easy to judge. The anxiety response pattern is exaggerated if circumstances involve no possibility of physical harm or the probability of or magnitude of the harm is much less than the way in which the individual is responding. For example, situations like social rejection and public speaking involve little or no physical harm, and airplanes and cars do crash, but the probability is low. Even where significant harm is involved and the event probability is either high or unknown, the anxiety is overreactive and debilitative to the extent that individuals consistently avoid the topic or situation, thereby making evaluation of the situation and planning to deal with it impossible. For example, avoiding talking about or having examined a lump in the breast is exaggerated, given the potential consequences of not approaching the situation. Severity is a more complex judgment based on the response characteristics of frequency, pervasiveness, duration, magnitude, and consequence. Generally, anxiety will be judged more severe and hence in need of treatment if the individual experiences:

- More anxiety attacks per unit time (frequency)
- Anxiety reactions across more situations (pervasiveness)
- Anxiety responses lasting for longer periods following termination of the stressor (longer recovery time) or prior to the stressor — longer history of anxiety (duration)
- Serious levels of involvement in a given response channel, such as very high heart rate, or high levels across multiple response modalities (magnitude)
- Serious consequences such as deterioration of cognitive or behavioral performances or the onset of psychophysiological or other physical disease processes (consequences)

If we use these parameters for examining the three response channels, we can see how the assessment of severity would operate. For the affective-physiological channel, severity might be seen in the frequency of autonomic arousal, the presence of a long latency before such arousal comes under control, the observation of high arousal such as high heart rate, and/or the development of psychophysiological disorders such as hypertension. For the cognitive channel, severity might be seen in the presence of severe attentional or memory disturbances, in the very early onset of cognitive ruminations, in the long continuation of ruminations after the stressor is over, and/or the number and variety of situations which involve catastrophizing. For the somatic-behavioral channel, severity might be judged if there are serious levels of muscle tension, if there are many incidences of behavioral disruptions and disfluencies, and/or if the stereotypy or avoidance behaviors are associated with diverse situations.

Once again, it is important to recognize that different persons may show the anxiety condition through different channels and to different degrees within each channel. Thus, one person may show anxiety reactions affectively and behaviorally, with more severe evidence being in the behavioral domain. Another individual might also react both affectively and behaviorally, but with affective symptoms dominating. Thus we would have different "anxiety profiles" characterizing each of these two persons.

SELECTING AN ANXIETY-REDUCTION APPROACH

While the topic of this book is self-control, self-control approaches are not necessarily the treatment of choice in all cases. The sources of anxiety and the responses are numerous, and knowledge of these should help in decisions about the selection of the most efficacious intervention, one that is most carefully turned to the source and nature of the anxiety. The rest of this section will offer some illustrations relating to this concern.

First, the anxiety pattern may be seen as a relatively natural by-product of high-level stressors in the persons' life. For example, it may stem from severe interpersonal disputes, financial concerns and problems, or a major life decision like marriage or career. In such cases the most appropriate interventions would be directed to providing the necessary skills and decision-making and/or environmental restructuring to reduce or minimize the external sources of stress. The individual might be referred to marriage therapy, a financial advisor, or to career counseling.

Another source of anxiety may be the presence of a skill deficit. If the individual is unskilled in an area, life is likely to continually punish the person for his or her inferior performance. Thus, the anxiety is realistic in the sense that the person continually endures punishment and aversiveness in that arena; life is continually conditioning anxiety. For example, if the person is socially or sexually unskilled or lacking in study skills, then the person is likely to perform poorly and experience failure and rejection, unless he or she withdraws from the contexts. Here the most appropriate interventions would be aimed at providing the necessary cognitive and/or behavioral skills. Referrals to assertion training, sex therapy, and study skills programs would be examples of appropriate interventions for these sources of anxiety.

Anxiety may also be elicited by informational deficits. That is, the person possesses the necessary skills with which to handle the situation, but does not have the knowledge with which to cue the behavior. For example, the individual may be verbally facile, but not know how to present information in a job interview. Or a couple may be very anxious about possible birth defects in an unborn child and not know about new techniques. For cases such as these, reasonably straightforward communication of information may be the most appropriate intervention.

Anxiety can also be a function of the individual not having the coping skills with which to decrease affective/autonomic arousal or cognitive interference from which anxiety is inferred. That is, the person is reasonably skilled and possesses the necessary information with which to handle the situation, yet still experiences significant (disruptive) affect arousal and cognitive-behavioral involvement. Such individuals appear to be experiencing a self-control or beta-control deficit in that they do not possess internal controlling responses which lower or moderate affective/autonomic arousal and/or cognitive-attentional disruptions. It would appear that self-management approaches would be most appropriate for these types of problems, as there is a set of empirically supported techniques (to be reviewed below in detail) which are designed to train individuals in affective, cognitive, or combined affective-cognitive coping skills with which to intercept and correct anxiety-related cognitive or affective-physiological dysfunctions.

Affective coping skills programs are designed to give individuals self-management skills, generally in the form of applied relaxation, with which to decrease affective/autonomic arousal and related phenomena. At least in theory, affective coping skills programs should be most appropriate when assessment has demonstrated major involvement in subjective feelings of anxiety (table 12.1, part I.A), heightened autonomic arousal (I.B), increased muscle tension (III.A), misdirected attention to autonomic arousal or muscle tension (II.C.4), psychophysiological disorders (I.C), and behavioral disruption and deterioration (III.B) to the extent it is due to heightened arousal and not skill deficit. Changes in the other arenas are seen to be primarily a function of reducing these sources of interference and allowing other skills and abilities to be implemented.

Cognitive approaches to the self-control of anxiety generally contain self-instructional training in coping skills with which to focus attention, alter sources of misdirected attention, and approach the situation in a task-oriented, self-rewarding manner. Such cognitive self-control approaches, therefore, would appear to be most appropriate when assessment has revealed significant attentional distraction (II.C.1), sources of misdirected attention (II.C.2–5), off-task behavior (III.C) which involved misdirection of attention, and learning, memory, and cognitive performance problems (II.A.1–2 and II.B.1–3) to the extent that these do not reflect basic skill deficits and/or neurological deterioration. With a given client, the cognitive self-control program should emphasize those elements which were shown by the assessment to be the key sources of the inference of anxiety.

Combined affective and cognitive coping skills programs would be suggested when assessment shows significant involvement in both domains as noted for each separately above.

Even for problems that do not directly derive from self-control deficiencies, self-control treatment might still be the treatment of choice. Such a decision relates to additional advantages which self-control training may provide. All things equal, self-control strategies might be preferred under the following conditions:

1. If there is limited time for therapy, then the most practical goal may be to start persons on self-control skill development so that the individuals can help themselves after treatment ends. Thus, the persons may not be trained to actually resolve their immediate problems, but be trained in strategies or principles of problem solving.

2. If there are multiple sources of anxiety or future stressors that are anticipated, then self-control training might provide the skills to control these other sources of stress, present or future. This recommendation is based on the research evidence (to be reviewed later) which shows that self-control treatments reduce not only anxieties targeted in treatment sessions, but other nontargeted anxieties as well. In addition, there is some evidence of a consolidation of anxiety reduction during follow-up intervals post-treatment.

3. If low self-efficacy is a problem, then self-control training may be helpful since as the client learns self-control, self-efficacy may improve along with the increase in self-mastery. The self-control approaches bring the additional benefit of enabling the person to prove his or her ability to control anxieties and the environment. Instead of the client perceiving that "I am better because the therapist helped me change," the client realizes "I am better because I have learned how to control anxiety myself; and I possess these skills."

Thus, self-control interventions would appear most appropriate for cases where the inference of anxiety is based primarily on self-control deficits and/or when the above advantages are present.

The following sections of the chapter will review, respectively, affective, cognitive, and combined cognitive-affective coping skills programs. Major procedures will be described and selected outcome research will be briefly summarized.

Affective (Relaxation) Coping Skills Programs

Relaxation is the dominant coping skill used for the self-control of affective-physiological arousal. Therefore, programs based on a relaxation coping model will be reviewed here, including cue-controlled relaxation (CCR), applied relaxation (AR), self-control desensitization (SCD), relaxation as self-control (RSC), and anxiety management training (AMT). All of these programs are designed to train clients in the application of relaxation to reduce anxiety. They all include training in progressive relaxation and at least one method of applying it *in vivo*. They also all at least discuss the applications of coping skills for the client's life circumstances. They do, however, differ in the degree to which they provide a clear, explicit self-control rationale; systematic training in using the proprioceptive cues of anxiety arousal as the cue for the application of relaxation coping skills; directed practice of self-control skills to reduce anxiety within sessions; and systematic transfer of relaxation coping skills from the therapeutic to the external environment (Denney, 1980).

A summary of the procedural steps for each procedure is found in table 12.2, and a comparison of the methodologies of each is found in table 12.3.

Cue-controlled relaxation (CCR). CCR was originally described by Cautela (1966) in the treatment of pervasive anxiety. He outlined it as a means of establishing verbal control over relaxation so that clients could verbally do relaxation in circumstances for which the person had not been desensitized in therapy. The procedure consists of two phases. First, clients are trained in progressive relaxation. Second, while clients are in a deeply relaxed state, they focus upon their breathing and subvocally present a cue word or phrase such as "calm," "relax," or "calm control" as they exhale. Initially, the therapist repeats the cue in synchrony with client exhalation, but after 10 or so trials fades the instruction, allowing clients to continue on their own. In this manner it was thought that the cue would be paired with, and classically conditioned to, the relaxed state. Future repetitions of the cue should elicit all or a portion of the relaxed state. Thus, if clients represented the cue when becoming anxious, they should be able to short-circuit and exert self-control over the anxiety response.

After the cue-control procedure has been demonstrated in the session, it is added to relaxation homework for more conditioning trials, and clients are instructed to self-produce the cue to elicit relaxation whenever they feel themselves becoming anxious outside the therapy setting. While efforts to apply cue-controlled relaxation appear to be discussed in subsequent sessions, little emphasis is placed on directed control of anxiety within or between sessions.

Several studies suggest the CCR is effective in reducing self-reports of specific anxieties. For example, in multiple case study reports, CCR reduced self-reported test anxiety (Russell, Miller, & June, 1974) and both self-reported and physiological measures of dental anxiety (Beck, Kaul & Russell, 1978). In studies comparing CCR and desensitization, both were equally effective and superior to untreated controls in reducing speech (Russell & Wise, 1976) and test anxieties (Russell, Miller, & June, 1975; Russell, Wise, & Stratoudakis, 1976). However, in the latter two studies in-

Table 12.2.   **Procedural Steps in Affective Coping Skills Programs**

Program	Procedures Within Sessions	Procedures Between Sessions
Cue-Controlled Relaxation (CCR)	1. Rationale given 2. Progressive relaxation training 3. Therapist pairing of cue word with relaxed state 4. Client pairing of cue word with relaxed state 5. Repeated sessions of above 6. In vivo application of CCR encouraged and discussed	1. Practice of relaxation with pairing of cue word with relaxed state at end of practice 2. Application of CCR when tension felt
Applied Relaxation (AR)	1. Rationale given 2. Progressive relaxation training 3. Introduction of one or more methods of applying relaxed state, e.g., CCR, pairing relaxation with deep breathing, etc. 4. Repeated sessions of above 5. In vivo application of relaxation skills concretely discussed and assigned with detailed discussion of progress in next session	1. Practice progressive relaxation procedures 2. Practice methods of cueing relaxation in nonstressful situations at home 3. Application of methods of cueing relaxation when tension felt
Self-control Desensitization (SCD)	1. Rationale given 2. Progressive relaxation training with added emphasis on tension 3. Introduction of three methods of applying relaxation: relaxation without tension, pairing with deep breathing, and CCR 4. Multithematic hierarchy constructed 5. Anxiety aroused and controlled via imagination of hierarchy items and application of relaxation 6. In vivo application of relaxation skills concretely discussed and assigned with detailed discussion of progress in next session	1. Practice of progressive relaxation procedure 2. Practice of methods of cueing relaxation in non-stressful situations at home 3. Application of methods of cueing relaxation when tension felt 4. Self-monitor and record trials of applied relaxation

Table 12.2. (Cont.)

Program	Procedures Within Sessions	Procedures Between Sessions
Relaxation as Self-Control (RSC)	1. Rationale given 2. Progressive relaxation training with added emphasis on tension 3. Introduction of several methods of applying relaxation, e.g., CCR, relaxation without tension pairing with deep breathing, etc. 4. Coordinate best methods into a written set of self-instructions 5. Anxiety aroused through simulated stress, e.g., test or speech, and controlled via applying relaxation 6. In vivo application of relaxation/skills concretely discussed and assigned with detailed discussion of progress in next session	1. Self-monitoring of anxiety and response-produced cues 2. Practice of progressive relaxation procedure 3. Practice methods of applying relaxation in nonstressful situations at home 4. Practice methods of cueing relaxation in mild-moderate stress situations 5. Practice methods of cueing relaxation in all stress situations 6. Self-monitor and record all applications of relaxation
Anxiety Management Training (AMT)	1. Rationale given 2. Relaxation image constructed 3. Progressive relaxation training presenting relaxation image 4. Anxiety images constructed 5. Introduction of three methods of applying relaxation: relaxation without tension, pairing with deep breathing, and relaxation imagery 6. Arousal of anxiety through anxiety imagery and therapist initiation of methods applying relaxation 7. Arousal of anxiety through imagery with client attention to response-produced cues of anxiety arousal 8. Client-initiated self-control; first by terminating anxiety imagery and applying relaxation, later while retaining the anxiety imagery and relaxing away tension	1. Self-monitoring of anxiety and response-produced cues 2. Practice of progressive relaxation procedures 3. Practice of methods of applying relaxation in nonstressful situations at home 4. Practice methods of applying relaxation in mild-moderate stressful situations 5. Practice methods of applying relaxation in all stress situations 6. Self-monitor and record all applications of relaxation

Table 12.3 Comparison of Relaxation Coping Skill Procedures

Dimension	CCR	AR	SCD	RSC	AMT
Self-control rationale	Present	Present	Present	Present	Present
Relaxation training	Present	Present	Present	Present	Present
Methods to cue relaxation state, e.g., cue word, relaxing image, deep breathing, etc.	Cue word	Multiple, varies with program	Deep breath, cue word, relaxation without tension	Deep breath, cue word, relaxation without tension, self-instructional set, etc.	Relaxation imagery, relaxation without tension, deep breathing, cue word
Anxiety arousal within session	Absent	Absent	In graded imagery	Simulation	Partially graded imagery
Anxiety control within session	Absent	Absent	Present	Present	Present
Attention to anxiety response as cues	Discussed in interview	Discussed in interview	Observed in session and self-monitoring homework	Observed in session and self-monitoring homework	Observed in session and self-monitoring homework
Homework:					
Application in vivo	Present*	Present	Present	Present	Present
Self-monitoring of applications	Absent	Absent	Present	Present	Present

*Less detailed assigning than in other procedures.

volving test anxiety, neither CCR nor desensitization led to improved performance.

Studies comparing CCR to attentional controls are confusing. One study (Counts, Hollandsworth, & Alcorn, 1978) found CCR, either in usual format or supplemented with EMG feedback training, to be superior to an attention control in changing both self-report and behavioral measures of test anxiety. Another study (McGlynn, Kinjo, & Doherty, 1978) found both CCR and attentional control conditions to be equivalent, but better than a no-treatment control in reducing self-reported test anxiety. A third (Marchetti, McGlynn, & Patterson, 1977), however, found no differences among CCR, attentional controls, and no-treatment controls on self-report, performance, or physiological indices of test anxiety. This latter study is the one published study which revealed no significant effects for CCR.

Six of these studies (Counts et al., 1978; Marchetti et al., 1977; McGlynn et al., 1978; Russell et al., 1975; Russell & Wise, 1976; Russell et al., 1976) included some index of nontargeted or generalized anxiety, and only one (McGlynn et al., 1978) revealed any evidence of nontargeted anxiety reduction, a finding which was revealed only at follow-up.

Together these studies suggest that CCR may be a valuable procedure for establishing relaxation coping skills that may be employed in fear-provoking situations. For some specific anxieties, it may be a sufficient treatment. Little evidence, however, was found for generalized or non-targeted anxiety reduction. Yet, there is a central prediction of the self-control model and the hallmark of the acquisition of self-control. It would therefore appear that more attention should be devoted to training in self-control within the session and transferring the skill to the external environment if full self-control effects are to be achieved by CCR. It may also be that while CCR is an effective technique for some, it is not for others. CCR may have its place alone for some individuals or be included as part of a more comprehensive relaxation coping skills program for others, but may not be a sufficient general treatment (Grimm, 1980).

Applied relaxation (AR). AR is a category which encompasses a number of programs which differ procedurally in small degrees, but contain a number of common elements. They have in common (1) a self-control rationale similar to that proposed by Goldfried (1971), (2) training in progressive relaxation, (3) additional training in one or more specific relaxation coping skills—for example, CCR, pairing relaxation with breathing (Deffenbacher & Snyder, 1976: Meichenbaum, 1972), tension-release exercises for specific muscle groups (Deffenbacher & Snyder, 1976), autogenic relaxation (Schultz & Luthe, 1959), differential relaxation (Davison, 1965) and relaxation without tension—and (4) greater emphasis on how to apply relaxation to control stress in the real world. Although AR may include CCR, AR is classified separately because these programs include a *clear self-control rationale*, and added steps for *in vivo* application.

Regarding the rationale, anxiety is explained in terms of heightened autonomic arousal. Clients are informed that the purpose of treatment is to teach them relaxation coping skills with which to relax away and cope with this autonomic arousal. Relaxation training is described as a means of bringing the relaxation response under voluntary control, and coping skills are introduced as ways of applying the relaxation *in vivo*. Clients are further told that with practice of these relaxation skills, they will be more proficient at voluntarily inducing relaxation to reduce anxiety. When progressive relaxation and coping skills training have established reliable coping skills, effort is made to encourage and discuss specific applications of relaxation in real life settings.

In an early study of AR, Zeisset (1968) showed that it effectively reduced targeted interview anxiety and other nontargeted anxieties in psychiatric inpatients compared to attentional and no-treatment controls, and that the effects of AR were equivalent to those of desensitization. He also found an interesting patient-by-treatment interaction. Specifically, patients who were more recently admitted responded better with AR, and patients who had been hospitalized longer responded more favorably to desensitization. Perhaps institutionalization extinguishes self-controlling tendencies. If so, the self-control rationale and procedures would have appealed more to the purportedly less-alienated new admissions, whereas those who were more used to institutionalization would have responded more readily to the therapist control inherent in desensitization.

Goldfried and Trier (1974) demonstrated that AR led to reduction of targeted speech anxiety and nontargeted anxiety in college students. This study was important in two other respects. First, the importance of the self-control rationale and detailed instructions in applying relaxation was demonstrated. Compared to a group which received a passive, counterconditioning rationale and no instruction in applying relaxation, the AR group showed more consistent reductions in indices of speech anxiety. Second, the self-control effects were more pronounced at follow-up, a finding similar to that noted in the McGlynn et al. (1978) study for CCR. Denney (1974; Chang-Liang & Denney, 1976) has also found that AR was as effective as desensitization in reducing test anxiety, but was the only treatment which led to improved test performance and nontargeted anxiety reduction.

AR programs have also been effective in reducing generalized anxiety directly. For example, Sherman and Plummer (1973), in a program which introduced a number of specific coping skills, showed some evidence of general anxiety reduction. A 2-year follow-up (Sherman, 1975) suggested that clients continued to use these self-control skills. Similar results for a less complex AR program were noted for treatment of anxiety neurotics (Canter, Kondo, & Knott, 1975).

While methodological problems and the small number of studies available limit strong conclusions, these studies suggest that AR, with its greater emphasis on a self-control rationale and *in vivo* applications, shows promise in reducing targeted anxieties, nontargeted anxieties, and general anxiety. Targeted anxiety reduction for AR appears to be as strong as for CCR and more traditional approaches such as desensitization. The self-control effects of AR on nontargeted and general anxiety appear more consistently than for CCR or more traditional approaches.

Self-control desensitization (SCD). SCD was first described by Goldfried (1971). As a result of conversations with his clients with whom he was using desensitization, he reported that many of them did not conceive of desensitization within the traditional passive, counterconditioning paradigm. Instead, they talked about it as helping them learn how to manage their anxieties in a number of situations; they were learning a means of relaxing away tension. Goldfried therefore reconceptualized desensitization as training in self-control; that is, desensitization trains clients to voluntarily reduce anxiety by teaching them to be aware of proprioceptive cues associated with anxiety and to apply relaxation whenever these cues are perceived.

Goldfried (1971) then offered several procedural modifications to enhance the self-control features: (1) An active, self-control treatment rationale replaced the passive counterconditioning one. Desensitization is described as a procedure which teaches clients to actively cope with anxiety by teaching them how to relax, how to recognize tension, and how to apply relaxation skills to relax away tension. (2) During the tension phase of relaxation exercises, clients are instructed to focus on feelings of tension and become more sensitive to them so these feelings may serve as cues for the application of relaxation. (3) Hierarchies are used, but include many different anxiety-arousing themes in order to increase the range of situations in which self-control is practiced and to maximize transfer of the coping skills. (4) Instead of a client signal at the first experience of tension resulting in the termination of the scene, clients signal, but continue imagining the scene and actively relax away the tension. When anxiety is brought under control and clients are once again deeply relaxed, they signal, and then the scene is cleared, representing a successful trial of coping with tension. (5) Applied relaxation homework is emphasized, with clients trying out relaxation coping skills between sessions. *In vivo* application is reinforced and modified in light of these homework assignments.

A number of studies have compared SCD with traditional desensitization. For example, Jacks (Note 2) found both forms of desensitization equivalent in reducing several measures of acrophobia; however, SCD subjects reported significantly less anxiety while performing the behavioral avoidance task than either traditional desensitization or control subjects.

Spiegler, Cooley, Marshall, Prince, Puckett, and Skenazy (1976) found both equally effective in reducing test anxiety and no evidence of non-targeted anxiety reduction for either. Denney and Rupert (1977) found the two equally effective in reducing debilitating test anxiety, but also found that SCD improved facilitating test anxiety, analog test performance, and grades. Again, neither treatment differed from the controls on nontargeted anxiety. Deffenbacher and Parks (1979), however, found a somewhat different pattern. Both SCD and traditional desensitization reduced state and trait test anxiety, but no performance differences, were found on the analog test. Additionally, evidence of nontargeted anxiety reduction was found on both measures for SCD and on one measure for traditional desensitization. Zemore (1975) compared the two models of desensitization in treating students who suffered from both test and speech anxieties. Half were treated for test anxiety and the other half for speech anxiety; thus, one anxiety was targeted and the other nontargeted in a counterbalanced manner. The two treatments were equally effective in reducing both targeted and nontargeted anxieties.

Other studies have compared SCD with other self-control interventions. For example, Deffenbacher, Michaels, Michaels, and Daley (1980) compared SCD and anxiety management training (AMT) in the reduction of test and nontargeted anxieties. Both SCD and AMT were equally effective in reducing state and trait test anxiety, though neither led to improved performance on the analog test. By 6-week follow-up, both evidenced nontargeted anxiety reduction on both indices of nontargeted anxiety. A 15-month follow-up (Deffenbacher & Michaels, in press a) revealed maintenance of both targeted and nontargeted anxiety reduction in this study. Harris and Johnson (1980) compared SCD and a covert self-control modeling program, and found that both reduced test anxiety, but that only the covert modeling program led to improved grades. Goldfried and Goldfried (1977) compared SCD with a target-relevant hierarchy to SCD with a target-irrelevant hierarchy and to a prolonged exposure condition. Within-group analyses for all three groups found reductions on most measures of targeted speech anxiety and nontargeted anxieties assessed by social-evaluative and general anxiety scales. Though no between-group differences were found, the trend favored the target-relevant form of SCD on both targeted and nontargeted anxiety. Finally, Kanter and Goldfried (1979) compared SCD, systematic rational restructuring (SRR), and a combination of SCD and rational restructuring to a wait-list control in the reduction of targeted social anxiety and other nontargeted anxieties. SCD evidenced some reduction of state and trait social anxiety, but little reduction of nontargeted anxiety. The comparisons with the cognitively oriented SRR also suggested that SRR was more effective in reducing targeted and nontargeted anxiety.

Overall, SCD appears effective in reducing targeted anxieties. Also, targeted anxiety reduction for SCD was equal to and, on some measures, superior to traditional desensitization (Denney & Rupert, 1977; Jacks, Note 2), was as good as AMT, another relaxation oriented self-control program, but may not have been quite as strong as more cognitively oriented coping skills programs (Harris & Johnson, 1980; Kanter & Goldfried, 1979). Evidence of nontargeted anxiety reduction for SCD is somewhat mixed. Of the eight studies reviewed which included nontargeted anxiety measures, five revealed nontargeted anxiety reduction for SCD, and three did not. Thus, the consistency of self-control effects on non-targeted anxieties is not clearly established for SCD.

Relaxation as self-control (RSC). RSC was developed in 1971 by one of the authors (Deffenbacher) in order to meet a deficiency of desensitization. A review of the existent literature on desensitization (e.g., Paul, 1969) revealed very few studies which showed significant nontargeted anxiety reduction for desensitization. That is, while desensitization was very effective in reducing the anxiety targeted in the hierarchy, it did not appear to help clients deal with other sources of anxiety or stress or provide training in preventing coping skills. RSC, therefore, was designed to overcome this deficiency by developing relaxation as a general coping skill for anxiety management.

The logic underlying RSC assumes that four conditions are necessary for the development of relaxation as a self-managed coping skill. First, clients must develop a relaxation response. Second, they must be able to self-induce this relaxation quickly and easily *in vivo*. Third, they must become skilled at detecting the internal cues related to the presence and build up of anxiety so that they will know when to apply the relaxation. Fourth, this sequence of discrimination of tension and the application of relaxation coping skills must be practiced sufficiently under stressful conditions so that clients have an established method of preventing or reducing anxiety. In addition, the skills become trans-situational as the cues for anxiety reduction come from within the individual.

The procedures of RSC mirror this logic. Progressive relaxation training is conducted to develop the relaxation response. In the second stage of coping-skills training, clients are introduced to a number of applied relaxation methods, such as CCR, relaxation tension, and deep-breathing procedures (cf. Deffenbacher & Snyder, 1976). These coping skills are practiced as part of homework. Clients select out the most effective methods for them and develop a set of personalized, written self-instructions with which to self-initiate their best procedure(s). The third phase involves discrimination training during which clients become sensitive observers of the response-produced cues of anxiety arousal. This is done by having clients note areas of tension during relaxation practice and by observing and logging their tension level at least three times a day, noting a "subjective units of disturbance" rating and physiological cues of arousal. After approximately four sessions, the discrimination of tension and application of relaxation is practiced under simulated stressful conditions within the session, such as when taking a test or giving a speech. Application to real life is transferred first to nonstressful conditions (e.g., riding a bus or watching television), then to mildly stressful situations, and then finally to more stressful conditions. Movement to progressively more difficult *in vivo* assignments is based on success in the simulated tasks and in less stressful real-life situations. Further *in vivo* assignments are then planned, contracted, and analyzed at the beginning of the next session to prepare for further assignments.

Initial multiple case reports of RSC (Deffenbacher, 1976; Deffenbacher & Rivera, 1976) revealed significant reductions in test anxiety, significant improvements in test performance, and reports of generalized anxiety reduction for college students and minority women taking civil service exams. In a study with a subjects-as-own-control design (Deffenbacher & Snyder, 1976), RSC led to significant test- and general-anxiety reduction. Two other studies (Deffenbacher, Mathis, & Michaels, 1979; Snyder & Deffenbacher, 1977) compared RSC to a SCD-like variant of desensitization and controls in the reduction of test and nontargeted anxiety. Both studies revealed significant reductions of state and trait test anxiety for both treatments. While no performance differences were found in analog testing, RSC subjects had better introductory psychology grades than did no-treatment expectancy controls (Deffenbacher et al., 1979). In both studies, active treatments revealed significant nontargeted anxiety reduction. Six-week (Deffenbacher, et al., 1979) and 1-year follow-ups (Deffenbacher & Michaels, 1980) revealed that reductions of targeted and nontargeted anxieties were maintained for RSC. Another study (Deffenbacher & Payne, 1977) compared RSC and the self-control form of desensitization in reducing communication apprehension in student teachers and found that both reduced communication apprehension and increased nontargeted assertiveness. In a more recent study (King & Deffenbacher, Note 3), RSC was compared to Anxiety Management Training (AMT) and a no-treatment control in the reduction of general anxiety in a medical outpatient population. Compared to the controls, RSC and AMT groups showed significant reductions in self-reports of state and trait anxiety, of anxiety in two personally stressful situations, and of physiological arousal and psychophysiological involvement. A 4-week follow-up revealed maintenance of these gains. No significant changes were noted for either systolic or diastolic blood pressure; however, by follow-up, RSC subjects showed lower resting heart rates than controls of AMT subjects. The self-control effects of both RSC and AMT appeared to generalize as reductions in hostility and depression were reported at both post-treatment and follow-up assessments.

RSC appears to be effective in reducing and maintaining reduction of specific anxieties. It, however, appears to involve more than situational anxiety reduction. RSC has led to nontargeted anxiety reduction, general anxiety reduction, and improvements in other areas such as assertiveness, depression, and hostility. Short- and long-term follow-ups reveal maintenance of these more general gains. Thus, subjects seem to be learning and employing more general coping skills as predicted by the self-control model.

Anxiety management training (AMT). AMT was developed by one of the authors (Suinn) in 1971 to resolve a major deficiency of desensitization. Desensitization requires that clients be able to specify concretely and hierarchically the stimuli which elicit their anxiety. Yet, many anxious clients cannot do this. Their anxieties are not elicited by specific external cues, but appear to be prompted by vague internal cues or by complex and often subtle patterns of external cues. Their anxieties are much more pervasive or "free floating," which makes desensitization either impossible or cumbersome. Thus, AMT was developed for cases of general anxiety, though it is applicable to single or multiple phobias.

The theory underlying AMT is that anxiety has drive or cue properties which, through self-control training, can become stimuli for relaxation coping behaviors. In practice, AMT teaches clients to identify their specific ways of experiencing stress, such as neck and shoulder tightening, upset stomach, or clenched fists, and to use these cues to prompt relaxation coping skills, thereby aborting or decreasing anxiety. Thus, in principle, AMT is very similar to that of RSC and SCD previously described.

AMT goes through five somewhat overlapping phases (Suinn, 1977b): (1) rationale and relaxation training; (2) guided rehearsal of anxiety arousal and reduction; (3) anxiety discrimination training; (4) training in self-initiated rather than therapist-initiated control of anxiety; and (5) transfer of relaxation coping skills to real-life circumstances. In phase 1, AMT is outlined as a means of learning relaxation as an active, general coping skill. The steps of AMT are described as a means of learning to be aware of the "early warning" cues of anxiety arousal and to apply relaxation whenever these are experienced. Relaxation training follows basic progressive relaxation procedures, and homework involves practice of this. Over the course of the first three sessions or so, clients are trained to acquire control over relaxation to a degree that relaxation can be quicky and easily self-initiated. Guided rehearsal in anxiety reduction (phase 2) employs anxiety arousing imagery to elicit anxiety to provide practice in controlling anxiety through relaxation. Clients develop moderately and intensely anxiety-arousing scenes from their past experiences. These scenes include all types of cognitive, affective, and behavioral cues which re-elicit anxiety. Unlike desensitization, these scenes need *not* be related in any way; they need only elicit the anxiety response so the cue properties are available for discrimination and self-control training. Attending to and becoming aware of these cues is the third phase. Starting with the moderately anxiety-arousing scenes and, a session or two later, moving to more anxiety arousing imagery, clients are instructed to imagine the scene and to focus upon the feelings of arousal and let them build. In early sessions the therapist terminates the scene and initiates the relaxation to reduce the anxiety. As clients become successful in this, the therapist fades out direction and shifts responsibility for anxiety control to clients (stage 4, or self-control training). For example, clients move from the therapist switching off anxiety arousal and instruction in relaxation retrieval, to self-termination of the scene and self-initation of the relaxation. In the last stage of AMT, clients totally control anxiety arousal and practice control of anxiety while continuing to imagine the anxiety scene. The increased self-control within sessions is paralleled in homework to transfer the coping skills to real life (phase 5). Throughout therapy clients track and record their "stress profile" — early bodily cues of anxiety buildup. When the basic coping skills are in place, clients first practice them in non-anxiety-arousing circumstances as in RSC. Then, they combine the tracking of early warning cues to apply relaxation in mild to moderate anxiety-arousing situations, and finally to the full range of stressful circumstances once they have been successful with less stressful conditions. These applications of coping are recorded and discussed in each subsequent session.

AMT has been shown to be an effective method of reducing situational anxieties. For example, in their initial study, Suinn and Richardson (1971) demonstrated that AMT lowered math and test anxieties and improved math performance, and that AMT was as effective as desensitization methods. Richardson and Suinn (1973) later replicated these findings for math anxieties. Deffenbacher and Shelton (1978) also found that AMT effectively reduced test anxiety in clients coming to a counseling center, and that it was as effective as desensitization. However, 1-month follow-up suggested that AMT was superior to desensitization in the reduction of test anxiety. Two subsequent studies have also used test anxiety as the targeted anxiety. In the first (Deffenbacher, Michaels, Michaels, & Daley, 1980), AMT was compared to SCD, no-treatment expectancy, and wait-list controls. The second (Deffenbacher, Michaels, Daley, & Michaels, 1980) compared AMT in homogeneous groups of test- or speech-anxious students to mixed groups of speech- and test-anxious students to a no-treatment expectancy control. Both studies revealed reduction of test anxiety and maintenance of reduction at short-term follow-up. Neither study demonstrated performance gains in the analog testing, but subjects receiving treatment in the first study had higher psychology grades than controls. AMT was also as effective in targeted anxiety reduction as SCD. Twelve-month and 15-month follow-ups (Deffenbacher & Michaels, in press a & b) have revealed long-term maintenance of test-anxiety reduction. Significant reductions of speech anxiety have also been demonstrated for AMT (Deffenbacher, Michaels, Daley, & Michaels, 1980; Edie, Note 4; Nicoletti, Note 5) with such improvements being maintained in 12-month-term follow-up (Deffenbacher & Michaels, in press b).

Evidence of generalized anxiety reduction for AMT comes from two types of studies. In the first, some specific anxiety is targeted, such as test anxiety, but measures of other or trait anxieties are included to assess nontargeted anxiety reduction. The second type picks general anxiety itself as the target — the populations treated are persons suffering general anxiety. Three studies of the first type (Deffenbacher, Michaels, Daley, & Michaels, 1980; Deffenbacher, Michaels, Michaels, & Daley, 1980; Deffenbacher & Shelton, 1978) have revealed significant nontargeted anxiety reduction, at least by the end of short-term follow-up. Yearly and 15-month follow-ups (Deffenbacher & Michaels, in press a & b) of the first two studies revealed maintenance of this nontargeted anxiety reduction for the most part. A similar study (Suinn & Bloom, 1978) found trait-anxiety reduction where Type A behavior patterns had been the target of AMT. Studies of the second type have found general anxiety reduction for college students (Edie, Note 4; Hutchings, Denney, Basgall, & Houston, 1980; Nicoletti, Note 5), anxious community volunteers (Berghausen, Note 6), anxious medical outpatients (King & Deffenbacher, Note 3), mental health center patients diagnosed as anxiety neurotics (Shoemaker, Note 7), schizophrenics (VanHassel, Note 8), and patients with essential hypertension (Houston, Jorgensen, & Zurawski, Note 9). Additionally, King and Deffenbacher (Note 3) found reductions in hostility and depression; Hutchings et al. (1980) found reductions of state anxiety and maladaptive cognitions in the face of evaluative stress and long-term maintenance of general anxiety; and Nally (Note 10) reported a decrease in antisocial behaviors and improved self-concepts in adjudicated adolescent offenders. Comparatively in these studies, AMT was effective as SCD (Deffenbacher, Michaels, Michaels, & Daley, 1980), AR (Hutchings et al., 1980), and RSC (King & Deffenbacher, Note 3), but more effective than desensitization (Deffenbacher & Shelton, 1978), implosion, or relaxation training (Shoemaker, Note 7).

Overall, such research suggests that AMT effectively reduces not only specific anxieties, but also other nontargeted anxieties as well. AMT also appears to be an effective intervention for persons with a generalized anxiety disorder or similar complaints. The specific and generalized anxiety reductions appear to hold over both short- and long-term follow-up. Thus, AMT appears to achieve reasonably stable self-control effects for specific and generalized anxiety disorders; clients appear to learn and employ relaxation as a generalized coping skill. Though the evidence is less complete, these effects appear to impact other psychological processes such as depression, hostility and maladaptive cognitions. Comparatively speaking, in the treatment of both specific and generalized anxiety disorders, AMT appears to be as effective as other self-control procedures and as effective, if not more effective, then desensitization and other more traditional approaches.

Cognitive Coping Skills Procedures

Cognitive coping skills interventions are based on the importance of cognitive mediators of anxiety. According to this way of looking at anxiety, it is not the stimulus conditions per se which elicit anxiety, but the ways in which the individual appraises or evaluates the situation that determine whether or not the individual will experience anxiety (Beck, 1976; Ellis, 1962). That is, external events prompt a set of anxiety-engendering cognitions which in turn produce affective-physiological arousal and/or behavioral disruption and avoidance. Anxiety arousal then is a function of idiosyncratic, faulty cognitions which are not reality based. For example, anxious clients may interpret situations as dangerous where no danger exists (Beck, 1976), or may evaluate them in absolutistic, catastrophic ways when reality is not nearly so absolute or catastrophic (Ellis, 1962). Yet, if events are cognitively processed in these ways, anxiety will likely be experienced.

If one's distorted thinking can prompt anxiety (Goldfried & Sobocinski, 1975), then it follows that changing this thinking to be more reality based or adaptive should lead to decreased affective-physiological arousal and somatic-behavioral involvement. This is exactly the goal of cognitive coping skills approaches which train clients to develop and employ more reasonable appraisals of themselves and the world when facing stressful circumstances. Generally, such programs are designed to assist clients in: (1) identifying their dysfunctional cognitive patterns; (2) generating alternative, more reality-based and self-reinforcing cognitive patterns; and (3) providing systematic rehearsal of more adaptive patterns in anxiety-arousing situations both within and between sessions.

Any discussion of cognitive coping techniques should acknowledge its roots in the rational emotive therapy of Albert Ellis (1962). Ellis described twelve irrational ideas thought to elicit negative affect, and outlined a directive means of therapy for identifying and changing such cognitions. While rational emotive therapy is not itself a self-control procedure, it has led to two cognitive self-control interventions which we will consider in detail: systematic rational restructuring and cognitive modification.

Systematic rational restructuring (SRR). SRR (Goldfried, Decenteceo, & Weinberg, 1974) presents rational-emotive therapy as a systematic, self-control procedure for anxiety reduction. In many ways, SRR parallels SCD, except that the coping orientation is cognitive rather than relaxation. SRR involves four phases designed to develop cognitive self-control of anxiety. In the first phase, a rationale is given which describes anxiety as a function of dysfunctional, unrealistic expectations, evaluations, and predictions. The notion of cognitive change of anxiety reduction is introduced: that by changing one's cognitions to be more appropriate and realistic, one can learn to lower anxiety. SRR is then described in terms of cognitive self-control. Specifically, SRR involves training in: (a) monitoring subjective experience of anxiety to know when anxiety is aroused and when to cognitively intervene; (b) identifying negative self-statements; (c) learning to self-instruct using more positive, realistic self-statements; and (d) practicing these adaptive self-statements in the external environment for self-controlled anxiety reduction. In the second phase, an overview of irrational assumptions is provided. The emphasis is on getting clients to identify their own irrational beliefs and to form their own arguments for the unreasonableness of these assumptions. In phase three, clients are then taught, in a Socratic-like manner, a rational-emotive way of analyzing problems. Specifically, they learn to analyze anxiety-arousing situations in terms of the probability that specific events would occur (such as imagined catastrophes) so as to point out the irrationality of such negative predictions and expectations. The fourth phase involves employing these cognitive, analytic skills to modify anxiety-arousing cognitions and reduce anxiety. A hierarchy of increasingly more anxiety-provoking situations is then constructed. The client then imagines the scene, engages in thinking through the problem aloud, and stays in the scene in this manner until the anxiety is reduced. During scene presentations the therapist models how to reduce the anxiety by changing inappropriate self-statements. Repetition of successful coping in this manner determines advancement to the next scene. In addition to practice within the sessions, clients are encouraged to utilize these coping skills when confronting anxiety arousing circumstances *in vivo*. Through this training within and between sessions, the internal cues of anxiety arousal become cues for rational reanalysis, hence cognitive self-control of anxiety.

Three studies are available in the literature which evalute SRR. Goldfried, Linehan, and Smith (1978) compared SRR to a prolonged exposure and wait-list control conditions. Both led to reductions of self-reported trait anxiety and state test anxiety, and SRR showed significant nontargeted anxiety reduction on four of six nontargeted anxiety measures. In the study previously described for SCD, Kanter and Goldfried (1979) demonstrated that SRR led to significant reductions of both targeted social anxiety and other nontargeted anxieties. Furthermore, the results suggested that SRR was generally a more impressive treatment than SCD. Linehan, Goldfried, and Goldfried (1979) found that both the cognitive coping skill training of SRR and the behavior skill training of behavioral rehearsal successfully increased targeted assertion and decreased nontargeted general anxiety and hostility. Thus, SRR appears effective in impacting targeted anxiety-related behavior, but also in affecting significant self-control effects in nontargeted areas as well.

Cognitive modification (CM). What we are labeling CM is really the cognitive portion of the combined affective-cognitive coping skills program of *stress inoculation* (SI) (Meichenbaum, 1972, 1977) which will be discussed shortly. It is presented separately because it can and often has been separated from the non-cognitive portion of the stress inoculation technique, and because there is a separate body of literature related to it.

CM is a three-phased program. In the education phase, clients are told that stress reactions come from the two factors of the Schachterian model of emotion: heightened arousal and anxiety-engendering cognitions. Then, much as in SRR, they are told that the lowering of anxiety can be achieved through changing cognitive patterns. This educational phase is concluded with a discussion that stress control will involve learning four sequential steps: preparing for the stressor, confronting the stressor, dealing with feelings of being overwhelmed, and lastly, reinforcing oneself for coping with the stressor. The second, or rehearsal, phase introduces the cognitive coping skills. Clients are assisted in identifying the set of negative self-statements which they make and to evaluate their validity. They are also provided with other more appropriate self-statements, which may be modeled by the therapist. Then, clients and therapist join together to shape a set of self-statements to guide the individual realistically through the phases of dealing with the stressor. This self-controlling cognitive set includes statements which focus on: (a) assessing the reality of the situation; (b) controlling and changing negative cognitions and images; (c) initiating task-oriented, problem-solving self-instruction, and (d) engaging in performance evaluation and self-reinforcement for coping. When these new cognitive patterns are developed, clients move to the third phase of application training. Stressors, often in the form of target-relevant imagery or simulations, are presented, and clients practice controlling their reactions with their newly formed cognitive sets. Problems are corrected, and clients are given more practice at recognizing their arousal and bringing it under control by self-instruction. Clients also apply these in the external world with progress and problems being discussed in subsequent sessions.

In an early study of CM, Meichenbaum, Gilmore, and Fedoravicius (1971) found that CM and desensitization effectively reduced speech anxiety relative to the controls. CM-treated clients also evidenced nontargeted anxiety reduction. Glogower, Fremouw, and McCroskey (1978) found similar targeted speech anxiety reduction for CM, but did not find the nontargeted anxiety reduction. Test anxiety has also been reduced by CM. For example, Holroyd (1976) found that CM reduced test anxiety and improved test performance and grades and that the effects of CM were generally equal to and in several cases better than those of desensitization or a combination of desensitization and CM. Hussian and Lawrence (1978) also demonstrated significant reduction of test anxiety and improved performance. However, they found no evidence of nontargeted anxiety reduction. Additionally, both Finger and Galassi (1977) and Deffenbacher and Hahnloser (in press) demonstrated that CM was as effective as relaxation coping skills or the combination of CM and relaxation coping skills in reducing state and trait test anxiety. Performance differences were not shown in either of these studies. Two studies which have compared CM to behavioral rehearsal of social-assertion skills have yielded somewhat different outcomes. Glass, Gottman, and Shmurak (1976) found CM alone to be equal to behavioral rehearsal or behavioral rehearsal plus CM in reducing self-reported dating anxiety in shy males. However, CM was superior to the other interventions on some behavioral measures of dating anxiety. On the other hand, Hammen, Jacobs, Mayol, and Cochran (1980) found CM and behavioral rehearsal generally equivalent on both self-report and behavioral measures of assertion.

In summary, CM appears to effectively reduce targeted anxieties of various sorts. These effects appear as strong as some other affective interventions, and in some cases CM appears to lead to behavioral-performance gains not found for some other interventions. Only a few studies were found which included measures of nontargeted anxieties or behavior to warrant any speculation about nontargeted effects for CM.

Combined Cognitive-Affective Coping Skills Programs

These programs integrate training in both cognitive and relaxation coping skills. That is, clients are trained to pay attention to the internal cues of anxiety arousal and to apply a combination of attention redirecting and relaxation coping skills to reduce anxiety wherever it occurs. Anxiety should decrease as major dimensions of the affective-physiological and cognitive, and to some extent somatic-behavioral, domains are directly altered by the client.

Stress inoculation (SI). The best known research of the combined cognitive-affective coping skills programs is that on stress inoculation (Meichenbaum, 1972, 1977). SI essentially is a combination of CM and a coping form of desensitization. As noted for CM, anxiety is explained in terms of heightened arousal and faulty cognitions. SI is explained as self-control training in altering both factors—relaxation coping skills for heightened arousal and self-instructional training for dysfunctional cognitions. Progressive relaxation training and training in relaxation coping skills, such as connecting relaxation with deep breathing and verbal self-instruction, are added to the rehearsal phase. During training, clients practice these relaxation coping skills in a form of desensitization similar to SCD, though hierarchies are not necessarily multithematic as in SCD. The relaxation coping skills are integrated into the repertoire of cognitive coping skills, and clients practice controlling anxiety both within and between sessions with a combination of skills. That is, clients feel the experience of anxiety arousal and then actively cue in their relaxation coping skills to reduce arousal and their cognitive self-instructional sets to change faulty cognitive mediation of anxiety.

Meichenbaum (1972), in the first report of SI, found it to be as effective as and in some cases more effective than desensitization in impacting on test anxiety. Additionally, SI improved performance, whereas desensitization did not. A recent component analysis involving test anxiety (Deffenbacher & Hahnloser, in press) revealed that the combination of cognitive and relaxation coping skills in SI was significantly better in increasing facilitating test anxiety than either the cognitive or relaxation coping skills components did alone, even though each alone was effective in reducing state and trait test anxiety. Interestingly, by 4-week follow-up, the individuals in the full SI program reported significantly less debilitating test anxiety than those receiving cognitive or relaxation components, even though these separately were each still effective compared to controls. Similar but somewhat weaker effects were found in another component analysis involving test anxiety (Cooley & Spiegler, 1980). Three studies where speech anxiety was targeted (Fremouw & Harmatz, 1975; Fremouw & Zitter, 1978; Weissberg, 1977) revealed significant targeted anxiety reduction and evidence of nontargeted anxiety reduction at least by the short-term follow-up assessments. A recent report of SI (Siegel & Peterson, 1980) showed that SI lowered physiological arousal and reported anxiety and increased cooperation in young dental patients. Other studies (e.g., Alden, Safran & Weideman, 1979; Carmody, 1978; Safran, Alden, & Davidson, 1980) have compared SI to behavioral rehearsal in increasing assertiveness, and found both to be equally as effective.

As with other self-control interventions reviewed, SI has been shown to be an effective treatment for targeted problems. Comparatively, it was as effective or more effective than other treatments in impacting the targeted problem. In the few studies that included nontargeted measures, SI typically led to nontargeted anxiety reduction as well. However, too few studies included such measures to draw more than tentative support of nontargeted anxiety reduction for SI.

KEY ELEMENTS IN DESIGNING A QUALITY SELF-CONTROL INTERVENTION

Based on the material reviewed in this chapter and on our own research and clinical experience with self-control approaches to anxiety reduction, we would like to offer our conclusions about necessary conditions for the design of a quality self-control intervention.

Importance of Assessment

As outlined earlier, assessment, both of the initial diagnostic impression and continuing case planning, is critical. The general decision to select a self-control approach should be based on a careful understanding of client data from three response channels and their subareas. Generally, self-control deficits in the cognitive and/or affective-physiological response channels serve as the central sources of the inference of anxiety. The selection of the specific type of coping skills training is then based on the data from these response domains. At an even more narrow level, the information from assessment should be used to individually tailor the self-control program to the specific characteristics of the anxiety problem. For example, a relaxation coping skills program might have a specific focus on stomach tension if interviewing, self-monitoring logs, and/or psychophysiological assessment suggested that this was a particularly important aspect of affective-physiological arousal. Similarly, a cognitive coping skills program might be specifically aimed at teaching "de-catastrophizing" cognitions, were this to be a salient element in assessment. On the other hand, a cognitive program might focus primarily on training in task-oriented self-instruction and problem-solving skills for the self-distracting client. In other words, the most effective intervention is likely to be the one that is most carefully tuned to the specific characteristics of anxiety revealed in assessment. Thus, assessment is critical for selecting a self-control approach generally, selecting the type of self-control program more specifically, and for individually tailoring treatment to best fit the needs of the client.

Self-control Rationale

Regardless of the nature of the coping skill training, clients must be helped to accept their roles through an introduction to a self-control rationale. This rationale should provide clients with a comprehensible explanation of anxiety and should logically describe how client problems may be resolved by their gaining and applying specific coping skills. These skills should be explained in lay terms and amplified by examples drawn from the assessment data so that clients see how the proposed intervention is intimately linked to them and their problems. A rationale should also give clients an orientation to the therapy such that they can understand what will be happening and be an active participant in designing and implementing their self-control training. The rationale can also capitalize on the self-help philosophy which characterizes many anxious clients. They want to help themselves and do not want to be seen as passive victims of anxiety. A self-control rationale is consistent with their world view and enlists their efforts to help themselves. The value of a self-control rationale is supported by research (e.g., Denney & Rupert, 1977; Goldfried & Trier, 1974) which has shown that such a self-control rationale significantly improved the effectiveness of intervention.

Coping Skill Training

Specific cognitive and/or affective coping skills should be developed and rehearsed in nonstressful circumstances within the session. This allows the therapist to make sure that the component elements of the skills are reliably trained prior to self-control applications in more stressful situations. This also ensures that clients have achieved familiarity and success with these behaviors before they are chained together and applied to the control of anxiety in the real world. This stage also allows for some individual tailoring of coping skills programs even though the intervention may be delivered in a group format. That is, individual differences in the need for coping skills can be discussed, and clients can be assisted in selecting the most appropriate coping skills for the nature of the anxiety problems they experience.

Training in the Discrimination of Response-Produced Cues of Anxiety

Self-control theory suggests that clients should gain the capacity to reduce anxiety whenever and wherever it is felt. In this way they will be acquiring the preventive skills with which to reduce future stresses on their own. Training clients to be aware of the internal cues of anxiety arousal appears critical to achieving these goals. If clients are going to be able to apply their coping skills whenever they experience tension, then they must know precisely when they are experiencing anxiety. Preferably, clients should know when they are experiencing even small amounts of anxiety so that they could abort those feelings early, before they become out of control. Some clients may already be aware of their cues of arousal; but many are not, especially of the "early warning" cues of arousal. Specific training in becoming aware of and monitoring these cues should greatly facilitate the transfer of coping skills across other anxiety-arousing situations. Three tasks are recommended to develop this discriminability: (1) attending to the feelings of tension during relaxation training, if an affective coping skill approach is used; (2) tracking the internal cues of anxiety arousal during induced anxiety in the sessions; and (3) self-monitoring and recording of the response-produced cues of arousal between sessions.

Anxiety Arousal and Control Within Sessions

Clients should be purposefully exposed to anxiety arousal within the session. This provides clients with the opportunity both to become more sensitive observers of the internal cues of anxiety arousal and to practice coping with anxiety within a relatively safe and controlled environment. It is insufficient for clients to simply "know" what they are supposed to do about anxiety; they must be trained directly in self-control of anxiety. The levels of anxiety arousal and/or degree of client responsibility for anxiety control should be graded so that clients experience increased probabilities of success before moving to the next step. For example, SCD, SRR, and SI do this through hierarchical presentation of anxiety-arousing cues; AMT, through faded therapist control.

Systematic Transfer of Coping Skills

Learning coping skills, even applying them within the session, is insufficient. Clients must be able to apply them in reliable ways in the external world. Systematic attention, therefore, should be given to having clients apply their coping skills in the external environment. It is suggested that clients be given clear, concrete homework in applying their coping skills. This homework should have clients first apply the skills in nonstressful situations, then mildly stressful situations, and finally in more stressful situations so that success in the external world is maximized. Clients should monitor their attempts at applying coping skills and record these in a log. These logs should be discussed in the next session, and skill application should be reinforced and further shaped in light of the new data.

Attention to Maintenance

This recommendation is more speculative, as little research has addressed this issue. There is some evidence (see discussion of the importance of follow-up below) that self-control effects may continue to consolidate after treatment is over. One may wonder if this effect might not be enhanced if attention were paid to it.

Two different elements of intervention are suggested. First is the issue of therapeutic set relative to post-treatment self-control. Rather than implying that anxiety has been reduced permanently by treatment, a philosophy of coping should be imparted. That is, anxiety and stress are likely to continue, and what clients have learned are methods of coping with the continued stress. Stress reduction will continue if clients continue to employ their coping skills. Coping may get easier and faster, but clients will nonetheless have to continue to employ their self-control skills. Clients need a realistic expectation that they can continue to cope, but that they will have to work at it. Possible discontinuation or disuse of coping skills should be addressed by having clients anticipate times when they may not be using the coping skills and concretely plan steps for how they will start again. The second direction is the employment of therapeutic contact to foster continued application of self-control. Clinically speaking, contact for a period of time after major self-control training has been accomplished seems to facilitate continued attention to self-control on the part of the client. The following types of activities seem to hold promise for continuing this contact without inducing unnecessary dependency: (1) spacing the ending sessions of therapy to perhaps two or three weeks apart; (2) assigning self-monitoring homework of progress in coping in between these sessions to ensure that clients observe their new successes; (3) scheduling specific check-in sessions on a monthly schedule for a few months and then lengthening the time interval; or (4) reporting self-control efforts over the phone or through the mail at regular intervals for a period of time, say once every 2 weeks for 10 weeks post-treatment. Sessions or contacts need not be of full length. All of these activities keep clients focused upon their continued efforts at self-control, reporting these to someone who is invested in their self-control and who can reinforce their efforts and help then reassess their coping efforts as needed.

ISSUES IN RESEARCH ON THE SELF-CONTROL OF ANXIETY

There are numerous papers and books which discuss the important issues in evaluating treatment outcome. We are therefore only going to touch on two issues which have particular relevance to the evaluation of self-control interventions. These are the importance of follow-up and the need for non-targeted measures.

The Importance of Follow-Up

Follow-up is important in evaluating the maintenance of treatment effects for any intervention. However, the inclusion of follow-up in research on self-control may be even more important if self-control effects are to be fully evaluated. If clients are truly learning sets of trans-situational coping skills, then they should continue to employ these and gain even greater competence after treatment is over. That is, self-control effects may consolidate after treatment. If follow-up is not included, such consolidation would not be assessed, and the extent of self-control effects would be underestimated. Differences among treatment groups not apparent at post-treatment would also be obscured. These comments would seem to hold particularly for nontargeted measures or for generalized anxiety. This is because it takes some time for clients to have the experience of employing the coping skills across situations and to report general anxiety reduction or other non-targeted effects.

While this argument appears logically sound, four different types of empirical data could be used to support this assumed "consolidation gain" effect during follow-up in self-control research. First, a statistical comparison of post-treatment and follow-up anxiety levels may reveal a significant reduction in anxiety from post-treatment to follow-up assessments for the self-control intervention. This would be direct support of the consolidation-gain effect. On the other hand, consistent nonsignificant anxiety reduction from post-treatment to follow-up could be interpreted as suggestive, but not conclusive support. Second, self-control treatments may show a greater number of significant differences in comparison to controls at follow-up than post-treatment. This too would suggest a consolidation effect for self-control therapies. Third, long-term follow-ups may also reveal greater effects than immediate post-treatment or at short-term follow-up. That is, post-treatment and short-term follow-up data for those retained in the long term may be compared against the long-term follow-up data. Significant continued reductions and/or a greater number of significant differences compared to the controls would support the consolidation-gain notion. Finally, differences among treatments favoring a self-control intervention may be found at follow-up which were not apparent immediately after treatment. Evidence along any of these four lines would support continued gain of self-control and would demonstrate the necessity of follow-up evaluations in self-control research. Data from several of our studies is provided below to elucidate these points and emphasize the importance of follow-up.

In an unpublished study of group AMT (Deffenbacher, Note 11), significant pre-post reductions were found on the two measures of general anxiety. A 4-week follow-up revealed significant post-test to follow-up reductions on both measures as well, suggesting continued gains. A number of our studies have used analysis of covariance and have not statistically compared post-treatment and follow-up means. However, means on both measures of nontargeted anxiety were always lower at 6 to 9 weeks than at post-treatment for AMT (Deffenbacher, Michaels, Michaels, & Daley, 1980; Deffenbacher & Shelton, 1978), for SCD (Deffenbacher, Michaels, Michaels, & Daley, 1980; Deffenbacher & Parks, 1979), and for RSC (Deffenbacher, Mathis, & Michaels, 1979). Furthermore, King and Deffenbacher (Note 3) found that means for RSC and AMT on measures of general anxiety and other non targeted behavior tended to be lower at follow-up than post-treatment. Thus, measures of general anxiety and other nontargeted behaviors tended, with a high degree of consistency, to be lower at follow-up than post-treatment. While other arguments can be invoked to account for this pattern, it is consistent with a consolidation-gain theory.

Several of our studies have shown a greater number of significant differences between controls and self-control interventions at follow-up than at post-treatment assessment. For example, in a study comparing AMT and SCD (Deffenbacher, Michaels, Michaels, & Daley, 1980), no nontargeted anxiety reduction was noted for AMT immediately after treatment, and SCD evidenced nontargeted anxiety reduction on only one of two measures. However, by follow-up, both AMT and SCD subjects reported less nontargeted anxiety than controls on both measures. In another study (Deffenbacher, Michaels, Daley, & Michaels, 1980), two forms of AMT were compared in two different samples. In one sample, one form of AMT evidenced no significant nontargeted anxiety reduction post-treatment, but such a reduction did show on one of two measures at follow-up. In the other sample, both forms of AMT showed no post-treatment differences from controls on one measure, but were significantly different by follow-up on this measure. Deffenbacher and Shelton (1978) found significant pre-post change on only one of two nontargeted anxiety measures for AMT, but found significant pre-follow-up changes on both for AMT. In these studies, had not the 6-week follow-ups been included, nontargeted anxiety reduction either would not have been evidenced at all or would have been underestimated.

Three follow-ups over 12- to 15-month periods also point to continued consolidation-gains of self-control training. In a 12-month follow-up of RSC (Deffenbacher & Michaels, 1980), attrition made the differences on the two nontargeted anxiety measures no longer significant between RSC and controls for post-treatment and 6-week follow-up. However, the 12-month follow-up revealed significantly less nontargeted anxiety on both measures for RSC than controls. A 15-month follow-up of AMT and SCD (Deffenbacher & Michaels, in press a) revealed a similar pattern. AMT and SCD were not different from controls on either measures post-treatment, and were significantly different on only one measure at short term follow-up. However, 15-month follow-up demonstrated that AMT and SCD reported significantly less nontargeted anxiety than controls on both measures. The pattern was not quite as clear in a 12-month follow-up of two forms of AMT (Deffenbacher & Michaels, in press b). Little nontargeted anxiety reduction was found across assessment for either form of AMT in either sample. However, when AMT conditions were pooled, nontargeted anxiety reduction was evidenced on one of two measures at the extended follow-up, whereas none was apparent at earlier assessments. Despite the relatively weaker findings in the latter follow-up, self-control interventions always reflected a greater number of significant improvements over controls at the extended follow-ups than at earlier assessments on the same subjects. Thus, once again, more powerful non-targeted anxiety reduction was evidenced for self-control interventions at extended follow-up.

Finally, two of our studies have revealed significant treatment differences at follow-up which were not apparent at post-treatment. Deffenbacher and Shelton (1978) compared AMT and traditional desensitization and found no differences among the two on targeted test or nontargeted anxieties post-treatment. However, the 6-week follow-up revealed significantly lower anxiety on one of two test-anxiety measures and on one of two nontargeted anxiety measures for AMT. In a component analysis of SI, Deffenbacher and Hahnloser (in press) found significant and equivalent post-treatment reductions of test anxiety for relaxation, cognitive, and combined relaxation-cognitive coping (SI) skill programs. On the other hand, the follow-up revealed that the combined group reported significantly less test anxiety than either component alone. Without the follow-ups, the synergistic effects of the combination of cognitive and relaxation coping skills and the relative superiority of AMT in targeted and nontargeted anxiety reduction would have gone unnoticed.

To summarize, four sources of evidence converge to underscore the need for follow-up in self-control research. Without them, the consolidation-gain effects, the greater long-term strength of self-control interventions, and important treatment differences favoring self-control may all have gone unnoticed. Thus, research on self-control interventions for anxiety must include at least short-term follow-up so that effects are fully assessed and unnecessarily discouraging or limiting conclusions are not drawn.

Importance of Nontargeted Measures

Demonstrating the effectiveness of self-control interventions with specific targeted problems is valuable and needed in its own right. However, research which includes only measures of targeted anxiety is missing the assessment of one of the most exciting possibilities of self-control approaches, namely, the development of general coping skills which cut across dissimilar sources of anxiety and stress. Without the inclusion of nontargeted measures, it is unclear whether the effects are target-specific or whether clients have truly learned generalized, preventive coping skills. As noted earlier, one of the key therapeutic advantages of self-control approaches is that they may teach such skills. To fully evaluate self-control programs and to contribute to the underlying theory of self-control, research designs must include strategies for assessing these nontargeted effects.

There are essentially three research designs which could test the value of a therapy for nontargeted anxieties. First, individuals with two distinctly different phobias (e.g., individuals with very high test anxiety and an animal phobia) may be found. They could then receive self-control training targeted to one of the phobias, and the effects on both the targeted and non-targeted phobias could be assessed. If reduction were noted on the non-targeted phobia, then the generalized coping skill hypothesis would be supported. This design, however, may be practically infeasible, as it is difficult to locate sufficient numbers of clients with high levels of anxiety in the same two areas. Zemore (1975) used this strategy with highly test- and speech-anxious subjects in an evaluation of SCD with success.

A second approach follows a similar logic, but is practically more feasible. A single source of anxiety is targeted because it is the presenting problem, and other anxieties of clients are allowed to vary from client to client. The design includes measures of general or trait anxiety and/or lists of specific fears, as in the various forms of the Fear Survey, to assess changes on these other sources of anxiety. Post-therapy reductions on these would confirm the reduction of general anxiety and/or nontargeted specific fears, thus implying that coping skills have generalized.

The third design option is to make general anxiety the focus of treatment. If clients are able to reduce their levels of general anxiety with self-control procedures, it suggests that they are learning general coping skills. Such a design may also include other nontargeted behaviors as well, such as hostility and depression (King & Deffenbacher, Note 3) or prosocial behavior (Nally, Note 10). This design, with or without measures of other non-targeted behaviors, is both practical and feasible with clients whose presenting problem is general anxiety or multiple phobias.

Self-control approaches theoretically offer the potential of making clients "their own therapists" by teaching them generalized coping skills for anxiety reduction. Research which is sound in other ways, but which includes measures of nontargeted anxieties and other behavior as well as follow-up, will vastly improve the understanding of the full possibilities of the interventions and the theories underlying them. The research reviewed above suggests that our designs may potentially have underestimated the effects of self-control interventions. However, until such time that adequate designs become the norm and sufficient data have been collected, we must be guarded in our optimism for self-control approaches to anxiety reduction.

REFERENCE NOTES

1. Deffenbacher, J. L., & Hazaleus, S. L. *Worry, emotionality, task-generated interference, and physiological arousal in test anxiety.* Unpublished manuscript, Colorado State University, Fort Collins, Colorado, 1981.
2. Jacks, R. N. *Systematic desensitization versus a self-control technique for the reduction of acrophobia.* Unpublished doctoral dissertation, Stanford University, Palo Alto, Calif., 1972.

3. King, M., & Deffenbacher, J. L. *A comparison of anxiety management training and relaxation as self-control in the treatment of generalized anxiety in medical outpatients.* Unpublished manuscript, Colorado State University, Fort Collins, Colorado, 1981.
4. Edie, C. *Uses of AMT in treating trait anxiety.* Unpublished doctoral dissertation, Colorado, 1972.
5. Nicoletti, J. *Anxiety management training.* Unpublished doctoral dissertation, Colorado State University, Fort Collins, Colo., 1972.
6. Berghausen, P. E. *Anxiety management training: Need for arousal-cued relaxation.* Unpublished doctoral dissertation, Colorado State University, Fort Collins, Colorado, 1977.
7. Shoemaker, J. *Treatments for anxiety neurosis.* Unpublished doctoral dissertation, Colorado State University, Fort Collins, Colo., 1976.
8. VanHassel, J. *Anxiety management with schizophrenic outpatients.* Unpublished doctoral dissertation, Colorado State University, Fort Collins, Colo., 1979.
9. Houston, B., Jorgensen, R., & Zurawski, R. *The effectiveness of anxiety management training in reducing hypertensives' blood pressure at rest and following stress.* Paper presented at the Society of Behavioral Medicine, New York, New York, November 1980.
10. Nally, M. *AMT: A treatment for delinquents.* Unpublished doctoral dissertation, Colorado State University, Fort Collins, Colo., 1975.
11. Deffenbacher, J. L. *Use of anxiety management training for stress reduction in large groups.* Unpublished manuscript, Colorado State University, Fort Collins, Colorado, 1981.

REFERENCES

Alden, L., Safran, J., & Weideman, R. A comparison of cognitive and skills training strategies in the treatment of unassertive clients. *Behavior Therapy*, 1979, *9*, 843–846.

Barrios, B., & Shigetomi, C. Coping skills training for the management of anxiety: A critical review. *Behavior Therapy*, 1979, *10*, 491–522.

Barrios, B., & Shigetomi, C. Coping skills training: Potential for prevention of fears and anxieties. *Behavior Therapy*, 1980, *11*, 431–439.

Beck, A. T. *Cognitive therapy and the emotional disorders.* New York: International Universities Press, 1976.

Beck, A. T., Laude, R., & Bohnert, M. Ideational components of anxiety neurosis. *Archives of General Psychiatry*, 1974, *31*, 319–325.

Beck, F. M., Kaul, T. J., & Russell, R. K. Treatment of dental anxiety by cue-controlled relaxation. *Journal of Counseling Psychology*, 1978, *25*, 591–594.

Borkovec, T. D., Weerts, T. C., & Bernstein, D. A. Assessment of anxiety. In A. R. Ciminero, K. S. Calhoun, & H. E. Adams (Eds.), *Handbook of behavioral assessment.* New York: John Wiley & Sons, 1977.

Canter, A., Kondo, C. Y., & Knott, J. R. A comparison of EMG feedback and progressive relaxation training in anxiety neurosis. *British Journal of Psychiatry*, 1975, *127*, 470–477.

Carmody, T. P. Rational emotive, self-instructional, and behavioral assertion training: Facilitating maintenance. *Cognitive Therapy and Research*, 1978, *2*, 241–253.

Cautela, J. R. A behavior therapy treatment of pervasive anxiety. *Behaviour Research and Therapy*, 1966, *4*, 99–109.

Chang-Liang, R., & Denney, D. R. Applied relaxation as training in self-control. *Journal of Counseling Psychology*, 1976, *23*, 183–189.

Cooley, E. J., & Spiegler, M. D. Cognitive versus emotional coping responses as alternatives to test anxiety. *Cognitive Therapy and Research*, 1980, *4*, 159–166.

Counts, D. K., Hollandsworth, J. G., & Alcorn, J. D. Use of electromyographic biofeedback and cue-controlled relaxation in the treatment of test anxiety. *Journal of Consulting and Clinical Psychology*, 1978, *46*, 990-996.

Daly, J. A., & McCroskey, J. C. Occupational desirability and choices as a function of communication apprehension. *Journal of Counseling Psychology*, 1975, *22*, 309-313.

Davison, G. C. Relative contributions of differential relaxation and grades exposure to *in vivo* desensitization of a neurotic fear. *Proceedings of the 73rd Annual Convention of the American Psychological Association*, 1965, *1*, 203-204.

Deffenbacher, J. L. Relaxation *in vivo* in the treatment of test anxiety. *Journal of Behavior Therapy and Experimental Psychiatry*, 1976, *7*, 289-292.

Deffenbacher, J. L. Relationship of worry and emotionality to performance on the Miller Analogies Test. *Journal of Educational Psychology*, 1977, *69*, 191-195.

Deffenbacher, J. L. Worry, emotionality and task-generated interference in test anxiety: An empirical test of attentional theory. *Theory of Educational Psychology*, 1978, *70*, 248-254.

Deffenbacher, J. L. Worry and emotionality in test anxiety. In I. G. Sarason (Ed.), *Test anxiety: Theory, research, and applications*. Hillsdale, N.J.: Lawrence Erlbaum Associates, 1980.

Deffenbacher, J. L., & Hahnloser, R. M. Cognitive and relaxation coping skills in stress inoculation. *Cognitive Therapy and Research*, in press.

Deffenbacher, J. L., Mathis, H., & Michaels, A. C. Two self-control procedures in the reduction of targeted and nontargeted anxieties. *Journal of Counseling Psychology*, 1979, *26*, 120-127.

Deffenbacher, J. L., & Michaels, A. C. Two self-control procedures in the reduction of targeted and nontargeted anxieties — A year later. *Journal of Counseling Psychology*, 1980, *27*, 9-15.

Deffenbacher, J. L., & Michaels, A. C. Anxiety management training and self-control desensitization — 15 months later. *Journal of Counseling Psychology*, in press. (a)

Deffenbacher, J. L., & Michaels, A. C. A twelve-month follow-up of homogeneous and heterogeneous anxiety management training. *Journal of Counseling Psychology*, in press. (b)

Deffenbacher, J. L., Michaels, A. C., Daley, P. C., & Michaels, T. A comparison of homogeneous and heterogeneous anxiety management training. *Journal of Counseling Psychology*, 1980, *27*, 630-634.

Deffenbacher, J. L., Michaels, A. C., Michaels, T., & Daley, P. C. Comparison of anxiety management training and self-control desensitization. *Journal of Counseling Psychology*, 1980, *27*, 232-239.

Deffenbacher, J. L., & Parks, D. H. A comparison of traditional and self-control desensitization. *Journal of Counseling Psychology*, 1979, *26*, 93-97.

Deffenbacher, J. L., & Payne, D. M. J. Two procedures for relaxation as self-control in the treatment of communication apprehension. *Journal of Counseling Psychology*, 1977, *24*, 255-258.

Deffenbacher, J. L., & Rivera, N. A behavioral self-control treatment of test anxiety in minority populations: Some cases and issues. *Psychological Reports*, 1976, *39*, 1188-1190.

Deffenbacher, J. L., & Shelton, J. L. A comparison of anxiety management training and desensitization in reducing test and other anxieties. *Journal of Counseling Psychology*, 1978, *25*, 277-282.

Deffenbacher, J. L., & Snyder, A. L. Relaxation as self-control in the treatment of test and other anxieties. *Psychological Reports*, 1976, *39*, 379-385.

Denney, D. R. Active, passive, and vicarious desensitization. *Journal of Counseling Psychology*, 1974, *21*, 369-375.

Denney, D. R. Self-control approaches to the treatment of test anxiety. In I. G. Sarason (Ed.), *Test anxiety: Theory, research and applications*. Hillsdale, N.J.: Lawrence Erlbaum, 1980.

Denney, D. R., & Rupert, P. A. Desensitization and self-control in the treatment of test anxiety. *Journal of Counseling Psychology*, 1977, *24*, 272–280.

Ellis, A. *Reason and emotion in psychotherapy*. New York: Lyle Stuart, 1962.

Finger, R., & Galassi, J. P. Effects of modifying cognitive versus emotionality response in the treatment of test anxiety. *Journal of Consulting and Clinical Psychology*, 1977, *45*, 280–287.

Fremouw, W. J., & Harmatz, M. C. A helper model for the behavioral treatment of speech anxiety. *Journal of Consulting and Clinical Psychology*, 1975, *43*, 652–660.

Fremouw, W. J., & Zitter, R. E. A comparison of skills training and cognitive restructuring relaxation for the treatment of speech anxiety. *Behavior Therapy*, 1978, *9*, 248–259.

Glass, C. R., Gottman, J. M., & Shmurak, S. H. Response acquisition and cognitive self-statement modification approaches to dating skills training. *Journal of Consulting and Clinical Psychology*, 1976, *44*, 520–526.

Glogower, F. D., Fremouw, W. J., & McCroskey, J. C. A component analysis of cognitive restructuring. *Cognitive Therapy and Research*, 1978, *2*, 209–224.

Goldfried, M. R. Systematic desensitization as training in self-control. *Journal of Consulting and Clinical Psychology*, 1971, *37*, 228–234.

Goldfried, M. R., & Sobocinski, D. Effect of irrational beliefs on emotional arousal. *Journal of Consulting and Clinical Psychology*, 1975, *43*, 504–510.

Goldfried, M. R., Decenteceo, E. T., & Weinberg, L. Systematic rational restructuring as a self-control technique. *Behavior Therapy*, 1974, *5*, 247–254.

Goldfried, M. R., & Goldfried, A. P. Importance of hierarchy content in the self-control of anxiety. *Journal of Consulting and Clinical Psychology*, 1977, *45*, 124–134.

Goldfried, M. R., Linehan, M. M., & Smith, J. L. Reduction of test anxiety through cognitive restructuring. *Journal of Consulting and Clinical Psychology*, 1978, *46*, 32–39.

Goldfried, M. R., & Trier, C. S. Effectiveness of relaxation as an active coping skill. *Journal of Abnormal Psychology*, 1974, *83*, 348–355.

Grimm, L. G. The evidence for cue-controlled relaxation. *Behavior Therapy*, 1980, *11*, 283–293.

Hammen, C. L., Jacobs, M., Mayol, A., & Cochran, S. D. Dysfunctional cognitions and the effectiveness of skills and cognitive-behavioral assertion training. *Journal of Consulting and Clinical Psychology*, 1980, *48*, 685–695.

Harris, G., & Johnson, S. B. Comparison of individualized covert modeling, self-control desensitization, and study skills training for alleviation of test anxiety. *Journal of Consulting and Clinical Psychology*, 1980, *48*, 186–194.

Henderson, J. G. Denial and repression as factors in the delay of patients with cancer presenting themselves to the physician. *Annals of the New York Academy of Sciences*, 1966, *125*, 856–864.

Holroyd, K. A. Cognition and desensitization in the group treatment of test anxiety. *Journal of Consulting and Clinical Psychology*, 1976, *44*, 991–1001.

Holroyd, K. A., & Appel, M. A. Test anxiety and physiological responding. In I. G. Sarason (Ed.), *Test anxiety: Theory, research and applications*. Hillsdale, N.J.: Lawrence Erlbaum, 1980.

Hussian, R. A., & Lawrence, P. S. The reduction of test, state, and trait anxiety by test-specific and generalized stress inoculation training. *Cognitive Therapy and Research*, 1978, *2*, 25–37.

Hutchings, D. F., Denney, D. R., Basgall, J., & Houston, B. K. Anxiety management and applied relaxation in reducing general anxiety. *Behaviour Research and Therapy*, 1980, *18*, 181–190.

Jenkins, C. D., Zyzanski, S. J., Ryan, T. J., Flessas, A., & Tannebaum, S. I. Social insecurity and coronary-prone Type A responses as identifiers of severe atherosclerosis. *Journal of Consulting and Clinical Psychology*, 1977, *45*, 1060–1067.

Kanfer, F. H. The maintenance of behavior by self-generated stimuli and reinforcement. In A. Jacobs & L. B. Sachs (Eds.), *The psychology of private events*. New York: Academic Press, 1971.

Kanfer, F. H. The many faces of self-control, or behavior modification changes its focus. In R. B. Stuart (Ed.), *Behavioral self-management*. New York: Brunner/Mazel, 1977.

Kanfer, F. H., & Karoly, P. Self-control: A behavioristic excursion into the lion's den. *Behavior Therapy*, 1972, *3*, 398–416.

Kanter, N. J., & Goldfried, M. R. Relative effectiveness of rational restructuring self-control desensitization in the reduction of interpersonal anxiety. *Behavior Therapy*, 1979, *10*, 472–490.

Lang, P. J. The mechanics of desensitization and the laboratory study of human fear. In C. M. Franks (Ed.), *Behavior therapy: Appraisal and status*. New York: McGraw-Hill, 1969.

Lang, P. J. The application of psychophysiological methods to the study of psychotherapy and behavior change. In A. E. Bergin & S. L. Garfield (Eds.), *Handbook of psychotherapy and behavior change*. New York: Wiley, 1971.

Leitenberg, H., Agras, W. S., Butz, R., & Wincze, J. P. Relationship between heart rate and behavior change during the treatment of phobias. *Journal of Abnormal Psychology*, 1971, *78*, 59–68.

Linehan, M., Goldfried, M. R., & Goldfried, A. Assertion therapy: Skill training or cognitive restructuring. *Behavior Therapy*, 1979, *10*, 373–388.

Magerey, C., Todd, P., & Blizard, P. Psychological factors influencing delay and breast self-examination in women with symptoms of breast cancer. *Social Science and Medicine*, 1977, *11*, 119–232.

Mahoney, M. J., & Avener, M. Psychology of the elite athlete: An exploratory study. *Cognitive Therapy and Research*, 1977, *1*, 135–141.

Marchetti, A., McGlynn, F. D., & Patterson, A. S. Effects of cue-controlled relaxation, a placebo treatment, and no treatment on changes in self-reported and psychophysiological indices of test anxiety among college students. *Behavior Modification*, 1977, *1*, 47–72.

Marx, M., Garrity, T., & Bowers, F. The influence of recent life experience on the health of college freshmen. *Journal of Psychosomatic Research*, 1975, *19*, 87–98.

Masters, W. H., & Johnson, V. E. *Human sexual inadequacy*. Boston, MA: Little, Brown, 1970.

McGlynn, F. D., Kinjo, K., & Doherty, G. Effects of cue-controlled relaxation, a placebo treatment, and no treatment on changes in self-reported test anxiety among college students. *Journal of Clinical Psychology*, 1978, *34*, 707–714.

Meichenbaum, D. H. Cognition modification of test anxious college students. *Journal of Consulting and Clinical Psychology*, 1972, *39*, 370–380.

Meichenbaum, D. *Cognitive behavior modification: An integrative approach*. New York: Plenum Press, 1977.

Meichenbaum, D. H., Gilmore, J. B., & Fedoravicius, A. Group insight versus group desensitization in treating speech anxiety. *Journal of Consulting and Clinical Psychology*, 1971, *36*, 410–421.

Mueller, J. H. Test anxiety, input modality, and levels of organization in free recall. *Bulletin of the Psychonomic Society*, 1977, *6*, 194–198.

Mueller, J. H. Test anxiety and the encoding and retrieval of information. In I. G. Sarason (Ed.), *Test anxiety: Theory, research and applications*. Hillsdale, N. J.: Lawrence Erlbaum, 1980.

Neeman, R. L., & Neeman, M. Cancer prevention education for youth—A key for control of uterine and breast cancer. *Journal of School Health*, 1974, *44*, 543–547.

Nottlemann, E. D., & Hill, K. T. Test anxiety and off-task behavior in evaluative situations. *Child Development*, 1977, *48*, 225–231.

Paul, G. L. A two year follow-up of systematic desensitization in therapy groups. *Journal of Abnormal and Social Psychology*, 1968, *73*, 119–130.

Paul, G. L. Outcome of systematic desensitization. II: Controlled investigations of individual treatment, technique variations, and current status. In C. M. Franks (Eds.), *Behavior therapy: Appraisal and status*. New York: McGraw-Hill, 1969.

Richardson, F., & Suinn, R. A comparison of traditional systematic desensitization, accelerated massed desensitization, and anxiety management training in the treatment of mathematics anxiety. *Behavior Therapy*, 1973, *4*, 212–218.

Rimm, D. C., & Masters, J. C. *Behavior therapy: Techniques and empirical findings*. New York: Academic Press, 1974.

Rimm, D. C., & Sommervill, J. W. *Abnormal psychology*. New York: Academic Press, 1977.

Russell, R. K., Miller, D. E., & June, L. N. Group cue-controlled relaxation in the treatment of test anxiety. *Behavior Therapy*, 1974, *5*, 572–573.

Russell, R. K., Miller, D. E., & June, L. N. A comparison between group systematic desensitization and cue-controlled relaxation in the treatment of test anxiety. *Behavior Therapy*, 1975, *6*, 172–177.

Russell, R. K., & Wise, F. Treatment of speech anxiety by cue-controlled relaxation and desensitization with professional and paraprofessional counselors. *Journal of Counseling Psychology*, 1976, *23*, 583–586.

Russell, R. K., Wise, F., & Stratoudakis, J. P. Treatment of test anxiety by cue-controlled relaxation and systematic desensitization. *Journal of Counseling Psychology*, 1976, *3*, 563–566.

Safran, J. D., Alden, L. E., & Davidson, P. O. Client anxiety level as a moderator variable in assertion training. *Cognitive Therapy and Research*, 1980, *4*, 189–200.

Sarason, I. G. Experimental approach to test anxiety: Attention and the use of information. In C. D. Spielberger (Ed.), *Anxiety: Current trends in theory and research* (Vol. 2). New York: Academic Press, 1972.

Schultz, J. H., & Luthe, W. *Autogenic training: A physiological approach in psychotherapy*. New York: Grune & Stratton, 1959.

Schwartz, R. M., & Gottman, J. M. Toward a task analysis of assertive behavior. *Journal of Consulting and Clinical Psychology*, 1976, *44*, 910–920.

Sherman, A. R. Two-year follow-up of training in relaxation as a behavioral self-management skill. *Behavior Therapy*, 1975, *6*, 419–420.

Sherman, A. R., & Plummer, I. L. Training in relaxation as a behavioral self-management skill: An exploratory investigation. *Behavior Therapy*, 1973, *4*, 543–550.

Siegel, L. J., & Peterson, L. Stress reduction in young dental patients through coping skills and sensory information. *Journal of Consulting and Clinical Psychology*, 1980, *48*, 785–787.

Snyder, A. L., & Deffenbacher, J. L. Comparison of relaxation as self-control and systematic desensitization in the treatment of test anxiety. *Journal of Consulting and Clinical Psychology*, 1977, *45*, 1202–1203.

Spiegler, M. D., Cooley, E. J., Marshall, G. J., Prince, H. T., Puckett, S. P., & Skenazy, J. A. A self-control versus a counterconditioning paradigm for systematic desensitization: An experimental comparison. *Journal of Counseling Psychology*, 1976, *23*, 83–86.

Spielberger, C. D. Theory and research on anxiety. In C. D. Spielberger (Ed.), *Anxiety and behavior*. New York: Academic Press, 1966.

Suinn, R. M. Treatment of phobias. In G. A. Harris (Ed.), *The group treatment of human problems*. New York: Grune & Stratton, 1977. (a)

Suinn, R. M. *Manual for Anxiety Management Training (AMT)*. Fort Collins, CO: Rocky Mountain Behavioral Science Institute, 1977. (b)

Suinn, R. M., & Bloom, L. J. Anxiety management training for Type A persons. *Journal of Behavioral Medicine*, 1978, *1*, 25–35.

Suinn, R. M., & Richardson, F. Anxiety management training: A nonspecific behavior therapy program for anxiety control. *Behavior Therapy*, 1971, *2*, 498–510.

Thoresen, C. E., & Mahoney, M. J. *Behavioral self-control*. New York: Holt, Rinehart, & Winston, 1974.

Weissberg, M. A comparison of direct and vicarious treatments of speech anxiety: Desensitization, desensitization with coping imagery, and cognitive modification. *Behavior Therapy*, 1977, *8*, 606–620.

Wine, J. D. Cognitive-attentional theory of test anxiety. In I. G. Sarason (Ed.), *Test anxiety: Theory, research, and applications*. Hillsdale, N.J.: Lawrence Erlbaum, 1980.

Wolpe, J. *The practice of behavior therapy*. (2nd ed.) New York: Pergamon Press, 1973.

Ziesset, R. M. Desensitization and relaxation in the modification of psychiatric patients' interview behavior. *Journal of Abnormal Psychology*, 1968, *73*, 18–24.

Zemore, R. Systematic desensitization as a method of teaching a general anxiety-reducing skill. *Journal of Consulting and Clinical Psychology*, 1975, *43*, 157–161.

13

Self-Management of Addictive Behaviors

G. Alan Marlatt and George A. Parks

This chapter presents a sociopsychological approach to the self-management of addictive behaviors. The material in the chapter is intended to provide a general discussion of self-control as it relates to addictive behaviors, with an emphasis on problem drinking (alcoholism) as a representative example. It is assumed here that addictive behaviors represent learned habits which are developed and maintained on the basis of a set of similar processes that apply across a variety of problems such as alcoholism, heroin addiction, smoking, overeating, workaholism, compulsive gambling, and some types of interpersonal relationships.

In the initial section of the chapter, addictive behaviors are analyzed from a self-control perspective that focuses on the paradoxical issue of "control" as applied to the development and treatment of addictive behaviors. The self-control model is contrasted with the disease model of addiction along a number of dimensions influencing decisions about the nature of addiction, the role of the client in treatment, and the goals of therapy. Finally, the introductory section proposes a set of criteria for the "ideal" self-control program for the treatment of addictive behaviors. This program is an integration of principles derived from learning theory, cognitive psychology, and experimental social psychology.

The treatment section of the chapter begins with a brief description of a cognitive-behavioral analysis of the process of initiation and maintenance of an addictive behavior cycle. The treatment of problem drinking is used as an illustration of the intervention program described, although the model has also been applied to other addictive behaviors such as smoking, over-eating, and compulsive gambling. The description of the treatment program begins with a general approach to clients that emphasizes self-management and active involvement in treatment. This orientation to treatment evolves into an individualized program of strategies tailor-made for a particular client. The treatment approach presented places great emphasis on the maintenance of behavior change or *relapse prevention* as well as on initial changes in behavior. Self-control interventions used in treatment are divided into two-classes. First, *specific* procedures are implemented to assess parameters of the addictive behavior, such as frequency, duration, antecedents, and situational patterning, and to determine the need for specific techniques such as skills training, stress management, and cognitive restructuring. The second class of self-control interventions includes *global* procedures designed to modify events that often set the stage for addictive behaviors such as an unbalanced lifestyle and covert psychological processes that act to "set up" a relapse. The overall goal of treatment is to teach the client a set of self-control skills which will enable choice and personal control over whether the client desires to abstain from an addictive behavior or to change an addictive behavior pattern to one of self-managed moderation.

The chapter ends with a brief discussion of the limitations and contraindications for the self-control approach to the treatment of addictive behaviors presented. Issues of ethics and training are also addressed in this final section. Much of the material presented in this chapter is drawn from a forthcoming book entitled *Relapse Prevention* (Marlatt & Gordon, in press); additional sources for this material include recent publications by Marlatt (Note 1); Marlatt and Gordon (1980), and Cummings, Gordon, and Marlatt (1980).

SELF-MANAGEMENT OF ADDICTIVE BEHAVIORS: BASIC ISSUES

Addictions and the Paradox of Self-Control

We are currently approaching a crossroads in our approach to the understanding and treatment of addictive behavior problems. Until recently, the primary approach has emphasized the importance of physical parameters of addiction with a focus on the drug or substance and its pharmacological effects. Implicit in this approach is the assumption that the "addict" cannot voluntarily control his or her drug-taking behavior due to the overpowering influence of internal forces such as compulsions, cravings, or irresistible urges. The fact that contemporary society embraces this view is reflected in dictionary definitions of addiction. *Webster's New Collegiate Dictionary*, for example, defines addiction as the "compulsive physiological need for a habit-forming drug"; a compulsion itself is defined as "the state of being compelled" or "an irresistible impulse to perform an irrational act." The basic thrust of these definitions is clear: the "addict" cannot control his or her addictive behavior.

Is it really the case that the addict is incapable of exercising control over the problem behavior? At first glance, behaviors traditionally defined as addictive appear to be under voluntary control. After all, aren't behaviors such as drinking, eating, smoking, or the use of other drugs all activities that we choose either to engage in or to refrain from performing? Viewed from the traditional perspective, excessive use of any substance (or excessive performance of any activity leading to immediate gratification) is seen as a problem in "impulse control" in which the individual is apparently lacking in "willpower" and is thereby unable to exercise appropriate control over the behavior. This line of thinking culminated in the "moral model" of addictive behavior, a view that dominated conceptions of addiction in the early decades of this century. An addict was perceived as someone who lacked the moral fiber to resist temptation. In the case of alcoholism, for example, society came to label the "drunk" as a person lacking in moral character or strength of will, someone who was unable to resist the temptation to give in to the evil spirits of alcohol. The moral condemnation of alcoholism reached its height in this country with the unsuccessful experiment with prohibition.

Following the failure of the moral approach, a less judgmental approach to addiction began to surface in the form of the "disease model." Addictive behaviors were viewed as a form of physical dependency and attention was focused on the physiological effects of drug use as the underlying cause of addiction. The definition of alcoholism as a disease exemplifies this approach. First introduced in the late 1940s by E. M. Jellinek and his associates at the Yale Center for Alcohol Studies (see Jellinek, 1960), this position was given sanction in 1956, when the American Medical Association officially declared alcoholism a disease. Certainly the disease concept of alcoholism offers a number of advantages over the moral model that preceded it. By attempting to remove the moral stigma associated with drinking problems, the diagnosis of alcoholism as a disease encouraged many individuals to seek medical treatment for their disorder. Perhaps one of the main reasons why the disease model led to increased numbers of individuals seeking help or assistance for their drinking problems is that this approach absolves the alcoholic from accepting personal responsibility for his or her condition. Alcoholics were told, in essence, that they were suffering from a disease similar to other diseases, such as diabetes. Is a diabetic to blame for his or her condition? No? Then neither is the alcoholic. The disease process is assumed to be latent even before the alcoholic takes the first drink (due to genetic predisposition) and to remain active (although temporarily in remission) even if the reformed alcoholic has not taken a drink in years.

There is a major paradox in the disease model of addictive behavior. The paradox involves the central concept of *control* and how it is defined within the model. On the one hand, the disease model assumes that the alcoholic is unable to exert control over drinking behavior because of the compelling influence of internal physiological factors which underlie the addiction. On the other hand, the alcoholic is told that the only way to curb the problem is to refrain from drinking, to maintain total abstinence for an indefinite period. Surely the intention or commitment to abstain is in itself a form of control. On this basis, an individual can only exercise control while maintaining total abstinence from drinking; to relapse is to *lose* control. the disease model thereby produces a dichotomous restriction on the possible range of treatment outcomes: one is either abstinent — exerting control, or relapsed — losing control. Thus, even though the etiology or cause of alcoholism is described as a disease process which is beyond the control or responsibility of the victim, the major *treatment* mode takes the form of a moral commandment: Thou shalt not drink!

It is ironic that the major strength of the disease model, which is that it absolves the addict of personal responsibility for the problem behavior, may also be its major shortcoming. If alcoholics come to view their drinking as a disease or physiological addiction, they will be prone to assume the passive role of a "victim" whenever they engage in drinking behavior which is a symptom of their disease. The disease model may be successful insofar as it convinces the alcoholic that he or she is sick, suffering from a medically recognized illness, and no longer capable of drinking without losing control. If the alcoholic accepts this diagnosis and agrees to never take another drink, *and doesn't*, all is well. Unfortunately, the ability to maintain total abstinence from alcohol is a rare outcome in the alcoholism-treatment field. A recent comprehensive study conducted by the Rand Corporation evaluated the outcome of over 700 alcoholic patients following their participation in a variety of typical treatment programs. It was found that less than 10 percent of the patients were able to maintain abstinence over a period of 2 years following discharge from the treatment program (Armor, Polich, & Stambul, 1978). These data demonstrate that *relapse* is the most common outcome of alcoholism treatment.

Relapse is the turning point where the disease model is likely to backfire. If an alcoholic has accepted the belief that it is impossible to control his or her drinking (as embodied in the Alcoholics Anonymous slogan that one is always "one drink away from a drunk"), then even a single "slip" may precipitate a total, uncontrolled relapse. Since drinking under these circumstances is equated with the occurrence of a symptom signifying the re-emergence of the disease, one is likely to feel powerless to control this behavior as one would feel powerless with any other symptom of disease (e.g., a fever or convulsion). The belief in the inevitability of loss-of-control drinking as a pathognomonic symptom of alcoholism is a strongly held dogma by adherents of the disease model and underlies much of the furor that surrounds the mention of "controlled drinking" as an alternative treatment goal to abstinence in the treatment of alcoholism (see Pattison, Sobell, & Sobell, 1977 for a more extensive discussion of this issue).

Addictions as Learned Behaviors

In recent years, an alternative approach to understanding addictive behavior problems has received increased attention. Derived from the principles of learning theory, cognitive psychology, and experimental social psychology, the self-control model based on social learning theory makes a number of assumptions that differ markedly from the disease model. From the social learning perspective, problem drinking is categorized as but one example of a general class of actions labeled addictive behaviors, including such other behaviors as smoking, substance abuse, overeating, and compulsive gambling. In terms of frequency of occurrence, addictive behaviors are viewed along a continuum rather than being defined in terms of a dichotomous all-or-none scale of abstinence versus excessive behavior. *All* points along this continuum of frequency of occurrence, from very infrequent to "normal" to excessive use, are assumed to be governed by similar processes of learning.

Addictive behaviors are viewed as overlearned *habits* that can be analyzed and modified in the same manner as other habits. This position does not imply that continued excessive involvement in an addictive behavior is free from any negative physical consequences, however. On the contrary, it is fully recognized by adherents of the social learning approach that excessive performance of an addictive behavior can lead to the development of disease states (e.g., cirrhosis of the liver in alcoholics, lung cancer in smokers, etc.). The fact that a disease state is the product of a long-term addictive behavior cycle does not necessarily imply that the behavior itself is a disease or that it is caused by an underlying physiological disorder. Does continual, excessive use of tobacco (along with high relapse rates among those who try to quit) constitute a disease in and of itself? It is informative to direct this same question to the excessive, habitual use of alcohol.

Those who subscribe to the social learning model are particularly interested in studying the *determinants* of addictive behavior, including situational and environmental antecedents, beliefs and expectations, and the individual's past learning history or prior experiences with the substance or activity. In addition, there is an equal interest in discovering the *consequences* of these behaviors, so as to better understand both the reinforcing effects that may contribute to increased use and the negative consequences that may serve to inhibit the behavior. In addition to the effects of the drug or activity itself, attention is paid to the social and interpersonal reactions experienced by the individual before, during, and after an addictive behavior is performed. Social factors are involved both in the initial learning of an addictive behavior and in the subsequent performance of the activity once the habit has become firmly established.

One of the central underlying assumptions of the self-control model, as mentioned earlier, is that addictive behaviors consist of overlearned, maladaptive habit patterns. These habit patterns can also be thought of as *indulgent behaviors*, since they refer to behaviors which are usually followed by some form of immediate gratification (the "high" state of pleasure or reduction in tension or arousal). In many instances, these behaviors are performed in situations perceived as stressful in some way (for example, drinking in an attempt to reduce social anxiety, smoking as a means of "calming the nerves," overeating when feeling lonely or bored, etc.). To the extent that these activities are performed during or prior to stressful or unpleasant situations ("high-risk" situations), they represent *maladaptive coping mechanisms*. Habitual indulgent behaviors are maladaptive to the extent that they lead to delayed negative consequences in terms of the individuals health, social status, and self-esteem. Performance of these activities per se is not necessarily maladaptive providing they are engaged in on an occasional basis, in moderation, and by individuals who choose to do so with a full awareness of the long-term consequences. Responsible moderate use of certain drugs, for example, is acceptable as long as the behavior does not become a habit or addictive behavior cycle (frequent, repetitive use with minimal awareness of the activity and its long term consequences).

Habitual behaviors characterized by immediate gratification and delayed negative consequences have been classified as "social traps" (Platt, 1973) and as "impulsive" behaviors (Ainslie, 1975). These behaviors are not limited to the use of drugs and other substances, since they include non-drug activities such as compulsive gambling, compulsive working ("workaholism"), certain sexual problems (e.g., exhibitionism), and some forms of interpersonal relationships such as "addictive" love (Peele, 1975). It is important to note that the source of the compulsion is often thought to be rooted in internal body chemistry, especially experiences like the "physical" craving for the effects of a particular drug. An overemphasis on internal physiological factors neglects the possibility that these behaviors are strongly influenced by the individual's *expectation* or anticipation of the desired effects of the activity. Recent research suggests that cognitive factors such as expectation and attribution play a more influential role in determining drug use than the pharmacological or physical effects of the drug itself (see Marlatt & Rohsenow, 1980). The major implication of this research is that cognitive processes such as expectation are learned and thereby more open to modification and change than are underlying physiological processes.

One final point needs to be discussed concerning the self-control of addictive behaviors. Some individuals have argued that to accept the fact that addictive behaviors are learned is equivalent to saying that an addicted individual is *personally responsible* for his or her condition (cf. Sontag, 1978). Viewed from this perspective, the social learning account represents a regression to the earlier moral model of addiction. This argument is based on the false assumption that individuals are responsible for their past learning experiences; that they "choose" to engage in these activities perhaps because of some lack of willpower or because of moral weakness. The fact is that an individual who acquires a maladaptive habit is no more "responsible" for this behavior than one of Pavlov's conditioned dogs would be responsible for salivating at the sound of a ringing bell. However, even though an individual's particular habit has been shaped and determined by past learning experiences (for which he or she is not to be held entirely responsible), the process of *change* does involve the active participation and responsibility of the person involved. Through involvement in a self-control program in which the individual acquires new skills and cognitive strategies, habits can be transformed into behaviors that are under the regulation of high mental processes, involving awareness and responsible decision making. As the individual undergoes a process of deconditioning, reeducation, and skills acquisition, he or she can begin to accept greater responsibility for the behavior. This is the essence of the self-control or self-management approach: one learns how to exercise control over one's behavior and its consequences.

Self-Control and the Disease Model: Alternative Approaches to the Treatment of Addictive Behaviors

As a means of summarizing the material presented thus far, let us review the major differences between the self-control model and the more traditional disease approach to the treatment of addictive behaviors. The differences are outlined in figure 13.1. Each of the major points will be discussed briefly.

Locus of control. The essence of the self-control model is that the individual moves from a position of being the "client," under the direction of a therapist, to a position in which the person becomes more able to assume responsibility for the process of change. It may be the case that a preference

Topic	Self-control Model	Disease Model
Locus of Control	• Person is capable of self-control	• Person is a victim of forces beyond one's control
Treatment Goal	• Choice of goals: abstinence or moderation	• Abstinence is the only goal
Treatment Philosophy	• Fosters detachment of self from behavior • Educational approach	• Equates self with behavior • Medical/disease approach
Treatment Procedures	• Teaching behavioral coping skills • Cognitive restructuring	• Confrontation & conversion • Group support • Cognitive dogma
General Approach to Addictions	• Search for commonalities across addictive behaviors • Addiction is based on maladaptive habits	• Each addiction is unique • Addiction is based on physiological processes
Examples	• Cognitive-behavioral therapy (outpatient) • Self-control programs • Controlled drinking programs	• Hospital treatment programs (inpatient) • Aversion treatment • AA + Synanon

Fig. 13.1. Alternative Approaches to the Treatment of Addictive Behaviors.

for a more active role in treatment is associated with an internal locus of control personality orientation (Lefcourt, 1976; Phares, 1976). The disease model, on the other hand, views the individual as a victim of forces beyond one's personal control. The addition is viewed as a physical illness or disease brought about by some biochemical, genetic, or metabolic disorder; forces that are not usually considered to be subject to the voluntary control of the individual. A preference for a more passive role in the treatment process may reflect an external locus-of-control orientation in which the individual perceives behavior as being under the regulation of uncontrollable inner impulses, external forces, or outside circumstances.

Treatment goal. The disease model strongly advocates abstinence as the only acceptable treatment goal. In the traditional alcoholism field, for example, total abstinence is considered as an essential step in the recovery process. Commitment to abstinence is not considered a cure, however, since any return to drinking is assumed to trigger the latent disease. In contrast with this view, the self-control model favors a more individualized selection of treatment goals ranging from abstinence to controlled or moderate use. One key implication of the self-control approach is that addictive behaviors are not always successfully treated by insistence upon excessive restraints over these behaviors. The emphasis in the disease model on the dichotomy of abstinence and indulgence (absolute control versus loss of control) tends to reinforce the oscillation of addictive behaviors from one extreme to the other by forcing the individual to adopt one or the other of these extreme roles. From the self-control perspective, there is an alternative "middle way" or position of balance between total restraint and total indulgence; that is, moderation based on awareness, skills, and responsible choice.

Treatment philosophy. The traditional disease model often tends to equate the person with his or her disorder: your excessive drinking indicates that you are an *alcoholic*, or your use of heroin indicates that you are a dope *addict*. It is as though the alcoholic is required to pin a Scarlet Letter on his or her chest for everyone to see, a large letter "A" for Alcoholic. Adherents of the self-control approach take issue with the notion that a person's *behavior* (e.g., excessive drinking) should be taken as an indication of the individual's entire *identity*. We don't label a person who has cancer as a "canceric." Why should we then label a person who drinks to excess as an "alcohol-ic?" In the self-control model, every attempt is made to foster a sense of detachment between the problem behavior and the person's identity or self-concept. This detachment facilitates an objective, nonevaluative approach to treatment in which the client is trained to become his or her own personal scientist-therapist using objective observation of the target behavior as the essential "data" to work with in treatment (Mahoney, 1977). The emphasis on social learning principles as the basis of modification of problem behavior illustrates the *educational approach* of the self-control model.

Treatment procedures. As should be evident from the foregoing material, the hallmark of the self-control approach to treatment is a combination of behavioral coping skills and cognitive restructuring techniques. It is assumed that the client will eventually be able to perform newly acquired skills and attitudes without the assistance of external aids such as the continued availability of the therapist or some other suppport group (e.g., Alcoholics Anonymous). In contrast, the traditional approach often attempts to change the basic personal orientation or belief system of the "addict" through a combination of confrontation procedures ("You must admit that you are an alcoholic before we can help you!") and/or conversion techniques ("Surrender your own sense of control, accept the guidance and control of a higher power!"). In some groups such as AA, the "higher power" is religious or spiritual in nature; in other groups, such as Synanon and certain therapeutic communities for addicts, the power is vested in the organizational hierarchy of the group itself. Once the required behavior change has occurred (e.g., a commitment to abstinence, admitting one is an "alcoholic"), it is then reinforced by conformity pressures from a peer group. Since members of such groups provide support and encouragement for continued adherence to the behavioral mandates and philosophy of the organization, any transgression of the rules is met with strict punishment and peer rejection. An attempt is often made in such groups to regulate members' behavior by the use of simple slogans, prophecies, and other "cognitive dogma" (e.g., "You are always only one drink away from a drunk," "drink, drank, *drunk*," etc.).

General approach to addictions. In the self-control approach, an attempt is made to search for *commonalities* across various addictive behaviors. Since addictive behavior problems are assumed to be acquired on the basis of learning maladaptive behavior patterns, there is general agreement among proponents of this model that common factors are involved in the acquisition and maintenance of these behaviors. The present attempt to develop a common model of addictive behaviors is consistent with the search for commonalities. In contrast, the disease model tends to favor the view that each addiction should be treated as a unique and separate disorder. The tendency to treat each addictive behavior problem as a unique entity is reflected in current American administrative and political policy which encourages the separation and independence of research and treatment programs with different addiction problems. The establishment of separate national institutes for alcoholism (National Institute on Alcohol Abuse and Alcoholism) and for drug addiction (National Institute on Drug Abuse) is an example of this policy, as is the generally accepted tradition of assigning clients with alcohol, drug abuse, smoking, and weight-control problems to different types of treatment programs for each "addiction."

From the above discussion, it is clear that the self-control and disease models differ in a number of fundamental ways. The two models hold contrasting basic assumptions about the etiology and treatment of addictive behavior problems on a number of dimensions. Does this mean that one theory is more "correct" than the other, or that the self-control model is beginning to replace the traditional medical approach as the beginning of a paradigm shift (Kuhn, 1970) in our basic understanding of addiction? Not necessarily. What seems to be more likely is that we are approaching a new synthesis of behavioral, psychological, and physiological factors that will give us a broader and more comprehensive perspective on the basic nature of addictive behaviors and how to modify them. What does seem clear is that we are entering a new era in our thinking about addiction, one that is characterized by a fresh empirical approach that dares to challenge the influence of untested myths and the rhetoric of dogma which have held a tight grip on the addictions field for the past several decades.

The preceding analysis may appear to exaggerate the differences between the self-control and disease models, suggesting that the self-control approach focuses exclusively on psychological factors and that the disease approach focuses entirely on physiological processes. In reality, however, the distinctions between the two models are not so clearly cut. Although the differences between the two approaches have been stressed in this discussion for expositional reasons, it would be an oversimplification to conclude that there are no areas of overlap or interaction involved. In most addictive behaviors, there is a significant interaction between the psychological state of the individual (expectations, attributions, individual differences in personality, etc.) and the pharmacological or physiological effects of the drug or activity. In the area of alcohol use, for example, the effects of alcohol itself (e.g., the depressive effects on central nervous system activity) influence both the individual's attributions and subsequent expectations concerning alcohol and its effects (cf., Maisto, Connors, & Sachs, 1981). The self-control and disease models do differ, however, in terms of the relative emphasis each model places on both the major determinant or "cause" of addiction and the recommended approach to treatment. Self-control theorists place primary emphasis on cognitive-behavioral variables, in contrast with proponents of the disease model who stress the importance of biological factors.

Some Criteria for the "Ideal" Self-Control Treatment Program

What elements comprise an ideal self-control program for the initiation and maintenance of behavior change with addictive behavior problems? Our cognitive-behavioral approach to self-control suggests that a combination of selected components from both the behavioral and cognitive domains will yield the most powerful intervention program. Although research on the effectiveness of various combinations of procedures is still in the early stages of development, the following characteristics emerge.

The ideal self-control program should prove itself to be effective in maintaining behavior change for clinically significant periods of time following initial treatment (as demonstrated by long-term follow-up) compared to the best available alternative programs.

The ideal program should enhance and maintain an individual's compliance and adherence to program requirements such as the continuation of required techniques such as record-keeping, relaxation training, and rehearsal of new skills.

The ideal program should consist of a mixture of both specific behavioral techniques (e.g., skill training, exercise, etc.) and cognitive intervention procedures (e.g., cognitive restructuring, increased attention to covert ideation such as rationalization and denial, use of coping imagery, etc.).

In addition to teaching cognitive strategies and behavioral coping skills, the ideal program should also facilitate the development of motivation and decision-making skills as applied to ongoing changes that occur during the maintenance phase of therapy.

To increase overall compliance and effectiveness, the ideal program should include a balance of "right brain" and "left brain" intervention components. Recent work on cerebral hemisphere specialization (Ornstein, 1977) suggests that the left and right hemispheres are associated with different mental operations: the left hemisphere (dominant in most right-handed people) is believed to be the center for linear thought processes such as verbalization and mathematical and logical thinking, whereas the right or nondominant hemisphere is more associated with nonverbal functions such as imagery, spatial ability, and intuition. One of the central precepts of the self-control model to be presented is that a combination of both verbal and nonverbal (imagery) procedures provides the best relapse prevention. Although the optimum sequencing of verbal and nonverbal materials has yet to be determined empirically, the most effective strategy may be to include nonverbal material as a means of illustrating (or providing imagery for) each verbal principle as it arises in the program.

The ideal program should replace maladaptive habit patterns with alternative behaviors and skills with an emphasis on substitute activities that provide the individual with at least some of the reinforcing consequences (gratification) associated with the old habit pattern. For example, a negative addiction may be replaced with a positive one, especially if engaging in the latter behavior also produces a subjective "high" or altered state of consciousness (as appears to be the case for some people who meditate or exercise frequently).

The ideal program should enable the individual to cope effectively with new problem situations as they arise to reduce the probability of relapse. To do this, an effective self-control program should have built-in generalization components designed to teach the client to identify and cope with problems that may not have been specifically addressed in the initial phase of treatment. Training in general problem solving, effective decision making, communication skills, and assertion training are some of the more general approaches that can be used to prevent relapse. In addition to these general coping behaviors, effective use of lifestyle engineering and stress management skills may increase the individual's capacity and energy to cope with new or unanticipated problem situations.

In addition to increasing generalization effects in new problem situations, the ideal self-control program should also teach the client new and adaptive ways of dealing with failure experiences. An attempt should be made to teach the individual that setbacks can be viewed, not as failures, but as mistakes that can provide valuable information which can then be used to develop more effective coping strategies for the future. A single mistake does not mean that treatment has failed unless the client is led to believe that this is the case. As we shall see, an essential component of the self-control model is a cognitive restructuring strategy to prevent the occurrence of a single "slip" (e.g., the first drink or cigarette after a period of abstinence) from snowballing into a total relapse. Since such "slips" occur as a typical outcome of most treatment programs, the self-control model presented in the next section makes *relapse prevention* its central focus of treatment.

The ideal program should attempt to increase the client's sense of self-efficacy in specific problem situations. As defined by Bandura (1977), self-efficacy refers to an expectancy of how effectively one will be able to cope with a forthcoming problem situation. Unlike the concept of self-esteem, referring to a more global or trans-situational sense of well-being or confidence in self, self-efficacy refers to expectations of performance capacity in specific situations. The relapse prevention self-control model recommends a series of efficacy-enhancement procedures to increase the client's sense of perceived control in high risk situations.

Finally, the ideal self-control program should make use of client support systems to enhance treatment generalization effects. Every attempt should be made to enlist the cooperative support of people who are likely to have contact with the client. Members of the client's family or individuals in the client's work place can often be recruited to provide support and encouragement. Recent research on the use of spouses and other family members as providers of support for clients with addictive behavior problems shows considerable promise (e.g., Brownell, Heckerman, Westlake, Hayes, & Monti, 1978; McCrady, Paolino, Longabaugh, & Rossi, 1979). In addition, clients with similar problems who share a common theoretical or philosophical orientation to addictive behaviors can be encouraged to get together in self-help groups where members join to provide support and encouragement in their collective efforts to maintain charge.

A basic assumption that underlies the foregoing points needs to be emphasized. We are assuming that the ideal self-control program for addictive behavior problems involves three major stages. The first stage, the *readiness* component, involves those factors that influence the client's willingness or readiness to change. Motivational factors, personal history, and current environmental forces combine in this stage to influence the client's initial commitment to change. In the second stage, the *intervention* component, the client either works alone or under the supervision of a therapist to execute changes in the target behavior (e.g., to become abstinent or to moderate use). The application of specific treatment or self-help techniques and strategies occurs in this stage, subject to the mediating influence of the individual's compliance and adherence to the requirements of the change program. The intervention stage itself can be broken down into two separate, although often overlapping, phases: the "unlearning" of old maladaptive habit patterns and the acquisition of new skills and cognitions. Client compliance with the demands of treatment is particularly important at this juncture, because of the conflict between the lure of the old familiar coping response (usually as "easy as falling off a log") and the difficulties of learning a new way of coping with stress and high-risk situations. In the third stage, the *maintenance* component, the individual who has mastered the new skills during the intervention stage will be able to strengthen these abilities through repeated practice and gain increased mastery as a result. In addition, the newly acquired skills will be reinforced and strengthened by the impact of both external events (improved health and stamina, increased social approval, etc.) and internal processes (self-reinforcement and increased self-efficacy). If the gains of the intervention stage are not consolidated during the maintenance stage for any reasons, it may be necessary to introduce additional intervention procedures in the form of booster sessions. For a comprehensive discussion of these issues, the reader is referred to a recent volume of this general topic area (Karoly & Steffen, 1980).

THE ASSESSMENT AND TREATMENT OF ADDICTIVE BEHAVIORS: FOCUS ON RELAPSE

In the self-control model of relapse prevention to be presented in the following sections, we are defining *relapse* as any discrete violation of a self-imposed rule or set of rules governing the rate or pattern of a selected target behavior. The criterion of abstinence, the most stringent rule one can adopt in this regard, is violated by a single occurrence of the target behavior. From this absolute perspective, a single slip constitutes a relapse (one cannot be a "little bit" nonabstinent just as one cannot be a "little bit" pregnant). Although violation of the abstinence rule is the primary form of relapse we have studied in our research, other forms of relapse would also be included within the above definition. Violation of rules governing caloric intake for someone on a strict diet would also constitute a relapse, as would the exceeding of alcohol consumption limits imposed in a controlled drinking program. Within this general definition of relapse, we are making the distinction between the first violation of the rules (the initial *lapse*) and the subsequent *secondary* effects in which the behavior may increase in the direction of the original pretreatment baseline level (a full-blown *relapse* — e.g., when the first drink is followed by a binge or uncontrolled drinking).

Although the following sections present relapse prevention as the focus of treatment, the treatment model is equally applicable to initial attempts to change the pattern of an addictive behavior cycle. Indeed, once the decision to enter treatment has been made, the entire treatment process can be viewed as an experiment in developing and maintaining self-imposed rules governing the rate and pattern of a target behavior.

The Relapse Model: An Overview of Immediate Determinants and Reactions

In the material to follow, we will present an overview of the relapse process focusing on the immediate determinants (precipitating circumstances) and subsequent reactions to the first lapse following a period of abstinence or strictly controlled use. An important constraint in the model is that it applies only to those cases in which the person has made a *voluntary* choice or decision to change; the implications of the theory for enforced or involuntary abstinence have yet to be determined. It may be possible, of course, to set voluntary change as the initial goal of therapy for clients who are otherwise unwilling to undergo treatment (Kanfer & Grimm, 1980; Karoly, 1980). Commitment or readiness to change is often a key problem area in working with addictive behavior problems. All too often, clients make a sudden decision to change their behavior based on external demands or a reaction to guilt or remorse over a recent binge or period of prolonged abuse. The therapist must take special care to ascertain all of the factors involved in a client's motivation to change.

In the following overview, only the highlights of the model are presented, since further details are presented elsewhere; background research and theory leading to the development of this model can be found in Cummings, Gordon, and Marlatt (1980), Marlatt (1978, 1979), and Marlatt and Gordon (1980). A schematic representation of the relapse model is presented in figure 13.2.

To begin, we are assuming that the individual experiences a sense of *perceived control* while maintaining abstinence (or complying with other rules governing the target behavior). The behavior is "under control" so long as it does not occur during this period; the longer the period of suc-

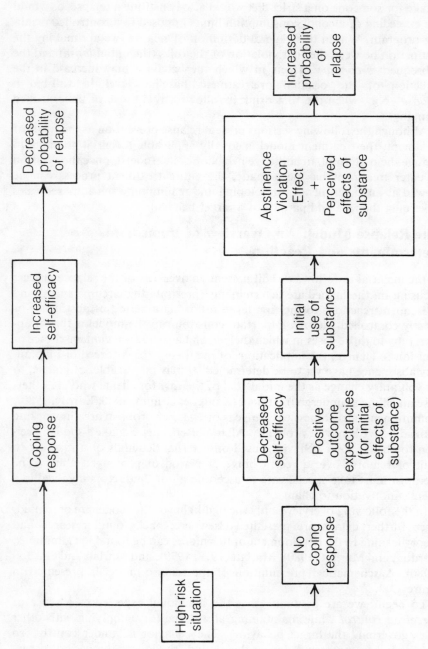

Fig. 13.2. Cognitive-Behavioral Model of the Relapse Process.

cessful abstinence, the greater the individual's perception of self control. This perceived control will continue until the person encounters a *high-risk situation*. A high-risk situation is defined broadly as any situation which poses a threat to the individual's sense of control and increases the risk of potential relapse. In a recent analysis of 311 initial-relapse episodes obtained from clients with a variety of problem behaviors (problem drinking, smoking, heroin addiction, compulsive gambling, and overeating), we identified three primary high-risk situations that were associated with almost three quarters of all the relapses reported (Cummings, Gordon, & Marlatt, 1980). A listing of high-risk situations adapted from the latter source is presented in table 13.1. A description of the three categories associated with the highest relapse rates follows. A complete description of all categories, along with scoring rules, is presented in Marlatt and Gordon (1980).

Negative emotional states. In these situations (35 percent of all relapses in the sample), the individual is experiencing a negative (or unpleasant) emotional state, mood or feeling such as frustration, anger, anxiety, depression, or boredom prior to or at the time the first lapse occurs. For example, a smoker in the sample gave the following description of a relapse episode:

> It had been raining continually all week. Saturday I walked down to the basement to do laundry and I found the basement filled with a good three inches of water. To make things worse, as I went to turn on the light to see the extent of the damage, I got shocked from the light switch. Later that same day, I was feeling real low and knew I had to have a cigarette after my neighbor, who is a contractor, assessed the damage at over $4,000. I went to the store and bought a pack.

In our scoring system, this category is classified under a major subdivision called *intrapersonal determinants*, which includes all situations that are primarily associated with intrapersonal factors (within the individual) and/or reactions to nonpersonal environmental events. Situations involving another person or group of individuals who are significantly involved in the relapse episode are grouped under the second major subdivision, *interpersonal determinants*. The two following categories both fall within this latter subdivision.

Interpersonal conflict. These situations (16 percent of the relapses) involve an ongoing or relatively recent conflict associated with any interpersonal relationship, such as marriage, friendship, family members, or employer-employee relations. Arguments and interpersonal confrontations occur frequently in this category. A gambler who had been abstaining from betting on the horses described his relapse in the following terms: "I came home late from a horrible day on the road and I hadn't stepped in the house five

Table 13.1. Analysis of Relapse Situations with Alcoholics, Smokers, Heroin Addicts, Compulsive Gamblers, and Dieters

RELAPSE SITUATION	Alcoholics (N=70)	Smokers (N=64)	Heroin Addicts (N=129)	Gamblers (N=29)	Overeaters (N=29)	TOTAL (N=311)
Intrapersonal Determinants						
Negative Emotional States	38%	37%	19%	47%	33%	35%
Negative Physical States	3	2	9	–	–	3
Positive Emotional States	–	6	10	–	3	4
Testing Personal Control	9	–	2	16	–	5
Urges and Temptations	11	5	5	16	10	9
TOTAL	61%	50%	45%	79%	46%	56%
Interpersonal Determinants						
Interpersonal Conflict	18%	15%	14%	16%	14%	16%
Social Pressure	18	32	36	5	10	20
Positive Emotional States	3	3	5	–	28	8
TOTAL	39%	50%	55%	21%	52%	44%

Source: Adapted from C. Cummings, J. R. Gordon, and G. A. Marlatt, Relapse: Strategies of prevention and prediction, in *The addictive behaviors*, ed. W. R. Miller (Oxford, England: Pergamon Press, 1980).

minutes before my wife started accusing me of gambling on the horses. Racetrack, hell! I told her if she didn't believe me, I'd give her a real reason for divorce. That night I spent $450 at the Longacres track."

Social pressure. In these situations (20 percent of the sample), the individual is responding to the influence of another person or group of people who exert pressure on the individual to engage in the taboo behavior. Social pressure may either be *direct* (direct interpersonal contact with verbal persuasion) or *indirect* (e.g., being in the presence of others who are engaging in the same target behavior, even though no direct pressure is involved). Here is an example of direct social pressure given by a formerly abstinent problem drinker in our sample: "I went to my boss's house for a surprise birthday dinner for him. I got there late, and as I came into the living room everyone had a drink in hand. I froze when my boss's wife asked me what I was drinking. Without thinking, I said, 'J & B on the rocks.'"

In our analyses of relapse episodes to date (Cummings, Gordon, & Marlatt, 1980; Marlatt & Gordon, 1980), we have found that there are *more similarities than differences* in relapse categories across the various addictive behaviors we studied. These same three high-risk situations are frequently found to be associated with relapse, regardless of the particular problem involved (problem drinking, smoking, gambling, heroin use, or overeating). This pattern of findings lends support to our hypothesis that there is a common mechanism underlying the relapse process across different addictive behaviors.

The fact that we have found commonalities in relapse episodes across a variety of addictive behaviors lends support to the notion that stressful high-risk situations frequently are involved as precipitants of relapse. Although information on the relapse episode is by necessity gathered after the event has occurred (relapses cannot be manipulated experimentally for obvious ethical reasons), the commonalities we have uncovered in our analyses with hundreds of subjects argues against the possibility that individuals are providing us with socially desirable "excuses" or otherwise spurious accounts of their relapse episodes. We make every attempt to minimize the negative aspects of recidivism in our interviews and other contact with subjects, in order to reduce the influence of social desirability as a potential source of bias. The validity of the relapse model presented here can, however, be tested in part by conducting treatment outcome studies that embody the basic elements of the theoretical model. The results of relapse prevention as an approach to treatment will be discussed later in this chapter.

If the individual is able to execute an effective coping response in the high-risk situation (e.g., is assertive in counteracting social pressures), the probability of relapse decreases significantly. The individual who copes successfully with the situation is likely to experience a sense of mastery or perception of control. Successful mastery of one problematic situation is often associated with an expectation of being able to cope successfully with the next challenging event. The expectancy of being able to cope with successive high-risk situations as they develop is closely associated with Bandura's notion of *self-efficacy* (Bandura, 1977b), defined as the individual's expectation concerning the capacity to cope with an impending situation or task. A feeling of confidence in one's abilities to cope effectively with a high-risk situation is associated with an increased perception of self-efficacy, a kind of "I know I can handle it" feeling. As the duration of the abstinence (or period of controlled use) increases, and the individual is able to cope effectively with more and more high-risk situations, perception of control increases in a cumulative fashion.

What happens if an individual is not able to cope successfully with a high-risk situation? It may be the case that the person has never acquired the coping skills involved, or that the appropriate response has been inhibited by fear or anxiety. Or, perhaps the individual fails to recognize and respond to the risk involved before it is too late. Whatever the reason, if a coping response is not performed, the person is likely to experience a decrease in self-efficacy, frequently coupled with a sense of helplessness and a tendency to passively give in to the situation. "It's no use, I can't handle this" is a common reaction. As self-efficacy decreases in the precipitating high-risk situation, one's expectations for coping successfully with subsequent problem situations also begins to drop. If the situation also involves the temptation to engage in the prohibited behavior as a means of attempting to cope with the stress involved, the stage is set for a probable relapse.

The probability of relapse is enhanced if the individual holds *positive expectancies* about the effects of the activity or substance involved. Often the person will anticipate the immediate positive effects of the activity, based on past experience, while at the same time ignoring or not attending to the delayed negative consequences involved. The lure of immediate gratification becomes the dominant figure in the perceptual field, as the reality of the full consequences of the act recedes into the background. For many persons, smoking a cigarette or taking a drink has long been associated with coping with stress. "A drink would sure help me get through this" or "If only I could have a smoke, I would feel more relaxed" are common beliefs of this type. Positive outcome expectancies are a primary determinant of alcohol use and other forms of substance abuse (cf., Marlatt & Rohsenow, 1980). Expectancies figure prominently as determinants of relapse in our model.

The combination of being unable to cope effectively in a high-risk situation coupled with positive outcome expectancies for the effects of the old habitual coping behavior greatly increases the probability that an initial lapse will occur. On the one hand, the individual is faced with a high-risk situation with no coping response available; self-efficacy decreases as the person feels less able to exert control. On the other hand, there is the lure of the old coping response: the drink, the drug, or other substance. At this point, unless a last-minute coping response or a sudden change of circumstance occurs, the individual may cross over the border from abstinence (or controlled use) to relapse (uncontrolled use). Whether or not this first excursion over the line, the first lapse, is followed by a total relapse depends to a large extent on the individual's perceptions of the "cause" of the lapse and the reactions associated with its occurrence.

The requirement of abstinence is an absolute dictum. Once someone has crossed over the line, there is no going back. From this all-or-none perspective, a single drink or cigarette is sufficient to violate the rule of abstinence: once committed, the deed cannot be undone. Unfortunately, most people who attempt to stop an old habit such as smoking or drinking perceive quitting in this "once and for all" manner. To account for the reaction to the transgression of an absolute rule, we have postulated a mechanism called the *Abstinence Violation Effect* or AVE (Marlatt, 1978; Marlatt & Gordon, 1980). The AVE is postulated to occur under the following conditions. Prior to the first lapse, the individual is personally committed to an extended or indefinite period of abstinence. The intensity of the AVE will vary as a function of several factors, including the degree of prior commitment or effort expended to maintain abstinence, the duration of the abstinence period (the longer the period, the greater the effect), and the subjective value or importance of the prohibited behavior to the individual. We hypothesize that the AVE is characterized by two key cognitive-affective elements: cognitive dissonance (conflict and guilt) and a personal attribution effect (blaming the self as the cause of the relapse).

According to Festinger's original theory (1964), cognitive dissonance is assumed to develop out of a disparity between the individual's cognitions or beliefs about the self (e.g., as an abstainer) and the occurrence of a behavior that is directly incongruent with this self-image (e.g., engaging in the forbidden act). The resulting dissonance is experienced as conflict or guilt ("I shouldn't have, but I did"). This internal conflict acts as a source of motivation to engage in behaviors (or cognitions) designed to reduce the dissonant reaction. To the extent that the problem behavior has been used as a coping response to deal with conflict and guilt in the past, it is likely that the individual will continue to engage in the previously prohibited behavior in an attempt to reduce the unpleasant reactions. An alcoholic, for example, who falls "off the wagon" for the first time may continue to drink after the first lapse in an attempt to relieve the conflict and guilt associated with the transgression itself—particularly if the person used to drink in the past when feeling guilty or conflictual. Continued drinking in an attempt to reduce feelings of guilt may be mediated by negative reinforcement (drinking to escape from unpleasant emotional states).

It is also possible that the individual will attempt to reduce the dissonance associated with the first slip by cognitively altering the self-image so as to bring this in line with the new behavior. Someone who takes the first drink, for example, may reject the former self-image of an abstainer in favor of a new image that is consistent with the emergence of the prohibited behavior: "This just goes to show that I am an alcoholic after all, and that I can't control my drinking once it starts." In either case, the result is the same: the probability increases that the lapse will escalate into a full relapse.

The second component of the AVE is a self-attribution effect (Harvey, Ickes, & Kidd, 1976), wherein the individual attributes the cause of the relapse to personal weakness or failure. Rather than viewing the lapse as a unique response to a particularly difficult situation, the person is likely to blame the cause of the act on such factors as lack of willpower or internal weakness in the face of temptation. People often draw inferences about their own personality traits, attitudes, and motives from the observation of their own behavior (Bem, 1972). To the extent that the person feels personally responsible for "giving in," attribution theory predicts that the person will attribute this failure to internal or personal causes. If the lapse is viewed as a personal failure in this manner, the individual's expectancy for continued failure will increase. If one feels weak-willed or powerless for giving into the temptation of the first cigarette, for example, the expectation of resisting the second or third cigarette is correspondingly lower. Again, the bottom line is the same: an increased probability that the lapse will soon snowball into a full-blown relapse.

A final factor to be considered in the relapse process is the subjective effect of the substance or activity experienced by the user following the first lapse. Although these effects differ with the type of drug or other activity, many drugs act in such a way as to produce an initial "high" or state of arousal which is interpreted by the individual as a pleasant or euphoric state. Both alcohol and tobacco, for instance, produce an initial state of physiological arousal (increased heart rate and other autonomic reactions) that may be subjectively experienced by the user as an increase in energy or power (cf., McClelland, Davis, Kalin, & Wanner, 1972). When this increased sense of power occurs, the use of the substance to counter the individual's prior feelings of personal powerlessness (low self-efficacy) in the high-risk situation is strongly reinforced.

General Approach in Working with Clients

Contrary to those traditional approaches in the treatment of addictive problems (especially those derived from the disease model), in which therapists often initiate treatment by using confrontation techniques designed to "break through the denial system" and force the client into accepting a particular diagnostic label, the Relapse Prevention (RP) approach attempts to foster a sense of objectivity or detachment in our clients' approach to their problem behaviors. By relating to the client as a colleague or co-therapist, we hope to encourage a sense of cooperation and openness in which clients learn to perceive their addictive behavior as something they *do* rather than as an indication of something they *are* (e.g., an "addict" or an "alcoholic"). By adopting this objective and detached approach, clients may be able to free themselves from the guilt and defensiveness that would otherwise bias their view of their problem. We also encourage our clients to take an active role in treatment planning and decision making throughout the course of treatment. Rather than treating the client as a passive victim of a disease, we try to facilitate active participation and to encourage the client to assume personal responsibility at every stage of the program. The overall goal of the RP program is to increase the clients' awareness and choice concerning their behavior, to develop coping skills and self-control capacities, and to generally develop a greater sense of confidence, mastery, of self-efficacy in their lives.

In selecting techniques from the material to be presented in the following sections, it should be kept in mind that the RP model can be applied either as an "add-on" program, in which techniques are introduced as an addition to an already existing treatment, or as a general self-control approach designed to develop and maintain a balanced lifestyle. In terms of the former application, the reader may wish to select procedures described in the first of the following two sections, since this section deals with *specific intervention procedures* designed to help the client anticipate and cope with the relapse episode itself. Material in the second section describes a variety of *global intervention procedures* designed to modify the early antecedents of relapse, including restructuring of the client's general style of life. A complete application of the RP model would include both global (lifestyle) and specific intervention techniques.

Relapse Prevention: Specific Intervention Techniques for Coping with Relapse

Figure 13.3 provides a schematic overview of the specific intervention techniques described in this section. The overall goal of the specific intervention procedures is to teach the client to anticipate and cope with the possibility of relapse: to recognize and cope with high-risk situations that may precipitate a slip, and to modify cognitions and other reactions so as to prevent a single lapse from developing into a full-blown relapse.

The first step to take in the prevention of relapse is to teach the client to

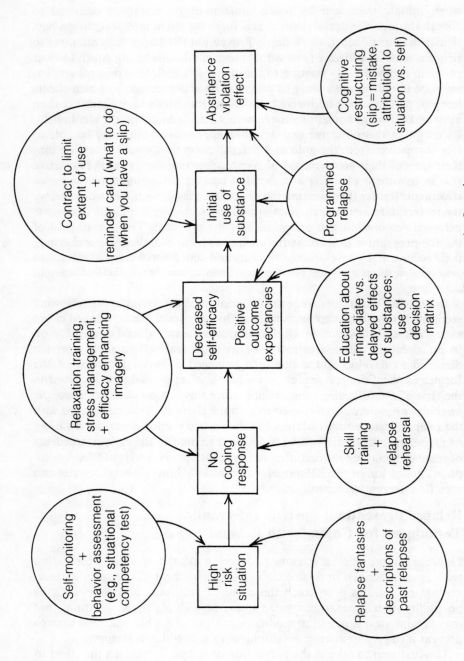

Fig. 13.3. Relapse Prevention: Specific Intervention Strategies.

recognize the *high-risk situations* that may precipitate or trigger a relapse. Here, the earlier one becomes aware that one is involved in a chain of events which increases the probability of a slip or lapse, the sooner one can intervene by performing an appropriate coping skill and/or recognize and respond to the discriminative stimuli that are associated with "entering" a high-risk situation, and to use these cues both as warning signals and as "reminders" to engage in alternative or remedial action.

To introduce a metaphor that we will return to in this presentation, imagine that the client involved in a self-control program is a driver setting out on a highway journey. The trip itinerary (i.e., moving from excessive drug use to abstinence) includes both "easy" and "hard" stretches of road (from the plains to mountain passes). From this metaphorical perspective, the high-risk situations are equivalent to those dangerous parts of the trip where the driver must use extra caution and driving skills to keep the car on the road and prevent an accident. The discriminative stimuli that signal a high-risk situation can be thought of as highway signs providing the driver with information about upcoming dangers and risks on the road (e.g., "Icy patches ahead: SLOW to 25"). The responsible alert driver is someone who is trained to keep an eye out for these signs and to take appropriate action to prevent mishap. So it is with the person who is attempting to refrain from engaging in a particular target behavior (smoking, drinking, overindulging, etc.): one must be on the lookout for cues that denote the proximity of potentially troublesome situations. These cues can serve as early warning signals that remind the individual to "stop, look, and listen" prior to engaging in an appropriate coping response. The sooner these signs are noticed, the easier it is to anticipate what lies around the next bend and take appropriate steps to deal effectively with the situation.

There are a number of different methods that can be used to help the client identify his or her own high-risk situations. The high-risk situations we have discovered as part of our research provide a general survey of various categories of relapse episodes, however, they do not necessarily reflect all of the situations which may be high-risk for any particular individual. Although the therapist may make use of the general categories of high-risk situations presented in table 13.1 as a starting point, it is important to highlight the need for an *individualized assessment* procedure to identify unique or idosyncratic situations that may pose a problem for a particular client.

The use of *self-monitoring* procedures (McFall, 1977) provides a very effective method of identifying potential high-risk situations where access to the ongoing behavior is readily available. In our own clinical work with problem drinkers and smokers, for example, we ask the client to record each cigarette or drink consumed for a period of two weeks prior to the target date for quitting. The client is asked to record the following information for each drink or cigarette: time of day (for both starting and ending the activity), a brief description of the situation (location, presence or absence of others), and a numerical rating of the individual's subsequent mood or feeling state. At the end of each week, the client and therapist together prepare a graph showing the average number of drinks or cigarettes consumed in each of the major situational categories emerging from the self-monitoring data (e.g., while working alone, at social gatherings, etc.). A thorough examination of this information frequently reveals a pattern of situations in which the behavior occurs with the highest frequency and/or is associated with the greatest psychological payoff.

In a recent study with male alcoholics who participated in an inpatient abstinence-oriented treatment program, Chaney and other members of our research team (Chaney, O'Leary, & Marlatt, 1978) investigated the effects of a relapse prevention program designed to help these clients cope with high-risk relapse situations likely to be encountered after discharge from the hospital. As part of the assessment battery developed to evaluate this program, we developed a test called the Situational Competency Test. In this test, administered either in written or oral (tape-recorded) form, the client is asked to respond to descriptions of high-risk situations. The situations are drawn from a pool of relapse episodes discovered in earlier research. A sample item: "You are eating at a good restaurant on a special occasion with some friends. The waitress comes over and says, 'Drink before dinner?' Everyone orders one. All eyes seem to be on you. What would you do?" The client's response is later scored along a number of dimensions, including the latency and duration of the response (for the tape-recorded version), the degree of compliance, and specification of alternative behaviors. The Situational Competency Test has shown itself to be a useful procedure for identifying the most problematic situations for individual clients, since it provides an indication of the client's actual coping capacity in a variety of situational contexts. The task can be adapted for use in different formats (e.g., it can be used as a role-playing assessment procedure) or with different addictive behavior problems. It is also useful as a pre-post measure in treatment outcome studies.

Another self-report measure that can be used to identify potential high-risk situations involves the use of *self-efficacy ratings*. In this procedure, the client is presented with a list of specific high-risk situations and is asked to provide a rating (e.g., on a 7-point scale) of how difficult or easy it would be to cope with the situation without engaging in the addictive behavior. The use of self-efficacy ratings over a variety of potentially problematic situations is a straightforward procedure that appears to have high utility as an assessment procedure. Recent research in the treatment of smoking, for example, has shown that self-efficacy ratings made on or near the date for smoking cessation are valid predictors of subsequent treatment outcome (Condiotte & Lichtenstein, Note 2; DiClemente, 1980).

Another useful technique is the use of *relapse fantasies* in which the client is asked to provide a fantasized account of a possible relapse that might occur sometime in the future. In this procedure, the therapist asks the client to sit back, close the eyes, and to imagine an actual relapse episode. The therapist can introduce this by saying:

> Although we hope that a relapse will not occur in your case, it still would be helpful in our work together if you would just pretend that you are having difficulty refraining from smoking sometime in the future. What kind of situation or event would it take to get you back to smoking? Try to imagine this scene as clearly as you can, and give me a description of the situation and your feelings.

Frequently, clients who have stopped using a particular drug or substance will report dreams in which a relapse occurred. A description of the dream can then be used as a starting point for a guided relapse fantasy.

Once the high-risk situations have been identified, the client can then be taught to respond to these situational cues as discriminative stimuli (highway signs) for behavioral change. In some cases, it might be best to simply avoid risky situations if possible (take a detour, to follow the highway metaphor). In most cases, however, the situations cannot be easily avoided, and the client must rely on coping skills or alternative strategies to "get through" the situation without a relapse.

The cornerstone of the RP approach is to teach the client coping strategies with *skill-training* procedures. A thorough behavioral assessment of the client's response capacity across the spectrum of potential high-risk situations will yield a profile of areas of strength and weakness for various coping responses. It is the therapist's responsibility to ascertain the extent to which a deficiency in responding to a given high-risk situation represents an actual deficit in past learning experience, or represents a current block in performance (of an already learned response) due to the inhibiting effects of anxiety, fear of evaluation, or other emotional reaction. For clients whose coping responses are blocked by fear or anxiety, the therapist should attempt to disinhibit the behavior by the use of an appropriate anxiety-reduction procedure such as systematic desensitization. For most clients who show deficiencies in their skill repertoire, however, we attempt to teach them new skills using a systematic and structured approach.

The approach we favor combines training in general problem-solving ability with specific skill training. Adopting a problem-solving orientation to stressful situations (cf. Goldfried & Davison, 1976) permits the client greater flexibility and adaptation to new problem situations, rather than having to rely on the rote learning of a number of discrete skills that may or may not generalize across various settings and situations. Our skill training methods are based on the work of McFall (1976), Goldstein (1973), and other investigators, and incorporate components of direct instruction, modeling, behavioral rehearsal and coaching, and feedback from the therapist. We find that the modeling of self-instructional statements (cf. Meichenbaum, 1977) to be particularly useful in teaching clients adaptive self-statements to use in conjunction with performance of the behavioral skills.

To take a specific example from our own skill-training research with alcoholic clients (Chaney, O'Leary, & Marlatt, 1978), the client's responses to the Situational Competency Test are first taken into account in planning the specific skill training program. For one particular client, the problem may involve an inability to resist social pressure to indulge; for another, the problem may involve a deficit in coping with feelings of loneliness or depression. In the skill training program described in the Chaney et al. study, alcoholics in treatment met together in a small group format for a series of treatment sessions. Each group was led by two therapists, who began by describing a particular high-risk situation. The group members then discussed the situation and generated various ways of responding to it. The therapists then modeled an appropriate coping response and practiced it in front of the group. Using this procedure, each client received individualized feedback from group members and specific coaching and instructions from the therapists. The client was then required to repeat the coping response until it matched the therapists' criteria for adequacy. This particular skill-training program was evaluated in a year-long follow-up study in comparison with two control groups: a group that spent an equivalent amount of time discussing their emotional reactions with regard to the same high-risk situations (as in psychodynamic group therapy), and a no-treatment control condition (regular hospital program only). The skill-training condition proved to be more successful than either control group, showing a significant improvement at the one-year follow up period for such variables as amount of post-treatment drinking, duration of time spent drinking before regaining abstinence, and frequency of periods of intoxication.

One additional procedure that may increase the generalization of newly acquired coping skills is to require the client to practice the adaptive behavior in actual high-risk situations. The therapist who is working with smokers or drinkers can, for example, take a group of clients to an actual bar or nightclub for a dry run session. The combined reactions and suggestions of the group members serve as the focus of discussion, while the clients meet together for a coffee or soft drink in a setting where they are surrounded by other people who are actively modeling the prohibited behavior.

In those cases in which it is not practical to practice new coping skills in real-life environmental settings, the therapist can again make use of imagery as a means of cognitively representing the high-risk situation. This procedure, called a *relapse rehearsal* is similar to the relapse fantasy technique described earlier. In the relapse rehearsal procedure, the therapist goes beyond the imagined scenario related to the high-risk situation and includes scenes in which the client actually imagines him-herself engaging in appropriate coping responses. The technique of covert modeling (Kazdin, 1978) can also be used to help clients to cope with their reactions to a slip, as it also provides an opportunity to rehearse cognitive restructuring techniques.

In addition to teaching the client to respond effectively when confronted with specific high-risk situations, there are a number of additional *relaxation procedures* the therapist can draw upon to increase the client's overall capacity to deal with stress. Relaxation training may provide the client with a global increased perception of control, thereby reducing the stress "load" that any given situation may pose for the individual. In this regard, such procedures as progressive muscle relaxation training, meditation, and various stress management techniques are extremely useful in aiding the client to cope more effectively with the hassles and demands of daily life. An increased perception of control often leads to improved self-efficacy over a variety of specific situations.

Positive outcome expectancies play an influential role in the relapse process. After a client has been abstinent for some period of time, a shift in attitudes and beliefs about the effects of the foregone substance or activity often occurs. Positive outcome expectancies for the immediate effects become an especially potent motivating force to resume use when the client is faced with a high-risk situation and is beginning to feel unable to cope effectively (low self-efficacy). An unbalanced lifestyle (marked by a preponderance of "shoulds") will also create an increase in need for immediate gratification. In either case, the temptation to "give in" and relinquish control by indulging in the formerly taboo activity is a powerful influence to contend with. As a reminder of its potent effects, we call it the Problem of Immediate Gratification, or the PIG phenomenon.

Education about both the immediate and delayed effects of the drug or activity involved may help offset the tendency to see the "grass as greener" on the other side of the abstinence fence. Information about the long-range effects of excessive drug use on physical health and social well-being may help counter the tendency to think only of the initial pleasant short-term effects (i.e., to counter the PIG phenomenon). Recent research and theory about the time-course of effects following the ingestion of many psychoactive substances suggests that the overall response may be *biphasic* in nature: the initial increase of euphoria and arousal (the "rush" or the "high") is frequently followed by a delayed effect in the opposite direction (increased dysphoria and other negative affective states). This biphasic reaction has been observed with alcohol (Docter, Naitoh, & Smith, 1966; Garfield & McBrearty, 1970; Mello, 1968) and other psychoactive drugs, and is often cited in association with the "opponent-process" theory of drug use motivation recently advanced by Solomon and his colleagues (Solomon, 1977; Solomon & Corbit, 1974).

One technique that we have found particularly helpful in teaching clients to look at both the immediate and delayed effects of returning to the old behavior is the use of the *decision matrix.* In the use of the decision matrix, the client is presented with the basic format in the form of a three-way table (2 × 2 × 2 matrix) with the following factors: the decision to resume the old behavior or to maintain abstinence; the immediate versus delayed effects of either decision; and, within each of the former categories, the positive and negative effects involved. The client is then asked (assisted by the therapist) to fill out each of the eight cells of the matrix, listing the effects which are thought to have the greatest impact. It is important that the client include *all effects* which are of subjective importance, regardless of whether the therapist agrees with the client's choices. An effect which the therapist may not see as objectively significant (e.g., fear of weight gain after smoking cessation) may have considerable psychological impact for the client. To emphasize the importance of this latter point, the client can be asked to assign numerical ratings to each of the positive and negative outcomes listed, to illustrate their relative strength. It should be noted that the values associated with each specific outcome will probably *change over time* (relative to the point of initial behavior change). The client should thus be reminded to revise the matrix at each significant choice point in the future, especially if the client is considering resuming the old behavior. Clients who are on the verge of relapse frequently will attend only to the immediate positive effects at this point (PIG phenomenon), and will overlook or deny the immediate and delayed negative consequences.

What if all else fails, and a slip occurs? The client can be prepared in advance to cope with this possible outcome, and to apply some behavioral and cognitive "brakes" so that the initial lapse does not "spin out" and become a full-blown relapse. A combination of specific coping skills and a cognitive restructuring approach offers the greatest advantage in this regard. First, we need to teach the client behavioral skills to moderate or control the behavior once it occurs. These coping behaviors can be specified ahead of time in a therapeutic contract. Second, if the controlled use skills are to be successful, we must instruct the client in cognitive restructuring procedures to effectively cope with the various components of the Abstinence Violation

Effect. Third, the use of a programmed relapse experience (in which initial use occurs under supervised conditions) may be an effective prevention technique to use in certain cases. Each of these interventions is discussed in the following sections.

The first step to be taken to anticipate a possible slip is to establish a working agreement or *therapeutic contract to limit the extent of use* should a lapse occur. The details of such a contract are best worked out in individual collaboration with the client.

The principal aim of *cognitive restructuring* is to counter the cognitive and affective components of the AVE. Instead of reacting to the first lapse as an indication of personal failure, characterized by conflict, guilt, and internal attribution ("This just proves that I am no good and that I'm a helpless addict after all," etc.), the client is taught to reconceptualize the episode as a single, independent event — to see it as a mistake rather than a disaster that can never be undone. As an additional aid to reconceptualization, the client can be given a summary of the cognitive restructuring material in the form of a *reminder card*. The client is instructed to carry this card at all times following initial treatment; it can be printed as a wallet-sized card in order to be carried conveniently in one's wallet or purse. The card is to be consulted immediately upon the first lapse experience.

As an example, let us examine a reminder card designated recently for a smoking control program developed at the University of Oregon by Edward Lichtenstein and his colleagues. The material presented in the card was adapted from one of our recent monographs (Marlatt & Gordon, 1980). This card measures 3-1/2 by 4-1/2 inches and is folded in half. The outside flap reads as follows: "DIRECTIONS: Please carry this card with you at all times. In the event that you smoke a cigarette, take this card out immediately, read it and follow the instructions given." The outside flap also contains the name of the treatment program and a phone number to be called for further information. The inside portion of the card contains the following message:

> A slip is not all that unusual. It does not mean that you have failed or that you have lost control over your behavior. You will probably feel guilty about what you have done, and will blame yourself for having slipped. This feeling is to be expected; it is part of what we call the Abstinence Violation Effect. There is no reason why you have to give in to this feeling and continue to smoke. The feeling will pass in time. Look upon the slip as a learning experience. What were the elements of the high-risk situation which led to the slip? What coping response could you have used to get around the situation? Remember the old saying: One swallow doesn't make a summer? Well, one slip doesn't have to make a relapse, either. Just because you slipped once does not mean that you are a failure, that you have no willpower, or that you are a hopeless addict. Look upon the slip as a single, independent event, something which can be avoided in the future with an alternative coping response.

In addition to the above information, a reminder card could include a list of "what to do next," summarizing the main points of the relapse contract described earlier. Having a phone number to call when a slip occurs is also a desirable addition, particularly if the treatment program includes a 24-hour "hot line" or other similar resource in which counselors are available to discuss the client's reactions to the potential or actual relapse episode (Shiffman, Note 3). Even a prerecorded taped message designed to help the client cope with the situation would be a useful aid in programs where it is not practical to provide around-the-clock counseling services.

The final intervention procedure to be described in this section is use of the *programmed relapse.* In this technique, the client is required to consume the first drink, smoke, or other substance under the direct supervision of the therapist. The goal of the programmed relapse is to help clients (particularly those who report that they are unable to maintain abstinence and plan to resume the old habit pattern) objectively experience the initial return to the target behavior under the guidance of the therapist. There are several advantages to this procedure. First, by scheduling the "relapse" at a time and place designated by the therapist, it precludes the otherwise dangerous possibility that the client will resume the habit under highly stressful conditions. To the extent that the client attributes his or her ability to cope with a stressful situation to the maladaptive coping response of drinking or smoking, the probability of a full-blown relapse increases. To prevent this outcome, the therapist should schedule the programmed relapse for a relatively neutral time and place. The therapist might say, for example, "Okay, I hear what you are saying about your wanting to resume smoking, but I want you to do me one favor: let's schedule your first cigarette for this coming Thursday, at noon in my office. I'll provide the cigarette. Do you agree to wait a little longer before you go back to smoking?"

In our own clinical use of this technique with smokers, we often find that there is a marked discrepancy between the client's pre-smoking expectations (usually quite positive) concerning the effects of the first cigarette and the actual experienced effects (e.g., "It makes me dizzy; is that all there is to it — blowing smoke out of my lungs!" etc.). Often this discrepancy will have a marked motivational effect in that the client may decide to resume abstinence, based primarily on this disconfirmation of expectancies. The use of programmed relapse thus seems to offer many advantages, compared to the alternative scenario in which the individual resumes smoking as a response to a stressful environmental event.

Relapse Prevention: Global Intervention Techniques for Modifying Lifestyle

In addition to providing the client with a set of specific skills and cognitive strategies as a means of coping with a variety of high-risk situations, the therapist can also impart several global strategies that provide a broader framework for the prevention of relapse. Simply teaching the client to respond mechanically to one high-risk situation after another is not enough. For one thing, it is impossible for the therapist to identify or work with all of the possible high-risk situations that the client may experience. For another, the skill training sessions described in the preceding section are by necessity quite specific in content, and generalization to other somewhat different situations may not always occur. Teaching the client general problem-solving skills (Goldfried & Davison, 1976) will enhance the generalization process to some degree. To develop a more complete prevention program, however, it is necessary to do two additional things: to intervene in the client's overall lifestyle so as to increase overall capacity to deal with stress and to cope with high-risk situations with an increased sense of self-efficacy; to train the client to identify and respond to situational and covert early-warning signals; and to exercise self-control strategies to reduce the risk level of any situation that might otherwise trigger a slip. We will describe each of these intervention methods briefly in this section.

Recently we worked with a client who illustrates the impact an unbalanced lifestyle can have on an addictive behavior problem. The client in question was a 35-year-old woman who came into therapy seeking help for a drinking problem. When asked to describe the pattern of her daily drinking, she gave the following details. She was employed as a school teacher and was currently living with a man who feared that she might develop an alcoholism problem. Because of his feelings, our client felt a great deal of guilt and usually avoided drinking any alcohol in his presence. As a result, almost all of her drinking was confined to a short period in the afternoon following work. A typical workday for her began at 7:00 in the morning when she got up to make lunch for herself and her living partner. Since she slept in until the last possible moment, the morning routine was rushed and frantic. She drove hurriedly to school to meet her first class, a group of rowdy second-graders. Instead of taking a lunch break, she chose instead to monitor the study hall during the noon hour, since doing so meant that she could get off work a bit earlier. The afternoons were much the same as the morning; she taught drama classes and frequently worked under the pressure of deadlines for upcoming plays she directed. By the time she got out of school at 3:00, she described herself as a "nervous wreck." Her means of coping with this stress was simple and direct: she was in the habit of keeping a fresh half-pint of vodka in the glove compartment of her car and would usually consume all of it on the half-hour commute home. Since she did not want to risk drinking at work, and since her living partner viewed her drinking with criticism and disdain, she squeezed all of her alcohol consumption into this one brief period each afternoon. Needless to say, she frequently arrived home in a "loaded" condition.

An individual whose daily lifestyle is characterized by a preponderance of "shoulds" and a dearth of self-gratifying "wants" may come to believe that some form of indulgence is justified as a payoff for responding to external demands and the hassles of everyday life. Our client illustrates this principle: she felt that she owed herself a "drunk" since that was almost the only form of self-gratification she allowed herself on a typical workday. She also said that she could hardly wait for the feeling of "release" that came from the rush provided by the gulped swallows of vodka (for her, the drive home was a "rush" hour that she eagerly looked forward to each day).

As an aside, it should be noted at this point that one of the most difficult issues clients are faced with is the rationalization that a desire for indulgence is justified. This justification is exemplified in the title of a book describing the drinking lifestyle of derelict alcoholics: *You Owe Yourself a Drunk* (Spradley, 1970). One of the key assumptions of our relapse model is that the degree of balance in a person's daily lifestyle has a significant impact on the desire for indulgence or immediate gratification. Here we are defining "balance" as the degree of equilibrium that exists in one's daily life between those activities perceived as external demands (the "shoulds") and those perceived as activities that person engages in for pleasure or self-fulfillment (the "wants"). Paying household bills, performing routine chores, or menial tasks at work would count highly as "shoulds" for many individuals. At the other end of the scale are the "wants"—the activities the person likes to perform and gains some immediate gratification from engaging in (e.g., going fishing, taking time off for lunch with a friend, engaging in a creative work task, etc.). We believe that a lifestyle that is weighted down with a preponderance of perceived "shoulds" is often associated with an increased perception of self-deprivation and a corresponding desire for indulgence and gratification. It is as if the person who spends his or her entire day engaged in activities that are high in external demand (often perceived as "hassling" events) attempts to balance this disequilibrium by engaging in an excessive "want" or self-indulgence at the end of the day. In order to justify the indulgence, the individual may rationalize it by saying "I owe myself a drink or two—I deserve a break today!"

Returning to our client, we began by focusing on two important aspects of her alcohol problem: her living mate's attitudes toward her drinking, and the client's daily lifestyle. Since it was decided on the basis of a careful assessment evaluation that the client would be a good candidate for a moderate drinking program, and since she did not want to give up drinking altogether, the goal of our approach was to bring about a marked change in her pattern of daily drinking. We agreed that a moderate drinking pattern would involve eliminating the afternoon vodka mini-binges, replacing this behavior with a moderate drinking pattern at home and in other social situations (using wine instead of distilled spirits), and limiting her drinking so as to avoid intoxication. In order to clear the way for her to drink at home, we brought in her boyfriend and discussed with him the possibility that his feelings and attitudes toward the client's drinking may have played an important role in establishing the current aberrant pattern. After some discussion, he began to see how his fears that she was becoming an alcoholic made her feel guilty to the extent that she had to conceal her drinking from him altogether, confining it to the single rush-hour experience. He then agreed to allow her to drink wine at home in his presence without reacting negatively. Almost immediately after her boyfriend came to accept her drinking without responding in a punitive manner, our client reported feeling much less guilt and concern over her consumption of alcohol. Her drinking self-monitoring data showed a drop in consumption of about 25 percent a week, even in the absence of any additional intervention.

Despite this advance, the client reported that she still felt the need for some form of release after a typical workday. To deal with this desire for immediate gratification, we began to modify her daily activities to restore a balance between her perceived obligatory duties (the "shoulds") and other activities that she found more self-gratifying (the "wants"). As a result of this intervention program, her typical daily routine changed in the following manner. Instead of getting up as late as possible and rushing to prepare lunches for both herself and her boyfriend, she now arises an hour and a half earlier in the morning, prepares her lunch (her boyfriend has now learned to make his own lunch), and then stops off on the way to school at a neighborhood health spa where she enjoys a leisurely whirlpool bath and massage. She arrives at school relaxed and refreshed to begin the day's work. At mid-morning break, she practices meditation for 20 minutes, sitting quietly in the school auditorium. At lunch, instead of monitoring the study hall students, she shares this time with a friend; she and her friend either have a pleasant lunch together or they spend time jogging around a nearby lake.

After the afternoon classes end, the client devotes an hour to what we call *body time*—time that is set aside exclusively for physical exercise and/or mental relaxation. Instead of rigidly adhering to an externally imposed exercise regime (e.g., "I must jog every day at 4:00 p.m., no matter what"), she first sits quietly and meditates for a few minutes in order to subjectively intuit what her body "needs" most. Depending on her mood (and often the weather conditions), she selects an activity from a menu of alternatives consisting of both aerobic activities (jogging, swimming, or bike riding) and meditation/relaxation exercises. In this manner, she chooses the activity best suited to her needs on any particular day. If she is feeling tense and wound-up from the day's work, she might select a vigorous exercise such as jogging. On the other hand, if she finds herself trapped in compulsive worrying, she may choose to meditate instead. Use of the "body time" concept is often a helpful strategy to overcome the reactance which often accompanies a rigid exercise program; to the extent that one feels that one *must* jog each day at a particular time, jogging may become a "should" instead of a desired form of self-indulgence. If the new behavior becomes a "should," the client will have difficulty maintaining the behavior over long time periods. With the body time concept, the client maintains a sense of freedom of choice, since the activity itself is not chosen until the designated hour arrives. Once our client made these lifestyle changes, scheduling them into her routine on a regular basis, her desire for the afternoon vodka rush subsided and was eventually replaced with a need for other more healthy activities. Her drinking decreased dramatically and leveled off at about two to three glasses of wine each evening.

The foregoing case illustrates the development of a balanced daily lifestyle. As indicated in figure 13.4, lifestyle intervention is one of the major global self-control strategies employed in the RP approach. A major goal for lifestyle intervention is to replace drinking or other potentially harmful behaviors with an activity that qualifies as a "positive addiction" (Glasser, 1976). If a "negative" addiction (e.g., excessive drug use) can be described as an activity that feels good at first but causes harm in the long run, a "positive" addiction (e.g., jogging) is an activity which may be experienced negatively at first (especially while one is in the early stages of exercise) but is very beneficial in terms of the long-range effects. Positive addictions often become "wants" as the individual begins to look forward to engaging in the activity, and/or misses the positive effects if the activity or exercise is not engaged in on a regular basis. In addition, since the individual usually must acquire new skills in the development of a positive addiction, self-efficacy often increases as a result. Similarly, since the regular practice of these behaviors is associated with a greater sense of relaxation or improved physical well-being, overall coping capacity is increased; high-risk situations may be more easily dealt with, rather than serving as precipitating triggers for excessive behaviors.

In our clinical work, we have found a number of activities that seem to enhance self-efficacy and provide alternatives to excessive drug use. One of the easiest activities to learn in this regard is meditation (Carrington, 1978; Marlatt & Marques, 1977). Meditation or the use of meditative-like procedures such as the "relaxation response" (Benson, 1975) provides a deep feeling of relaxation and is often described as a "high" experience by those who engage in it on a regular basis. Research on meditation has shown that continued practice is associated with an increased capacity to cope with a variety of stressful situations (Shapiro & Walsh, 1981).

Other lifestyle intervention procedures are recommended depending on the client's individual needs and abilities. A regular program of exercise, such as running or jogging, is a potent antidote to excessive use of drugs or related indulgent behaviors—particularly if the client substitutes running

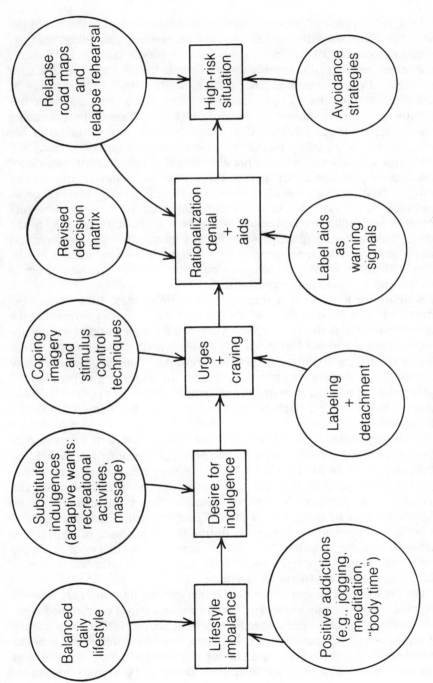

Fig. 13.4. Relapse Prevention: Global Self-Control Strategies.

479

for the usual "time out" with drugs (e.g., the cocktail hour) at the end of the workday. Other activities include working on hobbies, gardening, reading, attending concerts or the movies, learning to play a musical instrument, and other creative tasks. Learning to participate in "addictive" sports, such as skiing, skydiving, sailing, hang gliding, and automobile racing may be recommended for the more adventurous client since these activities frequently provide an intense alternative "high" experience. Programming periods of free time during the day, when the client can pursue his or her own interests (e.g., going shopping, having lunch with a friend, etc.) will help provide balance in an otherwise crowded schedule of "shoulds." Substitutive indulgences, or activities that provide an immediate form of self-gratification (e.g., receiving a massage, sexual activity, eating a gourmet meal, etc.) can also serve as last-minute alternatives or substitute forms of self-indulgence, especially when the temptation to "give in" to the lure of getting stoned on drugs is particularly intense. Lifestyle intervention may also involve therapeutic programs that have a major impact on the client's life, such as marital therapy, employment counseling, or changes in one's social or physical environment.

A desire for indulgence stemming from an unbalanced lifestyle may express itself in both affective (usually somatic) and cognitive forms. On the somatic side, the desire may express itself in the form of urges (sudden impulses to engage in the forbidden act) and/or craving responses (anticipation of the effects of immediate gratification). Alternatively, the desire may take the form of cognitive distortions that set the stage or "give permission" for a potential relapse, such as rationalization, denial, or apparently irrelevant decisions (AIDs). Each of these reactions can be countered with RP strategies.

To the extent that cravings and urges are elicited by external cues such as the sight or smell of cigarettes, alcoholic beverages, or other substances, the client can exercise a good deal of control by simply removing as many tempting stimuli as possible from his or her everyday living environment. The overall aim of such *stimulus control* procedures can be summarized in the old maxim "out of sight, out of mind." Employment of stimulus control techniques is particularly important during the early stages of abstinence. Along these same lines, the client can be encouraged to make use of simple *avoidance strategies*, staying away from high-risk situations which may elicit strong urges or desires to succumb.

The major point to emphasize here is that craving and urges are internal responses: just like any interoceptive response (such as a conditioned emotional response), they have a specific course of action, with a given latency of onset, intensity, and duration. The most important thing for clients to remember is that these urges and craving responses will arise and will then subside and *pass away* on their own. Individuals who give in to these urges may hold the mistaken assumption that the urge will continue to increase in intensity until it becomes impossible to resist. Giving in to the craving or urge at the peak of its intensity, however, increases the probability that the old habit or response will gain in strength; maladaptive coping habits are reinforced by the reduction in subjective tension or arousal associated with the buildup of the craving-urge, much in the same way as an escape or avoidance response is reinforced by a reduction in any aversive or unpleasant emotional state. On the other hand, if the individual is able to wait out the waxing and waning of the craving without engaging in the old habit pattern, the internal pressure to respond will eventually fade out through the process of extinction.

The most effective way of coping with craving and urge experiences is to develop a sense of *detachment* with regard to them. Instead of identifying with the urge (e.g., "I really want a cigarette right now"), the client can be trained to monitor the urge or desire from the point of view of a detached observer (e.g., "I am now experiencing an urge to smoke"). By *externalizing* the craving/urge, and "watching" it come and go through the eyes of an observer (much as a meditator learns to passively observe ideas, feelings, and images as they pass through the mind), there will be a decreased tendency to identify with the urge and feel overwhelmed by its power. The situation is analogous to that of an ocean surfer: the urge is similar to the swelling of a wave which the surfer hopes to "ride" without getting "wiped out." In a similar manner, we hope to train clients to "ride" the crest of an urge or craving, maintaining balance until the crest has finally broken and the wave of feeling subsides.

Many clients view repeated experiences of craving as an indication that treatment has been unsuccessful or that relapse is imminent. This defeatist attitude fails to take into account the fact that these responses are to be expected as a natural part of the recovery process: knowing that they are conditioned responses and that they will gradually weaken in intensity as the process of extinction continues frees one from the mistaken attribution that one is somehow responsible for their occurrence due to personal weakness or the existence of an "addictive" personality. Clients can be taught that the most effective point to intervene in the chain of events associated with a desire or craving to indulge is the associative linkage between the craving response itself and the subsequent urge or intention to engage in the consummatory response.

An additional technique to assist clients to cope with craving and urges is the use of *coping imagery*. Imagery can be used to help the individual externalize the urge and to cope with it with a greater sense of mastery and self-efficacy. As an example, we have used the following "samurai image" as a means of coping with urges to resume smoking. The samurai imagery is particularly useful as an antidote to the passivity and victimization that are often experienced by clients who feel easily overwhelmed by intense urges. In this example, the client is instructed to imagine that he or she is a samurai warrior who has assumed the duty of being on guard ("on watch") against possible enemy attacks. Here the "enemy" is identified as any urge to smoke; an urge, from the samurai's perspective, is viewed as an attack on one's life (a view which is not far from the truth, considering the serious health risks associated with resumption of smoking). The samurai's assignment is a simple one: to recognize an urge when it first appears, and to wield the "sword of awareness" to slay the urge before it can do any real damage.

Craving and urges do not always result in an immediate impulsive act. In many situations, for example, the consummatory response cannot be carried out immediately due to the limiting effects of situational constraints such as unavailability of the substance, the presence of others who may impose negative sanctions, or other such limitations. Here, the desire for immediate gratification may be temporarily sublimated, cast in the form of covert planning or fantasies concerning the performance of the taboo activity. Because of the potential for conflict and guilt associated with these covert schemes and plans, the client is likely to engage in the cognitive defense mechanisms of *rationalization* and/or *denial*. These defensive maneuvers may be directed toward obscuring the truth about certain choices or decisions that are covertly designed to "set the stage" for a potential relapse — namely, the tendency for one to make *apparently irrelevant decisions* (AIDs) that lead one closer to the brink of temptation. An AID is a decision that places a person at greater risk for eventual relapse, even though the decision itself appears to be an irrelevant or innocent one on the surface level. An example would be the ex-smoker who suddenly "decides" to sit in the smoking section of an airplane, only to find himself seated next to a passenger who offers him a cigarette the moment the "No Smoking" sign goes off after takeoff. Or the alcoholic who decides after three months of sobriety that it is now acceptable to have alcoholic beverages around the house "in case guests drop by who would like a drink." In the RP approach, the therapist attempts to train the client to "see through" the use of rationalization and denial, to recognize these cognitive defense mechanisms when they occur, and to use them as early warning signals or discriminative stimuli denoting the need for preventive action. In other words, the client is taught how to detect these cognitive precursors of relapse and to "red flag" them as signals that carry the message: "Stop/Look/Listen: Danger ahead; Use alternative route!"

Once the client is trained to recognize the early warning signals, what can be done to alter the course of events that might otherwise lead to a relapse? Here the client can first be instructed to slow down and stop before proceeding any further, to take a "time out" to gain a larger perspective on where all of these actions and thoughts must be leading. To continue the highway metaphor, the client can be encouraged to respond to the danger signals or red flags by pulling over into the nearest rest stop and to reconsider the route ahead. Two techniques are particularly helpful as aids to decision making at these important junction points: a review of the decision matrix, and consulting a personalized relapse "road map" to locate one's current position with regard to several alternative destinations. Hopefully, this break in the chain of events will enable the client to see the "big picture" of where his or her behavior may be leading, and to take corrective action (e.g., to make a "U-turn" and go back to an earlier junction, or to plan a "detour" that will avoid nearby or forthcoming high-risk situations, etc.).

The *decision matrix* can be reviewed and updated by the client during the time-out experience. Examination of the original decision and list of reasons for deciding to change one's behavior (in terms of both the immediate and delayed positive and negative effects) may have the desired effect of countering the cognitive distorting mechanisms. Since it is likely that the client may have previously ignored relevant components of the decision matrix, due to the combined influence of denial and rationalization, examination of the full matrix may permit the client to gain perspective and to see the entire "forest" instead of fixating in a biased manner on particular "trees." A review and possible revision of the decision matrix is an essential procedure to follow after a client has been abstinent (or otherwise changed a target behavior) for some period of time, since this temporal delay will usually create a shift in positive and negative effects associated with the initial decision to change (i.e., the negative physical effects of smoking will have subsided). A careful review of all the reasons leading up to the original decision to change, with an emphasis on the *delayed* effects, may produce a change in the client's expectations that will facilitate continued adherence to the original goals of treatment. The decision matrix analysis is closely related to the description of "decisional balance sheets" advanced by Janis and Mann (1977).

The *relapse road map* is an imagery technique that enables the client to both predict the occurrence of potential high-risk situations well in advance of their actual occurrence and to plan alternative "routes" or strategies to cope with these exigencies. In the clinical application of this procedure, the client is asked to prepare a map prior to embarking on the abstinence journey. Here the therapist might ask the client to make a list of all the possible high-risk situations he or she might encounter following initiation of the behavior change program. What problems might one expect to encounter in the next 3 months? In the next 6 months? Any important changes coming up in one's personal life (relationships, employment, living arrangements, etc.)? Any unusual or potentially disruptive changes in routine, such as vacation trips, celebrations or parties, financial difficulties, or health problems? Any unusual or potential trouble spots should be marked on the map, with the connecting highways representing the course of events over time that would lead one to any of these difficult destinations. By mapping out potential difficulties in advance, the client can be sensitized and forewarned to be on the lookout for various early warning signals and be prepared to take remedial action. Alternative "detour" routes can be identified in advance, along with other preventive strategies such as the use of rest stops for decision making and the availability of alternative coping responses at various stages along the route. Here again, it is helpful to have the client actually practice coping behaviors during a *relapse rehearsal* with the therapist. Finally, the client should be instructed in the use of last-minute *avoidance strategies* that can be employed whenever all other attempts to cope with high-risk situations have failed. Is there a "bypass" route that can be used to avoid the dangers of encountering a high-risk situation? If so, it should be marked clearly on the client's road map for use in emergencies. Just as Tolman's rats were thought to learn by means of "cognitive maps" to find the goal-box at the end of the learning maze (Tolman, 1948), clients can be trained in the use of relapse "road maps" to assist them in finding their way through the maze of everyday life events to reach their eventual goal.

Training, Contraindications, Ethics, Implications

We have now concluded our overview of the RP approach to the self-management of addictive behaviors. Before concluding the chapter, however, we will devote some space to questions concerning the practical implementation of a RP treatment program and the implications of the RP approach for the study of addictive behaviors in clinical psychology. First, with regard to training, the RP model can be applied by any member of the helping professions such as psychiatrists, physicians, clinical and counseling psychologists, and social workers. However, the therapist applying this self-control approach to the treatment of addictive behaviors must have a thorough knowledge of learning principles, cognitive-behavior therapy, self-control, and the various addictive behaviors. The supervision of an experienced cognitive-behavior therapist and/or advanced training in the application of self-control procedures is highly recommended.

Several factors, if present, would contraindicate the use of the RP treatment program. First, all potential clients should receive a thorough physical examination to determine if any organic or physiological disorders associated with the addictive behavior are present. If physical symptoms are present, they should be addressed prior to or concurrent with a self-control program depending on the nature and severity of the problem. Second, individuals experiencing psychotic or borderline symptoms are usually not good candidates for RP treatment and should be referred for treatment to an appropriate agency or therapist. Decisions concerning individuals with a *prior* history of psychosis or personality disorder should be made on an individual basis after appropriate assessment. Finally, perhaps the most important issue with regard to the appropriateness of a self-control treatment program for addictive behaviors is the locus-of-control or personal-causation orientation of the client prior to treatment.

Evidence is mounting that people can be placed along a continuum of "perceived personal causation," with those at one extreme believing that they are capable of exercising choice and "free will" to determine the direction and course of their lives, in contrast with those on the other end who believe that their lives are under the deterministic control of external forces, such as fate, chance, and luck. Most people, of course, fall somewhere between these extremes of internal or external control. It remains an open question as to the extent to which these personal differences in perceived control are modifiable for any given individual. Can we change the underlying belief orientation of an individual who is high on the "external" side of this dimension? Can a therapist facilitate a change in such a person by the careful application of procedures designed to enhance self-efficacy? Only future research can answer these questions.

In the meantime, it is tempting to consider the possibility of matching a particular treatment approach with the client's own expectancy system or locus of control orientation. For those client's who strongly hold the belief that their addiction problem is primarily a physical addiction, involving a "compulsive" behavior beyond volitional control, a traditional disease-model approach may be most effective. For these latter individuals, a conversion-like experience in which they "surrender" the notion that they are personally capable of exercising control in favor of a "higher" power or an authoritarian treatment program may be best. In contrast, clients who reject the notion that they are incapable of exercising control over their behavior and who would prefer instead to learn the skills and attitudes required to modify their lifestyle habits may be more suitable and appropriate for the self-control approach. The RP model is designed as an alternative for this latter group, for those who prefer a "do it yourself" philosophy. With these individuals, the role of the therapist may be similar to that of a more experienced colleague or guide. Although the therapist still retains responsibility for the client's welfare, the degree of structure or directiveness will be less compared to the approach taken with less independent clients. Individual differences in the client population must be taken into account when planning an intervention program and defining the role of the therapist (Karoly, 1980).

Issues concerning the ethics of applying the RP model are no different than in any other professional therapist-client relationship. Like most cognitive-behavioral treatment programs, the RP model adheres to strict

486   Self-Management and Behavior Change

confidentiality, respect for the personhood of the client, active involvement and full collaboration in treatment, client choice of treatment goals, and therapist dedication to the task of therapy. As stated in the previous sections, the RP model does not judge or condemn the individual with an addictive behavior problem with such labels as "alcoholic" or "addict," but allows the client to make his or her decision about how and to what extent to change a pattern of behavior.

Finally, we would like to close with a statement concerning the importance of addictive behaviors in the field of clinical psychology. Addictive behavior problems are a major issue in contemporary American society. We believe that by studying the commonalities of all addictive behavior patterns, a better understanding of a general principal of human motivation will be forthcoming. A generic model of addiction is becoming more of a reality today. It is hoped that such a general model will combine and integrate a wide array of observations into a single coherent picture. It is our hope that the RP model presented in this chapter represents a contribution in this direction.

REFERENCE NOTES

1. Marlatt, G. A. *Relapse Prevention*. Paper presented at the Annual Meeting of Association for the Advancement of Behavior Therapy, Banff, Alberta, Canada, 1980.
2. Condiotte, M. M., & Lichtenstein, E. *Self-efficacy and relapse in smoking cessation programs*. Unpublished Manuscript, University of Oregon, 1980.
3. Shiffman, S. M. *Analysis of relapse episodes following smoking cessation*. Paper presented at the Fourth World Conference on Smoking and Health, Uppsala, Sweden, 1979.

REFERENCES

Ainslie, G. Specious reward: A behavioral theory of impulsiveness and impulse control. *Psychological Bulletin*, 1975, *82*, 463–496.
Armor, D. J., Polich, J. M., & Stambul, H. B. *Alcoholism and treatment*, New York: Wiley, 1978.
Bandura, A. Self-efficacy: Toward a unifying theory of behavior change. *Psychological Review*, 1977, *84*, 191–215(b).
Bem, D. J. Self-perception theory. In L. Berkowitz (Ed.), *Advances in experimental social psychology* (Vol. 6). New York: Academic Press, 1972.
Benson, H. *The Relaxation response*. New York: William Morrow & Co., 1975.
Carrington, P. *Freedom in meditation*. New York: Anchor Press/Doubleday, 1978.
Chaney, E. P., O'Leary, M. R., and Marlatt, G. A. Skill training with alcoholics. *Journal of Consulting and Clinical Psychology*, 1978, *46*, 1092–1104.
Cummings, C., Gordon, J. R., & Marlatt, G. A. Relapse: Strategies of prevention and prediction. In W. R. Miller (Ed.), *The addictive behaviors*. Oxford, England: Pergamon Press, 1980.

DiClemente, C. C. Self-efficacy and smoking cessation maintenance. *Cognitive Research and Therapy*, 1981, in press.

Docter, R., Naitoh, P., & Smith, J. Electroencephalographic changes and vigilance behavior during experimentally induced intoxication with alcoholic subjects. *Psychosomatic Medicine*, 1966, *28*, 605–615.

Festinger, L. *Conflict, decision and dissonance.* Stanford, Cal.: Stanford University Press, 1964.

Garfield, Z., & McBrearty, J. Arousal level and stimulus response in alcoholics after drinking. *Quarterly Journal of Studies on Alcohol*, 1970, *31*, 832–838.

Glasser, W. *Positive addiction.* New York: Harper & Row, 1976.

Goldfried, M. R., & Davison, G. C. *Clinical behavior therapy.* New York: Holt, Rinehart & Winston, 1976.

Goldstein, A. P. *Structured learning therapy.* New York: Academic Press, 1973.

Janis, I. L., & Mann, L. *Decision-making.* New York: Free Press, 1977.

Jellinek, E. M. *The Disease concept of alcoholism.* New Brunswick, N.J.: Hillhouse Press, 1960.

Kanfer, F. H., & Grimm, L. G. Managing clinical change. *Behavior Modification*, 1980, *4*, 419–444.

Karoly, P. Person variables in therapeutic change and development. In P. Karoly & J. J. Steffen (Eds.), *Improving the long-term effects of psychotherapy.* New York: Gardner Press, 1980.

Karoly, P., & Steffen, J. J. (Eds.), *Improving the long-term effects of psychotherapy.* New York: Gardner Press, 1980.

Kazdin, A. E. Covert modeling: The therapeutic application of imagined rehearsal. In J. L. Singer & K. S. Pope (Eds.), *The power of human imagination: New methods of psychotherapy.* New York: Plenum, 1978.

Kuhn, T. S. *The structure of scientific revolutions.* (2nd ed.) Chicago: University of Chicago Press, 1970.

Lefcourt, H. M. *Locus of control.* Hillsdale, N.J.: Lawrence Erlbaum, 1976.

Maisto, S. A., Connors, G. J., & Sachs, P. J. Expectation as a mediator of alcohol intoxication: A reference level model. *Cognitive Therapy and Research*, 1981, *5*, 1–18.

Marlatt, G. A. Craving for alcohol, loss of control, and relapse: A cognitive-behavioral analysis. In P. E. Nathan, G. A. Marlatt, & T. Loberg (Eds.), *Alcoholism: New directions in behavioral research and treatment.* New York: Plenum, 1978.

Marlatt, G. A. Alcohol use and problem drinking: A cognitive-behavioral analysis. In P. C. Kendall & S. D. Hollon (Eds.), *Cognitive-behavioral interventions: Theory, research, and procedures.* New York: Academic, 1979.

Marlatt, G. A., & Gordon, J. R. Determinants of relapse: Implications for the maintenance of behavior change. In P. O. Davidson & S. M. Davidson (Eds.), *Behavioral medicine: Changing health lifestyles.* New York: Brunner/Mazel, 1980.

Marlatt, G. A., & Gordon, J. R. *Relapse prevention.* New York; Guilford Press, in press.

Marlatt, G. A., & Marques, J. K. Meditation, self-control, and alcohol use. In R. B. Stuart (Ed.), *Behavioral self-management: Strategies, techniques and outcomes.* New York: Brunner/Mazel, 1977.

Marlatt, G. A., & Rohsenow, D. R. Cognitive processes in alcohol use: Expectancy and the balanced placebo design. In N. K. Mello (Ed.), *Advances in substance abuse* (Vol. 1). Grennwich, Conn.: JAI Press, 1980.

McClelland, D. C., Davis, W. M., Kalin, R., & Wanner, E. *The drinking man.* New York: Free Press, 1972.

McCrady, B. S., Paolino, T. J., Longabaugh, R. L., & Rossi, J. Effects on treatment outcome of joint admission and spouse involvement in treatment of hospitalized alcoholics. *Addictive Behaviors*, 1979, *4*, 155–165.

McFall, R. M. *Behavioral training: A Skill-Acquisition approach to clinical problems.* Morristown, N.J.: General Learning Press, 1976.

McFall, R. M. Parameters of self-monitoring. In R. B. Stuart (Ed.), *Behavioral self-management: Strategies, techniques, and outcomes.* New York: Brunner/Mazel, 1977.

Meichenbaum, D. *Cognitive-behavior modification.* New York: Plenum, 1977.

Mello, N. K. Some aspects of the behavioral pharmacology of alcohol. In D. H. Efron (Ed.), *Psychopharmacology: A review of progress, 1957–1967.* Washington, D.C.: U.S. Government Printing Office, Public Health Service Publication No. 1836, 1968.

Ornstein, R. E. *The psychology of consciousness.* (2nd ed.) New York: Harcourt Brace Jovanovich, 1977.

Pattison, E. M., Sobell, M. B., & Sobell, L. C. *Emerging concepts of alcohol dependence.* New York: Springer, 1977.

Peel, S., & Brodsky, A. *Love and addiction.* Los Angeles: Taplinger, 1975.

Phares, E. J. *Locus of control in personality.* Morristown, N.J.: General Learning Press, 1976.

Platt, J. Social traps. *American Psychologist*, 1973, *28*, 641–651.

Rotter, J. B. Generalized expectancies for internal versus external control of reinforcement. *Psychological Monographs*, 1966, *80*, no. 1 (Whole no. 609).

Shapiro, D., & Walsh, R. (Eds.), *The science of meditation: Theory, research and experience.* New York: Aldine, 1980.

Solomon, R. L. An opponent-process theory of acquired motivation: IV. The affective dynamics of addiction. In J. Maser & M. E. P. Seligman (Eds.), *Psychopathology: Experimental models.* San Francisco: W. H. Freeman, 1977.

Solomon, R. L., & Corbit, J. D. An opponent-process theory of motivation: I. Temporal dynamics of affect. *Psychological Review*, 1974, *81*, 119–145.

Sontag, S. *Illness as metaphor.* New York: Farrar, Straus & Giroux, 1978.

Spradley, J. P. *You owe yourself a drunk.* Boston: Little, Brown, & Co., 1970.

Thoresen, C. E., & Mahoney, M. J. *Behavioral self-control.* New York: Holt, Rinehart & Winston, 1974.

Tolman, E. C. Cognitive maps in rats and men. *Psychological Review*, 1948, *55*, 189–208.

14
Self-Management in the Treatment of Sexual Dysfunction

Patricia J. Morokoff
and
Joseph LoPiccolo

Sexual dysfunction has gradually become recognized as a common problem in our society. As a result of this recognition, treatment of sexual dysfunction has undergone a demystification and subsequent inclusion in the battery of accepted therapeutic interventions. A concurrent trend in approach to therapeutic interventions has been the greater emphasis on self-management strategies in treatment of psychological problems. The self-management approach to treatment assumes a participant role of the client. The client is viewed neither as a passive recipient of a treatment nor as eager and nonresistant in the change process. The therapist plays an active role in facilitating motivation within the client to take increasing responsibility for the change process (Kanfer & Grimm, 1980). Three stages in therapy are conceptualized. In the first stage, the therapist focuses on helping the client to develop a commitment for change and establish clear objectives for therapy. In doing so, the therapist may work to incorporate incentives for change into the therapy program. A further aspect of this stage involves establishing an alliance between client and therapist and helping the individual to accept the role of client. In the second stage, the therapist structures circumstances under which the client may learn new skills designed to impact on the presenting problem and meet therapeutic objectives. Techniques such as self-observations, the use of a contract, and increasing the reward value of target behaviors serve the purpose of facilitating acquisition of the new skills. In the third stage, efforts are made to decrease the necessity of using such tactics. In doing so, the importance of the therapist diminishes and self-maintenance skills are emphasized.

In studying self-management strategies within treatment of a particular problem area, two broadly conceptualized routes are possible. One approach is to examine the ways in which self-management techniques can be employed within treatment of that problem area. In this chapter, we will look historically at treatment of sexual dysfunction, in terms of the trend toward increased focus on client responsibility within therapy. We will further look at current practice of sex therapy and identify ways in which self-management strategies are undertaken. A second broad approach is to look for ways in which specific syndromes in the problem area differentially make use of self-management strategies. We will examine in detail a treatment program developed at the Sex Therapy Center, Department of Psychiatry and Behavioral Science, State University of New York at Stony Brook, incorporating self-management methodology in treatment of primary orgasmic dysfunction in women.

HISTORICAL AND THEORETICAL FRAMEWORK FOR TREATMENT

Self-Management Components of Sex Therapy

Little attention was paid to the development of systematic treatment for sexual dysfunction prior to Freud's theoretical conceptualizations of the development of sexual disorder. Freud brought societal focus to the role of sexual desire in shaping global aspects of the personality, one component of which is sexual adjustment. Freud also originated a method of treatment focused on uncovering unconscious conflicts. Such conflicts were believed to produce fixation at a psychosexual stage of development. Thus the sexual symptom was viewed as a manifestation of neurosis. Bergler (1944) writes: "Frigidity is a symptom of a neurosis, a disease of the unconscious. It is curable analytically, the prognosis depending upon the type, that is, the depth of the regression." Analytic treatment of the sexual dysfunction is thus aimed at the treatment of the neurosis and as such requires an intense involvement between analyst and patient. Bergler (1944) suggests an appointment five times a week for a minimum of 8 months and a maximum of 2 years. Analytic treatment focuses on the interaction between the analyst and patient as the source of change and thus does not conform to a self-management model. In other words, responsibility for carrying out a treatment program is not placed on the client. The treatment rather occurs within the interaction of analyst and client.

Perhaps the first systematic break from this conceptual scheme occurred within the context of conditioning therapies. Salter (1949), later elaborated by Wolpe (1958), took the approach that sexual arousal is impeded by conditioned anxiety which may be deconditioned through desensitization. This approach to sexual dysfunction is noteworthy in that it does not conceptualize the dysfunction as symptomatic of a more pervasive problem that must first be cured. The treatment model proposed by Wolpe (1958) involves having the patient imagine a graduated hierarchy of sexual activities while maintaining relaxation. This approach, like analytic treatment, retains responsibility for therapeutic change within the therapist-client interaction. In this case, the therapist must teach the client how to relax and must present imaginal items in the hierarchy. The client may feel more in control of the change process than the patient in analysis, because the steps by which change is expected to occur are made explicit and thus can be later repeated by the client without the therapists' aid. When desensitization is structured *in vivo* rather than in imagination, the treatment begins to take the form of today's rapid treatment techniques. When a client is asked to engage in graduated sexual experiences with his or her partner, a higher degree of client responsibility enters the therapeutic equation. In this therapy format change is expected to occur as a function of engaging in "homework" sessions. Thus the client becomes overtly responsible for carrying out the treatment program. In Wolpe's application of *in vivo* desensitization to sexual problems, sexual arousal is expected to inhibit anxiety, and sexual experiences are graduated so as to begin with activities which would engender very little anxiety and gradually increase. Madsen and Ullmann (1967) reported a case study in which this approach proved successful.

The directed rapid treatment technique used today received its major impetus from Masters and Johnson's (1970) report of high success rates in treating marital couples with a heterogeneous package emphasizing structured sexual exercises. This kind of treatment package has been expanded upon by many practitioners (Kaplan, 1974). In order to identify the ways in which self-management is a part of the rapid treatment package, commonly referred to as sex therapy, it will be relevant to enumerate components of this treatment strategy and how each relates to a self-management conceptualization.

LoPiccolo (1978) has identified seven major underlying elements in the total treatment package. We will first discuss treatment components relevant to the first phase of therapy: developing a commitment for change and establishing objectives. A crucial aspect of this phase is structuring the clients' definition and perceptions of their problems so that change is possible. Current practitioners of sex therapy emphasize the necessity that both partners assume *mutual responsibility* as a first step in working on problems. A second component of this phase is *attitudinal change* related to altering cognitions which negatively affect sexuality. These attitudes typically result from parental or societal injunctions against sexuality and interfere with the individuals ability to fully and freely express sexual feelings. Such feelings impact directly on motivation for change. If a person feels that sexual activity is wrong, then he or she will probably be unwilling to take responsiblity for homework assignments designed to facilitate sexual expression. Thus attitude change may be conceptualized as one aspect of developing a commitment for change.

A third component is communication training on nonsexual topics or other aspects of *marital therapy*. Improving general satisfaction with the relationship may be conceptualized as preliminary to actual development of new sexual capabilities. The couple with severe relationship problems often find it impossible to put nonsexual problems aside for the purpose of working on sexual assignments together. Resolution of marital conflicts may be conceptualized as one aspect of developing a commitment for sexual change. In some cases, this phase may involve the most critical changes to be made in the course of therapy. Nonsexual communication training, contracting, or other aspects of marital therapy may also occur in the skill acquisition phase of therapy to the extent that sexual problems are a result of marital conflict, as will be discussed later. *Anxiety reduction* is a fourth component, which may involve techniques such as imaginal desensitization. Anxiety reduction may also be accomplished through attitudinal change (e.g., when the therapist helps the client to stop engaging in self-derogatory thoughts about sexual abilities), or may be accomplished through prescribed sexual behaviors (such as conditions arranged by the therapists to reduce performance anxiety). This treatment strategy thus encompasses heterogeneous techniques and may be a part of both the phase of developing a commitment for change and skill acquisition.

Before proceeding to therapy components related to skill acquisition, let us discuss in more detail how the elements just discussed interact to develop motivation. In developing motivation for change, it is important that the client see problems as being under his or her control. If individuals do not see themselves as choosing in some way to engage in activites which perpetuate their problems, the possibility of change may seem unrealistic and remote. This problem becomes particularly acute when treating marital dyads, for the person most motivated for change may be the nonsymptomatic one. Thus, in sex therapy, one of the first steps frequently is a communication to the couple that the therapist views responsibility for the problem as being mutually shared and that change will require the equal effort of both partners. Many times, people feel that their sexual functioning is unalterable. This is frequently a result of sporadic and ineffective attempts to make changes, as well as a belief that one has no control over one's body. Many areas of functioning that individuals wish to change fall under a general rubric of "self control." These are the types of changes that might be adopted as New Year's resolutions: smoke less, eat less, follow a regular schedule, write more letters, meet new people, and others. Sexual functioning is different in that it is not clear to people what they can do to attain their desired goals. Thus, an initial way by which the therapist facilitates change is by indicating that we do know of a series of steps the individual can take on his or her own to achieve improved sexual functioning. This constitutes a demystification of the problem. Appropriate explanation of why adequate functioning is not now occurring may be necessary to cement a belief that change is possible. Thus the client's self-perceptions may be changed from "I can't get an erection because there's something wrong with me" to "I'm not getting erections because I'm so worried about my performance that I'm not relaxing and letting myself enjoy sexual sensations." Thus the first goal of sex therapy is to communicate that the problem is each person's responsibility and that change is possible.

Concurrently, the therapist focuses on helping clients define therapeutic objectives. When presenting a sexual dysfunction the client often has a fairly well defined notion of what the goals for treatment are, such as reaching orgasm, maintaining erection, or lasting longer before ejaculation. Conceptualizing these goals in terms of acquiring new skills and attitudes, however, makes the goals seem more easily attained because it emphasizes the client's potential control over the situation (Heiman, LoPiccolo, & LoPiccolo, 1979).

Let us now turn to the skill acquisition phase of therapy. Most prominent in this phase is that the therapist prescribes changes in the couple's sexual behavior — *homework assignments* are given. These assignments take the hierarchical form of *in vivo* desensitization in that they typically begin in nondemanding sensual massage with no direct breast or genital stimulation. Gradually, assignments allow breast and genital carressing and eventually add intercourse. This component of the program clearly requires clients to take responsibility for completing assignments at home. The ability to complete homework assignments assumes that the client has accepted his role of client in therapy, that he has agreed on a definition of the problem toward which the homework assignments are directed, and that he is motivated to work on these problems. Another component of all sex therapy programs involves working with the couple on their *ability to communicate* and give each other feedback during sexual activity. Training in ability to communicate sexual feelings may include practice and role-play within the therapy session, as well as specific assignments prescribing feedback during sexual activity at home (Kaplan, 1974; LoPiccolo, 1977). It may further be facilitated by the therapist's modeling of frank, open discussion of sexuality. A final component of skill acquisition is *education*. Simply providing information and correcting misconceptions is a frequent aspect of therapy.

Acquisition of sexual skills may be facilitated by use of the same strategies designed to enhance skill acquisition in other problem areas. Directed homework assignments have already been discussed as a central aspect of the treatment program. Clients are given the expectation that their success in achieving therapeutic goals depends on their completion of homework assignments. As sex therapy is typically conducted, a variety of kinds of homework may be assigned. Most assignments prescribe the couple to engage in graduated sexual activities. Other assignments may prescribe each partner to work on individual goals or nonsexual, relationship goals. While directed sexual experience was originally conceptualized as activity that need be performed jointly by the two partners, a recent trend has been to ask each partner to work individually on developing comfort with his or her body, and to begin developing sexual skills during self-stimulation (LoPiccolo & Lobitz, 1972). These skills (e.g., learning to reach orgasm or learning to delay ejaculation) are hypothesized to be more easily learned via self-stimulation and may be gradually incorporated into lovemaking with the partner. Treatment programs which include masturbation have been found to be effective for female centered problems (Barbach, 1974; Kohlenberg, 1974; LoPiccolo & Lobitz, 1972; Reisinger, 1974; Riley & Riley, 1978) and male-centered problems (Annon, 1974; LoPiccolo & Lobitz, 1973). The inclusion of masturbation as a treatment component is significant because it increases the ability of the client to work on sexual problems on his or her own. When sexual assignments are designed for joint practice by the couple, they must be carefully limited so that neither partner feels that the other takes advantage. The marital dynamics of the dyad must be taken into account. However, assignments given individually to each partner may more easily be construed as practice or training which each individual may complete at his or her own pace. Thus, skill acquisition is more easily accomplished within the context of individual rather than dyadic assignments.

In addition to task assignments, Kanfer (1980) lists self-monitoring and contracts as methods of therapeutic change within the context of self-management. Both self-monitoring and contracts have been utilized within sex therapy. Lobitz and LoPiccolo (1972), in a discussion of new methods in behavioral treatment of sexual dysfunction, describe a modification of self-monitoring for keeping track of changes in sexual functioning. For each assignment given, the client is asked to write down what was done and what his or her reactions to the assignment were. As with other self-monitoring procedures, this record-keeping serves several functions. First, it allows baseline recording of target behaviors. In the beginning of treatment, the couple may be asked to simply engage in their normal sexual activities while beginning to keep records. This not only gives the therapist information about the dysfunction, but also provides a standard against which change may be measured. Secondly, the procedure concretizes completion of the assignment and permits the client to reflect on progress toward attainment of goals.

Lobitz and LoPiccolo (1972) further describe the use of contracts in sex therapy. The basic strategy outlined is to have clients contract with the therapist to engage in a set of behaviors (assignments) each week. An integral aspect of this strategy is that the client work together with the therapist to arrive at the set of homework assignments. Thus, the client participates with the therapist in determining the content of the contract. Lobitz and LoPiccolo (1972) describe use of negative consequences for failure to comply with the contract. These are in the form of a penalty deposit system. The client is asked to pay a monetary deposit at the beginning of therapy equal to their treatment fee. If part of the assignment is not completed, the client will be fined from his deposit. This strategy may be particularly effective for sexual dysfunctions resulting from skill deficits. The assumption is that once the client learns to become aroused, reach orgasm, or delay ejaculation, this activity will be reinforcing in and of itself and will not require external incentives. The client may feel inhibited or anxious about engaging in the self-stimulation and sensual massage exercises initially. Some people do not want their spouse to think them overly sexual, and hence feel obliged to turn down sexual advances. In each of these cases, a compelling external reason for engaging in the sexual behavior makes it easier for the client to comply. It is probably the case that it is not so much the actual prospect of losing money that motivates the client, but rather the fact that the reason for engaging in the behavior is not in a sense the client's responsibility. Those dysfunctions which are not based on skill deficits (such as low sexual desire) would be hypothesized to be less responsive to such external negative contingencies. While the client may engage in sexual behaviors as long as external contingencies are applied, the behaviors themselves are not sufficiently reinforcing to continue once contingencies are removed.

Sexual behavior differs from many targets of modification (e.g., smoking, eating, study behavior) in that the behavior itself, once shaped, is expected to be immediately reinforcing. Thus, there is no necessity (except possibly in low-sexual-desire cases) to pair other positive reinforcers with sex. However, postive consequences are frequently subtly included in sexual behavior-change programs. These take the form of self-statements or statements to the partner. The latter are most frequently employed: clients are asked to learn to reinforce each other by "letting the other person know when something feels good." Frequently, one or both members of the couple feel sexually unattractive or incompetent. Supportive statements of the partner's attractiveness or ability to provide good feelings are highly desirable. These statements are extremely important in making sensual massage assignments enjoyable. If such mutual reinforcement is not provided, it is usually doubtful whether clients will engage in such activities.

A final component used to facilitate skill acquisition is modification of the couple's environment. For those couples who have children, it is the rare instance in which children are not presented as a reason why it is difficult to complete sexual homework. Sometimes this is a rationalization masking deeper fears of sexual intimacy, while other times the client just requires "permission" to alter priorities. In either case, work on restructuring the environment may frequently be used as a way to approach the problem. A first step is to encourage the couple to spend time by themselves in their bedroom, even while older children are still awake. The environmental modification most appropriate in such situations is putting a lock on the bedroom door. The willingness of a couple to take such a step may tell the therapist much about the family structure, and often the prognosis for the case. If the couple is unwilling to set such clear boundaries, preliminary work on motivation for change is often required. Other modifications typically used involve making the environment in which sexual activity is to take place special and attractive. Placing flowers in the bedroom, putting fresh sheets on the bed, or playing soft music are suggestions often given to enhance the sensual attractiveness of the environment and thus facilitate enjoyment of assignments.

The third stage of self-management treatment is maintenance. In this stage the therapist is phased out so that the clients are able to arrange their own life to maintain newly learned skills. Lobitz and LoPiccolo (1972) and Heiman, LoPiccolo, and LoPiccolo (1979) describe such procedures within the context of sex therapy. The change from skill acquisition to maintenance may be brought about gradually. Initially, homework assignments may be determined solely by the therapist. As skills are acquired, the therapist may begin asking the couple to negotiate within the therapy session what homework assignments need be given. At this time, clients are asked to formally write out a *maintenance plan* in which they consider what changes they have made, what led to those changes, and how the changes can be maintained. Writing the maintenance plan is given as a homework assignment which each partner is asked to work on individually. Completing the assignment requires the client to think back over the course of therapy to determine what changes in behavior, attitude, or understanding led to changes in sexual functioning. Typically, clients cite increased communication about feelings related to sexual experiences and restructuring of schedules to give sex a higher priority. The couple is also asked to indicate how they may apply knowledge gained from the therapy to goals still remaining. In doing this, they are asked to identify areas they would still like to work on and structure a plan (based on factors identified in the course of therapy as important) for making these changes. This aspect of the maintenance plan is important because most couples have not completed all their goals. The assignment acknowledges this and fosters the attitude that maintaining a satisfying sexual relationship is a process which may require effort. Thus a goal of the treatment program is not only to effect changes in sexual functioning, but to teach clients strategies for how to make changes. Heiman et al. (1979) have described use of a 3-month follow-up visit. This session serves the clinical function of helping to increase motivation for working on goals following termination of therapy. Motivation is increased because clients know they will be meeting with their therapist again and often do not wish to come in with a bad report.

Differential Treatment of Sexual Dysfunctions

In the preceding section, the function of the various components of sex therapy was discussed in relation to overall treatment objectives. In this section, the argument will be developed that the process of treatment differs for different dysfunctions, such that some problems require more preliminary work in the first phase of therapy, focusing on reconceptualization of the problem, marital conflict resolution, attitudinal change, and anxiety reduction. Other sexual problems tend to require work centering specifically on skill acquisition. Those dysfunctions which fall in each category will be established in relation to etiology and treatment.

Etiological factors in sexual dysfunction. In order to elucidate how particular sexual dysfunctions are differentially treated (from a self-management perspective), we will look at differences in etiology among the dysfunctions. First, we will generally review potential etiological factors, then the classification of sexual dysfunctions, and then how etiology is related to specific dysfunctions.

Hogan (1978) presents an interactional model by which both historical and current factors are related in the etiology of sexual dysfunction. Kaplan (1974) conceptualizes organic and psychological etiological factors. Organic factors include physical trauma and disease processes such as those involved in diabetes or multiple sclerosis. Under psychological factors, Kaplan subsumes immediate causes, intrapsychic causes, and dyadic causes. Drawing from both models, we might propose the following etiological factors under the heading of psychological determinants of sexual dysfunction. The first factor is termed *intrapsychic conflict / early emotional trauma* and is meant to subsume all developmental experiences which lead the person to his or her current level of functioning. These may be conceptualized from more than one theoretical vantage (e.g., psychoanalytic or learning theory). Kaplan (1974) describes Freudian theory as implicating unresolved Oedipal conflicts which become activated by current adult experiences in the appearance of sexual dysfunction. Learning theory would suggest pairing of punishment or anxiety with sexual experience. Whichever model is adopted, rapid treatment techniques prescribe structured sexual experience, either to decondition anxiety (learning theory) or to provide opportunity for resolution of the previously repressed conflict by placing the client directly in the avoided situation (Freudian theory). While therapists of different orientations may focus to a greater or lesser extent on childhood material during the therapy session, the mechanism by which change is expected to occur in intrapsychic conflict is virtually identical, and highly consistent with a self-management format. A second factor is *anxiety*, which may result from several sources including: fear of evaluation—performance anxiety; fear of losing control—as when a woman holds back prior to orgasm for lack of trust of her partner or her own changing body sensations; or excessive need to please the partner—fear of rejection (Kaplan, 1974). Anxieties, like intrapsychic conflicts, may be dealt with in the graduated sexual experiences the couple is assigned to complete. Thus, again, this etiological component can be dealt with in a skill-acquisition format. Sometimes, anxiety-reducing procedures are utilized within therapy sessions if anxiety is so strong that a nonthreatening *in vivo* experience cannot be constructed. Such a procedure is systematic desensitization which may be conducted within the therapy session. Alternatively, the client may be taught relaxation and then asked to use this skill prior to beginning sexual assignments. The same effect is sometimes achieved by suggesting that the client have a drink or glass of wine before the sexual experience (Dengrove, 1971). Another anxiety-reducing procedure is attitude restructuring as described by Ellis (1967). Performance anxiety may be modified by altering the individual's self-expectations and self-statements. Thus, the etiological factor of anxiety may be treated either simply within the gradation of sexual homework assignments or with additional anxiety-reduction techniques. A third factor, *lack of sexual information*, can sometimes be a determinant of a dysfunction: a woman may be unaware of the desirablity of partner manipulation of her genitals and, in not engaging in this activity, may have difficulty becoming aroused. A man may believe that he should be able to get an erection simply by looking at his wife with no additional stimulation. If he fails to achieve an erection under these circumstances, he may feel he is dysfunctional. As indicated before, information may be supplied either directly by the therapist or in the form of books and movies. Dysfunctions based on misinformation tend to be the easiest to treat. *Skill deficits and lack of awareness of body* are again treated through the directed sexual experience with a focus on increased communication. When one is out of touch with one's own body, the commonly resulting symptoms are lack of sensation (such as women who have never experienced orgasm who often report a genital anesthesia) or the experience of all sensation focused in the genitals with no sensual pleasure derived from touching other parts of the body (more common in men than women). Clients are given homework exercises designed to help them focus on body sensations (Heiman, LoPiccolo, & LoPiccolo, 1976) or are instructed in communication of feelings to the partner (Kaplan, 1974; Lobitz & LoPiccolo, 1972b; Masters & Johnson, 1970; Prochaska & Marzilli, 1973).

Relationship problems (dyadic causes in Kaplan's terminology) impact on sexual functioning in a multitude of ways. On a basic level, one partner's sexual symptom may protect an intrapsychic conflict of the spouse. For example, a wife's inability to become aroused may serve a dyadic function in preventing the husband from dealing with his own sexual anxieties (Haley, 1963). In a similar fashion, sexual conflict between the couple may represent one manifestation of a dyadic power struggle. Such struggles generally take the form of disagreements over when to have sex (morning or night), how to have sex (should oral sex be included), or who is to initiate. Lack of emotional intimacy between partners often results in lack of physical intimacy as well as poor communication. Kaplan (1974) further specifies ways in which one spouse may sabotage the success of a sexual experience by creating pressure or tension prior to or during sex, initiating sex at a bad time, frustrating the partner's desires by disliking whatever the partner likes, and failing to make oneself physically appealing to the spouse. It is obvious that such marital issues cannot be dealt with solely through directed sexual experience and must be approached independently. Such direct treatment of the relationship may include features of skill training. However, theorists have emphasized the importance of the relationship between couple and therapist (Haley, 1963), in-session facilitation of communication training (Bolte, 1975), presentation of feedback on rules of the marital system (Haley, 1963), and defining and implementing behavioral goals (Hurvitz, 1975). Thus, even within the behavioral approach a high level of therapist intervention tends to be advocated, "once the counselor has elicited instrumental hypotheses which require change-affecting behavior, he teaches the spouses the appropriate change-initiating and change-supporting behavior by various verbal methods, modeling, role playing demonstrations and suitable behavior modification practices" (Hurvitz, 1975, p. 237).

In order to refer differentially to various dysfunctions, it will be useful at this point to adopt a classification scheme. The format to be utilized here is suggested by LoPiccolo (1977). In this scheme, dysfunctions are roughly separated into male-centered and female-centered problems. Male-centered problems include premature ejaculation, erectile failure, and ejaculatory incompetence. Definitions of premature ejaculation vary as to whether the locus of the response defining the disorder resides in the female or male. Masters and Johnson (1970) define premature ejaculation as the man's inability to delay ejaculation long enough for the woman to reach orgasm 50 percent of the time. In order to avoid separating out extent of female responsibility for her lack of orgasm, LoPiccolo has suggested using a more statistical approach, defining a premature ejaculation as one occurring more quickly than the lower threshold of an average latency range (roughly in less than 4 minutes). Both Masters and Johnson and LoPiccolo emphasize consideration of other relevant factors before diagnosis. Erectile failure refers simply to the inability of the male to attain or maintain an erection sufficient for intercourse (LoPiccolo, 1977). Ejaculatory incompetence refers to the inability of the male to reach orgasm through stimulation by his partner, and is a relatively rare phenomenon.

Female disorders include primary and secondary orgasmic dysfunction as well as vaginismus and dyspareunia. Primary orgasmic dysfunction occurs when a woman has never reached orgasm through any means of stimulation. Secondary orgasmic dysfunction is a quite heterogeneous category subsuming women who were previously fully orgasmic but who are currently nonorgasmic, women who reach orgasm only in some situations (e.g., with lover but not husband, via masturbation but not intercourse, etc.), and women who are reaching orgasm at a lower frequency than desired. Vaginismus refers to involuntary spastic contraction of the vaginal musculature preventing or impeding intromission. Dyspareunia refers to painful intercourse.

As is no doubt apparent, this classification scheme is not without problems. Kaplan's (1974, 1977) classification system is more comprehensive in subdividing sexual response into three phases: desire, arousal, and orgasm. Such a system permits diagnosing problems in desire separate from actual performance. This has given rise to the conceptualization of low sex desire which has received a good deal of recent attention (Kaplan, 1977, 1979; LoPiccolo, 1980). Kaplan's approach subsequently provided the basis for a more extended multidimensional classification scheme currently in use at the Sex Therapy Center, State University of New York at Stony Brook (Schover et al., 1980). Despite the clear conceptual improvement of the multidimensional approach, the original classification system will be employed here for two reasons. First, previous research equating etiological factors to particular dysfunctions tend to incorporate the older system, and second, the self-management program described at length here addresses a particular diagnostic group (primary orgasmic dysfunction) derived from the old system.

Relationship of etiology to dysfunction. *Organic etiology* has been most commonly related to erectile failure (Belt, 1973; Dengrove, 1971b; Masters & Johnson, 1970) as well as dyspareunia. For some reason, arousal and orgasm in the female do not seem to be as readily affected by organic pathology as in the male (Kaplan, 1974). It is entirely possible, of course, that the lack of observed effect merely reflects a lack of knowledge of vasocongestive and neural mechanisms in women.

Many theorists have hypothesized a relationship between *intrapsychic conflict or early emotional trauma* and sexual dysfunction. For example, strict religious training and poor sex education have often been impugned as causes of later sexual problems. Little research evidence substantiates such claims, however. Research relating childhood experiences to current sexual satisfaction has not succeeded in identifying variables which predict adult lack of satisfaction, much less specific dysfunctions (Morokoff, 1978).

Anxiety has been specifically implicated in many dysfunctions. Clinical observation has confirmed a relationship between anxiety and erectile failure (Annon, 1974; Cooper, 1969; Friedman, 1968). Masters and Johnson (1970) furthermore specifically conceptualize erectile failure as resulting from anxiety about performance or fear of failure. Some evidence exists suggesting that anxiety is also an etiological factor in premature ejaculation (Cooper, 1969). In reviewing the literature relating anxiety to premature ejaculation, Hogan (1978) concludes that, although this relationship is not conclusive, it is likely that anxiety plays a causative role in some types of cases and not others. Both Masters and Johnson (1970) and Lazarus (1963) present cases of female orgasmic dysfunction which appear to be mediated by anxiety. However, a differential role of anxiety in primary versus secondary orgasmic dysfunction has not been established. Anxiety has frequently been discussed as a causative factor in vaginismus (Fuchs et al., 1973; Haslam, 1965).

Lack of sexual information and skill deficits have often been implicated in causing primary orgasmic dysfunction (Annon, 1974; Heiman, LoPiccolo, & LoPiccolo, 1976; Hogan, 1978; Kaplan, 1974; McMullen & Rosen, 1979), and premature ejaculation (Kaplan, 1974; Masters & Johnson, 1970). Kaplan (1974) suggests that premature ejaculation results from lack of awareness of the sensations preceding ejaculation. Lack of focus on such sensation apparently interferes with learning to control ejaculation. Masters and Johnson have observed a different pattern also related to learning history. They found a pattern among their males presenting premature ejaculation in which early sexual experiences were hurried. They hypothesize that these men may be reinforced in their early sexual experiences for quick ejaculation. Thus, the learned skill of quick ejaculation becomes an established pattern. *Relationship problems* have been implicated in two diagnostic categories: secondary orgasmic dysfunction and erectile failure. McGovern, Stewart, and LoPiccolo (1975) compared etiological factors and treatment outcome in two groups of women. The groups ($N = 6$) were comprised of primary and secondary inorgasmic women. Treatment was found to be more effective in increasing orgasmic response of the primary orgasmic dysfunction group than the secondary orgasmic dysfunction group. Furthermore, it was found that the majority of the secondary dysfunctional women were dissatisfied with their marital relationships prior to treatment, as measured on the Locke-Wallace Marriage Inventory (Locke & Wallace, 1959). Primary inorgasmic women tended to have a higher level of marital satisfaction. The authors speculate that "primary inorgasmic women respond best to therapy focused specifically on sexual matters, whereas secondary inorgasmic women may respond better when traditional marital therapy is combined with sex treatment" (McGovern et al., 1975, p. 272). Such a recommendation has clear implications for prescriptive use of self-management principles. In comparing primary and secondary inorgasmic women, a picture emerges, supported by clinical experience, that primary inorgasmic women tend more to be out of touch with their bodies. This may be manifested by lack of perceived ability to become aroused or a lack of genital sensation. Secondary inorgasmic women tend to be aware of sensations, yet experience arousal more on some occasions than others. Their differential experience of arousal seems to enter into marital power struggles and sexual sabotage, making treatment of sexual dysfunction difficult to separate from treatment of marital conflict.

With respect to erectile failure, Masters and Johnson (1970) describe a variety of psychological determinants. The pattern they report as being most prevalent involves gradual loss of erectile functioning. They observed that erectile failure is frequently preceded by long-standing premature ejaculation. They hypothesize that over the years, the wife becomes more and more blatent in her expression of dissatisfaction with her husband's sexual performance. In the absence of a means for improving ejaculatory latency, the husband in this situation may experience feelings of inadequacy and desperation. He may become acutely aware of his own sexual functioning, monitoring his state of erection closely. This monitoring leads to taking the stance of observer of the sex act, rather than full participant (commonly referred to as spectatoring). Thus, in this syndrome, relationship problems lead to increased anxiety about sexual functioning. Lobitz et al. (1974) report a case study of erectile failure occurring in a second marriage for both husband and wife, who were in their fifties. The authors are explicit in describing the contribution of the wife to performance pressure by making hostile and derogatory remarks concerning her husband's sexual functioning. Thus, the marital relationship has been clinically observed to be etiologically relevant to erectile failure.

Self-Management and the Differential Treatment of Sexual Dysfunction

At this point, we may summarize those dysfunctions for which treatment focuses on skill acquisition versus those for which preliminary work is required. To begin with premature ejaculation, the primary etiological factors relate to skill deficits and lack of awareness of the body. The treatment strategy utilized to deal with these problems is homework assignments focused on directed sexual experience, thus making this dysfunction highly consistent with a skill-acquisition approach. Erectile failure, on the other hand, may be caused by physiological problems, relationship problems, and anxiety. While anxiety may be treated through structured sexual experience, it may also require attitudinal restructuring to develop an unambivalent commitment to change. Issues involved in physiological and marital problems seem to rely heavily on such preliminary work as well. Thus, treatment of erectile failure, while including some skill-acquisition components, is typically conducted with more emphasis on the preliminary stages of therapy. Ejaculatory incompetence is relatively rare and less well understood. Possible etiological factors are similar to those implicated in erectile failure.

In considering female dysfunctions, a clear difference in etiological factors exists between primary and secondary orgasmic dysfunction. Primary orgasmic dysfunction seems to have an immediate cause in lack of awareness of one's body and possibly lack of sexual information. It is thus amenable to treatment through directed sexual experience and education. Secondary orgasmic dysfunction seems related to anxiety and relationship problems, and thus, like erectile failure, relies much more on active involvement of the therapist in developing ability to change. Vaginismus, while etiologically related to anxiety and organic factors, is treated with a combination of relaxation training and a dilating program typically conducted under supervision of a physician. Dyspareunia also frequently has an organic etiology and in such cases is treated medically.

In summary, primary orgasmic dysfunction and premature ejaculation are conceptualized as resulting from skill/awareness deficits while other dysfunctions involve additional medical, relationship, or attitudinal factors. Because of this, primary orgasmic dysfunction and premature ejaculation are theoretically excellent targets for self-help programs, which function without the benefit of therapist involvement. As supplementary evidence that the development of commitment for change is less needed in treatment of these dysfunctions, successful use of self-help programs in their treatment will be presented. A self-help program, by definition, is one in which the skill acquisition phase of therapy is emphasized. Lowe and Mikulas (1975) report on use of a written manual in the treatment of premature ejaculation. Ten couples participated in the study. The couples met the criteria that (1) ejaculation occurred either prior to penetration, during penetration, or within 3 minutes after intromission, (2) both members of the couple agreed to participate, and (3) no interpersonal problems requiring initial treatment were present. Five couples were given the self-help manuals; five were placed on a control wait list. Both groups were given questionnaire measures assessing ejaculatory latency. The treatment program was self-paced, and took an average of 3 weeks to complete. The control group thus began the treatment program after an elapsed waiting period of 3 weeks. Contact with therapists involved an initial interview to determine whether the couple met the criteria, at which time they were given the questionnaire. They were then contacted twice a week by telephone to check on progress. No therapy sessions were conducted. The treatment manuals contained instruction in sensate focus, the squeeze technique, and coital positions. Results were highly significant, showing that as a result of the self-help treatment, men in the original experimental group increased their latency an average of 37.2 minutes while men in the control group reported no change. Following treatment, this group increased their latency an average of 18.6 minutes. The smaller latency gain for the control group seemed to result from one subject who gained only 4.5 minutes. The authors emphasize that care needs to be exercised in selecting clients for self-help programs.

Several self-help guides in treatment of primary orgasmic dysfunction have recently become available: *For Yourself: The Fulfillment of Female Sexuality* (Barbach, 1975); *Woman's Orgasm: A Guide to Sexual Satisfaction* (Kline-Graber & Graber, 1975); and *Becoming Orgasmic: A Sexual Growth Program for Women* (Heiman, LoPiccolo, & LoPiccolo, 1976). McMullen and Rosen (1979) experimentally examined the efficacy of a self-help masturbation training program — modeled after the LoPiccolo and Lobitz (1972) procedure — versus a waiting list control group in treating primary orgasmic dysfunction. Two training formats were compared: written instructions versus videotaped instructions in which steps in the program were modeled by an actress. Subjects in both formats came in once a week for 6 weeks to either view a 20-minute videotape or read a written booklet. Subjects in both groups were supplied with a vibrator during the fourth week of treatment, but no therapeutic contact occurred. Sixty subjects, of whom half were married and half were single, participated. Results showed that about 60 percent of women became orgasmic in masturbation and 40 percent became orgasmic in intercourse. These levels were significantly higher than the wait-list control group (in which none of the women became orgasmic). No differences in presentation format were found, but there was a trend for more married than single women to become orgasmic both in masturbation and intercourse.

Research such as Lowe and Mikulas (1975) and McMullen and Rosen

(1979) confirm theoretical predictions that skill training (as presented in their respective self-help guides) is effective without therapist input in treating premature ejaculation and primary orgasmic dysfunction for a sizable percentage of subjects. It should be kept in mind that, while latency to ejaculation and presence of orgasm are the most easily quantifiable aspects of the presenting problem for premature ejaculation and primary orgasmic dysfunction, respectively, greater overall satisfaction within the sexual relationship is usually a larger goal which may or may not be dealt with in such a self-help format. Additionally, a self-selection process undoubtedly occurs such that persons responding to a newspaper ad for a self-help program may not perceive their problems to be as severe as those who present for weekly treatment. Hence, optimism about effectiveness of such programs should be moderated with caution.

SELF-MANAGEMENT OF PRIMARY ORGASMIC DYSFUNCTION: A TREATMENT APPLICATION

To this point, the application of self-management principles in treatment of sexual dysfunction has been discussed from a theoretical vantage point. A more detailed look at practical aspects of this approach may be afforded by examination of the treatment program for primary orgasmic dysfunction currently under evaluation at the Sex Therapy Center, State University of New York at Stony Brook. This program combines a self-help package for treatment of primary orgasmic dysfunction with a limited number of therapy sessions. Normally, 15 sessions of therapy or more are utilized in treating dysfunctions at this center. Within the Minimal Therapist Contact (MTC) program, the number of therapist contacts are reduced to four sessions. Examination of this program may clarify the ways in which the couple learns to work on problems independently from the therapist.

The rationale for the MTC program is to utilize self-help strategies rather than the therapist-client relationship in treating primary orgasmic dysfunction. This particular dysfunction was selected for evaluation because, as previously detailed, treatment focuses on skill training and education, components particularly amenable to a skill-acquisition focus. Primary orgasmic dysfunction was selected as a starting point, rather than premature ejaculation simply because a step-by-step treatment program (Lobitz & LoPiccolo, 1972) had already been developed and was in place at the center. This should not be interpreted as suggesting that a self-help strategy is any less appropriate or easily applied to treatment of premature ejaculation, as Lowe and Mikulas' (1975) data confirms. It was thought that use of a minimal therapist contact program rather than full therapist-client involvement would be beneficial for three reasons.

1. *Responsibility for change.* Major responsibility for change is given to

the client couple. While an underlying focus of much traditional therapy involves a gradual working toward the clients' acceptance of responsibility for the problems they present, a limited therapist contact program forces this confrontation almost immediately. Thus, whereas a client's attitude of "I'm bringing this problem to you because you're the expert—you fix it" may be confronted gradually over many sessions in traditional therapy, in a self-help program, clients immediately face the prospects of "fixing" it themselves.

2. *Generalization.* Related to the issue of accepting responsibility for change is the issue of maintenance of treatment gains once therapy is complete. Because clients in a minimal therapist contact program are not "relying" on the therapist for rewards, encouragement, and motivation to continue behavior-change strategies, there is reason to believe that treatment gains will be less subject to relapse at the end of the program than at the end of a traditional therapy program.

3. *Cost-effectiveness.* A final advantage to a self-help strategy is that it requires less therapist time and costs the clients much less than regular therapy. This is particularly relevant in the field of sex therapy, where cost per hour of treatment is often much higher than corresponding treatment for a nonsexual problem (LoPiccolo, 1978). Thus, for these reasons, a Minimal Therapist Contact program for treatment of primary orgasmic dysfunction was developed.

The components of the program as developed include: (1) completing structured homework assignments presented in written form (Liss-Levinson & Morokoff, 1978); (2) reading the self-help book, *Becoming Orgasmic* by Heiman, LoPiccolo, & LoPiccolo (1976)—which is written in such a way that it may be used without the context of therapy sessions, and was used here because it describes in detail how and why to do the structured homework assignments; and (3) viewing a series of three films (LoPiccolo & Heiman, 1976) produced to accompany *Becoming Orgasmic.* Therapy sessions in this program are spaced about one month apart. The therapy sessions are spaced to encompass 14 weeks of homework assignments, making the actual directed sexual experiences completed by clients equivalent to those completed by clients in the standard 15-therapy-session format. The actual spacing of sessions allows 5 weeks to elapse between therapy sessions 1 and 2, 4 weeks to elapse between session 2 and session 3, and 5 weeks to elapse betweeen session 3 and session 4. Such a long interval between therapy sessions potentially increases dropout rate, and thus requires attention to methods for sustaining client motivation. These issues will be discussed, following a description of the program. The content of the first three therapy sessions includes showing one of the three segments of the film *Becoming Orgasmic,* assigning homework for the next 4 or 5 weeks, and discussion (in the brief time available) of relevant issues. The fourth session, marking termination of the program, is utilized to deal both with termination and maintenance issues. Sessions are designed to be 1 hour in length plus the time for showing a film.

Content of the homework exercises includes work on each of the seven change ingredients outlined earlier in this chapter, with particular focus on skill training and increasing awareness of the body. These are taught in the course of the directed sexual exercises. Education may perhaps be the next most important ingredient in the program, and both the self-help book and films were designed to provide information about what constitutes normal sexual functioning. Anxiety management and rational restructuring are included to a lesser extent. These are accomplished via relaxation exercises and suggestions for what to focus on attitudinally while doing each exercise. Sexual communication is also incorporated as part of the directions for engaging in sexual assignments.

Marital therapy (i.e. work on nonsexual relationship problems) receives minimal attention in this package. The only assignment directly addressing this area is an assignment for the couple to go out on a date together. This assignment is strategically placed at a point where some initial improvement in the sexual relationship is likely to have occurred and its goal is to help consolidate therapeutic gains by increasing intimacy in a pleasurable nonsexual experience. It should be emphasized here that active ingredient research has not been conducted, so that we really have no empirical evidence for believing that any one of these components is more effective than another. Empirical evidence indicates only that the whole package is effective when accompanied by weekly therapy sessions. The object of this program then is to see if the package will still be effective when therapy sessions are reduced and content is transmitted via film and written material.

The sequence of homework assignments in treatment of primary orgasmic dysfunction has been previously described (Lobitz & LoPiccolo, 1972). This nine-step program focuses on learning to reach arousal and orgasm via masturbation while incorporating the new skills into partner experiences. The program was designed to fit the 14 weeks of homework assignments and was consistent with the way treatment was normally conducted in weekly therapy. Every effort was made in constructing the weekly homework guide to make assignments reflect the average course of treatment in weekly therapy. This weekly sequence will be described here. Each week the couple is asked to read the sections from *Becoming Orgasmic* which are relevant to assignments they will be completing. They are also asked to record each assignment (no matter of what type) in which they engage. The assignments to be outlined below are preprinted in a weekly homework guide, but are not rigid. The therapist sometimes adds or deletes depending on individual needs of the clients.

MTC Program Outline

Therapy session 1. A basic overview of the program is presented to the couple. Each partner is asked to state his or her goals. Clarification of goals often focuses on the meaning of orgasm to each partner. The most important issue to be discussed in this session, however, is whether the couple's normal sexual relations will be restricted. In many sex therapy programs, the couple is initially asked to abstain from any sexual activity except that which is specifically assigned (Heiman, LoPiccolo, & LoPiccolo, 1979; Lobitz et al., 1974; Masters & Johnson, 1970). The purpose for this prohibition is twofold: to eliminate the pressure involved in an unsatisfying and frustrating relationship which, if occurring concurrently to other assignments, might undermine positive gains; and to facilitate the therapist's role in directing sexual experiences for the couple (the therapist, rather than the clients, now takes responsibility for what they do together sexually). Over the course of therapy, this responsibility is gradually shifted back to the clients. This strategy, however, becomes problematic in the context of a minimal therapist contact program. There is a strong probability that in the absence of weekly meetings with a therapist, couples asked to abstain from intercourse would find themselves reneging on their agreement. Therefore, in the MTC program, this issue is discussed at the outset as directly as possible. The couple is informed that it is our usual procedure to request that they abstain and that we feel this will be most helpful. However, if they feel this will be extremely difficult for them, they may continue having intercourse as they normally would, doing the assignments in addition. Sometimes abstention is difficult for inorgasmic women, either because the physical and emotional contact involved in intercourse is extremely important to them, or because they feel a great deal of guilt in denying the husband something important to him. Most nonorgasmic women, however, feel relieved at not having to engage in a sexual activity that is not gratifying. The couple is thus asked to set a goal they feel they will be able to achieve. A final topic to be considered in this first session is the husband's role in the program. This is an opportunity to reinforce the basic philosophy of mutuality of responsibility. At this session the couple is also shown part 1 of the film *Becoming Orgasmic* and is given homework assignments for 5 weeks.

Week one assignments. Most sex therapy programs begin with the taking of a sex history (Heiman, LoPiccolo, & LoPiccolo, 1979; Masters & Johnson, 1970). Although, in the course of a weekly therapy format, one function of this session may be to develop a sense of understanding between client and therapist, another function relevant to self-management is providing the client with a perspective on current functioning in terms of past experience, emphasizing the role of learning in sexual development. Thus, in the MTC program, sex-history taking is included, but left as the client's responsibility. A series of thought questions from a historical perspective are outlined in the book *Becoming Orgasmic*, and both partners are asked to write out answers then discuss them with each other. The couple is also assigned to discuss feelings about beginning the program with each other in a structured talk approximately one hour in length. Finally, the couple is asked to engage in and record whatever sexual activities they normally would over the week (i.e., take a baseline).

Week two assignments. In this and all subsequent weeks, assignments are divided into those to be completed by the female individually, those to be completed by the male individually, and those to be completed by the couple together. However, many weeks do not include an individual male assignment. No restriction is placed on male masturbation, whether or not other sexual activities are restricted. He is required to record all masturbatory experiences, however. Female and male individual assignments for this week include self-exploration in which each simply looks at his or her nude body. This is a first step in developing awareness of the body. The couple is asked to engage together in pleasuring sessions (sensual massage) modeled after Masters and Johnson's (1970) sensate-focus exercises. At the beginning, the couple is asked to abstain from touching each others breasts or genitals, as a way of preventing a sexual focus while retaining a sensual focus in the exercise.

Week three assignments. The female individual assignment here involves visual self-exploration of the genitals. Looking at the genitals is frequently a new experience for pre-orgasmic women. The same sensate focus assignment is given to the couple as in Week Two.

Week four assignments. At this point, relaxation exercises as described in *Becoming Orgasmic* are introduced in individual female assignments. The rationale for this is both to provide a means of self-control of anxiety and to increase awareness of sensations in the body. Vaginal exercises designed to increase the strength of the pubococcygeus muscle (Kegel, 1952; Kline-Graber & Graber, 1978) are also introduced at this time. Again, they serve the dual function of strengthening that muscle involved in orgasmic contractions and increasing awareness of body sensations. The vaginal exercises continue as homework throughout the remainder of the assignment weeks. In addition, the female begins self-exploration via touching her whole body, including genitals. She is asked to focus on discovery of whatever sensations she may experience, but not arousal. Relaxation exercises are presented as an optional male individual assignment, and he is also asked to engage in self-exploration by touch. The couple is asked to engage in sensual massage including breast but not genital stimulation. The couple is also asked to go out on a date to consolidate feelings of intimacy that frequently develop as a result of sensual massage assignments.

Week five assignments. In her individual assignment, the female repeats the touching exercise, this time focusing on discovering what sorts of touching produce pleasure. She also is asked to continue relaxation training. At this point, the male is encouraged to read sections in *Becoming Orgasmic* on increasing ejaculatory latency if he wishes to work on this. If this has previously been established as a goal, additional assignments may have been included as a means of working on pause or squeeze techniques. The couple continue sensual massage at this point, including genital touching, but with the caution to not focus exclusively on genitals.

Therapy Session 2. At this session, part 2 of the film *Becoming Orgasmic* is shown. In addition, several issues affecting upcoming homework assignments are discussed. One of these is a renegotiation of the "intercourse ban." The couple may decide to resume intercourse if they wish, although it will not be included in homework assignments until following the third therapy session. Two other issues are use of fantasy and use of a vibrator. Many pre-orgasmic women do not fantasize. Assignments include training in how to fantasize. This frequently raises fears in the husband that his wife will begin fantasizing about sex with another man. The therapy session is thus an opportunity to ask the couple to express feelings to each other on this topic. Similar issues arise in connection with use of a vibrator.

Week six assignments. In their individual assignments, both male and female are asked to complete exercises the goal of which is to increase ability to focus on physical sensations. Additionally, the female is asked to individually touch her body, specifically focusing on those genital areas which are most pleasurable. The couple continue sensual massage with no restrictions.

Week seven assignments. In her individual assignments, the female is again asked to focus on touching her genitals in the most pleasurable way, but this time including fantasy. A book of female fantasies (Friday, 1973) is usually assigned to provide examples of what a fantasy might be like and at the same time to suggest ideas that the woman might be able to continue imagining while doing assignments. The male is also encouraged to read the book on fantasies if he wishes to do so. The couple is asked to continue sensual massage including oral sex if they so desire, but not to the point of orgasm for either partner.

Week eight assignments. Clinical experience indicates that at this point in the program most women are starting to become aroused in their individual sessions. The object is thus to intensify this arousal to the point that orgasm may be triggered. A variety of intrapsychic reasons may prolong this stage. In order to facilitate orgasm, the woman is asked to role-play orgasm in her individual session. This involves acting out her fantasy of what an intense orgasm might look like, including such elements as pelvic thrusts, moans, or screams. The purpose is to help desensitize fears of appearing out of control. In the same session, she is asked to practice orgasm triggers including muscle tension, deep breathing, and throwing the head back. She is also asked to role-play orgasm in the couple session in order to begin working on the embarrassment that many pre-orgasmic women feel about displaying high levels of arousal or orgasm in front of their partner. At this stage, orgasm is permitted in the couple session, although the couple is still asked not to work toward orgasm.

Week nine assignments. At this stage, the vibrator is introduced. The rationale for use of the vibrator is that it is a fairly effective means of facilitating orgasm if it has not occurred at this point as a result of self or partner stimulation. The skill training and increase in awareness of physical sensation preceding its introduction guard against the woman becoming "hooked on" the vibrator as her only means of reaching orgasm. The vibrator is first experimented with nongenitally in both individual and couple sessions before being used genitally by the female in her individual session.

Therapy session 3. In this therapy session, part 3 of the film *Becoming Orgasmic* is shown. Issues that may be relevant to discuss include masturbation in front of the partner (to be included in assignments), intercourse if the couple has abstained, concerns of the male partner that he will not be able to control ejaculatory latency when intercourse is resumed, oral sex, the couple's progress if the woman has not yet reached orgasm, and fears of the male client that his partner's new found sexuality may be out of control. Naturally, there will be time only for the most salient issues.

Week ten assignments. In her individual assignments, the female continues manual self-stimulation if that has been effective in leading to orgasm, or vibrator stimulation if she has not yet reached orgasm. In the couple session, she demonstrates to her partner what she has done in her individual sessions. The male is also asked to masturbate in this session. Doing this facilitates partner learning of what types of stimulation are most effective and also increases trust between partners. In addition, the couple is asked to begin the first step toward intercourse: penile containment in the vagina. In the female superior position, the woman inserts the penis. Neither partner is to thrust or reach orgasm, and they stop after a couple of minutes. The purpose is to gradually return to intercourse, increasing the woman's sense of control over the process and decreasing the likelihood of premature ejaculation.

Week eleven assignments. Focus of assignments has now shifted from learning to reach orgasm to reaching orgasm with the partner. Individual sessions are still continued with vibrator stimulation if orgasm has not yet been reached. In the couple session, the couple is asked to have intercourse including intravaginal ejaculation with the woman on top and controlling the thrusting.

Week twelve assignments. Female individual sessions are continued. In their session together, the couple is asked to experiment with different intercourse positions and manual stimulation of the female (either partner or self-stimulation) during intercourse.

Week thirteen assignments. Individual and couple sessions continue as before, with possible inclusion of vibrator stimulation during intercourse.

Week fourteen assignments. The couple is asked to decide on their own what they would like to do. In addition, they are asked to make a maintenance plan focusing on how to maintain changes made, establishing what goals still remain, and structuring a plan to work on these goals.

Therapy session 4. Clients are asked to discuss their maintenance plans and any termination issues. If the couple is dissatisfied with progress made, this is naturally the focus of discussion.

From this treatment overview, it can be seen that the focus in treatment is first on teaching the woman to reach orgasm in whatever way she can by directing her to engage in certain behaviors (self-stimulation, stimulation by partner, role-play of orgasm, etc.) and to learn to focus on her sensations. Second, the treatment focuses on integrating this orgasm capacity into the sexual relationship. If orgasm is reached first through masturbation, the partner learns those types of stimulation that she finds most arousing. Similar work is done in learning to produce such sensations during intercourse. Anxiety management and rational restructuring play a secondary role in facilitating ability to follow the skill-training assignments. Work on the relationship is minimal. Self-management principles of helping the client in establishing goals, teaching self-monitoring and maintenance planning are central.

Implementing the Program

Procedures for gaining compliance with homework. As previously described (Lobitz & LoPiccolo, 1972), in weekly treatment, the client couple enters into a contractual agreement to complete assigned activities. They may lose money from a deposit if they do not. The same system is applied to the MTC program. While clients pay only for the number of therapy sessions they require, they make a deposit equal to 14 times their per-session fee. The incentive aspect of the treatment is maintained in the minimal therapist contact program on a week-to-week basis. To further facilitate weekly compliance with homework assignments, a procedure has been adopted which seems to work well. Clients are asked to mail in their homework records on a weekly basis. For each of the 14 weeks of homework assignments, they are given a due date. The records for each week's assignments must be postmarked by the due date in order to avoid penalty. This system has proved effective in keeping clients on track with the program despite infrequent therapist contact.

Selection of clients. It is relevant to discuss at this point restrictions determining for whom this program is appropriate. The criteria by which couples are selected for treatment in this program are fourfold.

1. Female diagnosis of primary orgasmic dysfunction.
2. No dysfunction present in the male.

Many couples present mixed dysfunctions. The only cases selected for the MTC program are ones in which males are nondysfunctional. A certain degree of leniency is permitted, however. A couple might still be eligible for MTC if the male describes a mild dysfunction, as long as neither partner defines it as a major problem. Opportunity to work on improving ejaculatory latency, for example, is built into the treatment program.

3. No major physical problems relating to sexual functioning are present.
4. Minimum reading and writing skills.

Because much of the program involves bibliotherapy, it is necessary that the clients possess adequate reading and writing ability. It may be apparent that in these few criteria, no restriction is related to marital satisfaction or psychopathology. These decisions are supported by lack of evidence that marital conflict or individual psychopathology are etiological factors in primary orgasmic dysfunction.

Our clinical impression in working with this program is that the techniques are extremely robust. That is, if the female client will wholeheartedly engage in the assignments, there is an extremely high likelihood that she will become orgasmic by some means and a good likelihood that she will become orgasmic with her partner. The issue then becomes the self-management question of how to best motivate clients to follow through on homework assignments. Preliminary evidence suggests that if initial impressions of the couple are that they will not be able to sustain motivation to carry through the program, weekly therapy in which the therapist can enlist motivation increasing techniques may be indicated. As previously discussed these include resolving nonsexual conflicts with the partner via marital therapy, changing negative attitudes toward sexuality, decreasing sexual anxiety, and helping each partner to accept the role of sexual being alone with other social roles (e.g. spouse, parent, worker).

Additional therapist contact and assessment. In order to assess whether a client meets the criteria for the MTC program, an initial intake interview is conducted. This is also an opportunity to have paper-and-pencil assessment instruments completed. As part of the larger research format for all clients, the couple serves as their own control by placement on a waiting list for 4 to 6 weeks, after which they again complete the assessment battery, and begin the MTC program. At the fourth therapy session, the assessment battery is again completed to provide a post-measure. The client couple are again offered an opportunity to meet with the therapist at a follow-up interview 3 months following completion of treatment. At this time, they are again required to fill out assessment forms. No telephone calls from therapist to client are structured as part of the program. However, calls from the client are handled according to the therapist's discretion, exactly as they would be in weekly therapy.

Preliminary Data

To this date, nine couples have completed the MTC program as outlined. A total of 13 couples began the program, representing a dropout rate of 30 percent (4 out of 13). This sample constitutes all couples meeting the requirements previously discussed who presented for treatment at the center. Clients are typically referred by a physician or mental health professional, but may also be self-referred.

Outcome Measures. As previously discussed, sexual dysfunction differs from many areas of distress in that clients frequently present their goals in behavioral terms. All women evaluated here presented a desire to reach orgasm as their primary goal in therapy. Unfortunately, treatment outcome evaluation is not as simple as implied by this unity of objectives. Orgasm can be reached as a result of a variety of different types of stimulation. Probably, the most important distinction is whether the orgasm is reached as a result of self- or partner stimulation. Furthermore, the orgasm does not by itself determine satisfaction with a sexual relationship, although this fact is sometimes overlooked by non-orgasmic women and their partners. It is desirable to measure general sexual satisfaction for both male and female partners. In order to measure occurrence of orgasm by different means of stimulation, female clients were asked to rate their frequency of orgasm on a 6-point scale for each of the following types of stimulation: masturbation, manual stimulation by partner, intercourse, intercourse with additional vibrator stimulation, and oral stimulation by partner. General satisfaction for both partners was measured in two ways. First, each partner answered the following question: "Overall, how satisfactory to you is your sexual relationship with your mate?" Ratings were made on a 6-point scale where 1 = extremely unsatisfactory, 2 = moderately unsatisfactory, 3 = slightly unsatisfactory, 4 = slightly satisfactory, 5 = moderately satisfactory, and 6 = extremely satisfactory. An additional measure of overall satisfaction was also made. Both members of the couple were administered the Sexual Interaction Inventory (LoPiccolo & Steger, 1974), an instrument designed to assess both sexual functioning and sexual satisfaction. Eleven clinically relevant scales are derived from ratings of 17 heterosexual behaviors. One of these (Total Disagreement) represents a summary scale measuring "the total disharmony and dissatisfaction in the sexual relationship being assessed" (LoPiccolo & Steger, 1974). It is important to emphasize that this score reflects ratings of both partners.

Results. As can be seen in table 14.1, all nine women in the MTC program became orgasmic through masturbation during treatment. All maintained this functioning at the 3-month follow-up. Two-thirds of the women were able to reach orgasm with their partners by some means of partner stimulation, a figure which had increased to roughly 75 percent by 3-month followup. Examination of table 14.1 further reveals that following the end of treatment, the women were increasing the diversity of ways in which orgasm could be reached. The number of women reaching orgasm increased in each type of partner-stimulation category from post-treatment to 3-month follow-up.

Examination of ratings of satisfaction with the sexual relationship show that initial ratings for both partners centered around "slightly unsatisfactory." Post-therapy and follow-up ratings center around "moderately satisfactory." While this shows a mean gain of only 2 points on a 6-point scale, all couples completing the program showed gains ranging from 1 to 5 points. On the Total Disagreement Scale of the Sexual Interaction Inventory, gains were likewise indicated. The averages presented represent standard scores (SD = 10). Thus it can be seen that there was over a one-standard-deviation increase in satisfaction between the partners both post-treatment and at follow-up.

Table 14.1.　Measures of Effectiveness of the Minimal Therapist Contact Program in Treating Primary Orgasmic Dysfunction

I. Percent of women reaching orgasm by different types of stimulation[a]

	Minimal Therapist Contact		
Type of Stimulation	Pre-Therapy (N = 9)	Post-Therapy (N = 9)	3-Month Follow-Up (N = 7)
Self-Stimulation			
Masturbation	0	100	100
Vibrator	0	100	86
Partner Stimulation			
(combined score)	0	66	77
Manual	0	11	71
Intercourse	0	33	57
Intercourse			
with vibrator	0	44	71
Oral	0	22	29

II. Sexual Interaction Inventory standard scale scores[a] pre and post Minimal Therapist Contact Treatment.

SII Scale	Pre-Therapy (N = 9)	Post–Therapy (N = 7)	3-Month Follow-Up (N = 7)
Total Disagreement	77.2	62.0	57.2

III. Sexual satisfaction ratings[b] pre and post Minimal Therapist Contact Treatment.

Spouse	Pre-Therapy (N = 9)	Post–Therapy (N = 7)	3-Month Follow-Up (N = 7)
Husband	3.2	5.3	5.3
Wife	2.4	4.6	4.8

[a]Mean score for the normative sample = 50, standard deviation = 10.
[b]Ratings were made on a 6 point scale ranging from 1 = extremely unsatisfactory to 6 = extremely satisfactory.

Dropouts. In evaluating these preliminary results, the dropout rate was quite high: 30 percent of couples beginning the program did not complete all four sessions (4 out of 13 couples). Additionally, it should be noted that this rate is much higher than the less than 10 percent dropout rate for weekly treatment at this center. Dropouts were not included in the statistics presented in table 14.1. It is interesting to note that early termination of therapy is not necessarily an indication of failure. Two of the four women who dropped out were able to reach orgasm at the point of termination. It seems likely that in a minimal therapist contact program, early termination is a much higher likelihood than in a program where clients meet weekly with a therapist.

Conclusions. From this preliminary evidence, strong support is provided for the efficacy of the MTC program. At this early vantage point, it would seem that ability to reach orgasm in MTC treatment is comparable to that of weekly treatment. It would also seem that relapse does not occur following the end of treatment, and if anything, improvement tends to continue. Finally, sexual satisfaction appears to be enhanced for both partners.

Training of Therapists and Ethical Issues

Therapists were fully trained in both general psychotherapy and sex therapy techniques. Thus, for this program, no attempt was made to utilize paraprofessionals. Much of what has been said here indicates that the therapist-client relationship is not important as a change factor — which is further confirmed by McMullen and Rosen's (1979) report of a successful self-help program with no therapist contact at all. Clients in the MTC program often report that this relationship is nevertheless subjectively perceived as important. Clients in this program do tend to call the therapist at some point during treatment, and report feeling helped by the knowledge that someone is going to be reading their written reports. The question of the effect of a therapist-client relationship is an empirical one which needs experimental exploration. It seems probable that this relationship is more important for some clients than others in enabling them to follow through a program and make behavioral and interpersonal changes.

An additional ethical issue centers on what to do if problems develop. This is of more importance when research consideration constrains how quickly additional sessions are offered to a couple experiencing difficulties. This could be an important clinical issue if minimally trained therapists are used, who may not be competent to provide additional marital-sexual therapy. In this case, a reliable referral network seems to be highly important. For research purposes, a policy was established for the MTC program that sessions additional to the four regularly scheduled appointments not be made unless the therapist judged a clinical emergency to exist. A clinical emergency was defined as a situation in which the well-being of either the individual or the couple's relationship was threatened. In one of the nine cases presented above, such an additional session was scheduled, and a decision was made with the couple to renew their therapy contract following the fourth MTC session. (No 3-month follow-up data were provided for this couple). In general, self-help and minimal therapist contact programs need to have well-thought-out procedures for dealing with client needs for additional treatment.

In addition to ethical issues involved in minimal therapist contact treatment, we may also address the question of ethics involved in sex therapy, with particular attention to directed sexual assignments. It is crucial when assigning an individual to complete a sexual activity that he or she have the advance opportunity to decline the assignment. Toward this goal, the nature of therapeutic assignments are discussed with prospective clients before therapy is begun (at an intake interview). Clients presenting primary orgasmic dysfunction are informed that our usual treatment program includes assignments involving masturbation. For those clients who do not wish to participate in masturbation or other structured sexual activities, important aspects of the program must be revised, thus potentially affecting success of outcome. It is important that such issues be discussed with clients. It is also important that therapists who treat sexual dysfunctions remain flexible in their conceptualization of a good sexual relationship. Typically it is assumed that comfort with nudity, touching the partner's body, and self-stimulation are important for overcoming dysfunctions. This may not always be the case, and therapists must guard against imposing their own values on clients. The Ethics Committee of the American Association of Sex Educators, Counselors, and Therapists (AASECT), has stated that nudity within the therapy session or observation of client sexual activity are beyond the boundaries of established therapeutic practice. Because of misconceptions related to sex therapy, we feel it is important to specifically inform prospective clients that these activities will *not* be part of their treatment.

SUMMARY

This chapter has attempted to provide an overview of ways in which self-management is incorporated in sex therapy. Self-management strategies including motivating the client for behavior change, teaching skills, and facilitating self-maintenance are integral components of rapid treatment sex therapy for all sexual dysfunctions. Inclusion of treatment components such as homework records, contracts, and maintenance plans further facilitate skill acquisition and acceptance by the client of responsibility for change. Treatment of some sexual dysfunctions, however, tends to focus more on these strategies than others. We have seen that the dysfunctions premature ejaculation and primary orgasmic dysfunction are specifically conceptualized as skill deficits, and thus are treated almost exclusively through skill-training procedures. In support of this, evidence is available that self-help programs (with no therapist input) have achieved success in treating these problems. A detailed look at the application of self-management principles in sex therapy is provided by discussion of a minimal therapist contact package for treatment of primary orgasmic dysfunction. This program has been found to be effective and offers us insight into the process of treatment which does not rely on development of a strong therapist-client relationship. It seems reasonable to conclude that similar prescriptive evaluation might be applied to problem areas outside of sexual dysfunction.

REFERENCES

Annon, J. *The behavioral treatment of sexual problems.* Honolulu: Kapiolani Health Services, 1974.

Barbach, L. G. Group treatment of preorgasmic women. *Journal of Sex and Marital Therapy,* 1974, *1,* 139–145.

Barbach, L. *For yourself: The fulfillment of female sexuality.* New York: Doubleday, 1975.

Belt, B. G. Some organic causes of impotence. *Medical Aspects of Human Sexuality,* 1973, *7,* 152–161.

Bergler, E. Problem of frigidity. *Psychiatric Quarterly,* 1944, *18,* 374–390.

Bolte, G. L. A communications approach to marital counseling. In A. S. Gurman & D. G. Rice (Eds.), *Couples in conflict: New directions in marital therapy.* New York: Jason Aronson, 1975.

Cooper, A. J. Clinical and therapeutic studies in premature ejaculation. *Comprehensive Psychiatry,* 1969, *10,* 285–295.

Dengrove, E. Behavior therapy of impotence. *Journal of Sex Research,* 1971, *7,* 177–183. (a)

Dengrove, E. The urological aspects of impotence. *Journal of Sex Research,* 1971, *7,* 163–168. (b)

Ellis, A. The treatment of frigidity and impotence. In H. Greenwald (Ed.), *Active Psychotherapy.* New York: Atherton Press, 1967.

Friday, N. *My secret garden: Women's sexual fantasies.* New York: Trident Press, 1973.

Friedman, D. The treatment of impotence by Brietal relaxation therapy. *Behavior Research and Therapy,* 1968, *8,* 257–261.

Fuchs, K., Hoch, A., Paldo, E., Abramovici, H., Brandes, J. M., Timer-Tritsch, I., & Kleinhaus, M. Hypnodesensitization therapy of vaginismus: Part I. In vitro method. Part II. In vivo method. *International Journal of Clinical & Experimental Hypnosis,* 1973, *21,* 144–156.

Haley, J. Marriage therapy. *Archives of General Psychiatry,* 1963, *8,* 213–234.

Haslam, M. T. The treatment of psychogenic dyspareunia by reciprocal inhibitions. *British Journal of Psychiatry,* 1965, *111,* 280–282.

Heiman, J., LoPiccolo, L., & LoPiccolo, J. *Becoming orgasmic: A sexual growth program for women.* Englewood Cliffs, N.J.: Prentice-Hall, 1976.

Heiman, J. R., LoPiccolo, L., & LoPiccolo, J. The treatment of sexual dysfunction. In A. S. Gurman & D. P. Kniskern (Eds.), *Handbook of family therapy.* New York: Brunner/Mazel, 1980.

Hogan, D. R. The effectiveness of sex therapy: A review of the literature. In J. LoPiccolo & L. LoPiccolo (Eds.), *Handbook of sex therapy.* New York: Plenum Press, 1978.

Hurvitz, N. Interaction hypotheses in marriage counselling. In A. S. Gurman & D. G. Rise

(Eds.), *Couples in conflict: New directions in marital therapy.* New York: Jason Aronson, 1975.

Kanfer, F. H. Self-management methods. In F. H. Kanfer & A. P. Goldstein (Eds.), *Helping people change.* New York: Pergamon Press, 1980.

Kanfer, F. H., & Grimm, L. G. Managing clinical change: A process model of therapy. *Behavior Modification,* 1980, *4,* 419–444.

Kaplan, H. S. *The new therapy.* New York: Brunner/Mazel, 1974.

Kaplan, H. S. Hypoactive sexual desire. *Journal of Sex & Marital Therapy.* 1977, *3,* 3–9.

Kaplan, H. S. *Disorders of sexual desire.* New York: Brunner/Mazel, 1979.

Kegel, A. H. Sexual function of the pubococcygeus muscle. *Western Journal of Obstetrics & Gynecology,* 1952, *60,* 521–524.

Kline-Graber, G., & Graber, B. *Woman's orgasm: A guide to sexual satisfaction.* New York: Bobbs-Merril, 1975.

Kline-Graber, G., & Graber, B. Diagnosis and treatment procedures of pubococcygeal deficiencies in women. In J. LoPiccolo & L. LoPiccolo (Eds.), *Handbook of sex therapy.* New York: Plenum, 1978.

Kohlenberg, R. J. Directed masturbation and the treatment of primary orgasmic dysfunction. *Archives of Sexual Behavior.* 1974, *3,* 349–356.

Lazarus, A. A. The treatment of chronic frigidity by systematic desensitization. *Journal of Nervous & Mental Disease.* 1963, *136,* 272–278.

Liss-Levinson, N., & Morokoff, P. J. *Minimal therapist contact manual.* Department of Psychiatry and Behavioral Science, State University of New York at Stony Brook, 1978.

Lobitz, W. C., & LoPiccolo, J. New methods in the behavioral treatment of sexual dysfunction. *Journal of Behavior Therapy & Experimental Psychiatry,* 1972, *3,* 265–271.

Lobitz, W. C., LoPiccolo, J., Lobitz, G., & Brockway, J. A closer look at simplistic behavior therapy for sexual dysfunction. Two case studies. In H. J. Eysenck (Ed.), *Case studies in behavior therapy.* London: Routledge & Kegan Paul, 1974.

Locke, H. J., & Wallace, K. M. Short marital adjustment and prediction tests: Their reliability and validity. *Marriage and Family Living,* 1959, *21,* 251–255.

LoPiccolo, J. Direct treatment of sexual dysfunction in the couple. In J. Money & H. Musaph (Eds.), *Handbook of sexology.* New York: Elsevier/North Holland, 1977. (a)

LoPiccolo, J. The professionalization of sex therapy: Issues and problems. *Society,* 1977, *14,* 60–68. (b)

LoPiccolo, J. Direct treatment of sexual dysfunction. In J. LoPiccolo & L. LoPiccolo (Eds.), *Handbook of sex therapy.* New York: Plenum, 1978.

LoPiccolo, J., & Lobitz, W. C. The role of masturbation in the treatment of orgasmic dysfunction. *Archives of Sexual Behavior,* 1972, *2,* 163–172.

LoPiccolo, J., & Lobitz, W. C. Behavior therapy of sexual dysfunction. In L. A. Hamerlynck, L. C. Handy, & E. J. Mash (Eds.), *Behavior change: Methodology, concepts, and practice.* Champagne, Ill.: Research Press, 1973.

LoPiccolo, J., & Steger, J. C. The sexual interaction inventory: A new instrument for assessment of sexual dysfunction. *Archives of Sexual Behavior,* 1974, *3,* 585–595.

LoPiccolo, L. Low sexual desire. In S. Leiblum & L. Pervin (Eds.), *Principles and practice of sex therapy.* New York: Guilford, 1980.

LoPiccolo, L., & Heiman, J. (film) *Becoming Orgasmic.* New York: Focus International, Inc. 1976.

Lowe, J. C., & Mikulas, W. L. Use of written material in learning self-control of premature ejaculation. *Psychological Reports,* 1975, *37,* 295–298.

Madsen, C. H., & Ullmann, L. P. Innovations in the desensitization of frigidity. *Behavior Research and Therapy,* 1967, *5,* 67–68.

Masters, W. H., & Johnson, V. E. *Human sexual inadequacy.* Boston: Little, Brown, 1970.

McGovern, L., Stewart, R., & LoPiccolo, J. Secondary orgasmic dysfunction: I. Analysis and strategies for treatment. *Archives of Sexual Behavior*, 1975, *4*, 265–275.

McMullen, S., & Rosen, R. C. Self-administered masturbation training in the treatment of primary orgasmic dysfunction. *Journal of Consulting & Clinical Psychology*, 1979, *47*, 912–918.

Morokoff, P. Determinants of female orgasm. In J. LoPiccolo & L. LoPiccolo (Eds.), *Handbook of sex therapy*. New York: Plenum, 1978.

Prochaska, J. O., & Marzelli, R. Modifications of the Masters and Johnson approach to sexual problems. *Psychotherapy: Theory, Research, and Practice*, 1973, *10*, 294–296.

Reisinger, J. J. Masturbatory training in the treatment of primary orgasmic dysfunction. *Journal of Behavior Therapy and Experimental Psychiatry*. 1974, *5*, 179–183.

Riley, A. J., & Riley, E. J. A controlled study to evaluate directed masturbation in the management of primary orgasmic failure in women. *British Journal of Psychiatry*, 1978, *133*, 404–409.

Salter, A. *Conditional reflex therapy*. New York: Creative Age Press, 1949.

Schover, L., Friedman, J., Weiler, S., Heiman, J., & LoPiccolo, J. A multi-axial descriptive system for the sexual dysfunctions: Categories and manual. *Archives of General Psychiatry*, in press.

Wolpe, J. *Psychotherapy by reciprocal inhibition*. Stanford, Calif.: Stanford University Press, 1958.

15
Self-Management in Depression
Lynn P. Rehm

The purpose of this chapter is to describe a model of depression which employs self-management concepts in several ways. The model in question is the self-control model of depression (Rehm, 1977), which is based on an adaptation of Kanfer's conception of self-control (Kanfer, 1970; Kanfer & Karoly, 1972a & b). Self-control in this chapter can be assumed to refer to a particular model of self-management.

One of the primary functions of the model is to provide an organizing framework for conceptualizing depressive psychopathology. Thus, the model is an attempt to identify logically the minimum features necessary to describe depressed behavior. It makes the assumption that multiple features are necessary for a full description. The model offers a way of structuring relationships between these features. The first part of the chapter is a review of current research on the psychopathology of depression, employing the model as an organizing principle. Research is reviewed concerning depressive behavior which can be categorized as self-monitoring, self-evaluation, self-attribution, or self-reinforcement behavior, and as the consequence of depressive self-control. The model is intended as a heuristic device for exploring interrelationships between constructs. The purpose of the review is to examine the empirical evidence with regard to possible alterations, additions, refinements, or expansions of the overall model of depression.

The second function which the model serves is to organize thinking about the treatment of depression. A therapy program has been developed which is structured around sequential attention to each of the potential depressive features or deficits identified by the model. The model serves both to organize the procedures of the therapy and as the rationale for the therapy which is presented to the participants. This program has been developed and refined in a series of studies which have evaluated it in comparison to control conditions and have attempted to identify its effective components. The second part of the chapter begins with a brief review of these studies in the context of the present status of behavior therapy for depression generally. Following this, the program is described together with a commentary on the clinical problems encountered, implications of current research for therapy, and recommendations for clinical practice. The chapter concludes with some comments on the status and utility of the model as a framework for research and therapy.

SELF-MONITORING IN DEPRESSION

In Kanfer's model, self-monitoring refers to the ways in which people observe their own behavior. The model presumes that when an individual perceives that some aspect of his or her behavior is dysfunctional, then attention is focused on that class of behavior. The individual may monitor the behavior itself and also the antecedents and consequences of the behavior. The events on which people focus in their personal environment may vary considerably. The focus of depression research has been on monitoring of pleasant and unpleasant events, positive and negative activities, and rewards and punishments. From the self-monitoring point of view, the question is: Do depressed individuals employ a deviant observation strategy in monitoring their behavior?

Beck (1972) sees cognitive distortion as the core component of depression. He describes specific forms of distortion such as selective abstraction, arbitrary inference, overgeneralization, magnification, and minimization. While the description of these methods is richly informative about the clinical phenomena of depression, it does not specify the psychological processes which underlie them. The self-control model of depression (Rehm, 1977) is one attempt to specify the process underlying one aspect of cognitive distortion. Depressed persons are hypothesized to attend more to negative than to positive events. That is, depressed individuals employ an observation strategy in which attention and time are devoted more toward detecting and observing negative events to the exclusion of attention and time devoted to observation and detection of positive events. Events include activities and their antecedents and consequences. "Negative" refers to an event which is personally aversive or a cue for a personally aversive event. Thus, a major component of cognitive distortion may involve self-monitoring. Other aspects of cognitive distortion may better be dealt with in terms of more complex judgmental processes in the self-evaluation stage of the self-control model. Both Rehm (1977) and Seligman (1981) have suggested that attributional processes may underlie other aspects of Beck's proposed forms of cognitive distortion.

Distortion in the self-monitoring processes of depressed individuals has been the focus of a number of recent studies. One can begin to get a clear idea of the processes by which distortion occurs by looking at the research literature in terms of the various ways in which distortion has been assessed.

Self-Monitoring of Daily Events

It has been fairly well established that daily mood is correlated with self-monitored events. Positive mood correlates positively with pleasant events (e.g., Grosscup & Lewinsohn, 1980; Lewinsohn & Graf, 1973; Lewinsohn & Libet, 1972; O'Hara & Rehm, Note 1; and Rehm, 1978). Positive mood correlates negatively with self-monitored unpleasant events (e.g., Grosscup & Lewinsohn, 1980; Lewinsohn & Talkington, 1979; O'Hara & Rehm, Note 1; Rehm, 1978). In those studies in which both pleasant and unpleasant events have been monitored (Grosscup & Lewinsohn, 1980; O'Hara & Rehm, Note 1; Rehm, 1978), it has generally been found that the number of pleasant events is uncorrelated with the number of unpleasant events, and thus they each contribute independently to mood variance. The primary instrument for assessing pleasant events is the McPhillamy and Lewinsohn (Note 2) Pleasant Events Schedule. The PES was constructed by having college subjects list pleasant and unpleasant events until an item pool of 320 nonredundant items were generated. For self-monitoring purposes, the PES or a subset of its items are used as a daily checklist for the occurrence or nonoccurrence of each event. The PES is also used in a retrospective report format in which subjects are asked to indicate the frequency of occurrence of each event in the last 30 days and to rate its enjoyability or reinforcement potential. Both ratings are done on 3-point scales. An activity level index is obtained from the sum of the frequency ratings. A reinforcement potential score is obtained from the sum of the enjoyment ratings. The sum of the cross products of these two ratings yields an obtained reinforcement measure. A similar instrument has been constructed for unpleasant events (cf., Lewinsohn & Talkington, 1979; Lewinsohn, Talkington, Falk, & Kikel, Note 3). Rehm (1978) had college subjects simply list daily pleasant and unpleasant events. Results were comparable to other studies using checklists, but such a listing methodology is more subject to various biases.

A study by Vasta & Brockner (1979) attempted to extend the findings of the self-monitoring and mood studies to covert events as well as overt events. Thirty-three undergraduates self-monitored positive and negative self-evaluative statements for 3 hours a day over 8 days. Mood was not monitored, but it was found that the number of negative self-evaluations, as well as the ratio of negative self-evaluations to total self-evaluations, were both correlated with self-esteem measures. Thus, there is some evidence that self-esteem, a major hypothesized component of depression, is related to monitored self-statements or at least to negative self-statements.

Self-Monitoring by Depressed and Nondepressed Subjects

A number of studies have looked at the differences between depressed and nondepressed samples, and have examined their self-monitoring behavior. Several different experimental paradigms have been used to explore this topic. The type of information to be self-monitored and the mode of self-monitoring have varied considerably.

Nonetheless, several conclusions can be drawn with regard to self-monitoring in depression. First, distortion appears to be a constructive process. Several studies show that depressed subjects are not deviant in perception per se. They are able to identify stimulus events accurately. It is only when some degree of ambiguity, interpretation or reconstruction is introduced that depressed subjects show evidence of distortion. Ambiguity may be introduced in the stimulus as in projective instruments or may occur because of the difficulty of the task. For example, recall of the number of correct trials on a long task becomes ambiguous in terms of the normal range of error expected. When ambiguity exists, subjects are called on to construct or reconstruct a response. In doing so, many factors other than perceptual memory accuracy come into play. Among these are expectancies, history of prior responses, the nature of the audience, and response biases.

Second, depressive distortion is an evaluative process. Distortion occurs in a *negative direction*. The experimental tasks do not call for explicit evaluation in the sense of asking for a response on a "good-bad" dimension. Nevertheless, there is an evaluation implicit in the task. Subjects are asked, for instance, to recall how often they were told they were right, or how many successful responses they made. Clearly, these are evaluative of the overall performance on these tasks in the sense that many correct is "good" and few correct is "bad." Distortion is most evident when actual good performance is distorted toward bad, though poor performance may be distorted to worse.

Third, negative distortion seems to be more apparent when the evaluation is of oneself or one's own behavior. There may be some instances where the performance of others is negatively distorted; but distortion is greater or more apparent when an evaluation is made with regard to depressed persons themselves or their relationships to the environment.

Fourth, distortion in depression involves the strategy or style with which the person observes or monitors himself or herself. One aspect of this style is the manner in which depressed persons distribute their attention. At least in some instances, depressed persons choose to expose themselves to negative information or aversive cues. This may be seen as a conservative response strategy designed to avoid errors involving erroneous identification of positive information or erroneous failure to identify negative information. Ferster (1973) has argued that depressed subjects are particularly vigilant in searching for cues for aversive events, as a form of overgeneralized avoidance. One possible reason for this vigilant avoidance may be a hypersensitivity to aversive stimulation. Several studies (Lewinsohn, Lobitz, & Wilson, 1973; Suarez, Crowe, & Adams, 1978; Baker & Jessup, 1980) have found depressed subjects more physiologically responsive to aversive stimuli. This is not a universal finding, however, since Davis, Buchsbaum, and Bunney (1979) found depressed subjects more analgesic to pain in a cold-stressor situation, using both threshold and signal detection analyses. Lewinsohn and his colleagues (MacPhillamy & Lewinsohn, 1974; Lewinsohn & Tarkington, 1979) have found that depressed subjects rate pleasant events as less enjoyable and unpleasant events as more aversive than do nondepressed subjects. Further research is necessary to evaluate the functions of vigilant avoidance in depressed individuals.

In general, there is a need for further research in the functional significance of distorted monitoring by depressed individuals. One factor that should be investigated is the possibility that distorted self-report might involve a form of impression management. The conservative response strategy demonstrated by Miller and Lewis (1977) might also extend in some ways to the social interactions of depressed subjects. It may be that depressed subjects want to avoid social criticism or other averse social reactions to their behavior, and thus they are very conservative in behavior which could be criticized. A negatively distorted description of one's self may also elicit sympathy, help, and other positive responses from others.

The Effects of Self-Monitoring on Mood

In a study on basic self-monitoring processes, Kirschenbaum and Karoly (1977) instructed college students who were working on math problems to either self-monitor the number of problems answered correctly or self-monitor the number of errors. Negative self-monitoring produced lower self-evaluation, decreased self-reinforcement, decreased accuracy, and increased anxiety. While the dysphoric mood assessed here is anxiety rather than depression, the study demonstrates that the strategy of self-monitoring can influence self-evaluation, self-reinforcement, and mood. Another study of self-monitoring (Hammen & Glass, 1975) reported two experiments investigating the effects of self-monitoring instructions on frequency of pleasant events and mood. In the first study, 40 depressed undergraduates were divided into four groups: the first group was instructed to increase pleasant events; the second group was an attention placebo condition in which subjects were asked to increase protein intake; the third group was a self-monitoring only condition; and the fourth group was a no-treatment condition in which subjects only received the initial and posttesting. All subjects in the monitoring conditions recorded pleasant events and food intake for 2 weeks. They also completed daily Depression Adjective Checklists (Lubin, 1965). The group instructed to increase pleasant events did indeed increase the number of events. However, no effects were found on mood. In the second experiment, depressed and nondepressed subjects were asked to self-monitor for 1 week. Half the subjects received instructions to attempt to increase pleasant events, whereas the other group was instructed only to self-monitor. In this study, no effect was obtained for the number of events reported. A mood effect was found in that the subjects who were asked to increase their activities ended up being slightly *more* depressed. Hammen and Glass argue that cognitive mediation or the significance of events rather than just the number of events influences depression. Lewinsohn (1975) replied to the paper arguing that no therapeutic effect was obtained for several reasons, including the fact that the experimenters had not ensured that subjects began with a low level of activity, that the events were not necessarily enjoyable, and that the initial correlation between mood and these activities was not obtained. It should also be pointed out that the subjects viewed the experience as part of an experiment, and not as something intended to benefit them personally.

O'Hara and Rehm (1979) divided a group of normal community volunteers into the following conditions: (1) pleasant-events monitoring, (2) unpleasant-events monitoring, (3) both pleasant- and unpleasant-events monitoring, and (4) mood monitoring only. The valence of events monitored had no effect either on activity level or on mood, despite the fact that correlations between activity level and mood were demonstrated. This study demonstrated that it was not activity level per se which mediated the effects, because activity level (as measured by pedometers) did not correlate with mood or with number of events daily. O'Hara and Rehm speculated that effects on events or mood were not obtained, partly because the subjects reported, for the most part, that they did not actively monitor during the day, but generally waited until the end of the day to record their events and assess their mood. Harmon, Nelson, and Hayes (1980) investigated this distinction. They had subjects monitor either mood or activity on a variable interval, 1-hour schedule for 11 recordings per day. In addition, all subjects filled out a Depression Adjective Checklist and a 139-item Pleasant Events Schedule at the end of the day. A replicated, single-subject reversal design was used. In this study, self-monitoring of either mood or activity produced an increase in mood and activity. Mood and activity were correlated. Self-monitoring of activity had a greater effect than self-monitoring of mood on both the Depression Adjective Checklists and the Pleasant Events Schedule. The authors concluded that activity and mood affect one another mutually, they also concluded that once-a-day global self-monitoring does not have a reactive effect, whereas frequent monitoring during the day does have a reactive effect. In this experiment, subjects were motivated for change because they were in treatment and the task was presented as a treatment assignment.

Finally, Evans and Hollon (Note 4) presented a study in which depressed and nondepressed college students monitored their mood in what was described as either an immediate (hourly) monitoring condition or a delayed (daily) monitoring condition. In addition, subjects filled out a Depression Adjective Checklist each evening for seven days. Depressed subjects differed from nondepressed subjects in daily, but not hourly, ratings. Daily checklist scores also differentiated between the groups. Thus, only in the daily monitoring were the mood ratings consistent with the Depression Adjective Checklist scores. The authors suggest that delayed (daily) monitoring may be distorted as may be all summary estimates. They recommend immediate or hourly monitoring as potentially more accurate. There is, however, no criterion for accuracy in this study.

The general conclusion from these studies appears to be that daily self-monitoring of events and mood is relatively nonreactive and can usefully be employed for assessment purposes. On the other hand, frequent monitoring during the day, under certain motivating conditions, may be employed as an intervention with potential effects on the number of monitored events and secondarily on mood.

SELF-EVALUATION IN DEPRESSION

In Kanfer's (1970) model of self-control, the self-evaluation phase deals with the manner in which people make judgements about the quality of ther performance. The model suggests that these judgements are made in terms of internalized standards against which individuals compare their performance. Standards for success may be independent of standards for failure. That is, they are not necessarily reciprocals. It is also assumed that there is temporal constancy and a degree of cross-situational generality in standard setting.

Consistent individual differences in standard setting are assumed to be based on a learning history of external reinforcement and modeling in similar situations. The distinction between self-monitoring and self-evaluation is somewhat blurred when one considers that estimates of performance often have a clear qualitative or evaluative connotation. This was noted in the review above of self-monitoring in depression. It is nevertheless useful to distinguish between perception of performance, usually defined for research purposes in terms of a quantitative estimate of the objective characteristics of behavior, and self-evaluation, usually defined in terms of a qualitative judgement of the performance as good, bad or indifferent, or as a success or a failure. Individual differences in evaluation exist for equal perceptions of performance; that is, the same level of performance may be a success for one person and a failure for another.

The self-control model of depression (Rehm, 1977) attempts to account for the self-depreciation and low self-esteem seen in depression in terms of self-evaluative standard setting. The studies that will be reviewed here will be those in which individuals explicitly made evaluative judgements of their behavior. A number of studies have examined the self-evaluations of depressed and nondepressed samples. A small set of studies has looked directly at standard setting behavior.

The self-control model as we have applied it to depression (Rehm, 1977) incorporates attributional processes into the self-evaluation phase of the model. Attributions are the judgements which people make about the causes of events in their lives. Helplessness and guilt are characteristics of depression which can be described in attributional terms. Like standard setting, attribution is a fairly abstract judgement about performance depending on prior experience, expectancy, and consistent individual differences. In our model, attribution is viewed as a modifier of self-evaluation.

Self-evaluation is more significant when behavior was judged to be caused by internal factors. Self-evaluation does not apply to externally caused events. Other dimensions of attribution may also influence the intensity or significance of self-evaluation. For example, performance can be judged in terms of narrow or broad classes of behavior; for example, a grade on a test may be evaluated narrowly against a standard for calculus ability or broadly against a standard for intellectual ability. Rehm (1977) described this difference in terms of the generality of the standard selected. Abramson, Seligman, and Teasdale (1978) describe the same factor as a "global-specific" dimension of attribution. Studies of attributions in depression will be reviewed here along with studies of self-evaluation.

Negative Self-Evaluation in Depression

In a study which assessed multiple dimensions relevant to self-evaluation in depression, Loeb, Beck, Diggory, and Tuthill (1967) assessed high- and low-depressed subjects in success and failure conditions on a card sorting task. One of their findings was that the more depressed subjects rated their performance as poorer even though they were objectively identical to low-depression subjects. Using normal subjects, Fry (1976) measured positive and negative adjective self-ratings before and after success, failure, and control experiences. Following success, subjects demonstrated greater gains on positive adjectives as opposed to negative adjectives. Following failure, larger changes were shown on the negative than on the positive adjectives—thus, the nature of the changes in self-evaluation was a function of the valence of the rating dimensions. Laxer (1964) had neurotic depressives, paranoids, and other hospitalized patients assess themselves under real-self and ideal-self formats. Real self can be assumed to be a form of self-evaluation and ideal self a form of generalized standard setting. Changes in real-self ratings correlated with changes in clinical improvement. No differences were found in ideal-self ratings. Using a similar assessment format, Wessman, Ricks, and Tyl (1960) followed 14 female subjects over 42 days in which they rated their mood on 10-point anchored scales and did a card sort evaluation for real and ideal self. Daily changes in mood correlated with real self, but not with ideal self. Both of these studies demonstrate that mood is correlated with changes in self-evaluation.

Gotlib (Note 5) compared depressed and nondepressed psychiatric and normal subjects in a study which found that depressed subjects showed a lower expectation for success, a lower estimate of performance, and a lower satisfaction with performance in comparison with normals. However, depressed patients were not different from the nondepressed psychiatric patients. Gotlib questioned whether negative self-evaluation is specific to depression or is generally an aspect of psychiatric disturbance.

Lewis, Mercatoris, Cole, and Leonard (Note 6) examined a number of self-control behaviors of depressed and nondepressed college students on a concept-formation task. Nonveridical feedback was given to standardize performance success. Of relevance is the finding that depressed subjects evaluated their performance as poorer, even though it was objectively the same as that of nondepressed subjects. Also, the self-evaluations were lower, despite the fact that recall of number correct was accurate and equal to that of nondepressed subjects.

Lewinsohn, Mischel, Chaplin, and Barton (1980) had depressed, nondepressed psychiatric patients interact at various points in therapy with normals in a group setting. All subjects evaluated their social performance on a series of rating scales. Depressed subjects rated themselves as less skillful than did the other subjects, and they were rated as less skillful by others. Interestingly, it was the nondepressed psychiatric and normal subjects whose self-evaluations were distorted. These subjects rated themselves as more skilled than others rated them. Depressed subjects self-ratings more closely corresponded to the ratings of others. Thus, the depressed subjects showed lower self-evaluation in a relative sense, but may have been more accurate in doing so. Ratings by self and others improved with treatment, but discrepancies between ratings did not change.

Shrauger and Terbovic (1976) had depressed and nondepressed college students assess themselves on a concept-formation task, and then again, one week later, assess a videotape either of themselves or of another subject who in fact was a model replicating the subject's own responses. Low-self-esteem (depressed) subjects rated themselves as lower than high-self-esteem subjects. Low-self-esteem subjects also rated themselves as lower than the model who was identical to the subject in performance. High self-evaluation subjects rated themselves as equal to the model. Thus, in this study, it was the low self-esteem subjects who distorted their self-evaluations.

A complex study by Garber, Hollon, and Seligman (Note 7) again pointed to the importance of the relationship between evaluations of self versus evaluations of others. In general, the results indicated that depressed females only set higher standards for themselves, evaluated themselves lower, and rewarded themselves less in comparison to their aspirations for others, their evaluations of others, and their reward of others. Taken together, these last three studies demonstrate that negative evaluations of performance by depressed individuals are specific to themselves and are not a generally distorted negative evaluation set. In general, this group of studies demonstrates that depressed persons do evaluate themselves negatively. In doing so, they may be more accurate than normals. One study raised the question of the specificity of negative self-evaluation to the depressed, though other studies indicate that nondepressed psychiatric subjects could be differentiated from depressed subjects on that basis.

Standard Setting and Expectancies

The self-control model of depression suggests that depressed individuals set stringent standards for themselves. This is reflected in the "perfectionism" which is often described as symptomatic of depression. High standards would account, in part, for the negative self-evaluations of depressed individuals. Selective self-monitoring of negative information would also contribute. In discussing self-evaluative standards, it is important to distinguish between different kinds of predictions which are made in research studies. To set a criterion is to describe one's level of aspiration. It is an evaluative process. Predictions of actual performance may be independent of such evaluation. The latter are often referred to as expectancies, but should be described as performance expectancies as opposed to success expectancies. Beck's (1967) theory of depression would predict that depressed individuals would have lower performance expectancies as well as lower success expectancies. For Beck, the defining characteristic of depression is a negative view of one's self and of the future. Thus, one would expect a depressed person to predict poor performance and failure.

A study which clearly makes this differentiation is one by Golin and Terrell (1977). College students high and low on a depression inventory were asked to predict their performance and also predict the level of performance to which they aspired in both skill and chance tasks. No differences were found in expected performance, but depressed subjects had an elevated level of aspiration, especially in the skill-task condition. Lewis, Mercatoris, Cole, and Leonard (Note 6) also made this distinction in their study with depressed and nondepressed college students. Their depressed subjects showed a significant discrepancy between the number of trials they predicted would be "correct" (performance expectancy) and the number with which they would feel satisfied (success expectancy). Depressed subjects set a higher standard, but expected the same performance as nondepressed subjects.

Attribution

Recently, a number of studies have focused on the manner in which depressed subjects attribute responsibility for their behavior. The topic has become important in the depression literature since Abramson, Seligman, and Teasdale (1978) reformulated the learned-helplessness theory of depression in attributional terms. The relevance of attributional processes to depression within the context of the self-control model was discussed in Rehm (1977) and in earlier version of the same paper (Rehm, Note 8). In the self-control model, self-attribution is seen as a modifier of self-evaluation. To make a self-evaluative judgment that a performance was either good or bad presumes that a prior judgment has been made that one was actually responsible for the behavior. Attribution to internal or external causes is a continuum of degree of responsibility, and the strength of the self-evaluation will depend in part on the degree of internal attribution.

Abramson, Seligman, and Teasdale (1978) argue that a dimension of *global-specific* attribution determines the generalization of depression. A similar dimension was discussed in Rehm (1977) with regard to the breadth of self-evaluative standards. The learned-helplessness model states that a dimension of *stability-instability* of attribution determines the persistence of depression. An attribution to a stable cause will have a more durable and persistent effect on mood. The learned-helplessness model predicts that depressed individuals will make internal, global, stable attributions with regard to failure, and external, specific, unstable attributions with regard to the causes of success. This combination of attributions leaves a person with a belief in his personal helplessness with regard to positive outcomes in the future.

SELF-REINFORCEMENT AND DEPRESSION

The self-control model suggests that self-monitoring and self-evaluating processes lead to and determine self-reinforcement. The model assumes that individuals control their own behavior by contingent rewards and punishments just as one organism would control the behavior of another organism. The concept of self-reinforcement has been the focus of considerable research (cf., Thoresen & Mahoney, 1974), but has been the center of much criticism (e.g., Catania, 1975; Goldiamond, 1976). The concept has also had its defenders (e.g., Bandura, 1976; Thoresen & Wilbur, 1976). Self-reinforcement is a relatively simple conceptualization of a mechanism by which covert processes influence behavior. More complex and sophisticated cognitive or social learning conceptualizations may prove to be superior means of explicating these phenomena. Unambiguous evidence for the reinforcing effects of self-administered reward has been difficult to produce. On the other hand, self-reinforcement procedures have been included in a number of successful behavior-therapy programs for diverse disorders (cf., Thoresen & Mahoney, 1974). This component has been retained in a self-control model of depression as a heuristic device useful in directing research and in developing therapy procedures.

Self-reinforcement has been suggested as a mechanism implicated in depression by several self-control theorists. For example, Marston (1964) suggested that a low criterion for self-punishment might be characteristic of depression. A similar suggestion was made by Bandura (1971). The self-control model of depression (Rehm, 1977) suggests that depressed subjects can be characterized as self-administering insufficient contingent self-reward and self-administering excessive self-punishment.

A study by Rozensky, Rehm, Pry, and Roth (1977) compared the self-reinforcement and self-punishment behavior of depressed and nondepressed VA psychiatric referrals. On a recognition memory task, depressed subjects self-reinforced less and self-punished more, despite no actual differences in memory accuracy. Roth, Rehm, and Rozensky (1980) used the same task with college students. In this instance, depressed subjects were found to self-punish more, but no differences were found in self-reward. Again, there were no differences in accuracy. A similar study by Nelson and Craighead (1977) found that depressed college subjects self-reinforced less, but found no differences in self-punishment. The difference in results between the two studies may be due to the different tasks involved. Ciminero and Steingarten (1978) used a digit symbol task, and found that depressed subjects both evaluated their performance as poorer and gave themselves fewer self-reward tokens. Nelson and Craighead (1979) used a marble maze task with depressed-anxious and nondepressed-anxious college students. There were no main effect differences between groups, but subjects who reached their goals self-reinforced less. Also, subjects who set more stringent standards self-reinforced less. Gotlib (Note 9) used the recognition memory task with depressed, nondepressed psychiatric and normal subjects. He found no effects for self-reward, but an effect for self-punishment whereby both depressed and nondepressed psychiatric patients self-punished more than nondepressed normals. Although these results are inconsistent with the Rozensky, Rehm, Pry, and Roth results cited above, they do suggest a need for discriminant validity studies in which deficits hypothesized to be associated with depression should be demonstrated to be associated with depression only. Sacco (Note 10) attempted to assess the self-reinforcement behavior of depressed, nondepressed, and normal subjects who had been subjected to helplessness-induction in public and private conditions. The only significant result was a complex subject group by public-private condition by sequence interaction. In general, when the sequence of reinforcement was from a high rate to a low rate, both depressed and helpless subjects self-reinforced more in the private condition, whereas the nondepressed subjects self-reinforced less in the private condition. While these results do not lend support to ideas about the association between self-reinforcement and depression, they again suggest that impression management considerations may be important determinants of depressive behavior.

An assumption of the self-control model of depression is that a typical form of reward or punishment self-administered by either depressed or nondepressed subjects is the self-statement. Positive self-statements presumably function as rewards, and negative self-statements are thought to function as punishments. Although none of the studies was done as a test of self-control conceptions of depression, three studies do demonstrate lower rates of positive and higher rates of negative self-statements by depressed subjects. Missel and Sommer (Note 11) gave depressed and nondepressed clinic patients questionnaires which described situations with positive and negative outcomes. Subjects were asked to indicate which of three multiple-choice statements would be more typical of them. Positive, negative, or external blame statements made up the choices. Depressed subjects chose more negative and fewer positive self-statements. The number of negative self-statements correlated .61 with the Beck Depression Inventory, and the number of positive self-statements correlated − .61. Vasta and Brockner (1979) had 33 undergraduates self-monitor positive and negative overt and covert self-evaluative statements. They found that a self-esteem measure correlated with the number of negative self-evaluations and with a ratio of the number of negative to the total number of self-statements. High self-esteem subjects recorded approximately equal numbers of positive and negative self-statements. It was concluded that self-esteem is related to self-statements and especially to negative self-statements. Hinchliffe, Lancashire, and Roberts (1971) analyzed 5-minute speech samples of depressed and control surgical patients. Depressed subjects demonstrated a higher number of "negators" (i.e., negative words such as "not," "never," "nor," or "nothing"). Depressed subjects also demonstrated a lower rate of speech, a greater number of personal references, a lower number of nonpersonal references, and a higher number of expressions of feelings. No differences were found on length of pauses or on the use of value judgments.

Overall, this research suggests that depressed subjects self-reward less and self-punish more, as these concepts are conventinally defined in laboratory research. Also, self-statements, which are presumably a typical form of self-reward or self-punishment, differ between depressed and nondepressed subjects in the predicted directions. Clearly, more research is necessary with regard to self-reinforcement in depression. The studies reviewed suggest that this behavior may not be unique to depression and that the nature of the social environment may influence the expression of self-reinforcement. The reinforcement function of these behaviors in depressed subjects has not been demonstrated. Results to date are positive and consistent with the model, but more complex models may be necessary.

PERFORMANCE DEFICITS

The self-control deficits identifiable with depression would be expected to produce certain specific deficits in performance. Since self-control behavior has to do with the ability to pursue delayed goals in the face of contingencies favoring incompatible behavior, it would be expected that: (1) Depressed persons would have more difficulty tolerating delay and would choose immediate over delayed reinforcers, even if the latter were of a greater magnitude; and (2) depressed persons would be less able to sustain effort in the absence of immediate reinforcement and would be less persistent. Several research studies bear on these points.

Immediate versus Delayed Reward

Rehm and Plakosh (1975) gave college students a questionnaire asking them whether or not they would endorse such statements as "I would rather get $10 right now than have to wait a whole month and get $30 then." Sentences were balanced so as to preclude the operation of various response biases. Subjects who scored higher on a depression scale had a greater tendency to express a preference for immediate as opposed to delayed rewards. O'Hara and Rehm (Note 1) attempted to assess the same question with an actual, as opposed to hypothetical, choice. Adult women who had been subjects in another experiment had been promised $20 for their participation. After the final experimental session, they were told that they had a choice between receiving $20 immediately or greater amounts up to $30 one month later. No correlation was found between choice and depression scores. In debriefing, subjects gave a large number of very pratical reasons for their choices which may have obscured any effect due to mood. Seeman and Schwarz (1974) assessed preferences for immediate versus delayed rewards with

9-year-old subjects. Mood differences were induced by a success-failure manipulation, which their pilot research had shown to induce dysphoria. Subjects in the success condition chose delayed reward more often than children in the failure condition. The authors argue that in a state of negative affect, subjects are reluctant to increase that negative affect with delay frustration. Three studies, two of which had positive and one had negative results, represent only a beginning effort at exploring the limits and implications of relationships between depression and preference for immediate versus delayed reward.

Persistence

The persistence of depressed and nondepressed subjects has been assessed in a number of studies coming from the learned-helplessness paradigm. A task frequently used in this research is solving anagrams with dependent variables, including average time for solution and average time taken to perceive a standard pattern in the anagrams. Hiroto and Seligman (1975) demonstrated that induced helplessness produced decrements in anagram solution and in learning to avoid an aversive stimulus in a shuttle box problem. Miller and Seligman (1975) replicated a portion of the prior study with depressed and nondepressed college students. Depressed subjects behaved like helpless subjects in that they were poorer at anagram solution and took longer to perceive the anagram pattern. Price, Tryon, and Raps (1978) replicated the same task with VA psychiatric and medical patients. Again, both depression and induced helplessness produced deficits in anagram solutions. Shrauger and Sorman (1977) assessed female college students who were high and low on self-esteem scales on a laboratory task. Following initial failure, low self-esteem subjects persisted less than did high-self-esteem subjects. The performance of low-self-esteem subjects was generally poorer.

Lewis, Mercatoris, Cole, and Leonard (Note 6), however, did not find differences between depressed and nondepressed college students in whether or not they chose to continue additional blocks of trials in a concept-formation task.

The self-control model would interpret the performance deficits of depressed subjects as being due to a lack of self-reinforcement for continued effort or persistence on these tasks. Lack of self-reinforcement in turn could be due to negative self-monitoring and stringent self-evaluative criteria. Inappropriate self-punishment might also be involved. An alternative explanation has been offered by Abramson and Alloy (Note 12). They demonstrated that depressed subjects may have a deficit in generating hypotheses for solving complex problems. When lists of hypotheses were provided, depressed subjects showed no deficit in problem solution. However, when they were not provided, depressed subjects did much poorer.

Summary

The research reviewed above suggests that depressed subjects do show deficits in self-monitoring, self-evaluation, self-attribution, self-reward, self-punishment, and self-control behavior generally. In many instances, this behavior may be more complex than originally stated by the model. Self-monitoring by depressed persons involves selective attention to negative events, in the sense of distributing attention to negative information; but other biases may also be operating. A bias toward negative self-evaluation seems to extend beyond goal setting into a negative bias in assessing performance (i.e., into self-monitoring behavior, according to the model). Goal-setting and attributional behavior both appear to be separable characteristics of depression with the potential for direct manipulation.

Self-reinforcement behavior has been demonstrated to differ in depression in some studies, but the parameters of this phenomenon have not been examined fully. It may be profitable to explore models for completing the feedback loop, other than through the use of the self-reinforcement concept. If self-monitored input is processed in the self-evaluation, output could be conceptualized in a variety of forms. Helplessness and deficient hypothesis testing are among the alternatives. Overall, however, evidence seems sufficient that the self-control model can usefully be applied as a framework for describing the behavior of depressed persons. It is therefore warranted to use the model as a framework for the psychotherapy of depression.

SELF-CONTROL THERAPY FOR DEPRESSION

This portion of the chapter will be devoted to a description of therapies for depression based on self-control conceptions of the nature of the disorder. It will begin with a brief review of therapy research. This review will include a variety of studies which have used aspects of self-control for the self-managed treatment of depression and will also describe a series of studies done by the author and his colleagues which have systematically investigated a therapy program built on the self-control model. Following the review, a more detailed description will be given of the self-control therapy program for depression. Each major component of this program will be described, followed by some evaluative comments and recommendations based on the psychopathology and psychotherapy reviews in this chapter.

Self-Management Strategies in Behavior Therapy for Depression

In the early 1970s, a number of case studies appeared which reported on self-management techniques used in therapy for depression. One of the most frequently reported techniques was the cueing of positive self-statements by requiring that the subject make the self-statements prior to frequent daily events. For example, Johnson (1971) had a male college student make statements about positive personal characteristics prior to certain events, and also had the client engage in more positive activities. Mahoney (1971) combined the positive self-statement strategy with a self-punishment technique for negative thoughts. Todd (1972) had a chronically depressed woman read one or two positive self-statements before smoking a cigarette, as part of the therapy program. Vasta (1976) used a single-subject design to assess the effectiveness of scheduled readings of postive self-statements on spontaneous self-statements. Todd (1972), in case studies, and Taylor and Marshall (1977), in a group study, used a technique of pairing positive thoughts with high-frequency behaviors as part of complex packages of behavior therapy.

Other case studies reported the use of additional self-control techniques. Jackson (1972) described the treatment of a 22-year-old woman in which the problems were explicitly conceptualized in self-control terms. The treatment consisted of setting realistic, objective goals for a variety of household tasks and developing a self-reinforcement program for the accomplishment of the tasks. Anton, Dunbar, and Friedman (1976) reported on the effectiveness of a treatment procedure in which nine depressed female volunteers were initially instructed to select and schedule pleasant activities. To facilitate participants' performance of these activities, subjects were taught to rehearse positive anticipation statements about the activities until the activity was performed. Tharp, Watson, and Kaya (1974) described the self-managed therapy programs developed by four depressed students who had completed a course in behavioral self-management. The techniques developed included self-monitoring of positive and negative activities, use of positive imagery, and self-reinforcement for positive statements and for the absence of depressive rumination. These programs were developed by the patients under the supervision of their therapists.

It should also be noted that self-control and self-management techniques have been used extensively in therapy programs which have had very different primary rationales and theoretical backgrounds. For instance, Peter Lewinsohn and his colleagues have developed a behavioral therapy program aimed primarily at increasing pleasant activities (e.g., Lewinsohn, Biglan, & Zeiss, 1976). The program involves extensive self-monitoring of pleasant events. Self-monitoring, in this program, is seen purely as an assessment modality and not as an intervention per se. On the basis of the self-monitoring information, target events are chosen for increase and are scheduled in subsequent weeks. Scheduling of activities in some ways is a self-evaluation procedure in that it involves setting explicit, limited, and realistic criteria for one's behavior during the week. Lewinsohn's program uses a variety of external reinforcers to encourage engaging in pleasant activities. Among these are self-reinforcement points, which are cashed in for rewards from a list developed by the patient as a part of his self-management program. Self-reward and self-punishment are also involved in methods aimed at controlling covert and overt verbal behavior. Lewinsohn's program also teaches a variety of other behavioral skills including specific social skills and relaxation.

Self-control techniques are also involved in Beck's cognitive therapy of depression (Beck, Rush, Shaw, & Emery, 1979). Beck's program involves both behavioral and cognitive techniques, and many of these techniques can be conceptualized in self-control terms. Self-monitoring is used extensively in Beck's program. Patients are given the assignment of keeping activity schedules which they record on an hourly basis throughout the week. In this program, the activity schedules are seen as both assessment procedures to gather data and as interventions per se.

For example, Rush, Khatami, and Beck (1975) described the use of activity schedules as a means of collecting information to counter unrealistic perceptions by the patients of the nature and quality of interactions with others. Self-monitoring of cognitions is also involved in Beck's program. Subjects are taught to identify and monitor what Beck refers to as "automatic thoughts." Automatic thoughts are negative assumptions which underlie depressive perceptions of situations. The recording of automatic thoughts is partly an attempt to make subjects more aware of the nature and extent of their use. It also allows the patient explicitly to counter the automatic thoughts with more rational counter-arguments. Self-evaluation techniques are also used in Beck's program. Specific activities are assigned and scheduled during the week, and in some cases these are assigned in the form of a graded task assignment. Activities are ordered from simple to complex under a particular heading. The idea is to establish realistic step-by-step criteria for accomplishment of a complex task. The program explicitly attempts to counter the cognitive perfectionism of depressed subjects by setting realistic fractional goals. Modification of self-attributions is also addressed in Beck's program. Explicit reattribution exercises are employed to help patients deal with excessive self-blame for negative events. Subjects are helped to make more realistic and objective evaluations and to search for alternative definitions and solutions of the problem. Attributional considerations are also involved in the self-monitoring of activities in what Beck refers to as *mastery* and *pleasure techniques*. The mastery technique involves recording the degree to which each activity on the daily record is one that the subject feels was performed competently. These mastery ratings imply the making of internal attributions for positive events. Self-reinforcement techniques are not used explicitly in Beck's program. However, making mastery ratings following activities and the stress in the program on positive self-statements to counter depressive thoughts can be seen as a means of encouraging contingent positive self-reinforcement. Beck's therapy program has been demonstrated to be effective in several studies (i.e., Rush, Beck, Kovacs, & Hollon, 1977; Shaw, 1977; Taylor & Marshall, 1977).

Self-control techniques can also be identified in the reports of a number of other programs. For instance, McLean's behavior therapy program involves use of multiple techniques selected to match the needs of individual subjects (McLean, Ogston, & Grauer, 1973). Considerable emphasis is placed on teaching social learning principles to patients so that they can develop and implement their own self-managed change programs. McLean and Hakstian (1979) demonstrated the effectiveness of this strategy in comparison to psychotherapy, relaxation control, and tricyclic antidepressant conditions. Dunn (1979) described a cognitive modification procedure which involves targeting positive self-evaluations and adaptive attributions regarding stressful events and responsibility for behavior. Self-monitoring is also involved in what is described as a "self-dialog diary." As in the other programs, these self-control techniques are part of a much larger overall package program. Hilford (Note 13) described a self-management behavioral program which he applied with depressed inpatients. This program involved self-monitoring the social consequences of one's behavior, setting goals for completing small tasks as a form of self-evaluative standard setting, and replacing depressive thoughts with positive and constructive self-statements. Again, the self-control techniques were part of a larger program. All of these programs have employed some self-control techniques. None has involved a full therapy program based on a self-control rationale independent of other behavioral and cognitive techniques.

Therapy Based on the Self-Control Model

Such a program has been developed by the author and his colleagues. Based on an explicit self-control model of depression (Rehm, 1977), we have developed a behavior therapy program which attempts to address depressive deficits in each of the areas of self-monitoring, self-evaluation, self-attribution, and self-reinforcement. The program is presented in a group format. It is partly didactic in that it involves the systematic presentation of self-control concepts about the nature of depression in each of the identified areas. These ideas are discussed in light of the experiences of individuals in the groups. In many cases, paper-and-pencil exercises are employed to help the subjects to understand the concepts. Homework assignments are made so that the participants apply the concepts in their daily lives. The program assumes that individual participants will have different patterns of self-control deficits contributing to their depressions, but that the program, by systematically covering major areas of deficit, will be relevant to each individual. In a series of studies, the program has been developed and refined. The format, in terms of the number, timing, and sequence of sessions, has varied somewhat across the studies. Overall, the research can be seen as attempting to assess the effectiveness of the program of a broad spectrum of criteria, and as attempting to make the program more effective by identifying and improving the contribution of its components.

To date, five studies have been concluded in our research program. In all of these studies, subjects have been depressed women volunteers who have been recruited from the general community. While the method of recruitment may imply important differences from clinical populations, demographic, diagnostic, and historical data suggest that our samples closely approximate clinical samples in personal characteristics, life situations, and in duration, course, and intensity of depression. The subjects have ranged in age from 20 to 60, with a mean in the mid- to late thirties. The average subject had a high school education plus some college. About half were married. Depression scores place the subjects in the moderate to severe range. Virtually all report a duration of depression of more than one month, and 50 percent report a duration of more than one year. About three-fourths report prior episodes of depression and two-thirds had previous treatment for depression.

The first two studies in the series were designed primarily to assess the efficacy of the self-control program in comparison to control conditions. Fuchs and Rehm (1977) compared a 6-week version of the self-control program to a non-specific group therapy control condition and to a waiting-list condition. Of the 36 subjects who met MMPI and interview screening criteria, 8, 10, and 10 completed the study in the three respective conditions. Screening in this study consisted of MMPI criteria plus an interview to rule out psychosis or suicidal crisis. Dependent variables included the MMPI, the Beck Depression Inventory, the MacPhillamy and Lewinsohn Pleasant Events Schedule, experimental questionnaires intended to assess self-control behavior, and measures of verbal activity in the first and last group sessions. On the major dependent variables, the self-control condition was the most improved and was significantly more improved relative to the nonspecific condition, which in turn was significantly more effective than the waiting list. Results were maintained on a 6-week follow-up. The results not only were statistically significant, but also represented a clinically significant improvement in terms of absolute scores on depression measures (i.e., most subjects score well within the normal range of post-test). The results of this study were quite encouraging and led us to a further evaluation of the efficacy of the therapy program.

Rehm, Fuchs, Roth, Kornblith, and Romano (1979) compared the self-control program to a behavioral assertion skills training condition. Subjects were assessed at four points at 6-week intervals, including screening, pretest, post-test and follow-up. Subjects were selected on the same criteria as in the first study. Two groups were seen in each condition, with a male and female pair of therapists seeing one group in each condition. Fourteen subjects completed the self-control condition and 10 completed the assertion skills program. Results indicated that on measures of self-control, self-control subjects did better than assertion-skills subjects. On behavioral role-play measures of assertions skills, assertion-skill subjects did better than self-control subjects. Self-control subjects did significantly better on measures of depression. The results were maintained at a 6-week follow-up. Once again, results were clinically as well as statistically significant. Again the results were encouraging, but it was also clear that results were obtained from a complex package procedure, much of which may well have been superfluous. The next two studies were designed to try to begin a disassembly of the therapy program in order to help identify the effective components.

Rehm, Kornblith, O'Hara, Lamparski, Romano, and Volkin (in press) conducted a disassembly study which attempted to evaluate the effects of major components of the therapy program. In particular, the self-reinforcement and self-evaluation portions of the program were eliminated individually and together. The study contained five conditions: (1) full self-control package; (2) self-monitoring plus self-evaluation—the package minus self-reinforcement; (3) self-control plus self-reinforcement—the package less self-evaluation; (4) self-monitoring only—the package less self-evaluation and self-reinforcement; and (5) a waiting-list control condition. Subjects in this study were selected on the basis of an MMPI-D score of 70 or more and an interview based on the Schedule for Affective Disorders and Schizophrenia (Endicott & Spitzer, 1978) which established a Research Diagnostic Criteria (Spitzer, Endicott, & Robins, 1978) diagnosis of non-bipolar, nonpsychotic Major Affective Disorder. A variety of alternative diagnoses were specifically excluded by the interview. In this study, 9, 12, 11, 9, and 15 subjects were seen in the respective conditions in a 7-week treatment format. Dependent variables included self-report and clinical ratings of depression (i.e., the MMPI-D, the Beck Depression Inventory, the Hamilton Rating Scale, the Raskin Three-Item Depression Scale), the Pleasant Events Schedule, the Self-Control Questionnaire, and some experimental measures of overt behavior during interview and during first and last therapy sessions. In general, all therapy conditions improved to a greater extent than the waiting-list control condition. However, no differences were found between conditions. This somewhat puzzling result suggests that the program was just as effective with either or both of two of its major components omitted. It was our feeling that the self-monitoring portion of the program may have had implicit in it suggestions of self-evaluation and self-reinforcement behavior. Also, we felt that the complete package program may have become too complex for the brief duration of therapy. The complexity of the program may have decreased the participants' sense of successfully mastering all aspects of the program.

The fourth study in this series, Kornblith, Rehm, O'Hara, & Lamparski (Note 14), extended the program to a 12-week format and attempted another form of disassembly. This study included a full self-control package condition, a condition which presented all of the rationale, presentations, discussions, and exercises, but omitted any explicit behavioral homework assignments; and a third condition, which replicated the self-monitoring plus self-evaluation condition in the prior study. In each of these three conditions, 11, 11 and 12 subjects were seen, respectively. Two groups were seen in each condition, with two therapists seeing one group in each condition. In addition, five subjects were seen by a different therapist in a group therapy control condition. Subjects in this study were selected on the basis of a Beck Depression Inventory score of 20 or more and on the same diagnostic interview as in the prior study. Again, in this study, all subjects in active therapy conditions improved on a variety of outcome variables. There were also no significant differences between the experimental conditions and the group therapy control. This latter condition was an active, structured, problem-solving program conducted by a talented therapist. The results were again somewhat puzzling to us. We had now a replication of the fact that the self-reinforcement portion of the program seemed to add little to the overall effectiveness of the therapy. In addition, it appeared that the explicit behavioral assignments did not contribute significantly to the outcome. It should be noted that the numbers of participants in this study were still rather small, so that real but very small differences might not have been detected. Also, there was anecdotal evidence that at least some of the subjects in the "rationale only" condition devised their own behavioral homework assignments. This study ruled out our hypothesis from the former study that subjects could make better use of the full condition in a longer, 12-week format. Intermittent Beck Depression Inventory probes suggested that the major therapy changes occurred within the *early weeks* of the therapy program.

A fifth study in the series compared three versions of the self-control program to a waiting-list control. One version of the program stressed a behavioral target of activity increase. Self-monitoring, self-evaluation, and self-reinforcement components were geared to this target. The second condition in the program targeted cognitive self-statements. Self-monitoring, self-evaluation, self-attribution, and self-reinforcement components of the program were geared to a cognitive self-statement conceptualization of depression. A third version of the program combined the other two rationales. Manuals were carefully written to establish presentations, exercises, and homework assignments within consistent behavioral target, cognitive target, or combined target versions of the program. In this study, 13 subjects were seen in the behavioral target condition, 11 in the cognitive target, 8 in the combined target, and 12 in the waiting-list condition. Subject selection was based on an MMPI-D score of 70 or more, a Beck Depression Inventory score of 20 or more, and the same interview criteria as in the previous study. Results of this study indicated again that all three active treatments were effective and superior to the waiting list. However, once again, no differences were found between the three treatment conditions. Results of this study have led us to a study presently underway, which is seeking to obtain a much larger sample in order to determine whether different variables are associated with positive outcome in the cognitive versus behavioral target therapy conditions.

Two studies have been reported which have independently evaluated the self-control therapy condition. Rothblum, Green, and Collins (1979) evaluated two versions of the self-control program. One version stressed self-generated activity goals, whereas the alternative condition stressed therapist assignment of activity goals. The third condition consisted of an attention placebo. On major dependent variables related to depression, all groups improved, with no significant differences between them. On two measures — the Pleasant Events Schedule pleasantness measure, and a peer assessment — the therapist generated goal condition was superior to either of the two conditions. These results suggest that it is desirable for the therapist to take an active role in, at least, aiding subjects in selecting and assigning therapy goals for homework.

Fleming and Thornton (1980) saw 13 subjects in a condition based on the Fuchs and Rehm manual and compared them to 13 subjects in a cognitive condition based on the Shaw (1977) manual. Nine subjects were also seen in a nondirective group therapy condition. Subjects were selected on the basis of a Beck Depression Inventory Score of 17 or more, a D-30 score of 14 or more, and an interview which established that depression was the major problem and that psychosis was absent. Subjects were volunteers solicited by media announcements. All three conditions demonstrated a positive therapeutic effect at post-test and at a 6-week follow-up. The self-control condition was superior on a number of variables, but was significant only on measures of negative self-references and overall depression (derived from the therapy sessions) when assessed at posttest.

The results of this series of studies need to be evaluated in the context of the overall results which have been obtained with behavior therapies for depression. Several recent reviews (cf. Rehm & Kornblith, 1979; Rehm, 1981) support the idea that there are now a number of therapy programs which have some evidence of efficacy in the treatment of depression. Beck's cognitive behavior therapy, Lewinsohn's activity increase program,

MacLean and Hakstian's behavior therapy program, and even Weissman's nonbehavioral therapy have good evidence for their effectiveness. The self-control program is certainly among these with evidence for the effectiveness of the program accruing from our five studies plus two independent replications. It is also clear that there is, at this point, little evidence to indicate the superiority of one of these therapy programs over another. While there now have been a number of studies comparing different therapy programs, these have generally been characterized by the use of small numbers of subjects over short periods of time. In addition, studies have involved mildly depressed "analog" subjects and quite diverse descriptions of procedures for what are nominally the same therapies. Overall, the results are equivocal. At present, we have no reason to be able to argue that any of these packages is more effective than another.

On the other hand, it should be noted that all of these programs consist of very complex packages and that there is much overlap between these treatment packages. While the theories behind the therapies vary, all of them seem to have common characteristics. For example, each has a clear rationale which is easily understood by participants. It is noticeable that a considerable stress is given in many of the therapy manuals or protocols on presenting the rationale in a careful, systematic, and convincing manner. The rationales are concrete, logical, and "scientific" and offer the participant a simple language for reconceptualizing the problem in a manner which has direct implications for change. Rationales also serve as overviews for the nature of the therapy. All the therapy programs instigate systematic behavior change. Directly deriving from the rationales, clear demands are placed on participants to perform certain assignments or behaviors between sessions. The required behaviors are usually relatively simple assignments which nonetheless demonstrate systematic step-by-step improvement back to the participant. Brown and Lewinsohn (Note 15) and Zeiss, Lewinsohn, and Muñoz (1979) proposed a similar analysis of current therapies for depression. It is probably not the case, however, that therapy for depression would be effective with virtually *any* rationale and any systematic instigation of new behavior. The rationale must be logical and must be accepted by the participants. Participants must be able to use the rationale to conceptualize what is happening to them in the program. Homework assignments must be effectively related to what the participant sees as his or her problem. The program needs to be flexible and comprehensive to be able to accommodate the diverse problems and the characteristics of individuals within the diagnosis for depression.

There are relatively few studies in the literature which attempt to evaluate separate components of larger package procedures. Two of our studies (Rehm, Kornblith, O'Hara, Lamparski, Romano, & Volkin, in press; Kornblith, Rehm, O'Hara, & Lamparski, Note 14) are examples of this strategy.

The results of our studies were puzzling, in that we found no evidence that components of the program which we felt were very important actually did not contribute significantly to the overall effectiveness of the package. It may be that the major effect of the program comes from the convincing presentaton of a functional rationale, instigation and reinforcement for effort at working on problems, and clear specification of progress. These factors may be so important that the details of procedure do not produce detectable additional contributions. Our feeling remains that these components are helpful for some aspects of the problems of some individuals. We also feel that systematic homework assignments are better than the unsystematic instigation of the "rationale only" group in the Kornblith, Rehm, O'Hara, and Lamparski study. Clearly, the field needs more studies to evaluate therapy components. Disassembly strategies are needed. Studies which evaluate therapy components singly are also needed. In addition, we need to look at new and different components of therapy programs. We need to evaluate the contribution of rationales and their acquisition, acceptability, and utilization by participants. We need to understand better *how* certain procedures are effective, and we need to be able to identify particular subjects *for whom* particular procedures will be effective. Ultimately, matching strategies may be the best means of maximizing the effectiveness of therapy programs for depression.

The comments above should be kept in mind during the description of the self-control therapy program which follows. Our therapy program is one of several which have demonstrated efficacy. It has many procedural components shared in common with other therapies, and it has the ingredients of a logical rationale and of systematic assignments which other programs have. We feel it has particular advantages in that it is *group administered* and thus *cost-effective*. Also, it is particularly comprehensive, in that *it targets for change multiple aspects of depressive behavior*. Over the course of our research during the last 5 years, the therapy program has been refined and modified in various ways. It has been lengthened to provide subjects more time to practice and consolidate skills after they have been initially presented. Presently, we are using a 10-week format, which we feel is sufficient in length. Exercises within the program have been expanded from the original protocol, but in recent revisions of our manual, we have streamlined and simplified some of the exercises. This was partly due to the fact that our research showed us that certain components were not adding significantly to the overall improvement of participants. Second, the streamlining was due to our feeling that the program had become too complex and thus too difficult for the participants to acquire and utilize. Finally, in our most recent work we have included a more explicit concern for cognitive (i.e., self-statement) as well as behavioral (i.e., activity level) targets of the therapy program. The description of the program to follow is based on a manual which has gone through a number of revisions from one study to another. It is the manual which combines cognitive and behavioral targets from our studies evaluating these separate versions of the program. The basic procedures involved in this manual will be described, and after each procedure, a commentary will be included with reference back to basic research on the nature of depression and, at times, to depression-therapy research. The commentary will include some recommendations for the most effective use of each component of the therapy program.

SELF-CONTROL THERAPY PROGRAM FOR DEPRESSION

Prior to describing the therapy program and its particulars, a number of points should be made about its general format and conceptualization. The first point is that the program is being conducted entirely in a group format. Seeing groups composed entirely of depressed persons is counter to traditional group-therapy wisdom, where it is assumed that depressed persons will reinforce one another's depression. Our impressions are quite the opposite. The group seems to be very helpful in establishing a sense in the participants that they are not alone and that they are fighting the same problems as others. The structure of the program focuses on discussion. Group members are often very helpful to one another in offering support, reinforcement, and encouragement; in offering suggestions for alternate ways to approach problems; and in serving as models for one another in their successful approaches to problems. Good clinical skills on the part of the therapist are necessary to allow these group processes to develop and to shape them in constructive directions. The therapist must maintain a difficult balance between allowing discussion and constructive interplay among participants and following a structured protocol which requires presentation of didactic material, exercises, and homework assignments.

Therapists in our studies have varied from advanced graduate students, to psychology interns, to psychology Ph.D.s with several years of experience. While it has not been a direct object of study, it seems fairly clear that even with a very structured protocol, clinical skill contributes to the success of the groups.

The program is organized around the self-control model of depression. Successive sessions focus on specific aspects of self-evaluation, self-attribution, and self-reinforcement. The model serves as the rationale for the program and is explicitly taught to the participants. The model is presented in an authoritative fashion as a way of understanding depression and as a strategy for modifying depression. It appears to have good participant acceptability. It is a relatively concrete and understandable model which participants can use and employ. The model is also flexible and multifaceted, allowing the program to cover individual circumstances and multiple aspects of depressive psychopathology.

Our experience with the self-control therapy program has been almost entirely in a research context. Thus the manuals we have developed are a detailed form of research protocol. They provide instructions to the therapists with regard to assessment and therapy procedures as well as to the timing and sequencing of the program. They provide script-like instructions for presenting the rationale, exercises, and homework. They are not meant to be read, however, and these materials are provided only as examples and guidelines to the therapists.

The population used in our studies has been depressed women volunteers. While we have worked only with women, there is no apparent reason why the program would not work as well with men. There have been clinical applications of the program with males in nonresearch contexts which suggest that positive results are not limited to women. As discussed above, despite the fact that our participants have been volunteers, their depression is of an intensity, extent, and duration comparable to depressed clinical outpatient populations. The fact that they have volunteered for the program may, however, have worked to our advantage in a couple of ways. Perhaps our participants are more highly motivated. On the other hand, in many instances, subjects have volunteered for our program because it was free or because it is a research project, when they would not have otherwise sought therapy through usual channels. Our subjects know that they are volunteering for a psychotherapy program, and a self-selection factor appears to be operating, in that many subjects have said that they were interested in volunteering because it did not involve drugs. In some ways, we may be tapping a broader population than usually comes to clinics. Recent epidemiological studies (e.g., Weissman, Prusoff, Thompson, Harding, & Meyer, 1978) suggest that only a fraction of depressed individuals seek treatment. In the long run, soliciting therapy participants through the media may be an effective mental health outreach procedure for reaching a larger portion of the population with depression.

The following sections will describe the major components of the therapy program. This includes the rationale, exercises done within the sessions, and homework assignments. The tone of the presentation reflects the manner in which the rationale is presented to subjects. It is didactic and somewhat informal. Ordinarily, each component of the program is done within one or two sessions, with a review of the homework experience in the following session. Clinical use would dictate some flexiblity in timing, and thus a weekly session-by-session schedule is not presented. As we use the program presently, we have tried to present all of the material in fairly rapid succession in the early weeks. This then allows several weeks at the end for continuation, review, and further development of the individual components. The program that will be described is based on our most recent studies, and as such, combines both behavioral and cognitive therapy targets. That is, the program explicitly attempts to change the statements which accompany self-monitoring, which express self-evaluation and self-attribution, and which can function as self-reinforcement. Multiple aspects of activity are targeted as our multiple aspects of cognition.

Self-Monitoring

Several major ideas are presented in the first self-monitoring component of the program. The first idea is that mood is a function of behavior. This is a central concept in the program on which all else is based. By behavior we are referring both to overt activity and to the self-statements which may accompany it. Both the activity and the self-statement may be events which influence mood. For instance, the activity of exchanging words with a rude and incompetent salesperson while shopping may be a negative event which has an effect on mood. The effect of the event may be magnified by the accompanying self-statements; for example: "I *always* run into people like this." "What did I do to provoke her so?" "Now I have made someone else mad at me." Self-statements nearly always accompany activities, although the person may not be aware of them. Often they are automatic or implied in the way in which the situation is construed. These events (activities or self-statements) may be either positive or negative. Negative events tend to depress mood and positive events tend to elevate mood.

Depressed persons often experience mood as being quite independent of activity or cognition. Depressed moods often seem to come from nowhere without a precipitating act or thought. We take the position that negative events are always the precipitant or concomitant of depressed mood, but that the relationship may often be difficult to perceive. In the groups, participants frequently express the view that depressed moods are caused by uncontrollable biological factors. It is important to acknowledge that biological factors may indeed be important in depression. There may be differences between individuals in susceptibility to events, based on a biological predisposition. There may also be variations in day-to-day biochemistry which affect mood; for example, the biochemical effects of the menstrual cycle. Biochemical changes, on the other hand, may also be an *effect of* behavior. The important point is that behavior (activity and self-statements) can effect changes in mood. The goal of this aspect of the program is to make participants aware of the relationship between their mood and concomitant activity and self-statements.

The second major point in the rationale underlying the program is that people who are depressed tend to focus excessively on negative events. People who are depression prone attend to negative activity to the exclusion of positive activity. They habitually make negative self-statements about their activities and ruminate in the form of repetitive negative self-statements. Depressed persons are inattentive to positive events which do occur in everyone's life. They are unlikely to make even the most realistic or accurate positive self-statements to themselves. The goal of this component of the therapy program is to make participants more aware of the positive events which occur in their lives on a day-to-day basis.

A third major point in the rationale is that depressed mood can be changed by changing activity and self-statements. The first step will be to increase awareness of the relationship, but later on, the program will focus on changing self-statements and behavior; that is, decreasing negative events and increasing and using positive events systematically. For the purposes of the program, we are assuming "mood" (a term which is usually used to describe fluctuations in daily affect) and "depression" (a term which is usually used to denote a persistent enduring emotional state) are equivalent. It is our assumption that if we can influence mood in powerful and consistent ways, then we are influencing and hopefully modifying depression.

The homework assignment for this first component of the program is to self-monitor positive activities and self-statements in the coming weeks. Subjects are given a self-monitoring log which consists of a sheet of paper for each day of the week. The day and date are written at the top of the sheet. The sheet contains a column of 20 numbered lines on which participants are to write brief descriptions of positive events which occur each day. Activities are described in a phrase or sentence which would be sufficient for the subject to recall the event. Self-statements are also to be entered on the log. To act as a guide and to prompt subjects, a list of 15 sample self-statements and 15 sample categories of positive activity is printed on the back of each sheet. Examples of positive self-statements include: "I really feel great." "I deserve credit for trying hard." "That was a nice thing for me to do." Examples of activities include going out for entertainment, playing a sport or game, and doing a job well. On the bottom of the self-monitoring log is a daily mood rating. Subjects are asked to circle a number from 0 to 10 corresponding to the "unhappiest day ever" to the "happiest day ever."

The importance of the homework assignment is stressed to subjects. Homework is an important device for therapy and behavior change. In addition, it provides information which is used in the next component of the therapy program. The components of the program and the homework assignments build one on top of the other. Participants are encouraged to keep their monitoring logs with them and make entries as frequently as possible during the day. Even the most trivial of positive activities and self-statements should be recorded. At a minimum, participants should try to record at lunch for the morning, at dinner for the afternoon, and at bedtime for the evening.

As we have used the program most recently, we have also had the subjects keep a parallel log of negative activities and self-statements. The negative logs are kept only during the first week of the program and then again during the last week of the program. They provide a contrast to the participant in terms of numbers of negative versus positive events during each of these weeks, and they provide a baseline and post-test for examining changes that have occurred as a function of the program. Since the emphasis of the program is on increasing the awareness and actual frequency of positive events, only the positive monitoring is continued throughout the program.

At the next session, homework assignments are reviewed and discussed. A number of experiences are common among the participants. They are often surprised at the number of positive events which they have on their records. Many participants anticipate that these will be quite few and far between; but in fact, they usually have a number of events for each day. Many participants are also surprised at the variation in their day-to-day mood which they detect. Their anticipation is that mood will be consistently poor with no day-to-day fluctuations. In fact, most participants can detect variations even if they are only a point or two on the 11-point scale.

The exercise for this component is conducted in this second session. The basic idea is to demonstrate to the participants the correlation between the number of daily events and mood. They are asked to go through their week's logs and graph their daily mood. They are provided with a graph which has days on the abscissa and mood ratings on the left-hand ordinate. After they have entered their mood ratings, they repeat the procedure, entering the number of events which occurred each day, using a scale provided on the right-hand ordinate. The result is two lines which, in most cases, do show a rough parallel with at least some common peaks and valleys. To reinforce the point, subjects are asked to look at their average mood ratings on their most active days and to compare them to their least active days. In instances where neither of these clearly demonstrates a correlation, the logs may be discussed to see if the items recorded are really positive and to determine whether other events were missed. A similar exercise can be done for negative events to show a negative correlation. Subjects are also given an extra set of the graphs to repeat the demonstration on the next week's self-monitoring log data.

Parallels with other forms of therapy are fairly clear. As in Lewinsohn's program, self-monitoring of activities is used to gather data which will later form the basis for attempting to increase activity. As in Beck's program, there is an attempt to help subjects to become more accurate observers of their own activity and to become more aware of automatic self-statements.

It is important to emphasize that in our program the self-monitoring is also seen as an intervention per se. The homework data are used as feedback to the subject to demonstrate the principles of the rationale and to convince the subject of their utility. In addition, the homework is an attempt to intervene in the self-monitoring style of participants. It is an attempt to make them more aware of a relationship between mood and daily events and of positive events that will later become the targets for change. The research review in the earlier part of the chapter identified aspects of the self-monitoring style of depressed persons which are maladaptive. Modification of this style is the goal of this component of the program.

Research on self-monitoring procedures similar to those used in our therapy program has demonstrated that correlations can be reliably obtained between daily events and mood. Also, research suggests that to have effect on mood, monitoring should be frequent across the day. Participants should not simply fill out the self-monitoring logs at the end of the day, but should keep them with them and record as the day progresses. Our therapy research has demonstrated that this component of the program alone is an effective therapy for depression. It may be that the presentation of a convincing rationale and the self-monitoring homework exercises have implicit in them sufficient motivation and direction so that the detailed presentation of the rest of the program is not usually necessary.

Immediate versus Delayed Effects of Events

The second component of the program focuses on the immediate versus the delayed consequences of events. Events are often complex. They may have both positive and negative, pleasant and unpleasant, aspects. We often define an event as positive or negative in terms of its consequences. Events are also complex in that they have multiple consequences. Some of these consequences are immediate and some are delayed. One of the problems in defining a positive event is to evaluate the relative weight of its various immediate and delayed consequences. As an example of this problem, a woman described a positive event on her log which involved taking her grandchildren shopping. She had wanted to do this in order to develop a closer relationship with her grandchildren. When she described the event more fully, however, it turned out that the stores were noisy and crowded, and she and the children had quickly become tired and irritable. By the time they got home, she was exhausted and the children were miserable. Clearly, the immediate negative effects of the situation had far outweighed the positive long-term goal of spending more time with them. In order to evaluate events and their effects on mood more accurately, it is necessary to assess both positive and negative, immediate and delayed, effects. The model holds that people who tend to be depressed are more likely to be affected by immediate than by long-term consequences of events,

partly because of a failure to recognize and to attend to the long-term consequences. Depressive self-indulgence occurs for this reason. A depressed person is likely to put off some difficult task because it is unpleasant in the
short run, despite the fact that it might have very important positive effects
in the long run. Depressed persons are also likely to indulge themselves in an
event with an immediate positive consequence; for example, eating the
chocolate eclair, despite the more delayed consequences of failure to maintain a diet. An exercise is done to make the point clear and to provide participants with experience in using the concept. Participants are asked to
select two positive and two negative activities from their self-monitoring
logs. These are filled in at the left-hand column of an exercise sheet. On the
right are two-by-two tables with the top margins labeled "immediate" and
"delayed" and the side margins labeled "positive" and "negative." Subjects
are asked to fill in all four quadrants for each example. For example, the activity "called a friend to come over for coffee" had the immediate positive effect of "enjoyed the talk," the immediate negative effect of "feeling nervous
about the call," the delayed effect of "a better friendship," and the delayed
negative effect of "less housework done." As the participants fill out these
exercises, they are asked to consider which consequences tend to come to
mind first and whether consequences occurred to them that they would not
have ordinarily thought of.

The homework assignment associated with this component of the program is to continue to self-monitor pleasant events and to use a third column on the self-monitoring logs to fill in at least one positive delayed consequence of a positive activity each day. It is also pointed out that one form of
positive self-statement is to note the positive delayed consequence of activities.

The earlier reviews of psychopathology and therapy research contribute
relatively little to an understanding of this component of the therapy program. The original rationale for including this component was to target the
hypothesized tendency of depressed subjects to attend insufficiently to
delayed consequences. The evidence that preference for immediate versus
delayed reward is related to selective attention does not exist. Our clinical
experience with this component is that many subjects find it helpful in
understanding and defining positive events for themselves. Several subjects
have used the two-by-two table idea as a simple problem-solving device in
making choices whether or not to engage in some activity. Further research
will be necessary to provide a more detailed evaluation of the contribution
of this component (cf., also Marlatt & Parks' chapter in this volume).

Self-Attribution

Self-attribution is the first component of the self-evaluation phase of the
therapy program. The immediate versus delayed consequences component

was conceptualized in terms of self-statements which people make about the *consequences* of events. Similarly, the attribution component is conceptualized in terms of self-statements which people make about the *causes* of events. An event can be positive or negative, or its positiveness or negativeness can be amplified depending on our judgment of its cause. Our model of depression states that people who are depressed distort events and make them negative by the way in which they attribute their causes. For example, after a minor quarrel with a friend, a woman feels depressed because, "I'm always making people mad at me." Another woman's work is praised by her boss, but she says to herself, "He's just trying to make me *feel* better after the criticism he gave me the other day." A woman who had just gone back to school gets an A on her first exam and says, "The exam was just easy, I'll never do well on a hard one." In each of these examples, the person has made a self-statement about the cause of an event. Each statement is depressive in that it made a positive event into a negative, or it made a negative event worse.

The therapist explains to participants that there is a pattern to the way in which depressed people tend to attribute the causes of success and failure (positive and negative events). Depressed persons tend to see their successes as external, specific, and unstable. A cause that is external is something outside of yourself; for instance, chance, luck, or someone else's efforts. A specific attribution means that the event is unique and its occurrence is unrelated to other events. People who are depressed tend to think that successes are isolated and unrelated to any other aspects of their lives. "Doing well on this doesn't mean I'll do well on that" is the logic. An unstable attribution means that is is unreliable; for example; "Just because I did it this time doesn't mean I'll be able to do it next time."

To some extent, we are all taught as children to make external, specific, and unstable attributions about successes. It is the "modest" thing to say, whether it is true or not. Undepressed attributions about successes are usually internal, general, and stable. For example, "I really did do a good job," "I can do a lot of things well when I try," and "I am confident in my ability to do this" are all immodest "self-statements," but when true, they contribute to a sense of control over one's life, to positive self-esteem, and to a lessening of depression.

By suggesting that positive self-esteem is based in part on making positive self-statements about the causes of events, we are not advocating immodesty nor bragging. Bragging is an attempt to publicize one's successes for the purpose of coercing others into recognizing them. We are suggesting only that it is important to recognize ones own skills, abilities, efforts, and accomplishments accurately and realistically. The majority of positive events or successes in life are events which we plan, work for, and deserve credit for. The exercise which accompanies this concept is shown in figure 15.1.

1. Select two positive events (successes) which occurred in the last week. They need not be major events. Trivial events can be successes too.

Event 1. _____

_____

Event. 2. _____

2. Rate the degree to which the causes of these events were External vs. Internal, General vs. Specific, and Unstable vs. Stable.

Event 1
Internal _____ External
100%   0%

General _____ Specific
100%   0%

Stable _____ Unstable
100%   0%

Event 2
Internal _____ External
100%   0%

General _____ Specific
100%   0%

Stable _____ Unstable
100%   0%

3. Write a positive self-statement about each event which reflects its cause or causes. These statements should be positive and true, i.e., realistic and accurate.

Event 1 _____

_____

Event 2 _____

_____

Fig. 15.1. Self-statements about causes of success.

After this exercise is completed, the therapist continues with a discussion of depressive attributions about failure. Depressed persons also show a pattern of making self-statements about the causes of failure that is the reverse of the pattern for successes. Failures are assumed to be caused by internal, general, and stable factors. Statements like "It is my fault" or "I let him down" are typical internal statements about failure. People who are depressed tend to accept guilt and responsibility for negative events. A general cause is one which covers many aspects of one's life. Statements like "I can't win whatever I do" or "I can't do anything right" reflect very general attributions about failures. People who are depressed tend to overgeneralize about negative events. A stable attribution about a negative event means that it is something which is relatively enduring or constant. Statements like "I'll never get this right" or "This always happens to me" are reflections of a depressive tendency to see negative events as constant and inevitable.

We may be taught as children to make these attributions about failure. We are supposed to accept the blame and be responsible for our errors. As a style of attribution, this can be maladaptive. First, it is often inaccurate or distorted to assume habitually that failures are caused by internal, general, stable factors. Negative events usually occur despite our efforts to the contrary and often for reasons which are specific and unstable. Even more importantly, this pattern of attribution eliminates ways of working on a problem. If a problem is due to a general and stable aspect of oneself, there is nothing one can do about it. If the cause is external, specific, or unstable, there is more likelihood something can be done.

As an example, a woman is hired on a job which requires selling a product. Her first customer does not buy. If she says to herself, "I'm just not cut out to be a salesperson" or "No one will ever buy from me," then she might just as well quit. If, on the other hand, she says "He wasn't really interested" or "I didn't try hard enough" or "I'll have to learn how to handle this type of customer," then there is room for improvement and something can be done for the future.

The exercise for attributions of responsibility for failure directly parallels the exercise concerning attributions about success. In both instances, the discussion of the exercise is aimed at helping participants to make more realistic and useful attributional assessments. The therapist attempts to encourage nondepressive attributions and to point out realistic ways in which these attributions can appropriately be made.

The homework for this component is to continue monitoring and each day to include at least one positive attributional self-statement about a positive activity and at least one positive attributional self-statement about a negative activity. The intent is to encourage participants to be aware of attributional self-statements and to practice making nondepressive attributions.

This component of the program is an attempt to modify in a fairly direct, didactic manner the attributional style which Seligman has termed learned helplessness. There is little research evidence available regarding the effectiveness of this or other modes of modifying attributional style with clinically depressed individuals. While some studies have demonstrated that attributional instructions or schedules of success experiences can overcome helpless behavior, such methods have not been evaluated as forms of therapy for depression with assessment of broad and clinically significant outcome. Our own research evaluated the contribution of the self-evaluation phase of our program, which included both the self-attribution and goal-setting components. Results of that study did not demonstrate an added effect for these components over and above the self-monitoring components alone. The design and measures, however, may not have been sufficiently sensitive to the potential effects of modifying self-attributions for at least some depressed individuals. To the degree that distorted attributions play a role in the pattern of depressed behavior in particular patients, some mode of attacking these distortions in a systematic fashion seems appropriate.

Goal Setting

The major idea presented by the therapist in this component of the program is that people who are depressed tend to set unrealistically stringent goals or standards for themselves. Depressed persons tend to be perfectionistic. They set goals which are distant, abstract, overly general, and unobtainable. Partial fulfillment is never satisfying, and the result is that these people are dissatisfied with themselves and are deprecating of their efforts. In order to overcome depression, it is important to set realistic and positive self-evaluative standards. For example, a woman might feel depressed if she were unable to complete all the work her boss has given her that day, even if it were an unreasonable amount. Another woman might feel she is a failure as a homemaker if dinner is not ready on time, even if she has completed many other tasks in the same day.

The way in which people define goals or standards for themselves determines their sense of success or failure, self-worth, or worthlessness. People compare themselves to internal standards constantly, and the result can be thought of as a form of self-statement. When goals are not set realistically, the result can be excessive self-criticism. The therapist is usually able to elicit examples from the group of stringent standard setting which the participants recognize in themselves.

The strategy for attempting to teach participants how to set standards more realistically is a goal-setting exercise in which participants are taught to define goals and subgoals in areas of interest. In part, the exercise involves teaching participants some basic behavioral concepts about goal setting.

Participants are asked to formulate a goal from their self-monitoring data. They are asked to find a class of activities which have been related to good mood. Important but infrequent activities may often give a clue to desirable goals. Participants are encouraged to choose something fairly minor to begin with, in order to practice with the ideas. Later on, the same principles can then be used to attack more serious problems.

Goals should have three properties. First, they should be defined in a positive fashion. That is, a goal should be something which can be increased in frequency or duration. Attempting to get rid of or decrease some behavior is a poor goal. Second, the goal should be attainable in a realistic fashion. It should be something which is well within the realm of possibility. A poor goal is one which is rare or highly improbable. Third, goals should be things that are potentially under your control; that is, within the span of your own abilities and efforts. Goals should not depend upon chance or the whim of others. For example, learning a new skill (such as painting, typing, using a computer, or gourmet cooking) could be a positive, attainable goal that is in a person's control. Being elected president of an organization may or may not be attainable, because it definitely depends on others, not just on our own efforts. Once participants select goals the next step is to establish a series of subgoals. The general idea is to break down the overall goal into a series of small individual steps. To begin with, a person may have to generate a long list of possible steps and then select out of this those subgoals which make the best and most orderly steps. Subgoals should be defined such that they are positive, attainable, in the individual's control, and concrete or operational. In other words, they should be defined in terms which identify specifically what behavior is to be performed that would allow *anyone* to recognize when it has occurred. This means that criteria for successful completion are built in. For example, if the person's goal is to lose 15 pounds, then a subgoal might be "to eat no more than 1,200 calories per day." This subgoal is formulated so that the person knows he or she has succeeded or not by comparing the calorie count to the criterion. On the other hand, "exercise more this week" is not formulated clearly or specifically enough to let anyone know whether or not a person has succeeded or failed. A better subgoal might be "to jog for 15 minutes per day."

Worksheets consist of a place to write out a goal, followed by spaces for subgoals. Criteria for establishing goals and subgoals are reiterated on the form. A considerable amount of time is spent in the sessions discussing and working on these forms. The homework assignment for this component is to continue monitoring and to consider the subgoal behaviors as target activities to be increased during the week. From this point on, the extra column on the self-monitoring logs is to be used simply to identify those positive activities which are subgoals.

In some ways, this component of the program forms a simple problem-solving algorithm for participants. It bears some similarity to problem-solving therapies which have been employed in therapy studies for depression (e.g., Shipley and Fazio, 1973). To the extent that specific behaviors are prescribed to be performed during the coming week, the component also bears a similarity to the activity scheduling exercises which are included in Lewinsohn's (e.g., 1976) and other activity increase programs (e.g., Anton, Dunbar, & Friedman, 1976).

The component is designed to help depressed individuals employ realistic self-evaluative standards in a number of senses. First, they are more realistic in the sense of being more positive and objective definitions. Second, there is a clear implication that accomplishing a *subgoal* is itself worthy of credit and positive self-evaluation. "You do not have to wait until the final goal is completed to feel good; you can feel good about progress toward a goal." This latter issue at times appears to be a revelation to some of our depressed participants.

Self-Reinforcement: Overt

As we are presently using the program, the self-reinforcement component is divided into two sections, one on overt self-reinforcement and the other on covert self-reinforcement. The therapist begins introducing the self-reinforcement ideas by relating them to earlier aspects of the program. One of the major thrusts of the program has been to identify and to increase positive activities. It becomes clear, however, that all positive activities may not be immediately pleasurable and rewarding. Some activities only lead to pleasurable or rewarding consequences in the future. Examples of this are probably among the positive activities which are listed as subgoals on the goal-setting exercise. In working on these exercises, participants are likely to have found that motivation is a problem. Therefore, this last component of the program attempts to deal with motivation as a problem which exists in depression generally and as a problem in implementing the earlier aspects of the program.

The therapist explains the concepts of reward and punishment in simple terms. A good deal of stress is put on the concept of contingency. The idea is then presented that people can control their own behavior by the use of rewards and punishments just as one might control the behavior of another person. It is asserted that people do in fact motivate and change their own behavior by the use of rewards and punishments. This can be done with overt tangible rewards or with covert (self-statement) rewards. The final point made is that people who are depressed tend to self-administer very little reward and a great deal of punishment. This follows directly from all of the prior points we have made about the nature of depression. The person who tends to self-monitor negative events selectively, who is unattentive to the long-term consequences of behavior, who sets stringent standards for herself, and who takes credit for failures but not successes is a person who virtually never sees herself as deserving a reward. The same person is likely to feel that she is frequently deserving of punishment, and indeed is likely to self-punish frequently. The consequences of frequent self-punishment are seen as guilt, self-depreciation, and inertia. Self-reward can motivate activity and ultimately lead to positive self-esteem and self-confidence.

The exercise for the overt self-reinforcement component is to develop a self-reward "menu." The menu is simply a list of material items or activities which can be self-administered as rewards. Rewards should be enjoyable, in the sense of bringing immediate pleasure; they should vary somewhat in magnitude from large to small, so that they can be matched to larger or smaller accomplishments; and they should be capable of free administration—that is, the participant should be able to decide when and where they will occur. Typical rewards are such things as buying oneself something, spending half an hour reading a book, going to a movie, swimming, watching a favorite TV show, or eating a favorite food. The overt self-reinforcement homework assignment is to use items from the reward menu to reinforce difficult subgoal activity from the goal-setting exercise. Participants are instructed to identify particularly difficult subgoal activities from their worksheets. Whenever these are accomplished during the week, they select an item from their self-reward menu and "consume" it contingently. These rewards should also be considered positive events and should be entered on self-monitoring logs. Another way of describing the assignment is that easy positive activities are being used to reward difficult positive activities.

Participants sometimes balk at the idea of rewarding themselves for something which is already being done for their own "gratification." To many, there seems to be something greatly improper about self-reward which appears to be "selfish" or "self-indulgent." The point needs to be stressed that we are not advocating a total orientation toward self-gratification and selfishness. We are arguing that it is legitimate to devote some portion of one's energies toward activities which are beneficial to one's self. Second, we are advocating a procedure for motivation and change, the end result of which is not simply giving oneself a lot of reward, but is the obtaining of a goal which is desirable and worthwhile. Some participants feel that self-reward should not be "necessary." Our argument is that it is a legitimate and effective tool for producing behavior change.

Self-Reinforcement: Covert

At the next session, the therapist presents the concept of covert self-reward. Here again we use the self-statement as a functional unit. In the earlier parts of the program, we spoke of self-statements as naturally occurring events of which participants should be more aware. In the next phase of the program we spoke of self-statements as conclusions or inferences drawn about events. At that point we tried to make participants more aware of stringent standards and unrealistic attributions which form the basis of depressive self-statements and tried to facilitate more accurate and realistic statements. In this final phase of the program, we treat self-statements as rewards and punishments which can be administered freely and contingently. People who are depressed tend to self-punish frequently by the use of negative self-statements. Negative self-statements can and do function as punishments which suppress behavior, decrease motivation, and make the depressed person inert and immobilized.

Again, participants may have some difficulty in accepting this concept, in that they may feel that covert self-reinforcement is "immodesty" or "bragging." Our response is that bragging is an attempt to coerce external reinforcement, whereas covert self-reinforcement is a realistic recognition of accomplishment and the basis for self-esteem and self-confidence. The healthy nondepressed person should not be dependent solely on external rewards or external praise for self-esteem or for motivation. People should be able to motivate themselves and one way to do so is through self-reward.

The exercise for this component is to make a list of positive self-statements. Participants are asked to list five positive attributes in the form of self-statements such as "I am good at . . . (my job, cooking, getting along with people, solving problems)" or "I am . . . (friendly, hard working, neat, honest, etc.)." In addition, subjects are provided with a list of general positive self-statements such as: "That was good." "I really do have some skill at this." "That took a lot of effort."

The homework assignment is to include on each day's log at least two positive self-statements which are explicitly used as contingent rewards following a subgoal. These can come from the self-reward list or can be any similar statements. Participants are encouraged to use covert self-reward as much as possible in all of their ongoing daily activities. Finally, they are also asked to try to add additional positive self-statements to their lists during the week as they think of other positive characteristics of themselves.

The review above demonstrated that depressed individuals do use less reward and more punishment in self-management on laboratory tasks. It is also evident that they make frequent negative self-statements and presumably fewer positive self-statements. Therapy programs have frequently used self-managed overt self-reinforcement programs for depression and for other behavioral problems. Covert positive self-statements have been encouraged in depressed individuals either as ends in themselves or as a means of reinforcing other behavior. Despite their frequent use, the evidence for the efficacy of these procedures, which are usually used as a component in larger packages, is not well demonstrated. Two of the studies in our research program failed to find a significant effect for the self-reinforcement component of our program over and above more basic components. The component may have an effect, but if it does, we have not yet detected it. We have retained the component in the program partly out of a desire to retain a conceptual coherence and partly because of clinical, anecdotal support for the procedure. It may be, for instance, that self-reinforcement is a procedure which helps participants to persist in applying the program, and thus may not show an effect until well after the usual post-test.

Conclusions

The self-control therapy program uses the self-control model of depression at several levels. First, it uses the model as a framework for conceptualizing psychopathology and identifying specific behavioral deficits in depression. Multiple deficits can be handled by the model. Second, the model becomes an organizing framework for the therapy program. Deficits are dealt with in a specific sequence, and each procedure builds on previous procedures. Third, the model is used as the rationale for the program as it is presented to the subjects. It may be that the most important aspect of the program is the manner in which it effectively teaches this rationale. In one sense, we are simply teaching subjects to be modifiers of their own behavior. We are teaching them problem recognition and definition, problem solving, and self-motivation. That each aspect of the program is tied specifically to depressive deficits makes the presentation more relevant and credible to depressed subjects. The therapists present, review, and summarize the model. They attempt to help participants rephrase and reconceptualize events in their lives in terms of the program's conceptual language. Homework assignments provide demonstrations of how the concepts can be put into operation and how they function according to the framework and predictions of the model. Success in carrying out the homework is success in understanding and utilizing the model.

The program involves the acquisition of cognitive and behavioral skills. In many ways, the program is didactic and is in fact more like a "course" than what is usually thought of as therapy. Participants frequently refer to sessions as "class" rather than as "therapy." The model provides an organization of the "curriculum." The intent of the skills-acquisition format is that subjects will acquire methods which they can use in the future to diminish or prevent depression which may be precipitated by future stressful life circumstances. In a 1-year follow-up of participants from our first two studies (Romano & Rehm, 1979), we found that while scores on depression inventories at 1 year did not differentiate self-control therapy participants from those who had been through control therapy procedures, two other factors did differentiate these groups. Self-control therapy participants reported having had significantly fewer episodes of depression in the intervening year, and significantly fewer of them had sought additional therapy during that year. One interpretation of this result is that subjects who had been in the self-control therapy program did acquire skills which helped them to circumvent episodes of depression and helped them to cope with problems without the necessity of "external" therapy.

SUMMARY

This chapter has reviewed depression research using a self-control model as a framework. Evidence for disorders of self-monitoring, self-evaluation, attribution, and self-reinforcement were reviewed. Also reviewed were deficits which would be expected as a consequence of dysfunctional self-control behavior. Deficits in self-control behavior do seem to characterize the behavior of depressed individuals. The evidence varies in terms of the number of studies which have been done with particular problems and in terms of the quality and degree of the evidence. It is clear that a more complex and articulated model may be necessary to understand behavior of depressed individuals at each of the phases of self-control. A more complex model and more thorough research may be needed to begin to understand the interrelationship between these deficits.

The use of therapy techniques predicated on self-control was also reviewed. As is true of behavior therapy for depression generally, there is evidence for the efficacy of self-control techniques in general, but little evidence to identify specific effective ingredients or to differentiate the utility of one program over another. Our self-control program has been found to be effective in at least eight studies.

The final portion of the chapter is a description of the procedures which make up our therapy program, together with a comment on each component procedure in light of the earlier research reviews. The model serves as the framework for organizing the therapy program into a coherent package which can be taught to depressed participants in a cost-effective and therapeutically effective manner.

REFERENCE NOTES

1. O'Hara, M. W., & Rehm, L. P. *Choice of immediate versus delayed reinforcement and depression.* Unpublished manuscript, University of Pittsburgh, 1979.
2. MacPhillamy, D. J., & Lewinsohn, P. M. *The measurement of reinforcing events.* Paper presented at the 80th Annual Convention of the APA, Honolulu, 1972.
3. Lewinsohn, P. M., Talkington, J., Falk, G., & Kikel, S. *Unpleasant life events and depression.* Mimeo, Univ. of Oregon, 1976.
4. Evans, M. D., & Hollon, S. D. *Immediate versus delayed mood self-monitoring in depression.* Paper presented at the meeting of the Association for the Advancement of Behavior Therapy, San Francisco, December, 1979.
5. Gotlib, I. H. *Self-control processes in depressed and nondepressed psychiatric patients: Self-evaluation.* Paper presented at the Convention of the American Psychological Association, New York, September, 1979.
6. Lewis, L., Mercatoris, M., Cole, C. S., & Leonard, A. *The self-control process in episodic depression.* Paper presented at the annual meeting of the AABT, 1980.
7. Garber, J., Hollon, S. D., & Seligman, V. *Evaluation and reward of self versus others in*

depression. Paper presented at the meeting of the Association for the Advancement of Behavior Therapy, San Francisco, December, 1979.

8. Rehm, L. P. A self-control model of depression. In W. E. Craighead (Chair) *Experimental/Clinical approaches to the study and treatment of depression.* Symposium presented at the Convention of the Association for the Advancement of Behavior Therapy. San Francisco, December, 1975.

9. Gotlib, I. H. *Self-monitoring and self-reinforcement in clinically depressed psychiatric patients.* Paper presented at the convention of the Canadian Psychological Association, Quebec City, Canada, June, 1979.

10. Sacco, W. P. *Self-reinforcement by depressives under public and private measurement conditions.* Presented at the meeting of the Eastern Psychological Association, Philadelphia, April, 1979.

11. Missel, P., & Sommer, G. *Depression and self-verbalization.* Paper presented at the World Congress on Behavior Therapy, Jerusalem, July 13–17, 1980.

12. Abramson, L. Y., & Alloy, L. B. *Depression and the role of complex hypotheses in judgement of response outcome contingencies.* Paper presented at the meeting of the Eastern Psychological Association, Philadelphia, April 20, 1979.

13. Hilford, N. G. *Let's help ourselves: Self-initiated behavior change by depressed women following verbal behavior therapy.* Unpublished manuscript, University of Auckland, New Zealand, 1977.

14. Kornblith, S. J., Rehm, L. P., O'Hara, M., & Lamparski, D. M. *An evaluation of the contribution of self-reinforcement and behavioral assignments to the efficacy of a self-control therapy program for depression.* Paper presented at the New Mexico Conference on Behavior Therapy, New Mexico Highlands University, September, 1979.

15. Brown, R. A., & Lewinsohn, P. M. *A psychoeducation approach to the treatment of depression: Comparison of group, individual, and minimal contact procedures.* Unpublished paper, University of Oregon, 1980.

REFERENCES

Abramson, L. Y., Seligman, M. E. P., & Teasdale, J. D. Learned helplessness in humans: Critique and reformulation. *Journal of Abnormal Psychology*, 1978, *87*, 49–74.

Anton, J. L., Dunbar, J., & Friedman, L. Anticipation training in the treatment of depression. In J. D. Krumboltz & C. E. Thoresen (Eds.), *Counseling methods.* New York: Holt, Rinehart & Winston, 1976.

Baker, L. L., & Jessup, B. A. The psychophysiology of affective verbal and visual information processing in dysphoria. *Cognitive Therapy and Research*, 1980, *4*, 135–149.

Bandura, A. Self-reinforcement: Theoretical and methodological considerations. *Behaviorism*, 1976, *4*, 135–155.

Bandura, A. Vicarious and self-reinforcement processes. In R. Glaser (Ed.), *The nature of reinforcement.* New York: Academic Press, 1971.

Beck, A. T. *Depression: Causes and treatment.* Philadelphia: University of Pennsylvania Press, 1972.

Beck, A. T., Rush, A. G., Shaw, B. F., & Emery, G. *Cognitive therapy of depression.* New York: Guilford Press, 1979.

Catania, A. C. The myth of self-reinforcement. *Behaviorism*, 1975, *3*, 192–199.

Ciminero, A. R., & Steingarten, K. A. The effects of performance standards on self-evaluation and self-reinforcement in depressed and nondepressed individuals. *Cognitive Therapy and*

Research, 1978, *2*, 179–182.

Davis, G. C., Buchsbaum, M. S., & Bunney, W. E. Analgesia to painful stimuli in affective illness. *American Journal of Psychiatry*, 1979, *136*, 1148–1151.

Endicott, J., & Spitzer, R. L. A diagnostic interview: The schedule for affective disorders and schizophrenia. *Archives of General Psychiatry*, 1978, *35*, 837–844.

Ferster, C. B. A functional analysis of depression. *American Psychologist*, 1973, *28*, 857–870.

Fleming, B. M., & Thornton, D. W. Coping skills training as component in the short-term treatment of depression. *Journal of Consulting and Clinical Psychology*, 1980, *48*, 652–655.

Fuchs, C. Z., & Rehm, L. P. A self-control behavior therapy program for depression. *Journal of Consulting and Clinical Psychology*, 1977, *45*, 206–215.

Goldiamond, I. Self-reinforcement. *Journal of Applied Behavior Analysis*. 1976, *9*, 509–514.

Golin, S., Terrell, F., & Johnson, B. Depression and the illusion of control. *Journal of Abnormal Psychology*, 1977, *86*, 440–442.

Golin, S., & Terrell, F. Motivational and associative aspects of mild depression and chance tasks. *Journal of Abnormal Psychology*, 1977, *86*, 389–401.

Grosscup, S. J., & Lewinsohn, P. M. Unpleasant and pleasant events, and mood. *Journal of Clinical Psychology*, 1980, *36*, 252–259.

Hammen, C. L., & Glass, D. R., Jr. Depression, activity, and evaluation of reinforcement. *Journal of Abnormal Psychology*, 1975, *84*, 718–721.

Harmon, T. M., Nelson, R. O., & Hayes, S. C. Self-monitoring of mood versus activity by depressed clients. *Journal of Consulting and Clinical Psychology*, 1980, *48*, 30–38.

Hinchliffe, M. K., Lancashire, M., & Roberts, F. J. Depression: Defense mechanisms in speech. *British Journal of Psychiatry*, 1971, *118*, 471–472.

Hiroto, D. S., & Seligman, M. E. P. Generality of learned helplessness in man. *Journal of Personality and Social Psychology*, 1975, *31*, 311–327.

Jackson, B. Treatment of depression by self-reinforcement. *Behavior Therapy*, 1972, *3*, 298–307.

Johnson, W. G. Some applications of Homme's coverant control therapy: Two case reports. *Behavior Therapy*, 1971, *2*, 240–248.

Kanfer, F. H., & Karoly, P. Self-control: A behavioristic excursion into the lion's den. *Behavior Therapy*, 1972, *2*, 398–416 (a)

Kanfer, F. H., & Karoly, P. Self-regulation and it's clinical application: Some additional conceptualizations. In R. C. Johnson, P. R. Dokecki, & O. H. Mowrer, *Conscience, contract, and social reality*. New York: Holt, Rinehart, & Winston, 1972. (b)

Kirschenbaum, D. and Karoly, P. When self-regulation fails: Tests of some preliminary hypotheses. *Journal of Consulting and Clinical Psychology*, 1977, *45*, 1116–1125.

Laxer, R. M. Self-concept changes of depressive patients in general hospital treatment. *Journal of Consulting Psychology*, 1964, *28*, 214–219.

Loeb, A., Beck, A. T., Diggory, J. C., & Tuthill, R. Expectancy, level of aspiration, performance and self-evaluation in depression. *Proceedings, 75 Annual Convention, APA*, 1967, *2*, 193–194.

Lewinsohn, P. M. Activity schedules in treatment of depression. In J. D. Krumboltz and C. E. Thoresen, *Counseling methods*. New York: Holt, Rinehart & Winston, 1976.

Lewinsohn, P. M. Engagement in pleasant activities and depression level. *Journal of Abnormal Psychology*, 1975, *84*, 729–731.

Lewinsohn, P. M. & Graf, M. Pleasant activities and depression. *Journal of Clinical Psychology*, 1973, *41*, 261–268.

Lewinsohn, P. M., & Libet, J. Pleasant events, activity schedules and depressions. *Journal of Abnormal Psychology*, 1972, *79*, 291–295.

Lewinsohn, P. M., Lobitz, W. C., & Wilson, S. Sensitivity of depressed individuals to aversive stimuli. *Journal of Abnormal Psychology*, 1973, *81*, 259–263.

Lewinsohn, P. M., Mischel, W., Chaplin, W., & Barton, R. Social competence and depression: The role of illusory self-perceptions. *Journal of Abnormal Psychology*, 1980, *89*, 203–213.

Lewinsohn, P. M., & Talkington, J. Studies on the measurement of unpleasant events and relations with depression. *Applied Psychological Measurement*, 1979, *3*, 83–101.

Lewinsohn, P. M., Biglan, A., & Zeiss, A. M. Behavioral treatment of depression. In P. O. Davidson (Ed.), *The behavioral management of anxiety, depression, and pain*. New York: Brunner/Mazel, 1976.

Lubin, B. Adjective checklists for measurements of depression. *Archives of General Psychiatry*, 1965, *12*, 57–62.

MacPhillamy, D. J., & Lewinsohn, P. M. Depression as a function of levels of desired and obtained pleasure. *Journal of Abnormal Psychology*, 1974, *83*, 651–657.

Mahoney, M. J. The self-management of covert behavior: A case study. *Behavior Therapy*, 1971, *2*, 575–578.

Marston, A. R. Personality variables related to self-reinforcement, *Journal of Psychology*, 1964, *58*, 169–175.

McLean, P. D., Ogston, K., & Grauer, L. A behavioral approach to the treatment of depression. *Journal of Behavior Therapy & Experimental Psychiatry*, 1974, *4*, 323–330.

McLean, P. D., & Hakstian, A. R. Clinical depression: Comparative efficacy of outpatient treatments. *Journal of Consulting and Clinical Psychology*, 1979, *47*, 818–836.

Miller, E., & Lewis, P. Recognition memory in elderly patients with depression and dementia: A signal detection analysis. *Journal of Abnormal Psychology*, 1977, *86*, 84–86.

Miller, W. R., & Seligman, M. E. P. Depression and learned helplessness in man. *Journal of Abnormal Psychology*, 1975, *84*, 228–238.

Nelson, R. W., & Craighead, W. E. Selective recall of positive and negative feedback, self-control behaviors, and depression. *Journal of Abnormal Psychology*, 1977, *86*, 379–388.

Nelson, R. W., & Craighead, W. E. Standard Setting, attribution, self-reinforcement, and depression. *Behavior Therapy*, 1981, *12*, 123–124.

O'Hara, M. W., & Rehm, L. P. Self-monitoring, activity levels and mood in the development and maintenance of depression. *Journal of Abnormal Psychology*, 1979, *88*, 450–453.

Price, K. P., Tryon, W. W., & Raps, C. S. Learned helplessness and depression in a clinical population: A test of two behavioral hypotheses. *Journal of Abnormal Psychology*, 1978, *87*, 113–121.

Rehm, L. P. A self-control model of depression. *Behavior Therapy*, 1977, *8*, 787–804.

Rehm, L. P. Mood, pleasant events and unpleasant events: Two pilot studies. *Journal of Consulting and Clinical Psychology*, 1978, *46*, 854–859.

Rehm, L. P., Fuchs, C. Z., Roth, D. M. Kornblith, S. J., & Romano, J. M. A comparison of self-control and assertion skills treatments of depression. *Behavior Therapy*, 1979, *10*, 429–442.

Rehm, L. P., & Kornblith, S. J. Behavior therapy for depression: A review of recent developments. In M. Hersen, R. M. Eisler, & P. M. Miller (Eds.), *Progress in Behavior Modification* (Vol. 7). New York: Academic Press, 1979.

Rehm, L. P., Kornblith, S. J., O'Hara, M. W., Lamparski, D. M., Romano, J. M., & Volkin, J. An evaluation of major components in a self-control behavior therapy program for depression. *Behavior Modification*, in press.

Rehm, L. P., & O'Hara, M. W. The role of attribution theory in understanding depression. In I. H. Frieze, D. Bar-Tal, & J. S. Caroll (Eds.), *Attribution theory: Applications to social problems*. San Francisco: Jossey-Bass, 1980.

Rehm, L. P., & Plakosh, P. Preference for immediate reinforcement in depression. *Journal of Behavior Therapy & Experimental Psychiatry*, 1975, *6*, 101–103.

Romano, J. M. & Rehm, L. P. Self-control treatment of depression: One-year follow-up. In A. T. Beck (Chair) *Factors affecting the outcome and maintenance of cognitive therapy*.

Symposium presented at the meeting of the Eastern Psychological Association, Philadelphia, April 18–21, 1979.

Roth, D., Rehm, L. P. and Rozensky, R. A. Self-reward, self-punishment and depression *Psychological Reports*, 1980, *47*, 3–7.

Rozensky, R. A., Rehm, L. P., Pry, G., & Roth, D. Depression and self-reinforcement behavior in hospital patients. *Journal of Behavior Therapy and Experimental Psychiatry*, 1977, *8*, 35–38.

Rush, A. J., Beck, A. T., Kovacs, M., & Hollon, S. Comparative efficacy of cognitive therapy and pharmocotherapy in the treatment of depressed outpatients. *Cognitive Therapy and Research*, 1977, *1*, 17–38.

Rush, A. J., Khatami, M., & Beck, A. T. Cognitive and behavior therapy in chronic depression. *Behavior Therapy*, 1975, *6*, 398–404.

Seeman, G., & Schwarz, J. A. Affective state and preference for immediate versus delayed reward, *Journal of Research in Personality*, 1974, *7*, 384–394.

Seligman, M. E. P. A learned helplessness point of view. In L. P. Rehm (Ed.), *Behavior therapy for depression: Present status and future directions*. New York: Academic Press, 1981.

Shaw, B. F. Comparison of cognitive therapy and behavior therapy in the treatment of depression. *Journal of Consulting and Clinical Psychology*, 1977, *45*, 543–551.

Shipley, C. R., & Fazio, A. F. Pilot study of a treatment of psychological depression. *Journal of Abnormal Psychology*, 1973, *82*, 373–376.

Shrauger, J. S., & Sorman, P. B. Self-evaluations, initial success and failure, and improvement as determinants of persistence. *Journal of Consulting and Clinical Psychology*, 1977, *45*, 784–795.

Shrauger, J. S., & Terbovic, M. L. Self-evaluations and assessments of performance by self and others. *Journal of Consulting and Clinical Psychology*, 1976, *44*, 564–572.

Spitzer, R. L., Endicott, J., & Robins, E. Research diagnostic criteria: Rationale and reliability. *Archives of General Psychiatry*, 1978, *36*, 773–782.

Taylor, F. G., & Marshall, W. L. Experimental analysis of a cognitive-behavioral therapy for depression. *Cognitive Therapy and Research*, 1977, *1*, 59–72.

Tharp, R. G., Watson, D. L., & Kaya, J. Self-modification of depression. *Journal of Consulting and Clinical Psychology*, 1974, *42*, 624.

Thoresen, C. E., & Mahoney, M. J. *Behavioral self-control*. New York: Holt, Rinehart & Winston, 1974.

Thoresen, C. E., & Wilbur, C. S. Some encouraging thoughts about self-reinforcement. *Journal of Applied Behavior Analysis*, 1976, *9*, 518–520.

Todd, F. T. Coverant control of self-evaluative responses in the treatment of depression: A new use for an old principle. *Behavior Therapy*, 1972, *3*, 91–94.

Vasta, R. Coverant control of self-evaluations through temporal cueing. *Journal of Behavior Therapy and Experimental Psychiatry*, 1976, *7*, 35–38.

Vasta, R., & Brockner, J. Self-esteem and self-evaluative covert statements. *Journal of Consulting and Clinical Psychology*, 1979, *47*, 776–777.

Wanderer, Z. E. Existential depression treated by desensitization of phobias: Strategies and transcript. *Journal of Behavioral Therapy and Experimental Psychiatry*, 1972, *3*, 111–116.

Weissman, M. M., Prusoff, B. A., Thompson, W. D., Harding, P. S., & Myers, J. K. Social adjustment by self-report in a community sample and in psychiatric outpatients. *The Journal of Nervous and Mental Disease*, 1978, *166*, 317–326.

Wessman, A. E., Ricks, D. F., & Tyl, M. M. Characteristics and concomitants of mood fluctuation in college women. *Journal of Abnormal and Social Psychology*, 1960, *60*, 117–127.

Zeiss, A. M., Lewinsohn, P. M., & Munoz, R. F. Nonspecific improvement effects in depression using interpersonal skills training, pleasant activity schedules, or cognitive training. *Journal of Consulting and Clinical Psychology*, 1979, *47*, 427–439.

Part IV:
Epilogue

16
The Psychology of Self-Management: Abiding Issues and Tentative Directions

Frederick H. Kanfer and Paul Karoly

The data that emerge from scientific investigations (whether the subject of analysis is organic or inorganic, cosmic or microscopic in nature) are the joint product of the methods employed and the investigator's purpose(s) and perspective. We tend to minimize the role of the latter, while seeking to strengthen the former—as though a powerful procedure for knowing could assure the "objectivity" and "high quality" of our facts. Yet, in ancient Egypt, Eratosthenes measured the circumference of the Earth with only a few sticks (and a lot of brains; cf., Sagan, 1980), while today's psychologists are deadlocked in debate on the value of multivariate statistics, the DSM III, the uses of personality testing, and the generalizability of laboratory findings. We do not know whether contemporary psychologists are less intelligent problem solvers than Eratosthenes; but we do know from the records of human achievement that the attempt to define human nature does not yield as readily to experimental procedure as have some of the ancient questions about the nature of the physical universe.

When we humans study ourselves, we do not simply observe, record, and note causal influences. There is a built-in bias and an inherent limitation involved whenever we try to use our knowledge and skills to seek to understand the operation of our knowledge and skills. Psychologists have sought to overcome their biases and limitations by developing nomothetic theories, reproducible methods, controlled experiments, and a strict separation between observer (experimenter) and observed (subject). The construction of a "Psychology of the Other" has been the debatable objective in which modern psychology has shown some modest success, but at the expense of criticism of its elitist, mechanistic, and condescending nature. A comprehensive psychology of human nature must account for the behavior of both the subject (client) *and* the experimenter (clinician). The history of our attempt to define and examine human self-directiveness (from within a "psychology of the other" framework) illustrates the excitement and challenge of behavioral science as well as the inevitable "pathology of knowledge" which Sigmund Koch (1981) describes as "our gift for the mismanagement of our own minds. . . . perhaps the ultimate genius of the race!" (p. 258).

THE ANTINOMAL TEXTURE OF SELF-MANAGEMENT

Koch (1981) has argued that the problem of "personal responsibility versus shaping or control from without" is one of the many *antinomies* (or meaningful questions which are rationally unanswerable) that preoccupy modern thought and contemporary psychological inquiry. Further, he suggests that the discipline copes with this and other antinomalities by "crawling into cozy conceptual boxes — any box, so long as it gives promise of relieving the pains of cognitive uncertainty" (p. 264). There have not been many safe boxes from which to seek an understanding of self-management (that is, of the tendency for people to either maintain or alter the course of their goal-directed behavior apparently independent of discernible external influence). But those that have been available have not lacked for interestingness.

Some writers have distinguished the human organism from other animal species by its propensity for overcoming the limits imposed by physical or environmental constraints, and for actively (knowingly) changing its own natural environment. Further, each generation's contribution toward changing the quality of life merges into the broader cultural heritage and is then passed on to the next generation. These contributions form the context within which each new generation must begin its own struggle to cope with life's new and recurring difficulties and conflicts. As an increasing storehouse of culture accumulates, human apprenticeship (often called *socialization*) becomes lengthier and more complex. Most importantly, adaptation comes to require *specialized competencies* of a social and intellectual nature (rather than merely hunting, fishing, farming, or fighting skills), competencies that are transmitted interpersonally, thus binding the individual to the group. And, hence, we encounter our Kantian "antinomy of pure reason" wherein a thesis and its antithesis can both be logically deduced: *the human organism is "basically" transcendent by virtue of its intellect and culture* while at the same time *the human organism is "basically" social by virtue of its intellect and culture.*

This theme of dependency versus autonomy has been highlighted by philosophers and psychologists for centuries. It is replayed as a continuing dialectic, from the level of individual personality development to the level of intersocietal relationships. The ideal is the achievement of an appropriate balance between unquestioning conformity to cultural norms and the attainment of total autonomy. It requires a blending of self-interest with a sense of personal control and the skills and attitudes with which to act as a responsible citizen in the absence of excessive surveillance (Kanfer, 1979). The difficulty of achieving such a balance has been discussed variously by personality theorists (e.g., with reference to the "adolescent period" of conflict, to pathologies of "self development" within object-relations theory, or to successful psychosocial development in Erikson's theory), by social psychologists (with reference to the development of morality), by philosophers (with reference to the concepts of free will versus determinism), and by sociobiologists (with regard to the notion of altruism).

At the sociopolitical level, since the time of the Ancient Greeks, debates have centered on the question of the proper form of government: that is, as a system of social control consistent with the presumed characteristics of "human nature." Throughout Western history, struggles between democracies and authoritarian regimes have reflected the clash of ideologies concerning the boundaries of influence of the state relative to the individual. Contemporary educational and legal practices as well as psychological theory building are born amid this continuing struggle and are strongly influenced by it. Thus, although the focus of the present book is on the psychological level of analysis of human self-determination, it is critical that researchers, clinicians, and students alike recognize the impossibility of separating the study of individual self-management from the larger systems within which all persons must operate (cf., also Feshbach, 1978).

THE DIALECTICAL ALTERNATIVE

No aspect of psychological inquiry need be stuck in an "either-or" (Aristotelian) mode of problem solving, despite the apparent strength of this tradition within science and formal logic (Johnson, 1946). Recent discussions in social psychology have highlighted the relativity of existing theories in relation to time, context, and the social forces acting upon the theorist. As Gergen and Morawski (1980) note, the dialectical approach offers both a method of understanding and describing action patterns over time. If we consider internal processes and environmental inputs as "opposites," then dialectics would have us look for interdependence between these processes and for a "transformation" in the person as a result of the "tension of opposites" continuously being exerted (in a constructive manner).

Clearly, investigators interested in the processes and variables that describe individual self-regulation (or self-control) and in the techniques for inducing the long-term adoption of these patterned activities must be cognizant of the setting factors, methodological prejudgments, and temporal constraints under which they work. While some of the chapters in this volume deal with biological, affective, cognitive, or social processes that appear relatively invariant over time and settings, the bulk of the material in the preceding chapters rests upon assumptions about cultural constancies which apply only within certain limits.

For example, subcultures within our society place differing emphases on the "virtues" of autonomy and independence. Individuals raised in a tradition which prizes an unassuming manner and respect for authority might be capable of "self-management" as patients only so long as a professional were nearby directing the action. Such people tend to object to self-rewarding their own actions or to making independent decisions. On the other hand, contemporary psychology champions the cause of the free and the responsible individual (e.g., in consciousness raising, the self-help movement, or continuous adult development); and the American ideal of "rugged individualism" is rarely questioned (cf., Sampson, 1977). These forces surely contribute to the widespread popular interest in self-regulatory processes (usually under the heading of "self-control") and the wide acceptance of self-management interventions by the therapeutic community.

Another important, yet all too often neglected, moderator of self-management processes is time — or, more correctly, the fluctuating internal (personal) and external milieu over time (Karoly, 1981). The link between the intention to change (to give up cigarettes or lose weight, for example) and the self-controlling behaviors that eventually bring about a desired outcome is, in reality, a series of time- and context-dependent links. No *static* model of behavior has as yet fully accommodated the flow and interdependence of behavior and events and of the person's history in relation to them. Success is forged in very small steps specific to the target, its context, and to the person's perception of the ultimate goal. When clients forget this, they tend to overestimate the importance of small often unavoidable failures (leading to what Marlatt calls the "Abstinence Violation Effect"). When investigators forget the role of temporal relativity they tend to inappropriately demean the predictive utility of the concept of intentionality (cf., Fishbein, 1980).

The role of biological "setting factors" is probably best illustrated with regard to the problem of obesity. As Rodin (1981) has noted, "people's metabolic machinery is constituted in such a way that the fatter they are, the fatter they are primed to become" (p. 361). Ignorance of the biologic background of obesity (particularly the role of metabolism) may lead to the design of clinical interventions that are destined to fail. For example, as a consequence of the fact that weight loss is tied to metabolic rate, clinicians typically encourage obese clients to "eat less and exercise more." Yet metabolic rate, which is already low in the obese (due to a disproportionate amount of fat tissue), is lowered still through food deprivation (dieting), thus making the process of energy expenditure during exercise more difficult. The obese person is thus being set up for frustration, a popular response to which is eating.

The consulting room itself is a social setting within which change or transformation is said to occur (according to dialecticians) as the result of "forces in conflict" opposing each other over time. As any reader with clinical experience knows, clients often seek out a practitioner who appears able to produce change by means of a powerful directive intervention, demanding a minimum of client effort or responsibility. Many individuals seeking help with weight or drug dependence problems expect behavior modifiers to forcefully manipulate them into giving up their habit as they passively allow the treatment to "take effect." Hypnosis is another oft-requested treatment for maladaptive patterns involving self-indulgence or avoidance. Thus, the development of motivation for self-directed behavior change represents one of the most challenging tasks of therapy. Not only must the client be made focally aware of the conflicting temporal outcomes associated with, say, overeating or alcohol abuse, but the subtle conflict between wanting to "take charge" of one's life versus "being cured" by the powerful therapist must also be resolved over the course of treatment.

It is through the influence of the skilled clinician that the client often learns to assume responsibility and control. Initially, clients will justify their very presence in therapy and their need for external intervention by pointing out what "a mess" they have made in trying to manage their lives. "If I could do *that*, I wouldn't be here," they report. The implicit Aristotelian message is "One either has self-control, or one doesn't." It is therefore neither uncommon nor surprising that the initial efforts by the therapist to involve the client actively in the resolution of the presented problems is met with resistance—from passive noncompliance to active opposition.

In the gradual development of greater reliance upon self-generated standards and instrumental solutions, the client does not "acquire self-management." All behaviors and decisions are influenced jointly and continuously by environmental, physiological, and cognitive-emotional variables. Self-management in therapy merely refers to the degree to which the influence by these three sets of variables on a particular sequence of behaviors, thought patterns, or emotional states is modified by the "editing" (organizing) actions of the client who (a) knows what the goal of treatment is, (b) knows how to make use of the feedback, (c) knows how to enlist environment support as well as self-generated tactics to obtain desired ends, and (d) arranges settings and actions for maximal effectiveness. In all instances, social and biological systems set limits on the full range of personal options.

In the preceding chapters, we have noted the discussions of human self-management based upon divergent theoretical models and data domains. Yet, despite the divergence, the various perspectives share the common assumption (as well as some empirical evidence) that humans are capable of and predisposed to direct their own behavior to an impressive degree. Obstacles do occur, however. Momentary environmental or biophysical conditions may be unfavorable to self-direction. Motivation for change (i.e., anticipation of favorable outcomes and a sense of personal mastery) may be undermined by short-or long-term emotional dysfunctions, skill deficits, or the inability to accurately perceive opportunities for self-managed behavior. When these problems affect the person's well-being or conflict with the interests, needs, or expectations of others, then outside intervention is often sought. The clinician must temporarily assume responsibility for the analysis of the problem situation and for stimulating the change process. Thus, in Part II, the methods of assessing individual strengths and deficiencies, and the techniques for enhancing self-management in children were described. In Part III the methods were applied to adults, with special emphasis on common features encountered when dealing with problems such as alcoholism, depression, anxiety, and the like. Having established our distrust of absolute pronouncements and generalizations without contexts, we now move on to some additional issues, consideration of which may assist the reader to formulate a practical framework for handling the complexities of self-management psychology. We shall emphasize the need for continuing efforts toward integration of research, theory, and practical methods — because it isn't really as simple as one (self-monitor), two (self-evaluate), three (self-reinforce)!

TOWARD A DEFINITION OF SELF-MANAGEMENT

A review of the preceding chapters makes it clear that in clinical usage, self-management, while covering a wide range of processes, generally signifies the gradual assumption of control by the individual over cueing, directing, rewarding, and correcting his or her own behavior. The term suggests active client participation in goal selection and evaluation, in attention to internal and external responses, and in the use of cognitive processes to increase adaptive effectiveness. This definition also suggests that for self-management to operate, there must be a shift in the client's repertoire relevant to problem areas in a direction away from well-established, habitual or automatic but ineffective responses toward systematic problem solving and planning, long-term affective control, and behavioral persistence. Continued change also requires alterations in the relationship between component skills and overcoming incompatibility with other concurrent behaviors.

Obviously, the processes involved in self-management are multileveled, and those who would employ the construct must be willing to acknowledge the power of what Dollard and Miller (1953) called "higher mental processes" (or what is today referred to as "controlled information processing"). Such a view does not make a theoretical commitment; nor does it reflect a mentalistic outlook. It merely recognizes the mass of data and experience indicating a powerful modifying influence over publicly observable behavior by various intrapersonal factors and activities. By its definition, self-management focuses upon the covert portions of the input-output sequences of human performance (Carver & Scheier, 1981).

In therapy, the problematic behaviors are often well established, "automatic," and overlearned — but lead to unacceptable consequences. The clinician's task is to assist clients in developing a new repertoire of well-learned, easily elicited responses that differ from pretherapy behavior(s) primarily in that they are more effective, more appropriate to the demands (situational and self-set) on the client, and instrumental in attaining desired goals. To achieve these goals requires first the disruption (and eventual extinction) of the habitual, but maladaptive behaviors. Next, the client must be helped to engage in complex cognitive (controlled processing) activities such as problem solving, imagining, or planning, and jointly (with the therapist) to evolve new and more satisfactory behavior patterns. Once these are well established, they in turn are "automatized." In addition, self-management therapy strives to impart to the client techniques for monitoring and (if need be) once again changing the new behaviors. Training of planning and of monitoring skills to deal with *transitional periods* in the client's life is the hallmark of the cognitive-behavioral approach. Thus, it should be clear that self-management therapies encompass processes during which both old and new modes of behavior are being "tried out," (re)organized, and (re)applied in the interest of self-directiveness — all under the guidance of the therapist. In this way the approach to treatment here called self-management can be seen to differ from a variety of self-help enterprises in that an experienced therapist actively participates in helping prioritize goals, in setting the optimum conditions for change to occur, in training the client in new (or reorganized) skills, and in monitoring progress over time.

The central concept in self-management psychology is *self-regulation*. The term is generally used to describe the integrated organization of a series of component processes that serve to achieve the person's objectives.

Beyond the specific definitions within various theories, the self-regulation construct has generally denoted psychological processes by which an organism *mediates* its own functioning. A broader, systems theory definition suggests two criteria for a self-regulatory living system: (1) it is goal directed; and (2) it develops a "preferential hierarchy of values that give rise to decision rules which determine its preference for one internal steady-state value rather than another" (Miller, 1978, p. 39). Our definition has been somewhat narrower (Kanfer & Karoly, 1972). Although self-regulation may apply to social or organizational systems, at the individual level it refers to the aggregate of processes by which psychological variables, both from the person's repertoire and biology and from the immediate environment, are interrelated in order to orient or sustain the organism's goal directed behavior. In the larger context, an individual's self-regulation is continuously affected by its dialectical interplay with the physical and social environment. Internal functions (and their observable products) affect the external world and are, in turn, modified by environmental input. While psychologists have not sought to systematically chart the evolution of social and ecological settings as a function of the input by human self-regulators, the organismic changes (growth, development) have been described by psychological investigators (cf., for example, the Piagetian descriptive concepts of *accommodation* and *assimilation*).

Many authors equate self-regulation with voluntary behavior. Unfortunately, the nature of the concept of "voluntary" has been burdened with exclusionary definitions (e.g., voluntary means *not reflexive*) and various added requirements, such as innate needs for acting competently upon the environment (Deci, 1980), demonstrations of intentionality, or the deliberate "slowing down" of automated reaction tendencies. According to Kimble and Perlmuter (1970), classical theory of "volition" assumes that self-initiated acts are the automatic result of images of the consequences of the act to be performed. These images are evoked by a process of association, and they have been learned in the context of previous experience. Finally, a feedback process enables the organism to make constant comparisons with the thought or image that initiated it. Kimble and Perlmuter further suggest that voluntary behavior develops initially by the acquisition of control over involuntary responses. Emergent voluntary behavior is practiced until supporting responses gradually drop out, and finally the voluntary reaction is performed without deliberate intent. "What was once involuntary and later became voluntary is now involuntary again, in the sense of out of awareness and free of previous motivational control" (Kimble & Perlmuter, 1970, p. 382).

The above definition parallels, at a different level, our suggestion that the process of therapy be conceptualized as a shift from overlearned, automatic (or automatized) responses that are maladaptive to deautomatized action via new learning and awareness, and from there to adaptive "habit reorganization" involving the gradual detachment of control mechanisms in favor of natural contingencies (cf., Karoly, 1977).

Perhaps the major difference between the learning-oriented approach to self-regulation and those of other psychological schools (particularly theories based on purely phenomenological models) lies in the belief of the former that (a) the content of self-regulatory processes, much as the content of other behaviors, is derived from social learning, and that (b) the mode of acquisition and development of these processes is not qualitatively different from the manner by which the child learns to understand the external world and satisfy his or her interpersonal needs. Neither the present authors nor most of the other contributors to this book are wedded to a belief in the reflex arc as the sole building block of human self-direction. Goal-directed behavior and its dysfunctions represent highly complex sequences of actions and counter-actions requiring the activation of units built upon the *feed-back loop principle* (a principle which has been articulated in various forms by the editors and a number of our contributors).

Contemporary theorists differ also in regard to the degree to which they view the self system as resulting from environmental shaping of the individual's potential. Many theorists give priority to those psychological phenomena which they ascribe to intrapsychic development, be they genetic, biological, or socially assisted. Secondary emphasis is given to the habit patterns the individual learns in order to conform to the demands of the social environment. On the other hand, S-R theorists characteristically have assigned causal priority to the environment — with the concept of "learning history" responsible for explaining differences in specific behavior patterns, social skills, and even the development of complex cognitive organization. In most of the humanist versus mechanist debates on the self (or causality or inner directiveness), there has been confusion between method and theory (Rychlak, 1976). Theorists avoid postulating internal determinants because they have been taught that psychology is best written for the convenience of a third-person observer. Even advocates of a cognitive-behavioral model, who espouse "reciprocal determinism" as a world view, continue to approach their subject matter from the perspective of an independent variable-dependent variable, factorial design, or efficient cause explanatory system, thus perpetuating the *theory-method confound*.

It is therefore important for us to reiterate our view of the nature of self-regulatory processes, to ensure that it not be colored by association with any singular or "main effect", linear model (such as *cognitive* or *behavioral*). The iterative process we have been discussing is best characterized as involving an ebb and flow of self-generated directives whose influence over behavior can only be determined across meaningful periods of time (meaningful in terms of the personal objective being pursued — such as practicing the violin or working one's way through medical school). It does not intrinsically rely upon internal (cognitive or imagined) processes nor upon external cues and contingencies. The systems or field theory view which we espouse stresses that self-management is not a sequence of "on-off" pulses—with cognition rising as environment wanes (or vice versa). Atkinson and Birch's (1978) approach to motivation as continuous rather than episodic provides a useful metaphor for conceptualizing self-regulation. As these authors point out, "a living organism is constantly active—that is, always doing something that must be conceptualized in a theory of behavior as an expression of the then dominant tendency—even when it is asleep or resting and when it superficially appears that activity has ceased (p. 23)." To be clinically, socially, or personally effective, self-management must, over the course of goal-directed pursuits, be a dominant tendency. But where do we start to uncover the specific sources of self-regulatory success or failure?

From the perspective of control systems (cybernetic) theory, the essential diagnostic question is "What is the organism's reference level?" To better grasp the meaning of this question, the reader should bear in mind the following: (1) higher organisms are believed to be activated by perceived deviations from self-set reference levels (or standards) that change over time, and (2) although goals or "reference conditions" are not directly observable, they can be *deduced* by the observation and measurement of an output which remains invariant over time and across changing environmental conditions (Jeffrey & Berger, in press; Powers, 1973). For example, a student attempting to regulate "study time" would be aroused by factors interfering with her evening study schedule (she would be detecting an "error"). To the extent that she made studying a "controlled quantity," her success at self-regulation would be indexed by her consistency at engaging in that activity. "The subject can be said to control a variable with respect to a reference condition if every disturbance tending to cause a deviation from the reference condition calls forth a behavior which results in opposition to the disturbance (Powers, 1973, p. 47)."

Problems in self-regulation (deduced, from among other things, by the fact of inconsistency, inaction, or excessive variability) could be a function of: a system (person) seeking to control too many or contradictory (mutually exclusive) reference signals; a system unable to detect errors or deviations; a system lacking the behavioral strategies necessary to rectify a deviation(s); a system trying to function with inappropriate reference levels; or any combination of these (and probably other) factors. Access to relevant data will continue to come, as might be expected, from direct observation of clients, interviews, structured tests, and the like (see Karoly, 1981; Kendall & Hollon, 1981; McFall & Dodge, in this volume) as well as research on self-management (cf., Kanfer, 1980; Mahoney & Arnkoff, 1978; Meichenbaum, 1977).

When an individual encounters situations in which it is necessary to alter a behavioral sequence rather than maintain it, then we say that *self-control* processes are required. The most commonly encountered types of conflicts in clinical settings that require self-controlling processes involve changes in behavior either because a strong habitual response needs to be inhibited or because a new response with some aversive features needs to be initiated. Self control is viewed as the end product of a set of processes in a specific situation rather than as an enduring personality trait or a series of skills (cf., also Karoly's discussion in Chapter 1 of this volume). Its important characteristics include the presence of one or more alternatives, the conflicting temporal consequences of the available options, and the initiation of a self-generated (but not totally *self*-dependent) controlling response (Kanfer & Phillips, 1970; Kanfer & Karoly, 1972).

The development of methods for the training of a self-control repertoire and the study of conditions which facilitate such learning has been of special interest to empirically minded clinicians over the last decade. While all the relevant variables and hypothesized processes of self-regulation also need to be addressed by those concerned about self-control, an additional task involves the generation of incentives for making the initial behavior change, since the goals or incentives in the "problem" situation are typically inconsistent with the "therapeutic" change. For example, a change in motivation is required of the would-be dieter, abstainer from alcohol, or modifier of a "type A personality" style. In each case, the person must learn to *move away* from certain occasionally rewarding goals (a process Klinger calls "disengagement from incentives") and *toward* other (supposedly more adaptive) ones.

A GUIDING FRAMEWORK FOR
SELF-MANAGEMENT THERAPY

In seeking to provide a useful framework for self-management therapy, it is important to decide what underlying assumptions (metatheory) about the human organism we should select as a basis for our clinical intervention. Failure to address the question of what kind of model (or models) to draw upon opens the door for an unhealthy reliance upon a fixed experimental worldview and relatively inflexible data reduction methods (scientism) to guide our assessment and behavior change efforts with individual clients (cf., Barlow, 1981). With respect to influential theories in human self-management, three candidates for a "guiding framework" include the biological, the cognitive, and the behavioral (see also Chapter 1, in this volume, for a historical review of self-management perspectives).

The biological approach draws heavily upon the assumption that even the most complex human functions (products of evolution and central nervous system flexibility) are best accommodated by the application of principles of homeostasis to all levels of analysis (see Rodin's chapter in Part I of this volume). Indeed, principles appropriate at lower levels are viewed as applicable to an understanding of higher levels and to the interface between levels. Research and theorizing in biofeedback (an area not strongly emphasized in this volume) illustrates the attempts to deal with the interconnectedness of autonomic, behavioral and attitudinal events (Budzynski, Stoyva, & Peffer, 1980). The biopsychical model is not necessarily built upon reductionism (from psychological to biological events), but argues rather for the generality of principles that span the gamut of living systems and their functions. In clinical practice and in social psychology, however, this approach has had only occasional representation (e.g., Rapoport, 1974). Far more widespread has been the restricted and selective use of the results of physiological research for the development of practical change procedures and models of psychopathology (such as depression or schizophrenia). The clinical yield has not been as impressive as was once anticipated (e.g., Turk, Meichenbaum, & Berman, 1979; Young & Blanchard, 1980).

The chapters in this volume, accurately reflecting the current emphasis, have tended to focus upon the relative merits of the cognitive versus the behavioral model in clinical psychology. Since considerable discussion and debate on the metaphysical, philosophical, and/or epistemological grounds upon which protagonists have erected their respective systems has already occurred, we will address ourselves primarily to a comparison of the two approaches in terms of their pragmatic utility in the development of therapeutic strategies.

Cognitivists have generally claimed greater comprehensiveness for their model, which encompasses not only observable input-output relationships, but also the intricate and interdependent relationships among the processes that mediate them. Cognitive psychology has also offered explanations of mediational systems that include the nature of sensation and perception as well as the evaluative (cognitive and affective) and selective processes that eventually result in the stream of integrated overt behaviors. As Hilgard (1980) noted, "Cognition is a generic term used to designate all processes in knowing. Hence it covers everything from perception to reasoning" (p. 6). Hilgard (1980) credits Miller, Galanter, and Pribram's *Plans and the Structure of Behavior* (1960) for introducing a "subjective behaviorism" into psychology. A successful integration of subjectivism and behaviorism would certainly qualify for the label *comprehensive*. But, how close have we come to a unified paradigm?

Neisser (1980) views cognitive psychology as a family of theories "deeply divided against itself." The major approaches are the information-processing model, the constructive approach, and the perceptual realism of J. J. Gibson. The information-processing model offers a detailed experimental analysis of perception, memory, and thought, yet "has curiously little to say about the kinds of experiences that bring patients to therapists" (Neisser, 1980, p. 364). While this approach, and the research developed from it, has been the most widely cited by the so-called cognitive therapists, the analysis of the components of the human information processing system has typically focused on the characteristics and capacities of persons to select, organize, and recall inputs. To date, the model has failed to address itself to the critical question of how such characteristics relate to human incentives, and the everyday interpersonal experiences with which clinicians deal.

The constructivist approach has as its objective the explication of the individual's structural model of the world. The model "both guides behavior and provides a structure for inferring the meaning of events" (Arnkoff, 1980, p. 340).

Finally, in contrast to the view that individuals construct their own experience and apply invariant rules or control structures to govern thought and action, is the view that *the organism does not need to add meaning to its encountered environment.* Gibson (1979) suggests that perceivers respond to the objectively available information from the external world. This approach is ecological in that it relates the given world directly to experience, and views knowledge as dependent upon the interaction of the person and the real characteristics of the environment. However, by leaving out the modifying (and distorting) influence of the person's action upon perceptual and sensory input, the ecological model remains too general to account for individual differences. Gibson's approach raises the question of how, in fact, misrepresentations of reality and memory can occur, if indeed perception is directly given.

Thus, the "cognitive model," whose star is on the rise in clinical assessment and intervention (see any issue of the journal *Cognitive Therapy and Research*), does not appear to be a unified point of view within experimental psychology. Neisser (1980) has suggested that the Gibsonian view may, when considered together with the constructive, have something to offer clinicians—odd as that possibility might seem. Basically, we need to consider the impact of both constructive and objective (direct information pickup) processes in understanding our clients—and replace one with the other "when it is appropriate to do so." Unfortunately, we are given no hints by Neisser as to how said "appropriateness" can be discerned, or by whom. Mahoney (1980) also acknowledges weaknesses in the cognitive therapy premises which have so strongly taken hold in clinical work. Among the theoretical issues he notes are the emphasis on rationality in adaptation, the downplay of emotional responses, and the disregard for inaccessible cognitive, imaginal, or associative processes. Procedurally, such problems lead to narrow intervention strategies, or techniques that are often "mechanically focused on the surface structure content of thought rather than its deep-structural themes" (Mahoney, 1980, p. 173).

On the other side of the conceptual mountain, the behavioral emphasis has been upon the critical role of the environment in shaping a person's experiences and actions. While other psychological processes are not denied, learning (rather than perception) is seen as the central mechanism for change. The focus has also been upon the learning of overt instrumental behaviors rather than on verbal learning (or language acquisition) and the many strategies a linguistically competent person can employ in his or her transactions with the environment and/or with oneself.

Both the cognitive and behavioral models and their variations have strengths and weaknesses vis-à-vis clinical work. Their major difference lies in the underlying approach to constructing a science of *human* behavior and experience.

Among the cognitive models, the information processing view, which has employed the computer as a basic analogue, certainly shares many assumptions (and often criticisms) with the behavioral approach. Both operate on the assumption that a series of general laws can be established relating the capacities of the organism and its specific behaviors to "objective" reality. Neither presumes that individual differences result in such unique constellations of organization that a thoroughly idiosyncratic approach is required to examine human activity. In both domains, laboratory research has been conducted in accordance with the operational rules inherited from the physical sciences.

The fundamental differences between the models involves the information-processors' search for interior mechanisms and structures, while the behaviorist has traditionally shunned the investigation of intra-organismic processes, focusing instead upon the functional analysis of observable stimulus-response relationships. As a consequence, the models vary in the degree to which central processes are favored in developing explanatory systems. They differ also with regard to the breadth of phenomena studied and in the level of analysis chosen. For example, some behavioral treatments have incorporated a *field* or *systems* theory perspective (Bandura, 1977; Kantor, 1959; Kanfer & Grimm, 1976, 1980; Karoly, 1980; Staats, 1975), and the comprehensiveness of the system considered has been quite diverse. Most often the system includes the organism as a unit in interaction with the social and physical environment in a wide range of activities. The information-processing theorist has been concerned with a more limited system, one which is bounded by operations within the individual and at the interface of person and environment. The contrast is most evident when comparing extreme representations of each of these approaches.

For example, in the analysis of self regulation, the radical behavioral positions of Ainslie, Rachlin, Goldiamond, and others (see Chapter 1) focuses its causal analysis on social and physical variables that act as efficient causes, while the position of Powers (1973) and Carver and Scheier (this volume) admit of self-regulatory events at the central (formal or final cause) level. Although we are aware of the limits in characterizing these two points of view in brief, it seems that the crux of the difference between them lies in the cognitivists' failure to deal adequately with *motivational* and *affective* variables (cf., Klinger, this volume) as well as with the *interpersonal exchange* (cf., DeVoge, 1980), while the behaviorists have tended to omit consideration of the uniquely human characteristics that determine selection, organization, and use of information (primarily symbolic) as powerful influencers of human adaptation. In what is called the *cognitive-behavioral* movement, recent attempts to develop a pragmatic combination of the two points of view illustrate that good practical results can accrue, although conceptual difficulties and vagaries can be bred when a fit between the two models is forced. The technical advances have thus far occurred at the expense of internal, systematic inconsistencies.

An extreme oversimplification of the difference between the behavioral versus cognitive approach would represent the former as interested only in performance and the latter only in the acquisition and organization of knowledge. However, doing and knowing are typically interdependent. Cognitivists make use of overt behavior to indicate knowledge, and behaviorists use knowledge as a discriminative stimulus. The current emphasis upon the broadening of paradigms has meant that cognitivists have placed greater stress on the cognition-behavior relationship (and its influencing variables), while behaviorists have attended to cognitive events and processes. It will be interesting to note, in the years to come, how the basic models are changed or modified. From the viewpoint presented here, both sides will need to give greater consideration to the dynamic time- and context-relativistic quality of human behavior (cf., also Karoly, 1981).

The point was made in Chapter 1 of this volume that the pure intrapsychic and pure environmental theorists have been steadily moving toward a conceptual middle ground. Contemporary interactionist psychology (e.g., Endler & Magnusson, 1976; Magnusson & Endler, 1977; Mischel, 1973) has sought (with varying degrees of success) to understand the person-environment "connection" without recourse to chicken-and-egg debates or to static methodologies. The concept of *skill*, which is so basic to the notion of self-management and to social adaptation (McFall & Dodge, this volume), has recently been conceptualized in a genuinely dynamic, cognitive-developmental model (Fischer, 1980). According to Fischer's (1980) skill theory, "environmental factors play a central role in determining the relative degree of synchrony between developmental sequences, and they also affect the specific developmental sequences that people show (p. 511)." Environmental enabling conditions, practice, direct feedback and a host of other noncognitive factors must be taken into account along with representational and transformational rules in order to build a comprehensive model of human adaptation, wherein "unevenness in skills across domains seems to be a fact of development" (Fischer, 1980). This view stands in sharp contrast to the bulk of cognitive theory in which internal structures are given causal priority in the explanation of behavioral organization.

On the other hand, developments in social learning theory have also begun to blur the boundaries between structural and functional models. Mischel's (1973) cognitive competencies, Kanfer's self-regulation model (e.g., Kanfer, 1971; Kanfer & Hagerman, 1981), and Bandura's (1977) self-efficacy construct illustrate attempts by social learning theorists to conceptualize behavioral organization on the basis of "within-person" operations. And, in a fascinating series of studies dealing with the interface of externally and internally generated memories, Johnson and her colleagues (Johnson, Raye, Wang, & Taylor, 1979; Johnson, Taylor, & Raye, 1977; Raye, Johnson, & Taylor, 1980) have demonstrated the robustness of the IFE effect (i.e., the Increase in apparent Frequency of External events as a consequence of internal events): a phenomenon that illustrates the power of covert processes to significantly influence estimates of the frequency of external occurrences. Johnson's work on what she calls "reality monitoring" may lead to further insights into the nature of self-generated events and personal schemata in both normal and maladjusted populations, and further the cause of a cognitive-behavioral integration. It also promises to permit the refinement of clinical methods (such as covert modeling, guided imagery, or role-playing) that make use of mixtures of cognitive and overt responses.

A genuine amalgam of cognitive and behavioral constructs and methodologies may offer a firmer platform for clinical intervention than either perspective by itself. A belief in this vision as a point of departure for assessment and therapy is providing the fuel for a tremendous outpouring of effort by numerous investigators (see Kendall & Hollon, 1979, 1981). As far as self-management is concerned, the future holds both promises and pitfalls.

For example, in the clinic, the differences in what level of analysis one focuses on can result in wide divergences in problem definition, selection of therapeutic goals and targets, and selection of observational or data-analytic methods. A theory rich in complex constructs often requires inferences and interpretations quite distant from observed events and an elaborate analytic network to make sense of inferred psychological processes. The pressure on clinicians to work quickly and effectively under conditions of great uncertainty, in the absence of controlled observations and with few individually tailored measurement tools, tends to increase the likelihood of *shortcuts via subjective estimates, conjectures, and inferences* and/or *measurement by unvalidated procedures that purportedly access cognitive mechanisms.* Certainly self-management, as we view it, will not yield to simple counting of responses in specific situations. But it is not likely to be clarified by the development of a host of new constructs either. As Davison (1980) points out, we must be extremely cautious in "populating the black box with a host of strange-sounding cognitive metaphors" (p. 206). We can safely assume, therefore, that neither the cause-in-the environment nor self-as-initiator views of self-management specify the domain of events to be measured. Where, then, do we look?

The distinction between measures reflecting self-processes versus environmental events might be replaced by attention to three sets of constantly moving and interacting variables. These variables include: (1) external cues and reinforcers; (2) well-established (automatized or overlearned) behaviors; and (3) self-mediated reactions, including plans, images, expectancies, and the like. With this triad in mind, broad questions such as whether the "ultimate" control of behavior resides in the "self" or the environment, or questions about the relative priority assigned to cognitive formulations (e.g., "insight", "awareness") over feedback reactions (as determinants of behavior change) resolve themselves into a series of more specific and detailed questions. These questions will hopefully enable researchers to formulate experiments and provide some meaningful answers.

A functional approach, for example, including both task and environmental determinant analysis, may raise questions about the degree to which particular setting events (cues) or social reinforcement practices support stereotyped, overlearned responses or activate self-regulatory sequences. In a specific case, the question may be rephrased to assess a client's self-management skills, the client's recognition of the need to put skills into operation, or the probable response of significant others. (Kanfer & Grimm, 1980; Karoly, 1977, 1981).

Although cultural forces posit self-discipline as an intra-personal moral structure and widely proclaim its self-evident virtues, the work discussed in the preceding chapters and our own point of view clearly suggests that one of the clinician's most difficult tasks may involve the rejection of such a model and the fostering in the client of a repertoire of skills to *realistically* cope with and appraise demands for delay of gratification, tolerance of unpleasant circumstances, or abandonment of unrealistic goals. In the previous chapters we have seen how such skills can be slowly built up by means of careful engineering for persons with limited experience (children) or capacity (intellectually handicapped) or can be developed rather quickly by the invocation of the full range of already existing cognitive and emotional control processes in many adults. In all cases, however, the constant interplay between the variables in the aforementioned *triad* suggests that the clinician must attend to the relationship between the client's changing repertoire and the fluctuating input of the social and physical environment. Further, the person's emotional state interacts both with the perception of the external world and the efficiency of execution of mediating responses. The practicing clinician whose source of data consists only of interview material will encounter as much difficulty in assessing and in treating self-management problems as will the clinician who takes and examines only frequency counts or self-monitoring records.

The most critical need in self-management psychology as far as the clinician is concerned is an integrated world view. It is far easier to talk to triadic variables, or put a hyphen between "cognitive" and "behavioral," or invoke the idea of reciprocal determinism, than it is to interpret action and thought in an internally consistent manner.

To caricature the extremes of this problem, we might find a behavioral clinician (who readily adds parts of a cognitive formulation to his or her own S-R view) who overinterprets the imitation of a verbal response modeled after the therapist (such as a positive self-statement) as an indication of a change in self-regulatory functioning, without any attempt to differentiate such a change from one due to long sequences of self-reactions, feedback from experiences, and/or relabeling under stimulus control. A cognitive theorist, who incorporates an S-R view, may likewise be tempted to equate new psychological organizing principles in an individual with simple behavior changes more parsimoniously ascribed to recent conditioning.

The integration of behavioral and cognitive methods and constructs demands caution in our bridge building efforts. Each builder is likely to proceed by use of raw materials taken exclusively from his or her side of the shore. For this reason, it is doubtful that the two bridge spans will ever meet. We can certainly try, as Kendall (1981) advised, to avoid conceptual and methodological *isolationism* and the errors of *specificity* (assuming that a specific cognitive leads to a specific dysfunction), *generality* (assuming that a cognitive distortion found in one group of clients is common to all), and *etiology* (assuming that successful treatment of a condition confirms the clinician's etiological explanation). However, until we reexamine and reorganize our epistemological commitments and the structure of our theories, we may find that, for the empirical clinician interested in self-management, the path out of the *lion's den* (see Kanfer & Karoly, 1972) may lead, not to improved clinical methods, but to *Fantasy Island*.

In this section, we have tried to describe some of the central differences between the cognitivist and behaviorist approaches to self-management. We have pointed out that integration appears desirable and is, in fact, already underway. However, we have taken pains to underscore the fact that the road to integration is fraught with problems at many levels. For the practicing clinician, the collection of information necessary for reaching decisions about therapeutic goals and methods is a crucial step. We have indicated that different systems lead to different foci of attention for both measurement and treatment. Epistemological considerations influence every step of the clinical process (cf. Kanfer & Nay, in press; Karoly, 1981). Specifically, conceptual formulations affect the clinician's definition of the task and the formulation of task-relevant hypotheses. In turn, these guesses relate to the selection and evaluation of therapy methods. The problem formulation and reformulation process is continuous, spanning the course of treatment and beyond.

A self-management approach in the clinic presupposes the goal of changing regulatory *processes* rather than just behavioral outcomes or products in a specific situation. While most of the clinical research in this area has focused on outcome (not inappropriately as far as assessment is concerned), repeated mention has been made by various investigators that the ultimate goal of self-management therapy lies in altering a client's skill repertoire for coping with problem situations and for maintaining, transferring, and generalizing therapy-based learning to new (nontargeted) behaviors and situations (Goldstein & Kanfer, 1979; Karoly & Steffen, 1980). It would, therefore, appear that the indicants of the effectiveness of self-management therapies must include *process measures*, not just *product* or outcome measures. Process measures would include: changes in the client's evaluational standards; changes in the client's ability to monitor incipient problem situations; changes in the relationship between intention statements and self-regulatory actions; improvements or alterations in planning or problem-solving style; adaptive changes in rates of self-reward and self-criticism; and an enhanced appreciation for the interactional nature of one's choices and the success of attaining them. In addition, the hypothesis that therapy involves a shift from the predominance of overlearned, automatized behaviors enacted in problem situations toward the invocation of "mindful" behaviors (cf. Langer, 1978) suggests that successful therapy should also result in increased variability of behavioral repertoires and coping skills at post-treatment combined with a reduced variability in the use of newly acquired and effective responses (directed at previously threatening or conflictful situations).

PRACTICAL CONCERNS
Self-Management of What?

Currently, self-management psychology deals with three different target areas. Clients may learn to develop control over their behavior responses to environmentally presented conflictful situations (as in resistance to temptation or engagement in short-run unpleasant activities). Or they may learn to control such physiological reactions as emotional arousal, anxiety, or the experience of pain. Finally, the purpose of self-management may be to help clients control their cognitive or imaginally mediated reactions, such as intrusive thoughts, negative self-reactions, or undesirable urges. In order to accomplish any change, most problems cannot be dealt with simply "as stated" or as first presented by clients. A thorough task analysis is required, one that focuses not only upon functional relationships, but also upon the status of component skills and the applicability of normative criteria (Karoly, 1977, 1981).

In their well-known schematization, Thoresen and Mahoney (1974) note two kinds of self-control strategy. In the first, the person is responsible in an ongoing fashion for the change of her own responses by rearranging self-generated consequences (often covert); this strategy is known as *behavioral programming*. However, perhaps the older approach is the one that Thoresen and Mahoney call *environmental planning*. In this approach, which makes use of stimulus control principles, the person essentially controls or manages what the environment does to him. A critical practical issue in environmental planning involves the decision about the onset of antecedents calling for the initiation of self-management. In other words, the client must know precisely, and in advance of their occurrence, what external factors are responsible for cueing adaptive and/or maladaptive behaviors. In practical terms, this means teaching the client that his or her therapeutic task extends beyond *self*-management. Control of inputs is as important as the control of output (or instrumental responses). The client should be trained (where deficient) to recognize cues in the environment, in biological functioning, or in cognitive or feedback events from one's own behavior that would signal the necessity for instituting self-controlling behavioral sequences. This position lies at the heart of cybernetic conceptions (Powers, 1973), but has been rather simplified in learning-theory accounts (cf. also Carver & Scheier's discussion, in this volume).

Self-Management – Where?

We have strongly emphasized the importance of defining the context in which self-management occurs. Yet, the theories and the bulk of supporting evidence for self-management practices have been derived from widely divergent settings. The extant theories of self-regulation are laboratory bred. The development of clinical practices has followed the laboratory model to a large degree. The apparent ease with which laboratory investigators have been able to assess the determinants of time-limited self-control or self-regulation (for example, see Mischel, 1974) has inspired clinical investigators in the design and evaluation of complex intervention programs built on the operant or social learning foundation. See especially, in Parts II and III of this book, Gross & Drabman; Litrownik; Rehm; Morokoff & LoPiccolo; Marlatt & Parks; and Deffenbacher & Suinn. A surprisingly coherent set of guidelines and procedures has developed from this mix of problem areas, populations, and procedures. Nevertheless, the factors *in the real world* that may alter the relevance of variables affecting self-management and the relative contribution of individuals and setting events toward the facilitation or disruption of effective self-management remain open questions. Such questions are of utmost importance, particularly in view of the scant data in support of the long-term effectiveness of most clinical self-control programs (Karoly, Note 1).

For example, we might inquire as to whether process analysis is affected by the fact that, in one instance, the subject is faced with a clearly defined task posed by the experimenter while, in another case, the therapy client confronts a task that is poorly defined and has uncertain outcomes. For the experimental subject, behavioral changes occur under the watchful eye of the experimenter, and can be limited in scope and temporal duration. A laboratory subject generally views the ultimate purpose of his or her self-management as a contribution to the experimenter's knowledge or as an activity for pay. The client in therapy should be primarily concerned with self-improvement and/or social adaptation. The range of actions in the laboratory is relatively limited, and a noncompliant subject can quit or be excused. In contrast, clients possess an almost infinite interpersonal repertoire for countering the clinician's influence. They can waver between terminating and actively working for change over many therapeutic sessions. Further, the highly personal content of clinical targets and the continuing contrary influences in the client's extra-therapy life often act in opposition to therapeutic goals (even though they are strongly endorsed by the self-aware client). Laboratory investigators are typically one-dimensional (in terms of *fixing* targets and setting factors), effectively sheltering the subject from interference by competing controlling agencies or events. Autonomy is, thus, differentially defined in the laboratory, the clinic, and the real world. The only true test of the power of self-management in the natural setting is one that permits reasonable countervailing influences to operate freely.

Self-Management — For Whom?

The experimental literature often gives the impression that self-control programs and self-management therapies consist of a set of procedures that can (and should) be applied equally across diverse client populations. This impression is most often fostered by omission — that is, by the investigator's failure to acknowledge the role of individual differences and environmental demands. Person variables are undoubtedly relevant to the evaluation of overall treatment outcome through their interaction with process variables across the various phases of therapy (Karoly, 1980). Furthermore, we cannot readily estimate the *strength* of an intervention, its *appropriateness*, or its *integrity* (the degree to which it is delivered as intended) without reference to the client's unique psychological status (cf. Yeaton & Sechrest, 1981) or the extent of environmental support for (or opposition to) the client's new strategies and behaviors.

We must be concerned not only with a client's previous learning history and the nature of the current target problem, but also with component skills and the current incentives that affect acquisition and execution of self-management routines. Individual difference factors affect and are affected by the purposes for which self-management training is sought as well as the structure of available social support systems.

A particularly important characteristic of self-control programs is the degree to which they demand changes in well-established life patterns. For example, while an exercise program may be difficult to initiate for several reasons, it may fit easily into one person's daily schedule without extensive readjustment while, for another person, work patterns, social engagements and other activities may need to be modified to accommodate the change. Some social skills programs may involve use of already available opportunities, while for other clients, a series of new strategies must be taught to allow them to meet people and try out newly acquired repertoires. Clearly, then, standardized programs will vary in suitability for individual clients not only on the basis of target behavior or personal skills but also as a function of factors beyond the client's control.

Self-Management — By Whom?

In principle, all therapeutic interventions that strive to achieve and maintain a behavior change independent of the therapist or an artificially controlled milieu require self-management (in varying degrees) by the client. While it is clear that "instigation therapy" (Kanfer & Phillips, 1970) requires client responsibility, most traditional therapies and many recent "humanistic" treatments also depend upon an active participatory stance on the part of the client. Any assignment of homework, self-observation, or diary keeping implies the client's agreement to initiate, direct, and evaluate his or her own behavior in accordance with guidelines worked out by mutual consent with a therapist. Most clinical techniques incorporate some method(s) for attaining cooperation for self-directed change. And a collaborative or cooperative "set" is another important and neglected individual difference factor: one that can vary both within and between therapy sessions.

When therapeutic interventions, whether they be initiated via individual interactions or in group programs, disregard the role of the client-therapist relationship, the plausibility of the treatment, the degree of client discomfort with "symptoms", and other factors that stimulate the client toward assumption of responsibility for change, then treatment outccomes are more likely to depend upon unforeseen and fortuitous circumstances. The extensive literature on the treatment of subassertiveness, habit disorders, and fears has failed to demonstrate that "one method fits all."

Research on the importance of expectations about the process and outcome of therapy has demonstrated the importance of client attributions regarding the success of therapy (Garfield, 1978; Goldstein, 1962). It is unfortunate that clients in self-management therapies often enter treatment with conflicts about the process as well as the goals, and with unrealistic expectations of a fast-acting, powerful intervention by the therapist, requiring only passive compliance on their part. Such expectations are enhanced by the general model of relationships with physicians, dentists, or other professionals who are paid to assume the major portion of the responsibility for a successful service.

As indicated elsewhere (Kanfer & Grimm, 1980), the therapist's early focus in treatment must center upon providing favorable conditions that help the client to shift gears — from passive to active participation. Various strategies have been proposed for achieving this goal. For example, challenging the inconsistencies in the client's behavior patterns or verbal statements, stimulating the client to formulate the presenting complaint as a problem to be solved, communicating confidence and esteem for the client's capacity for self-direction all serve to activate "latent" self-regulatory functions.

The important contributions of social influence theory have recently been brought to bear on the problem of creating a therapeutic atmosphere conducive to clients' willingness to assume an active role in therapy (e.g., Brehm & McAllister, 1980; Wilcoxon-Craighead & Craighead, 1980). Further, the variety of techniques to enhance client involvement have been described by Frank (1973).

Self-Management and the Self-Help Movement

Distinct from the empirical orientation and the procedures outlined in this book (although not inconsistent with some aspects of the underlying philosophy) are the various self-help movements in mental health. The main distinguishing feature lies in the fact that self-help groups are deliberately *not* conducted by professionals. Usually, individuals with common problems (self-assessed) meet with the goal of offering support and a group identity as the base from which to enhance the participants' resolve to change.

Ethics and Self-Management

Self-management approaches to therapy have often been hailed as truly egalitarian and democratic in advancing the principle of shared responsibility. In contrast to criticisms of behavior modification as being excessively directive, controlling, or authoritarian and of psychoanalytic procedures as being sexist, elitist, and dependency enhancing, the apparent *internal locus* of the self-management model(s) described in this volume would seem to render them immune to charges of being arbitrary or operating in the service of the status quo. In actuality, the self-management psychologist must be as careful as his or her colleagues working from other schools of therapy to avoid possible abuses of power—whether it be through subtle or obvious attempts at manipulation. On the other hand, self-management therapists might be accused of being unwilling to assume the clinician's responsibility for the outcome of treatment. Thus, therapists can be too directive or not directive enough. Is there a resolution of this dilemma?

Clients present themselves to therapists of all persuasions for help, direction, competent advice, and instruction. Even children recognize the "remedial function" of a therapist. The clinician (including the self-management psychologist) uses a variety of psychological techniques to enhance cooperation and/or to overcome initial reluctance to change. In all these ways, the therapist continues to maintain control (paradoxically) in the service of teaching the client self-control. Nevertheless, there are some significant differences among procedures that affect ethical considerations.

For example, in developing self-management, the client has an active role in establishing therapeutic goals, in specifying the various parameters of the treatment techniques, and in evaluating and reinforcing changes; client and therapist negotiate. They attempt to arrive at decisions that are compatible with the value system within which both parties operate. To this end, contracting, goal and value clarification, problem solving, and other methods enable the clinician to assist the client to achieve his or her own wishes and aspirations. Nevertheless, the important effective ingredient lies not in relinquishing control over the therapy process to the client, but in providing an attitude and outlook that is compatible with cooperation. Conceptually, "perceived control" may be the most important ingredient. As illustrated by a series of studies (Kanfer & Grimm, 1978; Langer, 1978; Perlmuter & Monty, 1978) participation, faster learning, and greater satisfaction is precipitated not by *actual* assumption of control but by the belief of it. Consequently, the therapist's task can be conceptualized as (a) helping the client to recognize the inherent benefits of change, and (b) helping the client to adopt strategies for executing behaviors that will ultimately shift control attributions inward. These considerations imply the need on the part of the clinician to be willing to compromise in his treatment approach and to remain flexible in accepting objectives and techniques that may not be totally satisfying. At times the clinician may have to interpose therapeutic maneuvers and practices that do not directly attack the client's problem, but are aimed at preparing the ground so that the client can accept goals and procedures judged appropriate by the therapist's assessment of the problem situation.

As stated above, applications of various self-control techniques are transitory in bringing about a change. This means that clients, who are often disturbed by the artificiality of technical routines (such as self-monitoring, self-reinforcement, problem-solving, decision-making heuristics, or various cognitive methods for enhancing motivation), need to realize that these procedures are temporary "crutches" in the service of restoration or of a new and more effective behavioral organization. Much as any other prosthetic devices, they should eventually be given up once the new behavior has stabilized and is supported by its natural consequences. At the same time, many of the self-management techniques can be called on again when clients confront difficult problems or when various cues signal the possible occurrence of familiar conflicts or difficulties.

Many of the clinical methods described in this book have been found to be effective in altering both emotional reactions and behaviors. In considering their utility in a therapeutic setting, it is important that the therapist evaluate the possibility that use of such methods may be beneficial for the client but disastrous for others. Similarly, undesirable side effects for the client may occur. For example, coping in order to endure stress situations that may be dangerous or life-threatening is ultimately less sensible than learning to anticipate them and to avoid or escape them. Similarly, applying self-control methods to control affectionate or positive reactions in order to aid a person to prepare for separation or dissolution of a partnership may, in the absence of joint planning, result in disastrous emotional effects on the "untrained" partner. Professional obligation requires that the therapist always assess the compatibility of the therapeutic program, not only with the client's own values and goals, but with *social* values and goals.

IN CLOSING

This epilogue was not intended as a summing up of the contents of the preceding chapters. Rather, we sought to provide some observations of the current clinical scene from both a theoretical and a practical standpoint. Nevertheless, our emphasis on unresolved (but not unresolvable) debates, continued definitional problems, the unfinished nature of the cognitive-behavioral integration, and the need for an enlarged clinical focus underscores the fact that the two-way road connecting theory to practice in self-management is neither complete nor toll free. Self-management is not a panacea. Rather, the psychology of self-management, when vigorously pursued with a full knowledge of its complexities and challenges, is but one promising means of enhancing the breadth and effectiveness of contemporary psychotherapy and, perhaps, our knowledge and understanding of human behavior in its historical and contemporary contexts.

REFERENCE NOTE

1. Karoly, P. *On the failures of self-control interventions: Review and speculation.* Manuscript submitted for publication. (Available from the author. Department of Psychology, University of Cincinnati, Dyer Hall, Cincinnati, Ohio 45221.)

REFERENCES

Arnkoff, D. B. Psychotherapy from the perspective of cognitive theory. In M. J. Mahoney (Ed.), *Psychotherapy process: Current issues and future directions.* New York: Plenum, 1980.

Atkinson, J. W., & Birch, D. *Introduction to motivation.* (2nd ed.) New York: D. Van Nostrand, 1978.

Bandura, A. *Social learning theory.* Englewood Cliffs, N.J.: Prentice-Hall, 1977.

Barlow, D. H. On the relation of clinical research to clinical practice: Current issues, new directions. *Journal of Consulting and Clinical Psychology,* 1981, *49,* 147–155.

Brehm, S. S., & McAllister, D. A. A social psychological perspective on the maintenance of therapeutic change. In P. Karoly & J. J. Steffen (Eds.), *Improving the long-term effects of psychotherapy.* New York: Gardner Press, 1980.

Budzynski, T. H., Stoyva, J. M., & Peffer, K. E. Biofeedback techniques in psychosomatic disorders. In A. Goldstein & E. B. Foa (Eds.), *Handbook of behavioral interventions.* New York: Wiley, 1980.

Carver, C. S., & Scheier, M. F. *Attention and self-regulation: A control theory approach to human behavior.* New York: Springer-Verlag, 1981.

Davison, G. C. And now for something completely different: Cognition and little *r.* In M. J. Mahoney (Ed.), *Psychotherapy process.* New York: Plenum, 1980.

Deci, E. L. *The psychology of self-determination.* Lexington, Massachusetts: D. C. Heath, 1980.

DeVoge, J. T. Reciprocal role training: Therapeutic transfer as viewed from a social psychology of dyads. In P. Karoly & J. J. Steffen (Eds.), *Improving the long-term effects of psychotherapy.* New York: Gardner Press, 1980.

Dollard, J., & Miller, N. E. *Personality and psychotherapy.* New York: McGraw-Hill, 1950.

Endler, N. S., & Magnusson, D. (Eds.), *Interactional psychology and personality.* Washington, D.C.: Hemisphere Publishing, 1976.

Feshbach, S. The environment of personality. *American Psychologist,* 1978, *33,* 447–455.

Fischer, K. W. A theory of cognitive development: The control and construction of hierarchies of skills. *Psychological Review*, 1980, *87*, 477–531.

Fishbein, M. A theory of reasoned action. Some applications and implications. In H. E. Howe & M. M. Page (Eds.), *Nebraska symposium on motivation 1979: Beliefs, attitudes and values*. Lincoln: University of Nebraska Press, 1980.

Frank, J. *Persuasion and healing*. Baltimore: Johns Hopkins University Press, 1973.

Garfield, S. L. Research on client variables in psychotherapy. In S. L. Garfield & A. E. Bergin (Eds.), *Handbook of psychotherapy and behavior change*. (2nd ed.) New York: Wiley, 1978.

Gergen, K. J., & Morawski, J. An alternative metatheory for social psychology. In L. Wheeler (Ed.), *Review of personality and social psychology*. Vol. 1. Beverly Hills, Calif.: Sage, 1980.

Gibson, J. J. *An ecological approach to visual perception*. Boston: Houghton Mifflin, 1979.

Goldstein, A. P. *Therapist-patient expectancies in psychotherapy*. New York: Pergamon, 1962.

Goldstein, A. P., & Kanfer, F. H. *Maximizing treatment gains*. New York: Academic Press, 1979.

Hilgard, E. R. Consciousness in contemporary psychology. In M. R. Rosenzweig & L. W. Porter (Eds.), *Annual Review of Psychology*, 1980, *31*, 1–26.

Jeffrey, D. B., & Berger, L. H. A self-environment systems model and its implications for behavior change. In J. Polivy & K. R. Blakenstein (Eds.), *Self-control or self-modification of emotional behavior*. New York: Plenum, in press.

Johnson, W. *People in quandaries*. New York: Harper & Row, 1946.

Johnson, M. K., Raye, C. L., Wang, A. Y., & Taylor, T. H. Fact and fantasy: The roles of accuracy and variability in confusing imaginations with perceptual experiences. *Journal of Experimental Psychology: Human Learning and Memory*, 1979, *5*, 229–240.

Johnson, M. K., Taylor, T. H., & Raye, C. L. Fact and fantasy: The effects of internally generated events on the apparent frequency of externally generated events. *Memory and Cognition*, 1977, *5*, 116–122.

Kanfer, F. H. The maintenance of behavior by self-generated stimuli and reinforcement. In A. Jacobs & L. B. Sachs (Eds.), *The psychology of private events*. New York: Academic Press, 1971.

Kanfer, F. H. Self-management methods. In F. H. Kanfer & A. P. Goldstein (Eds.), *Helping people change*. New York: Pergamon Press, 1980.

Kanfer, F. H. Personal control, social control, and altruism: Can society survive the age of individualism. *American Psychologist*, 1979, *34*, 231–239.

Kanfer, F. H., & Grimm, L. G. The future of behavior modification. In W. E. Craighead, A. E. Kazdin, & M. J. Mahoney (Eds.), *Behavior modification: Principles, issues, and applications*. Boston: Houghton Mifflin, 1976.

Kanfer, F. H., & Grimm, L. G. Freedom of choice and behavioral change. *Journal of Consulting and Clinical Psychology*, 1978, *46*, 873–878.

Kanfer, F. H., & Grimm, L. G. Managing clinical change: A process model of therapy. *Behavior Modification*, 1980, *4*, 419–444.

Kanfer, F. H., & Hagerman, S. The role of self-regulation. In L. P. Rehm (Ed.), *Behavior therapy for depression: Present status and future directions*. New York: Academic Press, 1981.

Kanfer, F. H., & Karoly, P. Self-control: A behavioristic excursion into the lion's den. *Behavior Therapy*, 1972, *3*, 398–416.

Kanfer, F. H., & Nay, W. R. Behavioral assessment: Toward an integration of epistemological and methodological issues. In C. M. Franks & G. T. Wilson (Eds.), *Behavior therapy and its foundations*. Vol. 1. New York: Guilford Press, in press.

Kanfer, F. H., & Phillips, J. S. *Learning foundations of behavior therapy*. New York: Wiley, 1970.

Kantor, J. R. *Interbehavioral psychology.* Bloomington, Ind.: Principia Press, 1959.

Karoly, P. Behavioral self-management in children: Concepts, methods, issues, and directions. In M. Hersen, R. M. Eisler, & P. M. Miller (Eds.), *Progress in behavior modification.* Vol. 5. New York: Academic Press, 1977.

Karoly, P. Person variables in therapeutic change and development. In P. Karoly & J. J. Steffen (Eds.), *Improving the long-term effects of psychotherapy.* New York: Gardner Press, 1980.

Karoly, P. Self-management problems in children. In E. Mash & L. Terdal (Eds.), *Behavioral assessment of childhood problems.* New York: Guilford Press, 1981.

Karoly, P., & Steffen, J. J. (Eds.), *Improving the long-term effects of psychotherapy.* New York: Gardner Press, 1980.

Kendall, P. C. Assessment and cognitive-behavioral interventions: Purposes, proposals, and problems. In P. C. Kendall & S. D. Hollon (Eds.), *Assessment strategies for cognitive-behavioral interventions.* New York: Academic Press, 1981.

Kendall, P. C., & Hollon, S. D. (Eds.), *Cognitive-behavioral interventions.* New York: Academic Press, 1979.

Kendall, P. C., & Hollon, S. D. (Eds.), *Assessment strategies for cognitive-behavioral interventions.* New York: Academic Press, 1981.

Kimble, G., & Perlmuter, L. The problem of volition. *Psychological Review,* 1970, *77,* 361–384.

Koch, S. The nature and limits of psychological knowledge. *American Psychologist,* 1981, *36,* 257–269.

Langer, E. The illusion of incompetence. In L. Perlmuter & R. Monty (Eds.), *Choice and perceived control.* Hillsdale, N.J.: Lawrence Erlbaum, 1978.

Magnusson, D., & Endler, N. S. (Eds.), *Personality at the crossroads: Current issues in interactional psychology.* Hillsdale, N.J.: Lawrence Erlbaum, 1977.

Mahoney, M. J. Psychotherapy and the structure of personal revolutions. In M. J. Mahoney (Ed.), *Psychotherapy process.* New York: Plenum, 1980.

Mahoney, M. J., & Arnkoff, D. Cognitive and self-control therapies. In S. L. Garfield & A. E. Bergin (Eds.), *Handbook of psychotherapy and behavior change* (2nd ed.). New York: Wiley, 1978.

Meichenbaum, D. *Cognitive-behavior modification.* New York: Plenum, 1977.

Miller, J. G. *Living systems.* New York: McGraw-Hill, 1978.

Miller, G. A., Galanter, E., & Pribram, K. H. *Plans and the structure of behavior.* New York: Holt, Rinehart & Winston, 1960.

Mischel, W. Toward a cognitive social learning reconceptualization of personality. *Psychological Review,* 1973, *80,* 252–283.

Mischel, W. Processes in delay of gratification. In L. Berkowitz (Ed.), *Advances in experimental social psychology.* Vol. 7. New York: Academic Press, 1974.

Neisser, U. Three cognitive psychologies and their implications. In M. J. Mahoney (Ed.), *Psychotherapy processes.* New York: Plenum, 1980.

Perlmuter, L., & Monty, R. (Eds.), *Choice and perceived control.* Hillsdale, N.J.: Lawrence Erlbaum, 1978.

Powers, W. T. *Behavior: The control of perception.* Chicago: Aldine, 1973.

Rapoport, A. *Conflict in man-made environments.* Baltimore: Penguin Books, 1974.

Raye, C. L., Johnson, M. K., & Taylor, T. H. Is there something special about memory for internally generated information? *Memory and Cognition,* 1980, *8,* 141–148.

Rodin, J. Current status of the internal-external hypothesis for obesity: What went wrong? *American Psychologist,* 1981, *36,* 361–372.

Rychlak, J. Comments on "The self as the person." In A. Wandersman, P. Poppen, & D. Ricks (Eds.), *Humanism and behaviorism: Dialogue and growth.* New York: Pergamon, 1976.

Sagan, C. *Cosmos.* New York: Random House, 1980.

Sampson, E. E. Psychology and the American ideal. *Journal of Personality and Social Psychology,* 1977, *35,* 767–782.

Staats, A. W. *Social behaviorism.* Homewood, Ill.: Dorsey, 1975.

Thoresen, C. E., & Mahoney, M. J. *Behavioral self-control.* New York: Holt, Rinehart & Winston, 1974.

Turk, D. C., Meichenbaum, D. H., & Berman, W. H. Application of biofeedback for the regulation of pain. *Psychological Bulletin,* 1979, *86,* 1322–1338.

Wilcoxon-Craighead, L., & Craighead, W. E. Implications of persuasive communication research for the modification of self-statements. *Cognitive Therapy and Research,* 1980, *4,* 117–134.

Yeaton, W. H., & Sechrest, L. Critical dimensions in the choice and maintenance of successful treatments: Strength, integrity, and effectiveness. *Journal of Consulting and Clinical Psychology,* 1981, *49,* 156–167.

Young, L. D., & Blanchard, E. B. Medical applications of biofeedback training: A selective review. In S. Rachman (Ed.), *Contributions to medical psychology* (Vol. 2). Oxford, England: Pergamon, 1980.

Author Index

Subject Index

About the Editors and Contributors

THE EDITORS

Paul Karoly (Ph.D., University of Rochester) is Professor of Psychology at the University of Cincinnati. His research and professional interests include self-management in adults and children, maintenance of the effects of psychotherapy, behavioral medicine, and the conceptual and methodological issues in bridging the scientist-practioner gap.

Dr. Karoly is on the editorial boards of several professional journals including the *Journal of Consulting and Clinical Psychology*, *Journal of Personality and Social Psychology*, *Behavioral Assessment*, and *Behavior Therapy*, and serves as a reviewer for numerous others. He also serves as a consultant to several hospitals in the Cincinnati area and maintains a small private practice of psychotherapy. Dr. Karoly is the senior editor of *Improving the Long-term Effects of Psychotherapy* and three volumes to date in the *Advances in Child Behavior Analysis and Therapy* series. He is currently writing a text on behavioral medicine. In addition, he has authored a number of book chapters and over 40 journal articles. Dr. Karoly is a member of the American Psychological Association and the Association for the Advancement of Behavior Therapy.

Frederick H. Kanfer (Ph.D., Indiana University) is Professor of Psychology at the University of Illinois. For many years his primary interest has been in developing the necessary conceptualizations and methods to provide a broad research-derived framework for application to personal, clinical, and social problems.

He was awarded a Diplomate in Clinical Psychology from the American Board of Professional Psychology. He is a Fellow of the American

633

Psychological Association and has held offices in the Division of Clinical Psychology and in the Association for the Advancement of Behavior Therapy.

Dr. Kanfer has taught at Washington University, St. Louis; at Purdue University; in the Department of Psychiatry at the University of Oregon Medical School; and at the University of Cincinnati. He was a Fulbright Scholar and has been Visiting Professor and Consultant to various agencies and universities, both in the United States and in Europe. In addition, he has served on editorial boards for several psychological journals and has published over 110 articles. He is coauthor of a book in *Learning Foundations of Behavior Therapy* and coeditor of *Helping People Change* and of *Maximizing Treatment Gains*. His research has focused on the areas of self-regulation, human learning, and motivation.

THE CONTRIBUTORS

Thomas A. Brigham (Ph.D., 1970, University of Kansas) is currently Professor of Psychology and Director of the Self-Control Research and Training Unit of Washington State University (Pullman, Washington). His major interests involve the analysis and teaching of self-management skills. He is co-editor of *The Handbook of Applied Behavior Analysis.*

Charles S. Carver (Ph.D., 1974, University of Texas at Austin) is currently at the Department of Psychology at the University of Miami (Coral Gables, Florida). His research centers on the behavioral consequences of self-focused attention. He is co-author (with Michael Scheier) of *Attention and Self-Regulation: A Control Theory Approach to Human Behavior.*

Anne P. Copeland (Ph.D., 1977, the American University) is currently affiliated with the Department of Psychology, Boston University. She is interested in verbal self-regulation of attention and emotion in normal and atypical populations.

Jerry L. Deffenbacher (Ph.D., 1975, University of Oregon) is currently Associate Professor, Department of Psychology, Colorado State University. His research interests include self-control and cognitive approaches to anxiety and anger management.

Kenneth A. Dodge (Ph.D., 1978, Duke University) is currently at the Department of Psychology, Indiana University. Dr. Dodge is interested in developing models for the assessment and training of social skills in children, and in exploring the role of skill deficiencies in the peer relationship problems of children.

Ronald S. Drabman (Ph.D., 1972, SUNY at Stony Brook) is currently at the University of Mississippi Medical Center as Professor and Director of the Clinical Psychology Training Program. His research has focused on the disordered behavior of children.

Alan M. Gross (Ph.D., 1979, Washington State University) is currently working at Emory University. He is interested in child behavior therapy and behavioral medicine and has conducted research on the training of self-management skills with delinquents.

Susan Harter (Ph.D., 1966, Yale University) is currently Professor of Psychology at the University of Denver. Dr. Harter's research concerns mastery motivation, competence, perceptions of control, self-esteem, and children's emergent understanding of emotions.

Philip C. Kendall (Ph.D., 1977, Virginia Commonwealth University) is currently in the Department of Psychology, University of Minnesota. His current research concerns cognitive-behavioral assessment and therapy with a focus upon self-control in children. Dr. Kendall is co-editor (with S. Hollon) of *Assessment Strategies for Cognitive-Behavioral Interventions*.

Eric Klinger (Ph.D., 1960, University of Chicago) is currently affiliated with the University of Minnesota (Morris), Division of the Social Sciences. His research has dealt with fantasy, thought flow, emotion and motivation, and their interrelationships. He is author of *Meaning and Void* and *Imagery*.

Alan J. Litrownik (Ph.D., 1971, University of Illinois, Champaign) is currently Professor and Chair, Department of Psychology, San Diego State University. Dr. Litrownik's clinical and research work deals with the application of social learning and information processing approaches to the understanding and treatment of distrubed children.

Joseph LoPiccolo (Ph.D., 1969, Yale University) is currently Professor of Psychiatry, School of Medicine, SUNY at Stony Brook. He is director of the Sex Therapy Center and co-author of *Becoming Orgasmic* and co-editor of the *Handbook of Sex Therapy*.

G. Alan Marlatt (Ph.D., 1968, Indiana University) is currently at the Department of Psychology, University of Washington (Seattle). Dr. Marlatt has published extensively on cognitive-behavioral approaches to the addictions and is co-author of the book *Relapse Prevention*.

Richard M. McFall (Ph.D., 1965, Ohio State University) is currently at Indiana University, Department of Psychology. Dr. McFall has pioneered the study of social competence and social skills and has investigated such populations as psychiatric in-patients, delinquents, depressed students, and anorexics.

Patricia J. Morokoff (Ph.D., 1980, SUNY at Stony Brook) is currently Assistant Professor in the Department of Psychology of Syracuse University. Dr. Morokoff's clinical and research interests include the treatment of sexual dysfunction and the psychophysiological study of the determinants of sexual arousal.

George A. Parks (Ph.D., 1980, University of Washington) is currently at the University of Washington's Department of Psychology. He has conducted research on alcoholism and smoking and is presently working on a book on intimate social relationships and love.

Lynn P. Rehm (Ph.D., 1970, University of Wisconsin-Madison) is currently Professor and Director of Clinical Training at the University of Houston. His interests are in psychopathology and the assessment and therapy of depression. He is the editor of *Behavior Therapy for Depression*.

Judith Rodin (Ph.D., 1970, Columbia University) is currently at Yale University. Dr. Rodin is internationally known for her work on obesity, aging, and the study of coping processes.

Michael F. Scheier (Ph.D., 1975, University of Texas at Austin) is presently at Carnegie-Mellon University. Professor Scheier has conducted research on the role of attention processes in the self-regulation of behavior. He is co-author (with Charles Carver) of *Attention and Self-Regulation: A Control Theory Approach to Human Behavior*.

Richard M. Suinn (Ph.D., 1959, Stanford University) is currently the head of the Department of Psychology at Colorado State University. Dr. Suinn's research has involved stress-management training for generalized anxiety disorders, Type-A behaviors, and athletic performance. He is the author of *Anxiety Management Training* and *Fundamental of Behavior Pathology* (3rd Edition).

Carolyn L. Williams (Ph.D., 1979, University of Georgia) is currently with the Adolescent Health Program—University of Minnesota. Dr. Williams' research and clinical interests focus on adolescents and children with somatic concerns and/or social skills deficits.

Pergamon General Psychology Series

Editors: Arnold P. Goldstein, Syracuse University
Leonard Krasner, SUNY, Stony Brook